Developing Ericksonian Therapy

State of the Art

Developing Ericksonian Therapy
State of the Art

Edited by

Jeffrey K. Zeig, Ph.D.

and

Stephen R. Lankton, M.S.W.

BRUNNER/MAZEL Publishers • New York

Library of Congress Cataloging-in-Publication Data

Developing Ericksonian therapy.

Proceedings of the Third International Congress
on Ericksonian Approaches to Hypnosis and Psychotherapy,
held in Phoenix, Ariz., Dec. 3–7, 1986.
Includes bibliographies.
1. Hypnotism—Therapeutic use—Congresses.
2. Psychotherapy—Congresses. 3. Erickson, Milton H.—
Congresses. I. Zeig, Jeffrey K.
II. Lankton, Stephen R. III. International Congress
on Ericksonian Approaches to Hypnosis and Psychotherapy
(3rd : 1986 : Phoenix, Ariz.) [DNLM: 1. Erickson,
Milton H. 2. Hypnosis—congresses. 3. Psychotherapy—
congresses. WM 415 D489 1986]
RC490.5.D48 1988   616.89'162   87-35533
ISBN 0-87630-501-X

89-1376

This book is dedicated
to the Erickson family members
who have been so supportive of
The Milton H. Erickson Foundation
throughout the years,
and to Shirley Bliss, patron of
The Milton H. Erickson Foundation.

" Each person is a unique individual. Hence, psychotherapy should be formulated to meet the uniqueness of the individual's needs, rather than tailoring the person to fit the Procrustean bed of a hypothetical theory of human behavior. "

Milton H. Erickson, M.D.

Contents

SECTION ONE: PRINCIPLES

Part I. Position Statements

Part II. The Utilization Approach to Strategic Therapy

Part III. Overviews

SECTION TWO: PRACTICE

Introduction

This volume presents the proceedings of the Third International Congress on Ericksonian Approaches to Hypnosis and Psychotherapy held in Phoenix, Arizona, December 3–7, 1986.

The First International Congress on Ericksonian Approaches to Hypnosis and Psychotherapy was held December 4–8, 1980, also in Phoenix. Milton H. Erickson was a member of the organizing committee of that Congress, and one of the purposes of the meeting was to give him an opportunity to see the impact of his work. Unfortunately, Erickson died eight and one-half months prior to the meeting. The proceedings of the first Congress were published in *Ericksonian Approaches to Hypnosis and Psychotherapy* (Brunner/Mazel, 1982).

Whereas the first Congress was organized to honor Erickson, the second Congress (November 30–December 4, 1983) was intended to broaden and advance Ericksonian methodology, and it had a different tone.

The second Congress was even larger than the 1980 Congress, probably making it the largest professional meeting held on the topic of hypnosis. More than 2,000 attendees came from 19 countries.

The third Congress brought many new people to the Erickson movement. Enthusiasm for this approach was quite high. Approximately 1,800 attended, a striking indication of the continuing influence and growth in the therapeutic legacy of Milton H. Erickson.

CONGRESS FORMAT

The program was academic, experiential and interactive. The academic program consisted of keynote addresses, invited presentations, accepted papers and panels. In total, more than 70 speeches were made. The faculty was composed of more than 150 members including moderators, co-presenters and special faculty.

It is the academic portion of the Congress that is reported in these proceedings. Most of the 66 presentations were submitted for publi-

cation. Of these papers, 30 chapters are included in the present text.
A special issue of the *Ericksonian Monographs* on the use of Ericksonian
techniques with special populations contains nine chapters which were
presented at the third Congress. Another issue of the *Monographs,
Research, Comparisons and Medical Applications of Ericksonian Techniques,*
contains an additional nine papers from the Congress.

The experiential component of the Congress consisted of three–hour
workshops. In total, 39 workshops were offered. A unique feature added
to the workshops was small group practicums. Each three-hour prac-
ticum consisted of no more than 12 students and was led by a faculty
member. These were experiential sessions on topics such as utilization
of hypnotic phenomena, habit problems and metaphor.

On the third day of the Congress, the format changed to allow for
interactive events; no workshops were conducted and no papers were
presented. Rather, that day consisted of one-hour clinical demonstrations, conversation hours, group discussions and panels on special topics.
A special feature of the 1986 Congress was the addition of 33 short
courses held on the last day of the meeting. These were one and one-
half hour mini-workshops on a wide range of topics concerning Ericksonian methods and hypnosis. The short courses were meant to enhance
the experiential nature of the meeting and represented a shift towards
the experiential component and away from academic presentations.

There were four keynote presentations including a keynote panel on
"Erickson's Use of Humor" with Kristina K. Erickson, M.D., Lance
Erickson, Ph.D., Stephen R. Lankton, M.S.W., and Ernest Rossi, Ph.D.;
a keynote address on "Objects, Language and Reality: Reflections on
an Operational Magic" with Heinz von Foerster, Ph.D.; a keynote debate
on "Indirect versus Direct Approaches to Psychotherapy" featuring Paul
Watzlawick, Ph.D., and Albert Ellis, Ph.D., and a keynote address on
"The Tools of the Therapist" by Virginia Satir, A.C.S.W.

The evening programs at the Congress included an Authors' Hour,
Media Events, a Hospitality Reception and a Banquet.

ACKNOWLEDGMENTS

The assistance of a great many individuals is instrumental in the
success of the meeting. I would like to take this opportunity to thank
them.

The following professionals reviewed abstracts of papers and short
courses submitted for presentation at the Congress: Jeffrey Feldman,

Ph.D., Ronald Havens, Ph.D., Melvin Hector, M.D., Stephen Lankton, M.S.W., Bill O'Hanlon, M.S., and Michael Yapko, Ph.D. Stephen Lankton also shared in all editorial decisions. This book bears the mark of his wisdom and precise, energetic and prompt input as co-editor of these proceedings.

The Editorial Review Board is listed in the front of the book. The editors made an important contribution in reviewing papers for publication in these volumes. Each paper was read by a minimum of two editors.

On behalf of the Board of Directors of the Erickson Foundation, I want to take this additional opportunity to thank the distinguished faculty of the Congress. It was their theoretical and clinical contributions that made the meeting a successful training event.

Special thanks are due to the following people for their contributions: Barry Shephard, SHR Communication Planning and Design, Phoenix, Arizona, who designed the logo for The Milton H. Erickson Foundation. Brent Geary, M.S., Scottsdale, Arizona, donated his time to assist the Foundation Staff.

The Staff of the Erickson Foundation worked endless hours in handling registrations, meeting arrangements and administrative tasks. Led by Sherron Peters, Administrative Director of the Foundation, the following staff deserve special recognition: Sylvia Cowen, bookkeeper; Greg Deniger, computer operator; Joyce Patzer, secretary; Lori Weiers, M.S., secretary; Linda Carr McThrall, registrar; and Barbara Egleston, receptionist.

A number of volunteers helped, both prior to and at the Congress, including Michael Munion, M.A., Martin Zeig and Ruth Zeig. Diane Keith served as Jeffrey Zeig's administrative assistant and was extremely helpful in compiling the proceedings. In addition, there were more than 50 volunteers who served as monitors and staffed the registration and continuing education desks.

The Third International Congress was cosponsored by the Department of Psychiatry, University of Arizona College of Medicine, the Department of Psychology, Arizona State University and the Phoenix Society of Clinical Hypnosis, and their efforts are gratefully acknowledged.

Elizabeth Erickson and Kristina Erickson shared in most executive decisions about the Congress. As members of the Board of Directors they have worked tirelessly on behalf of the Foundation.

I can never express enough appreciation to my wife, Sherron Peters, Board member of The Milton H. Erickson Foundation and Administrative

Director of The Milton H. Erickson Foundation from its inception in 1979 until 1987. The success of the Third International Congress and of the Erickson Foundation are, to a great extent, the product of her dedication and genius.

Jeffrey K. Zeig, Ph.D.
April, 1987   Director
Phoenix, Arizona   Milton H. Erickson Foundation

The Milton H. Erickson
Foundation, Inc.

The Milton H. Erickson Foundation, Inc. is a federal nonprofit corporation. It was formed to promote and advance the contributions made to the health sciences by the late Milton H. Erickson, M.D., during his long and distinguished career. The Foundation is dedicated to training health and mental health professionals. Strict eligibility requirements are maintained for attendance at our training events or to receive our educational materials. The Milton H. Erickson Foundation, Inc. does not discriminate on the basis of race, color, national or ethnic origin, handicap or sex. Directors of The Milton H. Erickson Foundation, Inc. are Jeffrey K. Zeig, Ph.D., Kristina K. Erickson, M.D., Sherron S. Peters, and Elizabeth M. Erickson.

ERICKSON ARCHIVES

In December 1980, the Foundation began collecting audiotapes, videotapes, and historical material on Dr. Erickson for the Erickson Archives. Our goal is to have a central repository of historical material on Erickson. More than 300 hours of videotape and audiotape have already been donated to the Foundation.

The Erickson Archives are available to interested and qualified professionals who wish to come to Phoenix to independently study the audiotapes and videotapes that are housed at the Foundation. There is a nominal charge for use of the Archives. Please write if you are interested in details.

PUBLICATIONS OF THE ERICKSON FOUNDATION

Books

The following books are published by Brunner/Mazel, Publishers:
A Teaching Seminar with Milton H. Erickson (J. Zeig, Ed. & Commen-

tary) is a transcript, with commentary, of a one-week teaching seminar held for professionals by Dr. Erickson in his home in August 1979.

Ericksonian Approaches to Hypnosis and Psychotherapy (J. Zeig, Ed.) contains the edited proceedings of the First International Erickson Congress.

Erickson Psychotherapy, Volume I: Structures, Volume II: Clinical Applications (J. Zeig, Ed.) contain the edited proceedings of the Second International Erickson Congress.

The Evolution of Psychotherapy (J. Zeig, Ed.) contains the edited proceedings of the landmark Evolution of Psychotherapy Conference.

Ericksonian Monographs Number 1: Elements and Dimensions of an Ericksonian Approach (S. Lankton, Ed.), 1985.

Ericksonian Monographs Number 2: Central Themes and Principles of Ericksonian Therapy (S. Lankton, Ed.), 1987.

Ericksonian Monographs Number 3: Treatment of Special Populations with Ericksonian Approaches (S. Lankton & J. Zeig, Eds.), 1988.

Ericksonian Monographs Number 4: Research, Comparisons and Medical Applications of Ericksonian Techniques (S. Lankton & J. Zeig, Eds.), 1988.

Newsletter

The Milton H. Erickson Foundation publishes a newsletter for professionals three times a year to inform its readers of the activities of the Foundation. Articles and notices that relate to Ericksonian approaches to hypnosis and psychotherapy are included and should be sent to the editor, Michael Yapko, Ph.D., Milton Erickson Institute of San Diego, 2525 Camino Del Rio S., Suite 225, San Diego, CA 92018. Business and subscription matters should be directed to the Foundation at 3606 North 24th Street, Phoenix, Arizona 85016.

The Ericksonian Monographs

The Foundation has initiated the publication of the *Ericksonian Monographs*, which appear on an irregular basis, up to three issues per year. Edited by Stephen Lankton, M.S.W., the *Monographs* publish only the highest quality articles on Ericksonian hypnosis and psychotherapy, including technique, theory and research. Manuscripts should be sent to Stephen Lankton, P. O. Box 958, Gulf Breeze, Florida 32561. For subscription information, contact Brunner/Mazel, Publishers.

Audio and Video Training Tapes

The Milton H. Erickson Foundation has available for purchase professionally recorded audiotapes from its meetings. Professionally produced video cassettes of one-hour clinical demonstrations by members of the faculty of the 1981, 1982 and 1984 Erickson Foundation Seminars and the 1983 and 1986 Erickson Congresses can also be purchased from the Foundation.

Audio and video cassettes from The Evolution of Psychotherapy Conference in 1985 are also available from the Foundation.

Audiotapes of Milton H. Erickson

The Erickson Foundation distributes tapes of lectures by Milton Erickson from the 1950s and 1960s when his voice was strong. Releases in our audiotape series are announced in the Newsletter.

Training Videotapes Featuring Hypnotic Inductions
Conducted by Milton H. Erickson

The Process of Hypnotic Induction: A Training Videotape Featuring Inductions Conducted by Milton H. Erickson in 1964. Jeffrey K. Zeig, Ph.D., discusses the process of hypnotic induction and describes the microdynamics of technique that Erickson used in his 1964 inductions. Length: 2 hours.

Symbolic Hypnotherapy. Jeffrey K. Zeig, Ph.D., presents information on using symbols in psychotherapy and hypnosis. Segments of hypnotherapy conducted by Milton Erickson with the same subject on two consecutive days in 1978 are shown. Zeig discusses the microdynamics of Erickson's symbolic technique. Length: 2 hours, 40 minutes.

Videotapes are available in all U.S. formats, as well as in the European standard. For information on purchasing tapes, contact the Erickson Foundation.

TRAINING OPPORTUNITIES

The Erickson Foundation organizes the International Congress on Ericksonian Approaches to Hypnosis and Psychotherapy. These meetings are held triennially in Phoenix, Arizona; the first two meetings were held in 1980 and 1983. Each was attended by over 2,000 professionals. The Third International Congress on Ericksonian Approaches to Hypnosis and Psychotherapy was held December 3–7, 1986. Departing from tradition, the Fourth Congress is scheduled December 7–11, 1988 in San Francisco and will feature an eclectic array of presenters who will address the topic "Brief Therapy: Myths, Methods and Metaphors."

In the intervening years, the Foundation organizes national seminars. The seminars are limited to approximately 450 attendees, and they emphasize skill development in hypnotherapy. The 1981, 1982 and 1984 seminars were held in San Francisco, Dallas and Los Angeles, respectively.

The Milton H. Erickson Foundation organized the landmark Evolution of Psychotherapy Conference considered by many to be a milestone in the history of psychotherapy. Presenting at the Conference were 26 experts each of whom made important contributions to the field. This was the first comprehensive gathering of master practitioners and theorists from major contemporary disciplines. The Conference was held December 11–15, 1985, in Phoenix, Arizona. Faculty included Beck, Bettelheim, Bowen, Ellis, M. Goulding, R. Goulding, Haley, Laing, Lazarus, Madanes, Marmor, Masterson, May, Minuchin, Moreno, E. Polster, M. Polster, Rogers, Rossi, Satir, Szasz, Watzlawick, Whitaker, Wolberg, Wolpe and Zeig.

Regional workshops are held regularly in various locations.

Programs held at the Foundation for local therapists include beginning and advanced ongoing training in hypnotherapy.

All training programs are announced in the Foundation's newsletter.

ERICKSON INSTITUTES

There are a number of Milton Erickson Institutes that have applied to the Foundation for permission to use Erickson's name in the title of their organization. Institutes provide clinical services and professional training. There are institutes in major cities in the United States, in Europe and in Australia. For information contact the Foundation.

THE MILTON H. ERICKSON CENTER FOR HYPNOSIS AND PSYCHOTHERAPY

The Center provides both psychotherapy to clients and training/supervision for professionals. The Center is equipped with observation rooms and audio/video recording capabilities. Clients are seen on a sliding-fee scale. Training and supervision programs for professionals are available. Inquiries regarding services should be made directly to the Center. (Telephone: (602) 956-6795.)

ELIGIBILITY

Training programs, the newsletter, audiotapes, and videotapes are available to professionals in health-related fields, including physicians, doctoral level psychologists and dentists who are qualified for membership in, or are members of their respective professional organizations (AMA, APA, ADA). They are also available to professionals with graduate degrees in areas related to mental health (M.S.W., M.S.N., M.A., or M.S.) from accredited institutions. Full-time graduate students in accredited programs in the above fields must supply a letter from their department, certifying their student status, if they wish to attend training events, subscribe to the newsletter, or purchase tapes.

Faculty of the 1986 International Congress on Ericksonian Psychotherapy: State of the Art

INVITED ADDRESSES

Daniel L. Araoz, Ed.D.
Mineola, NY
Human Sexuality, Hypnosis and Therapy

Joseph Barber, Ph.D.
Los Angeles, CA
The Erickson Legacy: The Power of Hypnosis

Ernst Beier, Ph.D.
Salt Lake City, UT
The Patient's Silent Rules

Richard J. Crowley, Ph.D.

Joyce C. Mills, Ph.D.
North Hollywood, CA
A Multi-Dimensional Approach to the Utilization of Therapeutic Metaphors for Children and Adolescents

Steve de Shazer, M.S.S.W.
Milwaukee, WI
Utilization: The Foundation of Solutions

Betty Alice Erickson Elliott, M.S.
Dallas, TX
Reflections on Training by Erickson: The Mirror Within

Helen Erickson, Ph.D.
West Columbia, SC
Modeling and Role Modeling: An Ericksonian Approach

Kristina K. Erickson, M.D.
Glen Burnie, MD
Individuation of Patient Management

Jeffrey B. Feldman, Ph.D.
New York, NY
The Utilization of Cognition in Psychotherapy: A Comparison of Ericksonian and Cognitive Therapies

David Gordon, M.A.
Lancaster, CA
Linguistics: Manifestation of Experience

D. Corydon Hammond, Ph.D.
  Salt Lake City, UT
  Hypnosis in Marital Therapy
Ronald A. Havens, Ph.D.
  Springfield, IL
  *Erickson's Wisdom Regarding Self-
  Hypnosis: Is This State a Neces-
  sary Part of the Art?*
Lynn D. Johnson, Ph.D.
  Salt Lake City, UT
  *Naturalistic Techniques and the
  "Difficult" Patient*
Alfred Lange, Ph.D.
  Amsterdam, The Netherlands
  *Combining Paradoxical and Con-
  gruent Assignments in Directive
  Family Therapy*
Carol H. Lankton, M.A.
  Gulf Breeze, FL
  *Task Assignments—Logical and
  Otherwise*
Stephen R. Lankton, M.S.W.
  Gulf Breeze, FL
  *An Eco-Systems Approach to
  Therapy*
Herbert S. Lustig, M.D.
  Ardmore, PA
  *So Whose Therapy am I Using
  Anyhow?*
Bill O'Hanlon, M.S.
  Omaha, NE
  *Solutions-Oriented Therapy: A
  Megatrend in Psychotherapy*

Madeleine Richeport, Ph.D.
  Santurce, Puerto Rico
  *Transcultural Issues in Erickson-
  ian Hypnotherapy*
Sidney Rosen, M.D.
  New York, NY
  *What Makes Ericksonian Therapy
  so Effective?*
Ernest Rossi, Ph.D.
  Malibu, CA
  *The Psychobiology of Mind-Body
  Communication and Healing*
Steven J. Sherman, Ph.D.
  Bloomington, IN
  *Ericksonian Psychotherapy and
  Social Psychology*
Kay F. Thompson, D.D.S.
  Carnegie, PA
  Motivation Through Language
Michael D. Yapko, Ph.D.
  San Diego, CA
  Individuation: Alone Together
Carlos Zalaquett, M.A.
  Santiago, Chile
  *A Personal Perspective on Becom-
  ing an Ericksonian*
Jeffrey K. Zeig, Ph.D.
  Phoenix, AZ
  *Aspects of Ericksonian Hypnotic
  Inductions*

INVITED THREE-HOUR WORKSHOPS

Daniel L. Aaroz, Ed.D.
  Mineola, NY
  Hypnodrama

Joseph Barber, Ph.D.
  Los Angeles, CA
  Hypnosis in Psychotherapy

Philip Barretta, M.A.
Norma Barretta, Ph.D.
San Pedro, CA
Language and Change
Franz Baumann, M.D.
San Francisco, CA
Hypnotherapy with Children in a Pediatric Practice
Richard Belson, D.S.W.
Great Neck, NY
Humor in Strategic Therapy
Yvonne Dolan, M.A.
Charles Johnson, M.S.W.
Denver, CO
The Legacy of The February Man: Erickson Age Regression Techniques
Albert Ellis, Ph.D.
New York, NY
Combining Hypnosis and R.E.T.
Richard Fisch, M.D.
John H. Weakland
Palo Alto, CA
Off the Pedestal: Advantages and Limitations in Erickson's Work
John H. Frykman, Ph.D.
Ron Cobley, M.A.
San Francisco, CA
Creating the Time When Change is Possible
Anthony Gaito, A.C.S.W.
Syosset, NY
Introducing Hypnosis in Psychotherapy
Stephen Gilligan, Ph.D.
Encinitas, CA
Symptom Phenomena as Trance Phenomena

David Gordon, M.A.
Lancaster, CA
Therapeutic Metaphor
Norman W. Katz, Ph.D.
Marc Lehrer, Ph.D.
Albuquerque, NM & San Francisco, CA
Living Hypnotically: Hypnosis As a Way of Living, a Path
Alfred Lange, Ph.D.
Amsterdam, The Netherlands
Combining Paradoxical and Congruent Strategies in Directive Therapy
Carol H. Lankton, M.A.
Gulf Breeze, FL
Hypnosis in Marriage and Family Therapy
Stephen R. Lankton, M.S.W.
Gulf Breeze, FL
Methods of Constructing Sophisticated Metaphors for Specific Outcomes of Affect, Attitude, or Behavior
Marc Lehrer, Ph.D.
Norman Katz, Ph.D.
San Francisco, CA & Albuquerque, NM
Living Hypnotically II (Children & Adolescents)
Camillo Loriedo, M.D.
Rome, Italy
Trance Induction and Utilization in Family Therapy
Herbert S. Lustig, M.D.
Ardmore, PA
Foundations of Ericksonian Psychotherapy

Marion R. Moore, M.D.
Deborah Ross, Ph.D.
  Memphis, TN & Los Gatos, CA
  Therapeutic Hypnosis and Change
Bill O'Hanlon, M.S.
  Omaha, NE
  Directive Couples Counseling
Noelle M. Poncelet, Ph.D.
  Menlo Park, CA
  Pain and Pleasure: Awareness and Trust
Sidney Rosen, M.D.
  New York, NY
  "Mind Reading" and Reading Body Language in Hypnotic Therapy
Ernest L. Rossi, Ph.D.
  Malibu, CA
  Creative Life Facilitation with Hypnotherapy
Charles R. Stern, Ph.D.
  Detroit, MI
  Storytelling/Metaphor Construction
Sandra M. Sylvester, Ph.D.
  Tucson, AZ
  Teaching the Self-Regulation of Autonomic Processes

Bruce Tanenbaum, M.D.
  Reno, NV
  Utilizing Ericksonian Techniques in Hypnotic Psychotherapy
Kay F. Thompson, D.D.S.
  Carnegie, PA
  The Language of Hypnosis
Lars-Eric Unestahl, Ph.D.
  Orebro, Sweden
  Systematic Auto-Hypnotic Training for Physical and Creative Performance
Paul Watzlawick, Ph.D.
  Palo Alto, CA
  Psychotherapy of "As If"
R. Reid Wilson, Ph.D.
  Chapel Hill, NC
  Strategic Interventions in Panic Disorder
Michael D. Yapko, Ph.D.
  San Diego, CA
  Ericksonian Approaches in the Treatment of Depression
Jeffrey K. Zeig, Ph.D.
  Phoenix, AZ
  Ericksonian Hypnotherapy

ACCEPTED PAPERS

Chiara Angiolari, Ph.D.
  Rome, Italy
  The Confusion Technique in Family Therapy
Juliet Auer
  Oxon, England
  Ericksonian Hypnosis and Psychotherapy in Clinical Settings

Dean Bathel, A.C.S.W.
Carlos Carreon, A.C.S.W.
  Globe, AZ & Tucson, AZ
  Cross-Cultural Ericksonian Techniques with Mexican-American Clients
Philip J. Booth, M.A.
  Oxford, England
  Strategic Therapy Revisited

Russell A. Bourne, Jr., Ph.D.
Ashland, VA
Promoting Readiness for Trance
Bob Britchford, M.D.
Lambourn, England
Ten-Minute Trance: Ericksonian Techniques in a Busy General Medical Practice
Robert A. Burnham, Ph.D.
Brookline, MA
Using Age Progression in Family Therapy: Hypnotic, Strategic, and Systemic Approaches
Nancy Czech, M.A.
Seattle, WA
Family Therapy with Adolescents Who Have Been Sexually Abusive
Richard E. Dimond, Ph.D.
Springfield, IL
Ericksonian Psychotherapy is the State of the Art: Suggestions for a Future Orientation
Janet S. Edgette, M.P.H.
Glenside, PA
Ericksonian Ethical Standards and APA Ethical Standards: Is There a Difference?
John H. Edgette, Psy.D.
Glenside, PA
"Dangerous to Self and Others": The Management of Acute Psychosis Using Ericksonian Techniques of Hypnosis and Hypnotherapy
Steven H. Feldman, M.A.
Seattle, WA
Applied Techniques of Ericksonian Hypnosis with a Family-of-Origin Approach to Psychotherapy

Jean Godin, M.D., Ph.D.
Paris, France
Evocation versus Suggestion in the Light of Erickson
Sandra Goldhaber, M.S.W.
Lakewood, CO
Strategic Consultation: "Nobody Wants to be a Consultee"
Steven Goldsmith, M.D.
Amherst, MA
The Application of Ericksonian Principles to the Use of Medication
Richard Hatten, Ph.D.
Citrus Heights, CA
Generating Effective Metaphors
David L. Higgins, M.A.
San Diego, CA
A Conscious Look at the Unconscious
Harriet E. Hollander, Ph.D.
Lynn Kilgallen, M.S.W.
Jack Atthowe, Ph.D.
Piscataway, NJ
Hypnosis: Innate Ability or Learned Skill?
John Jay Koriath, Ph.D.
Tempe, AZ
Milton Erickson in an Age of Therapy
Barbara B. LaRaia, B.S.
Tempe, AZ
The Ethics of Hypnosis
Jacques A. Malarewicz, M.D.
Antony, France
Ericksonian Techniques in Family Therapy

ACCEPTED SHORT COURSES

James M. Auld, B.D.S.
Inverell, Australia
Indirect Brief Therapy

Christopher J. Beletsis, Ph.D.
La Jolla, CA
Integrating Change: The Critical Task of Psychotherapy

Betty Blue, Ph.D.
Joan Hensley-David, M.A.
Long Beach, CA &
Santa Ana, CA
Play Therapy for the Bereaved Adult: A "Trance-sending" Approach Toward Grief Work

Paul M. Carter, Ph.D.
Encinitas, CA
Whole Parts Transformation

Lisa Chiara, M.A.
La Jolla, CA
Utilizing Dissociative Behavior with Ericksonian Approaches

Henry T. Close, Th.M.
Plantation, FL
Hypnosis as Nurturing

Gene Combs, M.D.
Jill Freedman, M.S.W.
Evanston, IL
How did Erickson get People to do Those Things? Utilizing Clients' Response Styles

Andrew Condey, Ph.D.
Stephen Goldbart, Ph.D.
Albany, CA
Access to the Unconscious: Ego-Psychological and Hypnotherapeutic Perspectives

Jill H. Freedman, M.S.W.
Gene Combs, M.D.
Evanston, IL
What to do with the Client's Metaphors as You Discover Them

Richard J. Gellerman, Ph.D.
Tucson, AZ
Conversational Unconscious Communication

Herbert L. Gravitz, Ph.D.
Julie Bowden, M.S.
Santa Barbara, CA
The Utilization of Trance States with Adult Children of Alcoholics

Alan N. Griffin, Ph.D.
Eric C. Steese, Ph.D.
Dallas, TX
Erickson, Humor and Healing

Brian Grodner, Ph.D.
Albuquerque, NM
Ericksonian Approaches to Permanent Weight Reduction and Non-Smoking

Linden L. Guthrie, M.A.
Templeton, MA
Co-utilization of Therapeutic Personalities in Hypnotherapy: An Evolving Model for Treating Dissociative Disorders

Carl A. Hammerschlag, M.D.
Paradise Valley, AZ
Erickson as Medicineman or: On the Spirit and Mystery of Mind Healing

Richard A. Leva, Ph.D.
Fredonia, NY
Hidden Hypnotic Communication in Therapeutic Situations not Defined as Trance

William K. Lombardo, Ph.D.
Claremont, CA
The Many Faces of Ericksonian Therapy

William J. Matthews, Ph.D.
Amherst, MA
Ericksonian Hypnosis in Couples Therapy: Theory and Practice

Michael J. Paulus, L.C.S.W.
Wendy Hurley, M.F.C.C.
Eureka, CA & Fortuna, CA
Hypnotic Unlocking of an Individual's Defensive Process During Family Therapy

Mark Reese, M.A.
Encinitas, CA
Somatic Learning: Integrating Feldenkrais and Ericksonian Approaches

Helmut Relinger, Ph.D.
Berkeley, CA
Indirect Suggestions in the Treatment of Depression

Ilana Rubenfeld
Paul Carter, Ph.D.
New York, NY & Encinitas, CA
Trance, Movement, and Touch

Gary Ruelas, M.A.
Terry Argast, Ph.D.
Richard Landis, Ph.D.
Santa Ana, CA & Anaheim, CA
Now, You Wanted a Trance Demonstration Today

George A. Sargent, Ph.D.
Bleema Moss, M.F.C.C.
Vista, CA & Hillcrest, CA
Ericksonian Techniques in Family Mediation: You Know Why I'm Waiting for . . .

Gunther Schmidt, M.D.
Wilhelmsfeld, West Germany
Circular Hypnotherapy–The Milan Systematic Family Therapy Approach Utilized as Ericksonian Hypnotherapy

Robert Schwarz, Psy.D.
Philadelphia, PA
The Use of Posthypnotic Suggestions in Hypnotic Pain Control

Jerrold Lee Shapiro, Ph.D.
Alan W. Scheflin, J.D.
Susan Bernadett-Shapiro, R.N., M.S.
Santa Clara, CA
Trance on Trial: The Legal Implications of Ericksonian Hypnotherapy

John C. Simpson, III, Ph.D.
Matthews, NC
Diagnosing: Reframing to Help Parents Establish a Context for Change

Thomas C. Walsh, Ph.D.
Liverpool, NY
Using Ericksonian Hypnosis with Adult Children of Alcoholics: Innovations in Treatment

Catherine Walters, M.A.
Springfield, IL
Building Inner Resources: Using Self-Hypnosis to Enhance Therapist Flexibility and Intervention Creativity

Ellen W. Williams, Ph.D.
  Tempe, AZ
  *Ericksonian Hypnotherapy/Be-
  havior Therapy: Weight Control
  in Groups*
J. Adrian Williams, Ph.D.
  Charleston, IL
  *Utilization of Classical Hypnotic
  Phenomena in Symbolic Psycho-
  therapy*

Rothlyn P. Zahourek, R.N., M.S.
Dorothy Larkin, R.N., M.A.
  New York, NY
  *"Nursing Hypnosis": Ericksonian
  Hypnotic Approaches in Nursing*

MODERATORS

Stephen Bacon, Ph.D.
  Greenwich, CT
Sally Franek, Ph.D.
  Williamsburg, VA
Robert N. Glenn, Ph.D.
  Richmond, VA
Scott M. Kamilar, Ph.D.
  Houston, TX
James R. Lane, Ph.D.
  Tempe, AZ
Jane Parsons, M.S.W.
  New York, NY

John Racy, M.D.
  Tucson, AZ
Reese Price, Ph.D.
  Tulsa, OK
Manfred Prior, Dip.Psy.
  Hamburg, West Germany
Zeva Singer, M.A.
  Laytonville, CA
Larry Stephens, A.C.S.W.
  Oak Park, IL
Lis A. Wells, M.S.
  Asheville, NC

SPECIAL FACULTY

Lance Erickson, Ph.D.
  West Columbia, SC

Robert Erickson, M.A.
  Phoenix, AZ

Developing Ericksonian Therapy

State of the Art

SECTION ONE: PRINCIPLES

PART I

Position Statements

Chapter 1

What Makes Ericksonian Therapy So Effective?

Sidney Rosen

Sidney Rosen, M.D. (University of Western Ontario), is in private practice in New York City. Rosen is an Assistant Clinical Professor of Psychiatry at New York University Medical Center and University Hospital. He has considerable background in psychoanalysis and is on the faculty of the American Institute for Psychoanalysis (Karen Horney). Founding President of the New York Society for Ericksonian Psychotherapy and Hypnosis, Rosen has been an invited faculty member of three International Congresses on Ericksonian Approaches to Hypnosis and Psychotherapy (1980, 1983 and 1986) and three national Erickson seminars. He has conducted workshops on Ericksonian approaches at various locations in the United States and Europe. Author of numerous professional publications, Rosen is the editor of My Voice Will Go With You: The Teaching Tales of Milton H. Erickson.

Rosen presents fundamental aspects of Erickson's approach and outlines factors which are effective in all forms of psychotherapy.

On Nov. 16th, 1986, *The New York Times* (Lindsey, 1986) featured a front-page article about a Mrs. Knight, who maintained that a 35,000-year-old man, Ramtha, "used her body to speak words of wisdom." This rather ordinary-looking, 40-year-old American woman commands a following of thousands and her long mesmerizing monologues are attended by hundreds of people who pay $400 each. Many of them feel that this is the best money they have ever spent.

After attending one of her seminars, George Hain, a millionaire businessman from Cheyenne, Wyoming, "returned to Cheyenne (the

5

next day), disposed of his five Burger King restaurants and moved to a rural area in northern California, where he is building a house that is shaped like a pyramid, he says, to 'manifest the energy' of the universe." However, one of her more skeptical observers reported, "She's either psychotic or she's a good actress. She's obviously a fake, but she sure is a spellbinder."

In our terms, she is able to enter into a trance, to do "automatic speaking," to influence large groups of people, and to voice oracular pronouncements, coupled with prophesies of doom for those who do not follow her advice. Can we, with all our education, training, hard work and sincere caring for our patients, inspire, guide and heal them more successfully than does Mrs. Knight or the hundreds of other gurus or the thousands of other "healers" and "channelers" who are offering their skills today? Mrs. Knight, with good old American entrepreneurial directness, says, "I'm not a guru. . . . This is a business." We claim that we are practicing a healing or a teaching profession. As professionals, we are constantly questioning ourselves and undergoing self-examination. We strive to improve our skills and help our patients more effectively.

I am not prepared at this time to discuss the intriguing question of our effectiveness in comparison with guides, healers, and gurus. Just comparing our effectiveness with other psychotherapists is enough of a challenge.

When I talk about "Ericksonian Therapy," I run into difficulties. I recall the comments that people would make to Erickson about hypnosis: "I know what hypnosis is now—it is suggestion!" "I know what hypnosis is—it is concern with body image." "I know—it is transference." "It is relationship." "It is regression." "It is dissociation." "It is focusing of attention." And Erickson would answer, "Is that a . . a . . a . . all?"

Probably every one of the hundreds of therapists and students who visited Erickson had his or her own idea of what was the central feature, the secret of hypnotherapy. At congresses such as this one, scholarly researchers and clinicians are still trying to pinpoint the true "jewel in the lotus." And we can imagine Erickson, saying to each one of us who believes that he or she has identified that central feature, "Is that a . . a . . a . . all?"

As I tried to put my finger on factors that make Ericksonian therapy so effective (and I realize that outside of meetings such as this Third International Congress I would not necessarily get universal agreement that it *is* "so effective"), I found myself coming up with the same kind of unsatisfying partial answers, answers such as these:

Ericksonian therapy is especially effective because it uses trance states which heighten suggestibility, and suggestion is a major element in all psychotherapies. Or, Ericksonian therapy is especially effective because it allows for and encourages experimentation on the part of therapist and patient. Because of the concept of reframing. Because of its emphasis on health and resources rather than pathology. Because of its focus on goals, rather than genesis. Because it applies "systems thinking." Because . . . because . . .

I despaired that, even if we could agree that there is such an entity as "Ericksonian psychotherapy" and that it *is* so effective, we would be unlikely to be able to pin down one or two elements that lead to its being "so effective."

In this chapter I will discuss some of the more demonstrable or observable elements in the therapies which each of us devises for himself or herself, based on what we think we have learned directly and indirectly from the writings and teachings of Milton Erickson. And, after finishing this self-indulgence, I expect Milton to have his voice go with me, asking, with a chuckle, "Is that a . . a . . a . . all?"

Still, I will proceed with my observations and theses, which are based on my own experience of almost 40 years of exploring the effects of many different approaches to psychotherapy. I also will take into consideration some of the reported experiences of others. It would be foolish of me to argue that other forms of psychotherapy are not effective. I propose, however, that, when they are effective, it is because of the elements that I will outline in this paper. In other words, I will take on the rather daunting task of outlining the main elements which make *any* form of psychotherapy effective.

NOVELTY

I create a new theory for each patient. (Erickson, personal communication, 1977)

"Practitioners of various forms of behavior therapy are also taking longer to obtain results" (Klein et al., 1969). "It is hard to believe that the lengthening of treatment reflects changes in the severity of patients' problems or symptoms. More probably it reflects a decrease in therapists' zeal with the disappearance of the novelty effect, and reduction of the need to proselytize as therapy gains recognition" (Frank, 1973). Several studies (Frank, 1973, p. 167) have shown that medical students obtain about the same improvement rates in short-term therapy as do psychiatrists. Certainly the zeal that goes with novelty applies here.

Since Ericksonian therapy is now in the forefront of some people's awareness, it will take us a while to determine whether this situation prevails here. In my own experience, I have found that whenever I have tried a new approach to therapy, I would get good results at first. Curiosity, zeal, enthusiasm, novelty . . . whatever it is, these are all very important factors which the therapist brings to the therapy and which are conveyed to the patient. Certainly, if, like Erickson, we approach each patient as a new challenge and create a new therapy for him, we will maintain this zeal.

THERAPIST ACTIVITY

If you do not do, I will do. (Erickson, personal communication, 1978)

Frank (1973, p. 186) also quotes Whitehorn and Betz (1954): "More successful therapists offered a therapeutic relationship characterized by active, personal participation rather than passive permissive interpretation and instruction or practical care." In this regard Erickson's degree of active involvement in his patients' lives was rarely seen in the work of other therapists of his day. Even today, especially in psychoanalytic circles, that degree of involvement is frowned upon.

For patients who did not have the initiative or the know-how to seek out community resources, Erickson would make arrangements for them to receive help and advice in all areas, ranging from help in dressing and grooming to advice on buying genuine, high-quality turquoise ("Go to the Heard Museum"). He would accompany patients on dinner dates and arrange for the waitress to treat them in a prescribed manner. He would stage fights in order to help desensitize a patient to anger. He would do whatever was necessary to promote therapeutic or growth experiences.

FLEXIBILITY AND ADAPTABILITY

Therapies may focus predominantly on the past, the present, or the future. Erickson's approaches—with age-regression, doing and experiencing on the present, and pseudo-orientation in time or age-progression—encompass all of these. Of course, if we simply use the hypnotic state in order to bring back memories from early childhood, as in hypnoanalysis, it might not be considered "Ericksonian," but on the other hand it is not prohibited within an Ericksonian framework.

Erickson was noted for developing and varying his approaches according to the existing climate and the uniqueness of the patient. In his early years, working with Lawrence Kubie, he used analytic understandings. In his later experimentation, he applied imagery and what could be called cognitive approaches. He constantly developed applications of nonverbal communication. He learned the language of psychotics, of children, of workers, and of mystics, speaking to each in their own language, even while apologizing that, "I know that I can never really understand the language of another person." He brought to his therapeutic approaches anything of value that he had learned from different areas of human knowledge—history, literature, anthropology, science, and, of course, medicine. In exploring ways of getting people to move or to change, he developed approaches which have been dubbed "strategic."

When I review the contents of a single issue of any psychotherapy journal, I am struck by many factors that might be considered *the* essential features which make therapy effective including production of dissociation, transference, corrective emotional experiences, and insight. Perhaps the strength of Erickson was that he did not exclude any of these, but rather included all of them and added his own innovations.

The technique of "reframing" has become identified with Erickson although other therapies also use it. Approaches which I have dubbed "corrective regression" are based on Erickson's "February Man" and are truly original; they do not seem to be included in any other therapeutic approaches. They involve the actual creation of new memories or, as somebody has put it, they prove that "it is never too late to have a happy childhood."

Erickson's own summation of "hypnosis" was that "hypnosis is the evocation and utilization of unconscious learnings" (Rosen, 1982a, p. 28). As he said, in order to do therapy, all you do is: "First you model the patient's world, and then you role-model the patient's world" (Rosen, 1982a, p. 35). The approaches mentioned above and dozens of others are applied within this flexible framework.

MULTILEVEL COMMUNICATION

We are all aware that a patient communicates with us on many levels. Erickson has made us more aware of the fact that we also communicate with the patient on many levels. When this communication is done with thought and intent, and when we are aware of the various ways in which we can communicate therapeutically, our results are bound to be better than if we simply rely on our desire to help, trusting that verbal interpretations, clarifications, and suggestions will be sufficient to enable us to help our patients.

A LEARNING APPROACH RATHER THAN A PATHOLOGY-FOCUSED ONE

Therapy is the substitution of a good idea for a bad idea. (Erickson, personal communication, 1978)

Erickson seemed to think of life's problems, including neuroses and psychoses, as arising from faulty or insufficient learning, or from inability to utilize the learning which we have already acquired. The therapeutic situation gives the opportunity for new learnings and for the utilization of helpful old learnings. The therapist guides the patient, acting as a model, as a teacher, and sometimes as a guru. Learning is generally more easily achieved when the patient is in a trance state. The therapist uses the trance state in himself in order to make the best contact with the patient, and to more completely understand him. And as Minuchin stated in his letter to Erickson (Rosen, 1982a, p. 18), Erickson was able "to look at simple moments and describe their complexity" and had "trust in the capacity of human beings to harness a repertory of experiences they do not know they have."

If what is learned is a result of therapeutic experiences that help the person to cope better with life, the new patterns and approaches will likely be retained and built upon so that the results will be long-lasting. They will be retained only if they can free the person to continue growing and learning.

MAGIC AND ENTERING A NEW REALITY

Every child likes a surprise. (Erickson, personal communication, 1970)

When a person entered into Erickson's sphere, he entered into a new reality—a world of magic, of childhood, and of whimsical humor. In this atmosphere we are likely to revert to childlike responses, to childlike openness to learning, and to the malleability of childhood. When a therapist can create a world of wonder, of freshness of view, his patients are likely to respond with the "suggestibility" of children. Therapeutic suggestions and role modelling are bound to be more effective than they would be if presented only to the conscious, logical, "left brain" mind.

Healing has always been associated with magic, as in the healing rituals and practices of so-called "primitive" groups, or the reported practices of the temple priests in biblical times. Hypnosis has also always been associated with magic, despite efforts by Erickson and others "to disassociate the study of hypnosis from mystical and unscientific connotations" (Rosen, 1982a, p. 192). In spite of our disavowals, when we do therapy under the aegis of hypnosis, we tend to arouse, in many patients, particularly the most desperate ones, overt or latent magical beliefs, and this may add power to our interventions, whether or not we ourselves believe in magic. We can benefit from the popular association between hypnosis, magic and mysticism. In scientific circles, it leads to hypnosis being viewed with scorn, but with desperate patients it adds power to our therapy and may, indeed, be one of the more powerful factors in making Ericksonian therapy "so effective."

ORACULAR PRONOUNCEMENTS, INTERPRETATIONS AND DIRECTIONS

You know much more than you think you know.

Your unconscious mind will protect your conscious mind. And, at an appropriate time, in an appropriate place, your unconscious mind will let your conscious mind know something that you already know, but don't know that you know. (Erickson, personal communication, 1970)

It appears that people are most helpful to themselves when they come to their own conclusions about the causes of their problems and discover their own solutions. The wheel does seem to have to be invented over and over again. In Ericksonian therapy, this inclination is encouraged by what I call "oracular" comments, predictions and interpretations. These are statements made in ways that access the patient's inclination to look into himself—to discover his own resources and his own explanations. They can be applied by almost every person to himself or herself: for example, "You have sometimes wished that your parents would die, yet you were terrified that your wish might be fulfilled" or, "you have some deep-seated feelings of inadequacy."

In dealing with a patient who has premature ejaculations, I might say, "I do not know anything about your background, your childhood, your family, your sexual history. But *you* know about these things. And you can, in a trance, get in touch with the things you know but don't know that you know and you can find attitudes and approaches that will enable you to enjoy sex in ways that you desire." The patient can do his inner searching and testing of solutions more quickly alone (especially with the aid of time distortion) than he could while verbalizing his thoughts and associations. I might add, "There are certainly good reasons for your sexual responses and these good reasons will be respected, won't they?" (The implication is that invalid reasons can be ignored or overridden.)

To the above I might add, "You can find ways of changing your sexual response so that you are able to achieve and give much more satisfaction than you have been able to up to this time." Evaluation of "how much is much?" is very subjective, of course. In other words, it will be done, again, according to the patient's needs and in keeping with his values, goals and understandings.

These types of statements, including truisms, "pacing" and an invitation for an inner search, are similar to the pronouncements at the Oracle of Delphi in that they are interpreted by each listener according to his own needs and understandings.

ENCOURAGING A MINIMAL CHANGE

Therapy is like starting a snowball rolling down a mountain. It builds up momentum and it can grow into an avalanche—and all the therapist has to do is start the snowball rolling. (Erickson, personal communication, 1978)

It has been noted that hypnotic subjects want to please the hypnotist. Paradoxically, with open-ended suggestions and directions, the patient can best please by pleasing himself, perhaps by interpreting his future responses so as to confirm the therapist's expectation that the patient can solve his own problem. He may also interpret his future responses so as to produce a positive effect of the therapist's open-ended, generalized "oracular" statements. Subsequently, he will have the feeling that he is making progress. This feeling of success leads to increased confidence, to a readiness to take risks, which may lead to still further progress, and so on.

As a patient is encouraged to value minimal changes, he is likely to expect to make further changes. At least the readiness to change and explore and experiment is increased when some changes, even minimal ones, are recognized.

ALTERED STATES OF CONSCIOUSNESS

Hypnosis is the evocation and the utilization of unconscious learnings. (Rosen, 1982a, p. 28)

Intrapsychically

If we examine all psychotherapies, we find that change is most likely to be initiated when the patient is in an altered state of consciousness. Some might even say that all healing is promoted with alterations in consciousness. Doctors have traditionally prescribed rest or a voyage or a change of scene for many chronic ailments. Medications such as hypnotics and tranquilizers, group experiences leading to emotional abreactions, sleep cures and activity cures, all lead to alterations of the patients' usual states of consciousness.

Simply helping a patient to enter into a state of consciousness which is different from that in which he is symptomatic may alleviate the symptoms or the disturbed mode of functioning. Rossi, in his outline of the stages of hypnotic induction, points out that the second stage is the interruption and depotentiation of the patient's usual mental sets (Erickson & Rossi, 1979). This depotentiation may apply not only to the set at the moment but also, with post-hypnotic suggestions, to the patient's "symptomatic mental set" which may be associated with compulsions, anxiety, depression, and so on. Thus, trance inductions, per se, may be very helpful for many patients.

The next stage of hypnotic induction—the "inner search," with or without guidance from the therapist—may lead to more specific therapeutic changes. Thus, on an intrapsychic level, the use of trance may expedite therapy.

Interpersonally

Contact between therapist and patient, which may lead to the patient's increased capacity to establish and maintain better contact with friends and intimates, is widely understood to be an important element in psychotherapy. It is often discussed under the rubric of "therapist-patient" relationship. In approaches such as Gestalt therapy it is specifically emphasized. Martin Buber has stated that it is only man with man who can be fulfilled or it is only in an "I-Thou" relationship that growth can occur. In other words, it is only in close or intimate relationship with others that one can grow. The therapeutic relationship should be one of these.

The trance state involves one of the most intimate relationships. In fact, in the trance state the barrier between the hypnotist and the subject is broken down and to some extent may even be eliminated. The subject then experiences the hypnotist's voice as coming from inside himself. In other words, it sounds and feels like his own voice. Obviously, the patient will not necessarily follow even his own inner vocalizations all the time, but they are certainly more influential than the voices of others.

In the trance state there really appears to be communication with the "unconscious mind" of the patient, communication on the deepest levels. As a result, the patient is most receptive to therapeutic interventions, whether they be strategic prescriptions, role modelling, indirect suggestions, behavioral instructions, or cognitive restructuring.

CHANGE OF SELF-CONCEPT

All successful therapies implicitly or explicitly change the patient's image of himself, as a person who is overwhelmed by his symptoms and problems to that of one who can master them. (Frank, 1973, p. 330)

Techniques such as self-hypnosis promote this sense of mastery directly. The patient will no longer feel so overwhelmed by anxieties, by phobias, by his limitations.

Changing "inner scripts" and "inner dialogues" can be accomplished most effectively when the patient is in a trance state. Ego boosting suggestions are routinely used.

"All forms of psychotherapy help the patient overcome his sense of alienation from his fellows" (Frank, 1973). In Ericksonian therapy this is especially likely to happen when patients are seen in a group, as in Erickson's teaching seminars. Here the element of commonly shared experiences and being able to relate more closely to one another was more likely to be experienced, particularly with the breaking down of barriers that occurs when people are in a hypnotic trance together.

EXPERIENCE COUNTS

You don't learn to do psychotherapy from books. You learn from experience. (Erickson, personal communication, 1978)

Our patients also learn to live from experience. Since the 1960s, the trend in psychotherapy has been to emphasize experiencing rather than insight. As Fromm-Reichman said, "Patients need experiences, not explanations."* Ericksonian approaches make experiencing, often with heightened emotions, more likely to happen than with the more intellectually oriented approaches. With a focusing of attention on them in a trance state, experiences in the therapeutic session are apt to be more vivid, whether they be a heightened awareness of present perceptions, thoughts and emotions or a "reliving," even in fantasy, of past experiences.

I have seen many patients who have undergone years of psychoanalysis or psychoanalytically-oriented psychotherapy and who have told me that they had never really *experienced* some early memories before doing so in a trance state. My own personal experience with Erickson confirms this.

Having an intense or dramatic experience, particularly one that has not been experienced before, is a real "convincer" of the power of the therapy. And the broadening of experiencing in the therapeutic session often makes possible a parallel, or even extended, broadening of experiencing in life.

In the dedication of his book, *The Language of Change*, Paul Watzlawick (1978) paid tribute "to Milton H. Erickson who heals with words."

---

* Quoted by Rollo May at The Evolution of Psychotherapy Conference, December, 1985, Phoenix, Ariz.

Elsewhere, Watzlawick (1982) writes, "What he taught us above all was a different use of language. Traditionally, the language of therapy is the language of interpretation, explanation, clarification and the like. It is an explanatory language and must be so because it stands in the service of consciousness-raising. By contrast, the language of hypnosis is injunctive, because its ultimate message, no matter how carefully veiled, is '*Do* something!' " (p. 149).

EXPLANATIONS AND PSEUDO-EXPLANATIONS

Any acceptable explanation can relieve anxiety and promote hope. This is probably the way "insight" helps in most psychotherapies. Sometimes it is difficult to differentiate between a "true" explanation and a pseudo-explanation, and from the point of view of the patient it seems to make little difference, at least for the purpose of relieving anxiety.

Watzlawick has pointed out the therapeutic value of naming a patient's condition. (Physicians call it diagnosing.) He quotes Gordon Allport's story of a dying patient to illustrate this. The patient had been informed that the physicians could not diagnose his condition. A bit of hope was held that a famous visiting specialist might have more luck. The visitor did not even pause at the poor patient's bedside. He simply strode past and proclaimed "moribundus"—on the verge of death. After hearing this "diagnosis" the patient made a rapid and complete recovery (Watzlawick, 1985).

If we reframe a situation into one which augments a patient's sense of worth instead of diminishing it (positive reframing), we are going a step further. For example, I am doing this if I tell a patient with premature ejaculation that he is suffering not from a lack of sexual strength, but from too much sexual energy. I am renaming his "premature ejaculation" as "excess sexual drive." Subsequently, we do not need to spend weeks or years in "uncovering" the "causes" of this "ailment." Instead, we can teach him to direct and control this energy— a much easier and quicker process.

SUGGESTION

Freud's fear that someday the pure gold of psychoanalysis would be polluted by the lead of suggestion was unwarranted. The "pollution" had already occurred! Expectations of the patient and therapist and suggestion are powerful elements in all psychotherapies, including psychoanalysis. In Ericksonian psychotherapy these elements are emphasized explicitly. Thus, our concern is not whether or not we will use suggestion, but to what end that suggestion is to be directed. What are the goals and values that the therapist is promoting and encouraging? Or, what goals do the therapist and patient evolve together?

Suggestions can be thought of as coming primarily from the patient (autosuggestions) or from the therapist (heterosuggestions).

Autosuggestions

These are generated by the patient's expectations, values, beliefs, inner images, scripts, and inner dialogues, all of which contribute to the patient's self-concept and emanate from it. As Paracelsus said, "Even as man imagines himself to be, such he is, and he is also that which he imagines" (Damon, 1971, p. 322).

Values, beliefs and life scripts may be thought of as long-term autosuggestions. They may also apply on a short-term basis. Erickson told a story (Rossi, Ryan, & Sharp, 1983) in which he described a patient at the Colorado Psychopathic Hospital who had announced, "I'm going to die next Saturday morning. I am dying on Saturday at 10 o'clock in the morning, on such and such a date." He said the man slept well and ate well. His blood pressure was fine. His blood chemistry was fine. Every index in his physical examination was fine. Saturday morning we all gathered around and watched that patient die at 10 o'clock. The autopsy showed no reason whatsoever for the patient's death. Erickson's conclusion was, "It shows the effects of thoughts and feelings and attitudes and beliefs on the functioning of the human body. (These same mechanisms are the ones you try to direct and utilize in a positive way in hypnosis)" (p. 180).

Working with patients on the deepest levels, such as the level of beliefs, may often make it unnecessary to deal with specific areas of their lives or with symptoms. Altering the roots or the foundation may lead to proliferation of the newer, healthier structures to the branches.

Heterosuggestions

These include the expectations and suggestions, direct and indirect, of the therapist. As we can clearly see now, psychoanalysis, along with all other psychotherapies, has, from its beginning, derived many of its successes largely from suggestion. The power of suggestions is heightened by the intense "positive transference" or "rapport" which is associated with a trance state. Psychoanalytic patients enter into a trance state as the result of undergoing the process of inner searching and free associating, while in the state of sensory deprivation, which characterizes the psychoanalytic situation. In fact, psychoanalysis is really a slower form of hypnotic therapy.

By hypnotic therapy I mean a therapy which aims at changing behavior, thinking and responses which we consider "unconscious." By "unconscious" I refer to parts of the mind which may, under certain circumstances, be dissociated from consciousness. And Erickson's definition, "Hypnosis is the evocation and the utilization of unconscious learnings" (Rosen, 1982a, p. 28), applies equally well to psychoanalysis. It is slower, that's all. And, sometimes, it may be better to be slower.

Psychoanalysts expect that if their patients can come up with and then "work through" "repressed material" they will get better. When these expectations are met, the patients are likely to value themselves more highly and have the courage to venture into other new behavior. Erickson also had expectations of his patients. When asked, "Why do patients do the crazy things you ask?" his answer once was, "Because I expect them to" (personal communication, 1978). He not only expected them to do as he asked, but he asked them to do things, such as surpassing their previous limitations, which would insure their getting well.

Working with his guidance, we therapists have more options than those allowed by any one "school" of therapy. Our patients also have more options. They can "get better" (I'm using this simple phrase to include relief of symptoms, overcoming of limitations, growth, capacity to cope) as a result of abreaction, relearning, self-understanding, imaging, carrying on new inner dialogues, or changing inner scripts. They can get better by going beyond their previous restrictions in behavior and thinking and feeling. And this transcendence of previous limitations may be engineered by the therapist with strategies which make it possible for new experiencing to occur.

I agree with Hammond (1984) that too much emphasis has been placed on Erickson's use of confusion techniques and of indirect suggestion. In most cases, it is probable that clear-cut direct suggestions and guidance are most appropriate and most effective. But, as Zeig (1980) has noted, "The amount of indirection necessary is directly proportional to the perceived resistance" (p. 25). The planning and use of interspersed suggestions, anecdotes, and word plays may make these suggestions more acceptable to some patients, but, as Erickson pointed out, they add to the "elegance" of the treatment, thus making the doing of therapy more interesting and more fun for the therapist and patient. Patients benefit more from being with a therapist who enjoys his work than with one who is bored.

Goals of the Therapist

Erickson's goals or expectations for his patients were that they would achieve a greater sense of mastery in their own lives, a sense of optimism, an ability to live in the present while relating well to others and contributing to the welfare of others.

Another way of outlining the goals of Ericksonian psychotherapy is that they are aimed at helping us achieve a sense of comfort, mastery and self-worth.

WHAT IS PATIENT CURED FROM? WHAT IS HE CURED TO?

We may not be able to compete with faith healers, gurus and quacks in terms of numbers. Hopefully we can offer better or healthier possibilities of growth, self-fulfillment and contributions to society. In order to do this, however, we must be cognizant of our own values and, like Erickson, strive toward expanding our own learning, growth and social contributions. "We all have our limitations," Erickson said. "We have to discover what those limitations really are" (personal communication, 1978).

HUMOR

Spread humor knee deep everywhere. (Erickson, personal communication, 1980)

The healing power of humor has been recognized more and more in recent years. Obviously it helps us and our patients when we can put things into perspective. We need to see the patient's dilemmas and our own problems in the light of the ultimate absurdities and with knowledge of the pitifully short time that we have in which to enjoy our life and fulfill some purpose. The distance that one needs in order to view systems is most easily achieved when we adopt a humorous or whimsical stance. And, with the feeling that everything is not necessarily a matter of life and death, we and, by example, our patients may have the courage to take the risks and make the changes that, as Shakespeare pointed out in Hamlet's soliloquy, we are so loath to do.

CONCLUSION

As I was finishing writing this chapter, my daughter hypnotized me and suggested that I follow the above advice and take a lighter view of the opus that I have just presented to you. In my trance I saw a bunch of people serving themselves from a smorgasbord. So, here it is. Serve yourself. Take what is useful to you. Chew on it, add your own spices and condiments to your taste. Digest it well . . . and eliminate any excesses or irrelevancies.

REFERENCES

Damon, S. F. (1971). *A Blake Dictionary: The Ideas and Symbols of William Blake.* New York: Dutton.

Erickson, M. H., & Rossi, E. L. (1979). *Hypnotherapy: An Exploratory Casebook.* New York: Irvington.

Erickson, M. H., Rossi, E. L., & Ryan, M. O. (Eds.) (1985). *Life Reframing in Hypnosis.* New York: Irvington.

Frank, J. (1973). *Persuasion and Healing.* Baltimore: Johns Hopkins U. Press.

Hammond, D. C. (1984, April). Myths about Erickson and Ericksonian hypnosis. *Am. J. of Clin. Hypnosis, 26,* 4.

Heine, R. W. (Ed.) (1962). *The Student Physician as Psychotherapist.* Chicago: Univ. of Chicago Press.

Hoffman, E. (1981). *The Way of Splendour.* Boulder, Col. and London: Shambala.

Klein, M. H., Dittman, A. T., Parloff, M. R., & Gill, M. W. (1969). Behavior therapy: Observations and reflections. *J. Consult. Clin. Psychol., 33,* 259–66.

Lindsey, R. (1986). Teachings of "Ramtha" Draw Hundreds West. *New York Times,* Nov. 16, p. 1.

Rosen, S. (1982a). *My Voice Will Go With You: The Teaching Tales of Milton H. Erickson.* New York: W. W. Norton.

Rosen, S. (1982b). The values and philosophy of Milton H. Erickson. In J. K. Zeig (Ed.), *Ericksonian Approaches to Hypnosis and Psychotherapy* (p. 468). New York: Brunner/ Mazel.

Rossi, E. L., Ryan, M. O., & Sharp, F. A. (Eds.) (1983). *Healing in Hypnosis.* New York: Irvington.

Turnbull, C. (1983). *The Human Cycle* (p. 45). New York: Simon & Shuster.

Uhlenhuth, E. H., & Duncan, D. B. (1968). Subjective change with medical student therapist: Some determinants of change in psychoneurotic outpatients. *Arch. Gen. Psychiat., 18,* 532–540.

Watzlawick, P. (1978). *The Language of Change.* New York: Basic Books.

Watzlawick, P. (1982). Erickson's contribution to the interactional view of psychotherapy.

In J. K. Zeig (Ed.), *Ericksonian Approaches to Hypnosis and Psychotherapy.* New York: Brunner/Mazel.

Watzlawick, P. (1985). Hypnotherapy without trance. In J. K. Zeig (Ed.), *Ericksonian Psychotherapy Vol. I: Structures.* New York: Brunner/Mazel.

Whitehorn, J. C., & Betz, B. J. (1954). *Am. J. of Psychiat., 111,* 321–331.

Zeig, J. K. (Ed.) (1980). *A Teaching Seminar with Milton H. Erickson, M.D.* (p. 25). New York: Brunner/Mazel.

Chapter 2

The Irony of the Ericksonian Legend: The Power of Hypnosis

Joseph Barber

Joseph Barber, Ph.D. (University of Southern California), Associate Clinical Professor at the UCLA Neuropsychiatric Institute, has a private practice in Los Angeles. With his wife, Cheri Adrian, he coedited Psychological Approaches to the Management of Pain, *which received the Arthur Shapiro Award from the Society for Clinical and Experiential Hypnosis as the best book on hypnosis in 1983.*

Barber is Assistant Editor for the American Journal of Clinical Hypnosis, *a fellow of the American Society of Clinical Hypnosis, and diplomate, American Board of Psychological Hypnosis. He has been an invited member of the faculty of Erickson Foundation Congresses and Seminars each year since their inception in 1980. He travels extensively, both nationally and internationally, to teach hypnosis and psychotherapy.*

Barber admonishes that we remain rigorous in our attempts to develop a solid basis for Ericksonian practice. Indirection and poetic interventions are not therapy per se. Technique is measured by effect, not by the cleverness of its structure. The concept of "trance" must have a verifiable basis, and should not be watered down. Followup studies clarify what methods are effective and limit self-deception. There must be accountability, clinically and experimentally.

Barber's arguments are persuasive and timely. The early phase of the Erickson movement has been one of proliferation. Barber calls us to enter a phase of consolidation.

EARLY ERICKSON, LATER ERICKSON, AND THE "ERICKSONIANS"

Beginning in the 1930s, Milton Erickson excited professional interest by demonstrating the power of hypnosis as a clinical tool. It was not, of course, that he invented the use of hypnosis in psychotherapy, but he did make innovations in the way that it was used, while developing his own unique approach. He brought widespread attention to the use of hypnosis in psychotherapy at a time when its use as a tool in psychotherapy had begun to decline.

Erickson demonstrated that hypnosis could produce alterations in an individual's consciousness, at times with dramatic clinical results. For instance, the phenomenon of reversible amnesia could be imaginatively applied in a clinical setting. An example is the case of the physician who had a lifelong difficulty with taking oral exams. Although he had been able to avoid oral exams through the kindness of his teachers and professors, he continued to apply to take various tests. After becoming a physician, he became certified in a number of specialty boards, but he needed yet one more. This time the head of the exam committee, with whom he had a long history of personal conflict, said, "You cannot take this exam in written form. This one is going to be oral." The young physician felt unable to continue; his reaction by this time was phobic. So he consulted Erickson who intervened with this hypnotic suggestion: He would not remember preparing for this exam, and he would not remember traveling to the exam setting or sitting through the exam. However, after the exam, while at the airport preparing to return home, he would suddenly remember that some weeks had gone by since he had seen Erickson. He would also remember that he had carefully and calmly prepared for the exam; he would remember going to the exam; and he would remember performing well at the exam. It was over, and he would be able to recall it all as a fait accompli. All this occurred as Erickson had said that it would. The power of hypnosis created a remarkable dissociation of memory.

The Early Erickson—by which I mean the Erickson in the 1930s, 40s, and 50s—wrote and taught that the hypnotic trance was a special condition. He pointed out that this state might occur in our daily lives, so in that respect it was a natural event. But the sustained, clinically useful hypnotic state was relatively rare. He wrote that hypnosis was not merely relaxation, nor a moment of inattention or confusion, but rather that it was an unusual extended state. It might last for minutes or sometimes even for hours.

Erickson also believed that some people could develop the hypnotic state more easily, readily, and competently than others. He wrote of guidelines to determine if someone was a "good subject." He discussed particular observable phenomena that one could notice, both ahead of time to determine if someone was likely to be a good hypnotic subject and during an induction to determine if someone was becoming hypnotized.

There are extant two very interesting films of Erickson in the late 1950s, but there is no visual or aural record of Erickson at work before that time. So we are left with a sizable number of papers from which we can understand the ideas and techniques with which the Early Erickson was working. But, we don't see and hear the Erickson whom we can see and hear in later years—the Erickson of the 1960s and 70s.

This Later Erickson, after decades of being ravaged by disease, disability and age, behaved differently as a clinician. He was no longer physically able to do the things he had once done. In his teaching he no longer distinguished the hypnotic state from the waking state as he once did. For instance, he no longer distinguished dissociation from momentary inattention or distraction, and he no longer separated hallucinations from mental imagery. The question of whether someone could be hypnotized or was hypnotized—the question of what characterized hypnosis—apparently was no longer of such special interest to him.

It is this Erickson—the Later Erickson—speaking with enormous difficulty, unable to express himself fully with movements or gestures in a way that he once had done with such grace and inventiveness, unable to exquisitely control the tones of his voice, who has come to be known as "the" Erickson. It is this Erickson who has inspired the multitude of "Ericksonian" therapists. The Erickson we have such powerful, vivid images of, the Erickson some of us knew, the Erickson we have heard and seen on videotape is a very different man from the Early Erickson. As a result of these compelling images of a still-compelling man, we seem unaware of the power of hypnosis in the way that Erickson once was able to demonstrate it. And, if you listen carefully to those of us who write about what is called Ericksonian hypnosis or Ericksonian hypnotherapy, you don't usually hear about demonstrations or cases of powerful hypnotic phenomena. You don't usually see such powerful phenomena demonstrated because, I believe, we don't know about them.

Jay Haley has remarked that Erickson in the early 60s declined to have himself filmed because he was well aware that his physical powers had waned, and he didn't like the idea that this significantly more limited self was the version that would be recorded. Much later he evidently changed his mind. It is only the much older, limited Erickson of whom we have videotapes. Haley has expressed regret that Erickson relented in his later years, specifically because this later image has so overshadowed the very important early work that he did.

THE POWER OF HYPNOSIS

It is ironic that the more traditional hypnotists like Ernest Hilgard and Martin Orne are called upon to demonstrate classic hypnotic phenomena, such as reversible amnesia or hallucinations. Although they learned from Erickson and appreciated him, they also developed their own ideas. By amnesia I mean not simply forgetting what was said a few minutes ago, but rather the ability to remember only after a releasing cue is given. Reversible amnesia is a remarkable phenomenon, and involves quite different cognitive processes from those that occur when someone listens to enchanting and/or boring stories . . . and then apparently forgets parts of the stories.* Amnesia is not the same phenomenon as forgetting.

Much of the hypnotherapy that is done by "Ericksonians" is relatively weak compared to the hypnosis done by Erickson in his early days. Moreover, it is weak compared to the hypnosis done by classical non-Ericksonians. The "Ericksonian" trend has been toward diluting the concept of hypnosis. Because hypnotherapy, by definition, cannot be successfully done in the waking state, dramatic hypnotic phenomena aren't typical of "Ericksonian" hypnotherapy. Relaxation is not hypnosis, and physical changes in the musculature do not necessarily reflect the complex changes in cognition associated with hypnosis.

As a result of inattention to this distinction, one can become unaware of the remarkable and dramatic power that can be tapped with hypnotic suggestions. By "power" I mean the power to quickly alter symptoms, the power to create amnesia, hallucinations or anesthesia, the power to create physiological change. To be able to use hypnosis as an effective way for a suffering patient to find comfort involves more than simply

---

*Editor's note: For a distinction between reversible amnesia and the clinical amnesia used by Erickson see "The use of therapeutic amnesia" by J. Zeig in *Ericksonian Psychotherapy, Vol. I: Structures*, J. Zeig (Ed.), Brunner/Mazel, 1985.

teaching a person how to deal with a problem, more than simply having the patient feel supported, and more than merely providing an opportunity for the patient to vent feelings. Using hypnosis involves creating a profound cognitive shift whereby the patient alters the feelings of pain or anxiety suffered only moments before the suggestions for comfort were given.

As a result of this lack of emphasis on the power of hypnosis per se to effect such changes, there has evolved instead an emphasis on language and technique. With the emphasis on indirect style and clever strategies, it is easy to forget that hypnosis can often allow the therapist to be quick, distinct and direct. In the 19th Century, Bernheim said that if a patient is in a normal waking state and you want him to follow a suggestion, you need to be indirect. But, he said, the value of hypnosis is that you can be quite direct in making such suggestions. It is easy to forget this at meetings such as this Congress or at workshops in which we see clever, sometimes very moving interventions, in which there is inordinate focus on cleverness of language.

THE NEED FOR EMPIRICISM

This raises yet another issue. When we see demonstrations at workshops, we don't know what the long-term effect will be. For instance, a professional told me about a patient I had worked with at a workshop several years ago. It had been his patient, and it was he who brought the patient in for the workshop. So I did some clever interventions, but this cleverness apparently didn't make any difference. There was no long-term change in the patient. And I had been so clever! It is interesting to watch a clinical intervention, but the question is, does it have clinical value? The only way you can know is to do follow-up.

Take, for example, a troubled family. Things seem to be better at the end of the therapy hour, and that is very interesting. But what if a month from now there isn't any change in the problem? Then it's not so interesting. And what if I work with someone in a workshop who has a pain problem and I demonstrate incredibly clever use of language by the way I construct suggestions? That may be interesting. But, if a week later the patient has no sense of control over the pain problem, then the demonstration is not so impressive. We need to attend to the long-term effects of what it is that we do.

It is natural that such a focus arises at these Congresses, partly because Erickson was so clever. Because he was so unusual and innovative, for a long time we focused on identifying principles of interventions while ignoring a number of things that we already knew about hypnosis and psychotherapy. When we become overly focused on issues like embedded metaphors, indirection or permissive language, what we often forget is that this is all just a vehicle to carry some kind of therapeutic change; if that change doesn't occur, then we have just been doing theatre.

In order to understand and replicate Erickson's work, we have simply tried to seek principles, tried to identify what is common in what he did between one case and another. But little effort has been made to actually investigate the validity of our hypotheses. Ironically, most of the investigation of Ericksonian therapy has been done by non-Ericksonians, with two notable exceptions, William Matthews and Jeffrey Feldman. Peter Sheehan and Kevin McConkey are non-Ericksonian hypnosis investigators who have investigated various Ericksonian claims, and it's not all pleasant news for Ericksonians.

Some aspects of psychotherapy need to be based on scientific principles. Psychotherapy is an art, but the principles of psychotherapy are based on something that can be shared in an objective way. If we don't use empirical methods to investigate what it is that we do and to challenge our own conclusions and our own allegations, then all we're really doing is literary criticism. We make transcripts of one another's work and we treat the transcript like a poem. We make interesting observations about the language of the poetry. But when there are exhortations to other people to believe these allegations, it is no longer even literary criticism. It has become religion.

Erickson did not respect any mystical or antiscientific bias. So it feels ironic to me, and not entirely delightful, that an antiscientific bias often seems to pervade the work that is being created out of Erickson's efforts. It is one thing to use an idea to clinically inspire a patient to make a change. For instance, it may be inspiring to a patient who is having difficulty experiencing hypnosis or believing in the value of hypnosis to say that "flattening of the facial musculature is an indication that you're going into a deep trance." It turns out, of course, that this is not necessarily true, but it may sometimes be a clinically useful thing to say. Or it may be useful clinically to say to someone who really lacks confidence that this therapeutic process is going anywhere that "the automatic movements of your fingers reflect unconscious impulses, and we can use these unconscious impulses to communicate directly with your unconscious." It is one thing to say that to a patient to inspire clinical change, because it can be effective and helpful. But it is another thing to believe it yourself, and yet another to teach it as fact. It may be clinically helpful, but there is no evidence to believe such things.

We need to be able to make a distinction between clinical interventions that we find useful and theoretical statements that may or may not be true. The progressive blurring of the distinction between the hypnotic state and the ordinary waking state exemplifies this problem. One can get the impression, if one reads "Ericksonian" authors, that we are always in a trance, or nearly always in a trance, or very often in a trance. And the difficulty with this, of course, is that it waters down the concept of trance; it dilutes the meaning of this very special state, and it makes it impossible to identify when this special state occurs.

I think this dilution has two important effects. First, it becomes theoretically impossible to understand what's going on. But, more importantly, we become handicapped clinically by our self-deception. We begin to believe that a patient is in a trance just because we have said he or she is. If it is clinically important for patients to be in a hypnotic state in order to achieve some kind of clinical change, then we need to know how to help them get into that state, and we need to know whether or not such a state develops. We need to have a criterion. If we don't know how to determine this, and if the person needs to be in a hypnotic state in order for change to occur, then how will we ever reliably create such change?

Personally, I use the following definition of hypnosis—which I didn't create, but for which I have source amnesia. *Hypnosis is a state or condition that is characterized by alterations in perception and/or memory, by the capacity for increased control of physiological function, and by increased accessibility of unconscious processes.* Hypnosis is a special state of consciousness that allows us under certain circumstances to change our memory so that we cannot remember something that we otherwise would be able to remember or we can remember something that we had forgotten, as in the case of releasing repressed memories. Hypnosis may also result in an alteration in perception so that we can hallucinate in order to see, hear, feel or smell something that we ordinarily could not. Hypnosis allows greater control of autonomic processes, in much more exquisite detail and to a much more dramatic degree, than otherwise possible. And we can access unconscious processes more easily and systematically by using hypnosis in the context of psychotherapy.

If you cannot demonstrate these phenomena in any given case, the patient in fact may be in a hypnotic state. But, if so, how do you know? It is certainly possible for someone to be hypnotized and not respond to suggestions. But if someone cannot demonstrate these phenomena, then how do we know he or she is hypnotized? If it is important, then we need to have some means of knowing. And, if it isn't important, then why do hypnosis? If it isn't important that someone be in a trance, then why not just do therapy and quit using the concept "hypnosis"?

For me, the challenge is to be inspired by Erickson's work, which was quite remarkable, and as a result of that inspiration to then test my own ideas. It is hard to examine the issue of how to sort out the clinical effects of hypnosis per se from the more general effects of the context of being in therapy with someone who does hypnosis. But it is important that we try. I think that I have made serious errors of judgment in the past about some of my clinical pain work by assuming that patients were hypnotized simply because they experienced a reduction in pain. I am now impressed by evidence that people can obtain those results without necessarily being hypnotized. This has significant implications, both for our theoretical understanding and for our clinical approaches. It is important that we test the ideas that we develop from our experience, and that we look at the long-range effects—that we look at follow-up results. And we must begin to insist on follow-up with each other. It is not enough to hear about a case or even 10 cases in which interesting interventions were made unless we also learn what happened some months later.

We will be better clinicians for this. And I think these issues are becoming increasingly important. Who will be interested in what we have to say if we do not attend to these issues in a scientific manner?

My personal concern is that Milton Erickson's remarkable work will be forgotten if all we do is maintain the memory of his last years. It will be a terrible irony if his earlier years—30 years of important work—are forgotten.

Chapter 3

Ericksonian Psychotherapy *Is* the State of the Art: Suggestions for a Future Orientation

Richard E. Dimond

Richard E. Dimond, Ph.D. (Kent State University), is in independent practice and consultation in Springfield, Illinois. He is also an adjunct professor at Southern Illinois University School of Medicine. Dimond has coauthored an introductory psychology text and written a number of publications on hypnosis, eclectic psychotherapy, and psychotherapy training.

In this chapter he presents some challenging issues facing practitioners of an Ericksonian approach. We are indebted to him for reminding us that Erickson was not merely a superb clinician; he was a clinical scientist. He emphasizes the importance of a future orientation toward client problems; pragmatism; and solution-oriented psychotherapy.

The theme of this Congress is, "Ericksonian psychotherapy: The state of the art." This theme implies a focus upon current thinking and practice among those of us who are devotees of Milton Erickson and his work. A similar emphasis is suggested by the publication last year of the first *Ericksonian Monograph* (Lankton, 1985b). Those excellent papers, along with those presented at this Congress, will contribute greatly to our understanding of the ways in which Ericksonian psychotherapy is being practiced and developed.

As the title of this paper suggests, I would like to take this opportunity to focus more broadly upon Ericksonian hypnosis and psychotherapy in an effort to provide an orientation for the development of our work. The central thesis of this paper is that Ericksonian psychotherapy, especially as practiced and described by Erickson himself (Rossi, 1980), *is* the state of the art across the range of psychotherapies which describe the enterprise today. As such, the learning that we can realize from our study of Erickson's work and from our own practices provides an opportunity for us to influence the entire field of psychotherapy.

This thesis will be developed by our first examining the position Ericksonian therapy has adopted vis-à-vis other approaches to psychotherapy. Next, some salient features of Ericksonian psychotherapy will be presented and discussed. Finally, suggestions for a future orientation will be presented. Throughout this discussion, I will incorporate personal observations made at The Evolution of Psychotherapy Conference (Zeig, 1987) and clinical examples to make my points.

TO BE OR NOT TO BE, THAT IS THE QUESTION

As students of the Ericksonian approach to hypnosis and psychotherapy, we are faced with a wonderful dilemma. We are all aware of Milton Erickson's position in reference to theories of human behavior, or to schools of psychotherapy. This is perhaps best exemplified by Erickson's now familiar "procrustean bed" statement (Zeig, 1983). Perhaps it is because we recognize that Erickson eschewed the development of "schools" of psychotherapy that we have developed our Ericksonian orientations with a "liberal attitude." This means that generally we do not proselytize, we respect other orientations to psychotherapy, and the orientation within our own ranks has become more permissive, valuing the way in which each one of us works in Ericksonian style.

This liberal attitude is, of course, laudatory, and certain benefits accrue from its adoption. However, the dilemma, which I mentioned, is that this attitude may inadvertently foster the development of an "Ericksonian school" of psychotherapy. In fact, I believe it will be nearly impossible to avoid developing as a school of therapy for at least two reasons. First, it is the natural tendency for people to perceive differences and to make comparisons. Consequently, those of our colleagues who are not interested in Ericksonian approaches will observe those of us who are and conclude, correctly, that differences exist between us and them. One example of this process could be seen to occur during the Evolution of Psychotherapy Conference (Zeig, 1987). Since panels contained representatives of an Ericksonian approach and various schools of psychotherapy, it is only natural that one might conclude that

Ericksonian psychotherapy is something distinct from, for example, Rogerian psychotherapy. Through such behavior, we wittingly or unwittingly, define ourselves.

Second, as we continue to share with each other our thoughts and practices of Ericksonian psychotherapy, we again define ourselves as an approach which is different from other therapies.

Consequently, I believe we cannot avoid defining Ericksonian psychotherapy as a distinct "school" of therapy. Perhaps we should choose to actively define it rather than permit it to be defined for us. The danger in adopting a passive position in this regard is the risk of losing both the uniqueness of Ericksonian psychotherapy and the inherent value of Erickson's work.

One way this loss of uniqueness can occur is when Erickson's approach is compared to another in an attempt to understand it by looking for similarities. Thus, it is possible to find in Erickson's work, similarities between his approach to psychotherapy and other approaches (Havens, 1985). This, in fact, not only destroys the uniqueness of Ericksonian psychotherapy but may actually misrepresent it by missing the unique points of his approach.

An anecdote may clarify this point. Recently an article was submitted to a well-known professional journal in an attempt to introduce Ericksonian psychotherapy and exemplify its usefulness on a specific client population (Hess & Dimond, 1986). In this article, several successful cases were described in detail and characteristics of Ericksonian therapy were presented in contrast to "traditional" therapy. The response from the reviewers was unexpected, yet quite revealing. The paper was accepted for publication with the proviso that each separate intervention, such as homework assignments, would be credited to "other" schools of therapy! In other words, the editor asked the authors to make it clear that Ericksonian therapy is "the same" as many other approaches. Once this was done, they would publish the article. This situation exemplifies the real difficulty in communicating the differences between Ericksonian psychotherapy and other approaches.

Just as the previous situation dealt with the Ericksonian approach as being obscured by its similarity to other approaches, the opposite is also possible. Another way in which Erickson's contributions may be lost is the tendency to reject that which does not fit with preconceptions and rigid conceptual sets. Specifically, some professionals will accurately conclude that Ericksonian therapy *is* different from other approaches, but may reach these conclusions for reasons which are not accurate.

These reasons, in turn, may lead to a rejection of the Ericksonian approach out of hand.

Dr. Erickson frequently approached therapy in unconventional ways. It is altogether possible that his material could be criticized due to its occasional lack of conformity to mainstream ideas. This very situation occurred with an introductory psychology textbook that is now out of print (Senter & Dimond, 1976).

This text was written to be easily understandable and contained material of interest to experimental, developmental, social, clinical and applied psychologists, but in an uncustomary manner. The major sections which divided the book were learning, perception, and motivation. Criticisms of the text all centered on one point: Psychology was not organized in this manner. Although the authors believed the book had merit, this merit was not seen because of the preconceived manner in which knowledge in psychology is thought to be organized. In short, a potentially good idea was rejected because it did not conform to a preconceived idea. Again, this example underscores a fear that Erickson's approach needs to be carefully and thoughtfully defined so it will not suffer a fate of a similar type of criticism.

My second anecdote concerns the rejection of ideas for misconceived reasons. In my experience in teaching Ericksonian approaches, a frequently raised issue is that of whether or not the approach is manipulative. That I have had people drop out of my seminars on this basis says something about my inability to deal constructively with this issue. However, since I probably did not provide adequate reasons in response to these questions, it is also an excellent example of rejecting ideas for misconceived reasons.

I believe Erickson provided us with an orientation toward psychotherapy which puts us in a unique position. In the following section I will further explain this unique position and offer a basis for defining Ericksonian psychotherapy. Following this, I shall discuss the future orientation implied in his definition.

CHARACTERISTICS OF ERICKSONIAN PSYCHOTHERAPY

There are several excellent papers which offer various perspectives on the elements or dimensions of an Ericksonian approach to hypnosis and psychotherapy (Lankton, 1985a; Matthews, 1985). My purpose here is not to duplicate these efforts. Rather, I want to focus attention on what I believe to be essential aspects of Erickson's work which contribute to the development of a future orientation for us, and define his work as unique. I define the future orientation as the therapist's focus on the observable results of interventions upon the behaviors of each client.

In considering Erickson's work from this perspective, I am in substantial agreement with my colleague, Ronald Havens (1985). He suggests that Milton Erickson's emphasis upon observation and pragmatism was the most salient feature of his work. Havens also warned us not to incorporate Erickson's ideas into existing theoretical frameworks.

An important aspect of Erickson's work was his ability as a superb clinician. Erickson focused upon outcomes, and his interventions were based upon his learning from previous observations and the impact they had during the course of psychotherapy. Throughout this process, he not only avoided theorizing, but also warned us to avoid it. Erickson was such a superb clinician because he was a clinical scientist. He continually performed experiments in therapy, drawing empirical conclusions from his observations. The literature which Erickson produced is replete with examples of his scientific work (Rossi, 1980).

I emphasize this point because it is important in developing a future orientation for Ericksonian psychotherapy and because the role of "clinical scientist" is, in my experience, not the emphasis currently adopted by most professional psychotherapists. My observations at the Evolution of Psychotherapy Conference led me to the conclusion that when psychotherapists *talk* about what they do, they frequently talk about their *theories, philosophies,* or *ideas* about how people behave, how they should behave, and the various ways to help people do so. At this level, I was, and always have been, impressed by the diversity of ideas represented by various "schools" of psychotherapy.

However, when I observed these therapists working, I became impressed with the *similarities* in their behaviors. These therapists were superb clinicians who "paced and led" their clients and created very powerful impacts with their behavior. From this point of view, psychotherapy begins to appear "all of one cloth."

Of course, the above observations and conclusions are open to debate. My point is, however, that if we become clinical scientists, we can better capture the essence of Erickson's work and put ourselves in position to contribute greatly to psychotherapy as a profession. Milton Erickson was the only major psychotherapist to emphasize observation, outcome and effect without attempting theoretical explanations. Consequently, we are freed to examine these dimensions in his work and in the work of others without being hampered by the need to explain. Herein lie implications for the future orientation I am suggesting.

TOWARD A FUTURE ORIENTATION FOR ERICKSONIAN PSYCHOTHERAPY

Defining Ericksonian psychotherapy as a clinical, scientific approach to psychotherapy offers, I believe, several immediate benefits. First, this definition captures the most salient features of Erickson's work—namely, his emphasis upon observation, outcome, pragmatism, and remaining atheoretical. Thus defined, these primary characteristics of his work are less likely to be forgotten in our own psychotherapy practice.

A second benefit is that we define Ericksonian psychotherapy as an approach to *therapy*, thus addressing the concerns presented earlier in this paper—the avoidance of theoretical frameworks. Such a definition preserves what is most unique about Ericksonian psychotherapy.

The major benefit from implementing this definition of Ericksonian psychotherapy is that we will build a basis for its future development. As we begin to operate as clinical scientists, our focus will be the elaboration of interventions in specific clinical situations and the reporting of the outcomes or effects of each intervention. This undertaking should be done, so far as possible, *without* theorizing or presenting a "framework" for conceptual understanding so as to minimize our falling prey to our own rigid conceptual sets (Dimond, 1985). Some examples will clarify this.

Margaret Mead (1977) wrote of Milton Erickson's originality, "that he maintains his own extraordinary freshness by seeing to it that he doesn't bore himself" (p. 5). She speculated that Erickson approached each clinical situation anew: "Instead of all the earlier solutions crowding his mind to shape the new venture, it is as if his mind had been swept clean of the debris of previous, and so perhaps intrinsically boring performances" (p. 4). While Mead's focus is upon Erickson's originality, she is also suggesting that there are *many* ways to solve a clinical problem.

Jay Haley remarked during one of his training seminars that therapists nowadays are being brought problems far more demanding than the "simple" neuroses of years ago. And, we are learning more about the nature of these problems. However, we do not need more theoretical elaboration of these problems, we need solutions and elaborations of the *process* of helping people move toward these solutions.

This, I suggest, is an example of a direction for us to take in the future, and certainly to some extent we are doing it now. However, there is a need to do it systematically and with the expressed purpose of developing *as many ways as possible* to solve a particular clinical problem. Each of us has in his or her files examples of outcomes created through fascinating events that may be planned or unplanned. We must share these with each other. The following brief case is an example.

Some time ago, I was consulted by a 25-year-old married woman who was in great distress with obsessive thoughts and ruminations, generalized anxiety, and panic attacks. She was also quite fearful of losing her mind and of discovering, in therapy, that something was, in fact, dreadfully wrong with her. Certainly, this woman was an excellent candidate for cognitive therapy.

What happened, however, fascinated me. I was able to help her calm down, but was unsuccessful in helping her beyond this. I decided on a variation of ordeal therapy (Haley, 1984), or paradoxical assignment. Prior to Christmas, I told her I knew the solution to her guilt and worrying, but that she would need to commit herself to carrying out an assignment if she wanted to know the solution. She was to think this over during the holidays. I also added that I had serious concerns about her "tolerance for enjoyment" and that, over the holiday, if she noticed herself enjoying some activity, she should observe how long it was until she felt obliged to undermine this enjoyment. The assignment gave her a great deal to think about.

She returned after the holidays quite angry with me and also quite changed. She had "misinterpreted" a part of what I had said and told me, in no uncertain terms, that she had no desire or need for me to tell her what was wrong with her. She further informed me that her "tolerance for enjoyment" was just fine, thank you, and that she had made certain basic decisions about her life. In fact, she told me, "There is never a time when everything is perfect and you just need to go ahead and do what you want to do."

I observed that her cognitions had changed. I was unaware of "teaching" her how to do this. I regret I had not collected pre- and post-measures on this phenomenon. This would be fascinating research to elaborate similar methods and to examine comparability of results. We all need to share and elaborate our cases in order to make those kinds of comparisons.

Along these lines, it is important to remember that Erickson's techniques are, essentially, empirically based. Many of his techniques have been identified and elaborated (Erickson, Rossi & Rossi, 1976; Haley, 1973). However, these techniques, such as paradox, double bind, and prescribing a relapse, have sometimes been left at the level of interesting "technique," and sometimes discarded or rejected, as mentioned earlier.

I would like to know more about what each of us is learning from the use of such apparently miniscule aspects of Ericksonian psychotherapy. Furthermore, we need to contribute to knowledge beyond our own group. It is interesting to note, for example, a recent article on relapse prevention in alcoholism which contains 158 references, but *none* regarding Milton Erickson's work (Brownell, Marlatt, Lichtenstein & Wilson, 1986). Many of us have examples drawn from Erickson's work on prescribing relapse, and I'm sad to see that none of these clinical experiences reached those authors.

Adopting the role of clinical scientist should not stop with sharing among practicing therapists. It would have a salutory effect upon the training and education in which various of us are engaged. My experience is that psychotherapists are not trained to be accustomed to thinking in terms of effects and solutions. I have come to enjoy hearing people ask Jay Haley questions about how to manage a case. His reply, now almost perseverative in nature, is a question: "What do you want to have happen?" This response stumps many therapists, and rightfully so.

CONCLUSIONS

I have taken this opportunity to suggest that Ericksonian psychotherapy *is* the state of the art because he was a clinical scientist who worked from a future orientation. We have not yet begun to plumb the depths of Erickson's contributions in this regard. I would also like to see psychotherapists contribute to this new definition of "clinical scientist" by working to share their collective accumulation of successful solutions to various clinical problems.

Finally, I am reminded that few individuals have changed therapy over the years as much as Milton H. Erickson did. I close with one of my favorite quotes from a delegate to an early training conference for psychologists, because I believe it to be as true today as it was in 1952: "I am afraid that in spite of our efforts we have left therapy as an undefined technique which is applied to unspecified problems with unpredictable outcomes. For this technique we recommend rigorous training" (Lehner, 1952, p. 547).

REFERENCES

Brownell, K. D., Marlatt, G. A., Lichtenstein, E., & Wilson, G. T. (1986). Understanding and preventing relapse. *American Psychologist, 41*(7), 765–782.

Dimond, R. E. (1985). Trials and tribulations of becoming an Ericksonian psychotherapist. In J. Zeig (Ed.), *Ericksonian Psychotherapy Volume I: Structures* (pp. 100–109). New York: Brunner/Mazel.

Dimond, R. E., & Senter, R. J. (1976). An organizational framework for the teaching of basic psychology. *Teaching of Psychology, 9*(3), 181–182.

Erickson, M. H., Rossi, E. L., & Rossi, S. I. (1976). *Hypnotic Realities: The Induction of Clinical Hypnosis and Forms of Indirect Suggestion.* New York: Irvington.

Haley, J. (1973). *Uncommon Therapy: The Psychiatric Techniques of Milton H. Erickson, M.D.* New York: Norton.

Haley, J. (1984). *Ordeal Therapy.* San Francisco: Jossey-Bass.

Havens, R. A. (1985). Erickson vs. the establishment: Which won? In J. Zeig (Ed.), *Ericksonian Psychotherapy Volume I: Structures* (pp. 52–61). New York: Brunner/Mazel.

Hess, J. L., & Dimond, R. E. (1986). Cognitive rehabilitation within the process of psychotherapy: I. Introduction to a collaborative effort with higher-order brain injured patients. *Journal of Head Trauma Rehabilitation.* submitted.

Lankton, C. (1985a). Elements of an Ericksonian approach. In S. Lankton (Ed.), *Ericksonian Monographs Number 1: Elements and Dimensions of an Ericksonian Approach* (pp. 61–75). New York: Brunner/Mazel.

Lankton, S. (Ed.) (1985b). *Ericksonian Monographs Number 1: Elements and Dimensions of an Ericksonian Approach.* New York: Brunner/Mazel.

Lehner, G. F. J. (1952). Defining psychotherapy. *American Psychologist, 7,* 547.

Matthews, W. J. (1985). A cybernetic model of Ericksonian hypnotherapy: One hand draws the other. In S. Lankton (Ed.), *Ericksonian Monographs Number 1: Elements and Dimensions of an Ericksonian Approach* (pp. 42–60). New York: Brunner/Mazel.

Mead, M. (1977). The originality of Milton Erickson. *American Journal of Clinical Hypnosis, 20*(1), 4–5.

Rossi, E. L. (Ed.) (1980). *The Collected Papers of Milton H. Erickson on Hypnosis: Vols. I–IV.* New York: Irvington.

Senter, R. J., & Dimond, R. E. (1976). *Psychology: The Exploration of Human Behavior.* Glenview, Ill.: Scott, Foresman.

Zeig, J. (Ed.) (1983). *Ericksonian Approaches to Hypnosis and Psychotherapy* (p. VII). New York: Brunner/Mazel.

Zeig, J. (Ed.) (1987). *The Evolution of Psychotherapy.* New York: Brunner/Mazel.

Chapter 4

Strategic Therapy Revisited

Philip J. Booth

Philip John Booth, M.A., is a certified psychiatric social worker. He teaches family therapy and hypnosis from an Ericksonian stance and conducts a private practice in family therapy and hypnosis in Oxford, England. He is the Founding Coordinator of the London Society for Ericksonian Psychotherapy and Hypnosis, Chairman of the Oxford Branch of the Association for Family Therapy, and member of the Editorial Board of the Journal of Strategic and Systemic Therapies.

Booth received the Milton H. Erickson Foundation Award for the most scholarly accepted paper presented at the 1986 Congress—this chapter. He reminds therapists that Dr. Erickson's work was based upon honesty and respect for clients and not on the deceitful and adversarial positions occasionally spawned from his work. Specifically, Booth illustrates how various strategic therapies have taken liberties with the spirit originally found in Erickson's work and often result in misinforming clients about the real intentions of the therapist. It is a thought-provoking chapter well worth digesting.

What can be said can and should always be said more and more simply and clearly. (Karl Popper, 1983a)

The aim of this chapter is to argue for the removal of "trickiness" and manipulativeness from strategic therapy and to rewrite the tech-

---

The title of this chapter is an allusion to the paper "Transference revisited" by Don Jackson and Jay Haley (Jackson & Haley, 1963). They were rewriting the techniques and concepts of psychoanalysis interactionally. My paper is an attempt to rewrite some of their ideas.

niques of strategic therapy according to commonsense and with non-technical terms. We take the definition of strategic therapy given by Haley: "Therapy can be called strategic if the clinician initiates what happens during therapy and designs a particular approach for each problem" (1973, p. 17).

Regarding the practice of strategic therapy, I am primarily referring to therapies such as those discussed by Madanes, Haley, and the Mental Research Institute in the United States and by the Family Institute in Cardiff,* in Britain. However, a strategic approach defined in this general manner has become a part of many family therapies, and ideas of this chapter also can be applied in part to various other schools of family therapy.

In this chapter I examine some philosophical trends that may have contributed to a decline in truth-telling among therapists and promoted increased manipulation of clients. Then, I rewrite and reformulate some specific strategic therapy techniques, properly placing emphasis on truth and honesty. This requires adopting a nonadversarial view of therapy contrary to that which is often promoted by strategic therapists.

I use Erickson's own words to couch the reformulations—and in that sense I am doing nothing new. I am "going back to the source" and tracing a different emphasis from that of the strategic therapists.† But a number of new formulations will also be made.

What emerges from this retracing is a way of thinking about work with clients that is straightforward and less technique-oriented. It is a psychology more related to commonsense which allows strategic work to be done in a relatively more candid way.

THE MANIPULATIVENESS OF STRATEGIC THERAPY

I want to begin with an anecdote. A colleague of mine, asking for hypnotherapy for help in giving up smoking, told me that I had been

---

* It is important to note that the Cardiff Institute's current attitude to lying and manipulation is now generally much closer to the one I advocate in this paper. See for example Speed (1985) and Speed (1987).

† I have been given greater confidence to do this by the recent appearance of the three volumes *Conversations with Milton H. Erickson* (Haley, 1985a, 1985b, 1985c), which are a record of some of the early conversations between Haley, Weakland, Bateson and Erickson which could be said to have greatly influenced strategic therapy. This has allowed me to review older and more original material to substantiate my points. The three volumes, *Changing Individuals* (1985a), *Changing Couples* (1985b) and *Changing Children and Families* (1985c), show the contrast between the thinking of the strategists, with their adversarial and pessimistic approach, and Erickson's optimistic and candid approach.

recommended by another colleague as someone who was particularly good with smokers. I had not seen a smoker before, in fact, and so my instant reaction was to say, "Really? Actually I have never seen a smoker before." To this he replied, "Oh, don't give me all that strategic stuff!" I protested my innocence, but to no avail. What the story reveals is that "strategic" has in some professionals' minds become synonymous with "lying."

The reason for this is simple: Strategic therapists have frequently disseminated misinformation or fabrications to clients when conducting therapy. Let me list some of the most common ways in which they have done this. In strategic family therapy, fabricated facts, misinformation, or lies are told when therapists, working with a team behind a one-way screen, tell a family that one member of the team thinks such and such and another member such and so when this is not the case; or when the therapist tells the family that there is a visiting expert behind the screen when there isn't, although such an expert was there the previous week; or when the team, during their break from the family, have pretended to have an argument within earshot of the family (for reasons relevant to the family's dynamics), are then asked by the family whether such an argument was real, and reply affirmatively (Cade, 1980). It happens when therapists tell families or individual patients that they should not change when in fact the therapist thinks the family or individual *should* change. It happens when therapists reframe patients' symptoms, behaviors or situations without believing in the validity of the new frame they offer.

The following is a lengthier but very specific example from the literature of strategic therapy. In *The Tactics of Change* (Fisch, Weakland & Segal, 1982), the authors point out the advantages of seeing members of a family separately:

> . . . the therapist has the freedom to engage in an open coalition with each person and can more easily enlist each person's co-operation. (p. 38)

They continue:

> Trainees have raised a legitimate question about this: What if a couple compares notes between sessions? Won't that expose the therapist's inconsistency?

Their answer is ingenuous:

While there is some risk of that occurring, we believe it is a small one.

The authors offer several reasons for saying this, but proffer the following advice should one of the parties later question the therapist about what he actually did say to the other party:

> . . . the therapist can always fall back on the statement: I can't control how people interpret what I say after they leave my office.

They then comment:

> The questioning party is likely to then discount the other spouse's report.

But the alternative, they conclude, is to tell the truth:

> As an alternative, the therapist can see both warring parties together, confess to double-talk, and explain that he felt forced to wheedle them both because they are so stubbornly locked into their vendetta that he could see no other reasonable way to get them to take any action necessary for the ending of their struggle. Thus his honest admission still can be used to apply pressure on them to cooperate with suggestions. (p. 38)

In other words, honesty is reduced to merely another strategy worth considering.

TRUTH AND REALITY

Manipulation, in the most concrete sense, is the act of controlling with the hands or the mind. But in the sense that it is being used in this chapter, it refers to managing affairs in an unfair, scheming or underhanded manner. Various forms of misrepresentation of the truth, trickery, deceit, lying, fabrication, and misinformation, therefore, qualify as manipulation of this type.

Although misrepresenting the truth is only one form of manipulation, I concentrate on it initially because of its central importance. How can it be that we have created a situation of having to argue for not lying in therapy? This seems outrageous. My speculation is that lying has been made easier because certain viewpoints have become prevalent in the strategic and family therapy field. Some of these viewpoints are thought to represent "the latest state of the art."

The most serious attack on the obligation to tell the truth when conducting therapy stems from an attack on the notion of "reality." Truth could be defined as correspondence with the facts, but then the question is asked, "What are the facts?" or "What is reality?" Arguments to challenge the existence of an objective reality are frequently brought to social science from the field of physics, in particular, but also from philosophy. Both in physics and philosophy these challenges are sophisticated. But in both there exist opposing camps whose arguments are rarely discussed in the strategic and family therapy literature.

Karl Popper's *Quantum Theory and the Schism in Physics* (Popper, 1983b) provides an example of this opposing view in the area of physics. In the area of *philosophy*, Karl Popper writes:

> In my opinion, the greatest scandal of philosophy is that, while all around us the world of nature perishes—and not the world of nature alone—philosophers continue to talk, sometimes cleverly and sometimes not, about the question of whether this world exists. (Popper, 1972, p. 32)

The arguments are important, because if the existence of an objective real world is undermined, the objective facts of that world become ephemeral. Regard for the facts is thereby undermined, and therapists can tell lies with philosophical impunity.

But, it might be countered, it is important to distinguish between the objective physical world and the subjective realities that we create for ourselves day to day. Watzlawick makes this distinction in his book *How Real is Real?* (1976, pp. 140–142) and again in the collection of essays he edited under the title of *The Invented Reality* (1984, pp. 236–237).

He talks of first-order reality for the objective physical world and second-order reality for the world of subjective experience or meaning. This is an important distinction to draw. But what is not emphasized sufficiently is the interplay between the two realities, for the realities that we construct for ourselves relate to the real objective world in which we live. Subjectively-held realities vary according to how they fit with the objective world. If they do not fit for the mentally healthy, subjectively-held realities change. For example, a child's attitude about himself and the meaning of his life is affected by his discovery of the objective fact of the finality of death. Also, personal beliefs, embodied in various theories about hypnosis and mind-body interaction have altered over time as knowledge of physiology, neurology, biology, etc., has developed (e.g., Rossi, 1986). Popper (1983b) further elaborates on this point.

Objective reality and subjective reality are not as divorced as Watzlawick perhaps assumes. He raises an important point, however, when he says we must be wary of claiming that our personal realities are *the* truth or *the* right view of the world. As he emotionally points out, this can lead to a world in which we witness "the acrid smoke rising from some auto-da-fé or the chimneys of crematoria" (Watzlawick, 1976, p. 222).

But how, in his scheme, can personally-held beliefs or realities be compared, if no reference can be made to something outside the individuals holding them? One personally-held reality becomes as valid as another.

Watzlawick, at times, even appears to give up a belief in his first-order objective reality. In *The Invented Reality* (1984) he writes, for example, "Constructivism [the view that he proposes] does not create or explain any reality out there; it shows that there is no inside and no outside, no objective world facing the subjective, rather, it shows that the subject-object split . . . does not exist. . . ." (p. 330). One is left confused.*

Watzlawick opposes rigidly held personal beliefs and the way some people impose these on others. His attack on objective truth and objective reality does not appear to further his goals in this area. My hypothesis is that these attacks have contributed to an undermining of respect for truth among certain strategic and family therapists.

Every therapist who fabricates is not necessarily influenced by the points of view I have criticized. It is possible to ignore physics and philosophy and to consider the issue of lying from a purely ethical point of view, as Haley, for example, has done in a chapter on ethical problems in *Problem-Solving Therapy* (1976, Chap. 8), or as Sissela Bok does in her book *Lying*. One might then point to mistaken ethical arguments that have supported lying.

---

* For elaboration of the constructivist view see Segal (1986). For a view which takes up many of the same scientific issues which Segal (1986) refers to but which comes to objectivist conclusions, see Popper & Eccles (1977). For further criticisms of constructivism, see the brief but excellent review of *The Invented Reality* by Wilk (1984). For a wider perspective on constructivism, as well as further criticisms of the subjectivist viewpoint, see Lukes (1977), particularly Chapters 6, 7 & 8, and particularly pp. 142–143 of Chapter 7.

There are still other sources of disrespect for telling the truth. The ones included here were selected because they are currently relevant to the field of therapy. It is my intention to promote the truthful alternative for those in the field who respect truth but who have been troubled by the arguments that have been put forward against it. I would like them to have the pleasure of feeling intellectually respectable in their truth-telling.

But, even if we accept the existence of objective truth, giving misinformation or lying might be justified on the basis either that this truth is difficult to define, or on other philosophical grounds, or simply in terms of the complexities of human behavior. All knowledge is tentative and subject to revision (e.g., Popper, 1972). We can never know, even in physics, and especially when we are trying to explain a client's behavior, whether what we are saying is true in any absolute sense. But we can distinguish between "speaking *the* truth" and "being truthful." Although objective truth is elusive, we *can* know when we are being truthful, that is, saying what we believe or what we know to be the case, and we *can* know when we are lying or fabricating, that is, saying, with the intention to deceive, things that we do not believe or what we know not to be the case. This is a central argument that is quite separate from any philosophical argument about the attainability of objective truth.

A JUSTIFICATION FOR BEING TRUTHFUL

What reasons could one give if one wanted to support the practice of telling the truth? We have already heard a pragmatic consideration in the passage quoted from *Tactics of Change* (Fisch et al., 1982) about the problems that might face you if you are discovered telling lies. But this merely argues for covering our tracks well; it is not an argument against misinforming.

Another pragmatic rationale for truth might be that therapy would otherwise be brought into disrepute. Also, families might get wise to what therapists are doing and therefore not believe anything therapists say, thus rendering therapy impossible. These are still stronger arguments—that if in a society at large the truth is not generally told, then communication becomes difficult and largely pointless since no one can give any credence to what is said.

But the strongest grounds are the simple moral ones, based on the "Golden Rule": Do unto others as you would have others do unto you.

The argument runs: I do not like to be lied to and so I choose not to lie to other people. An extra consideration is that I assume that they feel the same way about being lied to as I do, so that this becomes a further reason for my not lying to them. It is certainly the case that on a personal level trust disappears as soon as lies enter into a relationship such as that between client and therapist.*

ERICKSON AS MODEL

Did Erickson himself tell lies to his patients? There is a passage in the recent *Conversations with Milton H. Erickson* (Haley, 1985a, 1985b, 1985c) where Erickson objects to the practice. Weakland suggests to Erickson that Erickson should pretend in the case of a female client that the therapy is going well when Erickson has just told Weakland that it is not. Erickson replies: "She isn't going to believe that. I can't falsify the situation. That would be unethical" (Haley, 1985b, p. 98).

On the other hand what are we to make of Erickson's comments some few pages later about what he told a man who has suffered from premature ejaculation for years:

> I give a little song and dance in my most learned, erudite fashion, to the effect that there's always an unfortunate outcome with premature ejaculations. There is unexpectedly, one never knows when, usually after years—because my patient's told me it's been years he's been having premature ejaculations—there will be a sudden reversal. (ibid., p. 115)

And by this Erickson means that the man will have great difficulty in ejaculating at all. Here we see Erickson in a different light. He does not believe what he is saying.† It is clear, then, that Erickson was not always honest in what he said to his clients. But how manipulative was he?

---

* The moral arguments are more complex than I have presented them, of course. For a thorough analysis of them, see Sissela Bok's excellent book *Lying* (1980).

† In fact, Erickson, writing in 1954, admits in a published article to fabricating stories for one patient: "The whole discussion was then repeated, and to it was added (. . .) fabricated case histories" (Erickson, 1980, p. 152). I am grateful to Stephen Lankton for drawing this reference to my attention.

Manipulation

Manipulation is a charge that was often made against Erickson and it is often made against strategic therapy. (Manipulation, as stated previously, can involve lying but need not. I am dealing with the broader interpretation now.) Strategic therapy has defended itself against the charge of manipulation by pointing out that manipulation is involved in all forms of psychotherapy—it is just not so obvious in most forms. It is said that strategic therapists have merely come out into the open and explained how they do it.

In their further defense, strategic therapists would argue that manipulation is nothing more than influence and that the issue is how to influence or manipulate humanely. This is fine, but the problem with this view is that, thus defined, manipulation loses its ordinary meaning: the use of underhanded or unethical means to influence people. The illusion is thereby created that manipulation in the bad sense, that of abusing people, does not exist. Erickson himself compounds this illusion. Rosen (1982) writes:

> Erickson pointed out that he had often been accused of manipulating patients—to which he replied, "Every mother manipulates her baby—if she wants it to live. Every time you go to a store, you manipulate the clerk to do your bidding, and when you go to a restaurant, you manipulate the waiter. And the teacher in school manipulated you into learning to read and write. In fact, life is one big manipulation. The final manipulation is putting you to rest, and that is manipulation too. They have to lower the coffin, and then they have to get the ropes out—all manipulation. And you manipulate a pencil to write, to record thoughts. And you manipulate yourself, carrying around peanuts or cigarettes or Life-Savers." (pp. 470–471)

Erickson sounds rather impatient about the whole issue and Rosen seems to soften what Erickson says by adding: "In other words Erickson would equate what some people would call manipulation with what others call exploration, experimentation or mastery" (p. 471). One might guess that what Erickson had in mind when he uttered the statement was the denial by other therapies that they sought to influence their clients. But the statement remains nonetheless part of that obfuscation of the notion of manipulation that I am criticizing. It can be argued, however, that there were aspects of Erickson's work that distinguish it from the questionable manipulation of much modern strategic therapy.

ELIMINATING THE ADVERSARIAL EMPHASIS IN STRATEGIC THERAPY

There is a profound difference of attitude between Erickson and the strategic approaches referred to at the beginning of this chapter. Essentially, strategic therapy, as described here, is much more adversarial in its approach to people than Erickson was. Those strategic therapists talk as if therapy is a struggle—with a family, with "the system," with the individual client, or even with a part of a client. However it is construed, it is as if the client does not really want to change or is held back in some way from changing, and "plays dirty," as it were— psychologically, unconsciously, it matters little how it is construed—in order to keep things the way they are. And so the therapist is entitled to use similar tactics, albeit paternalistically, on the client's behalf.*

On one level this adversarial quality is seen in the language of strategic therapy in phrases such as strategy, tactic, the family game, maneuverability, being one-down, resistance, making interventions, "applying pressure on the patient to cooperate" (as quoted earlier), and so on. If the metaphors we use with our clients make a difference, as an Ericksonian approach suggests, then the metaphors we use to frame therapy also make a difference.

Beyond the words, however, are a whole range of techniques, clearly derived from Erickson, but which strategic therapists have purveyed in a very different spirit. I look at some of them now and reconsider them from a less adversarial perspective.

I refer mainly to the MRI Brief Therapy model. This is largely because they have been very explicit about what they do. But it is the style of thinking that I am criticizing, and this appears in many other places.

Taking a One-Down Position

One-downsmanship is a tactic recommended by brief therapists to help professionals avoid the all too common stance of one-upsmanship.

---

* This attitude is rarely expressed as openly as in *Provocative Therapy* (Farrelly & Brandsma, 1974): "In order to have a fighting chance in this kind of therapy, most of the maneuvers of patients must be available to the therapist to be used in the service of therapeutic change and strategy (. . .) The client's behavior is frequently seen as a ploy to control the relationship, and occasionally the therapist must counter it on a quite primitive level" (p. 57). But my contention is that the attitude is present in some form or other in a good deal of strategic therapy.

As with many of the tactics they recommend, an important goal is securing the patient's cooperation. One-upsmanship is seen as creating resistance with those clients who would be otherwise ready to cooperate with the therapist and it is therefore to be avoided. But, in general, taking the one-down position enhances the therapist's "maneuverability," in Brief Therapy terms. The aim of this, as they "put it bluntly" (Fisch et al., 1982, p. 23), is to maintain the therapist's options while limiting those of the patient, since it is the therapist who needs to maintain control of the treatment process.

I see one-downsmanship in a different light. It amounts to a certain modesty about what we are doing. It is an appreciation that, no matter how good we are at our job, we cannot be sure that we can help each new client who comes to see us. It amounts to not demeaning clients or imposing our point of view. It allows clients to reject what we are proposing. All this makes good sense without any reference to "maneuverability."

My comments on this as well as on other tactics relate to the therapist's attitude and not simply to some pragmatic criterion of whether that attitude "works" or not. The fact that it *does* is not the justification for it. The attitude cannot be reduced to a tactic or technique.

Therapeutic Pessimism

Therapeutic pessimism is a tactic whereby the therapist outdoes the desperate patient's pessimism so as to provoke the patient into being the more optimistic of the two. The following, from an article by Lynn Segal of the MRI, might be a typical exchange: the patient says, "Do you think you can help me, Doctor? I just can't take it any more," and the therapist replies, "Well, it's certainly understandable that you're feeling bad, but I don't want to give you any false hope. I haven't worked with anyone as depressed as you in a long time," etc. (Segal, 1981, pp. 217–218).

How can this be interpreted differently? Rather than seeing it as a tactic designed to avoid getting "caught" by the patient, I see this simply as a question of being realistic or not being unrealistically optimistic. Clients can come to therapy feeling desperate and therapists can be tempted to make promises about how much help can be obtained and how quickly it can be realized. However, a client's unconscious mind is not fooled by promises made on this basis any more than it is fooled by some affected protestation that the situation is even worse than he or she thought, such as this tactic suggests.

The Injunction to Go Slow

The "go slow" injunction is a tactic recommended for patients "whose main attempted solution is 'trying too hard,' or for clients who press the therapist with urgent demands for remedial actions while they remain passive or uncooperative" (Fisch et al., 1982, p. 160). It is also used with clients who return to the second session reporting "some definite and welcome improvement" (ibid., p. 160).

One nonadversarial explanation for this tactic is provided by Fisch et al. (1982) themselves when they say, "it removes a sense of urgency for the patient—an urgency that has probably been fueling his persistent attempts at 'solving' his problem" (p. 162).

Another way of understanding this is that clients can often come back after a first session flushed with the first successes and failing to appreciate that there may still be much work ahead. It may be realistic to warn them against being overly optimistic; otherwise, they may be overly discouraged by the first setback. How many therapists use the analogy of two steps forward and one backward?

Often, too, clients do not dare admit to themselves that they regard these first signs of improvement as rather fragile. The analogy Erickson gives can be a way of reminding them to "go slow" while reassuring them that this is a normal attitude: in *Changing Couples* (Haley, 1985b), he asks: "How do you really handle a brand-new set of dishes? Because you're worried about breaking them. . . . Handle with care because it's valuable" (p. 86). So the "go slow" is an empathic response to this feeling.

This is all rather different from the other rationale offered by the brief therapists when they write: "This tactic, we believe, is useful because it portrays the therapist as uncommitted to changing the patient, certainly quickly, and therefore induces implicit pressure on the patient to cooperate with any suggestions or advice the therapist may subsequently give" (Fisch et al., 1982, p. 162). We are back to an adversarial view that involves "inducing pressure."

Dangers of Improvement

Warning clients about the "dangers of improvement" can be used as an extension of the "go slow" tactic. It is seen as useful for certain kinds of resistance—for example, where the client fails to complete an assignment. It could be stated, for example, that maybe their unconscious is telling them that it would be dangerous for them to improve the present situation.

Here is another example: "A couple who fights constantly can be told that their problem is the only thing holding the marriage together, and that the therapist is reluctant to make further efforts at helping them stop their battles" (Segal, 1981, p. 128). Segal adds: "Of course, this is presented with the intention of having the couple resist such an interpretation."

The same points made about "go slow" can be made about "dangers of improvement." But in addition there is implicit in the thinking about dangers of improvement, and certainly in Segal's example, the idea that symptoms serve a protective function for people which may result in an "investment" in continuing the problem. Another view would acknowledge that when clients have been preoccupied for a long time with their problems and then those problems begin to disappear, there can be something of a vacuum in their lives and they should give some thought about how to fill it. I would not put this as a danger of improvement, but as one of the side-effects of improvement that it would be worthwhile thinking ahead about. For example, to parents who have been extremely worried about their child who has now shown improvement I often say that they should give some thought to what they are going to talk about together now. If I want to emphasize the point by hinting that even their sexual relationship may have been neglected because of their preoccupation with their child, I might ask them what they are now going to talk about *when they go to bed at night.*

After the presenting problem has been resolved, the adjustment period that follows can have its challenging aspects. The client or family often need help to prepare themselves. This is the point that Erickson makes in *Changing Couples* (Haley, 1985b) when Haley asks him the following question: ". . . when you see a patient with a reasonably severe symptom, do you assume that if he improves, there's going to be a reaction in the family that you have to take into account?" Erickson replies:

> Usually there *is* a reaction. The alcoholic [a case Erickson had mentioned earlier]—I asked his wife, I asked his daughter or son, "When father ceases to be an alcoholic, just how are you going to spend that time that you spent in the past devoting your energy to wishing he wouldn't, or avoiding him, or hammering away at

him that he better mend his ways? How are you going to spend that energy?" (pp. 137–138)

But those who still believe that people really do need their problems and want to hold on to them might consider the rather curious way Erickson described it (Haley, 1985a). He is talking about an inhibited patient called Ann who has a problem of gasping and choking:

> How many patients resent your taking their difficulty away from them? How many bottled up appendixes are there in the family treasures? Have you ever listened to someone tell you, "This is the appendix the doctor took out, and do you know how many attacks I had of appendicitis?" They treasure their problems, but they want to treasure them safely. (pp. 143–144)

Erickson has asked Ann to hold on to a part of her problem—to use the gasping and choking only when some particularly unpleasant friends come round to call, which she does to good effect. He continues: "What I was asking her was, 'Let's put your choking, gasping into a specimen bottle of some kind. And you can have it. It's yours.' " (p. 144)

Prescribing a Relapse

The concern about relapse after the problem is solved has led to the tactic called "prescribing the relapse." This is accomplished by telling clients to revert to the previous problematic behavior for a while, often with the request to see if there is anything they want to salvage from that behavior. This is purely an Erickson approach in one sense, but it may not be so in spirit. It is most frequently used "paradoxically" to show clients that they cannot in fact get the behavior back; or, if they do get it back, to emphasize thereby that they have control over the behavior.

But hear how Erickson replies to Haley (Haley, 1985b) when Haley asks him: "How do you keep them from going back to the previous pattern?" Erickson says:

> Oh, but you tell them that they really ought to go back to the previous pattern. . . . And select out of it that which needs to be salvaged. (p. 85)

His rationale is far more intriguing and subtle than a mere tactic, however:

> What are you doing? You're teaching them, "Don't be ashamed of that horrible past pattern, there's at least something worth salvaging." (p. 85)

He then links this to normal behavior:

> Just consider the small child with a favorite toy that he's got to discard, that he won't discard, which is all worn out. What do you do with him to get him to discard it? You salvage a part. And then he can discard it. (p. 85)

He then adds a final twist:

> When your couple goes back to that pattern, they really ought to go back to salvage some one little thing, because then *they* are earmarking it for complete disposal. (p. 86)

It is this kind of richness and naturalistic quality of Erickson's rationales that seem to be lost in the reductionistic tactics of the brief therapists who are derived from him.

I want to address now the related issues of paradox, resistance, and double binds, since all have figured prominently in strategic therapy.

Paradox

I suggest that what we refer to as "paradoxical" is often only the "unusual." Erickson says in the Foreword to Watzlawick, Weakland & Fisch's book *Change* (1974):

> I have viewed much of what I have done as expediting the currents of change already seething within the person and the family— but currents that need the "unexpected," the "illogical," and the "sudden" move to lead them into tangible fruition. (p. ix)

I think this is generally what paradox achieves. In Rossi's terms, it serves to "depotentiate habitual frameworks and belief systems" (Erickson & Rossi, 1979, p. 5). It challenges clients' beliefs and gets them to think anew about their problem.

The idea that we can get a "resistant" client to do something simply by telling them to do the opposite (the paradoxical injunction) is naive in the extreme. For example, when Erickson told patients at the beginning of the first session not to tell him more than they wanted to, was he using paradox? Why did the patients then tend to say more? The rationale lies much closer to the fact that they felt any pressure to reveal all taken off them. It is a frightening thought for clients to think they may have to reveal all, yet it is a common expectation when going to a psychiatrist or having hypnotherapy. The permission to withhold, when it is given genuinely by the therapist and not as a trick to get clients to say more, may free clients to feel more in charge about what they choose to say. It allows them to reveal things at their own pace. And the message of respect for clients' privacy implicit in the suggestion that they should withhold whatever they wish to can make them feel that this is a therapist whom they can trust.

Resistance

The word "resistance" does seem to be used less frequently now, largely because of Erickson and Ericksonians. Still it is important when encountering what may be considered resistance, to begin thinking about it as being something else.

For example, the classical situation of a client or a family not having completed an assigned task might be viewed as resistance. But there are a number of other commonsense reasons why they may not have completed the task:

1. They did not understand the task. We often assume too readily that clients and therapists understand each other. The room for misunderstanding is enormous and we should appreciate this.
2. There was something in the clients' views of things that prevented their accepting the task, something the therapist failed to take into account or did not even grasp. They may have kept quiet about this at the time; or it may be that, under the pressure of the session, they agreed, only to have second thoughts after leaving.
3. What seemed like a simple task to everyone at the time turned out to be more complex. When they got down to it, they discovered that they just were not equipped to carry it out in the prescribed way. Necessary skills were not available.
4. They didn't think it was possible and thus did not attempt it. It can take a lot to shift people's pessimism about their problems.

5. They understood, could have done it, thought it possible, but just did not want to do it right then, for whatever reason. We have all had difficulties and known what we should do about them, but postponed doing what was needed.
6. Any number of other reasons exist, none of which presuppose an adversarial view of clients' behavior. There is no need for the technical word "resistant" with its assumption that clients are unwilling in some sense to abandon their symptoms.*

The Double Bind

Finally I want to discuss Erickson's uses of the double bind, because it was in this area that he was most likely to be considered manipulative or "tricky." I refer specifically to his use of what has been called the "illusion of alternatives." For example, "Will you pay your bill this week or next week?" There is a choice, but what is presupposed in both parts is that the bill will be paid. One might think that this way of putting choices to clients could easily be used for the therapist's advantage. But I want to quote a passage from Erickson to emphasize the subtlety of his conception:

> You ought to help patients make their own proper decisions, and you ought to make those decisions as easy as possible for patients to make. (Erickson, 1983, p. 141)

This is the important context in which Erickson sets the discussion: helping patients make the decisions they need to make. He goes on:

> This brings us to the matter of using the double bind for your own selfish purposes. I know of some doctors who ask patients, "Do you want to pay your bill this week, or next week?" Patients unconsciously recognize the double bind and so decide, "I'll pay the bill this week, and find someone else to go to next week!"

And note here Erickson's faith in the patient's ability to recognize what is going on.

> In other words, the use of the double bind has to be in favor of the patient, never in favor of yourself.

---

* *Editor's note:* Erickson frequently discussed "resistance."

He then adds a vital comment about the therapist's attitude:

> In the use of hypnosis the very generosity of your attitude allows patients to feel utterly comfortable. Now I'm perfectly willing to put my patients in the double bind, but they also sense unconsciously that I will never, never, hold them to it.

And now comes a further layer:

> They know that I will yield anytime; they know that I will put them in a different double bind in some other situation so that they can make use of that new and different double bind that meets their needs more adequately.

This is a long way from manipulation: If the patient is not happy with either side of the alternative offered, he will resist the bind. (When I asked my five-year-old son once, for example, if he wanted to get ready for bed *before* having a story or *after* having a story, he sensed that my main interest was simply in getting him to bed because I was tired, and he accordingly replied: "I don't want to get ready for bed at all!") And Erickson finally adds:

> If you ever use the double bind selfishly, you will undoubtedly lose patients. (p. 141)

CONCLUSION

Strategic therapy grew out of Erickson's work, but only from one view of Erickson's work. Strategic therapy's techniques are so well-known and the association with Erickson so well established that it might be assumed that Erickson worked with the same rationales as strategic therapy does. By going back to Erickson's original words, however, I have shown that this may not be the case.

In general, he had a much more commonsense, optimistic and non-adversarial view of what he was doing. He *was* "strategic" in the sense that he was prepared to take charge of the therapy, be directive, and engage in problem-solving, but his rationales were straightforward. He avoided the "siege mentality" of much strategic therapy, and he thereby, I would argue, did not distance himself so much from his patients. He could be extremely playful, certainly, and he sometimes pitted his wits with his patients, but when he did so it was against the patient's problem and not against the patient.

REFERENCES

Bok, S. (1980). *Lying*. New York: Quartet Books.

Cade, B. (1980). Resolving therapeutic deadlocks using a contrived team conflict. *International Journal of Family Therapy, 2,* 253–262.

Erickson, M. H. (1980). Special techniques of brief hypnotherapy. In E. L. Rossi (Ed.), *The Collected Papers of Milton H. Erickson on Hypnosis Vol. 4* (pp. 149–173). New York: Irvington.

Erickson, M. H. (1983). *Healing in Hypnosis*. New York: Irvington.

Erickson, M. H., & Rossi, E. L. (1979). *Hypnotherapy: An Exploratory Guide*. New York: Irvington.

Farrelly, F., & Brandsma, J. (1974). *Provocative Therapy*. California: Meta Publications.

Fisch, R., Weakland, J. H., & Segal, L. (1982). *The Tactics of Change*. San Francisco: Jossey-Bass.

Haley, J. (1973). *Uncommon Therapy: The Psychiatric Techniques of Milton H. Erickson, M.D.* New York: Norton.

Haley, J. (1976). *Problem-Solving Therapy*. New York: Harper & Row.

Haley, J. (Ed.) (1985a). *Conversations with Milton H. Erickson, M.D.: Volume 1: Changing Individuals*. New York: Triangle Press.

Haley, J. (Ed.) (1985b). *Conversations with Milton H. Erickson, M.D.: Volume 2: Changing Couples*. New York: Triangle Press.

Haley, J. (Ed.) (1985c). *Conversations with Milton H. Erickson, M.D.: Volume 3: Changing Children and Families*. New York: Triangle Press.

Jackson, D. D., & Haley, J. (1963). Transference revisited. *Journal of Nervous and Mental Diseases, 137,* 363–371.

Lukes, S. (1977). *Essays in Social Theory*. London: MacMillan.

Popper, K. R. (1972). Two faces of common sense: An argument for commonsense realism and against the commonsense theory of knowledge. In *Objective Knowledge* (rev. ed.), pp. 32–105. Oxford: Oxford University Press.

Popper, K. R. (1983a). *Realism and the Aim of Science*. London: Hutchinson.

Popper, K. R. (1983b). *Quantum Theory and the Schism in Physics*. London: Hutchinson.

Popper, K. R., & Eccles, J. C. (1977). *The Self and Its Brain*. London: Springer.

Rosen, S. (1982). The values and philosophy of Milton H. Erickson. In J. K. Zeig (Ed.), *Ericksonian Approaches to Hypnosis and Psychotherapy* (pp. 462–476). New York: Brunner/Mazel.

Rossi, E. L. (1986). *The Psychobiology of Mind-Body Healing: New Concepts of Therapeutic Hypnosis*. New York: Norton.

Segal, L. (1981). Focused problem resolution. In E. R. Tolman & W. J. Reid (Eds.), *Models of Family Treatment* (pp. 199–223). Columbia: Columbia University Press.

Segal, L. (1986). *The Dream of Reality: Heinz von Foerster's Constructivism*. New York: Norton.

Speed, B. (1985). Can we justify strategic dishonesty? Unpublished invited commentary on M. Sheinberg. The debate: A strategic technique. *Family Process, 24,* 259–271.

Speed, B. (1987). Over the top in the theory and practice of family therapy. *Journal of Family Therapy, 9,* 231–240.

Watzlawick, P., Weakland, J. H., & Fisch, R. (1974). *Change: Principles of Problem Formation and Problem Resolution*. New York: Norton.

Watzlawick, P. (1976). *How Real is Real?* New York: Random House.

Watzlawick, P. (Ed.) (1984). *The Invented Reality*. New York: Norton.
Wilk, J. (1984, September). (Review of *The Invented Reality*). *The Underground Railroad,*
    5 (3), 5–7. (Available from The Brief Family Therapy Center, 6815 West Capitol
    Drive, Milwaukee, WI 53216.)

Chapter 5

Ericksonian Psychotherapy and Social Psychology

Steven J. Sherman

Steven J. Sherman, Ph.D. (University of Michigan), is Professor of Psychology at Indiana University. In addition to authoring numerous publications on the relation of attitude to behavior, he is Editor of the Attitudes and Social Cognition section of the Journal of Personality and Social Psychology, *ad hoc reviewer for National Science Foundation Grants in the social/developmental area, and Chair of the grant study section of the National Institutes of Health, Behavioral Medicine. He has served on the Editorial Boards of* The Journal of Experimental Social Psychology, The Journal of Personality and Social Psychology, *and* Social Psychology Quarterly.

This chapter is long overdue in the Ericksonian literature. Sherman describes major aspects of Ericksonian psychotherapeutic approaches from the perspective of social psychology principles. Research studies from social psychology shed light on Erickson's intuitive understandings about how change happens. Careful reading of this chapter should be required of all students of Ericksonian-influenced communications.

As a therapist, Milton Erickson was above all else an effective agent of social influence. In fact, this was clearly the way in which he viewed himself. His goal was to induce changes in the attitudes and behaviors of his clients that would allow them to feel better and function more effectively. In trying to achieve this goal, Erickson adopted an

I would like to thank Roberta Sherman and Eric Knowles for helpful discussions and for their comments on early drafts.

atheoretical approach and was willing and able to call upon a large arsenal of influence techniques in order to bring about change. His basic assumptions were simple—people are changeable, and powerful techniques are available to achieve change. He felt that it was not necessary or even desirable that clients gain insight into their feelings or behaviors or problems or that they understand the influence techniques that were being used to change them.

Clients did not necessarily participate equally in the change process. They were the targets of change, and Erickson was the social influence agent who set up the psychological and physical situations that would have the highest likelihood of success. Although his approach was rooted in hypnosis, his role was primarily as a source of influence communication, and he employed whatever powerful influence techniques he could devise.

This view of Ericksonian psychotherapy and the process by which it worked clearly identifies Erickson with the interests and research of social psychologists who have been concerned with understanding the processes of social influence and attitude change. It thus seems appropriate to try to interpret and understand Erickson's approach to therapy through social psychology theories, principles, and techniques of influence and to scrutinize and evaluate his ideas in light of these theories and principles.

As an experimental social psychologist who has been working in the areas of influence and attitude change for 20 years, I found reading Erickson's work and watching some of his video tapes to be an incredibly enlightening experience. It is remarkable how much Erickson appreciated existing principles of social influence without necessarily stating them explicitly. It is even more remarkable how he seemed to understand and use principles that had yet to be empirically demonstrated, but have been verified in more recent years. In addition, his work suggests general principles of influence that are testable but have yet to be researched. His ideas and techniques are thus able to provide social psychology with fertile ground for research.

The application of social psychology principles to Ericksonian psychotherapy is thus seen as being useful and helpful to both disciplines. The endeavor can help therapists (those of an Ericksonian persuasion as well as others) to understand how social psychology research and theory can be useful in the practice and appreciation of therapeutic interventions. For the Ericksonian-oriented therapist in particular, I hope to clarify the processes and mechanisms by which some of his techniques

work in the hope that this clarification will aid in the further development and application of these techniques.

The application of social psychology principles to Ericksonian techniques can be useful in another way as well. In some respects, the
current interest and excitement about Erickson's ideas and therapy
techniques have sometimes put Erickson in the position of a cult hero—
the charismatic and inscrutable guru. The mystery, myths, and exag-
gerations have often become larger than the man. His followers tend
to reify him rather than build upon what he has begun. It is hoped
that placing Erickson's work and ideas within the realm of experimental
psychology will humanize the work and demonstrate that rather than
being based on magic and intuition, it is understandable in terms of
solid psychological principles and processes.

For the social psychologist, the exercise should be equally useful. The
Ericksonian techniques not only exemplify what social psychologists
already know, but also suggest principles and processes that have not
been empirically tested or conceptually developed. It should thus be
an informative exercise for the psychotherapist and the social psychologist alike.

Although this is not the first time that social psychology principles
have been used in order to understand psychotherapy (Brehm, 1976;
Goldstein, Heller, & Sechrest, 1966; Weary & Mirels, 1982), it is noteworthy how seldom this has been done. The client-therapist relationship
is clearly one that involves social influence, with behavioral and attitude
change as its primary goals. One thus would think that training as a
clinical psychologist, counselor, or psychiatrist would involve a thorough
understanding of the principles of social influence. It seems reasonable
that work in the areas of attitude change, compliance, conformity, and
imitation would be indispensable for training as a psychotherapist. Yet,
unfortunately, most of the training involves learning about theories of
psychopathology and taxonomies of disorders. Learning about the techniques of influence that would improve the effectiveness of therapists
is rarely provided.

The present chapter will indicate the benefit and applicability of such
learning as it applies specifically to Ericksonian techniques. In addition,
I will focus on some of the newer and more specific areas of research
in social psychology (e.g., priming, automatism, scripts) rather than on
general theories where the direct relevance is less obvious.

Although it might appear that the application of social psychology
theories and principles to Ericksonian psychotherapy could easily be

done within a single chapter, I have discovered that even a book would probably not be sufficient. Thus, it will not be possible to consider all of Erickson's techniques in light of social psychological theory and research. Nor will it be possible to detail the vast array of research and theory that could be fruitfully applied. Rather, I shall have to pick and choose the techniques and the social psychological work that might be most useful and interesting. As an initial step in this pruning process, I will not consider hypnotherapy, although this was clearly a major technique used by Erickson. Instead, I will focus on the more specific principles and techniques that Erickson employed either within hypnosis or outside of it.

ERICKSONIAN TECHNIQUES

1. Indirection

If any single principle captured Erickson's general approach to therapy, it was indirection. He felt that communications need not be logical or concrete or direct in order to be effective. In fact, greater effectiveness could be achieved by communications that were paradoxical, meta-phorical, illogical, or indirect. Examples of Erickson's use of indirection are legendary, and the point should be clear to anyone familiar with these techniques. For those who are not familiar with specific examples of indirection, Haley's (1973) book is an excellent source.

When it comes to the use of direct vs. indirect approaches to social influence, social psychologists are very much in agreement with Erickson's assumptions about the advantages of indirection. To the extent that clients in psychotherapy or subjects in social psychology experiments that are concerned with influence and attitude change are aware of the change induction, the goals of the situation (i.e., to change them), and the techniques that are being used, these techniques are less likely to be effective. One cannot reveal to subjects in a conformity experiment that the other people are confederates who might give bogus judgments every so often. Nor can subjects in an attitude change experiment be told that the goal of the study is to try to get them to change their evaluations.

Such direct communication of goals and techniques is likely to be troublesome and ineffective for many reasons. Most important is the fact that motivations for mastery and control lead to the arousal of resistance or reactance when one's control is threatened. Thus, when another person is obviously trying to control and change your attitudes and behavior, a great deal of resistance is engaged. For these reasons, social psychologists who study conformity and attitude change often use deception in the course of the experiment in order to hide from subjects the fact that techniques are being employed that have the goal of social influence. Likewise, social psychologists often use nonreactive and unobtrusive measures so that subjects are not concerned with issues of control and change in the course of the experiment.

In a similar way, Erickson often did not make clients aware of the goals for change or of the techniques that were designed to achieve these goals. Such awareness would interfere with the process of change. Indirect techniques are clearly optimal in keeping subjects and clients alike from focusing on issues of control. And just as Erickson would predict, indirect techniques in the laboratory, such as overheard messages (Walster & Festinger, 1962) and messages received during distraction (Festinger & Maccoby, 1964), typically prove to be more effective than direct techniques.

It should be noted that the use of such indirect techniques and the decision not to fully inform subjects or clients about the techniques or goals of the experimenter or of the therapist is not incompatible with ethical practices. Deception or lack of full information is an acceptable ethical practice providing that the subject or client is in no way harmed by the practice and that the gain in knowledge or the gain in the ultimate happiness of the client more than balances the deceptive practice. It should be added that in Erickson's case the indirect communications that he provided were primarily errors of omission rather than commission. That is, Erickson did not seem to lie to clients about what was happening or why. He simply failed to share with them his goals and strategies.

Within his use of indirect techniques (which included the use of metaphors, anecdotes, and parallel talk), Erickson set forth an interesting and important principle. Zeig (1985a) formulated it as follows: The necessity of using indirect techniques (and the likely effectiveness of such techniques) was directly proportional to the amount of resistance experienced by the client. For nonresistant clients, Erickson could be quite direct and concrete. Only for resistant clients would he employ subtle, indirect, and paradoxical communications.

Social psychology tends to focus on general principles that are true for an entire population. On the other hand, therapists must rely on idiographic prescriptions, intuition, or heuristic rules as they deal with unique clients. Erickson's ideas about varying the indirectness of the therapy technique with the resistance of the client allows a blending of social psychological and clinical approaches by looking for personality modifiers of nomothetic relations.

The notion of varying indirectness with the amount of resistance represents an extremely important general statement from both an applied and a theoretical perspective about the relative effectiveness of different kinds of communications under different conditions. As far as I know, this proposition has not been empirically tested in social psychological research. However, there is one approach to attitude change that seems very relevant to this principle and might be used to support and to expand upon Erickson's ideas.

Katz (1960), in proposing a functional approach to attitude change, suggested that different attitudes and opinions served very different functions for different individuals. Even attitudes about the same object (e.g., toward authority figures) might be held for different psychological reasons by different people. Katz identified several such possible functions. In particular, let us consider two of these: the ego-defensive function and the knowledge function.

Attitudes that serve an ego-defensive function protect a person from acknowledging basic truths about himself or harsh realities around him. Attitudes serving a knowledge function are held in order to help the person give meaning to and correctly understand the social and physical world around him. Clearly, attitudes serving an ego-defensive function would show greater resistance to attempts at change. Erickson would thus suggest that these attitudes would respond better to indirect techniques, although attitudes serving a knowledge function would respond quite well to more direct approaches. Although it is difficult to classify the techniques used by Katz and his associates (e.g., Katz, Sarnoff, & McClintock, 1956), data do indicate that reality-oriented approaches were not effective with ego-defensive attitudes and more indirect techniques were far more effective.

Research should be done that directly manipulates the degree of resistance experienced by subjects or that selects subjects for their levels of resistance with respect to a certain attitude. Then the degree of directness of an attitude change technique could be systematically manipulated. Such a study would prove valuable in our understanding of attitude functions and of the techniques that are likely to be most appropriate for changing attitudes that are based on these different functions. The social psychology work does suggest, however, that therapists would do well to try to assess the function that is served by various attitudes and beliefs of the client. The best approach to therapy might well depend upon the function that is served by problematic attitudes and behaviors.

2. Seeding or Priming

The content of clients' thoughts is clearly important to the therapeutic process. So, too, is the way in which they think about and interpret events and outcomes. In fact, it is reasonable to maintain that it is people's subjective constructions and interpretations of reality that are more important to psychological functioning and happiness than are the objective realities of the situation. With this in mind, Erickson employed a number of techniques designed to affect the content of thought as well as the interpretation of events. One of the most important and prevalent of these techniques was seeding or priming.

In general, priming refers to the activation or change in accessibility of a concept by an earlier presentation of the same or a closely-related concept. Research in both social and cognitive psychology has demonstrated several important consequences of priming. For example, priming affects the speed with which lexical decisions (i.e., deciding whether a string of letters is a word or not) are made. Thus, following the presentation of words such as "orange" or "peach," a lexical decision about "apple" is faster than if no primes had been presented. The altered accessibility of primed category members accounts for results such as this. Priming also affects the speed with which subjects can generate category members and the speed of simply reading a word.

In addition to these simple effects of priming on latency, priming has other effects that are more relevant to the therapeutic situation. One is seen when subjects are asked to categorize an ambiguously described stimulus. In a typical study, Higgins, Rholes, and Jones (1977) passively primed subjects in the course of a color-naming experiment with words representing one or the other pole of a trait dimension (e.g., words connoting confidence vs. conceit, or risk vs. adventuresomeness). During a subsequent "unrelated" experiment, subjects were asked to form an impression of a character described in ambiguous terms (e.g., the character might be seen as confident or conceited). Subjects' interpretations were highly influenced in the direction of the trait terms that had been primed. In other words, the very interpretation of people and events can be affected by concepts and categories that are previously seeded.

Priming has also been shown to affect the content of "freely generated" thoughts and examples. Nisbett and Wilson (1977) initially gave subjects a list of paired associates to learn. For some subjects, the list included the pair ocean-moon. For others, the list did not include this item. Subjects were later asked to name a laundry detergent. Many more subjects named "Tide" if they had previously been exposed to the ocean-moon item. Interestingly, subjects were totally unaware of the effect and denied it as a possibility when asked.

The effects of priming may be even more general. Higgins and Chaires (1980) primed subjects with a relational construct emphasizing the separateness of items (e.g., "a box *and* cherries; a jar *and* pickles"). Subjects thus primed were far more able to subsequently solve the Duncker candle problem than were control subjects. In this insight problem, subjects have at their disposal a cardboard wall, a candle, a book of matches, and a box filled with thumbtacks. Their task is to affix the candle to the wall so that it burns properly without dripping wax on the table below. The difficult part of the problem is to think of using the box as a platform for the candle rather than as simply a container for the tacks. The solution to this problem thus depends upon the ability to separate the uses of thumbtacks from the box in which they are contained, a technique that was achieved by priming the "and" relational construct.

In a similar way, LaRue and Olejnik (1980) had subjects engage in either simple arithmetic tasks or complex logical reasoning. This presumably primed different ways of thinking. On a subsequent moral reasoning task, subjects who had engaged in complex thinking demonstrated more highly developed levels of moral reasoning. Finally, Wilson and Capitman (1982) primed subjects with a "boy meets girl" scenario by a radio broadcast while they were waiting for the experiment. Such subtle priming very much affected the subjects' behaviors toward a member of the opposite sex (communication, seating distance, etc.) during the subsequent experiment.

The extent of priming effects is thus remarkably comprehensive and general. Seeding concepts and ideas can alter what subjects later think about, how they interpret events, and how they act. Erickson often employed similar techniques by introducing ideas and examples at an early time during a therapy session so that clients would think in certain ways later in the session or after the session. For example, Haley (1973) reports Erickson's conversation with Joe, a terminally ill florist. Erickson introduced concepts relevant to plants and gardening and used concepts and ideas that Joe might later employ in thinking about his own life and situation in terms of growth, comfort, and beauty. The possible uses of priming techniques for altering clients' thoughts and behaviors have only begun to be appreciated. Understanding both the techniques for priming concepts as well as the likely consequences of priming should be of great value for psychotherapists.

The use of priming as a technique tells us something else that is important about Erickson's approach to therapy. Setting clients up for things to come implies that Erickson was always looking forward and planning ahead. He was always several steps ahead of his clients and predicated his current behaviors on the basis of what he knew was coming. In other words, he did not simply react to situations, but rather constructed the kinds of situations that he wanted. This is exactly what one must do to be effective at many tasks. A good chess player, a good baseball manager, and a good agent of influence share one thing in common—they structure the present in light of what is likely to occur in the future.

3. Use of the Unconscious

Erickson based many of his techniques and practices on the assumption that people had an active unconscious that was able to direct thoughts and behaviors independently of conscious processes. In fact, in many ways Erickson believed that it was more important to communicate with a client's unconscious than with his or her conscious mind. The unconscious better represented the true core of the person and could reveal the truth in ways that would be unencumbered by issues of social desirability or self-presentation.

I must admit that at times I have been skeptical of Erickson's true belief in the unconscious. It seems to me that having clients believe in an unconscious part of themselves frees them to communicate things that they might ordinarily inhibit—because it seems to come from their unconscious and not from them. It allows a third person (so to speak) to enter into the therapy session who is and at the same time is not identical to the client. This can make for a greater number of communication possibilities at many different levels of communication. It allows the therapist to choose "which client" to speak to and which to hear from.

Whether or not Erickson truly believed in the unconscious or whether he used his apparent belief as a technique to allow freer or deeper communication with his clients, the fact is that he did discuss at length the role of the unconscious in people's thoughts and behaviors. He maintained these ideas about the unconscious even at times when mainstream experimental psychologists were dismissing the possibility of unconscious cognitive processes or subliminal perception and persuasion. However, once again Erickson proved to be ahead of his time. It is now well accepted that quite complex cognitive processing goes on below the level of conscious awareness. Not only can information be received without awareness, but that information can be integrated and interpreted in the absence of conscious awareness.

As an example of such complex processing, Corteen and Wood (1972) demonstrated that semantic processing is possible at unconscious levels. In an initial task, the experimenters associated the names of various cities with the onset of a mild shock. Having established conditioned physiological responses in subjects to the city names, the experimenters proceeded to the second part of the study. In this phase, subjects were transferred to a dichotic listening task. This task involves delivering different auditory material to each ear at the same time. Subjects can be told to pay attention only to material that comes into one ear (the attended ear) and to ignore material that comes into the other ear (the unattended ear). Words presented to the unattended ear are not received at the conscious level, and subjects cannot report what they hear in the unattended ear. Yet whenever a city name was presented to the unattended ear, subjects produced a significant number of autonomic physiological responses—even toward city names that had not been included in the first part of the study. In other words, subjects processed these words below the level of awareness and even extracted the meaning and category representation of these words.

Other recent work has also demonstrated the important and general effects of stimuli presented below the level of awareness. For instance, Bargh and Pietromonaco (1982) did a priming study much like the one described earlier by Higgins, Rholes, and Jones (1977). However, rather than presenting the priming stimuli at a level where subjects could process them consciously, the experimenters presented subjects with priming stimuli tachistoscopically so that they could not be processed at the level of conscious awareness. Still this subliminal priming affected the way that subjects later interpreted the ambiguously described behavior of target individuals. Subjects saw greater hostility in a target person's behavior when they had been primed at the unconscious level by hostility-related words. Thus, the seeding of constructs and ideas can affect later interpretations even when such constructs are introduced below conscious awareness. This finding would certainly appeal to Erickson, who felt that ideas introduced at the unconscious level would be more effective because they would not engage resistance or counter-arguing.

In yet another interesting demonstration of subliminal effects, Kunst-Wilson and Zajonc (1980) took advantage of a well-known social psychological phenomenon, the frequency-attraction effect. This effect concerns the fact that we seem to like things better the more we see them. Kunst-Wilson and Zajonc showed that this effect held true even when the stimuli were presented below conscious awareness. Subjects were presented with a number of geometric shapes, and each shape was presented a different number of times. The presentation was done tachistoscopically so that conscious attention was not possible. The results indicated that subjects later preferred the shapes that had been presented the greatest number of times even though they could not recognize which shapes had been presented before and which had not. It is thus clear that attitudes toward objects can develop on the basis of information that is presented at the unconscious level. It certainly appears that Erickson was correct in suggesting the variety and complexity of processing that can go on at the unconscious level.

4. Cognitive Reactance

In discussing Erickson's use of indirect techniques, I have indicated how he was concerned with resistance or reactance expressed by his clients. He used indirect techniques to help get around the resistance. However, he was also able to use and arouse reactance to his own benefit. The term cognitive reactance was introduced by Brehm in 1966. He defined reactance as the feeling that is experienced whenever one's freedom is eliminated or is threatened with elimination. People will respond to reactance by attempting to reestablish the threatened behavior. This is the motivation, then, that can account for boomerang effects in social influence, for reverse psychology, and for counter-control ("Why did the children put beans in their ears when it's the one thing I told them not to do?"). In other words, people will be motivated to engage in restricted behaviors even when they might not have done so had the behaviors not been so restricted.

Erickson was clearly aware of the importance and usefulness of reactance. In the first place, he recognized the necessity of allowing people to resist control and to establish their freedom. Often he did this early in the therapy session during the induction of a hypnotic trance when he asked for a movement or a response that clients failed to give. Having expressed their freedom in this sphere, they were probably more likely to go along with requests in other areas that were far more important to Erickson.*

Erickson also used reactance more directly in order to achieve his ends. It obviously follows from reactance theory that when positive behaviors are threatened (behaviors that the therapist wants to see), these behaviors will become more likely to appear. Symptom prescription is an excellent example of using such a technique. When a client suffering from headaches is told to come to the next session with a huge headache or when a client is told to be extremely depressed, reactance can be resolved only by failing to have a headache or a fit of depression. Likewise, Erickson instructed his clients that they would have a positive experience on Monday or Thursday, but not on Wednesday. Often clients would come back the next week and report that they had the positive experience, but they had it on Wednesday. Of course, it was irrelevant to Erickson when the positive experience occurred, but his technique allowed subjects to express resistance and maintain some control over their behavior.

5. Control

It is clear from the above discussion of reactance that feelings of control are extremely important to healthy human functioning. People respond to a perception of lack of control with learned helplessness (Abramson, Seligman, & Teasdale, 1978; Seligman, 1975), a state that is characterized by depression and a lack of motivation and effort. It is probably of little consequence whether people actually have control over themselves or over the world around them—as long as they think that they do. Langer (1975) has demonstrated the importance of people developing an "illusion of control" even in situations that are clearly determined by random factors.

---

* *Editor's Note:* Examples of this technique can be found in two training videotapes available from The Milton H. Erickson Foundation: *Symbolic Hypnotherapy* and *The Process of Hypnotic Induction.*

Despite the fact that Erickson had rather tight control over the therapy sessions and the feelings and behaviors that the client would adopt both in and out of the sessions, he nevertheless went to great lengths to demonstrate to the clients that they did indeed have the ability to control things—even if this perception was an illusion. The client often controlled when or how much, but Erickson controlled the what.

In the example cited above, subjects who had their positive experiences on Wednesday felt that they had control, and this gave them a feeling of power and self-efficacy. Similarly, Erickson would often arrange for clients to have somewhat different symptoms than usual or to express them in a new place or at a new time. This could then be used to demonstrate to clients how they could exert control over their symptoms. Likewise, Erickson would often give the client the choice of two or more alternatives: They could take one or two or three deep breaths. Of course, any response among the alternatives would be acceptable to Erickson, but the feelings of choice and freedom would be maintained better than in a situation where the client is told exactly what to do. In fact, once the client chose a particular alternative, he/she would no doubt be committed to this choice.

6. Changing Perspectives

Stimuli, especially social stimuli, may have no objective position on many dimensions. How honest is someone? How good a ballplayer? How happy or sad? These are obviously relative judgments, and once again the important thing for therapy would be changes in people's perceptions or judgments of social reality rather than changes in objective reality. One thing that greatly affects judgments is the context in which these judgments are made. Social judgment theory (Sherif & Hovland, 1961) demonstrates how perceptions of identical stimuli can vary when different contextual stimuli are present. The classic example is the experience that tepid water feels hot when the other hand is immersed in ice water, but the same tepid water feels cold when the other hand is immersed in hot water.

In addition, when anchor stimuli are introduced, other stimuli may be assimilated toward such anchors or contrasted away from them. As an example of contrast effects, subjects judge their wives and girlfriends as less attractive after seeing pictures of beautiful movie stars (Kenrick & Gutierres, 1980). Similarly, it is easier to sell a customer an expensive belt after he buys a suit than before. After he has laid out so much money for an expensive suit, even a very expensive belt seems cheap in contrast (Cialdini, 1985).

Another aspect of context effects on judgment should be considered. We often develop an attitude toward an object, a person, or ourselves in a particular context. We arrive at a global judgment and label it. Later, this label may remain even though one's life circumstances and the context in which one lives have changed. Thus, we may continue to maintain our old beliefs and attitudes because we do not recognize the necessity of changing the label or the judgment in light of a new life context. An anecdote may help to clarify this process.

When I was a graduate student, special occasions were celebrated by eating at a particular restaurant near Ann Arbor. Given the year and the amount of money I had available, this was clearly a good restaurant—especially compared to most of the other restaurants that I frequented. This special restaurant was thus labeled "great" by me. A few years ago, I was in the Ann Arbor area and saw that this restaurant was still there. I raved about it to my wife and friends, and we went there for dinner. What a disappointment. The meal was clearly mediocre. At first I thought about how much the restaurant had gone downhill over the years. Only later did the real facts hit me. The restaurant had not changed at all. What had changed was my context, comparison restaurants, and set of experiences. In the intervening years, I had eaten at "truly" great restaurants. The label that I had applied as a graduate student took into account only my limited restaurant experiences at the time. Yet the label took on a reality of its own, and I failed to consider the context in which it had been originally applied. The same phenomenon occurs when we go back to visit our grammar school or high school. How could such a "huge" building have gotten so small over the years?

Erickson was very much aware of context effects in perception and judgment. In fact, he often used his own infirmities in this way. Compared to such an old and physically frail person, clients felt less handicapped. If he could function well with all his problems, certainly they could. Erickson thus often used himself as a standard of comparison for his clients. In addition, by establishing other particular objects of comparison and by manipulating contexts, Erickson was often able to affect clients' perceptions of their problems and their abilities. For example, he might direct a client concerned with her physical attractiveness to go out and look at all the ugly people in the street.

In a related way, Higgins and his colleagues have recently shown the importance of different standards of comparison (Higgins, Klein, & Strauman, 1985). According to this work, discrepancies between the self and what one wants to do ideally lead to sadness and dejection. Discrepancies between the self and what one should do lead to agitation and stress. By altering the standards of comparison or by manipulating salient standards, a client's degree of dejection or agitation can be affected. Such utilization of standards could be useful within an Ericksonian approach to therapy.

In line with his understanding of context effects on judgment, Erickson was also aware of the use of changing perspectives in other ways. Often the problem with clients is their rigidity of thought and behavior. They are stuck in characteristic ways of thinking and acting. Erickson believed that some change, *any* change, would be beneficial. A new way of seeing the world could only help. This is no doubt one of the reasons why Erickson had his clients bend over and look through their legs as they did when they were children or why he directed them to climb Squaw Peak or to go to the Phoenix Botanical Gardens and look at the boojum tree. These were experiences that would give one a different perspective on things. And this is often a critical step in psychotherapy.

In a similar way, Erickson's ideas about reframing are consistent with the benefits of changing perspectives. Tversky and Kahneman (1981) demonstrated how important the framing of problems is for judgments and decisions. Formally identical problems and situations will be responded to in different ways depending upon how they are framed. Thus, decisions about important medical choices will be different depending on whether the phrasing is in terms of the number of patients who will live as opposed to the number of patients who will die with each possible choice. The facts do not change, but the framing does.

Erickson was well aware of the power of framing. Impotence or premature ejaculation could be seen as an expression of great love for the partner rather than as a serious sexual problem (Haley, 1973). An inability to work or to travel could be seen as an opportunity to appreciate and enjoy one's life at home. The use of reframing was the technique that Erickson used most often in turning clients' deficits into assets. This is an extremely important technique because objective facts are often unchangeable, but the framing of those facts is quite easy to alter.

7. Effort Justification

One of the derivations of cognitive dissonance theory is that the harder people work at things the more they like these things and the more committed they are to them. This holds also for the process of psychotherapy. Axsom and Cooper (1985) have recently shown the application of this principle. Overweight subjects attempted to lose weight by one of two forms of "effort therapy." These therapies were bogus and were based solely on the expenditure of effort in tasks unrelated to anything that should produce weight loss. One of the therapies involved high effort and the other involved low effort. Reliable differences in weight loss emerged as long as one year after therapy, with high effort subjects losing significantly more weight.

The role of effort was not lost on Erickson. He often gave clients homework that involved a great deal of effort: climbing Squaw Peak, taking long drives, looking up many articles in the library. Clearly, expending such effort could commit clients to psychotherapy and to achieving the goals that were set—independent of any other benefits that might come from the particular homework.

Erickson's own handicaps may have inadvertently worked in a similar way. It was often difficult for clients to understand Erickson because of his slurred speech. One had to listen very carefully to understand what he was saying, and the outcome of this was increased attention and increased effort. In fact, I have heard that Erickson would at times make listening even more difficult for the client. When trucks or planes went by so that it was noisy in the office, most people would think of raising their voices in order to be heard. Not Erickson. He is said to have kept his voice the same so that clients would pay particular attention and expend even more effort listening (Zeig, 1985b).

8. Confusion

Another technique that Erickson used (often in conjunction with hypnosis or as a way to induce a trance) was confusion. By introducing plays on words or irrelevancies into his communications or by giving clients too much information to process or by talking in non sequiturs, Erickson hoped to bring about a state of momentary bewilderment. He did this for several reasons. First, he felt that this would prevent rehearsal of the past and would thus create amnesia for material processed right before the confusion, material that he did not want clients to dwell on or to process consciously (Zeig, 1985b). In addition, the state of confusion might require so much attention and feelings of ineptitude that subjects would lower their levels of resistance. This would make them more susceptible to subsequent attempts at influence. (See Erickson, 1964; Gilligan, 1986; Zeig, 1982 for discussion of the confusion technique.)

Although these are extremely interesting propositions, they have not been addressed experimentally to date. One of my students, Gina Agostinelli, is currently working on a dissertation project designed to assess the effects of inducing confusion. In particular, she will examine the effects of confusion on memory for prior and subsequently presented information, on comprehension of that information, on the ways in which information is processed under confusion (perhaps by using simple processing rules and principles), and on the extent to which subjects are vulnerable to influence attempts following the induction of confusion. An understanding of the processes involved in confusion and of the outcomes of a confused state would be useful in helping therapists to develop this potentially valuable technique.

9. Scripts

Scripts are defined as schemas or knowledge structures that we hold about behavioral sequences (Abelson, 1978). Thus, we all have our restaurant script, our day-at-the-beach script, and our being-at-a-therapy-session script. We know the typical behaviors involved and the sequencing of these behaviors. An interesting property of scripts is that once we are involved in a behavioral script, it is difficult to escape from it. We inevitably get carried along with the behaviors in a rather mindless, automatic way. Thus, if we can start a person in a particular script, the rest of the sequence will run off automatically, and we can gain a good deal of behavioral control in this manner. Cialdini (1985) refers to this as the click-whirr phenomenon and gives examples of both human and animal behavior that can be understood by the initiation of standard response sequences.

In a striking demonstration of this technique, Langer, Blank, and Chanowitz (1978) investigated the ability of an experimental confederate to break into a long line at a Xerox machine. When subjects simply asked if they could go to the front of the line, there was only 60% compliance. When they added a valid reason (they had an important meeting and were in a rush), the compliance rate increased to 94%. Most interesting, when they asked to break into line and added a meaningless reason ("because I have to make some copies"), compliance was at 93%. The presence of a request plus a reason seems to automatically trigger a compliance response, the endpoint of the behavioral script.

Such a technique is clearly useful in therapy. It allows the therapist to induce the client to think or act in certain desirable ways. One way in which Erickson found this technique useful was in the production of a "yes-set" response pattern. He would start with questions where the answer was obviously "yes" and would keep asking such questions to establish the pattern. Soon subjects would be agreeing to things that they might not have agreed to had the response pattern not been established.

Erickson would also induce behaviors and thoughts by subtly setting up the initial part of a sequence, knowing that the client would complete it. In one case, Erickson wanted the client to think about being warmhearted and kind.* By referring to her "cold hands," he knew that the rest of the response sequence would be established. Such a technique has the obvious advantage of being indirect. In addition, it is difficult to resist. The completion of a script or highly established response pattern is automatic and inescapable.

10. Predicting, Imagining, and Explaining the Future

Predicting the future or imagining and explaining hypothetical or possible future events can have important effects on actual judgments of those events and on one's behavior when the relevant situation actually arises in the future (Ross, Lepper, Strack, & Steinmetz, 1977). In other words, thinking about the future before it happens can actually affect what happens in the future. Thus, if we can control what a person thinks about or the particular outcome that is imagined, we can determine how this person will act in the future. In a demonstration of the effects of prediction, I (Sherman, 1980) asked subjects what they would do if someone called and asked them to devote an afternoon's time to collecting money for charity. Approximately 40% of the subjects predicted that they would agree to the request. From a normative perspective, their predictions were wrong (a separate group was simply

---

* *Editor's Note:* This case is described in depth in *Symbolic Hypnotherapy*, a videotape available from the Milton H. Erickson Foundation.

called and asked to devote time to charity and only 2% agreed to do this). However, having made this misprediction, subjects who had predicted the future acted in line with their prediction on a later, separate occasion when they were actually called and asked to help collect money for charity. In other words, volunteer rates rose from 2% to about 35% by simply asking a group of subjects to predict the future prior to making the actual request. It turns out that people tend to predict behavior that is far more socially desirable than they actually perform. But having thought about themselves and the future in this desirable way, they actually do act in a more desirable way. Can a better world be created through prediction?

In the realm of the future, subjects who imagine and explain a hypothetical victory by one football team over another in an upcoming game actually believe that the team that is imagined winning is more likely to win (Sherman, Zehner, Johnson, & Hirt, 1983). Subjects who imagine enjoying the benefits of cable T.V. actually sign up in increased numbers for this service (Gregory, Cialdini, & Carpenter, 1982). Subjects who imagined that they succeeded (or failed) at an upcoming anagram task and explained this outcome then judged the explained outcome as more likely to occur. In addition, those who explained hypothetical success actually went on to outperform those who explained hypothetical failure (Sherman, Skov, Hervitz, & Stock, 1981).

Indeed, thinking about the future in a particular way has important effects on that future. In a study that is more relevant from a clinical perspective, R. Sherman and Anderson (1987) asked first-time therapy clients to imagine staying in therapy for at least four sessions and to explain why they were able to do this. Premature termination from therapy by this group was substantially less than termination by clients who did not imagine or explain such an outcome.

Erickson often used imagination and explanation of possible circumstances in his therapy. Clients were asked to think about things as bizarre as floating through space or as mundane as what it would be like at home if some small thing were to change. Erickson would ask clients to respond to questions such as, "If you weren't so tolerant, what would you and your spouse disagree about?" This is precisely the kind of hypothetical thinking that engages the processes discussed above. By guiding clients' imagery and the kinds of outcomes that they were to think about and explain, Erickson no doubt affected how these clients behaved when the relevant situation arose. Once again we see the importance of a technique that stresses cognitive activity and tries to manipulate the way in which people represent and think about events.

11. Altering Accessibility

One mechanism through which hypothetical explanation tasks work is altering the accessibility of various facts in memory. When people think about possible situations or are asked to explain a potential outcome, they bring to mind concepts and ideas consistent with this outcome. When making subsequent judgments or making behavioral decisions, these ideas will then be most accessible and will serve as a basis for the judgment or behavior. For example, in the study by Sherman et al. (1981), some subjects were asked to imagine that they had tried an anagram task and had failed badly. Others were asked to imagine and explain success. No doubt as subjects were explaining the outcome, they brought to mind facts about themselves that were consistent with success (e.g., "I like games," "I have a good vocabulary"), or facts consistent with failure (e.g., "I'm tired," "I did poorly on the SATs").

Clearly, we all know things about ourselves that would be consistent with success and know other things about ourselves that would be consistent with failure. The task simply alters the accessibility of these facts. Subsequently, when subjects actually confront an anagram task and think about how well they will do, these specific accessible facts jump to mind and determine the expectations of the subjects. Thus, accessibility of thoughts can alter expectations and judgments; and, because expectations have an effect on later behavior, actual performance is also affected. People who imagine and explain success actually perform better than those who explain failure.

The general point is that accessibility of things in memory is an important determinant of judgments and behavior. To the extent that different kinds of facts are made accessible, different behaviors can be expected to occur. Salancik and Conway (1975) altered people's memory of either pro-religious prior behaviors or anti-religious prior behaviors simply by changing the way in which questions were asked. This created differential accessibility of past behaviors relevant to religion, and this affected subjects' subsequent assessments of their current level of religiosity.

Similarly, Strack, Schwarz, and Gschneidinger (1985) guided subjects to think about recent good or bad events or to think about good or bad events that occurred quite a bit in the past. Interestingly, when subjects thought about good recent events their feelings of satisfaction were greater than when they thought about bad recent events. However, exactly the opposite occurred when subjects were asked to recall past events. Thinking about bad past events led people to feel better and more satisfied in the present than did thinking about good past events. In this case, the past acted as a standard of judgment against which the present was measured. Thus, the present looked rosy when compared to how bad things used to be.

In another realm, Fazio (1986) has shown the importance of the accessibility of attitudes for the issue of whether behavior is consistent with feelings. When attitudes are accessible, the attitude object elicits these feelings spontaneously and automatically. Such feelings then affect perceptions and the definition of the situation, and thus guide behavior. When attitudes are not accessible, behavior is determined by things other than one's attitudes (e.g., norms) and will not necessarily be consistent with underlying attitudes. Fazio has identified the kinds of experiences that make attitudes accessible. One of these is direct experience. Thus, when our feelings toward a person or object are based on personal and direct experience rather than on simply reading or hearing about it, attitudes will be developed that are highly accessible. Subsequent behavior is then likely to be consistent with and predictable from these attitudes.

In short, accessibility of facts, concepts, and attitudes in one's mind is an important factor in judgments, feelings, and behaviors. There were many techniques that Erickson used where the outcome would be to alter accessibility of facts in memory. We have already discussed his use of seeding and of imagery. In addition, Erickson's use of metaphor and anecdotes served as a quite indirect way to alter the kinds of concepts that would be activated in his clients. He understood how ideas and categories were linked in memory (in a way similar to that proposed by current spreading activation models of memory) and knew how to alter the accessibility of various ways of thinking as well as of the specific content of thought.

12. Communication Techniques

An important point about Erickson is that he viewed therapy as a communication form between two or more people. He was intrigued by the process of communication and used many communication principles in his work—both verbal and nonverbal. He believed that a client could not not communicate, and he made sure that he received and sent the appropriate communications.

Part of his success as a communicator was based on his well developed powers of observation. He was able to pick up subtle messages from the words and gestures of his clients and send back to his clients messages in equally subtle forms. He believed in communicating to clients at several levels, and his messages were often intended to carry meaning at many levels at the same time. It has been said that Erickson had an actor's control of his communication. His communication patterns were complex, and words and gestures were usually carefully chosen. What appeared to be illogical or randomly chosen words and themes were often carefully designed communications.

Another important aspect of Erickson's communications was that he always used the language of the person with whom he was communicating. He would often adjust his tone, style of speaking, choice of words, and even accent to fit the linguistic style of the client. This allowed for more effective communication. A good example of Erickson using the language of the client is found in the case of Harold (Haley, 1973, pp. 120–148). Here Erickson used the language of a "damn dumb no-good moron" to help join his client psychologically.

In addition, Erickson would often communicate in global and ambiguous terms (much like reading a horoscope). The effect of this was to tap into the concerns that people might have as they interpreted his messages from the point of view of their needs. In fact, he might be able to tap into the concerns of a number of people at the same time. It has been said that when Erickson talked to a large group of people, individuals often felt that he was communicating with them personally.

Erickson also recognized that a communication consists of many elements. It involves behavior, feeling, and thought. In addition, one must consider the context of the communication, the relationship between the communicators, the duration of communication, and its ambiguity (see Zeig, 1980a, for an extended discussion of these ideas). Many therapists and other kinds of communicators fail because they focus on only one element of communication. Behaviorists are concerned only with behavior. Others, perhaps Gestalt therapists, are concerned only with the communication of affect. Erickson's success was in large part due to his ability to communicate to all elements—and to know when to speak to each element. Every client is primarily oriented to one element of communication, perhaps the affective element or the cognitive element in any particular case. Thus, a client might focus either on his behavior or on his feelings. The element the client focused on would often be avoided by Erickson in his communication forms. He would work on other elements, where resistance and personal investment were less, and the effects on these more peripheral elements would then spread.

With this in mind, it is interesting to speculate on the origins of attitudes as they are discussed by social psychologists. Attitudes can be developed on the basis of affective techniques (e.g., classical conditioning), behavioral techniques (e.g., role playing), or cognitive techniques (e.g., persuasive messages). The component that serves as the basis for attitude formation should be the strongest and the one most resistant to persuasion. This suggests that attitudes formed by classical conditioning might be best changed by techniques that hit at information or behavior rather than at emotion. Likewise, information appeals might do little to change an attitude that has a cognitive basis. Although I know of no such research that has been done, the ideas would be consistent with Erickson's principles. That is, in order to be an effective communicator and to induce change, one should aim the communication at the elements where the receiver has the fewest resources and the least resistance. Such an insight requires that we recognize the multilevel nature of communication.

Work in social psychology has established effective techniques for persuasive messages. Research on communicator, message, and receiver factors that influence the effectiveness of a message has been carried out for over 50 years. Erickson made use of many of these techniques. We have seen how he would ensure that clients carefully attended to him (when he wanted them to). Dropping his voice at key moments, using difficult phrasing, or employing confusing sentences were some of his techniques for getting attention. He was equally able to divert clients' attention away from himself when he so desired. In addition, he made sure that he had the attributes of an effective communicator. Clearly, his reputation and perceived expertise gave him credibility. Moreover, he tried never to lose control over the situation or the client. Many examples have been given in analyses of Erickson's techniques to indicate how he was able to stay "one up" on his clients.

Current work in the area of attitude change suggests that there are two general routes to persuasion via messages (Chaiken, 1980; Petty & Cacioppo, 1984). The systematic or central route depends on careful processing of the message content. The quality of the arguments is considered as one decides on the validity of the message. The heuristic or peripheral route depends on less effortful processing. Simple rules (e.g., attractive communicators are right; the length of a message indicates its strength) are used rather than in-depth processing. Although research has isolated these two routes to persuasion and has identified the factors that make a message effective in each case, it is not yet clear what kinds of factors instigate one or the other route to persuasion. I have the feeling that Erickson more often designed his messages to induce heuristic processing. The content was less important than the style and context of the message. Thus, the use of analogies was probably designed to give the message validity without providing a well developed set of arguments. He was also more interested in what cognitive responses his clients would make to his communications rather than to the content of the communications per se.

13. The Client as an Active Participant

Analyzing Erickson as a communicator, as well as considering many of his other techniques, shows how much he controlled what went on during therapy and how much he guided the direction of the interaction and the content of clients' thoughts. Nevertheless, this control was often indirect and left much room for an active role by the client. In fact, getting the client involved in the therapeutic process in an active way was one of the most important of Erickson's techniques.

It has often been demonstrated in psychological research that self-generated words, facts, or ideas have an advantage in memory and get greater weight in judgment compared to material that is presented from an outside source (Slamecka & Graf, 1978). Some of Erickson's most brilliant and effective techniques were designed in part to give the client this important active role in the therapy process. We have already seen the ways in which Erickson manipulated situations so that clients would adopt certain perceptions. Telling them how to think about or interpret things would obviously meet with great resistance. Thus, Erickson would not interpret things for the client or tell him/her how things were or should be. Rather he would allow clients to interpret and perceive things "on their own." He would simply set the stage (by techniques such as priming) to raise the likelihood of certain interpretations and perceptions.

Metaphoric stories were often used to achieve these ends. By using metaphors, Erickson would ensure that clients drew their own links and "aha" experiences rather than having an outside source interpret their life circumstances. Metaphors allow the client to actively develop a new perspective on a problematic situation while at the same time avoiding direct and open discussion of a sore topic. Metaphors allow the client to access relevant content from memory and develop new interpretations of that content. Because of the ambiguity of most metaphors, clients will also embellish and reconstruct their knowledge and understanding. All of this ensures that the client take an active role in thinking and problem-solving. Such techniques follow the basic principle of successful cognitive dissonance arousal and reduction—get people to do things without having them recognize that you got them to do those things. In line with this, Erickson typically did not advise people to behave any differently. Rather he arranged circumstances so that they *would* behave differently.

We also have seen how Erickson gave clients an "important" role in the process by inducing the illusion of choice or by giving them a choice between equally useful alternatives. Thus, they could choose whether to have a headache on Wednesday or Thursday, or whether to climb Squaw Peak or go to the Botanical Gardens. Such choices involved clients more in the therapy process, with its likely effects on commitment and perceptions.

With respect to making the clients active in the therapy process, there are certain specific examples from Erickson's cases that achieve this end in an especially clever and effective way. For example, Erickson usually took what the client said and built on it. He did not question or refute the client's reality. This allowed the client the sense of directing the interaction. The classic example is the client who claimed to be Jesus Christ. Erickson simply accepted this and thus communicated to the client the assumption that he must know a lot about carpentry. How could the client deny it? Soon Erickson had the client engaged in productive woodworking. Many other examples are given where Erickson allowed his clients to play out their own scenarios—with his indirect steering, of course.

Erickson also gave his clients tasks where they would determine the outcome and meaning. He might ask a depressed client to carry a heavy weight around until he or she "knew what to do with it." Knowing that the client would make something significant out of this task was enough for Erickson. They could interpret or choose whatever they wanted, and their active role made this an especially effective technique.

Finally, Erickson often employed a technique that is my special favorite. It is obviously beneficial at times to have a client think and talk about certain people or events—a spouse, early years in school, a former boss. Yet directly asking for such thoughts will likely meet with resistance. And any direct interpretation by Erickson about these people or events would not be as effective as if the client alone arrived at such interpretations.

How to get clients to think about these things "on their own"? Erickson used a simple yet little appreciated fact: The best way to get someone to think about his brother is to talk about your own brother (Zeig, 1985b). I have tried this with students in my classes. When I discuss my days in grammar school, they mentally think of themselves in school. When I discuss my relationship with my father, they think of their own father. Such egocentric thinking is done automatically and inescapably. By talking about his own life in certain ways, Erickson could subtly, but surely, affect the client's understanding and perception.

Of all his techniques, I find this the most elegant as well as the one that should prove to be among the most effective. Psychologists have not yet studied or appreciated egocentrism in thought or the tendency to personalize situations when others talk about their own situations, but this is likely to be an important kind of psychological phenomenon, with both theoretical and practical implications.

CONCLUSIONS

I have tried to select certain of Erickson's commonly used techniques and to analyze and interpret them in light of social psychological principles. Although I cannot come close to grasping all that Erickson did, I believe that it has been useful to look at some of his approaches and techniques in terms of principles of learning, cognition, judgment, decision-making, social interaction, communication, compliance, and attitude change. These principles of social influence are especially relevant to an understanding of Erickson because he was, as much as anything else, a directive and manipulative therapist. He understood and used many of these principles of influence. In fact, many of his techniques involved a combination of principles. For example, seeding was an indirect technique, it altered the accessibility of mental content, and it allowed the client to play an active role in the therapy process. Whether Erickson truly understood the precise psychological processes by which seeding or any other technique worked is not the point. What *is* important is that he saw the utility of these techniques—and he saw this at a time when much of the relevant theory and research on these social influence principles had not yet been developed.

Although Erickson was clearly an active intervener, he never had a set agenda or a fixed set of techniques. On the contrary, he was totally flexible and willing to try anything that he felt might work. The secret of Erickson's success was in his uncanny ability to know when to use which approach and which technique. He could use direct or indirect methods, symptom prescription or metaphors, reframing or seeding. There is obviously a certain amount of art in being a good scientist as well as in being a good therapist. As an artist, Erickson was a master.

During the course of this chapter, I have tried to give the reader a flavor for the practicality and pragmatism of Erickson's techniques during psychotherapy. I have also tried to discuss these techniques from the point of view of social psychologists or other agents of influence (e.g., advertisers, educators). Each approach has much to learn from the other. However, it is also important to point out some key differences between therapy clients as targets of influence and the kinds of targets of influence (often psychology students) who are used in social psychology experiments or the kinds of targets who are approached by sales people or politicians. These differences might suggest limits to the parallels between social psychology theory and research and principles of psychotherapy.

1. Clients have psychological problems, often in the nature of thought disorders. What might this imply about their information processing mechanisms or about our ability to understand their thinking by using psychological processes that have been uncovered during the study of "normal" subjects? After all, most of our knowledge of social psychology principles is derived from a rather normal, well-adjusted population.

2. Clients seek out change and ask to be influenced. Subjects in psychology experiments or consumers do not seek out the advice of experts in helping them to change.

3. Clients pay to be influenced. Often subjects in psychology experiments are paid for their participation.

4. Clients often go through changes in affect and thought as well as in behavior. Social influence in the laboratory or by advertisers is more often aimed at behavior. This raises some important questions that are relevant for both psychotherapy and social psychology. Are there differences at the conceptual level or in terms of the most likely effective

techniques for changing affect, cognition, and behavior? What are the relations among affect, cognition, and behavior? Some social psychologists see them as interconnected components (Breckler, 1984). Others see the affective system as separate and primary (Zajonc, 1980). Do therapists deal differently with affective disorders, behavioral problems, and thought problems? Did Erickson? On what basis?

A related issue concerns the distinction between cognitive and motivational bases for behavior. Some errors of judgment or psychological problems are best seen as motivational in origin, and others are perhaps best understood as based on cold cognitive processes. It is interesting that even such deviant symptoms as delusions have recently been interpreted by clinical psychologists as having a cognitive basis (Maher & Ross, 1984). This is very much in line with the recent emphasis in social psychology on cognitive processes. In any case, is the cognitive vs. motivational basis for a symptom of any importance to therapy? Although Erickson was not especially concerned with insight into the etiology of problems, he was interested in the functions served by the maintenance of symptoms. Is a different therapy strategy indicated when a presenting problem is motivationally maintained and need-related as opposed to cognitively based and maintained because of information processing mechanisms?

5. Clients often "want to" change but can't. Subjects in psychology experiments and consumers often do not want to change but can.

6. The situation is often more constrained for the client than for the target of influence in settings such as consumer behavior or political persuasion. The therapist can control much of the conversation, the time of the meeting, the context, etc. Therapists often have a degree of power and potential for control that few other agents of influence can attain.

7. The topic of influence is often different for the client as compared to other targets of influence. Attitudes toward nonsense syllables, laboratory games, or buying a car are quite different from attitudes about the self. The issues for a client are primarily self-relevant and of central importance.

8. The degree of awareness of the influence techniques may differ between clients and other targets of influence. People watching television or talking in a supermarket or participating in a laboratory study are usually not fully aware of all the social influence aspects of the situation. Clients, on the other hand, usually know that techniques of change are being employed. It is true that Erickson made these techniques as

subtle and indirect as possible. Yet the client's awareness of the possibility of social influence is still present.

9. The length of the social influence situation differs. Psychologists in the laboratory, politicians, and car salesmen must do the job quickly. Clients often stay in therapy for a rather extended period of time—although certainly less time with an Ericksonian approach than with others.

10. Social psychologists usually look for general principles of influence that are true across subjects. They seek to uncover general processes of attitude change. Therapy, however, is an individual endeavor. Each client is unique and must be understood and dealt with in unique ways. No one understood and took into account the uniqueness of the individual client as much as Erickson. His approach differed in significant ways from client to client. Thus, the goals of social psychology in spelling out general principles and the goals of psychotherapy in influencing individual people with individual circumstances, perceptions, and problems are quite different. Yet the nomothetic approach of social psychology offers hope for developing an understanding of when to use various specific techniques. It is an avenue out of intuition for the therapist.

11. There is, in addition, an important difference between therapy and other social influence situations in terms of the ability to assess the degree of change. In the laboratory, there are usually appropriate control and comparison groups. Measures of change are quite objective. Objective measures also exist for consumers and voters. However, judgments of change and success in therapy are very difficult. The therapist is obviously subject to biases in judgment as well, a factor that makes assessment still more problematic.

Given these differences, one should obviously be careful in either drawing general social psychological principles from Ericksonian psychotherapy techniques or from using social psychological principles as a way to understand Erickson's effectiveness as an agent of influence. Nevertheless, the similarities that the therapy situation has with other social influence contexts should also not be left unmentioned.

As an experimental social psychologist, I have learned a great deal by reading accounts of Erickson's techniques and by watching videotapes of him interacting with his clients. Many of the principles that I have learned about through laboratory research have been exemplified in his approach to therapy. In addition, his techniques have suggested new principles of influence not yet tested empirically in the laboratory. As these suggestions are researched, Erickson's work will contribute to social psychology knowledge in a direct way. On the other side, it is hoped that practitioners who use an Ericksonian approach can learn from this attempt to understand those techniques in terms of social psychology principles and processes. Such an understanding can be used to refine therapy techniques, to guide the development of new techniques, and to help the practitioner decide when different approaches are likely to be effective. If this occurs, both the social psychologist and the psychotherapist will benefit from this exercise.

REFERENCES

Abelson, R. P. (1978). *Scripts.* Paper presented at Midwest Psychological Association Meeting, Chicago.

Abramson, L. Y., Seligman, M. E. P., & Teasdale, J. D. (1978). Learned helplessness in humans: Critique and reformulation. *Journal of Abnormal Psychology, 87,* 49–74.

Axsom, D., & Cooper, J. (1985). Cognitive dissonance and psychotherapy: The role of effort justification in inducing weight loss. *Journal of Experimental Social Psychology, 21,* 149–160.

Bargh, J. A., & Pietromonaco, P. (1982). Automatic information processing and social perception: The influence of trait information presented outside of conscious awareness on impression formation. *Journal of Personality and Social Psychology, 43,* 437–449.

Breckler, S. J. (1984). Empirical validation of affect, behavior, and cognition as distinct components of attitude. *Journal of Personality and Social Psychology, 47,* 1191–1205.

Brehm, J. W. (1966). *A Theory of Cognitive Reactance.* New York: Academic Press.

Brehm, S. S. (1976). *The Application of Social Psychology to Clinical Practice.* New York: Wiley.

Chaiken, S. (1980). Heuristic versus systematic information processing and the use of source versus message cues in persuasion. *Journal of Personality and Social Psychology, 39,* 752–766.

Cialdini, R. B. (1985). *Influence: Science and practice.* Glenview, IL: Scott, Foresman and Company.

Corteen, R. S., & Wood, B. (1972). Autonomic responses to shock-associated words in an unattended channel. *Journal of Experimental Psychology, 94,* 308–313.

Erickson, M. H. (1964). The confusion technique in hypnosis. *The American Journal of Clinical Hypnosis, 6,* 183–207.

Fazio, R. H. (1986). How do attitudes guide behavior? In R. M. Sorrentino & E. T. Higgins (Eds.), *Handbook of Motivation and Cognition: Foundations of Social Behavior* (pp. 204–243). New York: The Guilford Press.

Festinger, L., & Maccoby, N. (1964). On resistance to persuasive communications. *Journal of Abnormal and Social Psychology, 68,* 359–366.

Gilligan, S. G. (1986). *Therapeutic Trances,* Vol. 1. New York: Brunner/Mazel.

Goldstein, A. P., Heller, K., & Sechrest, L. B. (1966). *Psychotherapy and the Psychology of Behavior Change.* New York: Wiley.

Gregory, W. L., Cialdini, R. B., & Carpenter, K. M. (1982). Self-relevant scenarios as mediators of likelihood estimates and compliance: Does imagining make it so? *Journal of Personality and Social Psychology, 43,* 88–99.

Haley, J. (1973). *Uncommon Therapy*. New York: W. W. Norton & Company.

Higgins, E. T., & Chaires, W. M. (1980). Accessibility of interrelational constructs: Implications for stimulus encoding and creativity. *Journal of Experimental Social Psychology, 16,* 348–361.

Higgins, E. T., Klein, R., & Strauman, T. J. (1985). Self-concept discrepancy theory: A psychological model for distinguishing among different aspects of depression and anxiety. *Social Cognition, 3,* 51–76.

Higgins, E. T., Rholes, W. S., & Jones, C. R. (1977). Category accessibility and impression formation. *Journal of Experimental Social Psychology, 13,* 141–154.

Katz, D. (1960). The functional approach to the study of attitudes. *Public Opinion Quarterly, 24,* 163–204.

Katz, D., Sarnoff, D., & McClintock, C. (1956). Ego-defense and attitude change. *Human Relations, 9,* 27–45.

Kenrick, D. T., & Gutierres, S. E. (1980). Contrast effects and judgments of physical attractiveness: When beauty becomes a social problem. *Journal of Personality and Social Psychology, 38,* 131–140.

Kunst-Wilson, W. R., & Zajonc, R. B. (1980). Affective discrimination of stimuli that cannot be recognized. *Science, 207,* 557–558.

Langer, E. J. (1975). The illusion of control. *Journal of Personality and Social Psychology, 32,* 311–328.

Langer, E. J., Blank, A., & Chanowitz, B. (1978). The mindlessness of ostensibly thoughtful action: The role of "placebic" information in interpersonal interaction. *Journal of Personality and Social Psychology, 36,* 635–642.

LaRue, A., & Olejnik, A. B. (1980). Cognitive priming of principled moral thought. *Personality and Social Psychology Bulletin, 6,* 413–416.

Maher, B. A., & Ross, J. S. (1984). Delusions. In H. E. Adams & P. B. Sutker (Eds.), *Comprehensive Handbook of Psychopathology.* New York: Plenum.

Nisbett, R. E., & Wilson, T. D. (1977). Telling more than we can know: Verbal reports on mental processes. *Psychological Review, 84,* 231–259.

Petty, R. E., & Cacioppo, J. T. (1984). The effects of involvement on responses to argument quantity and quality: Central and peripheral routes to persuasion. *Journal of Personality and Social Psychology, 46,* 69–81.

Ross, L., Lepper, M. R., Strack, F., & Steinmetz, J. (1977). Social explanation and social expectation: Effects of real and hypothetical explanations on subjective likelihood. *Journal of Personality and Social Psychology, 35,* 817–829.

Salancik, G. R., & Conway, M. (1975). Attitude inferences from salient and relevant content about behavior. *Journal of Personality and Social Psychology, 32,* 829–840.

Seligman, M. (1975). *Helplessness: On Depression, Development and Death.* San Francisco: W. H. Freeman.

Sherif, M., & Hovland, C. I. (1961). *Social Judgment: Assimilation and Contrast Effects in Communication and Attitude Change.* New Haven, Conn.: Yale University Press.

Sherman, R. T., & Anderson, C. A. (1987). Decreasing premature termination from psychotherapy. *Journal of Social and Clinical Psychology, 5,* 298–312.

Sherman, S. J. (1980). On the self-erasing nature of errors of prediction. *Journal of Personality and Social Psychology, 39,* 211–221.

Sherman, S. J., Skov, R. B., Hervitz, E. F., & Stock, C. B. (1981). The effects of explaining hypothetical future events: From possibility to probability to actuality and beyond. *Journal of Experimental Social Psychology, 17,* 142–157.

Sherman, S. J., Zehner, K. S., Johnson, J., & Hirt, E. R. (1983). Social explanation: The role of timing, set, and recall on subjective likelihood estimates. *Journal of Personality and Social Psychology, 44,* 1127–1143.

Slamecka, N. J., & Graf, P. (1978). The generation effect: Delineation of a phenomenon. *Journal of Experimental Psychology: Human Learning and Memory, 4,* 592–604.

Strack, F., Schwarz, N., & Gschneidinger, E. (1985). Happiness and reminiscing: The role of time perspective, affect, and mode of thinking. *Journal of Personality and Social Psychology, 49*, 1460–1469.

Tversky, A., & Kahneman, D. (1973). Availability: A heuristic for judging frequency and probability. *Cognitive Psychology, 5*, 207–232.

Tversky, A., & Kahneman, D. (1981). The framing of decisions and the psychology of choice. *Science, 211*, 453–458.

Walster, E., & Festinger, L. (1962). The effectiveness of "overheard" persuasive communications. *Journal of Abnormal and Social Psychology, 65*, 395–402.

Weary, G., & Mirels, H. L. (1982). *Integrations of Clinical and Social Psychology.* New York: Oxford University Press.

Wilson, T. D., & Capitman, J. A. (1982). Effects of script availability and social behavior. *Personality and Social Psychology Bulletin, 8*, 11–20.

Zajonc, R. B. (1980). Feeling and thinking: Preferences need no inferences. *American Psychologist, 35*, 151–175.

Zeig, J. K. (1980a). Symptom prescription techniques: Clinical applications using elements of communication. *American Journal of Clinical Hypnosis, 23*, 23–33.

Zeig, J. K. (Ed.) (1980b). *A Teaching Seminar with Milton H. Erickson.* New York: Brunner/ Mazel.

Zeig, J. K. (Ed.) (1982). *Ericksonian Approaches to Hypnosis and Psychotherapy.* New York: Brunner/Mazel.

Zeig, J. K. (1985a). The clinical use of amnesia. In J. K. Zeig (Ed.), *Ericksonian Psychotherapy Vol. I, Structures.* New York: Brunner/Mazel.

Zeig, J. K. (1985b). *Experiencing Erickson.* New York: Brunner/Mazel.

SECTION ONE: PRINCIPLES

PART II

The Utilization Approach to Strategic Therapy

Chapter 6

Solution-Oriented Therapy:
A Megatrend in Psychotherapy

Bill O'Hanlon

William Hudson O'Hanlon, M.S. (Arizona State University), founding editor of the Milton H. Erickson Foundation Newsletter, *maintains a private practice in Omaha, Nebraska. He is a world-renowned trainer of Ericksonian psychotherapy. An editorial board member of* The Ericksonian Monographs *and the* Journal of Strategic and Systemic Therapies, *his special area of interest is marital and family therapy. O'Hanlon authored* Taproots *and coauthored with James Wilk,* Shifting Contexts: Clinical Epistemology and the Generation of Effective Psychotherapy.

O'Hanlon presents tenets of his solution-oriented approach, a strategic therapy that builds on the utilization method of Erickson. He contrasts his method with traditional approaches. A therapist will alter his formulation of the client's problem dependent on his preexistent theoretical orientation. In this sense problems are cocreated by the therapist and patient. It is best to redefine problems so that they are solvable by the patient and therapist.

> The otherwise-impossible can be made to happen under the stimulation of a comprehensive plan and program focused on finding solutions instead of attacking a problem. By looking at the best that might be and determining how to get there, problems that might have been formidable are evaporated by the larger vision. (Rouse, 1985, p. 15)

Several years ago, John Naisbitt published his popular book *Megatrends* (Naisbitt, 1982) which detailed some sweeping trends that he saw emerging in our society but were, perhaps, not obvious to others. In a similar manner, I have observed and experienced a "megatrend" in psychotherapy that is detailed in this chapter. Stated simply, psychotherapy is moving away from explanations, problems, and pathology and toward solutions, competence, and abilities.

This megatrend has gradually emerged for me mainly as a result of my practice of "Ericksonian" therapy, that is, therapy in the tradition and spirit of Milton Erickson. Doing Ericksonian therapy has warped me in a particular direction. After some time, I noticed a similar warp in the work of others, most notably the recent work of Mara Selvini Palazzoli and her colleagues at the Nuovo Centro per lo Studio della Famiglia in Milan, Italy and that of Steve de Shazer and his group at the Brief Family Therapy Center in Milwaukee, Wisconsin. While they are not really Ericksonians, and in some ways work quite differently from the way in which Erickson did, there was something that smelled vaguely familiar in their work. Following that scent led to the articulation of this megatrend for me.

THE PATTERN WHICH CONNECTS

There is a thread which connects the work of Palazzoli, de Shazer, and Erickson (and perhaps others with whose work I'm not familiar). Here I will describe the work of Palazzoli and de Shazer that shows evidence of this thread.

Milan Invariant Prescription

Mara Selvini Palazzoli is an Italian psychiatrist who became interested in family therapy after she started working with anorexics. Her training was biologically and psychoanalytically rooted, but she found these approaches entirely inadequate to the task of treating these patients. The anorexics had an annoying habit of dying before their analysis was complete! Dr. Palazzoli's (1974) book about her work with anorexics is recognized as one of the seminal clinical works in the field. In the transition to working systematically, she gathered three psychiatric colleagues who worked as a team observing sessions from behind a one-way mirror.

After working with anorexics for a number of years, the team became bored because they were able to resolve most of the "hopeless" cases with their methods. So they turned their attention to schizophrenia and began to develop similar methods and report similar consistent successes.

As was bound to happen, they became quite well known, especially in Europe, and sought-after speakers and workshop presenters. This eventually led to the splitting of the team down gender lines, with the two men (Boscolo and Cecchin) choosing to do more teaching and training along with their clinical work and the women (Prata and Selvini Palazzoli) choosing to set up their own institute (the Nuovo Centro mentioned previously) to concentrate more on clinical research and practice.

The Nuovo Centro team once treated a family with an anorexic member with whom they were stuck. The 21-year-old eldest daughter, Mary, had made several suicide attempts, almost succeeding at times. The team saw little hope for curing this case and at best resigned themselves to rescuing the parents from the tyranny of their children, who constantly interfered in the parents' personal lives. Accordingly, they dismissed the children from therapy and saw the parents on their own. They gave the parents a directive that involved the parents going out together one night, not telling the children where they were going, but only leaving a note telling the children that they would be back at an appointed hour. The resulting disruption in the family system led to some amazing results. The daughter who had been anorexic began to improve dramatically, attending nursing school and becoming active in sports, eventually marrying a widower, and becoming a "good, happy wife and loving stepmother."

The team was flabbergasted by these reported changes. How had they come about? In an effort to investigate exactly which part of the intervention had the dramatic impact, they decided to use this intervention with every family that sought their help. They have to date given the intervention to 114 families. The dramatic results in many of these families have led them to develop an invariant prescription. (Selvini Palazzoli, 1986). One interesting aspect of this research is that the team is not interested in solution-oriented therapy. Although they have come across a widely applicable solution, they are on a quest to understand why the solution works—they are on their way back to explanation-land.

De Shazer's Skeleton Key Interventions

The recent work of Steve de Shazer has focused on interventions for solutions. In his latest book, *Keys to Solution in Brief Therapy* (1985), he details several invariant prescriptions that his team has found useful across a wide range of presenting complaints. He writes that he has become more interested in the nature of solutions than in the nature of problems. He gives five skeleton key interventions. They are:

1. The therapist tells the client (or clients) that "between now and the next time we meet, I would like you to observe, so that you can describe to me next time, what happens in your (family, life, marriage, relationship) that you want to continue to have happen."
2. The therapist tells the client that he does not know what will help, but that the client should do something, anything, different about the problem than what was done before.
3. The therapist tells the client to "pay attention to what you do when you overcome the urge to (binge, drink, yell at your children, get depressed, etc."—whatever the presenting complaint involved).
4. When a client is obsessed with some unhappy event (e.g., the breakup of a relationship), he or she is told to write about the subject for a certain amount of time on odd-numbered days, to read it over on even-numbered days and then burn it. If the obsessive thoughts occur at any other time, he or she is to put them out of mind until the "regular time."
5. Couples or families that have been fighting are told that they should have a structured fight in which each person gets to have their say for a set amount of time with no interruptions from the others. They are to toss a coin to see who goes first, then the other people get their turns. If they decide to go another round, they are to spend a certain specific amount of time in silence between rounds (de Shazer, 1985; de Shazer and Molnar, 1984).

Again, the team reports quite dramatic and impressive clinical results with these interventions. There is something afoot here.

The Birth of a Notion: Identifying the Common Thread

At first blush these interventions seem to be going in the exact opposite direction from Erickson, who emphasized not having an invariant approach to anything, much less clients in therapy. There was something familiar in these reports, however. It was the emphasis that Erickson placed on focusing on solutions rather than on problems. In conversation with Haley and Weakland (Haley, 1985a) in the 1950s, it comes across that Erickson had a solution orientation and Haley and

Weakland lived in explanation-land. When they would suggest that getting rid of a symptom would just lead to symptom-substitution because the interpersonal function was not taken care of, Erickson challenged that assumption: "Your assumption is that it served other purposes. Have you ever thought about symptomatology wearing out in serving purposes and becoming a habitual pattern?" (Haley, 1985a, Vol. 1, p. 15). Notice here that Erickson is not asserting that symptoms are habits, but challenging the "symptoms serve a function" idea and suggesting a more solution-engendering frame of reference.

This was the warp that I had gotten from working with Erickson and using his approaches for some time—the emphasis on solutions rather than explanations. It was what I responded to in the work of de Shazer and Selvini Palazzoli. Do not pass go; do not collect $200; do not go after explanations; proceed directly to solutions.

While I call this a megatrend, it may just be wishful thinking on my part, as I certainly hope this is a direction that therapy will take in the future. Time must be the ultimate judge, however, as to whether this is a trend or merely a phase or a fluke. Meanwhile, I will present a summary of how solution-oriented therapy developed and some of the differences in thinking and practice that this way of working entails.

FROM EXPLANATIONS TO SOLUTIONS: THE EVOLUTION OF PSYCHOTHERAPY

What follows is a brief history of the broad trends in therapy, a sort of *Cliff Notes* or *Reader's Digest* version of the history of therapy in my eyes. This will trace the steps we have taken to get where we are in the therapy field and point the way for the future trend that I am describing.

The Etiology of Therapy

Therapy was spawned in a sea of different disciplines, with tributaries from psychology, medicine, and philosophy. These disciplines very much concern themselves with explanations, diagnoses, and understanding the nature of human beings. While they are worthwhile endeavors, time has shown, and I have come more and more to suspect, that therapy involves a different set of assumptions and approaches than those provided by these systems. Therapy involves intervention to produce a change. As many of our clients can demonstrate, having a good explanation does not necessarily produce the desired therapeutic outcomes. Psychoanalysis is, of course, the archetypical approach that emphasizes that insight leads toward change. One assumes that sometimes it does indeed produce results, but more often it leads to situations like Woody Allen describes when he tells a friend that he has been in analysis for 13 years. As she expresses amazement that he has been in treatment that long with no results, he quickly counters by telling her that he intends to give it 20 years and quit if he has not gotten better by then.

The Emergence of Therapy as a Separate Discipline

Recently, since about 1960, therapy has emerged as a separate and distinct discipline practiced by nonphysicians and nonpsychologists. Perhaps those facts account to some extent for the trend that therapy is emerging as a separate discipline concerned with change and solutions rather than one concerned with understanding and explanation.

It is by now apparent that there are many different ways to do therapy. However, the advocates of the different methods and schools often are diametrically opposed to one another about the crucial elements and techniques involved in successful therapy. Witness the recent Evolution of Psychotherapy conference (Phoenix, December 1985). The faculty members for that conference represented a number of major schools and approaches to therapy and yet little agreement on assumptions or working methods was evident in the presentations. Some might think that this is the bad news, but I think it is the good news. There is no one right theory of psychotherapy. Many different theories and many different techniques and approaches seem to produce change and results. Perhaps we should search in another direction rather than for the right theory of therapy.

At first, therapy was primarily oriented to the past, searching in the client's childhood for the roots of present symptoms. Then, in the 1960s, a greater concern with the present prompted the emergence of behavior therapy, ego psychology, gestalt therapy, family therapy, and so on. Past-oriented therapy was dismissed as time-wasting and too speculative by these brash new approaches. These contemporary approaches were concerned with the generation or maintenance of the symptom in the present, with data that could be confirmed in the present. What I am suggesting here is that therapy has begun to evolve to a more future orientation that is unconcerned with how problems arise or even how they are maintained, but instead is concerned with how to resolve problems.

From the sea of psychology, medicine, and philosophy, we emerge into the dry land of intervention. In intervention-land there is no right or wrong diagnosis, no right or wrong theory, just data about what works or is useful in particular cases. The stress here is on the *particular*. Erickson's work shows a strong bias against general theories, explanations, and techniques and toward individualized treatment plans and approaches for each person. The latest data on successful results in therapy show that therapy does work and that each school seems to have approximately similar success rates (Gurman & Razin, 1977). The newest research therefore focuses on which therapists or approaches work best with which clients or types of problems. We have, in the words of Ashleigh Brilliant (1980), given up our search for truth and are now looking for a good fantasy.

THE UNCERTAINTY PRINCIPLE IN THERAPY: NEGOTIATING A SOLVABLE PRESENTING PROBLEM

As I have tried and believed different models and approaches for therapy, I have noticed that not only do I get different results with different models and approaches, but I get different data during the assessment process, which leads to different definitions of the problem. In other words, problem definition in therapy is a function of the assessment process. The assessment process is influenced by the therapist's metaphors and assumptions with regard to people, the nature of problems, and the theory of resolution he or she holds. It seems that the way one observes alters the data that is being observed. We could call this the Uncertainty Principle in Therapy.

At our house we make spritz cookies every year at Christmas—it's a family tradition. We use a cookie press to make these cookies. If you've never seen a cookie press, I'll explain it to you. Once the dough is made up, it is put into a tubular device with a mold on the end. The dough is forced through the mold at the end so that it comes out looking like a camel or, if the mold is changed, like a Christmas tree or a Santa Claus. The dough is the same, the shape changes. The cookies are then cooked and harden into that mold's shape. This is the type of process that I think happens in therapy. The raw data of the client's complaint is the same. It is shaped by the therapeutic interaction during and after assessment into a more solid "presenting problem."

If the client walks into a behaviorist's office, he or she will leave with a behavioral problem. If a client goes to a psychoanalyst's office, he or she will leave with unresolved issues from childhood as the focus of the problem. If a client seeks help from an Ericksonian, he or she is likely to get a problem that can be treated most effectively with hypnosis.

It is not that therapists randomly assign problems to clients. The problems are derived from the raw data of the client's complaints. They are interpersonally negotiated, or cocreated. It is uncanny, though, how similar the clients of a therapist of one particular persuasion will look and how different they will look from those of clients of a therapist from a different school. I remember chiding Ernest Rossi in a seminar I presented in which he was in the back of the room. I told him I thought that his clients probably talked about dreams very often in therapy, while my clients rarely discussed them. I wondered aloud about whether that might have had more to do with the fact that Dr. Rossi had been trained as a Jungian analyst and written a book about dreams (Rossi, 1985) than the differences in our client population. Of course, I think it does.

The implications of this point are exciting to me. If problems are negotiable, one might as well negotiate a problem that is easy or possible to solve. If you do not know how to do hypnotic pain control, it would be detrimental to negotiate a problem that requires that for a solution. It would be better to negotiate "stress" or problems in interpersonal relationships or something else that you know how to solve and that the client agrees fits the facts of his or her situation.

Usually clients have already come up with some sort of problem definition that has not sorted out the situation. I prefer to negotiate a problem definition that is both within the client's and my own power to solve. I often offer new, more workable problem definitions and/or listen for some hint of something in the client's complaint that can be solved.

A beautiful illustration of this principle of offering a new, more solvable problem definition is provided in an example taken from the book *Tea With Demons* (1985), written by Carol Allen with her psychiatrist, Herbert Lustig. Carol is afraid she is going insane and brings this concern to Dr. Lustig. (This excerpt has been edited for the sake of brevity. The points indicate where material has been deleted.)

"Last night I felt so out of control," I explained. "I was so afraid."

"Afraid of what?" he asked.

"Afraid that if all that force were released, I would disintegrate. Explode into a million pieces."

"That sure would be messy, wouldn't it?" Dr. Lustig answered cheerfully. He looked over to the wall across from us, motioned toward it with his head, and continued, "You—splattered over the whole universe."

. . . .

"Well, not really that," I said. "It was more of a feeling, really. The feeling that I wouldn't be able to contain the anger."

"Oh . . ." he replied musically, as if he was understanding the issue in a new light. "Not able to contain it? Well," he said, "that's different."

. . . .

He took out his wallet as he spoke, and removing a twenty-dollar bill, handed it to me. "I want you to take this money and go out and buy yourself a sweater." He glanced briefly at the navy-blue and red scarf around my head that day. "Buy either a dark blue or a red sweater. And make sure it fits very tightly. Get a sweater that fits so snugly that you can feel the edges of yourself—your physical limits. Then, anytime you feel that you're about to lose control of your feelings, or even if you fear losing control, go immediately and put on the sweater. This will allow you to accurately perceive your outer limits and to comfortably contain any emotion that you are experiencing—even if the emotion is a very frightening and powerful one."

. . . .

I did in fact go out and buy a tight, navy-blue sweater several days later. And on several occasions during the next month, I put it on to calm my alarm. But gradually I found that I didn't need it anymore. Dr. Lustig's words had given me some of the inner control that I sought. I no longer needed, for the moment at least, a symbolic container for my fears. (pp. 86–88)

THE ANSWER WITHIN: GETTING CLIENTS TO SOLVE THEIR OWN PROBLEMS

Starting from the End or Nothing Succeeds Like Success

Erickson used to have a task he would give to trainees. He would challenge them to read the last page of a book and then speculate on what must have come before to have led to that ending. In a similar manner, the solution-oriented therapist can start from the end-goal and work backwards from there until he connects with the current state of affairs in the client's life. Erickson's "pseudo-orientation in time" technique (Erickson, 1954) provides an example of this approach. Erickson would have the client hallucinate (usually in an imaginary crystal ball) meeting Erickson at some time in the future after his problem had been resolved. He would ask the patient to relate to him how the problem had been resolved and would inevitably get some description of the brilliant task or insight that resulted in the alleviation of the problem. Erickson would then suggest amnesia for the hallucination and send the client on his or her merry way. The client did not always use the hallucinated solution, but would often report success in resolving his problem.

Michele Weiner-Davis (1986), a solution-oriented therapist in Illinois, discussed a small research project she conducted recently in a report published in Steve de Shazer's newsletter, *The Underground Railroad* ("a newsletter for therapists who work . . . this way."). This report provides some preliminary data that is quite interesting. Reproduced below is her description of the project and the results.

> Clients come to therapy thinking that they have an insurmountable problem which occurs "all the time." Their "black and white" perceptions are very apparent. Our task then becomes to ask questions regarding when the problem *does not* occur and explore what is different about those times. Clients often realize for the first time that much of their life is problem-free *and* that *they* have, in some way, been doing something right to make that happen.
>
> Our research team noticed that clients would often mention changes they made in between the call for an appointment and the first session. Although they placed little significance on these changes, we wondered whether pre-session change could be viewed as the beginning of the change process. If so, this offered both client and therapist a great deal of information about exceptions to the problem. When clients begin to change prior to treatment, our job would simply be to help them continue the changes and avoid relapses.
>
> Since clients who told us about pre-session change placed little significance on it, we wondered whether there were many more

clients who did not think to mention their successful efforts to eliminate the problem. After all, clients do not expect to begin therapy discussing how well they are managing their lives. However, from our perspective, this is exactly the information we want.

We devised three questions and began to informally survey clients beginning therapy. (This survey was conducted with the help of the staff at the McHenry County Youth Service Bureau in Woodstock, Illinois.) We informed them that "our agency is doing some research, and before we begin our session, we have some questions we want to ask you."

1) Clients often notice in between the call for an appointment for therapy and the first session that things already seem different. What have you noticed about your situation?
2) Are these changes in the problem area?
3) Are these the kind of changes you would like to continue to have happen?

Of the 30 clients asked these questions, 20 reported experiencing changes prior to treatment. Of the 20 reporting changes, all answered "yes" to questions #2 and #3. Later in the session several of those who initially responded "no" to question #1 reported changes that had occurred before therapy had begun.

Perhaps the reader can make the connection between this report and Erickson's technique of "pseudo-orientation in time." Both start with getting the clients to provide the data that will lead to successful resolution and getting the clients to focus on solution. The work of Lankton and Lankton (1986) on ambiguous function assignments, an extension of some of Erickson's work, shows a similarity to these interventions as well. Clients are given an ambiguous task and challenged to find a therapeutic meaning for the assignment. When they come back to therapy with a meaning they have derived for the task, they are challenged again to come up with a deeper, more profound meaning. In this way, clients will often sort out their own problems without the interference of the therapist's interpretations.

CREATING A CONTEXT OF COMPETENCE

Accessing Abilities and Transferring Them Across Contexts

A woman who came in to see me was upset with her husband and the way he interacted with her. She attributed the problems in their relationship to his moodiness and felt helpless to do anything that would alter this. She happened to be a skilled horse trainer, one whose expertise was often sought to work with impossible-to-train horses. I asked her what her secret was for training "impossible-to-train" horses. She brightened considerably and proceeded to give me a detailed account of the principles of horse training. I took notes, as I quickly saw that not only could she use her know-how from the horse area in her marriage, but that I could use these same principles in psychotherapy with good result. I will list the principles she provided:

1. Be consistent.
2. Reward small changes and progress.
3. Give up some small controls to keep the overall control (e.g., let go of one of the reins if the horse is fighting you).
4. Do not get discouraged. Do not get hooked in unhelpfully (e.g., getting angry).

I told her that we should pretend that her husband is a horse, but not to tell him that as he might take it the wrong way (I think we were both thinking about what kind of four-legged animal he was, though). She went off with new enthusiasm and ideas about making changes in her marriage.

What Does the Client Do Well?

A colleague once asked me what contributions of Erickson's would last once the "Erickson fad" had passed. I responded without hesitation, "The utilization approach." Erickson cooperated with clients and discovered and used what clients were already doing well, even "resistance" and "symptoms." This principle seems to have been incorporated into many contemporary therapies, especially family therapies. In service of change, one of the therapist's tasks in solution-oriented therapy, then, is to discover and use what the client does well—even if it looks like it is useless or will be an impediment to change.

> A couple came to therapy with Erickson. They had been married less than a month and the husband was insisting on a divorce due to the "outrageous behavior" of his bride. Erickson accused the man of being a coward and ordered him to shut up while his bride talked. The woman gave an account of their sexual

relationship, which had to be done according to the husband's rather stringent standards of what constituted proper lovemaking. The lights had to be off, the curtains had to be drawn tightly, and she was to wear a nightie during the sex act. He would not kiss her or touch her in any way except to insert his penis in her vagina. The husband said that breasts were for babies only and served utilitarian purposes.

Erickson told the man that his sympathies were with the wife and that the man probably wouldn't like what Erickson said. Therefore he was to sit there and listen with his jaws clenched and his arms folded while Erickson discussed in some detail with the wife how a husband ought to approach sex with his wife and how she, as a healthy female, ought to enjoy it.

Erickson then pointed out that people have a tendency to give pet names to things. They name their guns "Old Betsy," their boats "Stay-Up," and their cabins "Do-Come-In." He suggested that the husband ought to come up with pet names for his wife's breasts, since he loved her. Erickson suggested that her twins really ought to have names that rhymed. If the husband did not name them by the next session, Erickson would name the first and the husband would be stuck with naming the second, which would immediately come to the man's mind. At the second session, the wife reported that her husband's sexual behavior had been more flexible, but that he had vowed he would never name the twins. Erickson then christened the right breast "Kitty." Six months later Erickson got a Christmas card from them, signed with both their names and K. and T., along with a note from the wife relating the great improvement in their sex life and relationship. (Haley, 1973, pp. 162–164)

In this approach, one assumes that the client has the know-how needed to solve the problem. The therapist's job is to create a situation in which the client can transfer that know-how from the context in which she or he already uses it to the problem area.

CHALLENGING ASSUMPTIONS: FURNISHING PREMISES FOR SOLUTIONS-ORIENTED THERAPY

To contrast an explanation- and pathology-oriented approach with a solution-oriented one, an examination of the assumptions of both is provided below. To make my point more clearly, I may have drawn the differences as too black and white and perhaps shortchanged some therapies in the process.

Assumptions of Many Contemporary Therapies

Deep, underlying causes for symptoms

A common assumption for many psychodynamic approaches and of many family/interactional approaches is that there is some underlying dynamic not readily perceived by the untrained eye that is creating the problem. Problems are thus "symptoms" of some deep, underlying cause, only the tip of the iceberg is seen, but the largest part of it is out of view. This "iceberg" theory seems to arise directly from medicine, where systemic processes give rise to specific symptoms. In medicine, it is often viewed as inadequate or even dangerous to treat only the symptom. Many therapies have transferred this notion and this caution to their models and approaches.

Awareness or insight is necessary for a change or symptom resolution

Following the medical metaphor again, it would be unwise to treat the "symptom" without an understanding of the underlying causes for the problem. Many therapies attempt to provide the client with an awareness of both the nature and the origin of the problem in order to resolve it.

Amelioration or removal of symptoms is useless or shallow at best and harmful or dangerous at worst

Jay Haley (personal communication, 1985) likes to say, perhaps only a bit tongue-in-cheek, that he thinks that psychoanalysts do not like to focus on eliminating the symptom because they do not know how to. I think that it is not necessarily so insidious. Again, it follows from the models of explanation- and pathology-oriented therapies that it is not only impossible to eliminate the real problem by removing the symptom, but that it could be dangerous, because it might mask the problem and reduce the client's motivation to seek "treatment."

Symptoms serve functions

Most therapists assume that symptoms occur because they serve some function or purpose in the person's life. If they did not serve a purpose, they would not persist. This idea persists in both individual and family therapies. The psychodynamically oriented therapist assumes that the symptom serves some intrapsychic function, and the interpersonally oriented therapist assumes a family or interactional function. Although they might not like to be lumped together, I find that both psycho-dynamically and interactionally oriented therapists around the world share this fundamental conviction. It follows from this belief that if the symptom is removed without somehow taking care of the function it serves, then symptom substitution can arise.

Clients are ambivalent to change and resistant to therapy

In supervising the teaching therapists of many persuasions, I have noted a fundamental attitude that holds that clients do not really want to change or that at least they are fundamentally ambivalent about the possibility of change. Therefore, one has to either wait them out or get around their defenses. This position lends itself to an adversarial model at times, with attendant military metaphors ("attacking the defenses," "being defeated by clients," "strategies to eliminate resistance," etc.). One recent author characterized "resistant" families as "barracudas" (Bergman, 1985).

Real change takes time and brief interventions are shallow and do not last

Since problems and pathology are deep-rooted or entrenched, rep-etitious patterns ingrained in individual or social systems, little can be expected with brief interventions and contacts, other than the possibility of better social or life adjustment. Brief intervention changes do not last. Real change takes place the same way the pathology arose, over a long period of time. In relationship-oriented therapy, where the relationship between the client and the therapist is the focus of treatment, it takes quite a while to build up this relationship.

Focus on identifying and correcting pathology and deficits

The emphasis is on pathology and deficits. I recently attended a workshop where a tape of solution-focused work was shown. It was a "one-shot cure" and the tape showed the techniques and follow-up very clearly. I was certain that even the skeptics in the audience could not fail to be swayed by the clear evidence and impressive results on the tape. After it was shown, a member of the audience commented on the rather bubbly mother in the family and inquired whether the therapist did not notice something strange about her affect. She appeared to the questioner as if she were "on uppers." I remember thinking that therapists look for pathology under every possible rock.

Assumptions of Solution-Oriented Therapy

It is not necessary to know the cause or function of a symptom to resolve it

Erickson was articulate on this topic. "I think that the cause of many problems is very often buried under an accumulation of a lifetime of experience, so that it is very difficult to excavate. . . . In many psychiatric cases the real problem is that of delivering the 'baby' of mental health to patients so that they can get along satisfactorily; the problem is not that of digging into the past in a frantic endeavor to discover possible causes" (Erickson in Rossi & Ryan, 1985, pp. 208–209). "Etiology is a complex matter and not always relevant to getting over a problem" (Erickson in Haley, 1973, p. 106).

Rapid change or resolution of problems is possible

One only has to have the experience of seemingly intractable situations being resolved rapidly with no symptom-substitution and no further occurrence of the difficulty to know that this is possible. Solution-oriented therapists not only think it is possible to rapidly resolve problems, but that the therapist can create the conditions to make it likely. Mara Selvini Palazzoli (1978, p. 199) has said, "If we change the rules, we change the organization. . . . It should, moreover, be stressed that this interaction does not demand hard or protracted work on the part of the therapist but only the ability to seize the right moment at the right time."

Focus is on what is changeable; focus on solution and abilities rather than pathology

> Our project elaborated the systems view as an explanation of human interaction in families and larger systems. As we applied the notion to families in therapy, it took the form of resistance to change. When we offered these ideas to Dr. Erickson, he responded with polite irritation. He thought, correctly I believe, that a theory that encouraged the notion that people resist change was a noxious theory for a therapist, since expecting resistance encourages it. (Haley, 1985b, p. 32)

Get the client to do something

"In therapy, the first thing I want to do with a patient is to get that patient to do something" (Haley, 1985a, p. 203). One of the things that I constantly get accused of when teaching workshops is being a behaviorist. At first this annoyed me a great deal, as I consider behavioral theory just as full of speculation as any other psychological theory and I do not agree with much of it. After a time I realized that any therapy that got people to take action was characterized by psychodynamic therapists as "behavioral." Erickson was very oriented toward getting people to do things that would encourage them to discover solutions. I follow his lead. My father used to say that if I wanted work, I would have to go out and look for it, because no one was going to walk up, knock on the door, and offer me a job. He was partly right. If you take actions to put yourself in the way of a job, you are much more likely to get one. I've noticed a correlation in my practice when working with the unemployed client. Those who go out and apply for jobs get them a lot faster than those who do not go out and apply for jobs, regardless of which clients work the hardest or have the most insight in the therapy room. (My father was partially wrong, as people often call up and offer me jobs teaching workshops, sometimes people I've never met. It took a lot of effort to get to that position, though.) In any case, there is an orientation toward getting people to take action, most often of the observable kind, but occasionally of the internal variety, in the service of change in solution-oriented work.

Find a trend toward positive change and encourage it

Out of the raw data of the client's complaint, there are often facts that can serve to create the frame that the client has been going in some positive direction. The therapist's task is to presume this trend and encourage the client to further this change. Just as I was writing this paper, I saw a client and had a supervisee sitting in. The client had been in once before, complaining of severe nightly headaches that would keep him awake; the problem I negotiated was two-fold: 1. The client was not getting enough sleep; and, 2. He was having headaches, perhaps made worse by the stress of not getting enough sleep. When he returned, he initially indicated no change. He reported that he had had several days of no headaches following the last session, but that the rest of the time he had had headaches pretty much daily. He did say that he had not had a headache at his usual time, however. They had moved to a different time of the day (to 9:30 A.M.). Since this was one of the possibilities I had suggested in the first session, I was quite happy with the response. Since he had also had some relief following the first session, I told him that it was now a matter of stretching out the results so that they lasted longer. I pointed out to the man that we had already taken care of one of the two problems he had sought help for. He was now getting a sound night's sleep every night. He agreed.

The supervisee later reported that when she heard the initial report, she had felt discouraged and worried that therapy would head downhill. She was surprised that I did not seem discouraged and in fact seemed quite encouraged. The client could have gone either way. I found a positive change trend and underlined it in my assessment. I encouraged this trend and tried to further it in the ensuing trancework.

SUMMARY

The purpose of this chapter is to make a case for a new, emerging positive trend in psychotherapy, one that I would like to encourage. It is a switch from a view that is focused on discovering the "real, underlying problem" and correcting the deficits and pathologies that give rise to the problem. There is another approach rising in the land that emphasizes the abilities that people have to solve their own problems. It is focused on creating solvable presenting problems and getting clients to continue to proceed toward the solution. This approach involves not only a new set of techniques, but also a different orientation and set of assumptions.

It is my fervent hope that this is a preliminary report of a new territory, as undreamed of as the creatures of the land were to sea creatures before land creatures evolved. Those first fish struggling out of the water could not have imagined eagles or elephants. In a similar manner, I hope that future generations of therapists continue to evolve in this direction, bringing forth new, previously undreamed of forms of effective therapy.

REFERENCES

Allen, C. (with Lustig, H.). (1985). *Tea With Demons.* New York: William Morrow.

Bergman, J. (1985). *Fishing for Barracuda.* New York: Norton.

Brilliant, A. (1980). *I Have Abandoned My Search for Truth and Am Now Looking for a Good Fantasy.* Santa Barbara: Woodbridge Press.

de Shazer, S., & Molnar, A. (1984). Four useful interventions in brief family therapy. *Journal of Marital and Family Therapy, 10*(3), 297–304.

de Shazer, S. (1985). *Keys to Solution in Brief Therapy.* New York: Norton.

Erickson, M.H. (1954). Pseudo-orientation in time as a hypnotherapeutic procedure. *Journal of Clinical and Experimental Hypnosis, 2,* 261–283.

Erickson, M.H. (1985). Life reframing in hypnosis. In E. Rossi & M. Ryan (Eds.), *The Seminars, Lectures, and Workshops of Milton H. Erickson Vol. II.* New York: Irvington.

Gurman, A.S., & Razin, A.M. (1977). *Effective Psychotherapy: A Handbook for Research.* New York: Pergamon.

Haley, J. (1973). *Uncommon Therapy.* New York: Norton.

Haley, J. (1985a). *Conversations with Milton H. Erickson, M.D.* (3 Volumes). New York: Triangle (Norton).

Haley, J. (1985b). Conversations with Erickson. *Family Therapy Networker, 9*(2), 30–43.

Lankton, S., & Lankton, C. (1986). *Enchantment and Intervention in Family Therapy.* New York: Brunner/Mazel.

Naisbitt, J. (1982). *Megatrends.* New York: Warner Books.

Rossi, E. (1985). *Dreams and the Growth of Personality.* New York: Brunner/Mazel.

Rouse, J. (1985). Commencement address. *Johns Hopkins Magazine,* October, p. 15.

Selvini Palazzoli, M. (1974). Self-Starvation: From the Intrapsychic to the Transpersonal Approach to Anorexia Nervosa. London: Chaucer. (American ed.: New York: Jason Aronson, 1978.)

Selvini Palazzoli, M. (1986). Towards a general model of psychotic family games. *Journal of Marital and Family Therapy, 12*(4), 339–349.

Weiner-Davis, M. (1986). What's new at BFTC? *The Underground Railroad,* (6)2: 7–8.

Chapter 7

Utilization:
The Foundation of Solutions

Steve de Shazer

Steve de Shazer is director and co-founder of the Brief Family Therapy Center/Wisconsin Institute on Family Studies, and editor and founder of its newsletter, In Brief. *In addition to his books,* Patterns of Brief Family Therapy: An Ecosystem Approach *and* Keys to Solution in Brief Therapy, *he has published numerous professional articles and chapters on strategic therapy, family therapy, and hypnosis. He is an approved supervisor and fellow of the American Association for Marital and Family Therapy. De Shazer is a member of the editorial board of* The Journal of Strategic and Systemic Therapies, Zeitschrift for Systemische Therapie *(German),* The American Journal of Family Therapy *and the* International Journal of Family Therapy.

De Shazer presents basic tenets of the model of brief therapy that he developed along with his colleagues at the Brief Family Therapy Center of Wisconsin. This is a utilization approach based on ascertaining and harnessing patient strengths—what the patient does right—rather than focusing on what the patient does wrong—the nature of the problem. De Shazer prods us to do things the simple way. Often, simple redirecting is all that is needed.

Let me preface my remarks, by telling you that I've been doing brief therapy since 1969 and, as a result, I have developed ideas that

---

The author wishes to thank the rest of the Brief Family Therapy Center team who have contributed to the development of the model: Insoo Kim Berg, Eve Lipchik, Elam Nunnally, Wallace J. Gingerich, Ron Kral, and Michele Weiner-Davis.

often seem rather simpleminded. I believe in simplicity and in systems theory. And I take both seriously. Therefore, I think that a small change is the *maximum* a therapist should help a client shoot for. Once that small change is achieved, the therapist ought to get out of the way and let that "beneficial" deviance amplify naturally. Since I have ideas like this, I have been called the "most minimal of the minimalists," which I take as a compliment even though it probably was not meant as one.

From the beginning, my work has been based on the principles I abstracted from Erickson's papers. As I see it, my work and the work of my colleagues at the Brief Family Therapy Center continues to use Erickson's work as a point of departure. Interestingly, after years of using hypnosis or trance-based methods in my practice (de Shazer, 1978; 1979; 1980), more recent work (since 1982) has been done without any deliberate efforts to induce trance. And yet, I see my work now as more hypnotic, further expanding the work Erickson initiated.

For instance, I see the consulting break we take during the session as almost like a trance induction since the client, while waiting, seems to become more receptive to what the therapist says when he or she returns to the room. This state is heightened and utilized by messages that start with complimentary statements from the therapist and team about what the client is doing that is "right," "good," and "effective." We continue to build the "yes set" begun during the interview phase of the session, which furthers the client's expectancy. Then we give the client our therapeutic suggestions. While delivering these compliments, we frequently see trance-like behaviors, that is, "unconscious head nods," changes in breathing rates, and the assumption of a more relaxed sitting posture. Clients tend to do some version of the task whenever the "yes set" has been established.

ERICKSON'S UTILIZATION

When Erickson talked about "utilization" he meant many things, including utilizing the problematic behaviors, thoughts, and feelings as part of a therapeutic solution. One aspect of this approach is a symptom prescription, a tool which certainly can be useful in some situations.

Symptom prescription is not the only thing Erickson meant by utilization. He had a second definition that is more general, " 'utilizing' a patient's own mental processes in ways that are outside his usual range of intentional or voluntary control" (Erickson, Rossi & Rossi,

1976, p. 19). My definition is related and yet different—at least in point of emphasis. From my perspective, utilization involves utilizing whatever the client does that is somehow "right," "useful," "effective," or "good" for the purpose of developing a solution.

Basically, I think therapists have gotten hung up on problems and how to solve them. Therapists talk about "the treatment of phobias," or "the treatment of bed wetters," or "the treatment of conflictual couples," or "the treatment of families," or "the treatment of couples," or "the treatment of individuals." Those therapists who talk this way seem to think that these are all somehow different and that the problem and/or the number of people involved determines the treatment. I am not going to go into it here, but I have come to the conclusion that "it ain't necessarily so."

Over the past four years we have been looking at "how solutions develop" (de Shazer, 1985) and have come to the conclusion that there are more similarities than differences between the treatment of phobias, the treatment of bed wetters, and the treatment of conflictual couples. And I am not sure that the differences make any difference! I suspect that some of you are as shocked by that idea, as I was at first. Don't let it keep you up nights like it did me. But it is the only conclusion my team and I could come to that fit our data.

DEFINITIONS

At this point it seems necessary to define some terms my colleagues and I at the Brief Family Therapy Center use idiosyncratically.

1. Complaints

Complaints seem to start with the common difficulties of everyday life. Let us say that a husband and wife have an argument. By itself, this is perfectly normal. Couples will have their differences, and they will disagree about things. If they consider this as "just part of life," then things go on—one damn thing after another. Unfortunately, under certain unknown and unknowable conditions, these arguments come to be seen as "problems." Sometimes this might be due to increased frequency or perhaps pressures from outside the marriage relationship, for example, difficulties at work. Whatever happens, the "one damn thing after another" switches to "the same damn thing over and over again." Their description shifts from "we have a fight now and then" to "we are always fighting."

As you all know from personal experience, these fights follow patterns, and both participants could predict exactly what steps any of their fights will follow. Of course, they will describe it differently: He might say that it starts with something she does, while she will say it starts with something he does. Neither of them are wrong about that. Once it becomes problematic, they both may try things to prevent and/or avoid these fights. Frequently, they have some bad luck and what they try doesn't work. For instance, if she typically withdraws by becoming quiet, she might try to stop the fights by leaving the room, thinking that this might help her cool off. Or, if he typically sticks to his point, repeating his view by using different words, he might start to become louder and louder. When their efforts don't work, those efforts become part of the fight. What we call a "complaint" has developed. I am over-simplifying a bit, but this point is reached when they say that "we have tried everything, but nothing works." Complaints, therefore, involve a rather circumscribed set of behaviors: the fights and their efforts to prevent them and, since they've tried everything to solve this, the expectation that the fighting is going to continue.

In spite of their statement that "we fight all the time," most fights take only a few minutes, frequently less than a half hour. I've asked hundreds of people about this; my sample includes both clients and therapists. This of course means that for 23 and a half hours that day they are not fighting. They may still feel bad, but nonetheless, they carry on their lives much as they would have had they not had the argument. They hang storm windows, cook dinner, go to the theater, go jogging, and so on.

As we see things, all complaints can be seen *as if* they develop in much that way. Even if this process is lost in the fog of the past, all complaints end up looking *as if* they had followed this path. This *as if* construction seems useful even if we cannot imagine what might have led to the complaint in the first place.

For instance, when a client complains of being depressed, this complaint includes the efforts she has made to not be depressed; efforts that haven't worked. Therefore, she expects to continue to be depressed. This might be why clients usually say that "I am depressed" rather than "I feel depressed." The "am" form of the verb implies a steady state, like "I am a redhead" and therefore suggests the impossibility of change.

2. Exceptions

As I see it, complaints and the rules they seem to follow are not very interesting, but any exceptions to those rules are very interesting. We define anything excluded from the rules of the complaint as *exceptions*. At times exceptions might be difficult to find, but even the most depressed people have moments when they are relatively "up" or become so distracted that they forget they are depressed.

Similarly, when the client's complaint involves alcohol abuse, this complaint description includes the efforts *he* has made and the efforts *others* have made to help him quit. *All* efforts are part of the complaint. Again, there are *exceptions*, times when the client is not abusing alcohol and times when he and the others are not working toward getting him to stop this abusive behavior.

Now, if you see yourself as "fighting all the time," or as "being depressed," or as "being a drug abuser," or as being "unable to stop smoking" and that complaint *includes* all the logical efforts to change you can think of, then further efforts are going to run into roadblocks if they seem like all the previous unsuccessful efforts. You won't go along with these efforts because they do not make sense. Many therapists misunderstand this idea and label such behavior as "resistant." From my perspective, this is just part of the normal course of events. If a client doesn't go along with the efforts of the therapist, it is simply a message that the way the therapist has suggested changing is *wrong*, it is just like all the rest of the efforts to change and is, therefore, a waste of time. The therapist thus needs to change and do something different so that client-therapist cooperation develops and the client can do something different and change.

Pretherapy change

One particular type of exception involves deliberate changes that the client initiated before starting therapy. With some frequency (perhaps as often as two thirds of the time), if you ask them in the correct manner, clients will report doing something different between the phone call and the first therapy session. And, from our perspective, it is exactly those differences that need to be utilized to develop a solution.

3. Solutions

Simply stated, *solutions* are what happens when the *exceptions* have become the rule. This might involve behaviors, thoughts, perceptions, and feelings that were *not* part of the complaint. From my perspective, anything that was outside the constraints of the complaint might be used to resolve the complaint. That is, the things you are doing when you are not fighting are exactly the kinds of things you should do more of. These exceptions might successfully be transferred into the fighting situation; in other words, what you are doing when you are not smoking might be useful in solving that complaint.

We spend most of the first session talking about "what happens when the complaint doesn't." With clients who say they are depressed, I will focus first on how they knew they were depressed, then on what they do on "up days," times they are not depressed. Almost none of my questions involve the complaint and the efforts they have already made. I assume that any complaint is self-maintaining; therefore, I think it is unnecessary to explore the details. Clients will give me these details anyway as they describe the difference between up days and down days. The particulars of the complaint are important only in how they contrast with the rest of the client's life—what the client does that works is important to the solution. Once you know what works, then you can do more of it. You can change the shape of the doughnut hole by changing the shape of the doughnut, and you can change the shape of the doughnut by changing the shape of the hole.

For instance, smokers might be asked to count the number of times they feel the urge to smoke and to observe what they do when they overcome that urge. The couple who fight might be asked to observe each other—what the other one does differently when a fight normally would have occurred. Or the wife of the alcohol abuser might be asked to observe how she acts toward her husband when she is not making the effort to get him to stop drinking. In any event, once we learn about these noncomplaint behaviors, thoughts, feelings, perceptions, and so on, then we at least have models for solution.

4. Utilization

The following detailed case examples will illustrate the way we use the term *utilization*.

Case example 1

A young lady came to therapy wanting to break her cocaine addiction. She had been injecting coke into her arm for 18 months, sometimes spending up to $1000.00 a night. In fact, she had discovered that she had spent more for coke in the previous year than she earned on her job. At the start of the session she presented herself as helpless with regard to coke. She saw no chance of quitting on her own. She requested that I use hypnosis to make her hate coke. I'm afraid I laughed at her, telling her that was just a silly coke dream. She wanted me to "make her stop," but again I laughed and said I couldn't do that, only she could do that! She again stated that she was helpless—that her coke use was beyond her control.

Before I could find out what she did when she didn't do coke, she told me that she had not had any coke for three days, her longest period without it in over a year. "But that ain't nothing!" she said. "I still crave coke." She thought these three days were a fluke, but I saw them as the start of the solution—*something to be utilized*. She knew how to solve the problem, but she did not know she knew. Therefore, I explored what she had done differently:

1. She unplugged her phone;
2. She refused to answer the door;
3. She came home, watched TV and went to bed early; and
4. She worked on her hobby of rug hooking.

Although she did not tell me about it at the time (5) she also turned over the management of her money to her aunt who worked in the same office.

When I told her for the third time that these were exactly the kinds of things she needed to continue doing, she agreed. She then told me about a major exception to her rule about being helpless in regard to coke: She had never stolen or sold her body to buy it.

In addition to complimenting her on what she had done during this three-day period and telling her to continue doing these things, I suggested that she "pay attention to what she does *when* she overcomes the urge to do coke." This is a handy task, because it

1. acknowledges that there will be urges;
2. suggests that the client will overcome some of the urges;
3. acknowledges that he/she might fail to overcome some urges;
4. focuses the client on "doing something"; and
5. suggests that the therapist expects the client to do something to overcome some urges.

Furthermore, the technique is transferable, for example, "pay attention to what you do when you overcome the urge to act depressed, or beat your husband, or suck your thumb."

Over the course of four more sessions (held over a period of three months), she found numerous things to do to overcome the urges, none of which I suggested. Throughout therapy, all of the interventions simply utilized what she was already doing and what she invented. By the final session (the sixth), six months after the first, her bet on success climbed from 50-50 to 80-20 in her favor. She doubted if these odds would ever change. Once again utilizing something she had done that had proved effective, I suggested that she probably could raise the odds to 99-1 by simply promising herself that she could have all the coke she wanted as long as she sold her body or stole to pay for it. She smiled and agreed. Six months later she was still coke free.

Case example 2

Another example involves a woman who described herself as "a phobic." She had made 10 different appointments for therapy, but the first session with me was the first one she had kept. I explored how she had developed that exception. Basically, she started to see herself the way she saw other people seeing her. That is, she started to think of herself as "unnecessarily crippled." Focusing on how other people saw her provided the central idea that she used to solve her problem. She decided on the kinds of tasks that she needed to work on between sessions. These were designed to help her see that other people saw her as "normal" when she behaved in a normal fashion. As a result, she gradually came to see herself as normal.

Case example 3

Some years ago, a woman brought her husband to therapy because she wanted him to stop abusing alcohol. He, of course, said he did not abuse it, did not want to stop drinking. As it turned out, he had promised her many times that he would stop drinking. Then, he would have "just one" when visiting his folks who ran a tavern, but that always seemed to lead to more because he felt bad for having broken the promise, which he hadn't really wanted to make in the first place. One of the first things I did was to suggest that he no longer make that promise. He agreed. I explored with him what he did when he wasn't drinking. And I explored with her what she saw him doing when he wasn't drinking. I also found out what she did when he wasn't drinking. In fact, I had them both keep records about what they each did separately and what they did together when he wasn't drinking.

In the second session, he explained that his drinking changed her tremendously. She was like a different person as soon as she even suspected that he had been drinking. When he wasn't drinking, she made his favorite meals, rubbed his back, reminded him of his household tasks, bought him little gifts, packed his lunch, initiated sex, and generally waited on him. There had been a period of two years when she behaved like this while he wasn't drinking. Both described this period as wonderful. But the minute she even suspected that he had had a drink, she stopped these behaviors, withdrew and complained about everything. As he put it, this was enough to "drive anyone to drink." And, when she knew he had had a drink, she would go to her mother's. Then he became lonely and drank more. Eventually, he'd make the promise; she'd return and things would go well until . . .

During the following session with her, I suggested that the next time she suspected he had been drinking, she was to pretend she did not suspect and to carry on as if things were fine. She was to go out of her way to serve a favorite meal and then to take him to a movie and initiate sex afterwards—all normal behaviors. She was to observe his reactions and then to observe the consequences. I also suggested that she think about what she was going to do differently if she came home and found out that he had been drinking before she got home. I suggested that she think about what he would *least* expect her to do, and then do it. Immediately, she said that he would least expect her to take him drinking, to her a repugnant idea.

Over the course of the next few months, she pretended a few times, and whether he had been drinking or not isn't known. His drinking behavior did not escalate and she did not go to mother's. Then one day she came home and saw his army buddy's car in front of the house. She *knew* that this meant drinking, so she went to the neighborhood shop and bought two six packs of the most expensive foreign beer she could find. Then she went home and placed the beer on the kitchen table where they had been sitting. She had been right, he had done a little drinking. She sat down and insisted that her husband drink the beer she bought him as a surprise, sticking to her normal behavior of bringing home a surprise now and then. He was shocked. His buddy, sensing trouble in the air, wisely left, and she continued to insist that as long as he was going to drink he should drink her beer. He would not. One year later, the two six packs were still in the refrigerator and he had not been drinking.

So, when she suspected that he had been drinking, she substituted her *normal* behaviors and his drinking did not escalate. When she knew he had been drinking, she again substituted *normal* behaviors, specifically, by bringing him a surprise (the foreign beer), and the drinking did not escalate. Now, he values her surprises. So, if he is going to drink again, he'll have to drink her surprise beer *first*—if he drank other alcoholic beverages, he'd be rejecting her surprise. This could ruin their marriage, something he doesn't want. Neither of them realize how central her surprises (and his responses to her surprises) are to the marriage and I wouldn't tell them. They don't need to know that they know that. One year after our final session, he does not abuse alcohol, and she continues to give him surprises, which he values.

Of course, one cannot generalize from this case to other cases involving abuse, that other wives can perform the same "surprise behaviors" and pretend in the same way because not all marriages depend on the wife's surprising behavior. Cases are not alike in that way. But, I do think that cases are alike in some other important ways.

First, the solution involves her doing something different from the usual complaint behaviors; second, these so-called "different" behaviors are really normal for her, they are already part of her repertoire; and, third, from his point of view, she is behaving in ways associated with good times, and so he has to respond with "good times behavior" since he values the marriage as much as she does: The intervention was designed to *utilize* their noncomplaint behaviors within the context of resolving the complaint.

If the marriage had been on the rocks, and he was no longer responding to her surprises during good times, then this approach probably would not have worked. The system has to be connected in order for systemic or interactional changes to be effective.

Case example 4

Now, let us see how the same ideas apply to an individual client. Late last year, a young woman who came in to see me had two complaints: 1) she abused food (bingeing and vomiting); and 2) she abused alcohol and sometimes other drugs. As it turned out, she had three kinds of cycles: 1) the good days cycle—usually two to seven in a row; 2) the bad days cycle, type A: She would feel bad one day and know, by the type of bad feeling she had, that she would binge and vomit on the next day; and 3) the bad days cycle, type B: She would feel bad and *know* that the type of bad feeling she had this time would lead to abusing alcohol. Importantly, she never drank during food-abuse cycles and she never abused food during booze-abuse cycles.

On the good days she took care of herself, eating well, exercising, visiting friends, going to church if it was a Sunday, calling her parents long distance, and so on. On bad days, she did not do these things. Somehow she could tell one type of bad day from the other. Although she could not define it so that I could understand, she knew. These two types of abuse had led to the breakup of her marriage. He left her because he was not able to help her—everything he tried only seemed to make things worse. They both said that they still loved each other but refused to see each other for the good of the other.

She was determined to cure both problems. We started to develop a catalogue of what she did during the good days cycle. While doing this, the good days continued: She had 30 in a row. She thought it was a miracle and stated, "Sometimes things do change overnight." But I was not so sure. I told her to continue doing what was working, but to watch out. Session four coincided with a down day, type A variety. She knew that the next day she was going to binge on food. She really did not want to do that! So she agreed to do whatever I told her, even before she knew what it was, just so she did not have to go through another binge. I told her that she had two options: 1) she could get up the next day and behave as normally she did during a good cycle; or, 2) since she knew a good abuse cycle was coming, she should start drinking *even though she did not feel like it*. And, the next time she thought a booze abuse cycle was coming, she had to abuse food instead.

She looked shocked but agreed to the assignment. A week later, she reported that she got up the day after this session craving chocolate cake but went out and bought some beer instead. She brought it home and sat there staring at it and shaking for three hours, after which she called her parents. Then, she went to her exercise class and by noon she had forgotten her urge to binge. Over the next six months she repeated the pretending to have a good day about once a month. Now, she has good days and "less good days," but no "bad days of either type A or type B." Of course, she might have a relapse, but I doubt it.

Again, the *key* is not in the details. Not every case can be solved by getting the client to blindly promise to do something. It's not the ordeal of promising to do the wrong, bad thing that counts. It is similar to the couple's case in that it involves the same elements of solution. In the problematic situation, she did something different. And, what she did differently was to *utilize* her noncomplaint behaviors within the context of the complaint. Buying beer, calling her parents, and going to exercise class are *all* behaviors from non-food abuse days.

CONCLUSION

As you well know, not every case involves clear and useful descriptions about what is going on. Sometimes the "up days" are seen by the client as "flukes" and are just further evidence that things are beyond control. That is, both good days and bad days just happen, and there is no accounting for them. Or clients are so focused on the down days that they cannot see the up days. Most simply put, the observer would not know from the client's description how to tell the difference between the movie of a good day and the movie of a bad one. What we have found useful in these situations is to help the client construct a picture of *how things will be when the problem is solved.* We might ask this question: "If there is a miracle one night while you are sleeping, and the problem is solved, how will you know it the next morning?" And, we would ask, "How will your spouse know? Your boss?" "What will you be doing differently that would let them know without your having to tell them?" Sometimes these questions can elicit wonderful descriptions that also provide measurable goals. And, at least once in a while, the client will go out and do these very things, finding that—and I am quoting a client—"When you act 'up,' people will think you *are* 'up,' and they will treat you like you are 'up,' and before you know it, you *are* 'up'." More often, however, this method gives you goals to shoot for, thus enabling you to find ways to figure out what to do. Goals also give you ways to measure success and failure.

This approach is not foolproof. Failures can develop when the therapist and client have different goals, when the therapist cannot find a way to help the client do more of what already works, or when the therapist cannot find a way to help the client see the significance of the exceptions. Clients, like many therapists, are hung up on the problem and think that the first step in solving a problem lies in understanding it. Therefore, they sometimes get the mistaken idea that solving it without under-standing it is not good enough. Perhaps, trying to understand the problem is actually the first step in maintaining it. I think that there are probably 1,000 ways to understand any problem. Erickson said (somewhere) to pick the explanation that has the most potential benefit, "the nicest one" for the client.

Of course, finding out what the client does that can be utilized to build a solution involves eliciting the right kind of talk during the session. If you don't ask about successes, the client won't tell you. After all, what they are concerned about is the problem which drove them to seeking therapy. But, as Erickson maintained, they often don't know what the problem is. Therapists do not know either, and we cannot know. All that both clients and therapists can know is how to recognize when the problem is solved. And, my conclusion at this time is that when the problem is solved, things will be much as they are during the time when the problem is not happening. Things will stop being "the same damn thing over and over" and revert to being "one damn thing after another." My colleagues and I tend to call this situation simply "life."

The Japanese characters for "therapy" include some of the same ones used for "teaching," and those characters can be taken to mean "tapping the student on the shoulder and pointing him in the right direction." The therapist cures nothing, all he does is tap the client on the shoulder and suggest that he look in a different direction from the one he was looking in before he came to therapy.

REFERENCES

de Shazer, S. (1978). Brief Hypnotherapy of Two Sexual Dysfunctions: The Crystal Ball Technique. *American Journal of Clinical Hypnosis, 20*(3), 203–208.
de Shazer, S. (1979). On Transforming Symptoms: An Approach to an Erickson Procedure. *American Journal of Clinical Hypnosis, 22*(1), 17–28.
de Shazer, S. (1980). Investigation of Indirect Symbolic Suggestions. *American Journal of Clinical Hypnosis, 23*(1), 10–15.
de Shazer, S. (1985). *Keys to Solution in Brief Therapy.* New York: Norton.
Erickson, M.H., Rossi, E.L., & Rossi, S.I. (1976). *Hypnotic Realities.* New York: Irvington.

SECTION ONE: PRINCIPLES

PART III

Overviews

Chapter 8

The Psychobiology of Mind-Body Healing: The Vision and State of the Art

Ernest Lawrence Rossi

Ernest Lawrence Rossi, Ph.D. (Temple University), has been an invited faculty member to every Erickson Foundation congress, seminar and conference. As well as maintaining a private practice, Dr. Rossi is a member of the editorial board of The American Journal of Clinical Hypnosis *and he is editor of* Psychological Perspectives: A Semi-annual Review of Jungian Thought. *Best known for his collaborations with Milton H. Erickson, he has coauthored three books with Erickson, edited four volumes of Erickson's collected papers and coedited three volumes of Erickson's early lectures. Current interests include the subjects of dreams and psychobiology, as evidenced by the books he has written:* Dreams and the Growth of Personality: Expanding Awareness of Psychotherapy *and* The Psychobiology of Mind-Body Healing.

This witty, easy-to-read chapter presents a three-year progress report on Rossi's effort to update Milton H. Erickson's initial explorations of the "neuro-psycho-physiological" foundations of therapeutic hypnosis. Rossi formulated the "mind-gene connection" as a visionary concept to guide hypnotherapeutic research and practice. The mind-gene connection consists of three major loci of information transduction: the mind/brain, *the* brain/body, *and the* cell/gene. *The ultimate task of any psychobiologically oriented hypnotherapy of the future is to develop clinical and experimental methods of integrating these three loci together as a single information loop to facilitate mind-body healing. The current practical state of this therapeutic art is presented in a number of instructional boxes. Research suggestions*

*are offered for the kind of clinical-experimental models that will be needed
to validate this psychobiological approach to therapeutic hypnosis.*

*The presentation from which this chapter was taken was the highest
rated of the 26 invited addresses at the Congress.*

THE MIND-GENE CONNECTION: A VISIONARY POSSIBILITY

It was at The Second International Congress on Ericksonian
Approaches to Hypnosis and Psychotherapy in 1983 that I first blurted
out the completely intuitive and unpremeditated idea of the "mind-
gene connection" as the ultimate basis of therapeutic hypnosis. Everyone
was remarkably kind at that time in not asking me for any details
about what I meant; most simply accepted it as a novel form of science
fiction. As I now look back at what I actually wrote about the mind-
gene connection, I am embarrassed by the naiveté of my exposition
(Rossi, 1985). I have pursued this vision, however, and have formulated
at least an outline of the psychobiological basis of the mind-gene
connection that is now grounded in solid experimental research (Rossi,
1986b). In this chapter I will give a progress report of my findings and
describe the new approaches to Ericksonian hypnotherapy that are
evolving from them.

In order to overview the range and limits of the mind-gene connection,
it is necessary to distinguish between the two major functions of genes
as 1) the fundamental *units of heredity,* and 2) the *blueprints for ongoing
cellular metabolism.* We are all familiar with the first role of genes as
the units within our chromosomes that transmit heredity from generation
to generation. Every high school student has learned about the genetic
experiments of Gregor Mendel more than 100 years ago that led to
our understanding of how genes from each parent are distributed in
sexual reproduction to their offspring. The mind-gene connection has
absolutely *nothing* to do with this role of genes in the transmission of
heredity.

If you have been out of school for more than 10 years or so, however,
you are probably not too familiar with the other main function of genes
as the blueprints that continuously regulate our cellular metabolism. *It
is in this stress sensitive role of mediating ongoing adaptive cellular
metabolism that I hypothesize a mind-gene connection is operative.* I believe
that recent remarkable progress in the psychobiology of memory and
learning, neuroendocrinology, and psychoneuroimmunology enables us

to outline a path of information exchange (transduction) between the mind and the genetic modulation of cellular metabolism.

If you are unfamiliar with these areas, recent newspaper reports of "genetic engineering" to produce natural body substances such as insulin and growth hormones are probably a bit puzzling to you. You may even be frightened by the many magazine reports of the *oncogenes* within each cell of our body that can produce cancer. You wonder how it can be that we have genes within us that can be "turned on" excessively to produce cancer. How could nature play such a mean trick on us?! Actually, it gets worse: The list goes on and on. It is estimated that there are at least 3,500 diseases that have been linked to variations in genes and the way they modulate our cellular metabolism (Baskin, 1984). It is now believed that virtually all the so-called psychosomatic problems are linked to such genetic variations. The chances are high that practically every patient in psychotherapy today has some type of gene-linked psychosomatic problem. The mind-gene connection, therefore, is not of theoretical interest alone; it is a vital and central concern of our daily psychotherapeutic work, about which most of us know almost nothing. To learn something about it, I believe, will lead us to a renaissance of Ericksonian therapy. This approach to therapy has a new, strong data base in the various fields of psychobiology: psychoneuroimmunology (Ader, 1981), neuroendocrinology (Guilleman, 1978), the psychosomatic networks based upon messenger molecules (Pert, Ruff, Weber, & Herkenham, 1985), and the neurobiology of memory and learning (Lynch, McGaugh, & Weinberger, 1984).

INFORMATION, FAMILY, AND MIND-BODY HEALING

It may seem initially overwhelming to most psychotherapists to be faced with the task of integrating such vast realms of apparently complex biology in order to understand the dynamics of mind-body healing as it is being developed here. This impression is correct. Psychobiological knowledge is currently distributed piecemeal, in an unintegrated fashion, throughout many apparently unrelated areas of psychological and medical specialization. Most researchers are so engrossed in their necessarily narrow fields of research that they do not synthesize an overview of the whole. This leaves the rest of us with a mass of interesting facts but no guiding theories that can provide a direction for our psychotherapeutic efforts. This is the difficult problem I have confronted during the past three years. I believe I have been able to discern a few integrative concepts, however, that may provide us with a theoretical outline for future research and clinical practice.

The most important integrative concept for us to consider can be found in *information and communication theory*. Many of us already feel somewhat burnt out by the abstract jargon, mathematics, and esoteric diagrams of traditional information theory. We are interested in people and do not want to put up any more rational and overly conceptualized barriers between us.

The flavor of the information theory that many psychobiologists are beginning to develop, however, is very different from that of mechanical "engineerspeak." *Family communication systems theory has come to psychobiology!* Many laboratory workers now blithely speak of "mother molecules" yielding a progeny of "messenger molecules" and "information substances" that flow throughout the mind-body to modulate all the emotions and behaviors that psychotherapists are traditionally interested in (sex, relationship, mood, growth, healing). This blending of vocabularies by the research people suggests to me that there need not be separate fields of sociology, psychology, and biology—they are all one. Mind, body, nerves, blood, flesh, bones, personality, family, and society are all one vast panorama of communicating networks. Just as we are able to recognize and facilitate manageable units of social communication such as nations, states, tribes, and families, so we can now also organize our understanding of the mind-body. One recent text, *Brain, Mind, and Behavior* (Bloom, Lazerson, & Hofstadter, 1985), in fact, provides a marvelous introduction to this entire field by using this social structure analogy. It is in this spirit that I offer the following outline of the future possibilities of mind-body healing.

AN OVERVIEW OF MIND-BODY COMMUNICATION

In Table 1 I have outlined the three major loci and pathways of information flow between mind, body, cells, and genes. From a technical point of view, Table 1 is an overview of *information transduction* throughout the mind-body. This new concept of information transduction greatly simplifies our task of understanding; it is the golden thread that stitches a seamless garment of the mind-body. Let us take a moment to explore its meaning and implications.

Transduction refers to the change in the form or structure of energy and information. Wind energy is transduced into mechanical energy by turning the blades of a windmill. This mechanical energy is in turn

Table 1

An Overview of Mind-Body Communication with the Three Major Loci and Pathways of Information Flow (Transduction).

Loci of Information Transduction	Pathways of Information Transduction	References
MIND-BRAIN	The *cortical-limbic system* pathways of the brain	Achterberg, 1985
	The sensory-perceptual languages of cortical mind (imagery, kinesthetic, etc.) are *ideodynamically transduced in the cross-modal association areas of the limbic system*	Bowers, 1977 Erickson, 1980 Mindell, 1982, 1985a & b Mishkin, 1982 Mishkin & Petri, 1984 Nauta, 1964
	Consciousness is a process of self-reflective information transduction	Rossi, 1986b
BRAIN-BODY	The *limbic-hypothalamic system* of the brain	Ader, 1981
	The neurally encoded languages of mind of the limbic system are *transduced into the messenger molecule languages of the body in the hypothalamus;* this involves *neuroendocrinal transduction*	Erickson, Rossi, & Rossi, 1976 Fischer, 1971 Overton, 1978 Rossi & Ryan, 1986
	State-dependent memory, learning, and behavior are encoded as "filters" in the limbic-hypothalamic and related systems	Selye, 1976 Weiner, 1977
	The autonomic, endocrine, immune, and neuropeptide systems are the major pathways from hypothalamus to all parts of the body	
CELL-GENE	The *cell wall receptor-gene system* of the entire body	Bulloch, 1985
	The messenger molecule languages of the body are *transduced into "second messenger systems" that move through the cell's cytoplasm to the genes in the nucleus*	Melnechuk, 1985 Olness & Conroy, 1985 Pert, Ruff, Weber, & Herkenham, 1985 Rossi & Cheek, 1988
	Messenger RNA carries the genes' blueprints out to the ribosome protein factories of the cell's cytoplasm where enzymes, proteins, and other messenger molecules are made	Schneider, Smith, & Witcher, 1984
	Many messenger molecules circulate back to hypothalamic-pituitary system to complete the information feedback loop	Smith, Harbour-McMenamin, & Blalock, 1985

transduced into electrical energy if a dynamo is turned by the blades of the windmill. This electrical energy can then be transduced into light energy if it is run through a light bulb. Light *energy* can be picked up by our eyes and transduced into chemical-molecular *information* in the retina. This molecular information is then transduced into neural information within the optic nerve that carries it to the hypothalamus as well as to the visual cortex of the brain. The subtle shift between the concepts of *energy* and *information* that is involved in the transition between sensory *stimuli* and mental *perception* is the fundamental problem of transduction between mind and body in the top row of Table 1.

This leads us to the interesting idea that the transduction between energy and information is one way of conceptualizing the essence of the life process. In the field of psychotherapy, we currently use the concepts of energy and information indiscriminately because we do not fully understand them. The concept of transduction will gradually help us to learn a great deal more about the special dynamics of mind-body energy and information exchange and flow. This more detailed understanding is needed to resolve the mind-body dualism that has plagued Western philosophy since the time of Descartes. In the history of hypnosis, this Cartesian dualism that separated mind and body into two different realms was bridged with the concept of the *ideodynamic:* Ideas could have dynamic effects on our sensory and bodily processes. Bernheim (1886-1957) believed that these *ideosensory* and *ideomotor* processes were the essence of therapeutic hypnotic suggestion. This view finds its most recent expression in Bowers's (1977) information approach to hypnosis, which he describes as "the transduction of semantic information into a form that is somatically encodable" (p. 222).

Ericksonian hypnosis involves more than semantic or verbal information, however. Virtually all our sensory-perceptual modalities of mind (visual, auditory, proprioceptive sense, etc.) function as languages that can be integrated and translated (transduced) into each other. Recent research (Mishkin, 1982) suggests that much of the mind-language transduction process takes place in the "cross-modal association areas" of the limbic system. This has led me to the interesting notion of defining *consciousness as a process of self-reflective information transduction* (Rossi, 1986b).

This view of consciousness is a way of integrating all the hypnotherapeutic methods that involve the use of imagery, emotions, felt sense, and so forth for accessing mind-body healing. Recent explorations of the relationships between the yogic use of breath meditation methods

(Rossi, 1986a) and cerebral hemispheric dominance, for example, have led me to develop the approach outlined in Box 1, "Shifting Cerebral Hemispheric Dominance and Mind-Body States" (Rossi, 1986b), which utilizes the cortical-limbic pathways in the top row of Table 1.

The second row in Table 1 outlines the process by which the neurally encoded languages of mind are transduced into the messenger molecules of the body. This is called the process of *neuroendocrinal transduction:* Information encoded in the nerves is transduced into the hormonal messengers of the body in the hypothalamus. The many specialized nerve centers of the hypothalamus integrate and modulate the four main branches of brain-body information transduction: the autonomic, endocrine, immune, and neuropeptide systems. I have hypothesized that the state-dependent memory, learning, and behavior (SDMLB) systems of the limbic-hypothalamus can function as "filters" that encode stress-related psychosomatic problems (Rossi & Ryan, 1986).

It was the fundamental contribution of Hans Selye (1974; 1976; 1982)

Box 1.
Shifting Cerebral Hemispheric Dominance and
Mind-Body States

1. *Identifying nasal dominance and mind-body state*
   When you are experiencing a mind-body state you would like to explore and transform, first determine which nostril is clear.

2. *Shifting nasal and hemispheric dominance*
   Lie on your side, with the clear nostril downward. This will shift reflexively your cerebral dominance within a few minutes to the hemisphere on the downward side. Simply receive and wonder about the sensory, perceptual, emotional, cognitive, or symptomatic shifts taking place all by themselves within the next five to 20 minutes.

3. *Ratify hemispheric and mind-body shifts*
   In an upright position, notice that the formerly blocked nostril is now clear, and vice versa. Record the mind-body changes that accompanied this nasal-cerebral hemispheric shift and study the characteristic patterns of your responses to guide yourself further.

Source: Rossi, 1986b, p. 123. Reprinted with permission.

to demonstrate how *stress* is the common denominator at the source of all psychosomatic illnesses. I recently integrated and summarized the contributions of Hans Selye and Milton Erickson for an understanding of the foundation of psychosomatic medicine as follows:

> Erickson's original contributions to the field of psychosomatic medicine are contained in four papers that were published together in the January 1943 issue of the journal *Psychosomatic Medicine* (1943a, b, c, d/1980). These papers on the *psychological* components of psychosomatic phenomena summarized the results of a decade of wide-ranging experimental and clinical hypnotic work that took place during the same time period when Selye was making his fundamental discovery of the *physiological* components. In a sense Erickson's and Selye's research was both complementary and reciprocal: Selye discovered the same physiological response to different stressors in what he termed the "General Adaptation Syndrome"; Erickson discovered psychologically different responses to the same stressor in what he termed "coincidental phenomena." Taken together, their work provides a comprehensive picture of the genesis and methods of resolving psychosomatic problems. (Rossi, 1986b, pp. 62–63)

As I studied these complementary contributions of Erickson and Selye in detail, I began to understand the limbic-hypothalamic system as the major information transducer between the brain and the body (outlined in row 2 of Table 1). The new neurobiology of memory and learning (Lynch, McGaugh, & Weinberger, 1984) is currently demonstrating how the hormonal messenger molecules of the body are encoding state-dependent memory and learning in a manner that gives rise to the mental sets and frames of reference that make up our phenomenological experience of mind in normal everyday life as well as in situations of stress and trauma. This research is laying the psychobiological foundation for understanding the state-dependent nature of our psychodynamic theories of mind and personality (Rossi, 1986b; Rossi & Ryan, 1986).

A broad range of holistic healing practices from acupuncture, massage, meditation, and the *relaxation response* (Benson, 1975; 1983a, b) to the *ultradian healing response* (Rossi, 1982, 1986a) may all utilize the brain-body transduction of state-dependent memory, learning, and behavior problems as outlined in the second row of Table 1. Box 2, "Naturalistic

Self-Hypnosis: The Ultradian Healing Response," presents one practical therapeutic approach that is consistent with this view.

Symptom prescription is one of the most specific Ericksonian approaches for accessing and reframing problems that have been encoded in state-dependent systems. I can well recall the despair I felt during the early part of my career when I was working exclusively within a psychoanalytic orientation and patients confronted me with their physical symptoms. Since I had been taught to *analyze* rather than *utilize* the symptoms, patients often got no better even after long periods of therapy. Now I actually have fun exploring an almost infinite number of hypnotherapeutic approaches to utilizing my patients' personal subjective experiences of their symptoms as a means of resolving them. Box 3, "Scaling and Symptom Prescription," outlines this approach.

Realizing that symptom prescription is the essence of paradoxical

---

Box 2.
Naturalistic Self-Hypnosis:
The Ultradian Healing Response

1. *Recognizing and facilitating the ultradian healing response*
   When you're tired, irritable, or simply feel the need to take a break, recognize it as a moment of opportunity to facilitate your natural ultradian healing response.

2. *Accessing and utilizing inner resources*
   Explore where the comfort is in your body. [Pause]
   Notice how it spreads and deepens, as you idly wonder about how your unconscious can utilize therapeutically your previous life experiences of optimal healing and deal with current problems all by itself.

3. *Ratifying continuing ultradian healing and coping*
   After a while you'll notice that you're awake and aware of yourself, but somehow you were not a moment ago. You look at the clock and notice that 10 to 20 minutes have gone by that you cannot account for. Recognize the comforting, healing changes that have taken place and resolve to do this again, a few times a day, whenever you need to.

Source: Rossi, 1986b, p. 139. Reprinted with permission.

Box 3.
Scaling and Symptom Prescription

1. *Symptom scaling and prescription*
   On a scale of 1 to 100, where 100 is the worst, what number
   expresses the degree to which you are experiencing that
   problem at this moment? Scale it right now.

2. *Problem prescription*
   Now let the problem get worse. Scale it. Now let the problem
   get better. Scale it. Etc.
   [Many ideodynamic hypnotherapeutic approaches utilizing
   imagery, active imagination, and Gestalt dialogue with the
   symptom are explored until the scaling is lowered to the
   diminishing point.]

3. *Ratifying the therapeutic response*
   [This therapeutic exercise is ended when the patient has made
   an obvious therapeutic gain by lowering the original scaling
   score of the problem, and by expressing confidence in being
   able to continue practicing this problem-solving routine for
   better and better resolution in the future.]

Source: Rossi, 1986b, p. 81. Reprinted with permission.

therapy, a most serendipitous insight came to me one day about the
apparently "mysterious" dynamics of how paradox works within a
psychobiological framework. I outlined it as follows:

> The so-called paradoxical aspects of this approach of problem and/
> or symptom prescription deserve further comment since paradox
> has generated so much interest recently as a new form of therapy
> (Seltzer, 1985; Weeks & L'Abate, 1982; Zeig, 1980a, b). From our
> psychobiological point of view, paradoxical therapy is not para-
> doxical at all: As we have seen, to prescribe a problem or symptom
> is actually the most direct path to accessing its psychobiological
> sources encoded within the state-dependent memory, learning, and
> behavior systems of the brain. Paradoxical therapy only seems
> paradoxical from a logical point of view wherein patients try to
> avoid the experience and expression of a problem in the hope
> that it will thereby "go away." Avoiding, resisting, or blocking a

problem, however, only prevents one from accessing and therapeutically reframing it. When a problem or symptom "haunts" a
patient, it is only because mind and nature are attempting to bring
it up to consciousness so it can be resolved.

As was indicated earlier, research in the neurobiology of memory
and learning indicates that the process of accessing and recall is
not simply that—accessing and recall are always a synthetic process
of reconstruction. As such, prescribing the symptom is actually a
process of reconstructing it. When we ask a person to experience
a symptom voluntarily rather than resisting it, we are drastically
altering the internal dynamics of state-dependent memory and
learning systems that allow the symptom to flourish. We have
changed it from a dissociated and involuntary action to a voluntary
action; we are undoing its state-bound character. When we ask a
person to scale the intensity of the symptom, we are changing it
further by adding a *novel, conscious, evaluative orientation* to it.
This new evaluative orientation immediately potentiates problem-
solving processes; it facilitates coping skills and self-efficacy; and
the patient's ego is strengthened in its relationship to the formerly
dissociated symptom. (Rossi, 1986b, p. 82)

I have also discussed the dynamics of symptom prescription as a process
that may involve the integration of left- and right-cerebral hemispheric
activity.

The cell-gene locus of information transduction in row 3 of Table 1
is the area with which most psychotherapists are least familiar. Yet it
is currently the most exciting area of breakthrough research in biology.
All the messenger molecules of the mind-body find their ultimate locus
of action here at the cellular-genetic level. If we were to think of each
microscopic cell of the body as an independent unit of life, we would
recognize that some channel of communication with them would be
needed. This channel of communication takes place at the molecular
level. All cells of the body have a myriad of doors in their walls in
the form of *receptor* proteins. These receptors have been compared to
"customized receiving docks" that pick up the messenger molecules
(hormones, neuropeptides, immunotransmitters, etc.) floating by in the
blood stream that fit them. This view has been engagingly dramatized
by Cordes (1985) as follows:

The findings are enough to send adrenaline levels of behavioral

sleuths soaring: Endorphins and other neuropeptides may be the
molecular bases of emotion.

"Right now," explains biochemist Candace Pert, "brain research
is colliding with psychology. And finally, with neuropeptides, I
think we can put the two together."

Many neuropeptides seem to meander through the brain, glands
and immune system like island-hopping cruise ships. They make
scheduled stops in the choicest locations, at only those cellular
ports with customized receiving docks. At these receptor sites—
including ones crowded into the most crucial brain processing
station for emotion—they sail in and unload their cargo of be-
havior-changing, mood-altering information. . . . .

Cells talking to cells through networks of neuropeptide-saturated
nodes connect the brain to the endocrine and immune systems.
And they may tie together the "internal milieu of the *whole
organism*," she [Pert] speculates.

"The striking patterns of neuropeptide receptor distribution in
mood-regulating areas of the brain, as well as their role in mediating communication throughout the *whole* organism, make
neuropeptides the obvious candidates for the biochemical mediation of emotion. Does each neuropeptide bias information processing uniquely when occupying receptors at nodal points within
the brain and body? If so, each unique neuropeptide's 'tone' might
produce a typical mood state."

So far, very little is known about what emotional mood most
neuropeptides may induce, [Pert] said. But they do ground theories
of psychoneuroimmunology in a molecular description of the bonds
between emotions and health. (pp. 18–19)

Once these messenger molecules signal the receptors in the cell walls,
their information is transduced into the so-called "second messenger
systems" within the cell. In turn, these second messenger systems
penetrate through the nucleus of the cell where they "unzipper" specific
segments of the genes to expose their information. This information is
transmitted as "messenger RNA," which then moves back out to the
cytoplasm of the cell. The messenger RNA carries the genes' blueprints
out to the ribosome protein factories of the cell where enzymes, proteins,
and other messenger molecules are made. These products of cellular
metabolism are responsible for the characteristic functions of each cell.
Digestive cells produce digestive enzymes; hormonal cells produce hor-

mones; muscle cells produce structural protein, and so forth. Many of the messenger molecules produced at this genetic-cellular level travel back to the hypothalamic-pituitary axis to complete the mind-brain-body-cell-gene information transduction loop. Thus there is no mysterious gap between mind, brain, and body: At the molecular level, there is a complete channel of communication continuously taking place between mind and body.

A CLINICAL CASE STUDY

The possibilities as well as the limitations of the current state of the art in mind-body healing is illustrated by the following personal account written by a patient who used the *ultradian healing response* as a form of self-hypnosis.

> After beginning psychotherapy with Dr. Rossi, I was informed by my gynecologist that I had developed a small polyp on my cervix. He said that I would probably need surgery but that the polyp was small and we could wait three months in order to see if it grew or decreased in size. I sought a second opinion, this time with a "top" O-B-G-Y-N. He confirmed the original diagnosis and recommended immediate surgery.
>
> I decided to wait the three months. During that time, I used a relaxation and imagery exercise that Dr. Rossi had taught me: I would relax and imagine the polyp as a small, round tumor or growth of cells. Then I would image a ray of light like a laser beam contacting the tumor and making it disappear. *When doing this visualization, I experienced a pleasurable sensation in the area of my cervix where I was visualizing the laser beam. The sensation reached a certain level of intensity and then I would stop the visualization naturally.* I did the exercise consciously about five or six times per day for about two to three minutes each time. But, after a week or so, I found that *the meditation was going on unconsciously most of the day. A great deal of my energy was withdrawn from involvement with social or emotional areas during this time as well. My focus was on being healed.*
>
> Three months later, on my 38th birthday, I returned to the gynecologist. He informed me that "Mother Nature had taken care of itself" and the polyp was gone!

The noteworthy features of this case may be conceptualized according to the mind-body model of Table 1 as follows.

1. The mind-brain locus

We may suppose that the planning functions of the prefrontal cortical areas of the brain were well integrated with the limbic cross-modal association areas when the patient and I initially explored the type of therapeutic imagery that would be *meaningful and pleasurable* for her. After trying out a number of different forms of imagery, we found that the healing laser visualization was the one that was most effective for her.

2. The brain-body locus

Since she was a highly orgasmic person, I utilized her interest and emotional investment in sexual pleasure by including it as another source of motivational energy for her therapeutic response. We may suppose that she was thereby led to utilizing those limbic-hypothalamic association areas that are involved with pleasurable orgasmic responses.

She was favorably impressed with my view of the *ultradian healing response* as a naturalistic form of self-hypnosis that she could use every 90 to 120 minutes throughout the day, when there was a normal, psychobiological shift in cerebral hemispheric dominance and a concomitant activation of many healing autonomic, endocrine, and immune functions. These ultradian cycles are regulated by the suprachiasmatic nucleus of the hypothalamus (Rossi, 1986a).

This patient was particularly interested in tuning in with great sensitivity to these natural periods of rest throughout the day and utilizing them as a self-hypnosis time. When people are doing this in an optimal manner, they typically report five or six short rest periods per day. I frequently give a posthypnotic suggestion that patients will reserve "about 5 to 10 percent of your life energy to be continuously involved with the inner healing process, even while you go about your daily life; and no one will notice anything different in your outer behavior." I also remind patients that the inner healing can continue in dreams that come every 90 to 120 minutes throughout sleep.

3. The cell-gene locus

All the rich neural and hormonal (messenger molecule) communication networks between the limbic-hypothalamic areas of the brain and the cervix were presumably involved in her meaningful and pleasurable visualization. The genital-sexual pleasure she felt during her healing laser imagery may have helped focus her mind-body information transduction systems on the area of the cervix that needed healing. I do not know that actual cellular-genetic mechanisms were involved in her healing of the polyp, but one hypnotherapeutic theory proposes that the blood supply serving the growth of the polyp could be cut off (Barber, 1984). A case could be made to support the possibility that all four of the major channels of mind-body communication (autonomic, endocrine, immune, and neuropeptide systems) were involved in the healing of this cervical polyp (Cheek, 1986).

The limitations of this essentially anecdotal clinical case is that at each of the above three major loci of information transduction, we can only speculate about what mechanisms are involved. The model in Table 1 is still only a theoretical vision; it is entirely consistent with all the well-known and scientifically validated psychobiological processes that *might* be involved, but no one has yet actually applied experimental controls to determine that these are, in fact, the *actual* healing processes involved. This is the task for future research.

The skeptic also could point out that perhaps the so-called mind-body therapy was not the healing agent since there is, after all, some natural base rate of spontaneous recovery with such cervical polyps. It is difficult to get an accurate estimate of the base rate for recovery from such polyps today, however, because O-B-G-Y-N specialists prefer to remove them immediately when they are discovered (Cheek, 1986). In any case, the base rate issue begs the question. One could say equally well that spontaneous remissions only take place because life smiles on the patients who experience them. A change toward favorable life circumstances would reduce their stress-hormonal levels and spontaneously activate the three-stage psychobiological healing model of Table 1 (especially via the limbic-hypothalamic-pituitary-*endocrine*-cellular-gene pathway [Rossi, 1986b]) in an unconscious manner. I have noted how spontaneous remissions, the placebo response, biofeedback cures, miracle cures, and shamanistic and holistic healing of every variety must have some sort of common denominator as outlined in Table 1 (Rossi, 1986b). The task of the future is to devise controlled clinical-experimental studies that can locate precisely where the mind-body locus of information transduction takes place in each specific type of mind-body healing.

THE ERICKSONIAN PSYCHOBIOLOGICAL RESEARCH TEAM

Throughout his writings and lectures on the neuro-psycho-physiological basis of hypnosis, Erickson emphasized the need for research on the actual mechanisms underlying mind-body healing. In one of his most significant discussions with many of his leading contemporaries (T.X. Barber, T. Sarbin, A. Weitzenhoffer, and others) about the nature of hypnosis research, Erickson had this to say:

> I do not think that hypnosis should be or can be investigated as a total phenomenon (whatever is implied by that global term). I think that hypnosis can best be investigated by a careful searching of the great varieties of human behavior which can be modified or changed or influenced by the hypnotic state. Learning, forgetting, sleeping, dreaming are but a few of the areas in which research on hypnosis needs to be done. I think research should focus on the various manifestations of hypnosis rather than a total hypnotic state. As for research on hypnotic techniques, one should never forget that these are only a means of attracting the subject's attention, and we should not lose sight of the purpose of these techniques because of fascination with the variations which can be employed. (1980, p. 325)

These words of Erickson's may prove to be prophetic. I believe that the golden era of research on hypnosis as a global phenomenon that took place during the 1960s and 1970s (Fromm & Shor, 1979; Sheehan & Perry, 1976) may be coming to an end. What we need now is a careful study and validation of the specific psychobiological mechanisms of therapeutic hypnosis. This is being developed currently by the new fields of psychoneuroimmunology, neuroendocrinology, and neurobiology of memory and learning (Rossi, 1986b). If Ericksonian therapeutic hypnosis is to survive into the future as a creative contributor to this newly emerging paradigm of clinical discovery, then it must adapt itself into new types of psychobiological research teams.

I see future research teams in mind-body healing consisting of essentially three specialists corresponding to the three loci of information transduction indicated in Table 1. I would like to believe, for example, that I could serve as the *mind-brain specialist* of row 1, who focuses clinical and research skills on helping patients utilize their personal repertory of inner experiential resources. I would help each patient explore, for example, how his or her unique ideodynamic and state-dependent memory, learning, and behavior processes activate and ameloriate the *stress response* that takes place within their cortical-limbic-hypothalamic systems. I would help each patient learn how to access and utilize their own imagistic, emotional, sensory-perceptual, dream, and cognitive processes to modulate the various psychobiological systems related to their problem.

I would need to coordinate my work with a *brain-body specialist* who knows what type of messenger molecules (in row 2 of Table 1) would be needed to mediate information transduction between the patient's cortical-limbic-hypothalamic systems and the cellular-genetic locus of the clinical problem. This member of the team would be able to monitor the activity of the autonomic, endocrine, immune, and neuropeptide systems and their unique interactions within each patient in mediating their *stress response*. This specialist would be able to measure the changes in the messenger molecule (ACTH, corticoids, endorphins, immunotransmitters, etc.) dynamics that are taking place as a result of my hypnotherapeutic facilitations.

The third member of the Ericksonian psychobiological research team would then be needed to help us determine what specific cellular-genetic mechanisms were evoking the clinical problem at that level. This specialist would be able to measure, for example, how *stress* was turning on the gene that sends out messenger RNA into the cells' endoplasmic reticular factories to make the protein called *"metallothionein"* and the effects of this metabolite in mediating the psychosomatic response. This specialist would tell us which messenger molecules the hypnotherapeutic work should be facilitating (see Box 4).

While this overall picture of the Ericksonian psychobiological research team may seem visionary, it is important to recognize that it is based upon well-documented scientific facts. What is still theoretical and remains for experimental demonstration is whether *hypnotherapeutic intervention at the mental level can really lead to a measurable metabolic change at the cellular-genetic level.* No one has done such an experiment

Box 4.
The Mind-Gene Operon

The value of a theory of science is determined by the extent to which it generates testable hypotheses. The mind-gene theory of psychobiological healing generates the testable hypothesis that *mind-gene operons* exist.

An *operon* is a new concept from molecular genetics that is of essence for understanding the mind-gene connection. An operon consists of a group of genes whose activity is regulated by stimuli or messenger molecules from outside the nucleus of the cell. The existence of genes that can be turned on by environmental stress, for example, is aptly described by Baskin (1984):

> An animal responds to stress and physical trauma on many levels, from mental to molecular. One of the most basic responses is the switching on of a gene that makes a protein called *metallothionein*, or MT. Chase a mouse around its cage for five minutes, dose the animal with high levels of toxic metals, or infect it with bacteria, and it will switch on the MT gene in tissues throughout the body. (p. 185)

The cellular-genetic level scientist on the Ericksonian research team would specialize in how the *mind-gene stress operon* can be accessed and modulated by hypnosis. We would hypothesize that many more mind-gene stress operons exist in addition to the MT operon described above. Each time we succeed in characterizing the existence of another mind-gene stress operon, we will be adding another bit of verification for the mind-gene theory of psychobiological healing.

Since we know that positive emotions, imagery, and placebos can theoretically facilitate healing at the genetic level (Rossi, 1986b), we can also hypothesize the existence of *mind-gene healing operons*. The unequivocal experimental demonstration of the activity of stress and healing mind-gene operons in humans should win researchers a Nobel Prize: they, at last, would be able to define the basic mechanisms of holistic mind-body healing.

yet because apparently no one has defined the mind-gene connection as the ultimate psychobiological basis of therapeutic hypnosis, mind-body healing, holistic health, and the placebo response, as is being done here.

This is my ideal Ericksonian research team. Do I have any takers out there? How much progress could we make if each Ericksonian institute throughout the world put together such a team?!

SUMMARY AND OVERVIEW

This summary is loosely adapted from my recent book on *The Psychobiology of Mind-Body Healing: New Concepts of Therapeutic Hypnosis* (Rossi, 1986b), which documents the major concepts of this paper in greater detail.

1. *Information theory* is capable of unifying psychological, biological, and physical phenomena into a single conceptual framework that can account for healing at the mind-brain, brain-body, and cellular-genetic levels.
2. *Information transduction* is emerging as the key concept in our psychobiological theory of mind-body communication and healing. The basic laws of biology, psychology, family systems and sociology are all essentially descriptions of different levels of information transduction.
3. There is no mysterious gap between mind and body. Ideodynamic processes and state-dependent memory, learning, and behavior processes encoded in the *limbic-hypothalamic and closely related systems* are the major information transducers that bridge the Cartesian dichotomy between mind and body.
4. Traditional *psychosomatic symptoms* and, perhaps, most mind-body problems are acquired by a process of experiential learning—specifically, the state-dependent learning of response patterns of Selye's *general adaptation syndrome*. Enduring mind-body problems are manifestations of these statebound patterns of learning that are encoded within a limbic-hypothalamic system "filter," which modulates mind-body communication. *Symptom prescription* is emerging as one of the most useful Ericksonian approaches to accessing and therapeutically reframing symptoms and problems encoded in these state-dependent filters.

5. This limbic-hypothalamic system filter coordinates all the major channels of mind-body regulation via the autonomic, endocrine, immune, and neuropeptide systems. *Messenger molecules* (neurotransmitters, hormones, immunotransmitters, etc.) flowing through these channels are the structural informational mediators of mind-body communication and transformation.

6. Ongoing research is clarifying the precise pathways by which these messenger molecules are mediating the *mind-gene connection* that is the ultimate basis of most processes of mind-body healing via therapeutic hypnosis, the placebo response, and the traditional practices of mythopoetic and holistic medicine.

7. The *new concepts of Ericksonian hypnosis* emphasize natural psychobiological processes of information transduction and state-dependent memory, learning, and behavior to access and facilitate the utilization of patients' own inner resources for problem-solving. This is in sharp contrast to previous methods of authoritarian suggestion, covert conditioning, and programming in hypnosis.

While there is a great deal of scientifically well-documented data that is consistent with this psychobiological view of mind-body healing, it still remains for future research to devise experimental paradigms that can document how a specific therapeutic intervention at the mental level can lead to a specific metabolic change at the cellular-genetic level.

REFERENCES

Achterberg, J. (1985). *Imagery and Healing.* Boston: Shambala.

Ader, R. (Ed.) (1981). *Psychoneuroimmunology.* New York: Academic Press.

Barber, T. X. (1984). Changing unchangeable bodily processes by (hypnotic) suggestions: A new look at hypnosis, cognitions, imagining, and the mind-body problem. *Advances, 1*(2), 7–40.

Baskin, Y. (1984). *The Gene Doctors: Medical Genetics at the Frontier.* New York: William Morrow & Co.

Benson, H. (1975). *The Relaxation Response.* New York: Avon.

Benson, H. (1983a). The relaxation response and norepinephrine: A new study illuminates mechanisms. *Integrative Psychiatry, 1,* 15–18.

Benson, H. (1983b). The relaxation response: Its subjective and objective historical precedents and physiology. *Trends in Neuroscience, July,* 281–284.

Bernheim, H. (1886/1957). *Suggestive Therapeutives: A Treatise on the Nature and Uses of Hypnotism.* Westport, CT: Associated Booksellers. (Originally published by Putnam.)

Bloom, F., Lazerson, A., & Hofstadter, L. (1985). *Brain, Mind, and Behavior.* New York: W. H. Freeman.

Bowers, K. (1977). Hypnosis: An informational approach. *Annals of the New York Academy of Sciences, 296,* 222–237.

Bulloch, K. (1985). Neuroanatomy of lymphoid tissue: A review. In R. Guillemin, M. Cohn, & T. Melnechuk (Eds.), *Neural modulation of immunity* (pp. 111–141). New York: Raven Press.

Cheek, D. (1986). Personal communication.

Cordes, C. (1985). Neuropeptides: Chemical cruise steers emotion. *APA Monitor, 16*(9), 18–19. Washington, D.C.: American Psychological Association.

Erickson, M. (1943a/1980). Experimentally elicited salivary and related responses to hypnotic visual hallucinations confirmed by personality reactions. In E. Rossi (Ed.), *The Collected Papers of Milton H. Erickson on Hypnosis. II. Hypnotic Alteration of Sensory, Perceptual and Psychophysical Processes* (pp. 175–178). New York: Irvington.

Erickson, M. (1943b/1980). Hypnotic investigation of psychosomatic phenomena: A controlled experimental use of hypnotic regression in the therapy of an acquired food intolerance. In E. Rossi (Ed.), *The Collected Papers of Milton H. Erickson on Hypnosis. II. Hypnotic Alteration of Sensory, Perceptual and Psychophysical Processes* (pp. 169–174). New York: Irvington.

Erickson, M. (1943c/1980). Hypnotic investigation of psychosomatic phenomena: Psychosomatic interrelationships studied by experimental hypnosis. In E. Rossi (Ed.), *The Collected Papers of Milton H. Erickson on Hypnosis. II. Hypnotic Alteration of Sensory, Perceptual and Psychophysical Processes* (pp. 145–156). New York: Irvington.

Erickson, M. (1943d/1980). Investigation of psychosomatic phenomena: The development of aphasialike reactions from hypnotically induced amnesia. In E. Rossi (Ed.), *The Collected Papers of Milton H. Erickson on Hypnosis. II. Hypnotic Alteration of Sensory, Perceptual and Psychosomatic Processes* (pp. 157–168). New York: Irvington.

Erickson, M. (1980). Explorations in hypnosis research. In E. Rossi (Ed.), *The Collected Papers of Milton H. Erickson on Hypnosis. Vol. II. Hypnotic Alteration of Sensory, Perceptual, and Psychophysical Processes.* New York: Irvington.

Erickson, M., Rossi, E., & Rossi, S. (1976). *Hypnotic Realities.* New York: Irvington.

Fischer, R. (1971). Arousal-statebound recall of experience. *Diseases of the Nervous System, 32,* 373–382.

Fromm, E., & Shor, R. (Eds.) (1979). *Hypnosis: Research Development and Perspectives* (2nd ed.). Chicago: Aldine-Atherton.

Guilleman, R. (1978). Peptides in the brain: The new endocrinology of the neuron. *Science, 202,* 390–402.

Lynch, G., McGaugh, J., & Weinberger, N. (1984). *Neurobiology of Learning and Memory.* New York: Guilford Press.

Melnechuk, T. (1985). Neuroimmunology: Crossroads between behavior and disease. Reports on selected conferences and workshops. *Advances, 2*(3), 54–58.

Mindell, A. (1982). *Dreambody.* Los Angeles: Sigo Press.

Mindell, A. (1985a). *River's Way: The Process Science of the Dreambody.* Boston: Routledge & Kegan Paul.

Mindell, A. (1985b). *Working With the Dreaming Body.* Boston: Routledge & Kegan Paul.

Mishkin, M. (1982). A memory system in the monkey. *Philosophical Transactions of the Royal Society of London, B298,* 85–95.

Mishkin, M., & Petri, H. (1984). Memories and habits: Some implications for the analysis of learning and retention. In S. Squire & N. Butters (Eds.), *Neuropsychology of Memory* (pp. 287–296). New York: Guilford Press.

Nauta, W. (1964). Some efferent connections of the prefrontal cortex in the monkey. In J. Warren & K. Akert (Eds.), *The Frontal Granular Cortex and Behavior.* New York: McGraw-Hill.

Olness, K., & Conroy, M. (1985). A pilot study of voluntary control of transcutaneous PO_2 by children. *International Journal of Clinical & Experimental Hypnosis, 33*(1), 1–5.

Overton, D. (1978). Major theories of state-dependent learning. In B. Ho, D. Richards, & D. Chute (Eds.), *Drug Discrimination and State-Dependent Learning* (pp. 283–318). New York: Academic Press.

Pert, C., Ruff, M., Weber, R., & Herkenham, M. (1985). Neuropeptides and their receptors: A psychosomatic network. *The Journal of Immunology, 135*(2), 820s–826s.

Rossi, E. (1982). Hypnosis and ultradian cycles: A new state(s) theory of hypnosis? *The American Journal of Clinical Hypnosis, 25*, 21–32.

Rossi, E. (1985). Unity and diversity in Ericksonian approaches: Now and in the future. In J. Zeig (Ed.), *Ericksonian Psychotherapy. Vol. I. Structures* (pp. 15–30). New York: Brunner/Mazel.

Rossi, E. (1986a). Altered states of consciousness in everyday life: The ultradian rhythms. In B. Wolman (Ed.), *Handbook of Altered States of Consciousness* (pp. 97–132). New York: Van Nostrand Reinhold.

Rossi, E. (1986b). *The Psychobiology of Mind-Body Healing: New Concepts of Therapeutic Hypnosis.* New York: Norton.

Rossi, E., & Cheek, D. (1988). *Mind-Body Therapy: Ideodynamic Healing in Hypnosis.* New York: Norton.

Rossi, E., & Ryan, M. (Eds.) (1986). *Mind-Body Communication in Hypnosis. Vol. III. The Seminars, Lectures, and Workshops of Milton H. Erickson.* New York: Irvington.

Schneider, J., Smith, W., & Witcher, S. (1984). The relationship of mental imagery to white blood cell (neutrophil) function in normal subjects. Paper presented at the 36th Annual Scientific Meeting of the International Society for Clinical & Experimental Hypnosis, San Antonio, Texas, October 25.

Seltzer, L. (1985). *Paradoxical Strategies in Psychotherapy.* New York: Wiley & Sons.

Selye, H. (1974). *Stress Without Distress.* New York: Signet.

Selye, H. (1976). *The Stress of Life.* New York: McGraw-Hill.

Selye, H. (1982). History and present status of the stress concept. In L. Goldberger, & S. Breznitz (Eds.), *Handbook of stress* (pp. 7–20). New York: Macmillan.

Sheehan, P., & Perry, C. (1976). *Methodologies of Hypnosis.* Hillsdale, NJ: Lawrence Erlbaum.

Smith, E., Harbour-McMenamin, D., & Blalock, J. (1985). Lymphocyte production of endorphins and endorphin-mediated immunoregulatory activity. *The Journal of Immunology, 135*(2), 779s–782s.

Weeks, G. R., & L'Abate, L. (1982). *Paradoxical Psychotherapy: Theory and Practice with Individuals, Couples, and Families.* New York: Brunner/Mazel.

Weiner, H. (1977). *Psychobiology and Human Disease.* New York: Elsevier.

Zeig, J. K. (Ed.) (1980a). *A Teaching Seminar with Milton H. Erickson.* New York: Brunner/Mazel.

Zeig, J. K. (Ed.) (1980b). Symptom prescription and Ericksonian principles of hypnosis and psychotherapy. *The American Journal of Clinical Hypnosis, 23*, 16–23.

Chapter 9

Motivation and the Multiple States of Trance

Kay F. Thompson

Kay F. Thompson, D.D.S. (University of Pittsburgh), maintains a private practice in dentistry in Pittsburgh, Pennsylvania. She is a Clinical Associate Professor in the Department of Community Dentistry at the West Virginia University School of Dentistry. Dr. Thompson is a member of the editorial board of the Ericksonian Monographs, and she is active in numerous professional organizations of dentistry and hypnosis. A colleague of Milton Erickson for more than 30 years, she travels internationally to present workshops on hypnosis. She has been an Invited Faculty Member of all Erickson Foundation-sponsored Congresses since 1980. Dr. Thompson has received numerous awards for her work in hypnosis from such organizations as the American Society of Clinical Hypnosis, the Society for Clinical and Experimental Hypnosis, and the Netherlands Society of Clinical Hypnosis.

Dr. Thompson's address was one of the most highly rated at the Congress. She is a powerful and sensitive communicator who understands how to reach her audience. One of the important contributions Dr. Thompson has made to Ericksonian hypnosis and hypnosis in general is her development of the importance of motivation in hypnosis. Many practitioners have enhanced their effectiveness by utilizing motivation as Thompson suggests. In her chapter she takes a phenomenological approach. She delineates six types of trance and distinguishes them according to the discrepant motivations of the subject in the respective situation.

As I prepared for the Third Erickson Congress, I reviewed and rejected a number of topics before I finally realized that my last three papers have covered everything I could say *about* Erickson. I could not begin what is already completed.

My tribute *to* Erickson is thus to go on, always acknowledging that my work is the result of what he taught me. Therefore, today, I come to bury Erickson, not to praise him.

It is time for me to go on, not go over, and over, and over Erickson's life and work in a fixed litany that I and my listeners may continue to repeat but will cease to hear or understand. Going over something that for me has so much emotion only desensitizes me to what was real about Milton H. Erickson and continues to be real about his work. There has already been too much talk about Erickson, too much trading on his name and reputation, and too little actual continuation of the work he started.

As Carlos Amantea (1986) said, in Part III of "The Lourdes of Arizona":

> A whole Industry has risen about visiting the Prophet of Phoenix. One comes for a day or two, and then advertises that one has "studied under Milton Erickson." This means you can charge $1000 a day for seminars. Few pay attention to the fact that the master himself charges only $25 a day for visitors . . . he doesn't care about making money, getting rich, making it in the American Dream Factory. He gives away information, knowledge, insights— gives them to all comers for so little. (p. 42)

As I see it, Amantea is speaking of all the self-proclaimed authorities on Erickson who came during those waning years, when he held "audiences," as Amantea so aptly titled them, and told stories. They came and they listened, but many did not hear and most did not learn.

It is interesting to note that those who did learn from Erickson in his "teaching" days have not chosen to, and have chosen not to, profess to understand or teach Ericksonian hypnosis—people such as Rossi and Haley and Weitzenhofer teach themselves.

Erickson taught thousands of therapists during the 1950s and 1960s in his "Seminars on Hypnosis." He accepted the responsibility of the teaching, knowing he was teaching, and doing it deliberately, masterfully, diligently, sometimes in a Machiavellian manner, but always effectively! He taught direct and indirect, basic and advanced, but always, he taught of trance!

And he did this in a way that allowed people to open their eyes, ears, and minds so that they could see, hear, and understand what was being given to them and then have the knowledge and the courage to use what they had learned to continue their work, not his. He did not leave it to his students to explain his approach, nor did he expect them to interpret his work. He expected them to learn in their own way and to present their own work, not his.

Erickson was a successful teacher who had both the arrogance to believe that what he had to say should be listened to, and the humility to understand that each would ultimately hear and use what he had heard in his own individual way. Erickson would be the first to insist that his way was the one true way, but he could paradoxically insist that each "student" develop the one true way that was true for him. He had a further gift that successful teachers must have: He motivated those who came to him to want to hear what needed to be said.

My tribute to Erickson is to continue the work he taught me how to begin. As I do this, one of the things I constantly learn and relearn is that listening, and hearing, is part of the ultimate communication skill, and of course, it is an art. But there exists a still more critical skill, which is making the listener *want* to hear what needs to be said. Erickson possessed these skills in abundance. He knew how to present ideas gift-wrapped so attractively that the intended recipient wanted to own the package. We all must learn this skill to begin to realize our own potential in communicating.

This sounds manipulative, but it is not necessarily a matter of actively doing something to change the situation so that the listener is more receptive. Often it is a matter of listening to ourselves so that we read the situation correctly and are able to go to where the person is and see the situation from the client's point of view. This putting oneself in the place of another creates a very different dynamic than is created when the practitioner is completely in charge, assumes a motivation for the client, and then imposes a schema which will fit that situation.

This is not to say that the practitioner should be passive. Listening and hearing may seem to be passive skills because on the surface they require little action by the listener. The "speaker" appears to be in control; the listener merely responds. In reality, listening must be very "active"; the listener must take in, analyze, and be prepared to act on a variety of inputs. Otherwise, he is simply allowing his eardrums to vibrate to sound. The practitioner who listens must indeed be skillful. He must be able to perceive the message even when the "speaker" is not consciously trying to send it, and he must be able to understand much more than simply what is said. Professionals in all health fields must know how to see and hear things that clients do not even know they are communicating.

As we listen, however, we must be constantly aware of our own assumptions and expectations regarding what we will hear. Listening and hearing may be blocked by assumptions, even valid ones. In the best instance, the assumptions may cause us to "hear" only what we already know to be "true." In the worst case, our assumptions distort sensory information into a preconceived notion of what it should be. Such assumptions can be limiting and dangerous if they are accepted as "truth."

I suspect that assumptions about the nature of listening—coupled with the practitioner's desire to control any given situation and common assumptions about trance—have had a crippling effect on research into the nature of trance. Such assumptions have led to projects in which the practitioner has an obviously active role as both the originator of the trance and its ultimate interpreter. In this type of "experiment," the practitioner induces trance using a prerecorded tape and then observes the outwardly measurable behavior of the subject. Because the method of induction is held constant, any variation in the subject's observable behavior is assumed to be a result of the action and intervention of the practitioner during the trance. The motivation of the subject and the level of his involvement in the trance are never even considered.

Professionals can sometimes lose sight of the fact that the primary moving force behind their work should be a positive therapeutic outcome and that the outcome must necessarily be defined in terms of the patient's motivation and needs in the situation. Our experimental goals, or even our own quest for knowledge, must be secondary. Paradoxically, when we put the concerns of the patient first and do so in a way that allows us to really listen and hear, we learn much more than we would by imposing a preset scheme. Both we and our clients benefit, and the state of knowledge is advanced.

In any clinical situation, there is always the matter of mixed motivations—ours, the clients, and those of the organizations for which we work. In effect, we and our patients enter into a marriage of convenience in which each hopes to gain by cooperating with the other.

This matter and manner of mutual motivational manipulation is manageable but mandates mastery of many methods. I believe that exploring trance more openly will open access to listening and hearing. In order to understand trance more thoroughly, we must begin to explore it with more liberal and inquisitive minds. I would like to propose that more research is needed and that the beginning point for the research is observation and listening. In that spirit, I would like to offer some of my observations about trance with a tentative schema for differentiating among the types of trance based on those observations.

All types of trance have the potential to be therapeutic. There is always the recognition of a learning skill acknowledged by the unconscious. We can enhance this by learning of ourselves as we observe the types of trance.

As a starting point, I would like to examine some widely held assumptions. First, trance is generally defined as an altered state of awareness. Second, generally such states are not discrete but exist on a continuum. And third, trance behavior, even of the same person, may vary from trance to trance. A general acceptance of these assumptions is an interesting example of the ability to readily and intuitively accept ideas without hearing or thinking through their implications.

Despite the general acceptance of the continuum concept, for example, many practitioners have postulated that hypnosis and the hypnotic trance state are one state, always the same. They propose that all trances are "located" in the same state, and that observable differences in behavior or outcome result from differences in the way people respond to the situation based on the suggestions given. Thus, the observable differences between trances are explained only by the behavior suggested by the practitioner and carried out by the client, not by possible differences in the states themselves. This would indicate that the power of the practitioner is the principal influence on the individual in trance.

These assumptions probably have their basis in two phenomena of human behavior: 1) our tendency to want to control whatever situation we find ourselves in; and 2) our tendency to prefer phenomena that can be measured to those that can be analyzed and understood but possibly never measured and therefore never "proved." Faith scares us. We work with the unconscious mind all of the time but are afraid to draw conclusions from anything but observable, measurable outward behavior.

If trance is an altered state on the continuum of awareness, should there not then be the possibility of different states of trance? Since theorists generally accept multiple states of awareness, why is trance designated as only one of those states, when it can represent a number of degrees on the scale of awareness? I propose that the term *trance* can be used to characterize a subset of states along that continuum of altered states of awareness and that the differences in these states may be accounted for by differences in the motivation of the subject.

The acceptance of the common concept of hypnosis as a single, simple state is fascinating. Consider just the outer appearance of the person in trance. Consider that some trances, when observed from the outside, look perfectly "natural" or normal; that there are others in which the person "looks" trancelike or even "zombielike"; and, that there is a range of other possible appearances. These outward differences are real, but they do not necessarily indicate the depth or type of trance involved. To get at this, we have to look at the aspects of trance that may not be clearly observable. I propose that we have to look at the purpose of the trance and the motivations of the practitioner and patient before we can begin to understand these differences.

When we examine the concept of purpose of trance, we realize that there are numerous possibilities. There are, for example, trances that have a hidden agenda, those that defend from other trances, trances for relaxation, trances for fun, trances for exploration, for physiological uses, for habit control, and so on. Is it reasonable to assume that trances that have such different motivational beginnings can be all the same?

I believe there are differences. I base this belief on clinical responses from patients who have experienced different types of trance; on subjective responses from patients and "subjects"; and on my own clinical, experimental, forensic, and demonstration experiences. Because of those many years of differing experiences, I have done some thinking about what I have actually seen and heard and what it might imply about *how* and *why* trances differ. The basic difference I see is *motivation*.

Differences in motivation, rather than differences in instructions, may account for differences in the aware states of consciousness observed in trance. In essence, the degree of attention the unconscious needs to focus on achieving and maintaining the trance will vary depending upon the use to be made of the trance.

This is easy to understand but difficult to measure for a number of reasons. For one thing, a motivating factor can have multiple origins. For another, there can be more than one motivating factor. It is also common for types of trance to be combined, which can make distinctions difficult. A further difficulty is that much of what occurs takes place in the unconscious and therefore is not highly accessible to either the practitioner or the client. The one constant is that the trance is determined by movement toward the result desired, or, in other words, by the motivation of the client.

Erickson understood and used these differences in his work. He was a master at determining how to skillfully monitor motivation so that the *unconscious* would maintain the many benefits manifest in the trance. He rarely decided to deliberately delineate the types of trances nor the nuances of nudges needed, and he could and would slip back and forth unnoticed using his multitudes of maneuvers. He would also combine and confuse the meaning in the messages with other communicative tools. His purpose, of course, was to produce therapeutic results rather than a taxonomy of trance. It was enough for him to understand and be able to use the variations himself, but it may be that we need a taxonomy to allow us to understand these variations before we can effectively use them.

Perhaps Erickson's mistrust of words, especially when they are arranged into systems and constructs that we accept (often uncritically) as truths, accounts for his willingness to use the differences in motivation without classifying or systematizing them. Words are, after all, merely symbols for experience, as Erickson's frequent use of the term *experiential life* reminds us.

Erickson stressed that words alone are poor and inadequate messengers. Tonal value and body/facial expression add to (which multiplies) or subtract from (which divides) the reliability of the message. It is interesting that Erickson, in his venture to use words accurately and meaningfully, used to write out his inductions. He did not, however, use these written inductions as formulas to be repeated verbatim, but as material to be learned and practiced until the pieces were so well known that they could be combined and used to improvise an appropriate script for a given situation. And, more than words were always used. The words finally selected were varied by expressions, intonation, and gestures. The written verbalizations were the starting point, not the end point. And, the use to which the script was put depended very much on the audience and the needed purpose of the trance. Perhaps Erickson constantly varied the performance to be as certain as possible that the messages he gave held the meanings the person before him at that moment needed to receive. The words were simply a starting point for the communication.

Still, there are those researchers who mandate an analysis of the hypnotic trance as induced only by the spoken word via tape recorder. They are missing an indispensable component of communication that is essential for understanding what is expected and for achieving the goal of the trance.

Reading, like trance, is a learned skill, mastered and used in different ways by each person who learns it:

Some persons learn slowly, then become proficient. Others take to it rapidly, and continue enthusiastically. Many learn just enough to satisfy their own selfish purposes, which often involve passing the necessary tests. Some persons read extensively for a while, then lose interest and proficiency. Of course, some people learn, but never really use the knowledge. (Pearson, Thompson, & Edmonston, 1970, p. 3)

People who learn trance may do it similarly: They may learn rapidly and well, or they may learn slowly but thoroughly. They might learn superficially. They can learn from good, bad, and neutral teachers. They may learn but choose not to use the knowledge. They may learn but be afraid to use the knowledge. Some graduate with a degree and go on to professional practice. Many, unfortunately, never progress beyond the kindergarten stage—they never understand the portentous potential of what they have learned.

Most neophytes are preoccupied with learning about how hypnosis affects them and what they can do with it. Their responses are influenced by their degree of learning, just as a beginning reader may not be able to make sense of fourth-grade books. At the other end of the spectrum, advanced learners develop their own internal cue systems so that when trance is appropriate, the mechanisms are activated through the autonomic nervous system. They have learned trance thoroughly enough that they can use it as a means to whatever end is appropriate at the moment.

The view that there is only one trance state may be correct in the sense that a given individual might enter trance consistently in the same way, and the observable behaviors that indicate that trance is present might be equivalent. Nevertheless, an individual might obtain different results from trance, and there must be some way to account for that. I think that the behavior in trance and the results of trance have not been thoroughly or systematically studied because of a preoccupation with studying trance induction. We are focusing on the vehicle, while the important aspect is the journey and, even more important, the destination. We may take many routes to the same destination, or conversely, we may take the same vehicle to many destinations. The destination and what we do when we get there is of ultimate importance.

When we first adopt a particular mode of travel—car, plane, etc.— we can be understandably obsessed with the details of it, but later the mode becomes so familiar that we see it for what it really is—a means to an end. We miss something very important if we continue to focus on the vehicle long after it has become routine and second nature.

As I go on, I want to emphasize that the types of trance I propose are a function of the sophisticated trance only. Sophisticated individuals are in a position to evaluate what is needed *by* them and *from* them both *for* this trance and *from* this trance. Sometimes an intense involvement is indicated, but at other times superficial participation will suffice. Patients ponder price, and once they buy the cost, they then weigh whether the work is worth the fee and the reward.

It seems reasonable for sophisticated individuals to establish their own internal cue systems, accessed through their autonomic nervous system. It also seems natural that once trance is learned, it becomes owned, to use (or not to use) according to choice. It becomes the goal of the practitioner to speak a language that will permit intrusion upon the hypnotic state with appropriate guidance and suggestions. The person entering trance determines both the mode of transportation and the destination. Examining trances from the point of view of the client's motivation leads to a proposal of six distinct types of trance:

1. *Clinical,* in which the chief motivation is self-control or self-help;
2. *Experimental,* in which the motivation is money, mankind, and self-learning;
3. *Demonstration,* in which the motivation is learning and/or teaching;
4. *Entertainment,* in which the motivation is the desire to entertain;
5. *Forensic,* in which the motivation is recall of past events; and
6. *Spontaneous,* in which the motivation is self-control and self-help.

The distinguishing characteristic in all cases is the motivation of the person entering trance, and the variations in motivation determine the variations in the quality and type of trance.

Each of these types of trance can contain within its subgroup light, medium, and deep trances. Each of them can include all or none of the phenomena of trance, depending on need. Each of them can be obvious or covert, based again on the sophistication and motivation of the person entering trance. All six types, and *all* types of trance, are defined by the significant behavioral, physiological, and emotional changes, which are, in turn, influenced by the motivational structures involved.

Let us first consider the *clinical trance.* In the clinical trance, the individual is motivated by a desire to increase his personal learning so that he can increase self-help or self-control. The learning and self-control may involve physiological, physical, or exploratory/emotional needs.

In clinical trance, the individual's only concern is himself; no outside element enters into consideration. For instance, the person about to utilize hypnoanesthesia and control of bleeding for surgery is only focused on that objective. Similarly, a woman who decides to use trance for labor and delivery in obstetrics focuses only on that. If a dental patient's bruxing (grinding his teeth) damages the temporomandibular joint, and he enters trance with the goal of controlling the bruxing, nothing else matters. If a psychotherapy patient wants to recover some traumatic memories that interfere with life adjustments, that is the purpose of that trance. There may be multiple factors responsible for the development of the problem, but the need is specific.

In each of these situations, the motivation is self-control and self-help. The importance of using trance for purely personal learning is paramount; nothing else matters! If the practitioner views this situation purely from the outside and as a product of how the trance was induced, he will miss most of what is actually happening.

An *experimental trance* may be induced in the same way as a *clinical* trance and may, in fact, look the same from the outside, but it is in reality different because the motivation is quite different. In the case of *experimental trance*, the motivation factors include money and mankind.

The individual goes into the experimental situation with full knowledge of the following facts: He has volunteered to participate in an experiment. He is informed about the experiment. He has been assured that the experiment cannot do him any harm, and further, that, if at any time he wants out, he can leave the experiment. He has also been assured that the experiment will be of benefit to mankind, that the results will help society in some way. In addition, he knows that he will receive some type of remuneration for his participation—if not financial, then some other reward.

So, this person goes into the experiment, which will be of a specific duration, knowing that he has nothing to lose. He can do anything asked of him, he cannot be harmed, he may learn something that will be of value, and he will be rewarded. He may walk out anytime he doesn't like it. His *motivation*, then, is *money, mankind,* and maybe some *personal learning.*

Contrast that with the individual lying on the operating table with a surgeon about to cut open his abdomen. Such a person cannot easily hold up his hand and say, "Stop, I've changed my mind." The differences in motivation probably lead to differences in the depth and nature of the trance.

The third distinct type is the *demonstration trance*. In this type of trance, the individual has a narrow range of requirements. The person volunteers to participate in a demonstration, knowing that the situation will be a fairly neutral one. Trance phenomena, and sometimes just "trance," will be demonstrated, either to him alone, as a learning procedure, or to a group, in a teaching situation. He may, in fact, be learning trance so that he can use it in a future clinical situation, but the learning is separate from the use of it; the trance is only a demonstration.

Demonstration trances are used routinely in classes teaching hypnosis, as the best way for practitioners to learn how to work with trance. Usually the volunteers are from within the group learning it, and the person who volunteers can both teach others by the demonstration and learn from the trance experience itself. In the *demonstration* trance, then, the *motivation* is either *teaching* or *learning*, or both.

The clinical, experimental, and demonstration trances are all recognizable as types that occur in therapeutic and teaching situations. The fourth type—the *entertainment trance*—is quite different. Understanding the motivation and use of this type of trance may help us to understand where our difficulties in utilizing clinical hypnosis first arose.

Years ago, stage and lay hypnotists were popular and were commonly used for stage performances, after-prom parties, etc. Even today we have popular, nationally known hypnotists such as Damon and Kreskin, and many lay hypnotists entertain for groups and private parties. Because these early entertainer/hypnotists were the only source of knowledge about trance, they became involved in teaching hypnosis to medical practitioners who sought this knowledge for its possible therapeutic value. As the doctors then began teaching hypnosis to other health practitioners, they taught it in the way they had learned it from the hypnotists. It thus retained its aura of magic and control. Trances were created so that subjects demonstrated "zombielike" behavior. It was not until the emergence of serious professionals like Erickson that we began to shed the "mystique" of hypnosis.

What about the people who make fools of themselves by following the commands of the lay hypnotist? Does this not demonstrate that the hypnotist (and *his* motivation) are in control? This situation does indeed demonstrate the skill of the hypnotist, but it is his skill in choosing subjects, not his skill in manipulating motivation, that we witness. He cleverly conceals the antecedent variables in the stage show, but they are there, and they influence events.

Consider this situation. The hypnotist gazes out on a crowd. When he asks for volunteers, he gets two types: He gets the extrovert, the ham, who really wants the opportunity to show off. And he gets the introvert, who is elbowed up by friends and is too intimidated to refuse. After a few suggestibility tests, the unsusceptible individuals are escorted off the stage by the assistant, and the audience promptly forgets about them. From the 16–20 people who volunteer, the hypnotist selects the best four or five and "uses" them.

But, they do stupid things! Doesn't this show that the hypnotist is in control? Yes, they go into a trance at the hypnotist's urging as part of the contract they made when they came on stage, and they crow like a rooster, or they run through the audience selling newspapers. They may even eat an onion and make it taste like an apple, knowing all the while that they are playing an enormous trick on the audience, since they do know what they are doing. It is a great opportunity for the subjects—the extrovert and introvert alike—to have the chance to show off. They can have a marvelous time!

But then the hypnotist says, "In a minute I am going to wake you up," and in their newly acquired sense of time distortion, the subjects immediately think, "I made a fool of myself, how am I going to go back and tell my friends I knew all these stupid things I did!" But then, the wily hypnotist finishes the sentence with, "And when I do, you will not remember a thing." The subject, of course, acquires a valid, instant amnesia, which solves his problem of going back to his seat with vivid memories of what he has just done. He can respond to the jibes of the audience with, "I didn't do a thing, he made me do it all," pointing to the hypnotist, who is quite willing to take the glory (or the blame) and look like the "magician" who controls people's minds.

But the contract and *motivation for the entertainment trance* is fulfilled— *to entertain.*

The next type of trance to consider is the *forensic trance*, a type which has aroused considerable controversy in both the courts and therapeutic circles. There are those who claim that hypnotically enhanced memory is valid, and others who claim that it is unreliable. An examination of the subject's motivation for entering this type of trance may help our understanding of the situation.

The *motivation* for the only valid forensic use of hypnosis is to *enhance recall*. Individuals in trance can still think, can still lie (often better with the aid of trance, since they are better able to control their responses), can still misremember, and can still enhance their memory with unconscious remembering. Enhanced recall can only be used as a guide or clue. Corroborating evidence must be the conclusive material used to make decisions or judgments.

Although courts are not ready to concede that hypnotic memories are as valid as memories recalled through "normal" means, we should begin to think about the nature and application of memory in forensic situations. We recognize that regular memory, especially of traumatic or long-past events, can be faulty. Yet those memories are routinely permitted in evidence with the understanding that they may not be complete or fully accurate but nevertheless present one type of evidence about the events in question. If we treat hypnotic memories the same way, hypnotically enhanced recall should be as valid as any other type of recall.

A further interesting point to consider is the distinct probability that individuals, particularly when they are under oath, can go into a self-induced trance caused by the stress of the situation. This type of trance is generally not recognized because it is not externally induced, and there may be no externally observable phenomena that can be identified as evidence of trance. This illustrates the urgency of understanding trance more thoroughly. Until we can measure trance, we cannot accurately predict who is in a hypnotic trance at any designated time.

The possibility of self-hypnosis under stress illustrates the next type of trance, a catchall category that we do not know how to investigate or even acknowledge: the *spontaneous trance*. This is the trance that individuals go into when the need to achieve or the need to survive automatically accesses unconscious resources not usually available to that person. The *motivation* for the spontaneous trance is the same as the motivation of the clinical type of trance, *self-control* and *self-help*, and so we come full circle. What then is the difference between the clinical and the spontaneous trance? The difference is that the spontaneous trance requires no outside person to introduce it. It is a trance that is entered as a result of an immediate, urgent need. Because none of the person's usual responses will meet the recognized need, the reserve potential of the unconscious is activated, and trance results. The "miracle feats of physiological control" which exist in the literature— the mother who lifts the 250 pound refrigerator off of her three-year-old boy, or the farmer whose arm is severed in a tractor accident who walks miles to the doctor's office without bleeding—may be instances of this phenomenon. Looking back on these events suggests that trance made the feats possible.

The possibility of spontaneous trance may have far-reaching implications. As we begin to explore and learn more about the immune system, and about the chemical components of thought, we should also examine the abilities that hypnotically skilled individuals possess in an attempt to determine the relationship between accessing altered states of consciousness and controlling bodily processes, organs, glands, and the immune system. Consider, for example, whether spontaneous remission is any less possible than superhuman feats of strength if we consider that trance and the access to the immune system may enhance physical capacity and capability.

All six types of trance I have described are patient- or individual-motivated. There is one further type of trance, however, that must be mentioned, the *involuntary trance*, which is *operator-motivated*. I know very little about this type of trance but have talked with some practitioners who have encountered it, and I do know that it exists. I first heard rumors of it back in the 1950s from an attorney member of the American Society of Clinical Hypnosis. Only now are some of the things that have been done with drugs and mind-controlling techniques involving hypnosis starting to become known.

At one time, I believed that nobody would do anything in trance that was against his will or beliefs. Since then I have encountered situations that lead me to believe there are trances that are induced utilizing other psychological techniques and/or drugs, and that these techniques result in undesirable consequences. Hypnosis is not the primary controlling factor, but is a technique used to create and to absolutely control the behavior. The drug-induced trance is involuntary and therefore dangerous. I do not know enough about it to discuss it in any detail, but it is a subject that we should all be aware of and one that certainly warrants further investigation. It exists; I know about it. I don't know enough about it, but there is a myth to be dispelled.

As health professionals, of course, we are primarily concerned with understanding the healing trance, and more research is also needed in this area. More research might be stimulated if motivation were considered as the basis for defining trance, categorizing it, and identifying the kinds of trance that individuals will go into based on their personal motivation. There could be parameters connected with each of the types of trance that people will understand.

I am proposing a research methodology for the study of the *utilization* of trance, rather than, as so often happens, the *induction* of trance. That method would involve using sophisticated individuals who already know how to go into trance, or even unsophisticated individuals who can learn how to go into trance. Criteria would have to be established for testing for the presence of *a* trance state that all individuals must attain, *any way and with any method of induction that will work for those individuals.* Once the individuals meet the criteria and after the trance-entering behavior is documented, standardized approaches can be used to test for the defined experimental criteria. The preliminary requirement would be that the person entering trance must be permitted to reach trance any way that is best for him. Then the experimental standardization can be established after the trance is achieved!

As we go on in our search both to enhance our understanding of the relationship of word to knowledge and behavior, and our understanding of the altered states of *awareness* of trance, we consciously and unconsciously pay tribute to Milton Erickson, who was forever curious about the ways of the How and Why and What. Today Erickson's influence on therapy is being acknowledged in a broader sense because of the sense, not the non-sense, of his techniques.

As we are motivated to look to the future with the knowledge gained from the past, we expect that more answers will lead to more questions, and the language of trance and motivation will continue to speak for itself.

REFERENCES

Amantea, C. (1986). The Lourdes of Arizona, Part III. *The Fessenden Review, 11* (3):42.
Pearson, R. E., Thompson, K. F., & Edmonston, W. E. (1970). Clinical and experimental trance: What's the difference? *American Journal of Clinical Hypnosis, 13:*3.

Chapter 10

The Role of Language in Therapy

David Gordon

David Gordon, M.A. (Lone Mountain College), is one of the original developers of Neuro-Linguistic Programming, and more recently is, along with Leslie Cameron-Bandler and Michael Lebeau, co-developer of a method for coding the patterns that underlie particular human aptitudes: The Emprint Method. *He has authored two books that are mainly based on Erickson's work,* Therapeutic Metaphors: Helping Others Through the Looking Glass *and* Phoenix: The Therapeutic Pattern of Milton H. Erickson *(with Maribeth Meyers-Anderson).*

Gordon teaches that it is crucial for the therapist to understand the patient's experimental model. Language can be used diagnostically as a "window to the subjective world," as long as one can maintain enough objectivity to avoid overlooking the obvious. Clear examples are provided in this informative, well-written chapter.

The Sufis tell a story about a man who was walking down a strange road one day when he came upon a large group of terrified villagers fleeing toward him. He stopped the panic-stricken mob to ask them what was the matter, and they cried that there was a monster in their fields. They pointed out to the fields, but all the man saw was a watermelon. He turned back to the villagers and, scoffing and sneering, told the ignorant people that there was nothing there but a watermelon. When the villagers insisted that it was indeed a monster, the suddenly wary traveler accused them of lying. The enraged villagers fell upon the man and killed him for being a fool.

A short while later, another, wiser man came down that same road, asked about the trouble, and, following the trembling fingers pointing

164

out to the field, also saw only the watermelon. The stranger drew his knife and, with a blood-curdling whoop, ran into the field, lept upon the watermelon, and hacked it to bits. The villagers were so transported with joy over seeing their enemy destroyed that they made the stranger the leader of their village, a position he retained until it came to pass that he was able to teach them the difference between a monster and a watermelon.

As the first traveler found out too late, reality is in the eye of the beholder. Though we may join with the first traveler in scoffing at the ignorance of the villagers, he is really no different than they are in terms of *how* he thinks—and neither are we. Their fear and flight were a function of their perceiving the thing in the field to be a monster. Had they seen the object as a watermelon, or merely an odd weed, their subjective experience and behavior would have been very different. Similarly, the first traveler considered the villagers' terror and panic to be either ludicrous or deceitful and, therefore, scoffed at them and accused them of lying. Had he instead considered them childlike, misguided, or interesting, his behavior toward them would have been different.

Like the villagers and the traveler, our experiences of the world, and behaviors in response to it, are largely functions of our cognitive and connotative processes. Our perceptions and the meaning that we make of those perceptions imbue our subjective worlds with form and texture. What is more, that form and texture can vary greatly from individual to individual.

Everyday you are presented with the perplexing and often vexing circumstance that seemingly intelligent, informed, and well-meaning people do not see the world as you see it: two politicians faced with the same situation and in possession of the same facts somehow disagree completely on the significance of those facts and about how to respond to them; your boss makes perfectly reasonable requests that you consider completely unreasonable; you are alarmed about your son's behavior at the table, while your spouse believes there is nothing to be concerned about. Generally, we account for these discrepancies by attributing to others maliciousness, ignorance, or incompetence. What is abundantly evident, however, is that you and all of those other people are responding sincerely, but through differing sets of perceptual and connotative filters.*[1]

Recognizing the idiosyncratic aspects of human experience is a crucial

---

* Notes are listed at the end of the chapter, starting on p. 180.

first step in understanding people; without taking this step, it will never be possible for those who would like to understand to get any further down the road than their own model of the world. This is, in fact, as far as most people go, peering out at the world through the sunglasses of their selves. If, however, we had a way to discover what was happening behind the shades of those around us, we would have the opportunity to truly understand others.

Two experiential windows available to us are analogue behavior and language. Analogue behavior, which includes complex behaviors, gestures, posture, and facial expressions, is a tremendously rich source of information about others, and in many popular and academic quarters is hailed as the only *accurate* expression of a person's true internal experience. This is not the case, as we shall see, because when language is attended to at the level of pattern and structure, it also accurately expresses the internal world of the individual, often with a richness of detail that analogue behavior cannot provide.

I. LANGUAGE AS EXPRESSION

Language is, perhaps, the most remarkable attribute of human beings. All human cultures have developed tremendously complex languages, each of which makes it possible for an individual to express his or her internal experiential world. What is within may be a need, an intention, or an abstraction, but whatever it is, language provides a medium for conveying internal experience to others. How close a connection there is between subjective experience and the language we use to express that experience is succinctly described by science philosopher Paul Feyerabend:

> From our very early days we learn to react to situations with the appropriate responses, linguistic or otherwise. The teaching procedures both *shape* the "appearance," or "phenomenon," and establish a firm *connection* with words, so that finally the phenomena seem to speak for themselves without outside help or extraneous knowledge. They *are* what the associated statements assert them to be. (1978, p. 72)

As the connections between phenomena and linguistic representations build, the experiential world shrinks, for each new connection distills or partitions the range of our perceptions and connotations. Because of the feedforward-feedback filtering effect of these distillations and partitions, the experiential world is self-perpetuating and remains relatively stable. In short, language both creates and *maintains* subjective coherency.

> We dissect nature along lines laid down by our native languages. The categories and types that we isolate from the world of phenomena we do not find there because they stare every observer in the face; on the contrary, the world is presented in a kaleidoscopic flux of impressions which has to be organized by our minds—and this means largely by the linguistic systems in our minds. We cut nature up, organize it into concepts, and ascribe significances as we do, largely because we are parties to an agreement to organize it in this way—an agreement that holds throughout our speech community and is codified in the patterns of our language. (Whorf, 1956, p. 213)

Language, then, is *essentially* expressive of an individual's subjective world. (I use "essence" in the sense of "a substance distilled or extracted from another substance and having the special qualities of the original substance.") If a person says to a friend, "I am feeling happy," all native speakers of English recognize immediately that this person is giving us information about her immediate subjective experience. The structure of the sentence explicitly informs us of this. What is not as evident to most of us is that if the speaker had instead made the statement, "He is feeling happy," she would also have been revealing information about her current subjective experience. The fact that she sees "him" as being happy—even if her judgment is corroborated by others—is no guarantee that that person is, in fact, feeling happy. In fact, the speaker's statement, "He is feeling happy," tells us more about her than it does about the person she is referring to. What she has revealed is that it is her current subjective experience that the person is happy. In other words, whatever perceptions it takes to satisfy her that the person is happy have somehow been satisfied. Again, language expresses the nature of internal experience: our perceptions, connotations, and emotions. It is, in a sense, a report of cognitive, connotative, and emotional activity.

Language is so much a part of our ongoing lives that we usually take for granted the subtleties of idiosyncratic expression that we use.

If we stop to listen, however, we soon discover that we do not all use the same words and phrases to express what are ostensibly the same experiences. The reason for this, as we discussed above, is that we are not having the same experiences. Consider, for example, two people talking about a trip to the movies:

Joe: It is great to be going to the movies!
Deb: Yes, it will be great to see that film!

These two people are not talking about the same experience. Joe is expressing that he is feeling great about going to the movies. Deb, on the other hand, is expressing that she is anticipating feeling great when she *sees* the movie. Joe's attention is on the experience he is having *now*, while Deb's is on the experience she *will* have when she gets there. The difference between their experiences is linguistically manifested in the verb tenses they are using. Joe is using the present tense, "is," Deb the future tense, "will be." The example is trivial in terms of its content but useful in that it illustrates the point that an individual's subjective experience is manifested in his or her language and is available to those attuned to hear it.

Let us briefly consider three examples of language distinctions that are readily identifiable verbal manifestations of perceptual and connotative processes.

Time Frame

Our Western culture allows us an experience of time that is made up of a discrete past, present, and future. Accordingly, the English language allows for time distinctions to be made between the past, present, and future through the use of verb tenses. We *have felt* happy, *feel* happy, and *will feel* happy.[2] Partitioning our experience of time in this way has certain consequences. Having a discrete past makes it possible for things to be over, and a discrete future creates an arena for planning and speculation. When someone says, "I was curious," he is saying that the experience of curiosity has occurred and is no longer necessarily a part of his ongoing experience. If instead that person says, "I am curious," we know that curiosity is part of his current experience. And, if he says, "I will be curious," we are informed that he is anticipating being curious at some time in the future (and is not necessarily curious now). All of this is so obvious to us as native speakers of English that it seems almost trivial. It is that very familiarity, however, that has bred neglect.

Verb tense can provide significant information regarding the internal processes of an individual. For example, a woman explains, "The reason I don't stick to a diet is that I just don't know if I will be able to successfully lose weight." This woman "does not know" (present tense) if she "will be able" (future tense) to lose weight. What she is revealing to us through her verb tenses is that her judgment about her *current* ability to diet is being based upon a search of her *future* for some sign of success. We now know something significant about the structure of this woman's experience within the context of motivating herself to go on a diet—namely, motivation for her is a function of generating (and probably maintaining) an imagined future in which she has succeeded. Her entire statement takes a cause-effect form in which, for her, "knowing I will be able to succeed" causes her to "stick to a diet." The "cause" is a convincing ("know") representation of the future ("will be able") in which she succeeds ("successfully lose weight").

Accordingly, we know that *it is useless to try to convince this woman that she has what it takes to diet by dredging up examples from her past.* She may well be able to find those examples, but they will not be meaningful or compelling to her, and any approach or technique relying on reassurance from the past, *no matter how successful it has been with other clients,* will be wasted on her. An approach that is far more likely to succeed with this woman is to assist her in building a sufficiently compelling image of a future in which she has successfully lost weight.

A more likely candidate for reassurances from the past might have expressed herself by saying something like, "I have never really stuck to a diet, so I don't know if I can." The therapeutic task would be to assist her to perceive past dieting "failures" as, in fact, examples of having stuck with it, or, more likely, by assisting her in finding examples of having stuck to outcomes in other contexts and then applying those examples to the context of dieting.[3]

Modal Operators

There is a class of verbalizations, called modal operators, that expresses the contingent relationships we believe to exist between ourselves, others, and outcomes. For example, to say, "I can't run away," is to say that there are some (as yet unstated) contingencies that make it *impossible* for the speaker to "run away."[4] What is being expressed here is a modal operator of *impossibility*, examples of which include "can't," "not possible," "impossible," and "unable." When an individual uses a modal operator of impossibility, he is expressing that he perceives contingencies that simply preclude something from happening (or, perhaps, from having happened). This perception is more than a mere statement of conditions, for along with it come certain subjective relationships that can greatly influence an individual's experiential and behavioral responses. Modal operators of impossibility, for instance, presuppose a cessation of action or engagement. As soon as you get to the point where you "can't" do or get something you want, striving ends.

The other modal operators are those of possibility, necessity, certainty, and desire. What follows is only a partial listing of the most common operators for each of the modalities:

Impossibility	Possibility	Necessity	Certainty	Desire
impossible	possible	necessary	will	wish
unable to	can	should	won't	would
can't	could	must	am	want
couldn't	might	have to	is	choose
	able to	need		
		ought to		

Like modal operators of impossibility, each of these other classes of modal operators presupposes a certain kind of contingent relationship between oneself, others, and outcomes. The nature of that relationship is given in the name for each of the classes; that is, that the outcome is impossible, possible, necessary, certain, or desired.

Each of the modal operators conveys certain qualities of subjective experience that makes them unique and indispensable in understanding the current psychodynamics out of which an individual is operating. These subtle, yet utterly compelling differences are immediately evident when you apply different modalities to the same content. For example:

- I can't have friends.
- I can have friends.
- I could have friends.
- I should have friends.
- I need to have friends.
- I will have friends.
- I want friends.

If you take a few moments to say each of the above sentences as though each were true for you (attending to your subjective experience as you do so), you will discover that each of the modal operators dramatically alters your perception of your relationship to the outcome of having friends. The experience of "I *want* friends" is quite different from the experience of "I *will* have friends." The first presupposes a contingency of desire, the second a contingency of certainty, and there is a significant difference between them in terms of the level of active involvement each presupposes. For most people "I *want* friends" is inherently a more passive experience than "I *will* have friends."[5]

Such differences in subjective experience associated with the various modal operators is not only true for modalities from different classes, but also for modalities within a class as well. For instance, although "need" and "should" are both modal operators of necessity, part of the subjective experience of "I *need* to have friends" is that the outcome of having friends is internally generated, while the subjective experience of "I *should* have friends" is that the outcome is externally generated (that is, has been somehow imposed from the outside).[6]

The perceived subjective experiences revealed by modal operators not only provide the clinician with yet another window into the speaker's subjective world, but may also hold clues regarding what that person needs in terms of a change. For instance, the client who concludes, "Yes, I'm sure with the work you have done with me, I could be considerate of other people's feelings," is not saying that he will be considerate, only that now it seems possible ("I *could* be considerate"). The therapist attuned to modal operators will recognize this, check whether the client intends to be considerate and, if not, move on to the next piece of therapeutic work, which is to help the client shift to an experience of commitment in relation to being considerate of others. This commitment will be manifested linguistically by modal operators of necessity or desire and of certainty: ideally, "I must/need to be considerate" (as already noted, *should* and *ought to* generally presuppose externally generated necessity and, therefore, often also elicit polarity responses), and/or, "I want to be considerate"; and, "I will be considerate."[7]

Criteria

We have considered the linguistic distinction of verb tense, which expresses our cognitive processes with regard to our perception of time frames, and touched on a connotative process regarding judgments about contingencies, which are expressed linguistically as modal operators. Connotative distinctions are also revealed by the *criteria* we use.

Criteria are standards applied within a particular context. (In using the word "apply," I do not mean to imply that criteria are imposed intentionally or consciously. In fact, it is most often the case that criteria are unconsciously invoked.) For instance, as you read this chapter, you are probably applying the criterion of "understanding," thereby evaluating whether or not you understand what you have read. Undoubtedly you are simultaneously employing other criteria as well, such as "usefulness," "clarity," "novelty," and so on. The particular criteria you are using right now (and, indeed, in any context) are not necessarily dictated by the context, but are more likely characteristic of you as an individual within that context. While most people will probably invoke the criterion of "understanding" when reading a psychology paper, there will also be those who are instead evaluating whether or not they find it "stimulating" or "properly organized."

The significance of the criteria you use is that your criteria determine what, out of the vast range of possible experiences, you are attending to at the time. Criteria both filter your perceptions and invest a particular situation with meaning and thereby inform your experience and behavior at the time. In *Steppenwolf*, Hermann Hesse (1963) described the significance of criteria perfectly:

> Man designs for himself a garden with a hundred kinds of trees, a thousand kinds of flowers, a hundred kinds of fruits and vegetables. Suppose, then, that the gardener of this garden knew no other distinction than between edible and inedible, nine-tenths of this garden would be useless to him. He would pull up the most enchanting flowers and hew down the noblest trees and even regard them with a loathing and envious eye. (p. 75)

When you know an individual's criteria within a particular situation, then you know what that person is attending to. Consider the following statements made by two men:

Frank: When you do a job, it's got to be done right.
Joe: Work isn't worth doing unless it's fun.

In the context of working, one standard that Frank will be holding and applying will be whether or not what is being done has "rightness." Accordingly, when Frank goes to see how his son is doing with mowing the lawn, he will inspect it to see whether the boy is doing it properly and is likely to correct his work and/or praise him for the fine job.

Joe, on the other hand, will be attending to whether or not he (or someone else) is having fun. When Joe steps out to see how his son is doing with mowing the lawn, he will want to know if his son is enjoying himself. Whether he simply takes a close look at the boy or asks directly, Joe's attention and behavior will be in service of satisfying his criterion of "fun." Joe will probably feel satisfied if he detects that his son is having fun, and if his son is not, Joe will probably feel dissatisfied and engage in responses intended to change the situation (e.g., suggesting ways to make the work more enjoyable; trying to convince his son that it is fun—or at least not so bad; telling him he can quit).

Criteria are manifested linguistically by those words representing standards applied to self, others, things, and events. Unlike time frame, which is overtly given by verb tense, criteria constitute a covert linguistic category, distinguished by context, inflection, and syntax. Though we do not have explicit, grammatically based rules for detecting criteria, nevertheless we are responsive to them. When the boss says, "From now on I want this done on time," we recognize that she is, and will be, applying a standard of "punctualness" to our work. Consider the criteria applied to these statements:

	Criteria
He was pretty smart about it.	*smart*
I like the naturalness of her movements.	*natural*
The trouble with me is I'm not friendly enough.	*friendly*
I want this done quickly.	*quickly*
How can I both learn and enjoy myself?	*learn*
	enjoyment

With enough content examples, criteria can become as explicitly and consciously recognizable as time frame or any other naturally expressive part of our language.

In the context of therapy, knowledge of a client's criteria is often essential. Your client's criteria specify what he or she is striving for and wants satisfied or fulfilled. Any change work that does not somehow address the client's criteria will not be recognized and responded to as meaningful by that person and, so, will not effect lasting change.

For instance, in a previous example a client stated, "The reason I don't stick to a diet is that I just don't know if I will be able to *successfully* lose weight." At least one criterion this person is using in trying to motivate herself to lose weight is that of being "successful." The time frames of this person's experience makes it most appropriate to help her motivate herself by helping her to construct a compelling future in which she loses weight. It can not be just any kind of future, however, but must be one in which she is "successful." There is little likelihood that helping this woman build a future in which she is *proud* of the weight she has lost, or is *flattered* about her figure, or is *relieved* that she made it will compellingly motivate her. These criteria certainly may be included as part of the imagined future for this woman, but the criterion that she wants fulfilled and the criterion that *must be addressed* in the work that is done with her is that of "success."[8]

In addition to the three we have just introduced, there are many other linguistic distinctions that provide information about the idiosyncratic, subjective world of an individual, including predicates, criterial equivalences, degree of influence, cause-effect, comparatives, lost performatives, and nominalizations. They are the patterns of expression through which we linguistically manifest our internal processes and representations and, so, are highly indicative of those internal processes and representations.[9]

II. LANGUAGE AS PRESUPPOSITION

It has become evident, through the work of linguists, anthropologists, and psychologists, that language and thought cannot be separated. As we discussed in the previous section, language is not an arbitrary set of symbols. It is, instead, a manifestation of perceptual and connotative processes. But it is more than that. Words and syntax not only reveal—they influence, as well.

> All our fundamental deeper knowledge must be, and can never be anything but, hypothetical, as what we see, hear, feel, speak about, or infer, is never *it*, but only our human abstractions *about* "it." What kind of linguistic form our inferential knowledge is cast in thus becomes of utmost importance. As Edward Sapir has put it, "We see and hear and otherwise experience very largely as we do because the language habits of our community predispose certain choices of interpretation." (Korzybski, 1951, p. 46)

Similarly, Whorf (1956) defines the lopsided balance between a language and its native speakers when he states, "Language thus represents the mass mind; it is affected by inventions and innovations, but affected little and slowly, whereas to inventors and innovators it legislates with the decree immediate" (p. 156). On a social scale, then, our shared reality is continually reified and maintained by the "linguistic system" we share. People operating out of linguistic systems different from our own perceive reality differently.[10] There are many examples of linguistically codified models of the world differing between cultures. For instance,

> Somehow we have managed to objectify or externalize our imagery of the passage of time, which makes it possible for us to feel that we can manage time, control it, spend it, save it or waste it. We have a feeling that the process of "becoming later" is real and tangible because we can attach a numerical value to it. The Hopi language does *not* do this. No past, present, or future exists as verb tenses in their language. Hopi verbs have no tenses, but indicate instead the validity of a statement—the nature of the relationship between the speaker and his knowledge or experience of that about which he is speaking. (Hall, 1983, p. 34)

The experience of reality and its linguistic counterparts are not likely to change at this level of culturally determined perceptual and connotative distinctions.[11] Running through the warp of our shared psycholinguistic reality, however, is the idiosyncratic woof of our personal realities, a pattern largely woven by our unique personal histories. Thus, the specific perceptions and connotations invoked in a particular context are not predetermined by our culture.

For instance, for us, as members of the American-European culture, our perception of time as linear and "always getting later" is a primary level pattern that is pervasive, axiomatic, and linguistically codified in the verb tenses that we use. But what particular time frame any one of us uses in a given situation is not so fixed but is determined (even if inadvertently) by the individual. These secondary, "woof" level patterns are those that stamp us as unique individuals and change when "we" change. It is lasting change at this level that is the aim (or at least the outcome) of therapy. What many therapists and researchers fail to realize is that they *do* change their clients at this level *whenever they speak to them.*

While paying attention to your own internal processes, ask and answer for yourself the following question:

1. When could I have been more effective?

It is very likely that upon asking yourself this question, you began searching through your past for examples of those times when you have considered yourself to have been effective and times when you considered yourself to have been ineffective. Taking your time, now ask and answer for yourself each of the following questions:

2. When will I be effective again?
3. When could I have been more purposeful?
4. When will I be purposeful again?
5. When should I be purposeful?

As with the first question, it is very likely that each of these questions altered your internal processes. Question 2 sent you searching into the future for examples of being effective. Question 3 took you into the past in search of personal examples of purposefulness, and question 4 took you back to the future. With question 5 you probably jumped about between the past, present, and future, trying to find those situations for which purposefulness is strongly recommended. In every case, the question was *presupposing for you* the time frame, modality, and criterion that you would use.

1. When could I have been effective?	*could:* MO* of possibility *have been:* past *effective:* criterion
2. When will I be effective again?	*will:* MO of certainty *will:* future *effective:* criterion
3. When could I have been purposeful?	*could:* MO of possibility *have been:* past *purposeful:* criterion
4. When will I be purposeful again?	*will:* MO of certainty *will:* future *purposeful:* criterion

---

* Modal Operator.

5. When should I be purposeful?   *should:* MO of necessity
                                              be: present
                                              purposeful: criterion

In other words, you responded with the same kind of perceptual and connotative processes that are naturally connected to the words, syntax, and semantics of each of the five questions. This automatic, analogical deciphering of language is so much with us, so rapid, and so much taken for granted that we are rarely aware that it is going on. But going on it is. It is how we (literally) "make sense" out of verbal communication. The process comes into consciousness only when it comes to a grinding halt, usually when we are suddenly presented with linguistic input that violates our experience with linguistic-representational connections. A sentence such as, "It is important to me to be a responsible person, so I will finish these reports last week," immediately makes us aware that we go along with the string of experiences being presented to us, revivifying their analogues in our own subjective experiences, until and unless there occurs an anomaly that disrupts the flow. Even then, our first response is to try to reconcile the anomaly. We try to make our own representations *fit the communication.* It is only after this fails that we may decide that we need more information, that we are, for some reason, not competent to decipher/represent the communication, or that the speaker is not competent.

Language, then, is essentially presuppositional in that *it presupposes for the listener how to think at that moment in time* (provided, of course, that the listener is a native speaker of the same language as the speaker). The significance of this must not be underestimated. At least for the moment that you are speaking, to a very great extent you are orienting the internal processes and attentions of your client. To that extent, you are determining your client's model of the world for that moment. If the object of therapy is to provide the client with compelling opportunities to experience and adopt more satisfyingly functional models of the world, then the direct link between language and the structure of perceptual and connotative processes must be respected and, when possible, exploited. We must recognize that when we, in all kindness and caring, ask a client, "How has your hostility made you unsuccessful?" we are imposing, for the moment, a constellation of internal processes that includes a personal history-based etiology with past-to-present cause-effects ("how have made"), nominalized experience ("hostility"), a modality of certainty ("has"), passive/"default" involvement ("made you"), and a criterion of "unsuccessful." When working with a client, the question that we need to ask ourselves is, "What might be more useful for *this* person to be perceiving and processing in this context?" Once we have answered this question, we have at our disposal the presuppositions of language—what we say to, and ask of, this person—in order to guide the client's thinking along different, more useful lines.[12]

The evidence is overwhelming that when you speak, you influence those around you at the levels of perception and judgment. Will it be haphazard, like the first traveler who came upon the crazed villagers, or will it be like the second traveler, who had an understanding of the samenesses that can be relied upon and used and of the differences that must be respected?

> During the intermission a question was put to me: "Are you aware of the way in which you use your words?" I certainly am, and I want to emphasize the importance of that awareness to all of you.
>
> In hypnosis you are going to use words to influence the psychological life of your patient today; you are going to use words to influence his organic life today; you are going to also influence his psychological and organic life twenty years from now. So you had better know what you are saying. You had better be willing to reflect upon the words you use, to wonder what their meanings are, and to seek out and understand their many associations. (M. H. Erickson in Erickson, Rossi, & Ryan, 1985, p. 32)

III. FROM PAST TO PRESENT TO FUTURE

The use of statistics came into its own in the 18th century when it was realized that numbers could render the mystifying births, deaths, and movements of the growing urban masses predictable to governments and insurance companies. Statistics were soon applied to human disease and behavior by physicians, and this was part of the inheritance endowed to modern psychotherapy when it adopted a medical model approach to treatment.

Essentially statistical thinking has filtered its way into our perceptions and created one of the greatest and most limiting of presuppositions—people can be categorized. The result of such thinking includes diagnostic categories, wholesale techniques, and endless theories of human personality and behavior based on generalizations. As good and structurally beautiful as many of these classifications, techniques, and theories are, all of them are inherently vulnerable precisely because they are based on statistical thinking. Sooner or later, all of them fall apart when they have to be applied to actual individuals.

The treatment of an individual can be a pretty messy affair. His symptomatic behaviors often fail to fall neatly into a category, techniques that have cured dozens before him seem to have no effect, and the dynamics of his psychology may not be explainable by the theory or theories in use. The reasons for these failures are variously given as client resistance, incorrect technique, therapist's lack of skill in using the technique, unreadiness of the client for change, inauspicious biorhythms, and so on. These explanations are demeaning to both the therapist and the client and serve only to implicitly maintain the fantasy that there are correct categories, techniques, and theories.

This is not to say that we do not as a species and as cultures and societies share many attributes. Of course we do. But, again, this sharing is at a fundamental level of distinctions (such as the "getting later" time of American-Europeans or the "durational" time of the Hopi). Beyond this level, shared realities can be said to be only statistical. Every member of a culture will have a constellation of attributes that is in some way different from every other member of that culture. You have only to trade a few minutes worth of ideas and opinions with a friend or neighbor to discover that, though you live on the same block, in the same country, and in the same era, your experiences of the world are in many ways different from one another.

The tragedy of statistically based thinking in the context of therapy is that it often leads to disregarding the client as an individual in favor of the reification of the theory and techniques held by the therapist. Too often, if the therapeutic suit does not fit, the client is stretched or trimmed, rather than the clinician taking the shears to the suit itself or, indeed, discarding it altogether. The result is a disservice to the client, who will eventually, inevitably burst or shed his ill-fitting therapeutic garment. It is also unsatisfying for the therapist, who wants more than the quick sale, preferring the satisfaction of having truly met and helped an individual to evolve toward a better life. Approaches to therapy that are ontologically based on a statistical view can hope to achieve only statistically significant levels of "cures," since ultimately the effectiveness of any such approach will be a function of whether or not the personal psychology of the client who has just walked in the door is congruent with the psychological constructs out of which the therapist is operating.

There is an alternative, however—to abandon the Procrustean beds of psychological theory and technique, replacing them with an approach based upon discovering, to the extent to which it is possible, the psychological model of the *individual*. Since each individual has his or her own model, it makes sense to proceed empirically, rather than theoretically, when working with a client, by endeavoring to discover that person's unique model of the world. Once the model is known, we can formulate a treatment approach that is *appropriate* for that person. Instead of generating interactions and interventions out of theories and models that are, at best, possible generalizations about people, we could be generating our approaches based on *a model of the individual we are working with* at the time. But does this make practical sense?

The answer is yes, as long as we have available to us sets of distinctions about individual subjective experience that allow us to generate useful models as well as ways of identifying those distinctions for each person. Language constitutes one such set. Its co-evolving, analogical, and metaphorical relationship with the private perceptual, connotative, and emotional worlds of human beings makes language a code of tremendous fidelity. To the clinician who learns the lexical, syntactic, and semantic ciphers for this code, language becomes a doorway to another world—the world of the person sitting right there.

NOTES

1. The effects of perceptual and connotative filters are not confined to the everyday experiences of the average person, but operate in everyone in all contexts:

   > An investigator who hoped to learn something about what scientists took the atomic theory to be asked a distinguished physicist and an eminent chemist whether a single atom of helium was or was not a molecule. Both answered without hesitation, but their answers were not the same. For the chemist, the atom of helium was a molecule because it behaved like one with respect to the kinetic theory of gases. For the physicist, on the other hand, the helium atom was not a molecule because it displayed no molecular spectrum. Presumably both men were talking of the same particle, but they were viewing it through their own research training and practice. (Kuhn, 1970, p. 50)

2. For a thorough discussion of time frames in our culture, and in other cultures as well, see Hall (1983) and Korzybski (1951).
3. The detection and elicitation of time frames, as well as the roles and uses of time frames in generating experiences and behavior, are described extensively in Cameron-Bandler, Gordon, & Lebeau (1985a, 1985b) and in Cameron-Bandler & Lebeau (1986).
4. "Outcome" does not imply *desired* outcome. The speaker might have the desired outcome of *running away* but is simply describing the "fact" that he cannot. Nevertheless, the speaker's use of "can't" expresses that he perceives contingencies that make running away impossible.
5. In our work with many hundreds of individuals, we have found some variation regarding the subjective significance of a particular modal operator (Cameron-Bandler, Gordon, Lebeau, 1985a, 1985b). (For instance, two friends of ours found themselves arguing about priorities until they realized that, for one of them, things that "need to" be done are to be done now, and things that "have to" be done go on a mental list to be done eventually, while for the other person, "need tos" went on the list and "have tos" were to be done immediately.) The exceptions are very few, however. The experiential impact of any one modal operator is remarkably consistent from one individual to the next.
6. You are encouraged to test out this difference for yourself. Select something that you "need," then tell yourself it is something you *should* have. How does your subjective experience shift? Next, select something you "should" have, then tell yourself that it is something you *need*. Again, how does your experience shift? Repeating this exercise with other pairs of modal operators will soon attune you to their differing impacts.
7. A thorough presentation of modal operators and their impact can be found in Cameron-Bandler & Lebeau (1986).
8. Normally, the criteria that you suggest to a client are your own. This is not surprising, since we tend to take it for granted that we are all operating out of the same model of the world. It is also not necessarily bad, since a brief, experiential brush with different criteria may be useful for your client. What is vital, however, is that you recognize the difference between your criteria and that of your client and that you are prepared to use *their* criteria in working with them. "Changes in *attitudes,* in our ways of evaluating, involve intimately 'perceptual processes' at different levels. Making us *conscious* of our *unconscious assumptions* is essential; it is involved in all psychotherapy and should be a part of education in general." (Korzybski, 1951, p. 40)

   The detection and elicitation of criteria, as well as the roles and uses of criteria in generating experiences and behavior, are described extensively in Cameron-Bandler, Gordon, & Lebeau (1985a, 1985b) and in Cameron-Bandler & Lebeau (1986).
9. For sources dealing with language as expressions of internal processes, see Bandler & Grinder (1975a, 1975b); Cameron-Bandler (1985); Cameron-Bandler, Gordon, & Lebeau (1985a, 1985b); Cameron-Bandler & Lebeau (1986); Gordon (1978); Gordon & Meyers-Anderson, (1981); and Grinder, Delozier, & Bandler (1977).

10. "All languages have a structure of some kind, and every language reflects in its own structure that of the world as assumed by those who evolved the language. Reciprocally, we read mostly unconsciously into the world the structure of the language we use. Because we take the structure of our own habitual language so much for granted, particularly if we were born into it, it is sometimes difficult to realize how differently people with other language structures view the world" (Korzybski, 1951, p. 22).

11. "The learning of language is . . . based on a phylogenetic programme which ensures that the child's innate power of abstract thought is integrated and reintegrated on every occasion with the vocabulary that belongs to its cultural tradition" (Lorenz, 1973, p. 231). See also Bickerton's (1983) paper on "Creole Languages."

12. Whether or not this moment of thinking in a new way is sufficient to effect change depends upon various factors. It is my experience that if it does make even a momentary difference for the client in accord with his or her outcomes, he or she will want to keep thinking in that way, and several content-specific repetitions of this changed way of thinking are often all that is needed to install it as a characteristic pattern.

REFERENCES

Bandler, R., & Grinder, J. (1975a). *The Structure of Magic, Vol. 1.* Palo Alto, CA: Science & Behavior Books.

Bandler, R., & Grinder, J. (1975b). *Patterns of the Hypnotic Techniques of Milton H. Erickson, M.D., Vol. 1.* Palo Alto, CA: Science & Behavior Books.

Bickerton, D. (1983). Creole languages. *Scientific American,* July, pp. 116–122.

Cameron-Bandler, L. (1985). *Solutions.* San Rafael, CA: FuturePace.

Cameron-Bandler, L., Gordon, D., & Lebeau, M. (1985a). *Know How: Guided Programs for Inventing Your Own Best Future.* San Rafael, CA: FuturePace.

Cameron-Bandler, L., Gordon, D., & Lebeau, M. (1985b). *The EMPRINT Method: A Guide to Reproducing Competence.* San Rafael, CA: FuturePace.

Cameron-Bandler, L., & Lebeau, M. (1986). *The Emotional Hostage.* San Rafael, CA: FuturePace.

Erickson, M. H., Rossi, R., & Ryan, M. (Eds.). (1985). *Life Reframing in Hypnosis.* New York: Irvington.

Feyerabend, P. (1978). *Against Method.* London: Verso.

Gordon, D. (1978). *Therapeutic Metaphors.* Cupertino, CA: MetaPublications.

Gordon, D., & Meyers-Anderson, M. (1981). *Phoenix: Therapeutic Patterns of Milton H. Erickson.* Cupertino, CA: MetaPublications.

Grinder, J., Delozier, J., & Bandler, R. (1977). *Patterns of the Hypnotic Techniques of Milton H. Erickson, M.D., Vol. 2.* Palo Alto, CA: Science & Behavior Books.

Hall, E. T. (1983). *The Dance of Life.* Garden City, NY: Anchor Press/Doubleday.

Hesse, H. (1963). *Steppenwolf.* New York: Bantam Books.

Lorenz, K. (1973). *Behind the Mirror.* New York: Harcourt Brace Jovanovich.

Korzybski, A. (1951). The role of language in the perceptual processes. In R. Blake & G. Ramsey (Eds.), *Perception: An Approach to Personality.* New York: The Ronald Press Co.

Korzybski, A. (1958). *Science and Sanity.* Lakeville, CT: The International Non-Aristotelian Library Publishing Co.

Kuhn, T. S. (1970). *The Structure of Scientific Revolutions.* Chicago: The University of Chicago Press.

Whorf, B. L. (1956). *Language, Thought and Reality.* Cambridge, MA: The M.I.T. Press.

SECTION ONE: PRINCIPLES

PART IV

Becoming an Ericksonian

Chapter 11

Erickson's Wisdom Regarding Self-Hypnosis: Is This State a Necessary Part of the Art?

Ronald A. Havens

Ronald A. Havens, Ph.D. (West Virginia University), is Associate Professor of Psychology at Sangamon State University in Springfield, Illinois. He also works as consultant to various organizations and has a private practice in psychotherapy and hypnotherapy. With interests in the training of mental health practitioners, hypnosis, and prescriptive approaches to psychotherapy, he has published numerous articles and chapters, and is author of The Wisdom of Milton H. Erickson.

Havens presents a manifesto on behalf of autohypnosis. Quoting liberally from Erickson, he admonishes us that the shortest distance to becoming an Ericksonian is to go straight into trance. Much of Erickson's clinical power was based on his personal ability to use autohypnosis.

Milton H. Erickson was a therapeutic wizard and a master hypnotist. It is not surprising, therefore, that thousands of professionals wishing to become better therapists or better hypnotists currently are attempting to learn how to do what he did.

This laudable desire to improve professional effectiveness by using a genius as a role model has been greatly facilitated by the impressive work of Erickson's remarkably creative and active followers. Detailed analyses of the microdynamics of his hypnotherapeutic procedures and broad conceptualizations of his overriding strategies and conceptual systems are available in a rapidly growing number of publications and workshops. As the presentations offered during the Third International Congress on Ericksonian Approaches to Hypnosis and Psychotherapy attest, the breadth and variety of conceptual analyses and techniques now being offered as Ericksonian is expanding at an almost exponential rate.

Everyone, it would seem, has yet another way to think about or extend Erickson's work in new directions. Indeed, it would be difficult to find another clinician whose unique influence has provided a more stimulating climate for the cross-fertilization and rapid proliferation of ideas and techniques.

Ericksonians appear to be the domestic rabbits of the therapeutic zoo. We are curious, active, incredibly prolific and no two of us look exactly alike. We seem destined to displace our plodding, unchanging, and outmoded ancestors, those ponderous dinosaurs of the species Psychoanalyticus, as well as those cute humanistic hamsters whose primary claim to fame is that they are soft, gentle, and cuddly. Whether or not we will displace our distant cousins, the behaviorist white rats, is of no real concern because they do not even inhabit the same planet we do.

Faced with the rapid proliferation of Ericksonian concepts and techniques, I am reminded of Erickson's frequent reply to those who attempted to offer theoretical explanations for one or another human phenomenon. He would look them directly in the eye and say, "Yes, but is that *all*?"

Obviously, conceptual analyses of Erickson's approach and catalogs of his techniques are useful and necessary. But is that all? Beneath this conceptual diversity it seems that there is an essential or core factor that cannot be overlooked, a kind of species-specific DNA that characterizes Erickson's work and that could link us all to him. As the title of this chapter implies, my hypothesis is that this core factor is the clinician's ability to enter into and function within a self-hypnotic trance.

ERICKSON'S AUTOHYPNOTIC EXPERIENCES

Erickson perceived, understood and responded to his patients in a different and more effective manner than any clinician before or since. I suspect that he was able to do so at least partially because he had spent much of his life functioning within a different and more effective reality, that is, an hypnotic reality.

Erickson had a uniquely unbiased perception of human functioning and an uncanny appreciation for what to say or do to elicit therapeutic and hypnotic responses. I believe that the unbiased and detailed quality of his observations, the intensity of his focus, and his mastery of hypnotherapeutic interventions derived directly from his personal immersion in a trance state.

This is hardly an original proposition nor is it even a very controversial one. Beahrs (1977) described in some detail his suspicion that Erickson utilized self-hypnotic trances to facilitate his work. When he asked Erickson about this suspicion, Erickson smiled and replied, "You're on the right track." Erickson himself once noted that "when there is a crucial issue with a patient and I don't want to miss any of the clues, I go into trance" (Erickson & Rossi, 1977, p. 42). He also once pointed out the general inattentiveness of his students to his trances by noting:

> You haven't been very attentive because I've been going in and out of trance while I have been talking to you. I've learned how to go into trance and I can discuss something with you and watch that rug rise up to this level. . . . I can go in and out of a trance without any of you knowing it. (Zeig, 1980, p. 191)

There is no doubt, therefore, that Erickson used self-induced trances to facilitate his work. The question remains, can we learn how to be Ericksonians without learning how to entrance ourselves, or are self-hypnotic experiences and abilities a necessary part of the art?

As mentioned previously, I believe that self-hypnosis is an essential component to the Ericksonian approach to psychotherapy and hypnotherapy. It may even be the identifying feature of an Ericksonian. Without it, I wonder if we can really appreciate or understand what Erickson tried to teach us. I doubt that we can accumulate the knowledge and unbiased observations that are the basic ingredients of Erickson's approach. I doubt that we can ever begin to develop the skills and creativity necessary to conduct hypnosis or therapy in a form that is not merely imitative and hence lifeless.

SELF-HYPNOSIS FOR HYPNOTISTS

The value and necessity of self-hypnosis is perhaps easiest to convey when discussing the skills and background needed to use hypnosis clinically. Erickson's comments and actions in this arena leave little room for doubt.

When Erickson trained others in the use of hypnosis, he did not just lecture to them; he hypnotized them. He did so for several reasons. First, as he repeated over and over in his lectures, "Experience is the only teacher." He recognized that the experience of an hypnotic trance is crucial to an understanding and appreciation of what is involved in the hypnotic process. He once stated:

> Indeed, long experience has disclosed that the easiest and quickest way to learn to induce a trance is to be hypnotized first, thus to learn the "feel of it." (1980, Vol. 1, p. 279)

His focus was upon experiential learning, not book learning. While working with a woman who wanted to learn about hypnosis Erickson remarked:

> Now S has been trying to get some rational understanding of hypnosis. She doesn't realize that to learn to swim you have to get in the water to actually experience it. Intellectual book knowledge about swimming won't do it. (Erickson, Rossi, & Rossi, 1976, p. 237)

It is obvious, therefore, that if we want to learn about hypnosis we should experience hypnotic trance ourselves. But what about learning how to enter a self-hypnotic trance. Where is the value in that?

One of Erickson's patients summarized his sessions with Erickson in the following manner:

> If you want to know the truth of the matter, Dr. Erickson puts himself in a trance. . . . The first thing you know I'm in there with him. (Haley, 1985, Vol. 1, p. 317)

Erickson was aware that his own entry into a trance stimulated trance in others. In fact, he felt that this was a crucial component to effective trance work.

> I was careful to emphasize the importance in inducing hypnosis, of speaking slowly, impressively and meaningfully, and literally

to "feel" at the moment within the self the full significance of what is being said. (1980, Vol. 1, p. 344)

How does one validate another's subjective experience? By participating, if possible! (1980, Vol. 1, p. 345)

The ability to enter into a self-induced trance allows the hypnotist to participate in or get the "feel" of the responses desired from the subject. By operating from within a trance, the hypnotist virtually guarantees that voice tone, inflection, timing, and wording will be consistent with the experience of trance, thus the resulting stimulus array will naturally lead the subject into a trance state.

The almost inherently hypnotic abilities of someone in a trance led Erickson to use hypnotized subjects as hypnotists on several occasions when confronted with resistant or difficult subjects (cf. Erickson, 1980, Vol. 1, p. 280). These were not people who had been trained as hypnotists. Rather, they were simply students who had proven to be excellent subjects. According to Erickson:

Anybody who has been hypnotized can employ it to hypnotize others, given cooperation and the patience to make use of it. (1941, p. 15)

It may be conclusively stated, therefore, that Erickson believed hypnotists should learn about hypnosis from first-hand experience and would be better hypnotists if they could conduct their sessions while in a trance themselves.

But what about the value of trance when hypnosis is not being used? Are there other situations within a typical therapy process when a trance state of mind is a necessary or valuable place to be for an Ericksonian?

SELF-HYPNOSIS FOR THERAPISTS

The inherent value of a familiarity with self-hypnotic trance may be relatively easy to appreciate with regard to those who wish to be hypnotists, but its relevance to the practice of general psychotherapy may not be as apparent. After all, if you do not intend to put your patient into a trance, why should you go into one yourself?

Erickson provided two answers to this question. First of all, he entered a trance to enhance his observational skills. Much of his therapeutic wizardry derived directly from his remarkable ability to perceive and understand minimal cues presented by his patients. Trance enabled him to focus his attention and to be undistracted by extraneous stimuli, thus allowing him to zero in on the important information that would guide his therapeutic efforts. In Erickson's words:

> At the present time if I have any doubt about my capacity to see the important things, I go into a trance. (Erickson & Rossi, 1977, p. 42)

Actually Erickson was so adept at entering trance that he tended to do so spontaneously whenever he began focusing his attention upon his patients. According to him:

> It (autohypnotic trance) happens automatically because I start keeping close track of every movement, sign, or behavioral manifestation that could be important. . . . It happened automatically, that terrible intensity, as I was looking at you. The word "terrible" is wrong, it's pleasurable. (Erickson & Rossi, 1977, p. 42)

Because this intensity of observation was a fundamental characteristic of Erickson's therapeutic approach, it would seem essential for anyone wishing to conduct therapy in a similar manner to master a similarly focused state of mind. In point of fact, it is highly likely that most practitioners have already experienced this shift into a highly focused trance state, though they may not have labeled it as such. Whenever we begin to pay close attention to what someone else is saying or doing and become totally absorbed by their words or actions, a trance state probably will occur. During the trance, the therapist may suddenly notice a kind of tunnel vision or an apparent shift in the brightness of the room. On the other hand, the spontaneous trance may only be recognized after the fact, when the therapist "comes to" with the realization that everything else had been forgotten for a time. Erickson himself described this experience in the following manner.

> Now and then I became aware that I had been so attentive to my patient that I had forgotten where I was, but I would comfortably and instantly reorient myself. (1980, Vol. II, p. 352)

The second use of self-induced trances proposed by Erickson may be somewhat more alien to the everyday experiences of most therapists. Erickson suggested that therapists plan and conduct their therapy from within a trance so that they can respond to patients on the basis of their unconscious knowledge rather than on the basis of their conscious decisions. To be specific, he offered these instructions:

> You go into autohypnosis to achieve certain things or acquire certain knowledge. When do you need knowledge? When you have a problem with a patient you think it over. You work out in your unconscious mind how you're going to deal with it. Then two weeks later when the patient comes in you say the right thing at the right moment. But you have no business knowing it ahead of time because as surely as you know it consciously, you start to improve on it and ruin it. (Erickson & Rossi, 1977, p. 44)

This is a rather straightforward admonition to avoid conscious analysis and to rely instead upon unconscious understanding. It also is a rather straightforward description of how therapists should use autohypnotic trance to facilitate therapy.

Although there were times when Erickson spent hours carefully and consciously reviewing a case and planning his interventions, it seems obvious that there also were times when he relied exclusively upon his previously acquired unconscious observations and understandings. Aspiring Ericksonians probably should be equipped to do likewise as the following quotation implies:

> Usually when a patient comes into your office and needs advanced psychotherapy or hypnotherapy, you do not have that time for preparation. You've simply got to rely upon your past experience and your past understandings. And I think that's the most important thing that you ought to bear in mind, that you do have a body of experience, a body of learning upon which you can draw. (Erickson, 1966)

The body of learning and experience to which he is referring is your unconscious mind, but it is a familiarity with autohypnosis that allows an effective utilization of that material, not merely intuition or hunches. It would be easy to conclude that all we need to do to be Ericksonian is to stay loose and to fly by the seat of our pants, responding to patients with whatever pops into mind or feels right at the time. That is *not* what Erickson is suggesting.

Erickson was an autohypnotic virtuoso, an individual who could enter a trance at will, who could allow his unconscious mind an opportunity to freely review a situation and decide how to respond to it, and who could subsequently differentiate between unconscious responses and conscious whims or wishes. Few of us have spent the time or energy needed to do likewise, though I believe it is imperative that we do so in order to increase our effectiveness with patients.

SELF-HYPNOSIS AND THE ERICKSONIAN PERSPECTIVE

Although it is apparent from the preceding discussion that a facility with autohypnotic trance would be valuable for prospective Ericksonian hypnotists and therapists, I have yet to establish that it is, as claimed earlier, the essential identifying feature of the Ericksonian approach. I have yet to demonstrate that the trance state is necessary for entry into and utilization of the Ericksonian perspective. In order to do this, it is first necessary to examine the fundamental features of Erickson's basic frame of mind.

To begin with, it is obvious that his approach was not built upon what he called a "Procrustean bed of hypothetical theory of human behavior" (Zeig, 1982, p. vii). As he noted in 1979, "I have no definite theory of psychotherapy, which some people say is very wrong" (The Milton H. Erickson Foundation Newsletter, 1986, p. 4). He rejected the notion that therapeutic understandings or responses could be based upon hypothetical constructs. In fact, he once stated that he did not know of

> anybody who has ever really understood the variety and purposes of any one patient's multiple symptoms despite the tendency of many psychiatrists to hypothecate, to their own satisfaction, towering structures of explanation often as elaborate and bizarre as the patient's symptomatology. (1980, Vol. IV, p. 202)

But if Erickson did not use theoretical constructs and inferences to decide what to do, what did he use? The answer is that he used the same thing he taught his patients to use: the information and learning he acquired by careful, unbiased observation of the realities he experienced directly.

According to Erickson, his approach was based solely upon observation. Not just any ordinary, run of the mill form of observation would do, however, because he realized that typical observations are distorted by a variety of conscious needs, expectations, biases, and values. Erickson accumulated only careful, detailed, and unbiased observations and he learned how to observe with such precision that it often seemed to others that he must be using special theories, intuitions or even mystical powers.

> Every time I demonstrate something before a professional audience, I tell them, "Now you didn't see, you didn't hear, you didn't think. These are the steps." It is so much easier to think there is something special about me than to learn how to really observe and think. "Erickson is mystical," they say. (Erickson & Rossi, 1981, p. 249)

Erickson observed with an intensity and clarity that is difficult for most therapists to imagine. He observed himself, he observed his family and friends, and he observed strangers. He filed away what he learned from these observations and used them as the basis for his general understandings of human functioning. He also observed each individual patient intensely, clearly, and from as many points of view as possible.

> You have to look at your patient as if you were sitting on a seat higher than his. You also have to look at him from a much lower seat. You need to look at him from the other side of the room. Because you always get a totally different picture from different points of view. Only by such a total look at the patient can you gain some objectivity. (Erickson, Rossi, & Rossi, 1976, p. 212)

An essential aspect of Erickson's approach, therefore, consists mainly of careful observation. But it must be emphasized that it is an atheoretical, unbiased multiperspective form of observation we are discussing, a form of observation that most of us would find difficult to carry out under ordinary circumstances.

Ordinarily we are easily distracted, tend to leap to unwarranted conclusions, and tend to overlook or ignore much of what the other person is doing or saying. We tend to translate the patients' words into our own language and to interpret their presentation into our own concepts and beliefs. This is exactly what Erickson did not do and exactly what he tried to teach his students not to do.

How was Erickson able to accomplish this remarkable feat? How was he able to observe so intensely with such an unbiased or flexible point of view? I suggest that he was able to do so by entering into a trance. Within trance, observation naturally takes on these qualities.

It already has been established that he used autohypnotic trance when he wanted to focus his attention and not miss any cues from his patients. It seems likely that he did the same thing when he wanted to carefully observe people who were not his patients or when he wanted to observe and explore the inner realms of his own mind. Whether Erickson did so or not, however, his basic perspective or frame of mind when he engaged in the therapy process was virtually identical to the frame of mind engendered by the trance state. This is true not only with regard to the focused nature and unbiased quality of his observations, but also with respect to his calm flexibility, his openness or receptivity, and his ready access to unconscious understandings, abilities, and communications. In fact, it is difficult to find a single quality or characteristic of his approach that could not be gained most directly and completely by immersion in and familiarity with the trance state.

BECOMING AN ERICKSONIAN

It would be difficult to overestimate the importance of autohypnosis in the acquisition and utilization of the Ericksonian approach to psychotherapy and hypnotherapy. In many respects, a trance state of mind may be a prerequisite to a genuine understanding of what Erickson tried to teach us about the conscious and unconscious minds, about observation, about the use of verbal and nonverbal cues, and about the nature of hypnosis and therapy.

Only from within a trance can we directly experience the validity of his statements. Only within a trance can we appreciate the characteristics or qualities of trance itself and of the unconscious mind. Only within a trance can we experientially learn about the impact of direct and indirect suggestions, metaphors, anecdotes, and plays on words. Only within a trance can we begin to observe in a truly focused and unbiased manner. Only within a trance can we begin to enter into a perspective on reality similar to Erickson's.

The ability to enter into trance is necessary for the conduct of hypnotherapy in an Ericksonian manner. It also seems to be necessary for the utilization of our own unconscious understandings and reactions to enable us to respond appropriately and therapeutically to each unique client.

I doubt that Erickson would have wanted us to keep repeating his techniques over and over again. The hallmark of his approach is not a collection of specific rules, techniques, or verbal tricks, but the constant development of new approaches with each new patient. In Erickson's words, "I've treated many conditions, and I always invent a new treatment in accord with the individual personality" (Zeig, 1980, p. 104). The only rule is this: there are no rules except those dictated by the needs and characteristics of each unique individual. To respond to this rule we must enter a realm of awareness, responsivity, and flexibility typical of a trance state.

We become Ericksonians, therefore, by entering into an Ericksonian state of mind, by learning about people, therapy, and hypnosis from within that state of mind and by responding to the individuality of our patients while in that state of mind. We do not become Ericksonians by trying to imitate Erickson's style or techniques. As Erickson himself stated:

> Remember that whatever way you choose to work must be your own way, because you cannot really imitiate someone else. In dealing with the crucial situations of therapy, you must express yourself adequately, not as an imitation. (Haley, 1967, p. 535)

This is not meant to imply that all we need to do to become more effective clinicians or to become effective Ericksonian therapists is to learn self-hypnosis. I wish it were that easy. Unfortunately, the hypnotic trance merely provides a new and more effective perspective from which to observe and to learn. It triggers our awareness of an enormous amount of previously overlooked information about human functioning and it offers an entirely new framework from which to operate as a clinician.

Admittedly, many of us may have spent numerous hours listening to lectures and presentations in a trance-like stupor, but that is not exactly what I am proposing. What I am proposing is that anyone who wishes to learn what Erickson had to offer should learn it the way Erickson did, from the inside out and with an open mind and a closed mouth. We should learn how to enter into a trance, how to observe ourselves and others within that trance, how to respond to others while in that trance, and how to let the reality we experience teach us what we need to know.

I believe that learning about Ericksonian concepts and approaches is a lot like learning about sex. You can think about it, listen to others talk about it, and even watch others do it. But I don't think you will ever really understand what it is all about until you actually experience it yourselves.

BECOMING BETTER PEOPLE

As a kind of footnote, I would like to suggest that there is a more compelling reason to learn how to use autohypnosis than any of those mentioned previously. A facility with self-hypnotic trance has much more to offer than merely an increased ability to engage in Ericksonian forms of hypnosis and therapy. It is, in fact, a skill that offers access to a richer and more meaningful existence. As such, it is something I believe every man, woman, and child should be taught as early in life as possible.

By learning how to enter into a trance, we can learn how to relax and experience the comfort of not needing to know how to make an effort to do anything at all for a time. We can learn how to allow our attention to become absorbed by subtle perceptions and internal images and become aware of a host of thoughts, sensations, and feelings that otherwise would go unnoticed. We can explore forgotten memories, reexamine childhood experiences, and enjoy a freedom from our ordinary cares, concerns, and fears. We can discover unconscious abilities and capacities we might otherwise never recognize, and we can realize how much control over ourselves and our lives we really have. We can reexamine old problems in new ways and allow our unconscious minds to find realistic ways to make our most precious hopes and dreams come true. We can do things we would never be able to do in any other way, and we can understand ourselves and others in ways we could never imagine at any other time. We can learn to use the remarkable gifts hidden in the vast reservoir of the unconscious mind as we learn how to lose our self-conscious minds' definitions of who we are, where we are, and what we can become.

Just imagine what the world would be like if everyone knew how to enter a trance. If nothing else, it certainly would be a lot quieter.

REFERENCES

Beahrs, J. O. (1977). Integrating Erickson's approach. *American Journal of Clinical Hypnosis, 20,* 55–68.
Erickson, M. H. (1941). Hypnosis: A general review. *Diseases of the Nervous System, 2,* 13–18.
Erickson, M. H. (1966). *Milton H. Erickson Classic—Cassette Series.* American Society of Clinical Hypnosis (Producers), 1980.
Erickson, M. H. (1980). *The Collected Papers of Milton H. Erickson on Hypnosis (4 vols.),* E. Rossi (Ed.). New York: Irvington Publishers.
Erickson, M. H., & Rossi, E. L. (1977). Autohypnotic experiences of Milton H. Erickson. *American Journal of Clinical Hypnosis, 20,* 36–54.
Erickson, M. H., & Rossi, E. L. (1981). *Experiencing Hypnosis.* New York: Irvington.
Erickson, M. H., Rossi, E. L., & Rossi, S. I. (1976). *Hypnotic Realities.* New York: Irvington.
Erickson, M. H. (1979). As quoted in *The Milton H. Erickson Foundation Newsletter,* 1986, 2, p. 4.
Haley, J. (Ed.) (1967). *Advanced Techniques of Hypnosis and Therapy: Selected Papers of Milton H. Erickson, M.D.* New York: Grune & Stratton.
Haley, J. (Ed.) (1985). *Conversations with Milton H. Erickson, M.D.* New York: W. W. Norton.
Zeig, J. K. (1980). *A Teaching Seminar with Milton H. Erickson.* New York: Brunner/Mazel.
Zeig, J. K. (Ed.) (1982). *Ericksonian Approaches to Hypnosis and Psychotherapy.* New York: Brunner/Mazel.

Chapter 12

So Whose Therapy Am I Using, Anyhow?

Herbert S. Lustig

Herbert S. Lustig, M.D. (Albert Einstein College of Medicine), is a psychiatrist in the Philadelphia area and a distinguished member of the Ericksonian community. He is Clinical Associate Professor of Psychiatry at Temple University School of Medicine. He has produced two videotapes, The Artistry of Milton H. Erickson, M.D., *and* A Primer of Ericksonian Psychotherapy, *and he is coauthor of* Tea with Demons.

Lustig's chapter is thought-provoking and his implicit message is timely. He challenges Ericksonian practitioners to define "whose therapy they are using."

I am uncertain of what "Ericksonian" means. I've always used "Ericksonian" to denote what Milton H. Erickson, M.D., actually did as a therapist. Other people, I understand, use the term "Ericksonian" to mean "in the style of," or "I dabble in what I believe Erickson did," or "I'm creative," or "I'm inventing it this very moment as I go along."

I began visiting Erickson after I had already established a private practice in adult and child psychiatry in suburban Philadelphia. During the six years I knew him, our relationship developed. Initially, I attended and participated in groups that Milton was teaching. Later we began having personal conversations; Milton began confiding in me as I had been confiding in him. During this time, I also came to be accepted by members of the Erickson family. It was a process that led from my being his student, to being his colleague, to being his friend. He was also my mentor.

During those six years, I do not recall hearing the phrase "Ericksonian"

198

uttered. Toward the end of his life, plans were being made for the 1980 First International Congress on Ericksonian Approaches to Hypnosis and Psychotherapy. It was around this time that Milton and I had the following conversation:

L: Milton, what exactly is it that you do in psychotherapy? What is the essence of your psychotherapeutic work?

In response, Erickson told me stories about psychotherapy. Later, I repeated the question more forcefully.

L: What is it that defines your clinical work, Milton?

His answer surprised me.

E: I can't define my work. I'll have to leave that for others.
L: Which others?
E: I don't know who they are right now.
L: But Milton, you are the only authority on your work who exists.
E: I can't do it. It would be too confusing, Herb.

Changing the subject slightly to focus on my own concerns, I responded:

L: Well, that's understandable at this stage in your career.

Pausing briefly, I continued:

L: Milton, you're the best at doing psychotherapy and hypnosis of anyone I have ever met or read about, and one of the most creative. But, now that I know and practice some of your work, Milton, what am I to call myself?
E: Herb Lustig, I hope. There's no need to change your name at this stage in your life.

Erickson was always quick to utilize another person's communication style.

L: Milton, people are beginning to call your clinical work and their copy of it "Ericksonian." How could people dare to use that term to describe their therapy when its originator still owns the phrase?

E: I don't own the phrase, Herb. I didn't even create it.

L: Well, if "Ericksonian" describes what *you* do, how does "Ericksonian" also relate to people who are *not you*?

E: I have taught many people and most of them have learned something from me. They're all "Ericksonian" when they use my techniques.

L: Is it necessary to use the term "Ericksonian," or can someone just use the techniques without using the term?

E: Use any term you wish.

L: Milton, what if people identify themselves to the public as "Ericksonian" even though they are not using any techniques that you have ever taught or used?

E: I can't stop them, Herb.

L: And what if they claim to be an expert in your techniques?

E: I can't stop them.

L: I'm confused, Milton. If I'm "Ericksonian" when I use your teachings, even though I might not use that same term to describe my clinical work, then what title am I supposed to use to identify myself professionally?

E: Whatever you like. Each title should be an accurate reflection of what it represents.

It was another frustrating, but informative, experience with Milton.

During the six years that I traveled to spend time with Milton, several qualities about his professional work impressed me greatly: He really wanted to teach others the therapeutic art that he had created. He was willing to share and demonstrate his work with others. He respected each person's special skills and abilities, accepting them for who they were. He delighted in fostering creative solutions to seemingly insoluble clinical problems. He had an impressive wealth of clinical knowledge and skills. He could simplify the complex so that it became manageable. His observational power made him aware of the most minute aspect of a communication or interaction.

Through all of this, I distilled the experiences that I had had with Milton and devised a triad that represented for me the hallmark of Erickson's clinical work. Those three items were creativity, effectiveness, and integrity: creativity being the ability to devise new or unusual methods for solving clinical or personal problems; effectiveness being a constructive outcome to a therapeutic intervention in an obvious manner and in a reasonable period of time; and integrity being the sincere respect accorded the patient, and the sense of personal honor displayed by the therapist in himself and his work. These were elements that I quickly absorbed into my personal life and clinical work. They resonated comfortably.

But I still don't know what "Ericksonian" means. How can we find out? And if we do find out, how can we discover the implicit obligations in using the term? Even if we accept being "Ericksonian," are we still ourselves, or are we representatives of someone or something else? If Milton didn't define the term, what is it that we say about ourselves if we call ourselves "Ericksonian"? And, since Milton never identified the cornerstones of his own therapeutic work, if we call ourselves "Ericksonians," must we also adopt the same ambiguity about our methodology as he did, or are we now compelled to do what Milton never did—and define *our* work? If we call ourselves "Ericksonians," are we labeled forever, even if we wish to resign from the affiliation? And what happens if we don't call ourselves "Ericksonian," are we ineligible to join this new and exciting mental health movement? What happens if we call ourselves "Ericksonian" and people ask us questions about "Ericksonianism" that we can't answer? Are we then reported to some higher "Ericksonian" authority?

I am not an historian nor even very familiar with the movements of humankind that have arisen over the past decades, but my impression is that when a movement took on the name of its founder or originator, there was usually something specific and demonstrable that could be identified as the foundation of the movement's philosophy or belief system. Commonly, this was based on the major theme of the originator's professional work or personal career. That is what is so confusing to me. Milton Erickson was alive when the term "Ericksonian" was first used, and he was still alive when the title for the First International Congress was being decided.* Yet, a definition of the term was never articulated.

Several years ago, I told a friend of mine that I could no longer distinguish between what Milton had taught me and what I was doing in my own clinical practice or, for that matter, what Milton had taught me and what I was doing in my own personal life. It made the question of being an "Ericksonian" redundant for me, since there was no dis-

---

Editors' note: Milton H. Erickson was a founding member of the Board of Directors of the Milton H. Erickson Foundation. He tacitly approved of the title for the First Congress when the idea was presented to him.

tinction. But it became a problem. When do I become myself as a clinician if I can't distinguish between my own skills and the teachings of my mentor? And if I don't honor him by calling myself an "Ericksonian," do I insult his memory? I reflected upon this for a long while and finally decided that he would be pleased, even now, at my independence and sense of self-worth and my professional effectiveness. So although I have still not completely resolved to my satisfaction this "Ericksonian" dilemma, I have found a solution that works well for me.

My name is Herb Lustig. I studied and loved a genius and a friend named Milton Erickson. However, the clinical work that I do now is "Lustigian."

Chapter 13

Becoming an Ericksonian, Becoming Yourself: A Personal Perspective on Becoming an Ericksonian

Carlos Zalaquett

Carlos Zalaquett, Licensed Psychologist (Catholic University of Chile), is Clinical Professor of Psychology and Vice-Chairman for Research at Catholic University of Chile. He is President of the Chilean Foundation for the Prevention of the Sudden Infant Death Syndrome. The recipient of many professional and academic honors, Zalaquett has published widely in professional journals in Chile. He is a member of the editorial board of Terapia Psicologica *(Chile).*

Zalaquett describes his personal process of becoming an Ericksonian. Key concepts of the Ericksonian method are presented and Zalaquett explains how he uses them personally.

I still remember my flight to Phoenix in 1983 . . . The roaring of the plane's turbines and the constant vibration of the cabin walls accompanied the ebb and flow of my thoughts.

Those thoughts centered on one of the most painful events of my life. The death of my first child, Carolina Andrea, had occurred only two months before as a result of Sudden Infant Death Syndrome. I was still depressed for I could not resign myself to her loss.

To escape the pain I carried on board with me, I allowed myself to imagine how it would be to attend the Second International Congress of Ericksonian Approaches to Hypnosis and Psychotherapy. I also wondered about what the organizers, the faculty and the other participants in this event would be like. Would I find myself surrounded by carbon copies of Erickson or by his severe and distant disciples? Would I learn things that I had not already read? Was it a good idea to have come at all?

I had heard from colleagues about this remarkable hypnotist and psychotherapist, Milton H. Erickson, and had read of his work and contributions to the development of psychotherapy in *Uncommon Therapy* (Haley, 1973). I went on to read other books explaining Erickson's thinking and techniques, until finally I presented a seminar on his approach in Chile.

We landed in Phoenix at midnight, and to my chagrin I learned that all hotels near the civic center were full. I had to spend this first night in the suburbs. I must confess that both my doubts and expectations increased due to waiting. I was very tired.

It was in this mood, exhausted and discouraged, that I arrived early the next morning at the location of the Second Congress. There I found 2000 participants from different parts of the United States and from many countries. I met Jeffrey Zeig and Mrs. Erickson. She surprised me when she asked whether Viña del Mar was still a very beautiful city. I also met Jay Haley, Paul Watzlawick and so many others during the next several days. They were kind to me, and I learned from every one of them.

During the Second Congress, I attended conferences, panels and demonstrations. And thanks to my friend, Bert Freeman, I even climbed Squaw Peak—a key side attraction of the event. I succeeded in inducing arm levitation and, in doing so, became aware of the importance of centering myself with the other individual, of establishing a significant communication that exceeds the mere repetition of suggestions or authoritarian orders. I grasped the relationship between hypnosis and psychotherapy, and the importance of the unconscious as Erickson conceived it. I felt that this represented the completion of a stage and the beginning of a new level of study and a deeper understanding of Erickson's work.

During the Congress, I lived surrounded by a warm and hypnotic atmosphere. Under the purple cast of the Phoenix sky, my spirit began to lift. I recognize today the influence of the experiences surrounding the Second Congress both on my personal life and on the work I have been doing since.

The purpose of this chapter is to present my own personal perspective of becoming an Ericksonian. "Personal" because I believe that each individual has his own unique way to learn about the Erickson approach, and I will submit mine. "Perspective" because I can describe my vision of Erickson's work and how I am influenced by his ideas only according to my subjective perception and experiences. Naturally, the aspects of Erickson's work that I will present are some of the most valuable for me, though Erickson himself may have visualized them differently. "Becoming" because this is a process that has only begun, but has not yet ended. Perhaps it will never end. It can only be portrayed at its current stage.

In this chapter I will present part of my process of becoming an Ericksonian both personally and as a therapist. Through studying Erickson, I experienced distinct personal changes, some of which my inner mind understands better than my conscious mind. Let me tell you something about my experience. In those days it amazed me to see that man, especially in his later videos when he was in his 70s, sitting in a wheelchair . . . slowly lifting his left hand and using it to raise his right arm . . . looking intensely into the eyes of the other person . . . and after greeting him with a handshake, lowering his sight . . . while the other person went into a deep trance. This was marvelous for me, the various methods he used to anchor people or to communicate at multiple levels.

This had always captured my immediate attention, but, upon looking at it more deeply, I fully recognized how he himself personified his ideas and methods. And I learned, likewise, how he himself was a testimony of the way in which he could make his afflictions and limitations become something positive. Even in consideration of his contracting poliomyelitis, his color blindness, and his being tone deaf, I could not see any traces of bitterness but only a strong orientation towards action and a vigorous orientation toward life. He was confined to a wheelchair as a result of physical problems and yet he was able to state that this disease had been a remarkable teacher of human behavior and human potential.

His method was one of personal reframing. I, too, experienced it. However, I realized this only after returning to my own country. At that point I founded the Chilean group for Prevention of the Sudden Infant Death Syndrome, which currently consists of more than 50 families. We can state that at least 18 children have survived due to our efforts. There were other changes, but for me the most impressive was that which occurred in my mood. Erickson's ability to turn his difficulties into an unprecedented opportunity to learn about himself and his surroundings allowed me to feel that I could do something too. Perhaps, in an analogous manner, as Erickson was able to overcome his physical pain, I could win the struggle against my emotional pain.

From the professional viewpoint, Erickson's ideas also had an impact on me, unconsciously at first and then in a more active conscious/ unconscious way. Very early in my career I realized that some ideas and attitudes about the psychotherapeutic process needed change, and I found myself drifting away from the traditional views of psychotherapy I had learned.

Upon my first acquaintance with Erickson's ideas in Chile, and then through the 1983 Congress, a seminar, and a workshop held by Jeffrey Zeig at the Universidad Católica de Chile, I found strong support for my own ideas. Erickson's approach supported the process I was experiencing and acted as a catalyst for it.

Let's think about therapy. We all agree that "therapy" is a highly significant word and such words often create realities and can lead to rigid approaches. In its Greek origin, this word meant only "service." So psychotherapy really means a service that one person can lend to another, in any way, with any technique, and amidst any culture (Masserman, 1968). This means that we need flexibility in our ideas about psychotherapy, especially since we are dealing with a process about which many aspects are not really understood. Watzlawick (1985) asserts in referring to the psychotherapeutic field that "many aspects are unclear, debated, esoteric and contradictory, and that especially its main vehicle—language—is insufficiently understood" (p. 5).

If we bear in mind these ideas, we see the absurdity in the statements of many authors or schools of psychology who claim to have discovered the *real way* to carry out psychotherapy. How many times have we heard a colleague saying that psychoanalysis is the only real psychotherapy, or that behaviorism is the only approach that creates change?

Erickson was a pioneer in demonstrating that the usual parameters and ways of developing a psychotherapeutic intervention had to be reconsidered and reformulated, though he did not do that in a confrontational manner. He just did his job and in so doing left traditional approaches trembling. His attitude is clearly illustrated in the following statement by Zeig (1980):

In regard to Erickson's professional approach, it is important to note that although he created many new permissive approaches to therapeutic hypnosis, he was quite adamant in being atheoretical. Erickson had no explicit theory of personality that he promoted. He was a firm believer that an explicit theory of personality would limit the psychotherapist and make the psychotherapist more rigid. Erickson was committed to the ideas of flexibility, uniqueness and individuality. He made that clear in his writings and in the way that he lived. (p. 44)

Undoubtedly these ideas promote a shift from traditional ideas to newer ones. This process is stimulated even more when we assume that the best measurement of psychotherapy is neither the theory on which it is founded nor the procedures, nor the time the therapy lasts, but rather its efficacy in helping the client.

Many of Erickson's interventions and those of some of his followers efficiently resolve the clients' difficulties. Frequently, the client continues experiencing changes far beyond the primary therapeutic goals. And today, from his writings, videos, films and audiotapes, and from those of his disciples, we are able to extract some of the basic values, attitudes, and techniques that form the foundation of Erickson's work and which therefore can be designated as "Ericksonian." These are the seeds of my own process.

From my point of view, to become an Ericksonian implies that the therapist must come to understand and integrate most of these values, attitudes and techniques into his or her own methods of work. But, paradoxically, the therapist should do this in a way that preserves the basic tenets of his or her own philosophy and individuality, and maintain an openness to share with others his ideas and learning in order to get dynamic and self-correcting feedback from more experienced colleagues. "Erickson deserves credit, not discredit, and tribute, not blame" (Thompson, 1985).

Let us now consider some of the Ericksonian elements which—from my own point of view—spring from his concepts of the person and of the psychotherapeutic process.

ERICKSON AND THE PERSON

One of the most profound assertions I ever heard about psychotherapy comes from Erickson. Within its content I found the basic philosophy of his work:

> Each person is a unique individual. Hence, psychotherapy should
> be formulated to meet the uniqueness of the individual's needs,
> rather than tailoring the person to fit the Procrustean bed of a
> hypothetical theory of human behavior. (Erickson, 1979)

From this beautiful statement we can appreciate that the person
occupies the starting point from which Erickson developed his ideas.
And this reference to the person implies both the person/client and
the person/therapist. Erickson's daughter, Kristina (1985), explains, "the
most important aspect of this (his) philosophy is the concept of the
individuality of the therapist and the individuality of the patient" (p. xi).

For Milton Erickson each human being was unique and possessed
the necessary attributes to develop himself in his life and to benefit
from himself, his family and his social surroundings. In the Ericksonian
view, each individual has the potential to develop his life in the most
satisfactory manner, just as do all those people who live happily and
fruitfully whom we never see in therapy. Even when confronted with
difficulties, they are able to overcome them.

But sometimes a person does not overcome his problems. Or the
people surrounding him decide that he has problems. In these situations,
either the person has the necessary elements within him and simply
cannot access them, or he lacks the necessary elements while still
retaining the possibility of creating them. With his own potential and
strength, he can develop the resources necessary to resolve his problems.

The person already has all that he needs, and psychotherapy or
hypnotherapy should be the key to help him realize his own possibilities.
For Erickson, clients did not need to become something new, nor should
they throw away the errors of the past. Rather, they need—here and
now—to use the abilities and potential abilities they have been developing in the various and multiple experiences of life.

We find the same idea when Erickson, while teaching hypnosis to
his students, told them, "I am not asking you to use a new skill that
you don't have. I'm only asking you to be willing to use a skill you
have but you don't know you have" (Carter, 1982, p. 50). The same
idea can be applied to the psychotherapist, who by no means should
be tailored according to a hypothetical theory of a psychotherapist's
behavior but should be helped to express his own individuality in the
therapeutic encounter. This implies, by necessity, the development of
uncommon training methods for therapists. Erickson seemed to have
uncommon methods to train himself, and Zeig (1985b) explained the
ways Erickson used to teach him.

This involves a positive view of the human being, who is recognized as a complete and integral system in which each element is considered valuable. According to Beahrs (1982), Erickson thought that all human beings—in all their aspects or parts—are basically adequate. This means that he held an approving attitude towards the basic being. From this positive view grows the idea that human beings will always make the best choice they can, using prior learning experiences regardless of whether they are conscious or unconscious (Lankton and Lankton, 1983).

Erickson tells us that no therapist wishing to help a client could despise, dismiss or reject any part of his client's behavior because that part appears to the therapist to be obstructive or irrational. He affirms that therapy can be firmly established on the utilization of foolish, irrational and contradictory manifestations (Haley, 1973).

Thus, he did not see any aspects of his client's reality as positive or negative; rather, he maintained that each therapy must work to guide the client in such a way that he finds his own solution and makes use of each of his parts in his own manner. This requires the understanding of the individual and of each of his parts, developing them, and achieving new and better forms of expression, so that the therapist can successfully help to satisfy all the client's needs. All this allows us to understand the meaning and the uses of techniques such as reframing which help the person to determine the positive intent of his behavior, and to achieve it to such an extent that even a symptom may become an ability.

Erickson tried to find the positive aspect of the part of the person that "sabotaged" his desire for a better life. If one wishes to come closer to Ericksonian psychotherapy, one must be able to discover the positive aspects even of the most "negative" characteristics within the client and to validate these so that positive results are obtained.

The concepts of uniqueness and wholeness imply that the therapist value each part of the client/system. Thus, even the unconscious—the source of conflicts in the analytical tradition—becomes the source of growth and life for Ericksonians (Beahrs, 1982). At the roots of Ericksonian work is reliance on the presence of a wise and intelligent unconscious mind which guides the client/system towards positive goals.

Though Erickson recognized the value of both conscious and unconscious aspects of the individual, he addressed his attention to the unconscious, seeking to activate this repository of learnings, memories, and resources (Erickson & Zeig, 1980). His working techniques were directed toward the unconscious in order to bypass the conscious mind, its biases, and its rigid patterns that tend to limit the experiences and learnings of the person (Lankton & Lankton, 1983).

In the Erickson perspective, the therapist must approach this human being, the client, and treat him not only by accepting him and respecting his behaviors, but also by actively trying to see the world just as the client sees it, by entering into the view of the client as such and adjusting to the different levels in which the client communicates. The therapist should always take into account and respect the client's family, vocation, and social system.

The positive view of the human being that Erickson held, his respect for uniqueness and individuality; and his consideration for all the person's aspects helped me to change the way in which I work with myself and my way of working with my clients, as well as my model of the psychotherapeutic process.

ERICKSON AND THE PSYCHOTHERAPEUTIC PROCESS

As a psychotherapist, I gained new understandings about the psychotherapeutic process and about how to train therapists. In brief, Erickson's work showed me an uncommon way for training therapists, which, as Zeig (1980) described, is consistent with this overall approach. It includes diagnosis and utilization of patterns, building of strengths, making predictions, developing a teleological orientation, giving assignments, observing cues, role-playing, reading good novels, and conducting anthropological field experiments (Zalaquett, 1986a).

In the psychotherapeutic process, "the integration of the total personality is the desired objective of psychotherapy" (Erickson, 1948). In order to be able to assume his therapeutic role, the therapist must be based in his own integrated individuality. Then the therapeutic task consists of finding a unique way of gaining access in each person to the resources he needs in order to solve his problems and continue his growth, allowing a new integration of the different parts of the personality in a direction advantageous to the client and his system.

Erickson looked at the behavior and actions of his clients intrapersonally, understanding the human being as a system in itself and its behavior as the way in which this individual interacts with others. In other words, the human being is seen as a system within a much larger system. In addition, there are phases or cycles in the individual's working, family and social life. Therefore, the therapist should help the person to move through each of these phases and to complete them appropriately. In this sense, termination of the treatment occurs when the individual achieves a new integration of his personality, a suitable interdependence with his family and social systems, and an adequate ongoing phase of development.

The distinctive aspects of Erickson's therapeutic approach that permitted him to undertake the therapeutic process were its strategic nature and the use of hypnosis.

THE STRATEGIC APPROACH

Erickson was considered the master of strategic psychotherapy (Haley, 1973; Zeig, 1985b). Consider the following description by Haley (1973):

> Therapy can be called strategic if the clinician initiates what happens during therapy and designs a particular approach for each problem. When a therapist and a person with a problem encounter each other, the action that takes place is determined by both of them, but in strategic psychotherapy the initiative is largely taken by the therapist. He must identify solvable problems, set goals, design interventions to achieve those goals, examine responses he receives to correct his approach, and ultimately examine the outcome of his therapy to see if it has been effective. The therapist must be acutely sensitive and responsive to the patient and his social field but how he proceeds must be determined by himself. (p. 17)

This strategic aspect of Milton Erickson made a great impression on me. It enriched my own view of the psychotherapeutic process and my role as psychotherapist, leading me to assume a more directive and goal-oriented stance.

My perspective was broadened exponentially by the addition of the other distinctive aspect of Ericksonian therapeutic work, i.e., hypnosis.

THE HYPNOTIC APPROACH

Milton Erickson developed, within the field of clinical hypnosis, an innovative style of hypnotic induction and utilization. All his communication was to a certain extent hypnotic. Even when Erickson did not formally apply hypnosis, his therapeutic work was to such a degree based on hypnosis that everything he did seemed to stem from it (Haley, 1976).

His work enabled me to recognize how natural a phenomenon hypnosis is in human beings. It is perhaps for this reason that many persons tended to view their contacts with Erickson as experiences in which it was not easy to distinguish when they were in or out of trance, and when he was using ordinary nonhypnotic conversation.

Erickson emphasized the interactional nature of the hypnotic process, where responsibility is shared between both participants. Thus, one considers the individual (both operator and subject), the relationship between the two of them, and the actual characteristics of the situation in which the induction has been carried out. Then the task of the hypnotist is to guide the client, and the task of the client is to decide when and how to respond to the communication of the hypnotist. From this perspective, each person has his own values and strategies to create his own experience. Therefore, the effectiveness of hypnotherapy depends on the therapist's ability to adapt his strategies to those of the client.

This approach was quite different from the hypnosis I had heard of and observed before. Erickson's hypnotherapeutic work aimed to establish a communication that would be significant for each person. It would help the individual to find solutions by himself instead of pretending to dominate his behavior through authoritarian orders.

Erickson assumed that the unconscious processes operated in an intelligent and creative way and that we could contact them and make use of them during the state of trance. According to Erickson, during induction the behavior of the subject is made up of both the conscious and the unconscious patterns, but the behavior during the state of trance is primarily of an unconscious origin (Rossi, 1980, Vol. IV). However, he often used the continuing activity of the conscious mind, casting aside the myth that hypnosis deals only with the unconscious mind.

These aspects obviously do not explain the whole complexity of Ericksonian hypnosis, but they enable us to differentiate his approach from authoritarian methods, in which the hypnotist takes on the posture of dominating and subjugating a client, and from standardized methods, where the hypnotic response is seen as a characteristic (trait) inherent to the client.

In this uncommon hypnotic approach, consistent with its view of the individual, the process of induction and treatment begins by accepting, matching and utilizing the client's reality so as to guide his subsequent behavior. Erickson was a master of the art of matching the reality of his client, becoming a complex system of biofeedback that described verbal and nonverbal behaviors of the subject. Once the person accepts, generally at an unconscious level, the descriptions of the hypnotherapist, the person's habitual behavior becomes less defined. This allows the therapist to induce the desired changes, guiding the thoughts and behavior of his client toward the solution of difficulties. This new conception produces a great flexibility in the forms of induction, many of which can be indirect with paralinguistic emphasis on words or phrases in a day-to-day conversation using the emitted behavior of the person.

THE ERICKSONIAN APPROACH

There are two ideas implicit in Erickson's strategic and hypnotic approach:

Utilization: Working with any person he usually used the actual behavior of the individual even when there were "resistances." The most difficult behaviors of a client can be viewed as their best effort to cooperate and as an expression of the person's needs. Erickson developed utilization techniques taking into account the needs underlying the behavior. Thus, the ensuing intervention could both provide change and gratify needs.

Indirection: Erickson used indirect communication such as metaphors, stories, and analogies to influence patients in a subtle manner. The underlying assumption was to obtain the person's own solutions which required moving beyond the conscious limits that had already been established (C. Lankton, 1985).

These ideas were new for me and showed me the need for an active attitude on the part of the therapist.

An Active Attitude

We, as therapists, can make ourselves comfortable in our chairs and let the client find his way through the forest of his mind. But such an attitude, as I am able to understand now, goes against the goal of strategic therapy and hypnosis. Accordingly, it frequently yields poor results. The clinician must assume the responsibility of directly influencing the client and, in some cases, the client's environment. He focuses himself on a problem, establishes goals, and intervenes actively and deliberately with the clear intention of exerting influence on the client's experience.

This does not mean that the therapist should change his personality in order to make a strategic intervention. Each person has his own way of being: Some are active and extroverted; others are quiet and reserved, and an active attitude does not fit their own way of being. But even the latter kind of therapist may have a degree of activity and an essential direction, and may be able to display interest in the client and in his vital and immediate problems, sharing with him his improvement, without the client relinquishing in any way his own responsibility and his obligation to act for himself.

Another form of active attitude is seen in the utilization of the elements in the client's environment. Milton Erickson actively searched for the establishment of a bridge between social and physical realities, returning the person to his or her own environment. Also, his attitude was to see other members of the client's family. This is quite understandable today, when we all know the communicative value and the interactional dimension of symptoms and behaviors.

But this active attitude leads us directly to the problem of influence and manipulation.

Influence and Manipulation

Erickson openly considered these matters, and he admitted that not to influence or manipulate was impossible. Therefore, he considered carefully the kind of effect he desired to have on his client. This does not imply seeking to manipulate the client so that he lives according to the therapist's standards and principles, because the goals of therapy are established in accordance with the client's own desire to change.

The therapist does not need to be coercive. Rather, he should seek an opportunity to co-create the conditions for achieving specific therapeutic results consistent with the client's values. Therefore, the client deserves all the credit for his responsibility in reaching his goals. In essence, this means that the client will change in ways that are significant to him.

Faced with a question about control and manipulation of his clients, Erickson answered that, like a professor who must have a certain control over his class, the psychotherapist should also have control over the psychotherapeutic situation and over his client in order to be effective.

He often clarified doubts about manipulation by saying that all mothers manipulate and exert control over their sons or daughters when they help them to live, and every buyer going into a store manipulates the seller in order to obtain what he wishes to buy. All of us were manipulated by our teachers when we learned how to read and write.

In psychotherapy we often tend to minimize this mechanism, but it exists. Many therapists are now concluding that they cannot do anything other than influence. Influence can occur subtlely—in the intensity of tone of the "mm"; the head nods of a therapist facing his client; or the sound of the pencil of the therapist when he is behind the client.

After analyzing Erickson's personality and values, as well as those of other well-known therapists, I have concluded that it is not only impossible not to transmit one's own values and ideas, but that it is beneficial. The open presentation of a new system of values can be advantageous, even essential, in order to educate the client to a more healthy orientation of life. As long as this is done without forcing the client to accept such ideas, it will be more valuable than exerting inadvertent influence, acting as if nothing had happened when we know that the client naturally assimilates many of our values. How many times have we been surprised when we hear the client saying that something mentioned by us in a past session was so important to him or had great effect.

Diagnosis

Erickson's work implies the strict development of a specific form of diagnosis. Obviously, diagnosis is a necessary step towards the planning and development of a psychotherapeutic intervention. It allows the possibility of determining what the person needs at this stage of his life, and what he believes will enable him to solve his current problem. At the same time, all this makes it possible for us to establish goals, to plan the treatment, and to carry it out. Thus, the therapist should evaluate the present patterns that make his client's present behavior idiosyncratic. This implies determination of client ideas, motivations, personal constructs, behaviors, and symptoms.

This kind or mode of diagnosis is different from the traditional diagnosis that looks for a diagnostic label. This difference cannot only be observed in the determination of the particular pattern or specific model of the client's reality. Rather, in the Ericksonian diagnosis, we attempt to ascertain resources and strengths on which the therapeutic intervention will be planned and based (Zeig, 1980).

Insight-Understanding

For a long time certain ideas have had primacy in psychotherapy. One of them was that even when the client had little time available for his treatment, it was important for him to understand the nature of his problem. We can see this quite clearly in Wolberg's (1968) statement that as soon as the patient grasps the idea that his troubles are not fortuitous but rather the fruit of concrete causes, he will be in a better position to use his energy towards the solution of his difficulties instead of wasting such energy in recriminations, resentments or self-devaluations.

Insight can be effective from a theoretical point of view, but most of the insights obtained through therapy are only a delicious series of shared fantasies elaborated between the client and the therapist. We can even arrive to the point at which a prolonged therapy results in provoking the same troubles it had intended to change. Erickson did not usually use insightful interpretations because of the limitations of the conscious mind. Instead, on several occasions he encouraged amnesia.

I am reminded of a case for which I had no explanation at the time, but now appears clear to me after considering the Ericksonian elements indicated above. The client consulted me in 1978 because he defecated uncontrollably. He had been suffering from this problem for more than five years in all types of stressful situations. Because of this problem, he could not accept a sales award granted by his company because at the moment in which the manager called him on stage to receive the award he had to run to the bathroom to change his underpants.

This problem had started in 1974, when he was arrested by the secret police because of some political problem. After he was subjected to psychological pressure and was not able to deliver any information, the police burned him on the leg with the cigarette lighter of his own car "in order that he would not live without a souvenir." Since that event, he had begun to defecate any time he saw a vehicle or a person belonging to the secret police, and had generalized this symptomatic response to other types of police, until finally he had this response when he faced any stressful situation, whether positive or negative.

During the first and second sessions, I was able to determine that:

a) nobody who knew him was informed about his problems; b) nobody in his company had learned about his socialist past; c) he was involved in an intense extramarital relationship. During the third session, I presented to him the metaphor of a lonely person living on a tight-rope, a person whose life was permanently at risk. I told him that there was no medication, no sorcery, no psychologist who would be able to take him safely out of his danger. In the following session, he reported the complete disappearance of his symptoms. In subsequent sessions, no relapses were reported. Instead, the patient made deep and far-reaching changes in his private life.

At that time I did not know how to explain what was done or what was happening. Now I have a clearer idea. The intervention worked to activate the inner constructive forces of the client, which resolved the critical tension of his life and stimulated a complete transformation of his personality.

In practice, any person who has worked in psychotherapy has experienced at least one situation in which the symptomatic patient begins to relax and become himself, changing towards a much more satisfactory and fulfilling life after only a few sessions. Today I can sometimes succeed in this kind of intervention in a way that is less intuitive and more the result of planning than on that occasion.

Duration of Treatment

Erickson challenged existing assumptions about treatment duration. Commonly, the psychotherapist's treatment plan reflects the belief that the longer the treatment, the better it will be for the client. However, this is not valid for every client.

It is often believed that brief psychotherapy is similar in philosophy to long-term psychotherapy: "To listen in a state of relaxation, to let this relaxation grow until it becomes a transference, waiting in an expectant attitude until the patient acquires motivation to direct himself and break through layers upon layers of resistance, until finally penetrating into the treasures of the unconscious" (Wolberg, 1968, p. 128). However, Erickson demonstrated that brief psychotherapy is not just a matter of repeating the canons of long-term psychotherapy. Brief treatment requires parsimony and tact, both of which can be acquired and delivered after long training and experience. From an Ericksonian perspective, the emphasis lies on the person and on the optimization of psychotherapy in relation to that person so as to make psychotherapy as brief as possible for each particular case.

The Problem of Deep Change

Therapists have been divided into two camps on this topic. There are those considered to be problem-solvers (symptom-based) and those considered as restorers or transformers of the personality.

However, from an Ericksonian view, psychotherapy is a human interaction which occurs within an immediate context and contains a series of dimensions both psychological and social, verbal and nonverbal. His psychotherapy and hypnotherapy constitute a special form of co-operative interaction between two or more persons, the goal being that, through the relationship established with the other individual, change is introduced in the person's model of the world which extends the outreach of his capacities. Although therapy focuses on behaviors and symptoms, the entire personality is influenced as well.

Delimiting the Target Problem

If we start from the perspective of long-term, laissez-faire therapy, it does not matter too much what we do because, sooner or later, we will arrive somewhere and, sooner or later, the symptoms of the client and the action of the therapist will be defined. They will jointly achieve advances or encounter difficulties, and little would be left without exploration.

At other times, we could do something to inform, to answer, or to confront a client with the eventual consequences of his actions and attitudes. But this implies limited therapeutic objectives. And it is usually taught that the client's problems continue even after he/she has understood that they are useless and prejudicial. Nevertheless, from an Ericksonian viewpoint, it is believed that the individual is a system, so that if we produce a slight modification unbalancing his adaptive equation, he will be able then to give birth to a more substantial transformation. Perhaps the person is allowed to doubt certain assumptions. This can be the seed for other, more important readjustments that contain all the adaptive phases and all the influential elements of the environment, of interpersonal relationships and even of the intrapsychic structure itself. These changes can occur at any stage in the process of change. It is possible that the client may observe only a slight change at termination of therapy. However, if the psychotherapy has been correctly carried out, one can predict added results in the future, perhaps after the client has completed the essential tasks he assumed during treatment.

Eclecticism

For the benefit of the client, we should combine therapeutic elements from different schools. This merging of methods, in which one utilizes tactics with proven merit from many different schools, yields the best results.

In order to apply this eclectic view, one needs a certain degree of flexibility in order to expand the limits of one's models and experiment with other methods. Let us not forget that each school has successes and failures. Our duty and commitment is toward our client; we are not committed to supporting a hypothetical theory of human behavior.

As can be seen, instead of focusing on Erickson's techniques, I have been interested in the elements emerging from his philosophy and approach. We can perceive a deep and positive consideration of the human being, visualized as a unique and complex individual involved in an ecological net of interdependence, with full respect for his abilities, his wise unconscious, and his capacity for self-correction. To help him, the therapist uses a strategic and a hypnotic approach tailored to fit the needs of that unique person, adapting any dimension required: duration, degree of activity, use of influence, goals, therapeutic methods. As Kristina Erickson explained: "My father encouraged others not to mimic him, but rather to incorporate into one's knowledge the skills and techniques that reflected one's personal abilities and interests" (1985, p. xi).

This means that to become an Ericksonian is, paradoxically, to become increasingly and more fully oneself.

CONCLUSIONS

It is easy to get the impression that one knows Milton H. Erickson's approach. That is not really the case, for his ideas are complex and far-reaching. It is necessary to go more deeply into the work of a man who—beyond any theoretical formulation or technical development—showed a high degree of respect and appreciation for his fellow beings.

He involved himself and committed himself in an active way to the task of helping people solve their problems and reach fulfillment.

Ericksonian ideas have led me to enrich my therapy in a creative way. The Ericksonian approach has influenced my way of understanding psychotherapy and of practicing it. A case in point is that of a young psychologist who had unsuccessfully undergone gynecological treatment for a year in order to become pregnant.

We worked through five sessions of therapy during which I learned about the history of her problem. We evaluated resolution patterns and implemented treatment. She had a five-year-old son. A second pregnancy was affected by German measles and led to an abortion. She rationally maintained that this had been the best medical determination; fetal examinations had confirmed the fact that the fetus had been adversely affected by her illness. Unfortunately, since that time she had developed an acidic intrauterine medium. Her own words were, "I am killing my husband's sperm. My uterus has developed an acid medium."

We decided to use images to work with her uterus and discovered that she saw maternity in orange and yellow colors, understanding it as protection, shelter, smoothness, and tenderness, but also as something that was in the distant past. She saw in black and white the physicians and the surgical board where the abortion had been performed and where she viewed herself as at the mercy of others, feeling sorrow, desperation, impotence, hopelessness, fear and loss. And last, she saw very near and in dark red her uterus which had been attacked by herself and was now active, negative, and with a strong drive for counterattacking. We contacted her uterus and encouraged it to express its pain for something that it described as the wickedness done against it and its rage which gave rise to the destruction it was now carrying out.

In our last session she translated her feelings into the following words: "I am calm, like a woman dressed in light colors."

I didn't see her for some time. This year she telephoned and told me that she was pregnant. She has since given birth to a beautiful baby, named Carolina Andrea.

This was another cycle that closed itself.

REFERENCES

Beahrs, J. (1982). Understanding Erickson's approach. In J. Zeig (Ed.), *Ericksonian Approaches to Hypnosis and Psychotherapy.* New York: Brunner/Mazel.

Carter, P. (1982). Almost 1984. In J. Zeig (Ed.), *Ericksonian Psychotherapy*, Vol. I. New York: Brunner/Mazel.

Erickson, K. (1985). Foreword. In Stephen Lankton (Ed.), *Ericksonian Monograph No. 1*. New York: Brunner/Mazel.

Erickson, M. H. (1948). Hypnotic psychotherapy. *The Medical Clinics of North America* (pp. 571–584). New York: W. B. Saunders Co.

Erickson, M. H. (1979). First International Congress on Ericksonian Approaches to Hypnosis and Psychotherapy (Conference brochure), Phoenix: Milton H. Erickson Foundation, Inc.

Erickson, M., & Zeig, J. (1980). Symptom prescription for expanding the psychotic's world view. In E. Rossi (Ed.), *The Collected Papers of Milton H. Erickson, Vol. IV*. New York: Irvington.

Haley, J. (1973). *Uncommon Therapy: The Psychiatric Techniques of Milton H. Erickson.* New York: W. W. Norton & Co.

Haley, J. (1976). *Problem-Solving Therapy. New Strategies for Effective Family Therapy.* San Francisco: Jossey Bass.

Lankton, C. (1985). Elements of an Ericksonian approach. In S. Lankton (Ed.), *Ericksonian Monographs No. 1*. New York: Brunner/Mazel.

Lankton, S., & Lankton, C. (1983). *The Answer Within.* New York: Brunner/Mazel.

Masserman, J. (1968). Raíces histórico-comparativas y experimentales de la psicoterapia breve. In L. Wolberg (Ed.), *Psicoterapia Breve.* Madrid: Gredos.

Rossi, E. (Ed.) (1980). *The Collected Papers of Milton H. Erickson on Hypnosis, Vols. I–IV.* New York: Irvington.

Thompson, K. (1982). The curiosity of Milton H. Erickson. In J. Zeig (Ed.), *Ericksonian Approaches to Hypnosis and Psychotherapy.* New York: Brunner/Mazel.

Thompson, K. (1985). Almost 1984. In J. Zeig (Ed.), *Ericksonian Psychotherapy, Vol. I.* New York: Brunner/Mazel.

Watzlawick, P. (1985). Hypnotherapy without trance. In J. Zeig (Ed.), *Ericksonian Psychotherapy, Vol. I.* New York: Brunner/Mazel.

Wolberg, L. (Ed.) (1968). Psicoterapia Breve. Madrid: Gredos. Originally published in 1965 as *Short-Term Psychotherapy.* New York: Grune & Stratton.

Zalaquett, C. (Ed.) (1986a). Una conversación con Jeffrey Zeig acerca de la formación de psicoterapeutas. *Fotocopia Psicológica* (paper accepted for publication).

Zalaquett, C. (1986b). Un acercamiento a la perspectiva Ericksoniana, *Cuaderno No. 7*, Escuela de Psicología, Pontificia Universidad Católica de Chile, Santiago.

Zeig, J. (Ed.) (1980). *A Teaching Seminar with Milton H. Erickson.* New York: Brunner/Mazel.

Zeig, J. (Ed.) (1982). *Ericksonian Approaches to Hypnosis and Psychotherapy.* New York: Brunner/Mazel.

Zeig, J. (Ed.) (1985a). *Ericksonian Psychotherapy, Volumes I, II.* New York: Brunner/Mazel.

Zeig, J. (Ed.) (1985b). *Experiencing Erickson.* New York: Brunner/Mazel.

SECTION ONE: PRINCIPLES

PART V

Individuation

Chapter 14

The Patient's Silent Rules

Ernst G. Beier

Ernst G. Beier, Ph.D. (Columbia University), Emeritus Professor of Psychology at University of Utah, is internationally known for his contributions to psychotherapy, especially in the realm of nonverbal behavior. He is active in professional matters and has served as president of a division of the American Psychological Association, a Chairman of its convention board and on its council of Representatives. He has been President of the Utah Psychological Association and a member of The National Institute of Mental Health Small Grants Committee. He also has served on numerous educational boards. Beier's publications are prodigious. His two most famous books are The Silent Language of Psychotherapy *and* People Reading.

Silent rules are derived as a compromise of the conflicting drives between the need for conformity and the need for identity. As the therapist recognizes the hidden meaning of a given compromise and responds to it paradigmatically, the patient is able to benefit.

All of us learned early in childhood to make compromises between our needs for conformity and our needs for identity. Patients who have psychological problems are no different from anyone else in that respect. Where they do differ is that their compromises are used to excess or result in bizarre behavior.

For example, a bright boy has learned to resolve his discordant motivations between expressing his need for identity and his need for conformity in the following compromise: He attends all his classes in school (i.e., he is conforming—he is not a truant), but instead of doing the required work, he doodles. In that way, he expresses his rebellion against conformity. He is not yet a patient when he doodles only occasionally. But the frequency of expression suggests he may eventually become a patient. If he becomes preoccupied with his doodles and, as an adult, continues to doodle instead of working, he will be seen as having a problem. He has selected doodles to express his sense of identity, and he expresses it often. Typically, as an adult he will have no awareness of his failure in conforming. Instead, he might argue that, after all, he shows up for his job and does his work.

Another person might show us that he will be a patient by exhibiting bizarre behavior. A 14-year-old boy conforms by going to school, but for the second time this year has set fire to his wooden desk and then urinated on it to extinguish the blaze. Here we have no need for frequency. The boy's compromise of going to school and then rebelling with a bizarre behavior earned him the title of patient.

All of us have attached our sense of identity to behaviors and thought processes that differentiate us from others. Freud described the learning of the variety of sexual behaviors in adult life by referring to "polymorphous perverse development of sexuality" during the first 10 years of life. This concept is instructive because it maintains that during these early years the child will attach his sense of pleasure to any possible behavior in order to experience that pleasure. Whenever this attachment (cathexis) is successful, the behavior to which the sexual impulse became attached will be sexualized in the adult. With this concept, we can understand the vast variety of pleasures people seek.

A similar development probably takes place with regard to the concept of identity. Just as in pleasure seeking, in seeking identity the young child learns to attach the feelings of being a person in his own right to certain types of behavior that are open to him. For example, a young boy is asked by his father to paint a garden fence. The boy does not like to paint the fence, but does not dare to rebel against his father. The father asked him to paint the fence, and the boy feels he has to conform to his father's wish. In order to express his identity, however, he also has to express his dissatisfaction with the required duty.

The result of these two motivational forces within the boy are largely determined by the history of interaction between the boy and his father. The boy already knows that simply saying "No" results in a beating. He also knows that if he accidentally spills the paint he will also get a beating. In other words, he has learned that father does not accept that type of accident as an excuse. This is not a conscious process in the boy. He simply "feels" that he cannot get away with these behaviors. He might have learned that stepping on his father's toes "accidentally" might result in a beating as well. For that matter, he would get the same results should he do a careless job of painting. He also has learned that just making a suffering face will be insufficient to persuade father to relent in his demands. Father is not sensitive to facial expressions. However, this boy has learned that when he hurts, when he is in pain, his father will relent from his demands. Therefore, it is quite possible that the boy will counter the demands for conformity by stumbling and hurting himself. In other words, he will attach his sense of identity to accident-proneness. This will become a silent rule in dealing with future demands. Originally, it was based on the boy's belief that father cannot conceive that anyone would willingly hurt himself to get out of a job.

Both a sense of identity and a sense of conformity are involved in this compromise. He hurts, but he has also shown his willingness to do the required task. Children learn very early in life to which behaviors they should attach a sense of identity in order to make a compromise between the two conflicting motivations. Some of these compromises occur when there are important issues involved, i.e., when they become "monumental." At this point, these compromises lead to silent rules which involve intense feelings and will govern the person's life.

A small girl may have learned that her mother hates even a modest attachment to father. Every time she is even close to father, mother comes between her and her father. This girl may develop a seductive style to express her identity. At the same time, she might say that she hates men, expressing the demands made on her by mother. The competitive feeling with mother may result in this particular compromise and consequently become a silent rule in the woman's life.

A compromise results in "half satisfaction" for each of the two conflicting motivations. That is why we cling to our compromises. Freud speaks of a sense of resistance to giving up one's problems and a sense of pleasure in the symptom. It is never a full pleasure, rather a half-pleasure, as there are conflicting motivations that are often mutually exclusive. It is true that most patients want to get rid of their problems when they come to a psychotherapist. But, the first thing the psycho-therapist must recognize is that their life-style also includes important half-satisfactions. The therapist has to learn to understand the silent rules which govern the person and the satisfactions that these silent rules give the person. It is because of the fact that silent rules give satisfaction that they are difficult to resolve. Silent rules give a person stability even though they may cause pain.

The critical issue is that a given compromise may become so monumental in a person's life that he becomes dominated by it. A person who is thoroughly depressed still might be in a bind of cross-motivations, not discounting the importance of concomitant physiology. Life is extremely unhappy for this person, yet there is likely to be gratification involved in that life-style. Perhaps this person in his past has learned to arouse guilt in others by expressing aggression in a passive way. It is the reward in the message of depression that maintains this symptom.

In another example, a young man had learned to cope with heavy social expectations by withdrawing into silence. He had attached his sense of identity to silence while at the same time maintaining his social interactions to the best of his ability. Before attaching silence behavior to his sense of identity, he had probably tried many different ways of dealing with social demands made on him, including becoming sickly, sulky, aggressive, or even destructive. None of these responses had the desired results. Apparently, it was the withdrawal into silence which had the desired impact. He could stay in a situation, conform, and at the same time, produce anger in the other person.

After he married, he became totally withdrawn and depressed while staying with his wife. It was noteworthy that this behavior occurred only in the presence of his wife, and not outside of the home. His silence drove his wife to helpless anger, as it probably was designed to do. The silent rule was operating; with this compromise, he could stay in the marriage, i.e., he could conform and yet maintain his identity. When the man began to carry his compromise outside of marriage, including in his job, his life became so stressful that he sought therapeutic help.

The expression of these compromises differs in length. A compromise can even be expressed in a single discordant message. For example, a person may giggle out loud when talking about his grief concerning a loved relative's death. Here, we have a direct discordant response, utilizing different channels of nonverbal expression. A compromise of longer duration is seen in a woman who compulsively seeks out situations which she can leave with a sense of making a "grand exit." Here, the compromise does not appear as a single message, but involves a brief action pattern that has a beginning and an end. In order to make a "grand exit," the lady has first to enter somewhere and establish herself. Only then can she walk out in a meaningful way.

A compromise that is a silent rule can extend, also, over a longer time. There is a man who had developed a complex system which involved him in five marriages in three years. He would woo a beautiful woman, bring her gifts, treat her with great care and love, be interested in her and be interesting to her, always showing a great deal of warmth. When she consented to marry him, he would go through with the marriage, bring her to his beautiful home, give her love and money—and then refuse further contact. He would no longer seek sexual contact, slept in a different room, and generally avoid her. The newlywed lady would at first be puzzled, then become angry. In due time, perhaps after some arguments, she would either threaten to leave, seek an affair, or actually run away.

The man followed this pattern in five marriages. After each episode, he felt deeply rejected by his wife and thought that he had nothing to do with the fact that he was rejected. He claimed he was innocent, that he was a concerned husband who had given his wife his love, his caring, his property. Women simply were not to be trusted. Even after his fifth divorce, he still maintained a self-concept of a sweet, caring husband, who was just a little busy. To the observer, it became clear that he was following a silent rule in which wooing and winning were important, but holding on and maintaining was downplayed in favor of experiencing rejection. This fixed pattern lasted for an average time of seven months.

His compromise gave him a sense of what I have called "delicious joy." He started out by being a gracious, wooing person, but ended up feeling betrayed and rejected. It turned out that he relived with his fixed pattern a monumental experience of joy and disappointment he had originally experienced with his mother. He would not have sought help but for the fact that his last wife had given birth to a son, a situation which was not accounted for in his fixed-action pattern.

How can silent rules be discovered? The most adequate way of understanding the silent rules a patient is operating by is by understanding the emotional expectations which are directed at the therapist during the therapeutic hour. The emotional expectations have to do with the type of emotional climate a patient is trying to elicit in the therapist. These expectations are expressed through nonverbal cues as well as with words.

All of us are skilled in creating in another person certain emotional climates that serve our purposes. As we stated earlier, we call a patient a patient when he uses his silent rules with high frequency or in a bizarre manner. He will use all his skill to elicit the type of emotional climate in the therapist which is most significant to him. One can assume that it is the silent rule which gets the patient into trouble.

There are, of course, a large variety of cues, each arousing a different emotional climate in a given respondent. These climates may range from simply attempting to bore the respondent with monotonous and conventional language to displaying violent emotions, such as love, hate, jealousy or anger. The patient will try to involve the therapist with these emotional bids, and when he is successful in obtaining the expected response, he will simply maintain his previous behavior pattern.

Among the many cues used by the patient will be facial expressions, eye contact or the lack of it, posture, gesture, the way he dresses, the way he washes, the way he touches himself, and, of course, the way he uses language, both nonverbal and vocal. He will try hard to elicit the emotional climate in the therapist which will permit him to reexperience a compromise he has made early in life. The emotional climate he is trying to create gives the disengaged observer information about the patient's vulnerability. Once the therapist understands the emotional climate the patient is seeking, he has the foundation to understand the patient's silent rules. The patient is most likely to use in the therapeutic session the silent rule which has gotten him into trouble elsewhere. And so, the therapist can discover early just where the patient hurts.

I once supervised a graduate student in clinical psychology who was working with a patient in the V.A. After his first hour, he came to see me and stated that he could not tolerate seeing that patient again. I got out of my chair, reached for his hand, shook it, and congratulated him that, within one hour, he had discovered the silent rule of his patient, at least the most predominant one. He had not yet sufficiently disengaged from the elicited emotional climate. He was still angry and still experiencing the feelings designed for him. He had to learn to disengage and discover the sort of cues the patient had used to make him angry.

We already know that the therapist should not permit himself to be angry or to reject the patient at this point, as this would only help the patient to maintain his problem. (We shall discuss the choice of a response in more detail later on.) The patient is often successful in emotionally engaging the therapist, particularly during the first hour, because the information given by the patient is in his territory, his battlefield. The therapist will become engaged; he cannot stay disengaged at all times. The therapist eventually has to use himself as an instrument, recognize the emotional climate offered to him by the patient, and discover the cues the patient is using for that end. The patient is likely to have had thousands of trials of using his cues. He has learned to arouse the type of emotional climate he needs with many different persons. He also knows how to impact the therapist.

When my student got angry at the patient, the question may be asked: To what extent did his anger come from his own experience? This is an important question and a good therapist should know his own predispositions in order to discount them. My student's feelings were not countertransference, nor were they deep-seated problems. It was more like what I have called "social transference" phenomena, a concept which is based on the observation that we all know how to use language and nonverbal cues to impact others in our culture. If we yell, we probably arouse attention. If we draw a gun, we probably arouse fear. It is the conventional use of cues in a given culture that is the basis of engagement processes. It is plausible to assume that the patient impacts the therapist as he impacts others. Most frequently, the patient is not aware of the impact he has on others, and most frequently he will not admit that he is motivated. The V.A. patient, for example, would not admit that he wants to make people angry and reject him.

The psychotherapist will learn about the patient's silent rules by using himself as an instrument, and he will analyze the social transference or engagement pattern. In a self-analysis, the therapist will ask: "How does this patient make me feel?", or alternatively, "How does the patient want me to feel?" The therapist must have a sense of self-awareness, a way of knowing just what his own contribution to experiencing this emotion might be. When he has identified the nature of the patient's impact, he now has the tools to help the patient to discover new choices.

All useful responses of the therapist act in three major ways: 1) They give the patient a sense of hope; 2) They create in the patient a sense of uncertainty (by extinguishing the customary and expected responses of the patient); and 3) They shift some sense of responsibility to the patient so that he can feel responsible for his own statements and actions. We can learn from Erickson that the tools of the psychotherapist are not effective when the therapist simply tries to provide insight or share his discoveries of the silent rules with the patient. In the processes of communication analysis, this sharing would probably be of little value, as it might have an entirely different meaning to the patient from that planned for him by the therapist. There is reason to believe that these insight-producing responses are likely to be perceived by the patient as helpful, but are also demands for greater dependency because the therapist knows so much more about the patient than the patient does himself.

There is one advantage to producing insight. It helps to clarify the therapist's own thinking. Insight also keeps the patient's interest alive; everyone wants to learn more about himself. However, rather than centering his attention on giving insight, the therapist should use effective tools to interrupt the use of the patient's silent rules.

The student therapist described earlier went back into the therapeutic hour and began to understand the patient's use of cues which were designed to elicit anger. It would not have been sufficient for the young therapist simply to tell the patient that he had recognized the nature of these cues. This would have resulted in an intellectual discussion rather than a significant impact on the patient.

After using himself as an instrument and recognizing his own sensation of anger, the young therapist will try to formulate responses which would communicate to the patient that disengagement has taken place. I have called these maneuvers of the therapist "unexpected responses" because they do not fall into the expectancy pattern of the patient. When a patient sends cues to a therapist to make him angry, the therapist could formulate a hypothesis about this. The existential facts are that this patient comes for help and yet spends his time to engage the therapist in feelings which are not much suited for giving help and, in fact, may result in rejection. From these existential facts, the therapist could hypothesize that the patient perceives someone whom he himself seeks out for help as a good object for a love test: "By my throwing in obstacles, I can test you and see how much you really want to help me." Such a hypothesis about a silent rule may be supported by further evidence, revised, or even rejected. But once such a hypothesis is assumed to be correct, the therapist will try to counter the automatic way with which it is being used.

To the casual listener, the silent rule mentioned here may sound insignificant, and perhaps not pertinent to the illness of the patient. However, if we assume that the use of this silent rule is automatic, we can recognize that the patient's testing behavior is likely to be of great importance, representing an element of the patient's lifestyle.

Now, the therapist would give responses to arouse "beneficial uncertainty" in the patient. All patients, including those who are thinking of themselves as anxious and uncertain, have painted themselves into a corner, a small and limited area in life where they feel certain and at home. The reduction in accepting uncertainty about the world may produce pain and suffering, but they want to maintain their little area of certainty where they can fully predict possible expectancies. They are not open to new information pertaining to that area (that is why advice does not work), nor are they able to learn. The unexpected response given by a caring and noncritical therapist can break into this limited area of certainty. It can give the patient new courage, and a sense of exploration and creativity. Beneficial uncertainty is a precondition for making new choices.

Unexpected responses are well established tools in the psychotherapeutic community. I divide the unexpected responses into three major types. Mini-responses such as nodding one's head or saying "uh huh" are the simplest forms of responses which, in a mild way, arouse uncertainty, provide responsibility to go on talking, and give the patient some hope of getting out of the quagmire of getting cornered. Midi-responses are more complex. They require that the therapist be more knowledgeable about the patient. For a midi-response, he would re-word the content or reflect the feelings of the patient's statement, and in that manner provide for the patient a sense of caring (increased hope), shift responsibility to the patient to expand further, and arouse uncertainty by withholding the expected response.

A somewhat rarer response is the paradigmatic or maxi-response, which has to be used sparingly because it helps to create a great deal of uncertainty. It conveys much hope and represents a significant shift of responsibility to the patient. In fact maxi-responses can be thought of as responses which often result in one trial learning. Here Erickson was particularly useful in leading the way.

A maxi-response is totally unexpected. It is a paradigmatic response and has to be stated in that manner; it cannot be a message representing the therapist's opinion. The paradigmatic response voices the underside of the patient's motivation, the very motivation the patient wants to hide. The response obviously has to be given carefully. A fairly common paradigmatic response is to tell a stutterer that, instead of improving his condition, he should stutter at least two hours at a time at high speed, or to instruct a patient who complains about fears that he should dwell on them often, not solely in the evening.

A patient said to a therapist, "I know you only see me for the money anyway," to which the therapist responded with a smile, "Why would anyone want to see a son of a bitch like you except for the money?" With a paradigmatic response, the therapist takes the wind out of the patient's emotional demand. It is a risky response because it may be misunderstood. The patient who believes he has been addressed seriously could become angry and the therapist should be prepared to dissolve any such misunderstanding. He should know his next move before he even starts using a paradigmatic response.

When we analyze a paradigmatic response, we find it is a maximal response with which to create hope, arouse uncertainty, and shift responsibility to the patient. It arouses uncertainty because it is totally unexpected, it creates hope because it is essentially a game response which, like humor and play, lessens the severity of the problem and shifts responsibility back to the patient because it tells him that his hidden motivation has become visible.

The process is similar to the one used by Alcoholics Anonymous. When the alcoholic is complaining that he hates to drink, the A.A. counselor tells him to admit that he really loves to drink. The patient has used drinking, and his statement that he hates to drink as a compromise of discordant motivation. By alerting the patient that everyone who continuously drinks obviously loves to drink, the A.A. counselor removes this convenient solution and forces the alcoholic to explore himself. By recognizing the hidden meaning of a given compromise and responding to it paradigmatically, the patient gets a very significant experience.

Such a response can be useful only when the setting in which it occurs is seen as being beneficial. If there is even the lightest hint of coercion or anger in the therapist's voice, the response is highly counterproductive. In such a case, the patient will misunderstand the intent of the therapist and get angry. No one allows others to uncover hidden meaning unless it is done with caring and without threat. If the patient misunderstands the therapist's response to his "I know you only see me for the money" statement, the therapist may end up with a black eye.

In the game of bridge, you should know your next bid before you make the first. In the paradigmatic response, you have to know how to respond to a possible misunderstanding. In the case cited, the patient may angrily respond: "You are calling me a son of a bitch." Upon this misunderstanding of his intention, the therapist should bring the relationship back into the therapeutic climate. The therapist should not apologize since an apology implies that he in fact had meant his statement as an insult. The therapist may respond with, "If I wanted only money, would I offend my customers?" Said with a smile, this may defuse the moment. Such a response implies a change of meaning altogether. The therapist creates a different emotional climate, tying his response to the patient's original message.

Erickson was a master of using the paradigmatic response. Erickson would send patients to climb a mountain or use hypnosis to bring across other metaphoric, symbolic exposures. Any of these maxi-responses is likely to create a maximum sense of uncertainty, because the consequences are unknown, create hope, represent an almost playful exploration, and shift responsibility for a solution to the problem to the patient. These responses do not have any inherent value, but they are messages, good-intentioned and unexpected. Technically speaking, these paradigmatic responses are effective extinction responses, in line with classical learning theory. As we can learn from animal studies, they may result in additional hard trials involving the behavior to be extinguished, but over time, extinction of the behavior will occur, or at least reduction in its frequency.

A beneficial climate in psychotherapy is established not simply by a friendly look or by the therapist's demeanor. The beneficial aspects of the therapeutic relationship are established message by message. The therapist's responses must show that he is caring, that he is listening, that he understands the patient's motivations, and that he is competent to provide for changes. In the following, I shall illustrate the concept of understanding the motivations of the patient.

A therapist counsels with a family where father is very upset about his son and uses all means of intimidating him. He yells and curses, and threatens to kick his son out. All this while mother is crying, "Please, Dad! Please, Dad! Don't do that!" The son, who had been engaged in several delinquent acts, is enjoying it all with obvious defiance on his face. The therapist gets up from his chair, goes over to the father, reaches for his hand. Then, he congratulates him and says: "I have never seen a man who is so concerned to be a good father and tries so hard to educate his son to be a good citizen. I want to let you know that I recognize your love for your son. Unfortunately, while your heart is in the right place, the methods you are using to teach your son are not very effective. So let's change them."

The father is quite shaken by this statement, but he is ready to explore new alternatives in dealing with his son because he has been understood, at least partially. Someone called this type of intervention the "alchemy of Erickson's work." He knew how to convey to the patient that his motivation might be very sound, but his methods would need improvement. Maxi, or paradigmatic, responses given in a beneficial climate can cut a large number of hours off the treatment process.

Erickson is known for his intuitive innovations in psychotherapy and hypnosis. There is generally a lack of theoretical conceptualization for his work. Communication analysis may provide such a theoretical underpinning. Within this theory, we assume that the therapist tries to understand the conflicting motivational forces operating within the patient. From this understanding, he formulates the silent rules by which the patient is guided and which are resulting in the compromises the individual has made. In order to provide the patient with new choices, the therapist will utilize significant, unexpected responses beyond the standard tools of listening. With those, he will create beneficial uncertainty and will interrupt the automatic functioning of the patient's silent rules. Hypnosis is an especially useful climate for this. In communication analysis, it is seen as a condition where the patient can temporarily "park" his sense of responsibility for his behavior with the therapist. The therapist can use this vacuum to suggest the exploration of new choices. While the conceptualization presented here is still tentative, it may be a start to translating the fundamental experiencing in Ericksonian writing into the rules governing it.

REFERENCES

Barker, P. (1985). *Using Metaphors in Psychotherapy.* New York: Brunner/Mazel.
Beier, E. G., & Young, D. M. (1984). *The Silent Language of Psychotherapy, 2nd Ed.* New York: Aldine.
Beier, E. G., & Valens, E. G. (1975). *People Reading.* New York: Stein & Day.
Erickson, M. H. (1980). *Innovative Psychotherapy. Collected Papers, Vol. IV.* L. Rossi, Ed. New York: Irvington.
Haley, J. (1973). *Uncommon Therapy: The Psychiatric Techniques of Milton H. Erickson, M.D.* New York: Norton.

Chapter 15

Individuation: Alone Together

Michael D. Yapko

Michael D. Yapko, Ph.D. (United States International University), practices clinical psychology in San Diego, California, where he is also Director of the Milton H. Erickson Institute of San Diego. Recently Dr. Yapko assumed the position of Editor of the Erickson Foundation Newsletter.

Yapko authored Trancework: An Introduction to Clinical Hypnosis *and* When Living Hurts: Directives for Treating Depression, *and edited* Hypnotic and Strategic Interventions: Principles and Practice. *He is a member of the Editorial Board of the* Ericksonian Monographs.

Individuation is the process of developing uniqueness. Six strategies are presented for facilitating this process.

Everybody has got to figure out experience for himself. I'm sorry. I realize that most people require externalized, objective symbols to hang on to. That's too bad. Because what they are looking for, whether they know it or not, is internalized and subjective. There are no group solutions! Each individual must work it out for himself. There are guides, all right, but even the wisest guides are blind in your section of the burrow. No, all a person can do in this life is to gather about him his integrity, his imagination and his individuality—and with these ever within him, out front and in sharp focus, leap into the dance of experience. (Robbins, 1976, p. 227)

A cornerstone of Ericksonian approaches to hypnosis and psychotherapy is Milton H. Erickson's guiding belief that "each person is unique." This chapter considers the relationship between personal values and the degree of autonomy one attains. Six strategies are presented that have been used successfully with clients experiencing difficulty in discovering and asserting their uniqueness as individuals. These strategies actively involve the client in assignments that permit a safe exploration of one's inner self. Greater self-awareness and self-acceptance are made possible when one can recognize and effectively use one's personal resources.

Psychotherapy is one arena in which the uniqueness of each person can easily become lost in a number of ways: 1) in the simplistic diagnosis of disorders according to a manual that is not particularly responsive to individual subjective experience, but rather is oriented to labeling symptomatic pattern clusters; 2) in the fitting of the client to the therapy rather than the reverse (accomplished primarily through the teaching of the language and concepts of the therapist's preferred theory concerning people's problems); and 3) through the intentional or unintentional imposition of the therapist's values and expectations on a client in an effort to control his/her thoughts, feelings or actions, in essence demanding conformity rather than accepting and rewarding individual differences.

The major underlying framework for subjective experience is that of "individuation," which has been defined in many ways: as the analytic, differentiating process in the person's development toward a stable unity (Jung, 1953), as the sense of psychosocial well-being produced by acceptance of one's appearance, clear goals, and recognition by others (Erikson, 1963), and as the ability to deal effectively with divisive polarities arising in the various developmental transitions of life (Levinson, 1980).

For the purposes of this chapter, individuation is defined as the awareness of, acceptance of, and acting upon those dimensions of self that define one as a unique, autonomous human being. This definition implies: 1) awareness of one's own thoughts, feelings, and behaviors, 2) acceptance of these as valid representations of one's self and one's experience, 3) their identification as separate, internal experiences existing within the boundaries of self, and 4) their serving as the basis for making choices in the course of daily living.

Individuation may be viewed as existing on a continuum, with the ambiguously-defined "self-actualized" person at one end and the chameleon-like borderline personality at the other. Self-actualization implies an inner-directed, efficient way of relating to ongoing experience. At the other extreme, the borderline individual has little or no sense of self so that whatever sense of self there is tends to be acquired through a "mirroring" process of mimicking the company one keeps. By examining the personality dynamics of those showing an extreme lack of individuation, treatment strategies for individuals who show blocks in attaining individuation to a lesser degree may be developed.

The concern of this chapter is in how the clinician can identify and treat the individual for whom issues of individuation are prominent enough to be troublesome, but not so prominent as to be diagnosed as personality disordered. Specifically, how can the clinician provide a context in which this type of client can discover, accept, and, most importantly, live effectively with him or herself?

There is a paradox evident in this line of thinking. The goal is individual autonomy, yet it is to be discovered in the context of a relationship in which the client is dependent on the clinician for directives. Is this dependency, used as a vehicle to independence, an unresolvable paradox? No, if one accepts each element of the paradox on its own terms. One can balance dependency as an inevitable part of existing in a world with other human beings with the autonomy that is reflected in the observation that no matter how interconnected we ever become with others, we are inevitably and ultimately alone in facing the events of our individual lives. No matter how much someone may love me or care for me, if *I* break my leg, *I* must wear the cast.

When component aspects of individuation are each valued as vital, each can be considered "alone together." In the relationship between clinician and client, who work "alone together," the dependency is idealistically one of a transient nature as is often the case in relationships. In a relationship, individual boundaries may become less clearly defined; at worst, a pathological enmeshment occurs. In such instances, mutual involvement can be intense and seem desirable or necessary to the involved parties. Later, a shift may occur at some level that precludes the relationship's continuance. This occurs in professional as well as personal relationships.

Haley (1973, 1984) provided a perspective on therapy in this light: That the person is even in therapy is a problem, and the goal is to get the person out of therapy. Progress can thus be measured in terms of when the client has reached a sufficient degree of individuation to no longer be interested in sustaining a dependent, reactive relationship with the clinician. The termination of a successful therapeutic relationship is evidence that the client has reached a level of individuation sufficient to accept and manage the ongoing interplay between self and the world.

Much of what occurs in the natural course of psychotherapy that facilitates individuation is the simple giving of permission. One manifestation of inadequate individuation is the excessive seeking of permission; another is the seeking of an acceptable justification by the client for behaving as desired. For example, a client may feel that a divorce is necessary and yet take no action to dissolve the relationship because of the inability to find a "good reason" that is personally acceptable. The result is a growing anxiety and a dread for the future that might well lead the individual to seek therapy. Through support for the client's feelings and a professional's different perspective about the indication and contraindication for divorce, the client may well receive permission to take action. What makes this typical scenario one reflecting a lesser degree of individuation is that self-validation is not sufficient grounds for action in doing what one perceives as being in one's own best interests. When one's choices are governed by guilt, intimidation, passivity, and other such controlling tactics, one is reactive rather than proactive. Individual choice is lost, at least temporarily, and the effect is one of giving up an aspect of one's self. The goal in facilitating individuation is to help clients maximize their range of choices and integrate their many aspects.

In a previously published chapter on the role of values in Ericksonian psychotherapy (Yapko, 1985a), the recognition of values as the basis for interpreting and relating to ongoing experience was briefly discussed. Values become the filter through which experience is subjectively evaluated. Values stabilize an organized sense of self. Values maintain one's sense of reality and apparently do not take kindly to efforts to tamper with them ("resistance"). Values enhance or restrict one's range of choices. Value systems, or the lack thereof, lead one to construct or seek out self-validating experiences, creating a self-supporting (even though possibly dysfunctional) system.

With the obvious role of values in the formation and maintenance of a sense of self, it seems equally obvious that values may also play a significant role in the *lack* of a sense of self. How does the socialization process facilitate such a condition? The value-based, subjective frame of reference used to interpret ongoing realities is limited by the range and quality of experiences one has. As will be discussed in the next section, specific values may be integrated which may preclude the full formation of an individual identity.

THE POTENTIAL FOR DEVALUING INDIVIDUATION

Elliot Aronson described what he called "the state of tension between values associated with individuality and values associated with conformity" (1984, p. 13). He pointed out that there are two main reasons why people generally conform to others: 1) In order to avoid punishment (i.e., rejection or disapproval) and gain rewards (i.e., acceptance or approval), and 2) as a reference point for determining the course of action to take at a given point in time. Aronson wrote that "when physical reality becomes increasingly uncertain, people rely more and more on 'social reality'—that is, they are more likely to conform to what other people are doing, not because they fear punishment from the group but because the group's behavior supplies them with valuable information about what is expected of them" (Aronson, 1984, pp. 25–26).

There is much literature in the field of social psychology that describes states of "deindividuation," those transient states of fusion with others characterized by perceived anonymity, inhibition of social conscience, and heightened impulsivity, as well as other related, identity-diffusing variables (Aronson, 1984; Goldstein, 1980). Throughout the literature describing what are only transient deindividuated episodes, there are many clues as to the types of circumstances that might engender an ongoing state of deindividuation. With a high level of responsiveness of individuals to others around them as a basic component of the socialization process, it is not difficult to imagine the social forces pulling and pushing one to the point of losing any (or never gaining any) genuine sense of self.

There are a number of arenas in which this type of ongoing deindividuating force has been explored, including politics (debates over the real or imagined consequences of socialism) and philosophy. In *Anthem* (1946), author and philosopher Ayn Rand described a futuristic society structured upon a collective identity. The words "I," "me," "my," and "mine" had disappeared from the vocabulary, so that even in reference to one's own self one would say "our," "us," or "we." One's own body is "our body," one's own face is "our face," and it is "we" who are thirsty. In the following passage, the story's main character, a person named Equality 7-2521, describes the order of things in his world devoid of individuals.

We strive to be like all our brother men, for all men must be alike. Over the portals of the Palace of the World Council, there

are words cut in the marble, which we repeat to ourselves whenever we are tempted: *"We are one in all and all in one. There are
no men but only the great WE, One, indivisible and forever."* (pp.
13–14)

Is the notion of a collective identity so far removed from social reality?
Many are socialized intensively to believe that self-worth is a direct
function of one's worth to others. Certainly, a glaring example is the
traditional female socialization that discourages the attainment of a
career or education in favor of being "a good wife and mother." It
does not seem to be mere coincidence that significantly more women
are diagnosed as suffering from dependent personality disorders and
major depression considering the social push for becoming other-oriented that still exists, although in only a slightly more disguised form
today than in previous decades (Davison & Neale, 1986). The implicit
message is a value-laden one that is evident in the following common
statements:

"You're only as valuable as you make others feel."
"You got a 'good catch.' Do whatever you can to hold on."
"Being a wife and mother is the only true meaning of a woman's life."

When the most intensely socialized values emphasize a social identity
over an individual one, an obvious potential is present for confusion
in making choices. A classic "approach-avoidance" conflict surfaces,
perhaps intensely, that effectively paralyzes one's ability to sort things
out in an orderly manner. The result is confusion over the "best" or
"right" thing to do, and, as Aronson pointed out, what others are doing
then becomes the reference point for guiding one's own actions. This
is one way dependency on others can become a lifestyle (social set),
just as indecisiveness and poor problem-solving capabilities can establish
a dysfunctional cognitive pattern. The following statements are common
examples reflecting valuing others over oneself:

"You're 'always' thinking of yourself. How can you be so self-centered,
    so selfish?"
"No matter how little you have, you always have enough to share."
"Count your success in life by the number of those who love you."
"Self-sacrifice is the peak of maturity."
"A friend in need is a friend indeed."

"Be a team player."
"Don't rock the boat."

What reactions did you experience to each of these statements? Did you experience an easily-accepting, comfortable internal reaction, or a surge of rejecting negativity? Can you find any manipulative tactics in these conformity-inducing statements? It should be apparent that the potential for enforcing and reinforcing values associated with conformity is a great one. These values, when out of balance with values associated with autonomy, are a major inhibition of individuation. While Rand's *Anthem* is an extreme and thought-provoking context for considering the liabilities of a collective identity, most people do, in fact, have individual identities. For them, the conflicts associated with attaining and maintaining an individuated self are lived out on a day-to-day basis with an underlying tension that maintains the heightened emotionality of such ongoing conflicts.

In the face of what Aronson (1984) termed the "tensions" associated with balancing values associated with conformity and values associated with autonomy, the mechanism that most people seem to evolve in order to manage is that of "control." Overt and covert attempts to control others through manipulative tactics are well described in the literature. Individuals aspire to a more comfortable balance between meeting their own needs for personal satisfaction and meeting the needs of others in order to enjoy the many benefits of belonging to a group. While manipulative tactics may involve such common patterns as inducing guilt, the use of intimidation, strong defensive reactions, and withdrawal, the common denominator is a high level of reactivity to others to the point of inhibiting access to a broader range of choices.

It is this point, in particular, that is the general theme of this chapter, coupled with an underlying emphasis on developing perspectives and therapeutic strategies to facilitate clients' access to those dimensions of self potentially valuable as resources to use in specific contexts. Such resources become self-validating through experience. With an integration of those values that engender a recognition and acceptance of the inevitable differences between individuals, the negative manipulative efforts aimed at controlling others can diminish with positive results. Thus, a "live and let live" approach to life can emerge, clearly the sort of "accept and utilize" philosophy that so meaningfully characterizes the nature of the approaches described throughout this book. In the remainder of this chapter are statements regarding ways of translating these concepts into clinical practice.

INDIVIDUATION: ALONE TOGETHER IN THERAPY

Equality 7-2521 from Ayn Rand's *Anthem* would probably have been one of those "difficult clients" psychotherapists frequently describe. Most clients are not so extreme in their lack of individuation, but rather are functional, competent people who experience varying degrees of discomfort with themselves for the way they experience their lives. For some, conflict surfaces as relationship problems, e.g., value conflicts, dependency, and boundary issues, while for others it seems more confined to immediate subjective experience, e.g., depression or anxiety. In either instance, the interpersonal and systemic nature of the individual's problems may become evident to the clinician, who is inevitably using the interpersonal context of the therapeutic interaction as the vehicle of treatment.

Goals of Therapy

The guiding definition for individuation presented earlier in this chapter was "the awareness of, acceptance of, and acting upon those dimensions of self that define one as a unique, autonomous human being." Inherent in this definition, the goals of therapy include promoting awareness and acceptance of one's self. More specifically, the general goals of therapy can be identified as the following:

1. *Identifying specific values within a client that are indicative of uniqueness.* In many individuals, perhaps most, personal values already present within are in a repressed form and are simply in need of a vehicle like therapy to facilitate access to them. In those individuals, the prognosis is excellent. For a second group of individuals, the ambiguity is so great and the sense of self is sufficiently missing that the task before the clinician is that of building a human personality. Those individuals will require longer-term therapy, and the prognosis is less favorable.

In yet another group of clients, a preexisting set of personal values may be readily identified by the clinician, but the values are externally focused on others to the detriment of the client. Such individuals maintain a value system that inhibits awareness of one's own rights and needs, a value system that emphasizes an other-directed orientation. A critical examination of their values is required, which includes strengths and limitations, relative functionality in having access to desired goals, and the balance of rigidity or flexibility in permitting changes to occur.

For this third group of individuals, the prognosis is also an excellent one, for like the first type of individual with repressed value expression, these people are already painfully aware of the consequences of their patterns. They are motivated, but lack knowledge of how to become "unstuck" from the paralysis of the "approach-avoidance" conflict discussed earlier.

2. *Accepting identified values as valid for one's self.* How does one integrate values into a lifestyle pattern? In Massey's (1979) model, it is through the Significant Emotional Event. In an earlier consideration of Erickson's work (Yapko, 1985a), it is through "The Erickson Hook." In any event, it is through direct experience and the subsequent establishment of a new frame of reference that individuals discover the limitations of the previous frame of reference. They also experience the expanded range of relief-providing personal choices associated with the new frame of reference. In this particular phase, various strategic approaches are powerful in their ability to generate meaningful changes due to their emphasis on subjective experience and experiential learning. The need to "accept and utilize" the client's preexisting belief system as the basis for knowing when and where to introduce a therapeutic shift acceptable to the client is well described in Ericksonian literature.

3. *Translating values into multiple dimensions of experience, particularly behavior.* Observation of the individual interacting with the other components of his or her world system can indicate the acceptance and integration of a particular value or set of values. Unless there is a shift in the client's experience of self in previously established systemic patterns, it is not evident whether or not the value works in the client's favor. The client evolves a recognition for dimensions of subjective experience previously unknown or avoided. Perhaps because they were framed as "wrong" or "bad" in some way, they now may provide new opportunities to discover a variety of aspects of him or herself, the potentials of each, and how to live competently "alone together" with them.

Values in Facilitating Individuation

The paradoxical nature of facilitating individuation in the context of a dependent relationship was briefly discussed early in this chapter. Every psychotherapeutic methodology has an inherent value system dictating its range of practical applications. In this respect, strategic methods are not unique. However, they are unique in their often powerful statements regarding the value of subjective experience. Many of these same statements will be found with little variation in wording in the writings of Ericksonian practitioners. Stated succinctly, these value-laden perspectives may be summarized as follows:

1. Each person is unique.
2. The client's experience is valid for him or her.
3. Each person relates to ongoing experience from his or her own frame of reference.
4. Join the client at the client's frame of reference.
5. The unconscious mind is rich in resources, is patterned from experience, and has positive capabilities.
6. People make the best choice for themselves at any given moment.
7. Respect all messages from the client.
8. Teach choice; never attempt to take choice away.
9. The resources the client needs lie within his or her own personal history.
10. The explanation, theory, or metaphor used to relate facts about a person is not the person (Yapko, 1986a; Lankton & Lankton, 1983, p. 12).

It is clear that there is a strong emphasis in the Ericksonian approaches on the value of the individual. Certainly, such an underlying value continually reinforces a recognition of personal worth. The message is a consistent one that says, in essence, "You are important. Your feelings matter. Your needs have a right to be considered." When a client is in a vulnerable position, particularly at the start of formal treatment, the client is often uncertain that his or her concerns are justified. Recall the earlier discussion regarding how frequently clients simply seek permission as a therapeutic answer.

Therapies may inadvertently encourage dependency and inhibit individuation. *Even the therapist who does not intend to be powerful will be.* Remember what was said earlier about people conforming to the social reality evidenced in others when physical reality is ambiguous. The therapeutic relationship involves being "alone together," and can influence clients for better or for worse. Therapists need a healthy awareness of their own values and how they affect the psychotherapeutic process.

When the clinician and client are "alone together," this is a valid time to ask: Can the client *individuate* from the clinician? When the clinician rewards conformity, via approval or acceptance, to his or her own views rather than encouraging independent thinking, individuation is not possible. The double bind for the clinician is that there must be at least enough conformity from the client to have an alliance in dealing with the treatment issue. Early in this chapter it was pointed out that the goal must be to get the client successfully out of therapy.

In this regard, Erickson's utilization approach is most effective. Erickson engaged people intensely and yet maintained a respect for the individual's need to save face, and the need to resist simply following directives blindly. His methods of redefining resistance as cooperation ("utilization of resistance") and giving multiple directives simultaneously (some to be followed, some to be resisted) are examples of a clinician who, through his very interventions, took care to preclude the possibility of long-term dependent relationships in his therapies. Strategic therapy by its very nature is not ordinarily intended to involve long-term treatment. Rather, it is meant to build and access resources of independence, knowing that the real living takes place out in the world, not in the therapist's office.

STRATEGIES FOR FACILITATING INDIVIDUATION

In general, the goal in using strategic methods is to provide experiences that help clients build newer, more adaptive frames of reference as a basis for their life decisions. Many clinicians are directive in the sense that they may offer specific advice or ideas to the client, but they do not appreciate that without an experiential frame of reference, the client has little or no basis for relating meaningfully to the clinician's input. Strategic therapies provide for such experience.

Each of the strategies described in this section has been used successfully by the author with a variety of clients needing a greater degree of individuation. Each strategy has been pared down to a rather simple form for presentation. It is assumed that the reader can readily infer the more complex variables associated with conducting a psychotherapy that might include such strategies as these.

An Exercise in Values Identification or "Me Mapping"

One approach to facilitating the client's identifying personal values involves listing specific issues about which one might have an opinion. For example, one might list topics such as capital punishment, abortion, legalization of marijuana, premarital sex, pornography, family importance, and so forth, in the direction of increasingly personal issues. A continuum of opinions regarding each issue is charted, with opposite opinions at each pole. The client is then directed to establish a point on the continuum describing each "significant other" in his or her life (e.g., mother, father, siblings, spouse, etc.). After everyone else's position has been "mapped out," the client is then instructed to place his or her own position on the continuum. In this first phase, both the client and the clinician can learn quite a bit about where there are overlapping values with others, or perhaps an ambiguity of values in the client's world. Virtually any positioning by the client, including no position, offers valuable input for treatment.

In the second phase, the client is instructed to map out 1) *specific* behaviors one would engage in if one were to "live" out that particular value, and 2) *specific* behaviors one would *not* engage in if one were to hold such a value. The client thus begins to evolve a cognitive framework for new experiences. This is consistent with the guiding definition for individuation given earlier that includes an awareness of one's own personal values. Other "values clarification" exercises are available in a variety of sources, some of which are listed in this chapter's references.

The Polling Ploy

One of the ways a client can discover the diversity of thought on value-laden issues is through the task assignment of conducting an informal poll. The client is directed to poll acquaintances or strangers, depending on which will have greater potential therapeutic value. The client is instructed to ask those polled in a neutral manner their position on issues that are particularly relevant to the client's problems, and to further seek out a brief rationale on the part of the person offering a perspective. The recognition that different people can have virtually opposite opinions on an issue and yet have what can be perceived as adequate justification for their opposing positions can enable the client to more easily accept his or her own values. The "approach-avoidance" conflict and ensuing paralysis can be minimized when the client discovers there is no need to fear being "wrong."

The Two-Faced Debate Assignment

In this task assignment, the client is asked to engage others in a discussion or debate regarding a specific issue. The client is instructed to continue the discussion over a period of time, and to switch to polar positions every 10 or 15 minutes. Thus, arguing in favor of a position is immediately followed by a period of arguing against a position, and so on repeatedly. The client is directed to notice which side of the issue is easier to assume and the feelings that accompanied both positions. This exercise provides the opportunity to directly experience conflict in a controlled atmosphere, the limitations of ambivalence, the justifications evident in either view, and the possibility that the client *really does* have an opinion rooted in personal values. For the type of individual who was described earlier as being ambiguous and lacking in a sense of self, this directive has been particularly valuable.

Metaphors Enhancing Individuation

More general in scope than the previous strategies, there are countless specific metaphors that can describe the evolution of self and the validity of self. Erickson (Zeig, 1980) offered many in the course of his teachings, two of which will be mentioned here. The first concerns his metaphorical discussion of how the infant discovers parts of its own body in early stages of development:

> Now, one thing about a child is that he is unacquainted with his body. He doesn't know that his hands are his. He doesn't know that he is moving them. He doesn't recognize his knees or his feet. They are just objects. So he has to feel them over and over again. And learning to recognize your body is really a difficult thing. (Zeig, 1980, pp. 235–6)

A second metaphorical example may be derived by describing to clients the case study Erickson offered regarding his patient named Will (Zeig, 1980, pp. 97–103). Will suffered terror when interacting with women. Through Erickson's unusual treatment methods, Will's terror of women evolved into a healthy assertiveness with his own mother, the lack of which had been the major dynamic in his problem. Describing Will, or clients like Will, in the context of a therapeutic metaphor can stimulate the associations necessary to begin evolving a sense of individuation.

The principles for formulating and delivering metaphors appropriate to the client's unique capabilities and needs have been well described (Lankton & Lankton, 1983; Gordon, 1978). In this instance, the general themes of establishing a sense of self and protecting it from intrusive demands and expectations of others is a basis for construction of appropriate metaphors. For example, with one client the author treated who had an interest in nature, it was particularly useful to offer a metaphor concerning the ongoing battle between conservationists and land developers. Embedded in the metaphor were suggestions for being able to *quickly understand the motives* for the developers' attempts to turn the natural beauty of scenic forestland into a shopping center, and for being able to *preserve one's own interest* in the face of those who would do damage to the environment in the name of selfish interests.

Another metaphor that builds on a point Massey (1979) made in his book *The People Puzzle* concerns differences in values regarding appropriate use of money across generations. Massey pointed out that the great majority of older Americans do not use credit cards, do not tend to spend money on leisure, and place a high value on financial security derived from their "value programming" during the Depression. Massey further pointed out that younger people tend to use credit freely, spend considerably on leisure, and generally place less value on saving for a later time. Using this information as a basis for introducing a metaphor concerning a value conflict between a grandfather and grandson, one might say something such as:

> . . . and you can imagine the 30-year-old grandson coming home and telling his 75-year-old grandfather that he'd taken his family to Disneyland that day and had lots of fun . . . and when grandfather asks how much he spent, and grandson replies "$200," one can easily understand how grandfather could become upset, even angry, at the seeming waste of so much money on a day of fun and games that leaves nothing to show for the money . . . but was it wrong for the grandson to spend the money on his family for a day at Disneyland? . . . What if he is unsure of his feelings about having gone? How will he react to his grandfather? What if he is confident he got his money's worth? . . . and you really can see how no one can know what's best for you the way you do . . . even when it's a loving grandfather . . . who sees the world from a different angle than you do . . . and why not enjoy being the ultimate authority on *you* . . . after all, no one will ever know your inner world the way that you do. . . .

As the client accesses answers to the rhetorical questions embedded in the metaphor, there is an opportunity to discover that each person's values are "right" *for him or her*. It is a part of the learning process of therapy to recognize and accept that whatever position one takes, there will be those who offer support, those who offer criticism, and those who just don't care. A metaphor such as the above helps build a resource of being able to withstand criticism or even rejection by those who view the world from a different value frame of reference. This is an especially important point in facilitating individuation, for it is the inability to cope with rejection or disapproval that so often pushes the client into the trap of being excessively other-oriented.

"Pretty Please" Permission Seeking

As stated above, the inability to cope with disapproval is perhaps the most frequent manifestation of a lack of individuation. What Satir (1972) called the "placater" is the individual who directly or indirectly makes the statement that "I'll do whatever you want me to do if only you'll like me." Often, there is a passive-aggressive element present since one's dependency needs from another can never be fully satisfied. Those unfulfilled needs cause inevitable frustration and anger which cannot be directly expressed for fear that the other person will leave.

In this strategy, the client is offered the behavioral prescription of asking others for permission to do whatever it is he or she wants to do (e.g., "Can I sit here?"). This exercise demands an extreme form of seeking approval. The client is required to get a positive reply from others before he or she can proceed with even the simplest tasks of going shopping, going to the bathroom, watching television, or going to sleep. The approval-seeking patterns of the client are thus exaggerated. It becomes easier to perceive the difficulties associated with having to have one's own needs validated by others, a practice which now becomes framed negatively. Others usually react with variations of "Why are you asking me such ridiculous questions?" Even those who may have previously encouraged dependency may respond with "Do what *you* want to do!" The client thus has the opportunity to experience firsthand that the excessive seeking of approval is not only a personal bother, but also taxing to others. The result is an establishment of a strong internal association that highlights approval-seeking behaviors which can then be noticed and altered appropriately at will.

The Self-Justification Shuffle

In using this strategy, the goal is to have the client discover that there is not likely to always be an adequate intellectually-based rationale for adopting a particular position. This directive involves directing the client to verbalize *at least three* reasons for doing whatever it is the client is doing. The client is told to state out loud or silently reasons why a particular route was chosen, why those particular clothes were worn, or why that particular food was ordered for lunch. The net effect is that the client rapidly reaches a "burn-out" point with the assignment. A simple "because I want to" can become sufficient justification for any decision.

It was pointed out earlier in this chapter that often clients come to therapy seeking permission to do something they want to do. Basically, such clients have failed to find a rationale or justification that eases anxiety about their situation. For clients who cannot seem to validate their own experiences by doing what they wish, this strategy teaches that despite a rational approach in gathering information to make a decision, the inevitable bottom line in the majority of cases is a subjective "because I want to."

For the nonindividuated person, what is personally wanted is less important than what others want. This strategy effectively teaches that what one prefers, what one chooses to do, and how one chooses to live are individual matters that need not be justified to anyone, not even to oneself. The acceptance of a willingness to act on one's own values has been emphasized throughout this chapter as instrumental to the individuation process.

SUMMARY

Individuation is ultimately the process through which all people come to recognize and assert their uniqueness as individuals. No one escapes the demands of being a member of society, and given all the potential benefits for such membership, the total avoidance of the disengaged "loner" is too costly a way of escaping such demands. For the majority of people, individuation is an ongoing process of becoming increasingly aware of the many choices one has in balancing the needs of the individual against the needs of the society of which one is a part. This chapter presented six strategies for facilitating the discovery of such choices, as well as concepts regarding ways clinicians can provide an atmosphere (the "climate" for change, as Erickson often said) for such discovery by their clients. Ultimately, this is when a client reaches the point of being able to live "alone together"—with his or her needs, values, feelings, and all the other aspects that collectively are the essence of the individual.

REFERENCES

Aronson, E. (1984). *The Social Animal.* (4th ed.). New York: W.H. Freeman and Co.

Biehler, R., & Hudson, L. (1986). *Developmental Psychology: An Introduction.* Boston: Houghton Mifflin.

Craig, G. (1986). *Human Development.* (4th ed.). Englewood Cliffs, N.J.: Prentice Hall.

Davison, G., & Neale, R. (1986). *Abnormal Psychology.* (4th ed.). New York: John Wiley & Sons.

Erikson, E. (1963). *Childhood and Society.* (2nd ed.). New York: Norton.

Erikson, E. (1968). *Identity: Youth and Crisis.* New York: Norton.

Gilligan, S. (1985). Generative autonomy. Principles for an Ericksonian hypnotherapy. In J. Zeig (Ed.), *Ericksonian Psychotherapy: Structures* (Vol. 1) (pp. 196–239). New York: Brunner/Mazel.

Goldstein, J. (1980). *Social Psychology.* New York: Academic Press.

Gordon, D. (1978). *Therapeutic Metaphors.* Cupertino, CA: Meta Publications.

Gunderson, J., Kolb, J., & Austin, V. (1981). The diagnostic interview for borderline patients. *American Journal of Psychiatry, 138,* 896–903.

Haley, J. (1973). *Uncommon Therapy.* New York: Norton.

Haley, J. (1984). *Ordeal Therapy.* San Francisco: Jossey-Bass.

Hall, C., & Lindzey, G. (1985). *Introduction to Theories of Personality.* New York: John Wiley & Sons.

Jung, C. G. (1953). On the psychology of the unconscious. In *Two Essays on Analytical Psychology. Collected Works.* (Vol. 7). Princeton, N.J.: Princeton University Press (First German edition, 1943).

Lankton, S., & Lankton, C. (1983). *The Answer Within: A Clinical Framework of Ericksonian Hypnotherapy.* New York: Brunner/Mazel.

Levinson, D. (1980). Conceptions of the adult life course. In N. Smelser & E. Erikson (Eds.), *Themes of Work and Love in Adulthood.* Cambridge, MA: Harvard University Press.

Massey, M. (1979). *The People Puzzle: Understanding Yourself and Others.* Reston, VA: Reston Publishing.

Masterson, J. (1981). *The Narcissistic and Borderline Disorders: An Integrated Developmental Approach.* New York: Brunner/Mazel.

Norwood, R. (1985). *Women Who Love Too Much.* Los Angeles, CA: Tarcher.

Rand, A. (1946). *Anthem.* New York: Signet Books.

Rathus, S., & Nevid, J. (1983). *Adjustment and Growth: The Challenges of Life.* (2nd ed.). New York: Holt, Rinehart & Winston.

Rokeach, M. (1973). *The Nature of Human Values.* New York: The Free Press.

Robbins, T. (1976). *Even Cowgirls Get the Blues.* Boston: Houghton Mifflin.

Rossi, E. (1985). Unity and diversity in Ericksonian approaches: Now and in the future. In J. Zeig (Ed.), *Ericksonian Psychotherapy: Structures* (Vol. 1) (pp. 15–29). New York: Brunner/Mazel.

Satir, V. (1972). *Peoplemaking.* Palo Alto, CA: Science & Behavior Books.

Simon, S., Howe, L., & Kirschenbaum, H. (1972). *Values Clarification: A Handbook of Practical Strategies for Teachers and Students.* New York: Hart Publishing.

Smith, M. (1977). *A Practical Guide to Value Clarification.* La Jolla, CA: University Associates.

Spitzer, R., Endicott, J., & Gibbon, M. (1979). Crossing the border into borderline personality and borderline schizophrenia. *Archives of General Psychiatry, 36,* 17–24.

Turner, J., & Helms, D. (1986). *Contemporary Adulthood.* (3rd ed.). New York: Holt, Rinehart & Winston.

Yapko, M. (1984a). Implications of the Ericksonian and Neurolinguistic Programming approaches for responsibility of therapeutic outcomes. *American Journal of Clinical Hypnosis, 27,* 137–143.

Yapko, M. (1984b). *Trancework: An Introduction to Clinical Hypnosis.* New York: Irvington.

Yapko, M. (1985a). The Erickson hook: Values in Ericksonian approaches. In J. Zeig (Ed.), *Ericksonian Psychotherapy: Structures* (Vol. 1) (pp. 266–281). New York: Brunner/ Mazel.

Yapko, M. (1985b). Therapeutic strategies for the treatment of depression. *Ericksonian Monographs, 1,* 89–110. New York: Brunner/Mazel.

Yapko, M. (1986a). Ericksonian hypnosis. In B. Zilbergeld, G. Edelstein, & D. Araoz (Eds.), *Hypnosis: Questions and Answers.* New York: Norton.

Yapko, M. (1986b). Hypnotic and strategic interventions in the treatment of anorexia nervosa. *American Journal of Clinical Hypnosis, 28,* 224–232.

Zeig, J. (Ed.) (1980). *A Teaching Seminar with Milton H. Erickson.* New York: Brunner/ Mazel.

SECTION TWO: PRACTICE

PART VI

Therapy Techniques

Chapter 16

Task Assignments:
Logical and Otherwise

Carol H. Lankton

Carol H. Lankton, M.A. (University of West Florida), maintains a private practice in Gulf Breeze, Florida, and is a renowned international trainer of Ericksonian psychotherapy and family therapy. She has been Invited Faculty Member to four Congresses and/or Seminars on Ericksonian Approaches to Hypnosis and Psychotherapy organized by the Erickson Foundation. She is coauthor of The Answer Within: A Clinical Framework of Ericksonian Hypnotherapy *and* Enchantment and Intervention in Family Therapy.

Erickson was well known for a variety of novel interventions. Among these were unusual assignments that ranged from methodical skill-building activities to elaborate symptom prescriptions and other, apparently irrelevant, tasks which may have seemed to clients to have no logical purpose. Erickson's choice of assignment dramatically changed the client's experience. Consequently, many questions arise when considering the use of these powerful interventions: What distinguishes the different types of assignments? Which ones are best assigned to which clients? How do assignments fit into a treatment regimen with various other interventions? Finally, what is involved in designing and delivering assignments, and how can clients' unique and unpredictable responses be utilized to further therapeutic gains? These questions are discussed in Carol Lankton's excellent chapter.

Though primarily known for his influence as a hypnotist, Milton Erickson is also widely known for his creative and often baffling use of task assignments. To say that he was unpredictable in his choice of therapy interventions is an understatement. For example, people would come to him requesting hypnosis for habit control and instead find themselves sent out to climb Squaw Peak. He assigned a husband the task of "properly" taking his wife to see a sunrise and even accompanied and supervised them so that they would complete the assignment correctly (Haley, 1973). A patient who had sought hypnotic help for agoraphobia was escorted through an elaborate (and all too real for his level of comfort) evening at a restaurant in the company of Dr. and Mrs. Erickson and an attractive young woman. Erickson even conspired with the waitress to create a context for the man to live through his worst fears (Haley, 1973). He gave paradoxical symptom prescriptions, assignments which clearly involved developing the client's deficit skills and transactions, and other assignments that inexplicably defied categorization.

In the wake of Erickson's influence, strategic therapies have flourished. Therapists have become more active and goal oriented in their treatment planning and selection of interventions designed to move clients toward stated and unstated goals. These interventions are frequently assignments that clients are to complete in and/or out of the therapy session. Some of these approaches favor paradoxical prescriptions (Fisch, Weakland, & Segal, 1983; Madanes, 1983, 1984; Weeks & L'Abate, 1982), some favor ordeals (Haley, 1984), while others favor more direct skill-building homework (Ellis, 1973; Lange & Hart, 1983).

There is some initial difficulty organizing and understanding homework assignments since they are so diverse in the literature. They range from keeping journals, to taking tests, to writing down dreams, to specific activities, to visualization, to listening to tapes, and to getting and losing erections, etc. Sex therapies have long been associated with giving couples assignments (Rosen, 1983). Yet, assignments have also been applied to depression, phobic disorders, habit control, stuttering, and family problems (Haley, 1984; Madanes, 1983, 1984; Wilson, 1986).

Therapists should offer some form of explanation to clients as part of the persuasion to perform assigned tasks, even though the explanation provided may be vague or general in character. Of course, clients usually approach therapy with an expectation that therapists will proceed in a logical, linear manner toward contracted therapy goals. Thus, they can be expected to react with some degree of confusion to whatever extent this expectation is unrealized. There is, nonetheless, therapeutic benefit to eliciting some degree of conscious confusion at times. This chapter emphasizes the therapeutic usefulness of such confusion as it occurs in three categories of assignments: 1) paradoxical; 2) skill building; and,

3) the category we have previously termed "ambiguous function assignments" (Lankton & Lankton, 1986).

Assignments from all three categories are given with some *logical* purpose in mind, that is, "in accordance with inferences reasonably drawn from preceding or surrounding or predictable facts or events or circumstances" (Webster, 1976). Yet with all three it is frequently desirable for the therapist to distract the conscious mind from that logical purpose in some manner. While this is true for many Ericksonian assignments, it is especially true for ambiguous function assignments. The ambiguous function assignment is unique in that its logical purpose seems particularly obscured, if not nonexistent to the client asked to perform it, and indeed to the therapist who can never be certain what intricacies and significance the client will project into the assignment. This intervention will be emphasized here as it is compared and contrasted to the other kinds of task assignments.

The use of interventions that bypass consciousness in strategic therapy do not imply a license to avoid treatment planning and ethical guidelines. The three types of assignments discussed below should be logically based on clearly defined goals that are part of a comprehensively designed treatment plan. Within this framework, the therapist can ethically encourage varying degrees of therapeutic confusion, regardless of the particular type of assignment being used. The next section will briefly examine the rationale for using therapeutic confusion when giving assignments.

THERAPEUTIC CONFUSION

It is well understood that limitations which bring a person into therapy are created in more or less complex ways by the individual in response to the system in which s/he lives. The client's conscious beliefs usually represent an understanding and deference to that social and private environment. Consequently, the person's conscious mind does not conceive of a solution to his or her difficulties, but most often continues or furthers problems by attempting to solve them. A typical example is the depressed person who does not express needs or anger, or enjoy social exchanges. Thinking that people do not like to be around him, the depressed person engages in a type of avoidance that furthers the problem of depression and seems to add evidence of his faulty problem-solving strategy.

In view of the self-imposed limits presented by the client's conscious mind, it is advantageous to work in a manner that minimizes the resistance or the faulty cooperation it offers. There are various hybrids of therapy methods for dealing with this problem. However, even those which propose to facilitate cure through insight seem to use confusion. Of course, each therapy approach will justify and explain the rationale for confusion according to the jargon and theory which describe the particular approach.

Perhaps there need not be so much concern associated with the idea of therapies using techniques which purposefully engender confusion in the mind of the client. Looking at various traditional and well-known approaches from this perspective provides an understanding of how certain aspects of therapeutic confusion have always been accepted. For instance, in psychoanalysis, "free association" is the first rule. Gestalt therapy avoids any explanation by staying in the "here and now." In psychodrama and related action-related approaches, the role of conscious mind activity is reduced to the use of fantasy-that-becomes-action. In Transactional Analysis and Rational-Emotive Therapy, the conscious activity is monitored by the therapist and judged to indicate different types of thinking, some of which are considered more effective or healthy than others. Often, therapeutic result seems to be enhanced to the extent that therapy can control or monitor conscious activity.

It may be useful to clarify the definition of confusion before proceeding. The first definition of "confuse" is "to bring to ruin" (Webster, 1976). Despite the fact that "confusion" is usually considered negatively, it is useful to operate on the premise that benefit often can occur in those moments when the client does not readily (consciously) understand the therapist's logic, meaning, or intention. This premise has been introduced and accepted in regard to paradoxical symptom prescriptions and other interventions involving paradoxical intention (Haley, 1973; Fisch et al., 1983; Madanes, 1983; Selvini Palazzoli et al., 1978; Watzlawick, 1976; Weeks & L'Abate, 1982).

An unexpected, ambiguous, or apparently irrelevant behavior prescription can be expected to be received by the client as an unconditioned stimulus. As such, there is no automatic or previously conditioned response to it that the client can initiate. Conscious understanding is depotentiated and unconscious "searching" is stimulated as the client works to find the significance implied by the request and to determine a satisfactory or appropriate response (Lankton & Lankton, 1983). Regardless of the specific response the client demonstrates overtly, the existing conscious frame of reference has been suspended. Thus, an "appropriate" and potentially therapeutic response already has been initiated with a shift in his or her frame of reference about the problem and what constitutes "therapy" for the problem. This process is based on a second and more benign definition of "confusion": "to make unclear in mind . . . bewilder, perplex" (Webster, 1976).

The premise upon which this discussion is based is that therapeutic results are often facilitated when conscious understanding is depotentiated. Erickson suggested that where problems are concerned the client's conscious mind is usually occupied with biases, prejudices, and limiting beliefs about why change is impossible (Erickson & Rossi, 1980a). Consequently, his therapy frequently involved various techniques (confusion, indirect suggestion, metaphor, paradox, ambiguous behavior prescriptions, etc.) designed to bypass, overload, confuse, or otherwise depotentiate the conscious mind so that he could elicit and reassociate the person's unconscious abilities and understandings.

Insight is occasionally a desirable result of therapy, but in most cases where clients have consciously analyzed the history of and reasons for an existing problem it comes to little avail in actually changing the problem. At those times, more indirect, apparently "irrelevant" or illogical interventions are indicated. Erickson made it clear that direct suggestions work well only when clients know exactly what they want, are congruent about wanting it, and have the resources readily available to accomplish that goal (Erickson & Rossi, 1980b).

Operating from a logical and comprehensive treatment plan, the strategic therapist must, nonetheless, expect a wide range of response unique to each client. This range of response may be even larger to the extent that interventions bypass the client's conscious understanding. In any event, the therapist must be able to observe, understand, and utilize the client's unique responses to each intervention. With regard to specific interventions, let's look now at what distinguishes the three types of assignments, comparing goals, design, delivery, and utilization of client responses.

PARADOXICAL ASSIGNMENTS

Paradoxical assignments are founded on the therapist's conviction that there is no such thing as "resistance" from clients, but simply misguided cooperation and incongruence about changing. Every behavior presented by every client is something that an Ericksonian therapist can work to incorporate into therapy in some way. Paradoxical interventions are one excellent method for utilizing client behaviors and problems. They typically are used to prescribe the continuation or increase of some aspect of a symptom, personality orientation, or family dynamic. Symptom prescriptions are used to serve a purpose which has been described by the therapist as beneficial or as somehow furthering the goals of therapy. Furthermore, the therapist avoids the role clients may be expecting as goals are reframed and thinking redirected.

A major goal of paradox is to free clients for problem solving by facilitating a shift in the frame of reference about the problem. Typically, clients think about their problems only in negative terms. This results in devaluing their own effort and actually misdirecting their problem solving. For example, one of Erickson's clients presented the problem of phantom limb pain. Erickson encouraged the man to continue to have phantom sensation, and suggested that, because he was able to do this, he could learn to experience phantom pleasure (Erickson & Rossi, 1979). By positively labeling the "problem" as an ability or value, the therapist can congruently redirect the client's misguided efforts. In order to accomplish this, the therapist views the development of any behavior as an adaptive learning which was appropriate to the unique context in which it was learned and which the client still continues to use. In short, the development of problem behaviors is the best choice available to clients responding to needs and responsibilities demanded by the current system.

Thus framed, that "problem" (or at least the useful intention behind the problem behavior) can be prescribed to continue, but in a way that disrupts or alters the client's typical experience of the problem. Alterations in the exact pattern of continuance may include a worse alternative version of the problem, changes in the time, intensity, or location of the problem, or a splitting of the problem between its physiological and psychological, or conscious and unconscious aspects. By so altering the pattern, a "doorway" to more comprehensive therapy is opened. We might look at this as a process of disorganization and reorganization, initiated by the unconditioned stimulus created when the therapist appreciates, praises, and prescribes the "problem." When unconditioned stimuli are presented, conscious associations are depotentiated and a resulting unconscious search renders the client more receptive to therapeutic input. That input, of course, is designed to stimulate thinking about new understandings and resources with which the client can better respond to situational and developmental demands.

Providing Reasons and Redirecting Attention

When giving paradoxical directives which promote disorganization through confusion of roles, cognitive interpretation, family organization, sequence of symptom events, etc., the therapist must give acceptable reasons to clients so they can perceive the assignment as worthwhile and respond in a positive manner. There must be a balance between the resulting confusion and an understanding that the therapist can be trusted and is suggesting something sensible, albeit somewhat unusual and unexpected.

Paradoxical assignments are given for strategically logical purposes but it may be preferable not to share with clients what these purposes are. The ultimate purpose behind paradoxical directives is to continue to have the symptom or problem in such a way that it is disrupted; the disruption becomes a means to no longer continuing it. Yet, the assignment is intended to maintain a "handle" to guide clients in the direction of beneficial change. This often involves finding resources for resolving developmental demands.

This process could be called maintaining "therapeutic leverage" when giving the prescription. The problem in explaining this straightforwardly to the client, as Frankl (1960) suggested, is that it places clients in a bind between continuing, even exaggerating, their behavior and simultaneously believing and hoping that this will alleviate the behavior (Lange & Hart, 1983). Clients need to have a good reason, but it need not be "the" strategically designed reason the therapist has in mind.

Reasons frequently given by therapists for a client to volitionally continue a problem behavior include developing awareness about the problem, helping another person, or gaining control of a situation previously considered involuntary or beyond control. Suggesting that the symptom represents the client's best choice at accomplishing certain age-appropriate tasks presupposes movement toward healthy adaptation at the current stage of development, as well as successful transition into the next. The therapist may then urge the client to continue the symptom (or the value it represents) for whatever gratification it currently accomplishes while alternative means to satisfy and meet developmental demands are retrieved or learned.

For example, consider a newly married couple who presented a symptom of the wife's eczema which "flared up" at times of emotional stress. The symptom was developed when she was a child, apparently in response to a family organization that failed to model or reinforce methods of appropriately experiencing, accepting, and expressing various emotions. As a teenager, when she explored the possibilities of expressing anger toward her father, he died from a heart attack shortly thereafter. She married but remained considerably fearful of self-revelation and emotional intimacy, especially when this concerned anger. Resulting communication problems caused stress and her eczema became worse. The symptom has represented her best, though inadequate, choice for dealing with emotion since childhood and is now being complicated by the demands and pressures that are part of the new stage of development she has entered. She sought hypnosis to stop scratching.

This client was sincerely complimented by the therapist for being a young woman who, because she was seeking therapy at this pivotal time in her life, had clearly indicated a great caring for her husband and obviously attached the proper significance to the commitment of marriage. That the symptom predictably occurred around times of emotional stress communicated to the therapist how sensitive and caring the woman was and indicated how much potential for emotional depth she had with her husband. Furthermore, she was told, no matter how uncomfortable the eczema became, it would be a shame to stop scratching until she had been willing to thoroughly "scratch more than the surface" of this situation and do so in such a way that her emotions could appropriately mature at this important time.

"After all," she was told, "there is no reason why a woman of your age—with the feelings you are entitled to have by virtue of being alive—should continue to age chronologically and yet allow your emotions to remain immature. So, continue to scratch the surface as you look more deeply to really understand just what it is that you need and want to express to your husband. And with each itch and urge to scratch, there can be another idea—but you wouldn't want to begin to express them to him too soon. And, there are other people as well. So, with each urge to scratch, take out a pad and write down at least two feelings that you wouldn't dare to share with anyone but which are important to you. Because as a woman who will one day be teaching her children how to understand and accept their feelings, you really ought to proceed cautiously and scratch very thoroughly as you stimulate your thoughts, feelings, and ideas."

This paradoxical prescription accomplished more than having the client continue symptoms in the same way. The customary functioning of the symptom was disrupted. This can be accomplished in one of several ways: 1) by changing the pattern of the symptom with regard to its frequency, rate, intensity, duration, location in the body, location in the environment, time of occurrence; 2) by changing the context or surroundings for the symptom to occur out of context, reframing the meaning of the symptom such that it is occurring for a beneficial outcome, arranging for a change in the environmental response to the sequence; and 3) by changing the sequence of events in the symptom with irrelevant components, confusion in the sequence, performing part of the sequence and leaving out the symptom, adding a worse alternative to the symptom sequence, or changing any other quality of the symptom.

In the preceding example, the routine occurrence of the symptom was altered in two ways: The prescription encouraged the symptom for its positive intent, and added to it an associated behavior (identifying and writing feelings) which was to occur each time the client produced the symptom. In any case, the alteration and the reason given for continuing the symptom legitimized subsequent therapy to explore and develop resources such that symptom development would no longer be necessary and she would be equipped to handle emotional relations in her marriage. Thus, the therapeutic confusion/searching and receptivity that result from the paradoxical prescription are enhanced by the provision of other interventions to focus thought, retrieve affect, build behaviors, etc. Paradoxical interventions do not necessarily cure in and by themselves. Rather they disrupt the usual course of problem behaviors and refocus attention, thus creating a context for retrieving and associating needed resources.

Retrieving and Associating Resources

The retrieving and associating resources phase follows a paradoxical directive. This phase may be accomplished with a variety of other interventions, including skill-building assignments, metaphor, indirect suggestions and binds, and hypnosis. Metaphor is particularly useful for illustrating needed behaviors to the client. Furthermore, metaphor has proven effective for developing affect, challenging limiting beliefs, and stimulating thinking to expand self-image and alter family structure (Lankton & Lankton, 1986). For example, the paradoxical directive in the case described above was given during the first portion of the session. For the remaining hour, the therapist related metaphors that detailed aspects of giving and getting nurturance, experiencing and expressing anger, dealing with issues of sexuality, curiosity, fertility, intimacy, mature responsibility, and self-image. The metaphors fostered a kind of inwardly directed concentration in the session. This type of thinking can be effectively supplemented with skill-building assignments which can be suggested during either the previous or subsequent phase of delivery. Thus, the complete session helps the client solidify the paradoxical assignment into actual behaviors which enhance appropriate problem solving.

Paradoxical directives may be given elaborately as an organizing framework for the therapy session(s) to follow, as the preceding example illustrates. They may be used in a briefer manner in a session to encourage and utilize any behaviors, personality orientation, or "problem" that develops in the course of any therapy session or becomes an issue of interview management. As such, they may be frequently used with most clients by simply framing positively whatever they are doing and urging that they continue doing it even though it might have been considered problematic. For example, Erickson instructed a client to remember the pain of a spanking: "Go ahead and feel that pain . . . it proves that you are alive and have a healthy nervous system. It would have been a shame if you couldn't have felt that pain" (Erickson & Lustig, 1976).

To a client who is angry at the therapist or someone in his family the therapist might suggest: "Go ahead and continue to experience that anger because to the extent that you are able to know your anger, the more you are going to be able to have and appreciate all of your feelings." To a client displaying a critically managerial personality orientation the therapist might say: "Please manage your responses today and continue to monitor and evaluate everything I say during this session so that you make certain you respond only to those suggestions that will be relevant for you." With this last example, the suggestions which follow will, of course, be most relevant if they educate and illustrate nuances of behavior, such as comfortable dependency and objectivity, that seem to be less available to such a person.

In each case, the client is told to continue to make the best choice available for whatever intention or gratification it represents; meanwhile, the therapy will be devoted to making better choices available.

SKILL-BUILDING ASSIGNMENTS

This category of assignments is featured in many types of therapy and is usually known as simply "homework." It is usually a task that the therapist designs so that clients, by performing it, will develop some impoverished area of learning—social skill, emotional skill, physical behavior, or otherwise. Erickson distinguished his use of such assignments in several ways. Most notably, this involved his characteristic creativity and willingness to assign the unusual. Another characteristic way Erickson constructed these assignments included distracting, bypassing, confusing, or overloading the conscious mind with regard to the subtle purpose of the activity.

The homework assignments he gave were often quite specific and were designed to help clients learn small, component parts of larger, more complex behavioral and attitudinal patterns. As mentioned earlier, he would at times even accompany a client to make sure the assignment was done according to his specifications. There was the man for whom Erickson elaborately demonstrated, as part of teaching appropriate intimacy with his wife and family, how to shop for lingerie, how to appreciate his wife wearing it, and even how to buy and decorate a Christmas tree and "properly" give the gifts to his family (Zeig, 1980). In another case, a self-effacing woman was sent, with post-hypnotic suggestion, to the library to study *National Geographic* magazine to notice how even disfigured women could still have husbands. This assignment was a very small component part of helping her develop an ability to appreciate herself and develop feelings of self-worth. Her conscious mind was so opposed to this attitude that she was instructed to have amnesia for receiving the suggestion and to have no immediate understanding as to why she would find the magazine so fascinating (Haley, 1973).

In another case a couple came to see Erickson after continually fighting over the management of their restaurant; the wife demanded that her husband become more managerial. Erickson intervened with one specific assignment that created a context for many specific skills to be learned by both husband and wife: The wife was to "see to it" that her husband arrived at the restaurant half an hour before her each morning to open and set up operations (Haley, 1973). Erickson, in this instance, utilized the woman's managerial orientation, paradoxically prescribing that she oversee her husband's compliance with performing the homework assignment that would result in his having an opportunity to learn the management skills he was missing. The wife, without ever having to realize it consciously, had an opportunity to learn behaviors related to comfortable dependency while letting someone else be in charge. This case illustrates the possibility of interconnecting paradoxical and skill-building assignments.

Setting Goals and Designing the Assignments

Before designing skill-building assignments for clients or families, it is imperative to have clearly defined treatment goals. These goals can be delineated by answering some relevant questions: What are the developmental tasks which have not been successfully completed? What are the missing experiences and transactions needed to improve adjustment in the current developmental stage and/or to begin the next stage? When these questions have been answered, the therapist then should identify a context where those skills can be learned or find an activity that is a component part, or metaphor, for the needed skill. Then, appealing to the client's strengths, "resources," or interests, assign the task.

Perhaps because these kinds of assignments are so straightforward or logical with regard to needed benefits to be obtained, it is especially useful to distract the client's conscious mind from the potentially threatening purpose of the activity. Most therapists are all too familiar with the kind of "resistance" or reluctance they meet when they straightforwardly assign a logical task that the client should do. If clients could comfortably negotiate this kind of situation, they wouldn't be in therapy to learn more appropriate ways of coping with developmental demands. Distracting the client's conscious mind from the notion that the strategic homework intervention is connected to something that they need to learn, but believe to be too difficult, vastly improves the likelihood that the assignment will be performed and the needed skill gained without threat.

For example, a shy, single, 23-year-old woman came to therapy and contracted goals of "getting close to people." Being able to show interest in someone else, share personal information, sit comfortably with another person, smile and make eye contact, affectionately touch the other person, etc., were missing experiences and transactions this client needed in order to improve adjustment in her current developmental stage of courtship. Sending her to a party to initiate a conversation with someone she considers attractive or interesting might provide a context for those skills, once learned, to be successfully displayed, but this would be an unlikely context for her to learn them. It would be too threatening. The component pieces are not specific or small enough for her to learn easily and her conscious mind would certainly raise objections about the difficulty of the task and/or her ability to do it.

Sending her to visit a nursing home to talk to one of the patients, however, as a "favor" for the therapist provided a context for the desired learning while removing the perceived threat. After all, in the nursing home she was not supposed to be learning anything for herself. She was ostensibly "just" helping the therapist who had a contract with the nursing home to periodically send volunteers to provide company for lonely patients. The desired learning could occur in this "safe" context and later be associated and applied to the client's proper developmental context.

Indications for Treatment Approach

Given that the behavioral goals have been clearly defined, the concern for treatment planning becomes whether to facilitate the development of the specific behaviors through metaphor and other forms of in-session instruction, through skill-building activities, or both. There are several factors which help determine the treatment. One of these is the resourcefulness of the client and the other is available time and motivation for therapy. When time is limited and the client has rich resource experiences, assigning skill-building activities is not necessary. In these instances, stimulation of the client's thinking through metaphor is an excellent method for expanding the internal map of options in a short period of time. The selected stories might well detail the experiences of other clients who were assigned and did complete skill-building activities outside of the therapy office. Erickson's case stories contained many descriptions of clients who were previously sent or accompanied on some skill-building activity. Behavioral repertoires can be significantly increased with this alternative, especially with those clients who communicate well.

When clients do not communicate well and have poorly developed resources, or when therapeutic contact is not limited, frequent use of behavior-building activities is recommended. Preceding and following these interventions, metaphor and suggestions can further help clients frame the experience, shape perception, develop feeling states, and form attitudes which support the designed activity. As with any intervention, the client's unique and idiosyncratic responses to the assignment must be considered, framed positively, and utilized, if only diagnostically, to understand more fully the scope of needed skills.

AMBIGUOUS FUNCTION ASSIGNMENTS

Ambiguous function assignments are those in which the client is asked to perform a highly specific, often extremely unusual, and apparently irrelevant behavior for which no purpose is given by the therapist. From the client's perspective, it seems that the logical purpose is something that will remain undiscovered until the task is performed. Erickson's assignments seemed to include a large number of these "ambiguous function assignments," though he never referred to them as such. Consider, for example, the countless clients and students sent to climb Squaw Peak or find a Boojum tree growing in the desert. Once Erickson suddenly asked a client with whom he was talking to "go over and pick up that large rock by the door" (Lankton, 1979). In another case, Erickson asked a man to take off his shoes and socks and then roll Erickson's wheelchair up onto his foot (Lankton & Lankton, 1986). In each example, the assigned task was specific, but the purpose of the task was ambiguous. Comparing this type of assignment to paradoxical prescription and skill-building assignments may clarify a definition.

Paradoxical assignments are often a way of utilizing current behaviors, while skill-building assignments develop or retrieve specific behaviors that have been identified as desirable. Ambiguous function assignments, however, are made with the understanding that the client's response to the task will include much more than what can be predicted. The goal in initiating ambiguous function interventions is not limited to simply helping clients shift cognitive frames of reference or develop a particular skill. The client's novel response will, in fact, provide further assessment information for the therapist. This additional information is supplied by the client's interpretation of the outcome of the task and, to a lesser degree, by the actual behavior which the client produced.

Performing an ambiguous function assignment disrupts the typical conscious mind-set and acts as a catalyst that stimulates the unconscious to reorganize perceptions and understandings that may have been previously addressed in therapy by other, more conventional therapeutic interventions. It facilitates the process of integrating the therapy, both physically and cognitively, though conscious understanding about the relevance of the task itself is not necessarily included. Stimulation of curiosity, hope, and interest is usually accomplished. Perhaps it is a need for closure or meaning that strengthens the responsiveness to subsequent therapy.

For example, an excessively dependent and self-effacing client was asked to wear comfortable clothing and walking shoes and to "be prepared to change" when she arrived for her session. At the door she was greeted by the therapist who was holding two 14-lb. barbell weights.

The client was asked whether she would prefer to carry one or both with her as she walked around the half-mile block outside the office. It was explained that she was to walk until she could give the correct answer as to why she had been sent on the walk and what the therapist thought she needed to learn. The client became increasingly involved each time she rounded the block and stopped in to give her latest understanding. With each useful learning she presented, her interest and curiosity about the "real" meaning continued to grow. At one point the therapist took the weights and gave the client a weightless crystal vase filled with delicate seashells to carry instead so as to finally understand the "real" meaning. The client returned to the office in a state of conscious confusion and yet she displayed many new ideas, unaccustomed feelings (for her), and, as she termed it, "excitement." The assignment proved to be the turning point in her therapy—the point at which she recognized the power of her own answers and abilities.

Designing Ambiguous Function Assignments

Though Erickson offered neither definition nor guidelines for designing this type of assignment, he did indicate the importance of creating a context in which clients can spontaneously change themselves. This "context" can be in the therapist's office and during the therapy session, but we usually prefer to use the larger environment, as Erickson frequently did. Thus, we design assignments that the client is to do between sessions, away from our office. The setting may be a park, the beach, a restaurant, a shopping mall, the client's home, etc., but the assignment always involves the client in actively doing something, usually with some physical object. We have given a variety of assignments that range from brushing teeth with the nondominant hand for a week to emptying out a drawer on the floor and leaving the mess undisturbed except to study it five minutes each day, to putting a smiling jack-o-lantern on the porch at Christmas time, to carrying a hammer everywhere the client goes for a week.

The only limit we impose on ourselves in designing these assignments is that the activity be possible, safe, legal, and ethical. The assignment can be designed to occur only once, or at specific intervals, or continuously. The therapist can select the object to be used arbitrarily or because it is expected to have some symbolic relevance for the client. Those objects selected arbitrarily can have just as much (if not more) significance attributed to them by clients as those objects selected due to anticipated symbolic relation to the client's problems. Furthermore, those objects selected for their likely symbolic relevance will usually be attributed a different meaning or significance than the therapist had expected.

Regardless of the object or the activity that has been selected, the assignment is best designed to include a bind on performance. This element tends to distract the client's conscious mind from whether or not the task will be done and focuses on the manner or the choice of object. The illusion of intended meaning is also furthered. For example, asking the woman in the example above whether she preferred to carry one or both weights while she walked was a bind of comparable alternatives that presupposed she was going to be walking carrying at least one weight. The therapist suggested that the client might learn more rapidly if she carried them both, but "on the other hand maybe you'll be able to understand more comfortably if you just carry one." Other binds of comparable alternatives would be whether to empty out the kitchen "collect-all" drawer or the drawer from the desk, whether to carry a small hammer or a large hammer, or whether to climb Squaw Peak at sunrise or sunset. In each case, the therapist's manner should imply that it is an important decision, and that although the therapist has some ideas on which would be best, it is really up to the client to decide. In this manner, conscious attention is even more strongly distracted.

Delivering the Ambiguous Assignment and Utilizing Responses

Whether this type of assignment is being used to gain additional diagnostic information or as a catalyst for integration of previous therapy, it is best to make it only after rapport and credibility have been established. This may well be accomplished early in the first session or only after substantial contact time. When therapy is being slowed by client's beliefs or actual manipulations, giving an ambiguous function assignment will disrupt conscious mind-sets and expectations about therapy and frame it as something the clients do, not something the therapist is to do or "give."

One of the aspects most crucial to the success of this assignment is its delivery to the client and the utilization of all resulting behavior. It is important to deliver any intervention in such a manner as to inspire the client to believe it is going to be worthwhile. Even though confusion about how it will be worthwhile is central to the design of ambiguous function assignments, a therapist can still imply value with an attitude of "compelling expectancy," as Erickson said, or by acting on a firm conviction that carrying out the task will be beneficial. When an assignment is given that otherwise appears to be totally irrelevant, this conviction is especially important. The conviction, in this case, is founded not on knowing exactly what benefit the assignment will create but on knowing that it will yield benefit beyond what the therapist can expect. Giving such a specific task with such a degree of value implied tends to create the illusion that the therapist has a very specific outcome in mind. One can further this illusion, in fact, by telling clients to do the assignment until they are able to tell the therapist what the "intended" learning had been.

The therapist's readiness to utilize any response creates a context in which it is possible for clients to give only "right" answers or have appropriate learnings. An ideal therapeutic situation results when each response is reinforced and utilized for its inherent value, while simultaneously being used as a "springboard" to additional, even more significant, learnings. The learnings come from the projective reports of clients when they are asked to explain what they got from the task. Deepening of associations and thoughts is fostered by the therapist's continuing to suggest that while the initial understandings are certainly worthwhile, there is still more to be discovered. Repeating the question, "Yes, but what did you *really* learn?" conveys an expectancy that the client can probe more deeply until optimal benefit has been derived.

Telling clients something about what the "intended" meaning is can stimulate additional searching if the revelation is phrased metaphorically, or with other abstraction and lack of specificity so as to allow clients to formulate their own answers. For example, when the man had picked up the heavy rock, following Erickson's instruction, and had fallen forward a bit, surprised by the heaviness of the rock, Erickson said, "Remember that next time you suck your thumb" (Lankton, 1979). The man might well wonder what he was supposed to remember and what "sucking his thumb" meant. Likewise, the man who rolled the wheelchair up onto his bare feet was asked, "Does it hurt?" to which he replied, "Not very much." Erickson then informed him that "It wouldn't hurt at all if you didn't do it" (Lankton & Lankton, 1986). With that "interpretation," certain ideas or understandings undoubtedly occurred to that man. Yet, what was the "real" purpose and why had Erickson chosen that method to stimulate thinking about it? These questions have remained a mystery to many of Erickson's students and probably even more so to his clients who were most likely engaged indefinitely in discovering new learnings set in motion by a cryptic intervention years earlier.

One might wonder how Erickson was consistently able to design what always seemed to be the perfect assignment that held such a special meaning or unlocked such an important understanding for his clients and students. But perhaps the learning he intended for his students involves a willingness and ability to observe and utilize anything given by the client. As a result, the "perfect" understanding is co-created in the process, not anticipated and prearranged by the therapist before the assignment is given. The therapist anticipates only that the client will project relevant understandings into any randomly selected ambiguous function assignment. So the therapist prearranges a context and waits to discover which "right" answer the client will discover. Even not doing the assignment can become the right answer. However, when assignments are given in a manner that expresses the therapist's conviction that they will be valuable, clients usually carry out the directed activity, although perhaps modifying it in selected ways.

For example, a quarreling couple was sent, following their therapy session, to a playground where they were to sit on separate ends of a "seesaw" until they were able to balance it and remain stationary. Then they were to remain in this position for five minutes, maintaining eye contact. Unbeknownst to the therapist, the playground did not have this piece of equipment and there was also an unexpected rainstorm at the time they were to do the assignment. Nonetheless, they returned to the next session with an atypical camaraderie and were excited to relate their "adventure." They had been only slightly discouraged by the rain and had ventured to the park where they were surprised to find no "seesaw." They reported that as they talked about what the therapist might have wanted them to learn, they "realized" that since this "problem" situation was something that neither one could blame on the other, the therapist must have wanted them to learn that they could make a decision without arguing. With that, they began to explore the "adult playground" of renovated houses and shops in the vicinity of the park and were excited as they shared how "fascinating" it had been to see those "old buildings so beautifully restored." This alternative activity and their interpretation were interesting in light of the fact that this couple had been married 20 years but had come to therapy considering divorce. The assignment seemed to motivate them to focus their resources toward "restoring the original beauty" of their marriage, rather than blaming each other.

In the positive reframing and the utilizing of any response from the client, a context emerges for more relevant understandings to follow. This process is enhanced by the use of paradoxical directives to continue feelings or behaviors the client might have considered negative, by suggestions and binds that continue to focus the client inward for the answers, by metaphors that stimulate additional thinking, and perhaps by skill-building activities that are themselves enhanced by the special receptivity and motivation to resolve the mystery that has been created with ambiguous function assignments.

COMPARISON AND CONTRAST

In the preceding sections, I have discussed distinguishing features of three types of assignments. Table 1 (pp. 276–277) is included to clarify and summarize the similarities, differences, and interconnectedness of these several assignments with regard to the aspects listed.

The three interventions discussed in this paper can be used frequently by therapists of various orientations regardless of whether therapy primarily involves strategic family therapy or individual hypnotherapy. There are clear similarities and differences, especially with regard to what the therapist hopes the interventions will accomplish. With all three, these distinctions are intended to be used only as guidelines for designing unique interventions for unique clients, delivering them in accordance with how those clients can be motivated, and utilizing idiosyncratic responses toward goals valued by each client.

Table 1

Aspects of Assignments	Paradoxical	Skill Building	Ambiguous Function
Frequency Indicators			
Use frequently during a session	Yes, especially for openers or closings	No, rarely during session	No, rarely during session
Use frequently between sessions	Yes	Yes, especially with impoverished resources	No
Use sparingly	No	No	Yes
Use Indicators			
After credibility and rapport	Yes, especially empathy	Yes	Yes
After resources retrieved	No	No, primarily do to develop skill	Yes, acts as integrative catalyst
Diagnostically	No	No, though some may occur	Yes, either initially or later
When client claims no control	Yes	Yes	No
When client tries to control therapy	Yes	No	Yes
Builds behaviors, skills or communication	No, but opens a channel for discussing them	Yes	Not intentionally but perhaps incidentally

Motivates client to action	No	Yes	Yes
Frames symptom as positive	Yes	No, doesn't mention symptom	No, doesn't mention symptom
Disrupts habitual conscious sets	Yes	No, but disrupts habitual behaviors	Yes
Frames therapy as participatory	Yes	No, seems to be an "aside" from therapy	Yes
Develops receptivity to other interventions	Yes	Not especially	Yes
Delivery			
Sincerely	Yes	Yes	Yes
With added empathy	Yes	No	No
Consciousness is distracted	Yes	Yes	Yes
Assignment is clear	Yes	Yes	Yes
With conviction that implies therapeutic value	Yes	No	Yes
Casually and objectively	No	Yes	No
Challenging	If necessary	If necessary	If necessary

REFERENCES

Ellis, A. (1973). *Humanistic Psychotherapy.* New York: McGraw-Hill.
Erickson, M. (1980). *The Collected Papers of Milton H. Erickson on Hypnosis: Vol. 1. The Nature of Hypnosis and Suggestion; Vol. 2. Hypnotic Alteration of Sensory, Perceptual and Psychophysical Processes; Vol. 3. Hypnotic Investigation of Psychodynamic Processes; Vol. 4. Innovative Hypnotherapy.* Edited by Ernest Rossi. New York: Irvington.
Erickson, M., Hershman, S., & Secter, I. (1961). *The Practical Application of Medical and Dental Hypnosis.* New York: Julian Press.
Erickson, M., & Lustig, H. [Producer]. (1976). *The Artistry of Milton H. Erickson, Part I.* [Film]. Ardmore, PA.
Erickson, M., & Rossi, E. (1979). *Hypnotherapy: An Exploratory Casebook.* New York: Irvington.
Erickson, M., & Rossi, E. (1981). *Experiencing Hypnosis: Therapeutic Approaches to Altered State.* New York: Irvington.
Erickson, M. & Rossi, E. (1980a). The varieties of double bind. In E. L. Rossi (Ed.), *The Collected Papers of Milton H. Erickson on Hypnosis: Vol. 1. The Nature of Hypnosis and Suggestion* (pp. 412–429). New York: Irvington.
Erickson, M. & Rossi, E. (1980b). The indirect forms of suggestion. In E. L. Rossi (Ed.), *The Collected Papers of Milton H. Erickson on Hypnosis: Vol. 1. The Nature of Hypnosis and Suggestion* (pp. 452–477). New York: Irvington.
Erickson, M., Rossi, E., & Rossi, S. (1976). *Hypnotic realities: The Induction of Clinical Hypnosis and Forms of Indirect Suggestion.* New York: Irvington.
Fisch, R., Weakland, J., & Segal, L. (1983). *The Tactics of Change: Doing Therapy Briefly.* San Francisco: Jossey-Bass.
Frankl, V. (1960). Paradoxical Intention. *American Journal of Psychiatry,* 14, 520–535.
Haley, J. (1973). *Uncommon Therapy: The Psychiatric Techniques of Milton H. Erickson, M.D.* New York: Norton.
Haley, J. (1984). *Ordeal Therapy.* San Francisco, CA: Jossey-Bass.
Haley, J. (1985). *Conversations with Milton H. Erickson, M.D., Vol. 2: Changing Couples; Vol. 3: Changing Children and Families.* New York: Norton.
Lange, A. & Hart, O. (1983). *Directive Family Therapy.* New York: Brunner/Mazel.
Lankton, S. (1979). Personal Communication with Milton H. Erickson, August.
Lankton, S., & Lankton, C. (1983). *The Answer Within: A Clinical Framework of Ericksonian Hypnotherapy.* New York: Brunner/Mazel.
Lankton, S., & Lankton, C. (1986). *Enchantment and Intervention in Family Therapy: Training in Ericksonian Approaches.* New York: Brunner/Mazel.
Madanes, C. (1983). *Strategic Family Therapy.* San Francisco: Jossey-Bass.
Madanes, C. (1984). *Behind the One-Way Mirror: Advances in the Practice of Strategic Therapy.* San Francisco, CA: Jossey-Bass.
Perls, F. (1947). *Ego, Hunger and Aggression: The Beginning of Gestalt Therapy.* New York: Random House.
Perls, F. (1979). *Gestalt Therapy Verbatim.* Lafayette, CA: Real People Press.
Perls, F. (1973). *The Gestalt Approach & Eye Witness to Therapy.* Ben Lomond, CA: Science and Behavior Books.
Perls, F., Hefferline, R. & Goodman, P. (1951). *Gestalt Therapy: Excitement and Growth in the Human Personality.* New York: Dell-Delta Books.
Rosen, R. (1983). Clinical issues in the assessment and treatment of impotence: A new look at an old problem. *Behavior Therapist,* 6 (5), pp. 81–85.
Rossi, E., & Ryan, M. (Eds.) (1985). *Life Reframing in Hypnosis: The Seminars, Workshops, and Lectures of Milton H. Erickson; Vol. 2.* New York: Irvington.
Rossi, E., Ryan, M., & Sharp, F. (Eds.) (1983). *Healing in Hypnosis: The Seminars, Workshops, and Lectures of Milton H. Erickson; Vol. 1.* New York: Irvington.

Selvini Palazzoli, M., Cecchin, G., Prata, G., & Y. Boscolo, L. (1978). *Paradox and Counterparadox*. New York: Jason Aronson.

Watzlawick, P. (1976). *How Real is Real? Confusion, Disinformation, Communication*. New York: Vintage Books.

Webster's Third New International Dictionary, Unabridged. (1976). Springfield, MA: Merriam-Webster.

Weeks, G., & L'Abate, L. (1982). *Paradoxical Psychotherapy: Theory and Practice with Individuals, Couples, and Families*. New York: Brunner/Mazel.

Wilson, R. (1986). *Don't Panic*. New York: Harper & Row.

Zeig, J. (1980). *A Teaching Seminar with Milton H. Erickson*. New York: Brunner/Mazel.

Chapter 17

A New Way of Motivating Clients to Carry Out Paradoxical Assignments: The Combination of the Paradoxical and the Congruent

Alfred Lange

Alfred Lange, Ph.D. (University of Amsterdam), is Lecturer at the University of Amsterdam in the departments of Social Psychology and Clinical Psychology. He coauthored Directive Family Therapy *and has published three Dutch-language books on directive therapy, family therapy, and behavior therapy. Lange serves on the editorial boards of the* American Journal of Family Therapy, *the* Journal of Family Psychology, *and the* Dutch Journal of Directive Therapy and Hypnosis. *He is a board member of the Dutch Society of Family and Couples Therapy and the Dutch Society of Psychotherapy.*

A new way of motivating clients to accept paradoxical assignments is introduced. This consists of a combination of congruent and paradoxical assignments. Five cases are described and analyzed. In the discussion, the indications for using this method of intervention are discussed, as are the problems sometimes encountered when classifying an intervention as having either a paradoxical or a congruent approach.

In 1977, in their chapter on pitfalls, Van Dijck and Van der Velden cautioned against giving clients paradoxical and congruent assignments simultaneously. Unless the combination is given within a carefully planned framework, they said, it leads to confusion, with the result that no changes take place. This warning is, of course, correct. But in my view, it applies to all combinations of assignments. For example, two learning assignments issued simultaneously will, generally speaking, not have much chance of success unless they are well-planned and clear to the client.

Van Dijck and Van der Velden do not say whether their warning applies only to issuing two assignments to one client, or if it also applies if they are issued to more than one family member, one client being approached in a paradoxical manner and the other in a congruent manner. Selvini Palazzoli et al. (1978) are explicit on this point. In their view, the whole family, or the whole system, must be subjected to the same paradoxical yoke (see also Tomm, 1984a, 1984b).

Hoogduin et al. (1977) were among the first therapists to forge a link between paradoxical and congruent advice. In the view of these authors, the symptom-bearer is prescribed the symptom, while others in the social environment are taught, in a congruent manner, how symptomatic behavior can be extinguished. Rijntjes (1982) deals with children in this way. With both Hoogduin and Rijntjes, the symptom-bearer is the central figure. He may continue displaying the symptom, or even increase it in order to get more of a grip on it. The environment "finishes it off" (acting as if it were a co-therapist) by reacting differently, thereby extinguishing the symptomatic behavior.

In this chapter, the combination of paradoxical and congruent interventions is examined once again, but this time from another vantage point. Using five cases, we shall see how it is possible to select and then introduce congruent and paradoxical elements in such a way that there is an extremely powerful motivation paradigm which, to my knowledge, has not been previously described. Seltzer (1986), for example, does not mention it in his thorough overview on paradoxical strategies in psychotherapy.

The essence of the motivating strategy presented here is as follows. One party (A) receives an assignment, for example to practice reacting to the other partner (B) in a different manner. B is asked to continue his symptomatic behavior (paradoxical instruction), because, if he did not, A would not have enough opportunity to practice. In the following sections, the cases will be described briefly and evaluated. In the discussion, special emphasis is given to formulating the indications for using this paradoxical paradigm.

THE CASES

Marg and Ralph Wilburn

Mr. and Mrs. Wilburn (Table 1) were in their 30s, in a high-income bracket and similar social class. They had been together for about seven years and did not want children. Mrs. Wilburn was strikingly attractive and vivacious. Mr. Wilburn was also very pleasant, but somewhat quieter. They had referred themselves for "marital problems." These consisted, in particular, of escalating quarrels emanating from a struggle for power. The pattern was as follows: Mrs. Wilburn would make sarcastic remarks to her husband, who would feel deeply hurt and humiliated. He would react, in the first instance, with resentful silence, after which he would enter into a confrontation, intended to hurt her in retribution. This process of escalation would go on for a while. Generally, they were affectionate towards one another, although Mr. Wilburn seemed fonder of his wife than she of him.

After the first two sessions, the picture was reasonably clear. The therapist had thought hard about how to break this common, but fairly difficult pattern. He was not very keen on prescribing the symptom or on issuing "fractionated quarrelling advice," i.e. instructing the clients to quarrel every day at a fixed time and for a fixed period (Van Dijck & Hoogduin, 1977), because the husband still felt hurt and humiliated. Perhaps the most obvious course of action would have been to have examined Mrs. Wilburn's behavior. Could she have been a little kinder and more considerate of her husband's feelings? On the other hand, Mr. Wilburn could have been less vulnerable and less dependent on his wife's being well-disposed towards him. The disadvantage of the

Table 1
Marg and Ralph Wilburn

Age	30s
Education	high
Living together	seven years, no children
Presenting Problem	power struggle
Assignment	congruent for husband, paradoxical for wife
Length of therapy	five sessions
Results	positive

former approach was that even if certain things changed, the pattern would have been no different. The husband would still have been dependent on his wife's moods, the only difference being that she would have been trying to spare his feelings a little more. For this reason, the latter strategy was chosen and introduced as follows:

> Mrs. Wilburn, we could try to help you to be less sarcastic and aggressive towards your husband, but . . . (long pause) . . . I'm afraid that would be missing the point. I think that we should first find out why you, Mr. Wilburn, get so depressed when your wife is unkind to you, why you don't defend yourself immediately, why you take everything so personally instead of shrugging it off and saying, "That's Marg and her sarcasm again." I'd like to suggest that during the next two weeks, as soon as Marg makes a remark which hurts you, you go into another room to be on your own for ten minutes. When you are alone, you are to make yourself feel the hurt as keenly as possible. You are to think about the terrible thing she has *said*, how it has humiliated you, and ask yourself whether this has anything to do with your family background. (This had been discussed during the second session.) At the end of ten minutes, you are to write all this down. In order to make the most of the next two weeks, would you, Mrs. Wilburn, make sure that your husband has enough material to work on so that he is able to gain insight into what it is that is making him feel this way. Strange as it may seem, this means that over the next two weeks, you will have to make as many sarcastic remarks as you possibly can. You know the sort I mean.

The instruction was the first instance of the new style combination of a paradoxical and congruent assignment. It was accepted without objection, although with a degree of surprise. The result was perfect. Two weeks later, they came in laughing: Mr. Wilburn had tried to carry out the assignment to start with, but after two minutes had decided that he would not allow himself to be humiliated any longer and that he did not care what she said to him, and he had then gone back into the sitting room. Mrs. Wilburn had tried several times, with increasing difficulty, to stick to the assignment. However, it no longer made any impression on her husband, so she stopped. The therapist complimented Mrs. Wilburn on her efforts, but asked her to continue the assignment as, unfortunately, her husband had not used the opportunity to withdraw to another room very often. The assignment was, therefore, reissued, with similar results, i.e., Mr. Wilburn had not gone off to sit on his own at all and Mrs. Wilburn had made hardly any sarcastic remarks. The pattern appeared to be broken.

The assignment to Mrs. Wilburn was withdrawn and Mr. Wilburn was advised to watch himself in the future and, if necessary, to withdraw to be on his own. There were three more sessions spread over a long period in which the couple received guidance in sustaining and using the changes which had taken place. At the last session, now eighteen months ago, there had been no relapse.

Observations

As there was no clear symptom-bearer, it was up to the therapist to indicate whose role in the above-described pattern he considered most problematic. He opted for Mr. Wilburn as this provided him with the best leverage for turning the existing system upside down. As the therapist had exposed the husband's weak attitude by means of a learning assignment, he was able to give Mrs. Wilburn a paradoxical assignment which made her previous behavior unappealing. This produced the desired effect.

The question of whether the assignment given to the husband was congruent is debatable. After all, his symptomatic behavior was tolerated during this period. He was not to try and resist it, but rather to use it to achieve a certain end, which was to learn and to gain insight from it. This leads us to a general problem concerning the classification of monitoring assignments. These often have a congruent content (gathering information before changes take place), but because of the reactivity (Lange & van der Hart, 1983), they often have a paradoxical effect, i.e., the client would rather stop the symptoms than monitor and record them. In any event, it seems clear that the wife, who was asked to continue to display her "old" behavior, was approached by the therapist in a more paradoxical manner than was her husband. We shall return to this question in the discussion.

Mr. and Mrs. Barclay

Mr. and Mrs. Barclay (Table 2) were in their 40s and had two sons, aged 13 and 14. Mr. Barclay was a chemist and Mrs. Barclay did not work outside the house. During the initial telephone conversation, Mr.

Table 2
Mr. and Mrs. Barclay

Age	about 45
Education	high
Married	about 20 years, two children
Presenting Problem	marital crisis
Assignment	congruent for husband, paradoxical for wife
Length of therapy	eight sessions
Results	negative

Barclay had said that their marriage was in crisis. As the children were regularly involved in the conflicts, an assessment session with the whole family seemed advisable.

During this session, it became apparent that there were no specific problem areas. Any chance remark could lead to a gigantic escalating quarrel during which both spouses in turn held a shouting monologue. They had had therapy several years previously and they said that this had been "no picnic." Subsequently, the situation had deteriorated progressively. The husband, in particular, accused his wife in a loud voice of all manner of sins, upon which she took out a notebook, observed him critically, and nervously made notes from time to time. She was gathering ammunition to use against him later. Despite this, she said that she loved him. His feelings were not quite so clear. He was grudging towards her and was not sure if it was worth all the effort. There were also problems with the older son, Dirk, who was not doing well at school.

The second session was with the parents alone. Their struggle for power was further examined. Once again, it was the husband who was most agitated. He ranted and raved about his wife for more than fifteen minutes—about how she treated him like a child, how she never agreed with him and was awkward about everything, how she sabotaged all his plans, and, above all, how she had systematically humiliated him over the years. He said that he would no longer allow himself to be humiliated. Although he certainly did not give a humiliated impression, the therapist decided, as he did with the Wilburns, to take this up as a theme. It would perhaps be possible to find out why he felt humiliated when his wife disagreed with him.

To begin with, he was given an instruction like Mr. Wilburn's, i.e., every time his wife treated him like a child, he was to go and sit on his own for 15 minutes and think about what had taken place. Mrs. Barclay was asked to provide him with as much opportunity to do so as possible by behaving in a humiliating and contrary fashion. They did not like the idea, but they were, nevertheless, prepared to try the assignment.

Two weeks later, it emerged that Mrs. Barclay had tried to carry out the assignment, even though she had found it extremely difficult, but that her husband had not tried at all. He was no longer interested in therapy and had decided he wanted a divorce as, according to him, there was no hope that his wife would ever change. Mrs. Barclay was very upset and tried in a touching but awkward way to refute his arguments.

The therapist introduced the idea of a trial separation (Lange & van der Hart, 1983). Naturally, Mrs. Barclay preferred this to the idea of a divorce, but Mr. Barclay did not see the point of a trial separation. The therapist once again explained exactly what a trial separation meant and they agreed that they would think about how they should go about it and on what particular matters they could make agreements.

Three weeks later, the situation had become more complicated. Mr. Barclay still wanted a divorce, but they had become closer again because there was a crisis with their son, Dirk, who had run away from home and spent several days with a friend. In dealing with this crisis they worked together. They talked about it reasonably, supported one another, and were even a bit affectionate. The husband nevertheless wanted a divorce. He could see no point in a trial separation.

The therapist offered to assist them with a divorce. After considering this for several days, Mr. Barclay refused the offer for the time being. A month later he contacted the therapist again, saying that they wanted to come and discuss Dirk who was becoming unmanageable. Things were going better between them again and the divorce plans had been scrapped. From their accounts of Dirk's behavior, it was clear that the hierarchy in the family was seriously disturbed. They agreed to work together to achieve a consistent approach, including using feasible sanctions, where necessary (Haley, 1980). After this, the relationship between the parents could be dealt with once again.

Observations

As with the Wilburns, in the case of the Barclays there was no single symptom-bearer. Here too, the therapist tried to convince the partner who saw himself as the more hurt of the two, i.e. the husband, that he was probably the party who had to change most. Once again, the therapist issued a congruent monitoring assignment which also contained paradoxical aspects. Although the final results of treatment were not negative, the combination of a paradoxical and a congruent assignment did not have the intended effect.

The following factors may have played a role in this. During the phase in which the assignment was issued, the relationship between therapist and client was not very good. Mr. Barclay, in particular, was not enthusiastic about being involved in the treatment. He was in the process of "getting rid of his wife" and was not amenable to the idea that he could perhaps change in some way. In view of the continually escalating struggle for power, it might have been possible, at a later stage to opt for a strategy in which both husband and wife were approached paradoxically (for example, by advising them to "take no nonsense" from each other for a while or by giving them "fractionated quarrelling advice") instead of using an approach in which one of the two was "persuaded" into temporarily being the main problem-bearer. The motivation behind the assignments issued, which was based on the advice that Mr. Barclay should think about why he felt so hurt, contained fewer elements from reality than the similar motivation presented to Mr. Wilburn.

Mr. Fulbright's Aggression

Mr. Fulbright (32) (Table 3) had referred himself for treatment because of obsessive compulsions, or rather a disorder of impulse control. He had the almost uncontrollable urge to do dangerous things, such as running out in front of cars to see if he could make it across the road without being run over, balancing on ledges and high buildings to see if he could manage to stay on, and strangling himself until he almost suffocated. When he was not doing these things, he was thinking about them continually. He displayed aggression not only towards himself but also towards his family. Everyone at home—his wife, his two young children, and even the cat—was afraid of him.

Things were reasonably smooth at work (although he did have compulsive thoughts there), but at home he behaved like an aggressive egoist and hardly ever did or said anything pleasant. He was mainly occupied with himself and his hobby, jogging. This had become increasingly difficult because of his strangling himself. He did not par-

Table 3
Mr. Fulbright and His Wife

Age	32
Education	middle
Married	10 years, two children
Presenting Problem	obsessive compulsions and aggression
Interventions	response prevention program congruent assignment for wife, paradoxical for husband
Length of therapy	32 sessions including follow-up sessions
Results	positive

ticipate at all in household chores. He had tried quite a few forms of therapy, including "primal scream."

To begin with, therapy was directed at treating individual complaints (in the presence of his wife). The relationship with the therapist was good. His behavior was labelled positively (the therapist said that he was a perfectionist and that he was trying to make up for past mistakes), which was not an impediment to a sound response prevention program (Emmelkamp, 1982; Rachman & Hodgson, 1980). This method of response prevention does not require elaboration in this chapter.

The approach began to bear fruit after about ten sessions. After some fifteen sessions, the obsessive thoughts and compulsive behavior had almost disappeared. There were, however, still many other problems in the family. The husband continued to occupy a peripheral position. Improving family relations was therefore added to the treatment contract. The children (8 and 10) attended several sessions. Problems in bringing them up were discussed, as was Mrs. Fulbright's fear of opposing her husband on any matter at all. That had been understandable in the past, but he had not been dangerously aggressive for quite a while and did nothing worse than swear a little. He was also getting along with the children much better although the cat was still afraid of him.

During the 22nd session, at which the children were present, a behavior reenactment was carried out (Lange & van der Hart, 1983). The immediate reason for this was an agreement, previously made between husband and wife, that if he had dinner alone after his jogging, she would serve him only once. He could help himself to second and third helpings in the kitchen if he wanted any more. He had not kept his part of the agreement and had continually ordered his wife to get him second helpings.

They reenacted the last time that this had taken place. While the children played at watching television, husband and wife readied themselves for battle. What was striking was that the wife was extremely unassertive. This had come up before. In many situations, including some in which her husband was not involved, she found it difficult to stand up for herself and chose the line of least resistance, which was to be self-effacing. Her husband had an aversion to this as he disliked submissive behavior.

The wife's unassertive behavior was chosen as the point of departure. The family was told that the father would be a fool not to try to get his own way when he succeeded every time, and that the mother should learn to apply some counterpressure. The therapist was a model for her in the scene and demonstrated how not to be put off by the husband's shouting (the husband acted superbly) and how to make it clear in a calm but compelling way that he was definitely not going to be served a second plate of soup, but would have to get it himself.

Mrs. Fulbright accepted the proposal to practice this every evening (her husband went jogging every evening) in the coming weeks. The husband was asked to help his wife by pressuring her as much as possible by not giving in too quickly, or "she wouldn't learn anything from the exercise."

The results were positive, if less dramatic than with the Wilburns. The pattern was not yet broken, but it had changed. Mrs. Fulbright's unassertiveness and her position in the family of origin were to remain on the therapy agenda for quite some time. After 22 sessions, another ten followed, including follow-ups every six months. Attention was also devoted to their sexual relationship, which had been quiet for some time on the therapist's advice.

On conclusion of the therapy, there was no relapse as far as the compulsive behavior was concerned and the situation in the family was satisfactory from everyone's point of view. The husband occupied a more central position. The wife still found it difficult to stand up for herself, but she was trying her best and her husband was not abusing her weakness as much as he had done previously.

Observations

As the wife's unassertiveness was the central aspect in the episode which took place before the intervention, it is not unreasonable to view her as the symptom-bearer, despite the fact that originally the husband was, with good reason, the identified patient. Here too, the person who in this particular respect was the one with the most symptoms received the congruent side of the advice, while the person labelled as having no symptoms (at that particular moment and in that particular respect) received the paradoxical advice. It will, however, be clear from the therapy as a whole that Mr. Fulbright's aggression played a considerable role in his wife's inability to stand up for herself where he was concerned. This situation had not yet been entirely rectified but it had improved. The paradoxical assignment given to the husband was intended to inhibit his aggressive behavior. But, should it nevertheless arise from time to time, it would be easier for his wife to respond to it as his verbal aggression now was a form of compliance with a therapeutic assignment.

In considering the positive results of the above approach, it is worthwhile noting that the intervention took place in the 22nd session, following a period of intensive therapy with positive results. Both clients were highly motivated to follow the therapist's advice.

Mr. Rose's Tics

Mr. Rose (Table 4) was a tall, thin man (33) who referred himself for what he called compulsive behavior. He lived on his own, but had a girlfriend with whom he often spent the weekend. He was referred by the social worker at his girlfriend's children's school. During the first session, at which his girlfriend was present, it became clear that he did not suffer from compulsive behavior, but a range of tics (such as blinking, finger-tapping and cracking of the knuckles), which increased in direct relation to the degree of insecurity he felt. He hid his insecurity and lack of social skills behind a considerable amount of verbal aggression, which emerged whenever anyone had the nerve to disagree with him or say anything which he thought was stupid. Although he had had hardly any education after primary school and did not have an interesting job, he was certainly not stupid and he was often right in the many conflicts he became involved in.

At the end of the first session, the therapist proposed directing initial treatment at his aggression and the problems this led to with the people around him. This was, after all, the reason for his referral. His girlfriend had given him the choice between therapy or ending the relationship.

Drawing up the treatment contract was not easy. The therapist was given a taste of Mr. Rose's suspicious nature and cutting remarks. The same fate had befallen his predecessor, an amiable psychiatrist, whose

Table 4
Mr. Rose and His Girlfriend

Age	33
Education	low
Unmarried	has a girlfriend
Presenting Problem	tics and aggression
Interventions	working through traumatic past
	congruent assignment for him,
	paradoxical assignments for her
Length of therapy	14 sessions
Results	negative

treatment was ended abruptly after two sessions. In the light of the above, the therapist decided to "play it cool." There was, after all, no rush. "Perhaps, Mr. Rose," he said, "it would be best if you were to take your time to think about whether you like this approach and want to carry on with me." Several weeks later, Mr. Rose telephoned to say that he did want to go on, but without his girlfriend. The therapist agreed to this, as it had become obvious during the first session that her part in the problems was relatively small and that Mr. Rose alone provided enough material to work on.

To begin with, the therapy was directed towards the past and the therapist was careful with Mr. Rose's resistance and disqualifying behavior. For example, he tried using positive labelling (pointing out Mr. Rose's honesty, sincerity and integrity) and presented him with options (Erickson & Rossi, 1975).

Mr. Rose's childhood had been miserable. He was the only child of parents who lived an isolated existence and nipped all his social activities in the bud. He had not learned the sort of social skills necessary for sustaining relationships and, understandably, he did not have much self-confidence. By writing a series of letters and by talking to both his mother and his father, he managed to express some of the resentment he felt about this.

At the end of eight sessions, this phase of the therapy was concluded. He had become calmer and did not display many tics during the sessions. His relationship with his parents had improved and he no longer allowed them to treat him like a child. The next step was to devote attention to the way in which he conducted himself in company. He agreed to have his girlfriend and her children rejoin the sessions.

One session with the children present followed. The problem areas within the "family" were inventoried. The central theme was the excessive anger Mr. Rose felt when anyone disagreed with him, or when things did not go quite as he had expected. It should be noted that his girlfriend was an expert at provoking him with her "mother-knows-best" attitude, which infuriated him and set him frantically finger-tapping and knuckle-cracking.

At the eleventh session, a response prevention program was begun. *Whenever he felt angry, he was to go and sit alone for fifteen minutes and think about how unpleasant it was to feel unsure about the matter which had caused his anger. While he was doing this, he was to squeeze a bodybuilder's hand grip so that he could not tap his fingers or crack his knuckles. He was to use the last few minutes to write down his conclusions. His girlfriend was instructed* (as the reader must have come to expect by now) *to assist him by providing him with plenty of opportunity for practice. She was to treat him like a child and disagree with him frequently.*

The results were not particularly successful. His girlfriend reported having been too busy to argue with him, but on the occasions when she had done so, he had not carried out his assignment. Instead, he had controlled himself and had not tapped his fingers. The therapist complimented him but urged him to carry out the assignment nevertheless. He did not want to, nor did he want his girlfriend involved in the therapy any longer. He said that it was an unnecessary burden for her. She disagreed with him completely and wanted to continue coming to therapy. No decision was made.

The therapist asked him to think about how therapy was to be continued—by following his own approach or by going along with the suggestions of the therapist. During the following session, it emerged that his girlfriend had said that, for the time being, she did not want him spending the weekends at her house. The situation was discussed, in particular its uncertainty for Mr. Rose. For him the situation was like trying to pass an examination all the time. The therapist offered him two alternatives. Either there was to be a trial separation for about six months, during which they were not to see each other at all and during which Mr. Rose was to work at solving his problems on his own, or they were to stay together for six months without threatening separation. The compromise his girlfriend suggested, i.e. seeing each other from time to time, did not seem to the therapist to be conducive to peace. They were to give the matter some thought.

At the following session, which was the fourteenth, the girlfriend said that she had chosen to continue the relationship with Mr. Rose as it was too deep to break off in such an abrupt manner. The therapist asked her to explain what it was about Mr. Rose she liked so much. As her answer was somewhat vague, the therapist asked her to be more specific. Mr. Rose suddenly became very angry, began pacing back and forth, accused the therapist of making life difficult for his girlfriend, and threatened to walk out. His girlfriend had no objection to the therapist's questions, but Mr. Rose said that he did not like his "psychological tricks."

After 13 sessions using the judo approach to motivate Mr. Rose (Lange, 1985c) and achieving very little, the therapist now pointed out that if Mr. Rose wanted to leave, he was free to do so and could still return within two weeks if he had any regrets. If he did not contact the therapist, the therapist would consider the treatment finished. Mr. Rose walked out, never to come back.

Observations

Unlike the Wilburns and the Barclays, in this case, there was a clear symptom-bearer who received the congruent part of the interventions. The question is whether or not such a response-prevention program may be classified as congruent.

As with Mr. Fulbright, Mr. Rose's girlfriend was asked to help him by providing him with sufficient opportunity to practice. The difference between the two cases is that Mr. Rose's girlfriend could hardly be called symptomatic and she had little influence on and was certainly not the cause of his compulsive behavior. The assignment to help him in that particular manner could, therefore, hardly be called paradoxical and neither did it really turn the system upside down. With the Fulbrights, this was the case, because the aggressive husband was seen as "the animal" and therefore as the only patient.

The final result in the case of Mr. Rose cannot be explained by the above alone. The relationship between him and the therapist was also troubled. At the end of ten sessions, Mr. Rose was still providing a steady stream of disqualifying remarks about the therapy, the therapist and therapists in general. In such circumstances, it is probably not much use presenting a relatively congruent response-prevention program, requiring a large amount of effort on the part of the client, whether it is accompanied by a paradoxical assignment for the partner or not.

The Michaels Family and Their Problems in Bringing Up Their Children

Mrs. Michaels (50) referred herself and her family as her younger son, Mark (14), was unmanageable. There were two other children at home, Josephine (15) and Nico (18). The parents had been divorced for a number of years. (See Table 5.)

The most important conclusion drawn from the first session was that the mother was not in control. She swung from one extreme to the other, sometimes trying to be "friends" with her children and then, when matters got out of hand, becoming unreasonably strict or losing her temper with them. Nico and Josephine appeared to be worriers and they were both having trouble at school. Mark, however, was the most urgent problem. He was threatening to fill the "authority vacuum" by not accepting anyone's authority, making a fuss about everything and generally trying to lay down the law.

The therapist conveyed his impression of the family to them at the end of the first session. They agreed on a treatment contract in which the restoration of authority was the most important part. The only person who objected was Mark, but the therapist ignored him. He was now concerned with the mother. In the second and third sessions, there was no explicit intervention with homework assignments. The emphasis was primarily on the divorce: how they went about it, how the children felt about it, the mother's feelings of guilt, and the resulting difficulty she was having finding a "niche" in the family. The therapist suggested indirectly that she should perhaps go for a walk with Nico and talk about herself. This would show her that being close to one's children need not necessarily mean failure as a parent or as a figure of authority.

Table 5
Michaels Family

Composition	mother (50), 3 children Mark (14), Josephine (15), Nico (18)
Education	middle
Presenting Problem	disciplining Mark
Strategy	restoring hierarchy
Intervention	congruent assignment for mother, paradoxical for Mark
Length of therapy	16 sessions
Results	positive

The suggestion was accepted gratefully. The atmosphere seemed to have improved already and Mrs. Michaels seemed determined to take the therapist's advice. In her case, a congruent approach was the most obvious choice.

During the fourth session, the fact that Mark was unmanageable came up once again. During the two weeks preceding the session, he had been extremely disobedient on several occasions, which had led to heated and unproductive outbursts from his mother. She complained that she had lost control of the situation and was at her wit's end. The therapist asked about several events in greater detail until he had a clear and concrete picture of what had taken place. He then said:

> "Mrs. Michaels, may I give you my impression of the situation in your family? When I hear that there is a constant fight going on, I can't help thinking that people can fight constantly only when the parties involved are equal. If one side were stronger, the fight wouldn't last long. In your case, Mrs. Michaels, this means that you are not stronger than your children and you should be. The problem lies not with Mark—you can't blame him for trying to find out how far he can go." Then he said to Mark: "The problem is that your mother does not exert her authority enough."
>
> The therapist continued: "I think, Mrs. Michaels, that it is your job to win this battle and your responsibility to discipline Mark. You could try to gain more insight into the situation. You could try to find out how often these clashes take place, in what circumstances, and how exactly you react. I would therefore like to ask you to monitor this for a while. In the evening, you will spend half an hour reading through the notes you have made that day and thinking about how you could have done things differently." The therapist then turned to Mark again and said, "Mark, you are to carry on being difficult. Behave exactly as you have been doing up to now."

During this introduction, Mark looked more and more uncomfortable. He said that he would much rather try to be nice in the coming weeks. The therapist said:

> "I am pleased to hear that, but I think being nice will have to wait for a couple of weeks. You see, it is important for your

mother to practice on the difficult Mark, and not on the nice Mark. So please, make a concerted effort to misbehave for two more weeks."

The above was agreed and written down. The mother was enthusiastic. Two weeks later, during the following session, it appeared that they had had an extremely pleasant time. The atmosphere at home had begun to change. Mark had hardly carried out his assignment; on the contrary, he had behaved well. The therapist asked him to try it again anyway, which he did, with the same result. Mark's paradoxical assignment was therefore withdrawn, and the therapist began working on increasing the family's problem-solving capacity (Lange & van der Hart, 1983). A good deal of use was made of registration and behavioral contracts, not only with respect to Mark's problems, but also in the relationships between the other members of the family.

After fifteen sessions, the therapy was more or less concluded. The mother was perfectly able to fulfil the role of parent, particularly where Mark was concerned. Mark also changed. As he was an intelligent and inventive boy, he enjoyed finding solutions to problems and he often succeeded.

Contact with the family did not end entirely, as Josephine was having problems regarding her position in the family and with her peers. Her fears and insecurity had previously been well-camouflaged by her somewhat symbiotic relationship with her mother. As the mother had changed, she had lost her special position. In order not to relieve the mother of too much responsibility, it was decided to end the therapy in principle, but to hold follow-up sessions once every two months. These were intended primarily to "supervise" the mother's guidance of the daughter. These meetings were satisfactory and when therapy was terminated, the positive changes in the family had been sustained for over a year.

Observations

The intervention described with Mrs. Michaels and her son, Mark, may be seen as a prototype. All the prerequisites were present. Although at the outset there was a more or less "identified patient," it is reasonable to say that the mother was symptomatic in her role of the inadequate parent. Nevertheless, results were surprising for everyone concerned, and the existing system, with a bullying, attention-seeking Mark and a nagging, ineffectual mother, was turned upside-down. Another factor was the good relationship which existed between the therapist and the mother. She was given a congruent assignment (there was not even a hint of the paradoxical about it) which required a good deal of effort. A less motivated client would not have put it to such good use. At the time of this session, the relationship with Mark was reasonable, although he was critical of the therapist. This made it very appealing to saddle him with a paradoxical assignment. By continuing to be a bully, he would be helping his mother and the therapist, which was the last thing he wanted to do at that moment.

DISCUSSION

An article with a title such as this may lead one to think that the author is easily able to distinguish between a paradoxical and a congruent assignment. This is, however, not always the case. Naturally, there are interventions, such as Mrs. Fulbright's and Mrs. Michael's learning assignments which are manifestly congruent. There are also assignments, such as those given to Mrs. Wilburn, Mrs. Barclay, Mr. Fulbright, and Mark Michaels which are manifestly paradoxical. There are, however, assignments which contain both congruent and paradoxical elements. Van Dijck, van der Velden and van der Hart (1980) pointed this out in their article on classifying directive interventions. As an example, they mention the "fractionated quarrelling advice" which we discussed above and which is generally considered paradoxical. Because of its regulating aspect, however, it may be said to contain congruent aspects as well.

Monitoring assignments can frequently also be viewed in two ways. On the one hand, there is the gathering of information which is to serve as the basis for further strategies designed to bring about change; on the other, it is customary (and rightly so) to warn the client that he should not change his behavior during the monitoring period. This in itself is something of a paradox and I think it would be wise not to classify this sort of intervention as either congruent or paradoxical by definition, but to examine in each case what the therapist's intention was and where the emphasis lay (Lange, 1985a, chapter 9).

The assignments to go off and be alone given to Mr. Wilburn and Mr. Barclay both contained a paradoxical element. At that stage, they did not have to fight their feelings of being hurt and humiliated. There is, however, a great deal to be said for attaching greater importance to the congruent aspect. Their symptomatic behavior was, after all, certainly not being encouraged. No one was saying that to feel hurt served a purpose, not even for the time being. They were, however, being advised to put those feelings to some use when they arose, and this was clearly intended to combat the symptoms. The "time out" which was linked to the monitoring may, moreover, be seen as an aversive consequence which, in terms of learning theory, may certainly be classified as congruent.

The response-prevention program for Mr. Rose was a borderline case, too. He received congruent instructions to react in a manner to which he was not accustomed when he felt bad moods and tension coming on. These instructions were designed to prevent his usual response (Emmelkamp, 1982), but, at the same time, his symptomatic behavior was tolerated. To begin with, he was not asked to prevent it. Viewed as a whole, therefore, the instruction also had a paradoxical aspect.

Hoogduin et al. (1977) also discuss treatments in which the distinction between the paradoxical and the congruent is difficult to draw. Their client, Mr. Donkers, was given permission to continue his compulsive asking of questions (paradoxical), but he knew that people around him would react aversively. The approach in cases reported by Rijntjes (1982) resembles that of Hoogduin et al.

To summarize the above: Certain interventions may be seen as both paradoxical and congruent. The choice depends on the therapist's intention and on nuances in the way the intervention is presented.

In the formal sense, there is a similarity between the cases described by Hoogduin et al. and Rijntjes and the situation described here in the Michaels family. In both situations there is an identified patient with whom the environment is at a loss to deal. With Hoogduin and Rijntjes, the identified patient remains labelled as such. His behavior is tolerated but the system remains unchanged. The environment is provided with a set of measures which equips it to react differently to the patient. The environment becomes a kind of co-therapist.

In the approach described above, for example, with the Michaels family, the environment was also coached, with the help of congruent advice, on how to react to the referred patient. There is, however, a surprising new aspect involved, that is, the identified patient is not all that crazy, and it is the environment (in this case the mother) which is odd for accepting the situation and responding so inadequately. This reasoning provides the opportunity to saddle the symptom-bearer with a cast-iron paradoxical assignment. His behavior is not only tolerated, *it is encouraged in order to help other people.* This provides motivation which is more convincing than the well-known paradigms, such as the "honest explanation," "positive labelling" and "becoming aware" (Lange, 1985a). Furthermore, the system is turned upside-down. Such motivation is, of course, possible only in cases where there are no people with extreme individual disorders. Furthermore, there must be some kind of inadequate behavior in the environment which requires change.

All the examples described above concern a combination of instructions, one half of which is given to one person and the other half to the other. The "help paradigm" in the form of a combination of the congruent and the paradoxical can also be used if there is only one person involved. A clear example of this is provided by Lange (1985b) in his description of the approach used with agoraphobic patients. After they have been taught to control their breathing by means of hyperventilation provocation and breathing exercises, they are instructed to practice what they have learned, i.e. cutting short an attack of hyperventilation, in the situation they fear. In order to carry out this congruent assignment, it is necessary that they have an attack. They are, therefore, asked to try to induce an attack (a paradoxical instruction) in the street. In doing so, they are helping themselves to carry out the congruent part (i.e. the practicing) of their program.

In three of the five cases described, the intervention had a decidedly positive effect. In one case, that of Mr. Rose, the outcome was definitely a failure. With the Barclays, the therapy was satisfactory, although this was not at all so at the outset. Do these cases provide any insight into the question of when this approach is indicated?

Mr. Rose was clearly and to an extreme degree the identified patient, while his girlfriend had very few shortcomings. The criterion of encouraging him to display symptomatic behavior was therefore not met. For this reason, he was given the congruent assignment (response-prevention) and his girlfriend, in order to help him, was given a paradoxical assignment, which, in view of the fact that she did not display any symptoms, cannot really be described as paradoxical. In retrospect, we may conclude that in this case, in which the two above described indications were not present, it was not wise to try to combine the paradoxical and the congruent. A method similar to that of Hoogduin et al. would probably have worked better.

Apart from this, both Mr. Rose and Mr. Barclay had objections to the therapist and to therapy in general. It was, therefore, not a good idea to give them congruent assignments requiring a great deal of effort.

To summarize, we may say that this method of motivating clients to accept paradoxical assignments is indicated particularly in the following cases:

1. *If there is a conflict situation between two people where the obvious course of action is to instruct one person to do something about his or her part in the conflict.* This will preferably be the person who was not referred (for example, a parent), while the referred patient, who is frequently also the most recalcitrant, is given the paradoxical instruction in order to help the other person.

2. *If the relationship between therapist and clients is good.* As long as there is no clear acceptance of a treatment contract, particularly on the part of the person who will have to carry out the congruent part of the assignment, this method has little chance of success.

In conclusion, it should perhaps be emphasized, that should the paradoxical side of the assignment lead to a reduction in the symptomatic behavior, the therapist should not be too jubilant. As with paradoxical assignments which are not combined with congruent assignments, a concerned attitude is more appropriate, as well as a repetition of the assignment, accompanied by an earnest request to try even harder to carry it out. Only when the symptomatic behavior has been absent for quite some time, as in the cases of Mrs. Wilburn and Mark Michaels, should the paradoxical assignment be withdrawn and a completely congruent strategy pursued.

REFERENCES

Emmelkamp, P. M. G. (1982). *Phobic and Obsessive-Compulsive Disorders: Theory, Research and Practice.* New York: Plenum.

Erickson, M.H., & Rossi, E.L. (1975). Varieties of the double bind. *American Journal of Clinical Hypnosis, 17,* 143–157.

Haley, J. (1980). *Leaving Home.* New York: McGraw-Hill.

Hoogduin, K., van der Hart, O., van Dijck, R., Joele, L., & van der Velden, K. (1977). De interactionele behandeling van dwangmatig controleren. In K. van der Velden (Ed.), *Directieve Therapie I.* Van Loghum Slaterus, Deventer.

Lange, A. (1985a). *Gedragsverandering in gezinnen.* Fifth revised edition. Wolters Noordhoff, Groningen.

Lange, A. (1985b). Een multidimensioneel behandelingsmodel voor agorafobie. *Directieve Therapie 5* (4), 319–341.

Lange, A. (1985c). Motivating clients in directive family therapy. In J. K. Zeig (Ed.), *Ericksonian Psychotherapy. Vol. II, Clinical Applications.* New York: Brunner/Mazel.

Lange, A., & van der Hart, O. (1983). *Directive Family Therapy.* New York: Brunner/Mazel.

Rachman, S. J., & Hodgson, R. J. (1980). *Obsessions and compulsions.* Englewood Cliffs, NJ: Prentice Hall.

Rijntjes, E. (1982). De combinatie van paradoxale opdrachten en leeropdrachten bij de behandeling van kinderen. *Kwartaalschrift voor Directieve Therapie en Hypnose, 2* (2), 119–126.

Seltzer, L. F. (1986). *Paradoxical Strategies in Psychotherapy. A Comprehensive Overview and Guidebook.* New York: Wiley.

Selvini Palazzoli, M., Boscolo, L., Cecchin, G. F., & Prata, G. (1978). *Paradox and Counterparadox.* New York: Jason Aronson.

Tomm, K. (1984a). One perspective on the Milan systemic approach: Part I. Overview of development, theory and practice. *Journal of Marital and Family Therapy, 10* (2), 113–125.

Tomm, K. (1984b). One perspective on the Milan systemic approach: Part II. Description of session format, intervening style and interventions. *Journal of Marital and Family Therapy, 10* (3), 253–271.

Van Dijck, R., & Hoogduin, K. (1977). Ruziemakende paren. In K. van der Velden (Ed.), *Directieve therapie I.* Van Loghum Slaterus, Deventer.

Van Dijck, R. & van der Velden, K. (1977). Valkuilen voor directieve therapeuten. In K. van der Velden (Ed.), *Directieve therapie I.* Van Loghum Slaterus, Deventer.

Van Dijck, R., van der Velden, K., & van der Hart, O. (1980). Een indeling van directieve interventies. In K. van der Velden (Ed.), *Directieve therapie 2.* Van Loghum Slaterus, Deventer.

Chapter 18

A Multidimensional Approach to the Utilization of Therapeutic Metaphors for Children and Adolescents

Joyce Mills and Richard Crowley

Joyce C. Mills, Ph.D. (International College), maintains a private practice in marriage, family and child therapy in Encino, California, where she trains psychotherapists.

Richard J. Crowley, Ph.D. (United States International University), is a psychotherapist with a private practice in North Hollywood, California.

Mills and Crowley have special expertise in the use of Ericksonian techniques with children. They have coauthored an excellent text, Therapeutic Metaphors for Children and the Child Within.

Mills and Crowley describe successful metaphorical interventions for adolescents and children. Therapists can create metaphors by entering the child's world and using existent strengths; the metaphors serve as "threads" around which dormant strengths can crystallize. Techniques must be tailored to the individual and strike a responsive emotional chord.

In the last two decades an important shift has taken place in the field of psychotherapy from insight analytically oriented approaches to those which emphasize the use of strategic interventions to activate behavioral changes in clients. This shift was pioneered by Erickson's maverick utilization approaches, which went largely unnoticed until his later years. Jay Haley's publication of *Uncommon Therapy* (1973) was instrumental in initially bringing Erickson's unusual methods to a wide audience. In attempting to describe how Erickson worked, Haley wrote:

It is easier to say what Erickson does not do in therapy than to say what he does, except by offering case examples. His style of therapy is not based upon insight into unconscious processes, it does not involve helping people understand their interpersonal difficulties, he makes no transference interpretations, he does not explore a person's motivations, nor does he simply recondition. His theory of change seems to be based upon the interpersonal impact of the therapist outside the patient's awareness, it includes providing directives that cause changes of behavior, and it emphasizes communicating in metaphor. (p. 39)

Erickson's use of metaphor has served as one point of inspiration and change in a substantial segment of family and growth-oriented therapies. An impressive body of literature describing and evaluating the use of metaphor as a form of therapeutic intervention already exists (Barker, 1985; Erickson & Rossi, 1979; Gordon, 1978; Haley, 1973; Lankton & Lankton, 1983; Madanes, 1984; Mills & Crowley, 1986; Ritterman, 1983; Zeig, 1980). We will address two facets of metaphors which relate to child and adolescent therapy. One facet focuses on the use of specific multidimensional techniques (storytelling, artistic, interactive, and living metaphors). The second facet highlights inner perspectives that can provide subtle yet profound enhancements of the techniques being utilized.

It is beyond the scope of this chapter to elucidate all the factors that ultimately contribute to the creation of any type of metaphorical intervention. In general, we use a *multisensory framework* for viewing, assessing and resolving psychogenic and psychophysiological problems. In this framework we utilize behavioral minimal cues, eye movement patterns, and verbal descriptive language to determine each child's *sensory profile* (kinesthetic, visual, and auditory sensory interrelationships). This sensory systems approach functions both as a resource indicator and as a diagnostic tool for retrieving the *out-of-conscious* sensory system (Heller & Stelle, 1987) that is implicated in the problem area. The goal of *sensory integration* serves as the underlying matrix of all our work.

FIRST FACET: METHODS AND TECHNIQUES

Previously we have presented the use of what we have termed *artistic* and *living* metaphors as multidimensional extensions of the *storytelling* metaphor (Mills & Crowley, 1986). In this chapter we will provide further elaborations of these approaches and, in addition, introduce the use of the *interactive* metaphor and its placement within the larger context of the other techniques.

Storytelling Metaphor

A major developmental aspect of adolescence is the movement out of the world of childhood fantasy and into the word of adult concrete thinking. Because of this shift, it would seem natural to limit or disregard the use of metaphor as a therapeutic approach for this age group. However, we have found that the opposite is often the case: The use of metaphor with adolescents can actually enhance communication and therapeutic outcome. Perhaps this is due to the fact that adolescents typically are deluged by commands, instructions, and judgements regarding their behavior and activities. Since metaphor is indirect and implicative by its very nature, a message can be "transmitted" on a level in which it is more likely to be accepted.

Indeed, some clinicians (Gardner & Olness, 1981) have speculated that the disuse of metaphor arising from our Western culture's devaluation of fantasy probably contributes to the problems that emerge during adolescence. Providing support and elaboration to this notion is Pearce's (1977) theory that metaphor represents a specific developmental right-brain process that is intrinsic to the stage of childhood. As the child grows into adolescence, left-brain functioning becomes dominant since right-brain abilities are less and less utilized in the educational system. Pearce goes so far as to speak of a left-brain overload of education which robs adolescents of a familiar and natural form of communication. The consequence of this imposed imbalance is a diminution of problem-solving abilities. Certainly Pearce also would acknowledge a concomitant diminution in creative and imaginative processes.

We have found that while remaining aware of an adolescent's concern with concrete reality, the therapist nonetheless can present meaningful metaphorical messages to even the "toughest" of teenagers. One of the strongest issues of adolescence is that of individuality and the need to control. Metaphor is respectful of this crucial developmental process because it provides a new, nonthreatening perspective: The therapist is not telling adolescents to do something but is, rather, presenting back to them what they have given the therapist.

Masks

Dressed in black, with spiked black-and-red hair, eyes and lips blackened with make-up, 16-year-old Lori was brought—no, practically dragged—into my (J. M.) office by her mother. Lori was an honor student and had many friends. Recently, however, her mother had become greatly disturbed by the remarkable change in Lori's personality, attitudes, and personal appearance. She was certain that Lori smoked marijuana and drank alcohol, but was not certain if she was also using other drugs.

While Lori's mother was describing her version of the problem, Lori sat glaring at me with hands folded belligerently across her chest as if creating a "silent dare" for me to cross the boundaries she was setting. In reply to the mother's comments and description of the problem, I acknowledged, "It is very difficult to watch someone you love change dramatically before you and not understand what those changes are about."

Shifting slightly in my chair, I asked Lori with genuine interest how she managed to do such a fine job of dyeing her hair, because it was so perfectly balanced with red and black. I asked her if she had done it by herself or if someone had helped her. Lori's face began to soften slightly as she proudly proclaimed, "I did it myself." I then went on to ask what brand and colors of dye she had used to get such an interesting effect; how long it had taken her to do it; and if she used anything special to create the spiked look. I was intentionally choosing to utilize Lori's "punk" appearance by entering her world and accepting it as meaningful rather than judging it negatively. By the end of this first session, her demeanor had relaxed; however, she was still clearly "on guard."

In the second session, Lori's behavior vacillated markedly from her initial hostility to one of inquisitiveness and receptivity.

In the third session, Lori sauntered into my office and plopped down into my overstuffed chair. Her demeanor exuded anger as she blurted out, "This therapy stuff is stupid"—followed by a string of profanities. As she ranted and raved on and on about not wanting to be here, my perceptions about her behavior began to broaden. I saw a young, bright teenage girl putting on layers of different masks: There was her makeup mask, her anger mask, her hair mask, her clothes mask, her drug mask. I realized that at this volatile moment she was giving me a valuable metaphor about herself that I could utilize. *Clowns* came into my mind, and I waited patiently for her pace to slacken.

When she finished her diatribe she flounced back in the chair. Unexpectedly and in a seemingly irrelevant way, I began talking about clowns at the circus. In order to capture her attention, I leaned forward, looked directly into her eyes, matched her breathing, and spoke in rhythmic tones. For the next half-hour, the theme of clowns and masks unfolded in a storytelling metaphor that both paralleled and reframed Lori's problems. Following is a condensation:

"You know, Lori, clowns are rather interesting. I remember taking a class of young children to the circus one day. They were most fascinated with the clowns. I arranged to take the children backstage to see how the clowns put on their make-up. But the children first wanted a chance to try on the colorful clown make-up, so one of the clowns named Bingo said that he'd be delighted to show them how to do it. He showed them all his tricks in making up different expressions. Boldly from the back of the group, one little girl spoke up and, pointing to her chest said, "I want a scary clown face." Bingo helped her with all of his colors. The children watched with wonder in their eyes as each of their friends was transformed. After the make-up was in place, I encouraged the children to act out their mask characters. Each one did so with surprising enthusiasm.

"Now the clowns began to put on their own makeup. One clown painted his face with a big red smile; another clown painted her face with a big tear in the corner of her eye; another clown painted her face with a 'tough-guy' scar. There must have been seven or eight different clowns, and everyone had different masks. One little boy asked the clown with the big tear if she really felt sad. Surprised, the clown replied, 'Why, no. I just paint that tear on, but inside I feel happy.'

"The clown with the big red smile spoke up and said, 'Sometimes I feel unhappy, but I put on this happy face which hides the unhappy feeling. No one really knows those times when I feel unhappy inside.'

[Lori was quiet as the clown story continued.]

"Remember, makeup masks are fun. Sometimes they even help us pretend we are someone we are not. But underneath those masks is the real YOU, so it's important to take off the mask at the end of the day, look in the mirror, and say to that reflection, 'Hello, I want to be your friend.' "

Lori was still listening intently as I finished the story about clowns and masks. At the end, her anger had softened into tears and she allowed herself to cry for a few moments.

This storytelling metaphor about masks seemed to act as a turning point in this early stage of Lori's therapy. She soon opened up and talked about the pressures to take drugs and "belong" with the other kids. I suggested she join Alateen for added support, and she did so. Lori continued in weekly therapy for eight months. Throughout her therapy, I found that the use of metaphor seemed to absorb her attention easily and in a nonthreatening way. Over a period of time, many of her masks were removed. While she still dressed "punk," *she* had become a different person—far more authentic and present. She had learned to be in touch with her feelings and to express them directly rather than through the indirect, harmful vehicles of drugs and alcohol. The punk dress, too, had taken on another meaning, a different purpose. Now it was not a method to keep people away but a statement of her individuality—and she was having fun with it.

Artistic Metaphor

Since research indicates that the right brain mediates imaginal and emotional processes (Erickson & Rossi, 1979; Galin, 1974; Gazzaniga, 1967; Rossi, 1977; Sperry, 1968), we have developed a concept of the *artistic metaphor* for children which incorporates a variety of multisensory drawing strategies specifically designed to access the abilities in that part of the brain. With this technique the hypnotic phenomenon of dissociation is utilized to help children resolve common childhood experiences such as separation and loss, anger, pain, and fear. The drawings act as "visual keys" to the unconscious, depicting and evoking the child's intrinsic but untapped healing processes. In the following case, the artistic metaphor was used to evoke strengths and resources in a nine-year-old girl going through another round of custody and visitation battles.

Denise's bridge

One day I (J. M.) received a distressed call from a client with whom I had worked some time ago. It seemed that Cristina's ex-husband wanted to change the visitation schedule they had agreed upon with regard to their two daughters. He now wanted one of their daughters to live with him for alternating weeks. He also was taking Cristina back to court to get reduced alimony payments. Nine-year-old Denise became quite upset with this new upheaval in her life; she was crying continuously and was not sleeping well at night. Since I had seen the family during the divorce process, I had already established a good relationship with the girls. When Denise asked her mother if she could come to see me about this problem, her mother readily agreed.

When Denise came into the office, she immediately walked over to the art table. Looking downward with a saddened expression on her face, she told me how things were "a big mess." She didn't know what to do. She loved both of her parents and was feeling pulled apart by their struggle over her. Since Denise was fully in touch with her feelings regarding her current situation, I decided to utilize the dissociative approach of the *artistic metaphor* in order to shift her perspective onto her strengths and resources. I asked Denise to draw a picture of the way her problem looked to her (see Figure 1). I then asked her to draw a picture of how the problem would look "all better" (see Figure 2). For the third picture, she was asked to draw what would help change Figure 1 into Figure 2 (see Figure 3).

As can be seen, Denise's first picture was graphically representative of her present state. She was feeling "broken up" and "pulled apart," and didn't want to hurt either parent. The second picture was drawn with great enthusiasm; Denise was smiling and humming as she sketched the happy homelife for which she was so urgently wishing. The third picture provided an amazing depiction of her inner healing process as she unconsciously knew it to be. This picture was particularly profound because this third step in our drawing technique is referred to as a "metaphorical bridge" (Mills & Crowley, 1986, p. 179) in the healing process. I had never used this term with Denise, since it would have had little or no verbal meaning for a nine-year-old. In Denise's picture, as can be noted, she actually drew a bridge to help her get from the unhappy, broken household to the happy, stable one.

Denise's dilemma of feeling pulled apart is a common one for children of divorcing and divorced parents. Certainly we are not suggesting that this drawing strategy can change the outer, real-life dramas these children encounter. However, it can serve as a catalyst for activating their own inner resources which can help them better cope with their fears, anger, and confusion. Moreover, the drawings provide rich information for the therapist that can be incorporated into later storytelling, living, and interactive metaphors.

Storytelling, Interactive, and Living Metaphors

As mentioned, we have described the storytelling and living metaphors in greater detail elsewhere (Mills & Crowley, 1986). In the *interactive*

Figure 1

metaphor, the therapist initiates some form of symbolic, playful activity with the child which requires a full range of movement and response from both child and therapist. Although the interactive metaphor appears similar in its outward appearance to many forms of play therapy (Axline, 1969; Capacchione, 1979; Jernberg, 1979; Kramer, 1971; Moustakes, 1953; Oaklander, 1978), its point of differentiation lies in the particular aspects of behavior which the therapist seeks to observe and utilize. In most applications of play therapy, the focus is on the acting out of

Figure 2

Figure 3

the psychodynamic processes surrounding the child's problem. In our development of the interactive metaphor, we emphasize a focus on sensory system functioning as it is manifested in both healthy and problematic areas of the child's life. The purpose of the interactive metaphor is to provide the child with an opportunity to experience his or her inner resources in an active process uniting body, emotion, and thought in a movement experience that imparts a therapeutic, metaphorical message. A simultaneous benefit occurs through the continued integration of the child's sensory systems as intrinsic sources of strength and healing.

The following case demonstrates a progression of levels within which the metaphor is operating. The therapist begins with a simple storytelling metaphor about bicycles which allows the child to remain in an apparently passive position. In reality, however, this is a kind of "warm-up" stage that activates the child's internal resources as the story is heard and visualized. Next the therapist brings the metaphor into a second, interactive level when participation is elicited from the child. The interaction between child and therapist literally helps to bring the child's internal resources outward into the therapist's office. Finally, the living metaphor which is given to the child as a homework assignment completes the progression by anchoring the resources into the child's actual life environment.

Mr. Forgetful . . . nevermore

One day in treatment an elderly client mentioned that her six-year-old grandson, Jimmy, had had a problem of wetting and soiling his pants. The problem had been unsuccessfully treated with home remedies and with recommendations from the pediatrician. Recently Jimmy's pediatrician referred him to a specialist in pediatric gastroenterology, whose findings were negative. The pediatrician and the gastroenterologist had concluded that Jimmy's problem was due to unexpressed anger that he was acting out in a passive-aggressive manner by wetting and soiling his pants. They viewed Jimmy's soiling as a "behavioral manifestation of an underlying emotional difficulty . . . not yet overcome." It was recommended that Jimmy receive psychiatric help in order to discover "the unidentified and as yet unknown motives for [his] self-damaging behavior."

Jimmy's parents had reacted with great reluctance to the suggestion of psychiatric intervention. Because the grandmother and I (R. C.) already had established an excellent therapeutic relationship, I suggested that Jimmy's parents make an appointment. I knew that my client had told them about how her chronic chest pain symptoms had subsided completely with hypnotic intervention, and so it seemed likely that they would be less reluctant to bring Jimmy to see me for a session.

The next week Jimmy and his parents came to my office. They sat on the couch, with Jimmy in the center. I found Jimmy to be a cute little boy who reminded me of a Raggedy-Ann doll as he slumped limply in the center of my large leather couch. I did not mention Jimmy's presenting problem in front of him but instead began with simple questions to elicit mention of some of his favorite things. He was extremely unresponsive and I realized that he was already in his own trance state without my needing to facilitate one! I then mentioned different types of favorite things such as television shows, cartoons, animals, sports, riding bicycles, going to the circus, and so forth, until I got nods from Jimmy. I began to talk slowly and rhythmically about bicycles (which had netted the most animated response) by interweaving themes of being *in control* and *out of control*, as well as *holding on* and *letting go*. My methodical talking further reinforced Jimmy's trance and he collapsed even more into a Raggedy-Ann posture.

My therapeutic focus was on discovering which sensory system was malfunctioning in Jimmy's problem area rather than on discerning the psychological dynamics of the problem as they had been described in the pediatrician's report. As I saw it, Jimmy needed to "reopen" his out-of-conscious kinesthetic sensory channel that apparently was failing to transmit normal bladder and rectal signals.

At one point Jimmy began telling me about one of his toys, which simultaneously triggered a therapeutic metaphor as well as a visual memory in my mind of favorite toys I had played with as a child—Lincoln Logs and a red crane truck. I got down on the floor with Jimmy and pretended that my arm was a crane and my fingers were metal claws. Slowly I created a story as I involved Jimmy in participating in my metaphorical drama. It seemed we were in the woods together, working as loggers. Many trees had been cut so that they could be turned into building materials. The crane was needed to hold the logs in place for a while and then to drop them into the nearby river to be taken downstream. As the crane, I acted as though I had several logs to hold onto until the right time. I asked Jimmy, "Should we let go of the logs now?"

"Yeah!" he replied enthusiastically.

"No, not yet," I cautioned. "We're too far away from the river where the logs belong." I moved my hand in a jerking motion (like a crane) over to the right.

"How about now? Should we drop them here?"

Jimmy again answered affirmatively and again I responded slowly and in a deliberating manner, "No, only let go when the logs are over the river and nowhere else."

As the "crane" was positioned over the "river," I rhythmically bobbed my head up and down saying, "How about letting go of the logs here?"

Jimmy eagerly responded, "Yeah!"

"That's right," I said. "You know exactly where and when to let go of your own logs, don't you?" He nodded yes, smiling proudly.

Four other main elements of Jimmy's treatment were incorporated into the same session: 1) anchoring him with a touch in order to establish an unconscious association between his kinesthetic channel and his memory; 2) having him tighten and relax various muscles, including the abdominal and buttocks muscles; 3) having him differentiate between smooth and "not smooth" objects in my office to increase his awareness of his kinesthetic sensory channel; and 4) assigning two living metaphors (Mills & Crowley, 1986) that he could carry out at home.

1. *Anchoring* is "any stimulus that evokes a consistent response pattern from a person" (Lankton, 1980, p. 55). I use it frequently in my work as a means of bringing a therapeutic association directly into the three main sensory channels (visual, auditory, kinesthetic). The idea to use anchoring with Jimmy came spontaneously while I was repeatedly receiving the same monotoned response of "I don't know, I forget," to my questions. After my fourth inquiry Jimmy responded, "I don't know, I forget. My parents even call me Mr. Forgetful."

Since Jimmy had just given me his nickname of Mr. Forgetful, I wanted to make use of it as another pathway into his symptom area. I immediately responded by simultaneously touching his knee (kinesthetic anchor), looking at him with a bright smile on my face (visual anchor), and saying in an uplifted voice (auditory anchor), "That's fantastic! You have a good memory to remember that your parents call you Mr. Forgetful, don't you?" A puzzled "Uh-huh," and a nod of the head was Jimmy's response.

I then asked a barrage of questions I knew he would be able to answer such as, "Do you remember which door of the two doors in my office you came through today?"

"Yeah, that one."

"You're right! You have a good memory," I commented as I again employed the triple anchor of my touch, facial expression, and voice. "Did Santa Claus have any animals that pulled his sleigh? . . . Was Santa Claus's beard white or purple?" Now Jimmy would laugh at my silly questions and respond with delight at all my positive reinforcements. Through my irrelevant questions, the intent was to anchor Jimmy back into the experience of remembering—since the issue for him involved, in a sense, a relearning of how to remember to notice the feelings within his body that were associated with his natural processes of elimination.

2. *Muscle experience* was my next focus. I directed Jimmy to flex and release a variety of muscles in his legs, arms, stomach, abdomen, and buttocks. I continued to anchor him to his abilities to *hold onto* and *let go* of his muscles. We even "walked" across the floor using our buttocks muscles.

3. *Differentiating textures* provided our next sensory lesson. I had Jimmy touch several objects in my office and tell me whether they were "smooth or not smooth." This became a rambunctious game for both of us in which I continued to reinforce Jimmy's responses via the triple anchor of kinesthetic-visual-auditory reinforcement. In addition, the game was described to his mother (in the waiting room) as a homework assignment they could do together.

4. A *living metaphor* was created to conclude the session and as a means of extending the interactive metaphorical experience into Jimmy's daily life environment. He was told to "tear off three pieces of paper and imagine that they are the logs. This time, Jimmy, you'll be the crane. Each day, you have to let your crane drop your logs at whatever times you decide into the toilet bowl (the river) to be flushed downstream." Jimmy readily accepted the assignment and showed no indication of comprehending any personal meanings or parallels.

Two weeks passed and Jimmy, his mother, and grandmother returned. In the outer office his mother happily reported that Jimmy's presenting symptoms had disappeared. He was finally toilet trained! When I met with Jimmy alone in the office, he conscientiously described to me how he had carried out his homework assignments. We then moved on to discussing swimming and other activities he had participated in since he had last seen me. If I had needed a sign of Jimmy's new found well-being, he provided it for me. After answering one of my questions correctly, he looked up mischievously and said in a matter-of-fact tone, "I have a good memory!"

The banishment of the bunny monster

I (R.C.) had the opportunity of treating a 33-month-old boy named Alex who was experiencing monsters in his bedroom. He would scream and cry "for hours on end," refusing to enter his bedroom. His father, who accompanied him to the office while his mother remained home with an infant girl, described Alex as "a little Jekyll and Hyde": "One minute he is hysterical and nothing we do can stop him. Then, when I'm ready to leave the house, he's all smiles—all set to leave with me as if nothing had happened for the last two hours of screaming." The parents were becoming agitated by their response to Alex's often un- relenting behavior; they had begun to identify with the abusive parent syndrome, as they were finding it increasingly difficult to restrain from physically acting out their frustrations.

Prior to his painful and disruptive behavior, Alex had been ill with a temperature of 105° which had lasted for three days. During this time, he became delirious and hallucinated. In fact, he apparently was hallucinating a monster at the very time his parents were present in his room—which gave it all the more credence, as far as Alex was concerned. Whenever he was questioned about why he was so scared, he would offer no information but would sink deeper into his hysterical state.

I had met Alex a year before when I treated his parents for transitional issues. When Alex heard he was going to come to my office, he gave out the first bit of information: "Does Dr. Crowley have a bunny monster in his office?" His father's and mother's inquiries into the bunny monster yielded only a stubborn "Won't talk about it" from Alex.

Even though Alex had met me before, he entered my office reticently and climbed up into his father's arms while I talked about everything except the bunny monster. I attempted to gather information for later metaphorical intervention but had difficulty eliciting from Alex some of his favorite things. His father helped me by mentioning that Alex was a fan of the "Yellow Bird" character (Big Bird) on Sesame Street. I became animated as I described how wonderful Yellow Bird was and placed drawing paper and magic markers in front of Alex to begin the artistic metaphor.

When I asked Alex to draw Yellow Bird, he obliged with a squiggly mark. His father then reminded him of the other television characters he liked. Interestingly, Alex chose to draw the succeeding characters on the same piece of paper, over Yellow Bird. He stacked up one favorite character upon the other as he giggled in pleasure. I praised Alex enthusiastically as did his father.

Now that Alex had gained momentum in his drawing, I asked him to draw his house (he squiggled), his livingroom (he squiggled), and, finally, his *forbidden* bedroom—which he drew with the same liveliness he had exuded while drawing all the other images. Now I had an accumulation of positive associations (anchors) cushioning Alex's previous negative feelings about his bedroom.

At one point, Alex's father encouraged him to "Tell Dr. Crowley about what you told me on the way to his office—you know, about the bunny. You wanted to know if he had a bunny here." I quickly handed Alex the box of markers and responded with the same positive auditory spark as earlier, "Yeah! That would be great—draw the bunny monster."

Although Alex responded with continued enjoyment of the drawing process, both his father and I noted the heavier movement of the markers and the extra time Alex took to produce his rendition of the bunny monster.

As Alex finished the drawing, I thought for a moment and then spontaneously decided to toss the "bunny monster" in the air. Alex giggled as I did so. I tossed the drawing to him and he threw it in the air with all his strength. Alex continued to take control of his artistic metaphor of fear, tossing it again and again in the air with delight (interactive metaphor).

I then suggested, "Let's make the bunny disappear." Immediately Alex tossed the bunny monster drawing up in the air and it floated downward, literally disappearing between three inches of space separating my couch from the wall. Surprised, his father and I looked at each other, not quite believing how the bunny monster had truly disappeared. Laughingly, we both hummed a few bars from the eerie theme of *Twilight Zone!*

To conclude the session, I instructed Alex's father in our three-step drawing technique (as described in Denise's case) and told him to use it at home with Alex whenever he became fearful. A few days later, the father phoned to tell me that he had forgotten about the assignment, but that Alex had reminded him by asking to draw. Over the next two weeks, Alex's fear dwindled significantly but did not disappear completely. He was no longer becoming hysterical, but still felt uneasy in his bedroom.

Coincidentally, the family was in the process of moving to a new home during this time. To utilize this ongoing reality for Alex, I instructed the parents to create a kind of "goodbye ritual" to their old house whereby each of them would leave behind anything that was scary or unwanted. Alex was eager and energetic when his turn came to say farewell to his old bedroom and, upon arriving at the new house, he went straight into his new bedroom without incident.

The use of metaphor as a strategic therapeutic technique places new demands and tasks upon the therapist. It requires acute behavioral observations and rapid utilization of what is presented by the client. Erickson was the consummate expert at perceiving a rich array of minimal cues which he would then spontaneously utilize in the creation of highly effective interventions that stimulated rapid change. With Erickson as the model, most of us have struggled long and hard to gain some of the level of facility he achieved. And while the strategic use of metaphor has opened a multitude of therapeutic doorways for both clients and clinicians, it also presents its own pitfalls. The most common trap could perhaps be called the "cleverness trap," because the therapist becomes unwittingly seduced by the technique as a novel manipulation in itself. Rossi and colleagues (Rossi, Ryan, & Sharp, 1983) have warned against the use of technique disconnected from the deeper chords of personal experience and genuine feeling:

> Patients rightly resent it when they feel they are being manipulated by the "empty technique" employed by an operator who has no personal connection and knowledge of the shared sources of problems and illness within all of us. Such operators attempt to use technique as a means of power and prestige to control others. But of course the patient's unconscious can pick up the shallowness of this empty charade, and nothing really changes . . . Even if a symptom is changed, there still has been no deepening association with the inner sources of illness and creativity that are the true quest of all healing work. (p. 58)

SECOND FACET: INNER PERSPECTIVES

Our experience of using metaphor with children has gradually crystallized three guiding principles that we believe must complement the therapist's knowledge of technique and strategy:

1. the child's natural use of metaphor as the developmental "language of choice";
2. the child's ability to spontaneously create his or her own therapeutic intervention via the use of metaphor;
3. the importance for the therapist of entering the world of the child.

In working with children, we are frequently presented with unexpected demonstrations of their spontaneous "deepening associations with the inner sources of illness and creativity that are the true quest of healing work" (Erickson & Rossi, 1979, p. 79). These experiences remind us in forceful and touching terms of the core therapeutic premise upon which all forms of strategic intervention must be based: that the child, adolescent, or adult possesses all the experiential resources necessary for change and growth. The point of strategic intervention is simply to give these resources a nudge upward and outward into daily experience.

We have found that it is extremely important to remain receptive to the client's active abilities in producing these resources. At times it is easy to get bogged down with figuring out what intricate interventions we therapists need to create in order to elicit the client's inner problem-solving capacities. In the following two cases, we were presented with profound experiences of children spontaneously creating their own healing interventions.

The tiger who didn't stand a chance

Little three-year-old Christopher walked briskly into my office one day, and with assurance and boldness in his voice asked, "Joyce, do you know what I dreamed last night?"

"No," I answered curiously.

Stretching his arms open to match his statement he said, "I dreamed about a B-I-G tiger. He came into my room to scare me, and do you know what I did?"

Again I said, "No," in a questioning tone as I squatted down to Christopher's size. Gazing unblinkingly at me, he took a deep breath and with a proud voice said, "I put him on a cloud and I B-L-E-W him away!"

Amazed, I replied, "Really? How wonderful!"

"Yes," he went on. "Then I dreamed he came back and breathed fire on me."

"What did you do *then?*" I asked.

Wide-eyed and smiling, Christopher answered in his big voice, "I S-N-E-E-Z-E-D him away and he never came back!"

I sat back for a moment and reflected to myself how utterly amazing children can be. They possess an uncomplicated and intuitive grasp of how to help themselves feel better. From a traditional analytical frame of reference, Christopher's image of the tiger would be more typically representative of, for example, unexpressed anger. In making that assumption, however, the therapist must *impute meaning* rather than *receive meaning* from the child. From our point of view, Christopher, in discovering his own resolutions to the problem of the tiger, was demonstrating his ability to self-create strategic interventions on a metaphorical level. He was also demonstrating the natural use of metaphor as a child's language of choice. Children do not have to be taught metaphorical language; it is the language they bring into the session.

This and the following case further underscore the third important learning for therapists: By entering the world of the child, we make it possible for them to *give us* the metaphors they need; they will give us a wealth of information about themselves that can greatly reduce the therapist's feeling of having to "figure everything out."

The goodbye party

I (J. M.) had been seeing a bright, precocious five-year-old boy for some six months because of his aggressive behavior at home and at school. His mother reported that Billy had been a difficult child from birth, but after the arrival of his baby sister he had become virtually unmanageable. Throughout my work with Billy, I employed storytelling and artistic metaphors as methods of intervention. When Billy's behavior had improved significantly at home and in school, I began to talk about picking a time to say goodbye. In my mind I assumed we would pick a date and then deal with the termination in the usual therapeutic manner. However, Billy knew more than I did about when and how he was ready to terminate.

As I opened the door to the waiting room to welcome Billy for his session, he leaped off the sofa excitedly. Carrying a big white bag in his little hand he said, "Today is my Goodbye Day, and I brought a party." His eyes were gleaming and he was smiling from ear to ear. His mother looked at me with a questioning expression and said, "Is that all right?"

Perceiving the completely confident expression on Billy's face I replied,

"Well, of course! Children know a lot about when it's time to say goodbye and just how to do it." My reply was a spontaneous response not just to the words Billy used, but to his overall body cues and unconscious communications that expressed what seemed to be an integrated and viable confidence.

I then held out my hand and we walked into my office together.

As Billy, his mother, and I shared in the goodies he had brought for

Figure 4

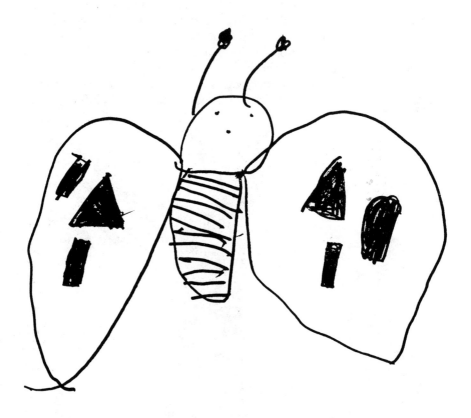

Figure 5

the party, I became aware of a telltale questioning part within myself that was still concerned about the abruptness of Billy's decision to end therapy. Each time saying goodbye was brought up, Billy would change the subject. Traditionally, this behavior could be interpreted as indicating that Billy was not truly ready to terminate his therapy. I decided to explore the issue in an indirect manner. Knowing how much Billy loved to express himself through artwork, I asked him if he would draw me a "Goodbye Picture." Immediately he bounded to the art table and began drawing.

His mother and I sat quietly observing. Billy picked up the brown marker and was happily humming as he drew. When he finished the first picture of a cocoon hanging from a tree (see Figure 4), he surprised me by adding, "I'm not finished yet—I want another paper."

I handed it to him gladly. Without pausing he then drew a butterfly (see Figure 5). As we looked in wonder at the images of the cocoon and butterfly, both his mother and I became deeply satisfied that this child truly knew his timetable for ending therapy. I recognized again how powerful and informative the child's unconscious use of metaphor can be when given room for spontaneous expression in a creative manner.

REFERENCES

Axline, V. (1969). *Play Therapy*. New York: Ballantine. (Originally published in 1947.)
Barker, P. (1985). *Using Metaphors in Psychotherapy*. New York: Brunner/Mazel.
Capacchione, L. (1979). *The Creative Journal*. Athens, Ohio: Swallow Press.
Erickson, M., & Rossi, E. (1979). *Hypnotherapy: An Exploratory Casebook*. New York: Irvington.
Galin, D. (1974). Implications for psychiatry of left and right specialization. *Archives of General Psychiatry, 31,* 527–583.
Gardner, G., & Olness, K. (1981). *Hypnosis and Hypnotherapy with Children*. New York: Grune & Stratton.
Gazzaniga, M. (1967). The split brain in man. *Scientific American, 217,* 24–29.
Gordon, D. (1978). *Therapeutic Metaphors*. Cupertino, Calif.: Meta Publications.
Haley, J. (1973). *Uncommon Therapy*. New York: Norton.
Jernberg, A. (1979). *Theraplay*. San Francisco: Jossey Bass.
Kramer, E. (1971). *Art as Therapy with Children*. New York: Schoken Books.
Lankton, S. (1980). *Practical Magic*. Cupertino, CA: Meta Publications.
Lankton, S., & Lankton, C. (1983). *The Answer Within: A Clinical Framework of Ericksonian Hypnotherapy*. New York: Brunner/Mazel.
Madanes, C. (1984). *Behind the One-way Mirror*. San Francisco: Jossey Bass.
Mills, J., & Crowley, R. (1986). *Therapeutic Metaphors for Children and the Child Within*. New York: Brunner/Mazel.
Moustakes, C. (1953). *Children and Play Therapy*. New York: McGraw Hill.
Oaklander, V. (1978). *Windows to Our Children*. Moab, Utah: Real People Press.
Pearce, C. (1977). *Magical Child*. New York: Bantam.
Ritterman, M. (1983). *Using Hypnosis in Family Therapy*. San Francisco: Jossey Bass.
Rossi, E. (1977). The cerebral hemispheres in analytical psychology. *The Journal of Analytical Psychology, 22,* 32–51.
Rossi, E., Ryan, M., & Sharp, F. (Eds.) (1983). *The Seminars, Workshops, and Lectures of Milton H. Erickson. Volume I. Healing in Hypnosis*. New York: Irvington.
Sperry, R. (1968). Hemispheric disconnection and unity of conscious awareness. *American Psychologist, 23,* 723–733.
Zeig, J. (1980). *A Teaching Seminar with Milton Erickson*. New York: Brunner/Mazel.

SECTION TWO: PRACTICE

PART VII

The Utilization Approach

Chapter 19

Symptom Phenomena as Trance Phenomena

Stephen G. Gilligan

Stephen G. Gilligan, Ph.D. (Stanford University), is an internationally recognized authority on Ericksonian hypnotherapy who practices in San Diego. He is a popular teacher of Ericksonian methods whose workshops are widely acclaimed. Gilligan has been Invited Faculty Member for all of the Congresses and Seminars organized by the Erickson Foundation. He has authored a book entitled Therapeutic Trances: The Cooperation Principle in Ericksonian Hypnotherapy.

Gilligan develops the idea that symptom phenomena are versions of classic hypnotic phenomena. He discusses similarities between symptom phenomena and trance phenomena, and then he contrasts symptom contexts and therapeutic contexts. This chapter summarizes the invited workshop that Gilligan presented at the 1986 Erickson Congress.

The major thesis of this chapter is that inherent in symptom phenomena are naturalistic versions of classical hypnotic phenomena. The interactional sequence leading to symptomatic expressions is viewed as a hypnotic induction, and the resulting symptom phenomena are acknowledged as hypnotic trance phenomena. This view allows therapists to accept symptoms as legitimate hypnotic expressions already being practiced by the client, and thus to work to transform such admittedly self-devaluing acts into self-valuing, flexible solutions.

The approach taken here is based on the utilization principle pioneered by Milton Erickson. Erickson (1948, 1952, 1959, 1965) advocated accepting and amplifying the client's processes as the means for therapeutic changes. His special emphasis on the relevance of hypnosis in this

327

regard continues to be developed by his students, and one of the major contributions of Ericksonian psychotherapy has been to elucidate the relationship between hypnotic processes and symptomatic processes.

SIMILARITIES OF SYMPTOM PHENOMENA AND HYPNOTIC PHENOMENA

A central assumption is that a person expressing a symptom is a person immersed in a naturalistic, albeit self-devaluing, trance. The therapist's task is to join the hypnotic processes inherent in the problematic expression and to cooperate in ways that allow their transformation into self-valuing solutions. To effectively do this, the therapist must be clear about the elements shared by symptomatic trances and therapeutic trances. Following are the eight shared characteristics we will explore in this section.

1. Paradoxical injunctions
2. Both/and logic
3. Ideodynamicism
4. Intensified experiential involvement
5. Sustained attention
6. Temporal variability
7. Somatic changes
8. Other phenomenological alterations

Paradoxical Injunctions

Induction of trance, like all communications, emerges within a relationship context. It is therefore important to consider the transactional patterns that give rise to this experiential state, one of which is the paradoxical injunction, wherein two seemingly contradictory directives are presented simultaneously. For example:

1. Hear what I say/Don't pay attention to me.
2. I want you to go into trance/I want you to stay out of trance.
3. I want you to let that hand lift/I don't want *you* to lift that hand.

Figure 1 illustrates the general form of this pattern, which is assumed here as fundamental to the development of trance states. The figure also indicates how the resulting trances may be generative or symptomatic, depending on the relationship context.

The idea that paradoxical injunctions create altered states is rooted in the Bateson group's formulation of the double bind hypothesis (Bateson, Jackson, Haley, & Weakland, 1956; Haley, 1963). In studying schizophrenics within a family systems context, the Bateson group

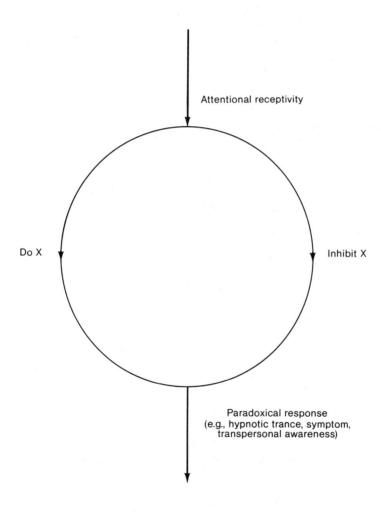

Figure 1. The generation of altered states from paradoxical injunctions.

observed that their altered states developed in response to contradictory parental "suggestions." For example, a parent may repeatedly communicate messages of this sort:

1. "This is funny/This is not funny."
2. "Listen to me/Disregard what I say."
3. "Love me/Don't express your love."

These contradictory messages are typically delivered simultaneously, though usually in different channels (e.g., verbal and nonverbal).* Bateson et al. (1956) proposed that the repeated offering of such statements stimulates (schizophrenic) altered states in a person who is unable to leave the context, comment on the communications, or respond to just one or the other side of the message.

Haley (1963) extended this hypothesis by applying it to the contexts of hypnosis and psychotherapy. He noted that a person expressing symptoms is a person giving paradoxical directives. For example:

1. I am communicating this (symptom)/It is not *me* who is communicating this (symptom).
2. I want to change/I don't want to change.
3. Come closer/Stay away.

Haley further observed that psychotherapists would typically use their own paradoxical injunctions when communicating with clients. For example:

1. Follow my directives/I am non-directive.
2. I cannot help you/I can help you help yourself.
3. Our relationship is personal/Our relationship is impersonal.

Haley (1963) suggested that such therapeutic paradoxes were effective precisely because they mapped into the contradictions inherent in a person's symptomatic behavior. Thus, psychotherapists may be suc-

---

* Double binds may be distinguished from paradoxes in that the former involves messages at different logical levels, whereas paradoxes contain messages at the same logical level. While Bateson and his group made much of this distinction (e.g., see Haley, 1955, 1963), I do not think it so important for practical concerns.

cessful to the extent that they execute judo-like counter-inductions to the "hypnotic inductions" of clients (cf. Watts, 1961).

Erickson and Rossi (1975) elaborated these ideas further in the context of hypnotherapy. They discussed techniques of therapeutic double bind wherein naturalistic hypnosis could be utilized via paradoxical communications such as:

1. I want you to respond (unconsciously)/I don't want you to respond (consciously).
2. You can be all alone in trance/You can be alone with me in trance.
3. You can remember to forget OR forget to remember.

As Figure 2 illustrates, each of these examples involves asking the subject to respond simultaneously to both sides of a complementarity. In contrast to the paradoxical injunctions underlying symptomatic communication, such "suggestions" also convey an underlying support for the individual. But in common with symptomatic communications, the respondent is expected to remain in the context, to respond to both sides simultaneously, and to not comment on (e.g., try to explain or talk about) the paradox. To reiterate, it is this formula which seems to be dramatically effective in inducing altered states of consciousness characterized by the emergence of trance phenomena, whether they be symptomatic or therapeutic in nature.

Paradoxical injunctions are inherent in most of the techniques developed by Erickson. Metaphorical stories include the paradox of "This story is not about you/This story is about you." Symptom prescription and "encouraging resistance" techniques instruct the person to change

Figure 2. Examples of paradoxical injunctions.

by not changing. Dissociation involves asking the person to respond spontaneously (i.e., unconsciously), but to deliberately not respond (consciously). In these and other techniques, paradoxical directives depotentiate the linear orientation of the conscious mind and amplify the circular and systemic orientation of the unconscious mind, thereby giving rise to trance and its symptoms. Haley (1963) proposed that the effectiveness of such techniques may arise primarily from their ability to join and recontextualize the paradoxical injunctions inherent in the client's symptomatic "trance."

Paradoxical messages occur in many contexts. Bateson (1954) and Haley (1955) have described their relevance to play, humor, fantasy, and dreaming. Watts (1961) and Rossi and Jichaku (1984) elaborated on their use in transpersonal contexts such as Zen Buddhism. Since this communicational form is prevalent in various contexts but produces extended trances in only some, it should be appreciated as a necessary but not sufficient condition for trance development. Other factors must also be present for a sustained trance to occur.

Both/and Logic

A corollary to the communication of paradoxical directives is the experience of both/and logic in entranced individuals. Both/and logics allow for something (X) and its opposite (X') to simultaneously be true, in contrast to the more traditional either/or logic which postulates that if X is true, its opposite (X') is not. This experience of "trance logic" (Orne, 1959) was beautifully illustrated in hypnosis experiments described by Beahrs (1982). Subjects actually hypnotized ("reals") and subjects merely pretending to be hypnotized ("simulators") were both given suggestions to not see ("negatively hallucinate") an individual actually standing in the room. Another person was then placed directly behind this individual, and subjects were asked to walk a direct path to the other person. The experimental question was thus one of how subjects would respond to the individual standing in their path, since they were asked to not perceive him. As expected, simulating subjects did what they thought a negatively hallucinating person would do: They bumped into the individual standing in their path. However, subjects actually experiencing trance responded quite differently: They walked around the individual they were told to negatively hallucinate.

In extensive post-test interviews, a fascinating story emerged. When asked if they "saw" the person standing in their path, hypnotized subjects insisted they did not. When asked why they forged a circuitous path, they claimed not wanting to bump into the person standing there whom they did not see! In short, entranced subjects entertained two experiential states without contradiction: They did not "see" the person AND they did see the person. Thus, the experience of trance seems to allow for an organizational state wherein opposing states or values can co-exist simultaneously.

We can see from these data a natural function of trance: It allows individuals an opportunity to experience both sides of a relationship simultaneously. The relationship can be distinguished in many ways: subject/object, observer/observed, self/other, conscious/unconscious, and so forth. This capacity for the experience of both/and logic may contribute to problems in a variety of ways. For example, problems often develop and persevere when a person dissociates from (e.g., denies) a relationship at a conscious level even while identifying with it deeply at an unconscious level. A person may claim to not want to eat (smoke, drink, take drugs, etc.) even while vigorously engaging in a systematic abuse of that activity. A marital relationship might be painfully balanced by the simultaneous feelings of love and hate, approach and avoidance. In these and other problems, individuals may be observed to express both sides of a relationship simultaneously. As they do so, other characteristics of trance discussed below also show up.

Both/and logics may also play a central role in solutions. For example, a pregnant mother being trained in hypnotic pain control for natural childbirth was told she could experience herself "apart from while a part of" her body when needles were inserted into her arms and hands. She later reported having felt a curious sensation at the insertion sites while simultaneously wondering (in a detached and comfortable state) whether this was what "they normally referred to as pain." With another client, a change in a behavioral pattern of overeating was achieved by hypnotically training the woman to experience a "phantom body" that could step outside of her physical body and binge when needed "even while her unconscious could take care of all the REST needed." (This "phantom body" technique has been used successfully in a variety of cases involving addictions.) Finally, significant therapeutic progress was made with a couple via "mutual hypnosis" exercises wherein partners learn to develop a "together yet apart" trance state. The both/and logic of trance may allow for creative interaction between normally conflicting parts.

Ideodynamicism

Self-expression in trance states is felt to occur independently of normal conscious mediation. Feelings, thoughts, behaviors, etc., just seem to happen, without planning or effort. In hypnotic terminology, this phenomenon is called *ideodynamicism* ("ideas" into "dynamics" without conscious interference), which may involve ideo-motor, ideo-sensory, ideo-cognitive, ideo-affective, ideo-perceptual, or ideo-imaginal expressions. As Bernheim (1895) noted, ideodynamicism is intensified by trance.

Ideodynamicism is a primary feature of symptomatic trances. Problem descriptions invariably contain some references to being "out of control," in terms of interpersonal (e.g., behaviors) or intrapersonal (e.g., cognitions) communication. While traditional therapy typically attempts to bring these "out of control" processes under the dominance of the conscious mind, the approach in Ericksonian therapy is often different. Such expressions are acknowledged as legitimate processes however they occur in self-devaluing or socially unacceptable fashions. Thus, therapeutic efforts are focused on recontextualizing or reframing such processes in ways that allow change. For example, a client complained of recurrent internal dialogue that "suggested" imminent failure. After his attention was suitably absorbed, intense and repetitive use of the "failure" theme was used as the basis for hypnotherapeutic communications:

> Now, John, I'm going to ask you to do some things here which I am confident you will succeed in failing to fully do even now. Now what do I mean by that? Simply this: You're thinking a lot about failure. You're thinking about failing at work. You're thinking about failing at home. You can think about failing to fully respond here in the office. So what I will not fail to continue to remind you to do is to wonder and wander unconsciously in terms of how much you can enjoy that failure as you hear now my words. I want to suggest that your hand will fail to lift up. I want to suggest that your eyelids will fail to blink or not blink. I want to suggest that you may fail to not wonder about how you will continue to wonder. I want you to fail to fully relax only part ways. . . .

Hypnotic elaboration on this "failure" theme served to absorb attention, elicit a therapeutic trance, and develop a variety of therapeutic trance phenomena.

This utilization approach to "out of control" processes in Ericksonian therapy stems from its hypnotic roots. The hypnotic subject is encouraged to "just let things happen." This may involve a hand lifting without a sense of conscious volition; a memory being recalled in a surprising way; a feeling of not being able to move; or a sense of thoughts "thinking themselves." In short, *the hypnotist encourages the development of self-expressions independent from the control of the conscious mind.* It is thus a natural step to appreciate symptoms as spontaneous ideodynamic processes that may be accepted and utilized as legitimate hypnotic phenomena.

In utilizing ideodynamic phenomena, it is important to recognize that they may be attributed to a variety of sources, including the devil, the unconscious, the deceased, or family members. Actually, all such ideodynamic processes are naturalistic expressions for which a person is responsible (i.e., has the ability to respond to). Thus, naming the source (e.g., "the unconscious") is relevant only to securing a person's cooperation in participating in the process of accepting experience.

Intensified Experiential Involvement

As discussed earlier, trance amplifies experiential involvement. Ordinary psychological processes are intensified to the extent of seeming phenomenologically different. Remembering becomes hypermnesia; forgetting can be experienced as amnesia. Memory deepens to regression, future projection to age progression. Detachment evolves into dissociation, attachment into full identification. These amplified phenomena are present in both therapeutic and symptomatic trance processes; as such, they may be experienced as self-valuing (e.g., revivifying a happy childhood event) or self-devaluing (e.g., internal dialogue intensifying into haunting voices). Trance augments the basic processes by which experience is generated.

Amplified expression in trance means deeper immersion in the experience. Just as would happen if the radio you were listening to were turned up or the colors you were watching grew more intense, the sense of involvement increases as trance augments whatever "shows up" in experience. At the same time, attention diminishes to stimuli outside the psychological field of the trance. Thus, if you were to go into trance with a friend in a crowded room, you might grow oblivious to all the neighboring stimuli. Or if you were to develop a symptomatic trance around a sense of anxiety in your chest, awareness of the surrounding environment (including the rest of your body) might fade away.

Trance increases absorption in stimuli inside the established psychological field and decreases it in stimuli outside of the field. In self-valuing states, this is quite an asset: Artists may become totally immersed in their artistic works; therapy clients can experience full absorption in a feeling of self-acceptance; thinkers may develop complete involvement in letting thoughts unfold. But in self-devaluing states, this same skill becomes a liability: A person victimized by incest remains deeply withdrawn into the horror of the experience; a couple in an argument can literally see nothing but each partner's cues indicating mistrust. Flexibility and other skills must be available if increased experiential absorption in trance is to be advantageous.

Part of the reason that experiential absorption is deepened in trance is that critical processes are dampened. Awareness becomes less laden with analytical processes and more filled with "concrete" phenomenological experience. As with any development, this may help or hinder, depending on the relationship context. On the one hand, less critical processes allow more creative and spontaneous processes to unfold; on the other hand, a person stuck in a symptomatic trance may require critical faculties to recognize what's happening. As we shall see, it is therefore important to develop trances that have error-correcting capacities available within them.

Sustained Attention

In addition to deeper experiential absorption, trance enables more sustained attentional orientation to a given idea or experience. This is in contrast to a normal waking state, where attention usually shifts across different facets of the environment. The ability to focus attention in trance was noted by James Braid in the 18th Century, who replaced his original term of *monoideism* ("single idea" state) with the term *hypnosis* ("sleep" state). It was also noted by Bernheim in the 1890s, who described psychological problems in terms of "idea fixations" and proposed the use of repetitively suggesting other ideas via hypnosis.

These "idea fixations" distinguish both symptomatic and therapeutic trance states. In symptomatic trances, individuals organize their experience around some recurrent stimulus. Possibilities include the voice of a parent, a feeling in part of the body, and the expression of some ritualized behavior (e.g., handwashing, smoking). This same sustained attention to a stimulus characterizes therapeutic trances. Here the focus may be on the hypnotist's voice, a thumbtack on the wall, a mantra, or a rhythmic dance. Thus, the sustained absorption of trance may make for ruts or grooves, depending on the relationship context.

Temporal Variability

As trance intensifies experiential involvement and sustains attentional focus, a person's sense of time changes. In particular, the linear sense of time as having a beginning and end (thereby creating "past," "present," and "future") often disappears, giving way in trance to a "timeless" quality. This development makes sense when we think of psychological time as a construct of analytical thinking, useful for organizing goal-oriented actions and sequencing events (cf. Ornstein, 1969). As analytical thinking dissipates in trance, individuals are less inclined to process experience in sequential terms, and the ability to accurately estimate the temporal duration of the experience is thus reduced. This seems to be true both for hypnotic trances (Schwartz, 1978) and symptomatic trances (Melges, 1982).

One consequence of the disruption in temporal sequencing is that individuals are less able to distinguish the order in which events transpired (Evans & Kihlstrom, 1973). Alternatively stated, individuals in trance are more able to "jumble" the order of a sequence, thereby freeing behavior from a rigid linear chain of events. Since this rigidity seems to distinguish problem sequences, where A automatically triggers B which automatically triggers C, trance can thus facilitate the use of "scramble techniques" (Lankton & Lankton, 1983) and other interventions designed to alter invariant sequences (see Haley, 1976).

Another consequence of "timelessness" is difficulty in distinguishing a past and future from the present (Melges, 1982). Thus, individuals in trance are less inclined to represent a "future" distinct from "now" (Zimbardo, Maslach, & Marshall, 1972). This state enables more aliveness, creativity, and spontaneity in the present.

At the same time, timelessness in a symptomatic trance may be quite problematic. Individuals engulfed in a "depressive trance" have extreme difficulty in sensing the possibility of a future different from their present state. Likewise, couples engaged in an altered state sequence of arguing have little access to other "times" that may provide resources for the present challenge.

The temporal variability of trance can be used for therapeutic advantage. For example, a client may be trained to experience a minute as an hour, or an hour like a minute. Thus, a few moments of relaxation in between labor contractions or before a public performance may provide a person with "all the time in the world" to retrieve and integrate needed resources. Alternatively, several hours of pain (e.g., following a surgery) might be psychologically felt as involving only minutes of clock time. As Cooper and Erickson (1959) and Masters and Houston (1972) have elaborated, time distortion can facilitate development in many areas.

Somatic Changes

Any significant shift in psychological experience will be accompanied by a shift in somatic experience. It is therefore not surprising that a variety of bodily changes are felt in the course of trance experiences. A person may feel relaxed and drowsy (the body becoming heavy and warm), or perhaps alert and immobilized (cataleptic). As such changes develop, a person may feel greater association with and/or greater dissociation from the body; for example, a person may feel oriented within the body or observing it from a distance. Either way, there will generally be less of a sense of active control over the movements or experiences of the body; expression will be felt as being initiated from some other source (e.g., "the unconscious," an enemy, the hypnotist).

These alterations will be accompanied by shifts in the person's patterning of physical expressions. As trance develops, changes may be observed in behavioral patterns of breathing, movement, eye focus, talking, pulse rate, and so forth (Erickson, Rossi, & Rossi, 1976; Gilligan, 1987). Observation of such cues thus reveals the onset of trance. As we will see, the behavioral patterns involved in therapeutic trances are clearly distinguishable from those accompanying symptomatic trances.

The variability of somatic experience during trance can be therapeutically utilized. For example, an obese client desiring weight loss reported in trance that her body felt like an expanding round balloon. Over time, elaborate suggestions to experience the "balloon body" expand and contract gently, along with specific breathing suggestions, enabled the gradual shrinking of the body image, which correlated with weight loss.* Thus, the therapist may utilize spontaneous bodily changes in trance as naturalistic "techniques" useful in establishing desired changes.

Other Phenomenological Alterations

In addition to the changes thus far discussed, other phenomenological alterations occur in trance. For the open-eyed person, vision may become blurry, light patterns may change, a face may distort or turn into that of another person (familiar or unfamiliar). When eyes are closed, unusual images may develop: geometric patterns, void-like spaces, archetypal characters, or dream-like figures.

As with all trance characteristics, such phenomenological alterations may be symptomatic or therapeutic. For example, a client described a recurrent symptomatic trance in which she felt imprisoned by a circular brick wall that rose high to the sky, leaving her with a painful sense of disconnection. A similar "hallucinated wall" technique was spontaneously developed by a hypnotized psychotherapy client interested in developing ways to experience safety and solitude. Thus, any of the many unusual phenomenological developments that occur in trance may be exhilarating and satisfying or frightening and debilitating, depending on context.

CONTEXT DIFFERENCES: SYMPTOMATIC TRANCES VS. THERAPEUTIC TRANCES

As we have seen, symptom phenomena and hypnotic phenomena share numerous characteristics. Both are developed from paradoxical injunctions and involve paradoxical (both/and) experience; both feature the principle of ideodynamicism, whereby expressions (thoughts, behaviors, feelings, etc.) develop outside of conscious control; and both involve intensified experiential absorption, sustained attention, temporal alterations, somatic changes, and other phenomenological shifts. In short, a person expressing a symptom is a person in trance.

In this view, the variable of therapeutic interest is the relationship context in which trance processes occur. The following are seven context variables that will be discussed:

---

* It may be assumed that people regulate their body weight partly by unconscious body images that serve as "homeostats" (Pribram, 1971). Thus, modification of this fixed image facilitates modification of the actual physical body (Achterberg, 1985).

1. Self-valuation process
2. Level of trust
3. Biological context
4. Content variability
5. Frame variability
6. Context sensitivity
7. Relationship style: Cooperation vs. competition

Self-Valuation

In any experience, two levels of participation may be distinguished. The first is phenomenological—the expressions that actually appear in the experience. The second is psychological—how a person chooses to relate to the experience. For example, a client complained that when she closed her eyes to relax, a pair of disembodied eyes would be staring at her intensely. Coincidentally, a therapy trainee reported a similar image of disembodied eyes appearing during a group trance some months later. The client felt afraid and attempted in various ways to negate the experience, while the trainee felt comfortable and chose to welcome the unusual development. Thus, different relationships were established toward the same trance phenomenon.

As might be expected, the experience was a problem for the client and a solution for the trainee. The claim here is that the "difference making the difference" was the valuation process. Whether aware of it or not, every person "votes" on each life experience: This vote is to either value or devalue the experience, thereby establishing it as either ally or enemy, resource or deficit. *A self-valuing vote enables a therapeutic trance, while a self-devaluing vote makes for a symptomatic trance.* Thus, a major task for the therapist is to validate symptom phenomena, thereby paving the way for a translation of problems into solutions.

This valuation process underlies the cornerstone principle of utilization in Ericksonian psychotherapy. This principle, which advocates accepting and using whatever a person is doing as the basis for change, seems to have emerged from Erickson's personal challenges with polio, dyslexia, tone deafness, and color blindness, phenomena normally devalued as major deficits (Erickson & Rossi, 1977). As Erickson demonstrated with himself and others, such "problems" can be appreciated as opportunities for unique learning and self-development.

This appreciation does not require trying to frame an experience as "good" or "pleasant," since many experiences are naturally unpleasant. Rather, it involves viewing each experience that arises as a viable human expression that can be integrated into the overall fabric of a person's developmental tapestry. To develop such an appreciation, the therapist often needs to "deframe" perceptual orientation, such that a phenomenon can be observed independently of its ascribed value (Gilligan, 1987). A therapist can recognize this neutral state by an ability to equally generate ways in which the phenomenon could be socially desirable or undesirable. For example, the process of withdrawing may be a problem or a solution, depending on the context.

Once the therapist is able to value the client's expression, various methods can be used to promote the client's doing the same. One technique is to simply feed back in a self-valuing way those aspects of a symptomatic experience in which a person is especially absorbed. For example, a client began to recount multiple childhood experiences of sexual and physical abuse. As she became increasingly upset and self-absorbed, I tried to reassure her. After about 30 minutes, I finally "heard" her repeated chants about feeling "crazy" and thus immediately proclaimed in an intense fashion, "You're crazy!" The woman's demeanor became centered and focused, and asked, "Do you really think so?" Maintaining the same intensity and sincerity, I continued to validate that her experience was indeed "crazy," while periodically wondering how this craziness was going to be approached in a way that would allow new choices. Thus, joining and valuing the person's dominant experience of feeling "crazy" was a first step in the therapeutic task of transforming her relation to it.

A similar technique is symptom prescription, which in its simplest form directs a person to continue to do what they are doing (Erickson, 1965). Thus, a depressed person might be asked to practice his depression. In traditional therapy, this strategy may seem unusual or paradoxical. It is straightforward and commonsense within the Ericksonian approach. The assumption is that joining an ongoing process allows one to gradually modify that process. Symptom prescription enables the client to shift from a self-devaluing strategy of attempted negation to a self-valuing process of choosing (and thereby accepting) the recurrent process.

Another way to value symptomatic experience is to re-language and develop it as a hypnotic skill. For example, a person complaining of overeating reported experiencing a burning sensation in her stomach shortly before binging. I accepted and defined this phenomenon as the

spontaneous development of hypnotic sensations, then worked with
the woman to "allow the unconscious" to amplify this trance phenomenon in ways that led to different responses.

The above methods assume that the way a person relates to a
phenomenon determines its value and the response to it. Such methods
seek to translate problems into solutions by changing the way a person
"votes" on the experience. When the relationship is shifted from self-
devaluation to self-valuation, a symptomatic trance can be translated
into a therapeutic trance.

Level of Trust

Another major difference between symptomatic and therapeutic trances
is the level of trust. A person immersed in a problematic trance experiences little trust in self and others, while someone engaged in a
solution-oriented trance experiences enhanced trust. Trust is crucial to
the quality of a trance, since without it a person will be unable to "let
go" and allow unconscious expression. An untrusting individual will
"fight" the trance experience, which can distort it and make it painful.
Thus, the therapist interested in joining and working with symptomatic
expressions must first secure the person's trust.

For example, an incest survivor requested hypnosis in hopes of
"reconnecting with feelings," but warned of a strong need to establish
boundaries. Accordingly, I emphasized the need for safety and trust as
paramount to the process, then asked her to reflect on what might
allow her to satisfy that need. After some contemplation, she reported
with mild embarrassment a recurrent sense of needing to be all alone
in the room. Contemplating this "hypnotic koan" of how to stay in
the room while leaving it, I imagined myself sitting in the doorway to
the office, with nothing but my feet visible to the client. I did a brief
hypnotic induction in this unusual position, and the client felt tremendously relieved that her considerations were being respected while her
needs were met. Further work gradually decreased the physical distance,
so by the end of several sessions she felt comfortable with me in close
physical proximity, though it was important for her to keep her eyes
open during this time.

With the client who had reported disembodied eyes staring at her,
the following communications helped to develop trust:

Now Joan, you are experiencing a lot of different things, some of which you are concerned about. Your conscious mind is participating in various ways, and so is your unconscious. And your unconscious is expressing a lot of different things, all the way from the way you're breathing, the way you're feeling, and other ways you can learn naturally to allow changes to occur comfortably. And so what I'd like you to do is simply look at me here, because it's important to know safely that you can feel grounded and secure as your unconscious begins to communicate. Because even while you look at me here, no matter what I say or don't say, your unconscious can feel safe and secure in the knowledge that you can continue to sit there comfortably and let your unconscious operate according to *your* needs as an individual. . . . And you have plenty of needs as an individual. . . . You have a need for safety . . . you have a need to operate at the rate which is appropriate to you . . . you have a need and a right to experience comfort in your breathing . . . you have a need to experience security . . . you have a need to be able to know that you can withdraw and stay here simultaneously . . . you have a need to know that even as you look at me and my eyes remain here with you, other meaningful changes can happen in accord with the needs of the entire self . . . my face may begin to change, and you have a need and a right to know that you can continue with that security even as the eyes remain and the identity and the relationship and the feeling and the sense of the ability of the eyes to transform as you develop that integration at your rate. . . .

Delivered in a soft yet absorbing manner, these communications served to experientially secure Joan's attention in a way that allowed rapport to develop. This context of trust was then used to elicit and recontextualize the trance phenomena of the disembodied eyes.

Trust is essential to transform a symptomatic trance into one that is therapeutic. The therapist seeks to find those conditions that will enable clients to realize that it is safe for them to explore their experience.

Biological Context

One of the most striking differences between symptomatic and therapeutic trances is in physical patterning. In symptomatic trances, individuals are typically distinguished by arrhythmic and nonfluid motor patterns, chronic muscular contractions (especially in the neck and stomach), irregular and shallow breathing patterns, and overall tension (i.e., physical holding patterns). In contrast, individuals in therapeutic trances tend to exhibit a greater sense of grace and rhythm in movements, balanced muscular tonicity, deeper and more rhythmic breathing patterns, general flexibility, and relaxed eye movements.

As the most rudimentary experimentation or observation will show, these different ways of organizing biological experience dramatically influence the perceived value of a psychological experience. A person with disrupted rhythms, poor breathing patterns, and chronic muscular tension will be hard pressed to accept and interact with hypnotic experience. On the other hand, an individual with balanced rhythms, breathing patterns, and muscle tonicity is generally willing and able to integrate experiences of all sorts. In short, the biological patterning of the self may determine whether a psychological event is experienced as a problem or a solution.

One of the most critical tasks of the therapist is thus to develop and maintain balanced biological states. This is especially important at the outset of hypnotic exploration. Since it involves transactions at a primary (nonverbal) level, the therapist should begin by ensuring a balanced, centered state within him or herself. As I have described in detail (1987), this orientation is then extended to include the client. Only when attention has been experientially absorbed in a fashion that allows rhythms to be synchronized does the therapist proceed with hypnotic directives.

Once hypnotic explorations are underway, the therapist continues to monitor nonverbal patterning. Changes in expression (rhythm, breathing, muscle tone, posture, etc.) signal changes in psychological orientation, thereby suggesting modifications in therapeutic communications. Specific interventions are needed if any changes involve sustained holding patterns (e.g., in breathing or muscles) or arrhythmic expressions, since this indicates a fundamental shift in biological context (from self-valuing to self-devaluing). For example, a man complaining of recurrent nightmares was directed to (hypnotically) redream the nightmare with a new ending. Halfway through the dream the man's nonverbal patterning abruptly shifted: His face paled, breathing stopped, muscles contracted (especially in his throat), and posture stiffened. The following direct suggestions were immediately given:

That's right . . . and there is that experience again. . . . So I want you to *breathe deeply* and automatically now, Bob . . . *breathe* and let the tensions move through you . . . breathe and let the fears dissipate . . . breathe and allow that new dream to complete itself . . . and you don't know and I don't know how your unconscious will and is now going to dream a different dream from here on in . . . but I do know that it is important that you *breathe*, Bob, as you develop that new relationship . . . that's it . . . *breathe* . . . and as you do, feel free to hear my voice in the background as much as is needed to recognize that you can feel safe here and now and there and then and here and now, a part of and apart from . . . and all the while, breathing, Bob, as you hear my voice and let your muscles relax and really enjoy that surprise of watching and feeling those integrations developing even more now . . . you can feel it, Bob . . . breathe . . . that's it . . . you can feel it . . . breathe . . . that's it . . . you can watch and feel those integrations . . . that's it . . . that's it . . . that's it. . . .

While these hypnotic directives were being given, Bob appeared to move through an array of intense emotional experiences, including anger, fear, sadness, and (finally) relief. From a pragmatic perspective, these emotional processes were of little concern to me; of primary importance was the biological context in which they developed. As with most clients, Bob had developed a way of intensely rigidifying his nonverbal patterning during the experience, thereby ensuring an unpleasant experience and undesirable outcome. With hypnotic "coaching" regarding new biological patterns (especially breathing), a new response developed. He dreamed a different ending to the dream, and experienced no further nightmares.

Sometimes additional interventions are needed to balance nonverbal patterns. With one mesomorphic client, who upon entering trance would develop intense muscular contractions, I did a great deal of hypnotic work while relaxing and supporting his neck muscles with my hands. With another client, a woman who complained of intense jealousy of her husband, I interrupted the extreme "tunnel vision" involved in the jealousy pattern by having her go into trance by looking at her husband while simultaneously seeing her own hands in peripheral vision. This strategy redistributed her attention in a way that disabled the focal intensity while enabling her to connect with her own body. With many other clients, I have found it useful to have them hold my hand and/ or keep their eyes open while in trance. These are some of the different ways in which the therapist can satisfy the major responsibility of ensuring that hypnotic explorations occur within self-valuing biological contexts.

Content Variability

For a process to remain generative, its content must periodically change. Conversely, for a process to remain problematic, some of its aspects must be invariant. Thus, while the content of a person's therapeutic trances varies over time, an individual's symptomatic trances feature the same focal content again and again. Consider the general hypnotic process of ideosensory phenomena. It might appear recurrently in a symptomatic trance as a migraine headache or a burning in the stomach. Regardless of the selected content, it would tend to repeat itself across successive symptomatic trances. In contrast, an individual experiencing a series of therapeutic trances might develop warmth in the hands during one trance, a tingling in the chest in the next trance, and heaviness in the feet in another trance. In short, a general skill or process will tend to be expressed in different times, depending on the situation.*

Looked at in this way, a major role assumed by the hypnotherapist is that of variety generator. The dictum in this regard is, "Where singular fixity was, flexible variability shall be." To function as a variety generator, the therapist identifies repetitive content in a person's symptomatic trance. For example, a depressed man complained of an overwhelming "feeling of emptiness" in his chest. A series of therapeutic trances were used to vary the content of this trance phenomena, such that successive experiences included a vision of emptiness, a picture of emptiness, a symbol of emptiness, a feeling of emptiness in the stomach, a feeling of emptiness in the head, a feeling of emptiness in the feet while noting a "full symbol" develop in the head, a comfortable feeling of full emptiness, a suggestive vision of empty fullness, and "a surprising dream integrating fullness and emptiness in regard to the whole body of experiential learnings." By using multiple trials to generate a variety of possible modifications of the focal content of the symptom, new

---

* In this sense, a person in symptomatic trance is engaging in idolatry ("an idea frozen into a specific image"). Just as God is not the statue on the dashboard, an idea is not the content used to represent it in a given situation. When content is invariant, this distinction is forgotten.

possibilities emerged. A symptom can only be maintained when certain parameters (what, where, when, with whom, how, what called, attributions) are fixed in content. When the content is varied, the process begins to shift and changes can be made.

Frame Variability

Individuals usually operate in relationship with (1) goals or intentions and (2) reference structures or frames for achieving those goals. This means that (1) the contents of consciousness are usually represented within a matrix or network of other associations, and (2) the person views this frame from a certain perspective (e.g., goal orientation). These frames serve as filters for experience, ensuring selective orientation and biased interpretations. Far from being undesirable, frames are essential for achieving specific goals. However, frames must be altered in accord with changing values and situations, so a person must periodically set aside frames to allow new structures to develop.* If this is not done deliberately, it will happen "spontaneously." For example, symptomatic trances may develop when the conscious mind is no longer able to handle a situation with its activated frames, thereby prompting the unconscious mind to become dominant (via spontaneous trance development) as a means to generate new possibilities.

How a person responds to this deframing process can determine whether a trance is symptomatic or therapeutic. In general, a person in a symptomatic trance maintains rigidity in regard to psychological frames, while a person in a therapeutic trance is highly flexible. Frame invariance thus makes for a self-devaluing trance, while frame variability enables a self-valuing trance.

Frame variability occurs in at least three ways. First, the person in a symptomatic trance tends to repeatedly view a psychological event from the same perspective. For example, a man in therapy attributed his troubles to his alcoholic father's abuse of him as a child. He recalled

---

* Historically, such frame transformations have occurred at developmental transitions such as initiation into adulthood, marriage, war, death, etc. In the present view, it is not coincidental that hypnotic processes usually played a central role in rituals marking these shifts. With the modern (Western) emphasis on individual development, it seems that frame transformation occurs more often and at different times for different people, thereby requiring additional ritualistic contexts wherein individuals can "deframe to reframe" (i.e., develop a trance to allow new structures to emerge). Psychotherapy seems to have arisen as the social institution for guiding persons through the altered states inherent in such transformations.

such abusive events often, each time viewing them from the same self-defeating, depression-inducing perspective. In contrast to this fixed position, a person in a therapeutic trance is capable of relating to an event from multiple perspectives. Thus, the above client was guided in therapeutic trance to successively examine a key abusive event from the perspectives of the young boy, the father, the father 20 years later, the mother, a kindly and wise stranger, and the boy as an old man. In a different set of trances, a series of emotional states (sadness, then anger, then contentment) were developed before having the man again access the key experience. This variability in perspective freed him from responding to the event as the "cause" of his unhappiness, and new ways of being became available.

Second, symptomatic trances typically involve rigid attachment to a frame, while therapeutic trances are often distinguished by a deframed orientation.* For example, consider a person reporting a recurrent symptomatic trance featuring hallucinated imagery. Investigation will likely reveal that such imagery occurs each time along with a "family" of other associations, e.g., specific eye accessing patterns, postures, cognitions, social partners, and so forth. A symptom is expressed within a static complex or fixed frame of other distinctions. In contrast, a person in a therapeutic trance is more able and willing to deframe experience. A person in therapeutic trance can experience this deframing experience in such a way that thoughts, feelings, and other associations drift in and out of awareness even as attention absorbs in a single distinction. The person hallucinating within a fixed frame can be guided to experience hallucinations within a drift of changing frames while grounded in relationship to the therapist, with the result that the fixed frame (and hence invariant meaning) normally binding the hallucination is deframed. This allows new possibilities to develop, since a distinction has no value independent from a frame of reference. Thus, the therapist first deframes a distinction, then uses the therapy context to promote new frames that reflect the present needs and values of the person.

A third distinction regarding the operation of frames in trances concerns their relationship to intentions or goals. Symptomatic trances usually involve a condensation (or enmeshment) of intentions and frames, whereas therapeutic trances enable intentions to operate independently from frames. For example, typically the desire for safety

---

* It is in this sense that therapeutic trance seems paradoxically to be a "state that is no state" or a process that is not "static."

in a symptomatic trance automatically activates the same frame or program used previously to achieve safety (e.g., withdrawal, substance abuse, violence). In contrast, the person in therapeutic trance may contemplate a goal without committing to a specific structure for achieving it. This allows multiple possibilities to be examined, and only those most appropriate for the present situation to be actualized. Thus, a client needing security (or any other outcome) may take time in therapeutic trance to "allow the unconscious" to serve up a variety of possible ways to achieve the goal according to the present needs. By "deframing" goals from structures, the intentions or motivations underlying problem processes can be acknowledged and satisfied in self-valuing fashions.

To summarize, therapeutic trance allows a much greater flexibility in relationship to psychological frames. In contrast to symptomatic trances, therapeutic trances enable variability in terms of (1) the perspective from which an event is viewed, (2) the unbinding (or deframing) of a distinction from a matrix of other associations, and (3) the independence of an intention from a frame to satisfy that intention. The therapist can translate problems into solutions by introducing variability in these framing parameters.

Context Sensitivity

The experience of trance has traditionally been associated with increased suggestibility. This is misleading to the extent that it depicts the hypnotized person as somehow gullible. However, trance does influence sensitivity to new relationships in the social or environmental fields. Interestingly, it seems that context sensitivity is enhanced by therapeutic trance and decreased by symptomatic trance. That is, individuals in therapeutic trances are open to new possibilities and generally willing and able to experiment with new ways of being. In contrast, persons in symptomatic trances tend to close down to new possibilities while trying to avoid potentially threatening changes.

Since context sensitivity is essential for adaptive behavior, the therapist works to transform the insensitivity of symptomatic trances into the sensitivity of therapeutic trances. Given that a person will generally be closed to "outside" influences around the symptom area, this is accomplished by joining a person's verbal and nonverbal patterns to first get "inside" the system. Once pattern matching has allowed the therapist to join a system, gradual pattern modification enables the experiential changes necessary for renewed context sensitivity.

Relationship Style: Cooperation vs. Competition

Trance allows both sides of a relationship to be experienced simultaneously. This can be a problem or a solution, as it requires an appreciation of differences as well as the realization of "commonunities." For example, a husband and wife (or two different "parts" of an individual) are "a part of yet apart from" each other, and thus must discover how to acknowledge not only both "sides" but "the middle third" as well. The quality of experience in this paradoxical "both/and" relationship depends partly on the relationship style used to guide transactions. In this regard, symptomatic trances tend to be dominated by competitive relationships while therapeutic trances are distinguished by cooperational strategies. Suppose a person has both an urge to smoke and an injunction to not smoke. That person can develop a symptomatic trance by attempting to have one side (e.g., not smoke) dominate the other side (smoke). Since negation is impossible at a primary level (e.g., "don't think of blue"), the competitive style produces at best a splitting of the self into a conscious and unconscious experience. If the situation continues, a symptom usually projects out of the struggle of these opposing injunctions (e.g., an identified patient emerges from the conflict between parents).

The therapist is thus faced with the task of transforming competitive "win-lose" relationships into cooperative "win-win" relationships. The challenge is to solve the "hypnotic koan" (see Gilligan, 1987) of, "How can X and X' be equally acknowledged?" While a straightforward answer or an immediate integration is usually not forthcoming, a therapeutic trance will allow a cooperational context wherein "opposites" or "enemies" can find common ground and generate solutions. Thus, the "smoker/non-smoker" relationship can be contemplated in trance as a "hypnotic koan": How can you satisfy the smoker's needs and the non-smoker's needs? When this question was posed in therapeutic trance recently to a man struggling with this complementarity, he responded with a variety of experiential processes. Later inquiry revealed that the koan triggered an experience of (hallucinated) mist and fog enshrouding the man. From a distant observer position he realized after awhile that both "sides" really needed to be "lost in the clouds" now and again during the day. In other words, his unconscious developed a symbolic solution (withdrawing into a cloudy daydream) that satisfied both sides of himself. Thus, a cooperative relationship in therapeutic relationship allowed a "win-lose" relationship to be translated into a "win-win" creative solution.

SUMMARY

We have proceeded from the naturalistic view that trance is a cross-contextual process by which unconscious processes are amplified. As we have seen, this process features paradoxical injunctions and paradoxical experience, ideodynamic expression, intensified experiential absorption, sustained attention, temporal alterations, somatic changes, and other phenomenological shifts. Trance may or may not be useful, depending on contextual factors such as self-valuation, trust, biological patterning, content and frame variability, context sensitivity, and relationship style. In other words, the relationship context provides the value for any experience; the therapist's task is to recontextualize symptoms so that solutions emerge. As Erickson (1948, 1952, 1959, 1965) emphasized, there are many ways to accomplish this task. The success of any method generally derives from its capacity to join and empower the client's reality. Modification and even outright rejection of a method will sometimes be necessary, depending on the unique needs and patterns of the individual client. Whatever the case, the main idea to remember is that solutions are inherent in the client's ongoing processes, not in the therapist's cleverness.

REFERENCES

Achterberg, J. (1985). *Imagery in Healing: Shamanism and Modern Medicine.* Boston: Shambhala.

Bateson, G. (1954). A theory of play and fantasy. Paper presented to the American Psychiatric Association Meeting on Cultural, Anthropological and Communication Approaches. March, 1954, Mexico City. Reprinted in G. Bateson, *Steps to an Ecology of Mind.* NY: Ballantine, 1972.

Bateson, G., Jackson, D. D., Haley, J., & Weakland, J. (1956). Toward a theory of schizophrenia. *Behavioral Science, 1,* 251–264.

Beahrs, J. O. (1982). *Unity and Multiplicity: Multilevel Consciousness of Self in Hypnosis, Psychiatric Disorder, and Mental Health.* NY: Brunner/Mazel.

Bernheim, H. (1895). *Suggestive Therapeutics: A Treatise on the Nature and Uses of Hypnotism.* New York: Putnam.

Cooper, L., & Erickson, M. H. (1959). *Time Distortion in Hypnosis* (2nd ed.). Baltimore: Williams & Wilkins.

Erickson, M. H. (1948). Hypnotic psychotherapy. *The Medical Clinics of North America* (pp. 571–584). New York: W. B. Saunders Co. (Reprinted in E. L. Rossi (Ed.), *The*

Collected Papers of Milton H. Erickson, Volume IV: Innovative Hypnotherapy. New York: Irvington, 1980).

Erickson, M. H. (1952). Deep hypnosis and its induction. In L. M. Lecron (Ed.), *Experimental Hypnosis.* NY: Macmillan.

Erickson, M. H. (1959). Further clinical techniques of hypnosis: Utilization techniques. *American Journal of Clinical Hypnosis, 2,* 3–21.

Erickson, M. H. (1965). The use of symptoms as an integral part of therapy. *American Journal of Clinical Hypnosis, 8,* 57–65.

Erickson, M. H. & Rossi, E. L. (1975). Varieties of double bind. *American Journal of Clinical Hypnosis, 17,* 143–157.

Erickson, M. H., & Rossi, E. L. (1977). Autohypnotic experiences of Milton H. Erickson, M.D. *American Journal of Clinical Hypnosis, 20,* 36–54.

Erickson, M. H., Rossi, E. L., & Rossi, S. I. (1976). *Hypnotic Realities: The Clinical Hypnosis and Forms of Indirect Suggestions.* New York: Irvington.

Evans, F. J., & Kihlstrom, J. F. (1973). Posthypnotic amnesia as disrupted retrieval. *Journal of Abnormal Psychology, 82,* 317–323.

Gilligan, S. G. (1985). Generative autonomy: Principles for an Ericksonian hypnotherapy. In J. K. Zeig (Ed.), *Ericksonian Psychotherapy, Volume I: Structures.* NY: Brunner/Mazel.

Gilligan, S. G. (1987). *Therapeutic Trances: The Cooperation Principle in Ericksonian Hypnotherapy.* NY: Brunner/Mazel.

Haley, J. (1955). Paradoxes in play, fantasy, and psychotherapy. *Psychiatric Res. Rep., 2,* 52–58.

Haley, J. (1963). *Strategies of Psychotherapy.* NY: Grune & Stratton.

Haley, J. (1976). *Problem-solving Therapy: New Strategies for Effective Family Therapy.* San Francisco: Jossey-Bass.

Lankton, S. R., & Lankton, C. (1983). *The Answer Within: A Clinical Framework for Ericksonian Hypnotherapy.* NY: Brunner/Mazel.

Masters, R., & Houston, J. (1972). *Mind Games.* New York: Dell Publishing.

Melges, F. T. (1982). *Time and the Inner Future: A Temporal Approach to Psychiatric Disorders.* NY: Wiley.

Orne, M. T. (1959). The nature of hypnosis: Artifact and essence. *Journal of Abnormal and Social Psychology, 58,* 277–299.

Orne, M. T. (1966). On the mechanisms of posthypnotic amnesia. *International Journal of Clinical and Experimental Hypnosis, 14,* 121–134.

Ornstein, R. (1969). *On the Experience of Time.* Baltimore, MD: Penguin Books, 1969.

Pribram, K. H. (1971). *Languages of the Brain: Experimental Paradoxes and Principles in Neuropsychology.* Englewood Cliffs, NJ: Prentice-Hall.

Rossi, E. L., & Jichaku, P. (1984). Therapeutic and transpersonal double binds: Continuing the legacy of Gregory Bateson and Milton Erickson. Paper presented at the Annual Scientific Meeting of the American Society of Clinical Hypnosis. October, San Francisco.

Schwartz, W. (1978). Time and context during hypnotic involvement. *International Journal of Clinical and Experimental Hypnosis, 4,* 307–316.

Watts, A. (1961). *Psychotherapy East and West.* NY: Random House.

Zimbardo, P. G., Maslach, C., & Marshall, G. (1972). Hypnosis and the psychology of cognitive and behavioral control. In E. Fromm and R. Shor (Eds.), *Hypnosis: Research Developments and Perspectives.* Chicago: Aldine.

Chapter 20

An Ericksonian Phenomenological Approach to Therapeutic Hypnotic Induction and Symptom Utilization

Jeffrey K. Zeig

*Jeffrey K. Zeig, Ph.D. (Georgia State University), is Director of The Milton
H. Erickson Foundation. He maintains an active private practice and
regularly conducts teaching seminars on Ericksonian psychotherapy around
the world. He has edited five books and authored one. Zeig organized all
the yearly Erickson Congresses and Seminars since 1980, including the
landmark Evolution of Psychotherapy Conference. He serves on the editorial
boards of two foreign and three American journals, including the* Ericksonian
Monographs.

  *Zeig's chapter presents a phenomenological perspective on hypnosis. Five
responses are commonly reported by patients. The therapist works to elicit
them by using techniques such as ratification, incorporation, hypnotic redefinition and seeding. Hypnotic induction can be tailored to the individual
by the therapist's utilizing the mechanism by which the patient maintains
his symptom.*

    This chapter has two theses. The first is that the mechanism
by which a problem is maintained is a mechanism of solution that can
be used during hypnotic induction. In other words, the hypnotic induction of successful symptom amelioration should be structurally analogous to the way in which the patient "induces" his symptom. A
second interwoven thesis, in contradistinction to traditional views of

induction, is that an Ericksonian induction is more than a means to an end. It is a therapeutic method in itself.

The chapter consists of five parts:

1. In discussing hypnotic induction, there is an initial concern to define hypnosis. As will be seen, one's induction is influenced to an extent by one's definition.
2. Five induction responses will be discussed from the phenomenological perspective of the patient. Just what is the induction of hypnosis to the patient? Not to an impartial observer. Not to the therapist. But how does the patient experience it? Under what five conditions is trance reported? A number of techniques used by the therapist to establish these five induction responses will be presented: ratification, incorporation, positive attribution, surprise, hypnotic redefining, and seeding. Illustrative examples will be provided from my own clinical practice and from Erickson's work.
3. Ericksonian and traditional methods, especially as concerns induction, will be contrasted.
4. A way of viewing the fundamental nature of psychological problems will be considered in a brief overview.
5. The similarities between the processes of induction and symptom maintenance will be discussed, indicating how the induction of hypnosis can recapitulate the process of symptom maintenance and thereby enhance its therapeutic efficacy.

WHAT IS HYPNOSIS?

When defining a process such as hypnosis, one can be either objective or subjective. Moreover, a phenomenon such as hypnosis can be defined according to its appearance, its function, its etiology, its history, or in terms of its relationship to other phenomena. The phenomenon is usually defined from the perspective of a preexistent theory. Subsequently, a specific theoretical lens (which has its own special language) is used in order to maintain the established definition.

Definitions are neither benign nor "neutral"; on the contrary, they influence, and usually limit, subsequent action. For example, a therapist's definition of hypnosis will influence treatment planning: If a therapist takes an objective approach to hypnosis, most likely he will use a preset script for induction and programming as a method of therapy. Most experts have attempted to define hypnosis objectively from the perspective of their preexisting underlying theory of personality and its language. In current literature, there are six traditional definitions of hypnosis, all of which can be summarized succinctly.

1. Pierre Janet around the turn of the century and Ernest Hilgard more recently (Hilgard, 1978) have defined hypnosis in terms of dissociation. There are multiple cognitive controls in human behavior.
2. Social psychologists Sarbin and Coe (1972) have described hypnosis in terms of role theory: Hypnosis is the role that people play; they act "as if" they were hypnotized.
3. Barber (1969) has defined hypnosis in terms of nonhypnotic behavioral parameters such as task motivation and the act of labeling the situation as "hypnosis."
4. In his early writings, Weitzenhoffer (1953) conceptualized hypnosis as a state of enhanced suggestibility. This followed on the pioneering work of Bernheim (1888, cited by Hilgard, 1978).
5. Psychoanalysts Gill and Brenman (1959) have described hypnosis by using the psychoanalytic concept of "regression in the service of ego."
6. Recently, Edmundston (1984) assessed hypnosis as being merely a state of relaxation.

Each expert has constructed a theory of hypnosis and set of techniques that follow logically from the proposed definition. In these traditional schools of hypnosis, induction is a formalized procedure that attempts to create a hypnotic experience in accordance with the proposed definition: That is, depending on one's theoretical orientation, induction will be used to create dissociation, "as if" behavior, relaxation, and so forth. Traditional induction is usually conducted in a rote manner as a means to establish the theorist's preordained effect (the "definition"). Therapy is also programmed (usually in an authoritarian manner) according to the tenets of the school to which the therapist subscribes (psychoanalysis, behaviorism, etc.).

When one considers hypnosis as it is actually used in the clinical setting, more possibilities arise, and one can see readily that, taken alone, not one of the six traditional theories constitute the essence of hypnosis. In fact, one can view the six positions as *goals* that the therapist works to establish, whether via an Ericksonian or a traditional approach. When inducing hypnosis, one works to establish the role of the hypnotized subject, facilitate dissociation, enhance task motivation, define the situation as hypnosis, increase responsive suggestibility, and so forth. In other words, *all six traditional perspectives are established simultaneously.*

If none of the six objective definitions is the essence of hypnosis, how can an Ericksonian define hypnosis and how does an Ericksonian definition differ from established theories?

Erickson's solution (Erickson, Rossi, & Rossi, 1976) was to discuss hypnosis as a distinct state. In addition, I propose that we take a subjective stance by primarily defining hypnosis *phenomenologically* from the perspective of the patient. An Ericksonian posture does *not* seek to establish an objective, quantifiable definition. It is well known that Erickson was adamantly atheoretical because he was acutely aware of how the theoretical lens of the therapist can distort the patient's reality. Therefore, he used numerous descriptions of hypnosis depending on the unique constellation of variables present in a given clinical or demonstration setting. He created a new precedent in the process of definition whereby interactional variables as well as the needs, goal, expectations, and responses of the patient played a determining role.

Such a fluid approach is the bane of objectivists who want to know "the real thing" in operational terms. But, flexibility in approach is absolutely necessitated in clinical practice where the "blinders" that are an inevitable concomitant of a preordained position work against both the clinician and the patient.

Hypnosis shares a qualitative affinity with other subjective emotional experiences. The personal experience of love, for example, differs from person to person. What is love to one is not to the next. Most people would avoid attempts to objectify "love." I propose that we treat hypnosis similarly. It might be more beneficial to have multiple definitions that reflect the complex psychodynamic and situational variables.

For example, depending on the circumstances, one could define hypnosis from the point of view of the observer, the patient, or the therapist. From an observer's position, hypnosis could be defined as *a context for effective communication.* Alternatively, from the subject's point of view, hypnosis could be viewed as *a state of focused awareness on whatever is immediately relevant, in which previously unrecognized psychological and physiological potentials* are accessed to some avolitional extent. For example, in hypnosis a patient may be surprised to discover an ability to modify the experience of pain.

From the position of the therapist, hypnosis might be viewed as a *dissociative responsiveness to injunction in a context that is defined as hypnosis.* (For more information about injunctive communication, see Zeig, 1985.) In Ericksonian hypnotherapy, the operator presents injunctions to the patient which also can be called *minimal cues, indirect suggestions,* or *multiple-level communication.* The purpose of injunction is to facilitate the phenomenological experience of trance induction.

Minimal Cues

For example, a therapist working with a patient in trance does not usually present an authoritarian command such as, "Move your head to a level position!" Moreover, if the patient responded to such a command, it might not be considered hypnosis at all. However, if in the context of an induction, the therapist talks about the importance of being *level-headed,* and then the patient unconsciously makes a physical, dissociated adjustment to the verbal minimal cue of *level-headed,* that would be considered hypnosis. To accomplish hypnosis and hypnotherapy in this framework, the therapist asks himself, "What idea do I want to present?"* Then, the therapist presents that back to the patient *"one step removed,"* as an indirect injunction.

The therapist knows that the induction of hypnosis is over when the patient manifests consistent avolitional (dissociative) responsiveness to minimal cues (injunctions). If the patient does not manifest this type of responsiveness, the therapist continues the induction; it is not yet time to enter the phase of utilization which normally begins only after one has "unlocked" the door to the unconscious. Unlocking the door to the unconscious is a matter of developing the patient's response to minimal cues to the maximum extent possible.

Indirection Suggestion (Injunction)

This approach is used in hypnotic and nonhypnotic therapy. In both cases, it is a process of communicating a message on a covert rather than overt level. If one has a patient who is depressed, one message to communicate is, "Cheer up." However, if the therapist were to say that directly, he would not achieve much of an effect. The challenge is to present the advice "cheer up" so that it can be utilized readily by the patient—so the patient can "reawaken" his own ability to change

---

* Erickson often conceptualized hypnosis as a presentation of ideas that stimulates the patient's own inner learnings.

his mood. The Ericksonian therapist increases response potential by using indirect techniques of communication such as *metaphor, symptom prescription, anecdotes,* and so forth. Couched within these techniques is the injunction "Cheer up." Eventually, enough associations are activated within the patient so that he comes in contact with his innate capacity for responding to the injunction as an internal ability rather than simply as a superficial exhortation.

In this sense, *the success of the therapy in general is proportional to the degree of responsiveness to minimal cues developed within the patient.* The more responsiveness to minimal cues that can be established, the more effective the therapy. *Indirection* is the essense of developing responsiveness, and, it also can be considered the essence of hypnosis.

FIVE INDUCTION RESPONSES

There are certain subjective experiences that occur when a person realizes that multiple-level communication is being used. In response to a hypnotic induction—especially one in which the therapist purposely uses injunctive (multi-level) communication—five preeminent subjective experiences are reported.

Induction

Induction is reported by patients when there exists some combination of subjective events: *modified awareness, altered intensity, avolitional experience* and/or *avolitional response.* Additionally, the situation must be *defined as hypnosis.* In fact, from the subject's point of view, hypnosis could be defined as a constellation of these five experiences. I will discuss each in turn.

As a result of induction, patients often report alterations in their process of attending and concentrating; somehow, *modified awareness* has occurred. Actually, awareness is modified in a number of different directions. For example, it can become focused or diffused, internal or external, and, in addition, it can assume any of the four possible combinations. In any of the cases, patients may report trance. For that matter, patients will report trance if awareness is "split" and occurs on multiple levels. For example, hypnotized patients often say, "I was listening to you but part of me was aware of being somewhere else." The important ingredient seems to be that awareness is significantly *modified. It is not necessary for awareness to be focused internally* as is customary in traditional approaches.

Altered Intensity

A second response commonly reported by successfully hypnotized patients is one of *altered intensity* from the "normal" state of consciousness. This alteration in vividness could be in the direction of relaxation, whereby patients often report hypnosis. However, more vivid relaxation is not essential to hypnosis. If there is significant alteration in intensity of any sensory experience as, for example, an alteration of visual perception or feelings of depersonalization, patients will indicate the experience of hypnosis. Similarly, if memories (or some aspect of a memory) become more vivid, or if the involvement in trance is more vivid than "normal" levels of absorption, hypnosis will often be acknowledged.

Avolitional Experiences

A third response that is almost mandatory if patients are to report hypnotic experience is the occurrence of some degree of *avolitional experience*—that something "just happens." The avolitional experience can be physical or mental. An example of physical avolitional experience would be an arm levitation in which the patient feels dissociative movement, that is, the arm lifts "by itself," and conscious volition differs from customary experience. An avolitional mental experience commonly can occur mentally in the process of visualization. For example, the therapist uses a guided fantasy induction and instructs the patient to imagine walking down a beach. Subsequently, he asks the patient, "Look down the beach. Who is that walking toward you?" The patient then has a "spontaneous" image of the approaching person and can answer the question as though it were valid in terms of external reality.

The avolitional experience does not need to be directly or indirectly suggested by the therapist. It can occur spontaneously, either in self-hypnosis or in hetero-hypnosis as, for example, when a patient suddenly manifests a classical hypnotic phenomenon such as amnesia. To reiterate, *in order for patients to report hypnosis*, it is important that the patient experience some kind of avolitional process.

Avolitional Responsiveness

A fourth experience interrelated with the third is that of *avolitional responsiveness*. In hetero-hypnosis, the patient's responsiveness to the therapist must be different in hypnosis than it is in the waking state. For example, the patient may not know that he is responding to a specific suggestion. Also, the patient might be unaware of the extent to which he is responding to the therapeutic evocations. As previously mentioned, the suggestion may be couched in indirect language as a minimal cue. The patient has the hazy realization that, "I am responding, but I am not exactly certain to what I am responding" (or "why my responses are different"). That sense of responding and not knowing why gives the person a clearly *different* experience from normal, waking states.

It should be noted that patients do not need to achieve all four of these responses in order to report that hypnosis has occurred. The minimal number and combination of experiences required varies from patient to patient.

These first four responses are actually goals of the therapist. Within the context of hypnosis, the therapist works to modify awareness, alter intensity, promote avolitional experience, and enhance avolitional responsiveness. In addition, he consolidates these naturally occurring phenomena in such a way that they are experienced by the patient as "trance."

Defining the Situation as Hypnosis

The fifth induction response/goal, *defining the situation as hypnosis*, definitely alters the quality of subsequent responses. It can be easily understood that we exhibit all of the first four responses regularly. But, when they are consolidated in a context defined as hypnosis, then patients report being hypnotized. For the most part, hypnosis exists when patients say that it has occurred. *It is the patient who defines the situation as hypnosis, and the therapist works to help create that effect.* As the patient defines his experience as being in hypnosis, he further modifies his awareness, alters intensity, and responds avolitionally.

In traditional hypnosis, a therapist might overtly offer a definition of the situation by saying, "Now we are going to do hypnosis." Erickson, however, more often worked indirectly by defining the situation to the patient as hypnosis via minimal cues. For example, he would speak more slowly and change the direction of his voice by turning his head down and away from the patient. These minimal cues could indicate to the patient, "This can now be considered hypnosis." However, the actual words were rarely spoken; rather, the message was implied. As the patient reacted to the implications, he naturally enhanced avolitional responsiveness. By contrast, when a patient responds to the direct message, "Now we are going to have a formal induction," there are fewer opportunities for avolitional responsiveness.

What is the reason for establishing the five induction responses? Basically, they add up to one word—*cooperation*. The purpose of induction is simply to facilitate cooperation (Zeig, 1985). The main problem with psychotherapy is achieving compliance so the patient can use his latent resources and abilities. Induction is a method to get this type of patient compliance.

We can use the problem of cigarette smoking as an example. If the therapist simply tells the smoking patient, "You will no longer have the urge to smoke," he should not expect a high percentage of success. However, if those suggestions are given to the patient after a successful hypnotic induction, there would be a higher degree of success. The induction of hypnosis—even traditional hypnosis—enhances compliance and increases the ability of the patient to cooperate in achieving his therapeutic goals. It is a tenet of this chapter that Ericksonian hypnotherapy is even more effective than traditional suggestions at evoking patient potentials and achieving effective therapy.

In Ericksonian hypnosis, an induction is an *application to influence*. It is similar to a legal contract. The therapist applies to the patient for the right to influence and the patient "signs on the dotted line" (agrees to be influenced) by responding to minimal cues (indirect suggestions). It is as if, at that point, the patient says, "Alright you can influence me, I will respond." Subsequently the patient is more open to eliciting latent potentials.

In traditional models, direct suggestions are used to establish aspects of the five induction responses, but in a way that is in line with the therapist's proposed definition and theoretical lens. In the Ericksonian approach, indirect suggestion is used and the definition of achieving trance is determined subjectively by the patient. The therapist works indirectly, rather than directly, instructing the patient via minimal cues to experience aspects of modified awareness, to alter intensity, to have avolitional experience and avolitional response, and to define the situation as hypnosis.

INDIRECT UTILIZATION TECHNIQUES

To create the five phenomenological induction responses/goals, the Ericksonian therapist uses indirect (injunctive) utilization techniques such as *ratification, incorporation, positive attribution,* and *surprise.* Advanced techniques include *hypnotic redefining* and *seeding.*

Ratification

Ratification of a change can be a simple, straightforward process. It was frequently utilized by Erickson in the early part of an induction. He maintained that a simple formula for inducing trance was to help absorb the patient in a memory and then ratify (report back) the changes that happened as the person became absorbed. Ratification can be effected through declarative sentences that feed back to the patient the changes that have occurred since the beginning of induction, all the while implying that these changes are happening in response to therapist's communication.

For example, Erickson often would begin the hypnotic process by absorbing the patient in a memory of learning to write letters of the alphabet. Then, pointing out actual responses, he would reflect back to the patient, "As you have been listening to me, your eye blinking has lessened; your pulse rate has slowed; your motor tone has changed; your reflexes have changed," and so forth. The implications of these statements can be, "You are responding. These are the behaviors to expect in hypnosis." Erickson would thereby utilize the patient's ongoing behavior and shape it in the direction of evoking avolitional responsiveness and defining the situation as hypnosis.

Incorporation

Another related technique is the use of *incorporation* whereby aspects of the environment or changes in patient behavior are woven into the induction patter. For example, the sound of a ringing telephone could be incorporated into the hypnosis. The therapist could immediately reply, "Some important ideas *can ring true* for you." If the patient moves one of his fingers the therapist can comment, "Your unconscious mind *can put its finger* on important and valuable understandings." By using incorporation, the therapist indirectly alerts the patient to the idea that multiple-level communication is being used which at the same time modifies the intensity and flow of the patient's awareness.

Positive Attribution

Often used in conjunction with incorporation and ratification is the technique of *positive attribution*, which is a more overt process than ratification. Customarily, passive behaviors are "ratified"; positive attribution is used to redefine behaviors that are more volitional and could be considered by the patient as resistant or nonhypnotic. Say the patient makes a small movement of his head during the induction. The therapist can describe how this movement is "more an unconscious variety of experience," thereby implying avolition. Alternately, the therapist can say to the patient, "You are turning an ear toward me so that you can hear me more clearly. Your ear has turned toward me because your unconscious mind is really interested in hearing what I say." The latter technique defines the same behavior as avolitional responsiveness.

Surprise

Surprise is also an effective technique to establish induction goals. One method of surprise used by Erickson was that of altering the order of the session. Erickson often would encourage his students to conduct hypnosis first. Rather than talking with the patient the first half hour of the session and conducting the induction in the second half hour as patients might come to expect, Erickson admonished students to "induce first and talk later." Perhaps this is inadvisable for the beginning therapist, but it can be valuable for those working at an advanced level.

An example of doing an induction first can be found in *A Teaching Seminar with Milton H. Erickson* (Zeig, 1980). In this induction (discussed in detail in the Appendix to the book), Erickson *initiated interaction* with a student who entered the room after the seminar had already begun by using a confusion technique to promote trance. His method did not reduce tension; rather, it momentarily increased the student's tension. However, it was quite effective in helping the student achieve hypnosis by disrupting her habitual set. Her expectation when entering the seminar room could not have been to be immediately confronted with the task of entering trance. Another example of a surprise induction was my initial meeting with Erickson (Zeig, 1985). His very first in-

teraction with me was to induce trance, using a nonverbal technique—
something I did not expect. I never forgot the introduction. In the
process, Erickson learned about my responsive style.

There are a number of reasons for doing an induction first. It is
easier to alter intensity when there is a great deal of initial intensity.
Also, when one does the induction first, psychodynamics can become
clear. This is because induction is not only a method of therapy; *it is
also a method of diagnosis.* The response that the patient manifests to
induction provides important diagnostic information. To an extent, an
induction is similar to a projective diagnostic method such as a Ror-
schach. The therapist puts pressure on the patient to respond, and then
the style and direction of patient responsiveness becomes clear. The
therapist learns the way in which the patient responds to tasks and
challenges. It is often difficult to clearly observe and identify specific
psychodynamic processes in an interpersonal situation such as psychotherapy. However, when one triangulates in a technique such as a
projective task, a puzzle, a gestalt technique, or a hypnotic induction,
the latent dynamics are more obvious and perceptible.

Utilization is a hallmark of the Ericksonian approach. The therapist
uses what the patient brings to the session—even including the symptom
itself and the strategy for maintaining it. This can be thought of as
"economical therapy": Whatever can be used is salvaged. Many en-
dogenous patient processes can be used to increase therapeutic effectiveness, including hypnotically redefining the words and metaphors
used by the patient to describe his or her problem. In this section, I
describe the two advanced induction techniques of *hypnotic redefining*
and *seeding.*

ADVANCED ERICKSONIAN INDUCTION METHODS

Hypnotic Redefining

The psychotherapeutic technique of *reframing* is well described and
understood (see, for example, Watzlawick, Weakland & Fisch, 1974).
In its most basic form, the therapist supplies a new, more benign
definition of the problem or its circumstances, thereby altering the
patient's attitude. For example, the therapist might say to a phobic
spouse, "It is good that you have your fears because if you were not
fearful, your husband would have to cope with his own problems, and
he really is not strong enough to do that yet." In this manner a new

"valence" is associated with the problem. It is now redefined as a sign of strength and an attempt to provide protection. Sometimes this technique can be quite effective.

In the induction of hypnosis, we can use Ericksonian methods to accomplish a *hypnotic redefinition*. Hypnotic redefinition can be more powerful than simple reframing. Not only can one attach new meaning to concepts, one also can *symbolically create helpful sensations and experiences by using the patient's symptoms*. In the following example, redefinition was accomplished by using the patient's words and symptoms and attaching new, more positive meanings.

In the initial interview, a depressed middle-aged male patient explained that his symptom was experienced as a "weight" on his chest. When queried, he explained that in order to depress himself, he would engage in self-criticism for not doing a good enough job and then "isolate." Customarily, he felt "inadequate" and "not worthwhile." He said he was the subject of his own "unrelenting" self-criticism.

In the third session, a hypnotic induction was created to use the very words that he had presented: namely, *isolate, inadequate, worthwhile,* and *unrelenting*. The departure point for induction was an aspect of the patient's symptom—the weight that he felt on his chest. Hypnosis was induced by having the patient gradually create a pleasant feeling of *heaviness* in his hands. Eventually, the developed heaviness was moved to the patient's chest. It was pointed out that his unconscious mind could find certain aspects of the heavy feeling *worthwhile*. Gradually, *in adequate* ways, the heaviness could develop into a feeling of *unrelenting* comfort. All of this would happen as his unconscious mind continued to *isolate* the heavy feeling in his chest.

These themes were developed in many different ways to create the complete induction. The patient's complaint of weight was induced as "heaviness." However, the induced heaviness had a different valence than the depression; it had the aura of hypnotic comfort. The heaviness was an avolitional *experience* that altered in intensity from the normal state of consciousness; it was an avolitional *response* to the injunctions in the induction. Hypnosis would be defined by the patient because of the perceived existence of heaviness. Previously, "weight" was only a problem.

Also, the patient's symbolic words were given new meaning: "Isolate," "inadequate," "not worthwhile" and "unrelenting" were presented in a favorable light. Patients have rigid and idiosyncratic meanings for special words and concepts that actually limit their choices. By using their special words and evoking new meanings, more flexible use of options can be promoted.

Seeding

Another important technique is *seeding*. Haley (1973) first described the concept of seeding and indicated that it was one of Erickson's most influential techniques. Unfortunately, little work has been done on developing this concept. Seeding basically entails priming subsequent behavior by alluding to the goal well in advance of its presentation.

Nonhypnotic forms of seeding are powerful influence devices. For example, in literature there is the concept of foreshadowing: Before an idea is presented, the novelist alludes to it in subtle ways. Erickson (Zeig, 1980) would instruct his students to read a book and speculate how "dangling threads" would be developed and used in subsequent chapters. In conjunction with seeding, the therapist builds toward the goal by moving in small steps.

Patients commonly seed concepts to their therapists. Before presenting a problem, they might symbolically allude to the difficult subject. For example, prior to crying and in the course of conversation a patient might unconsciously point to his eye, as if symbolically alerting the therapist to where subsequent action will occur.

Seeding is commonly used in Ericksonian therapy. Let us say that the therapeutic goal is to help the patient establish a more positive mood—to make things a bit rosier. If a therapist wants to present that idea in the utilization phase of hypnosis, it is desirable to seed it early in induction and then develop the idea in small steps. For example, the induction could be established by having the patient visually imagine a red color. Gradually the red color could take shape and the patient could see a rose, either as a projected hallucination or as an internal mental image. Eventually, the therapist could have the closed-eyed patient imagine seeing things through a red veil, as if looking through red-colored glasses. The patient could do the same with eyes open. Then, the patient could be instructed to memorize this effect.

Erickson had deep and subtle ways of using seeding. Once, when working hypnotically with a female patient, he asked her a question that seemed like a *non sequitur*: "If a blond woman were sitting across from you, you wouldn't be jealous, would you?" When the patient agreed, Erickson reverted back and continued the patter previous to the question. A few days later, he brought in a blond woman and did a double induction with both of them. Erickson seeded a concept for the future, and through that process he avoided adding an emotional charge to the subsequent event and, possibly, client jealousy and competition for his attention.

Erickson also used seeding as a step in establishing induction goals. I can remember an example of his seeding an arm levitation. Prior to suggesting the levitation, Erickson touched the patient's hand lightly. Then, he mentioned that the touch was light. Next, he induced light feelings and arm levitation. Erickson worked methodically. He focused the patient's attention on the arm; established the idea of lightness tactilely; suggested lightness verbally; and then developed it. All along, he used minimal cues so that the patient's experience and responses would be as avolitional as possible.

Seeding can be used whenever the therapist has strategically thought out therapeutic goals. It is a valuable technique that adds drama and sparks altered intensity that can energize hypnotherapeutic processes.

CONTRASTING TRADITIONAL AND ERICKSONIAN METHODS

Let us compare and contrast the traditional and Ericksonian models. In traditional hypnotherapy, the rituals of change are interpretation, explanation, ventilation and confrontation; induction is a means used to achieve those ends. In Ericksonian hypnotherapy, therapists elicit and co-create resource experiences, and induction is an important ritual of change. It is an end in and of itself.

In the traditional model, induction is merely "tilling the ground" so that fertile seeds can be planted. The amount of tilling is dependent on the number of seeds that exist in the therapist's pouch. The traditional induction is a sort of "psychological massage" that lulls the patient into a receptive state. Induction and termination "frame" the therapy, but the frame has no other intrinsic value; the "real" value is the picture, i.e., the therapeutic suggestions.

In the Ericksonian model, induction is intrinsically therapeutic; it is not discrete from therapy. Rather, it naturally feeds into therapy. There are no neat "rows to hoe." One hoes in accordance with the "ruts" that the patient has already developed; one plants seeds as one tills the soil. Also, the frame is part of the art. It can be equally ornate and equally interesting.

In the traditional model there are specific induction methods which are memorized. The Ericksonian model does away with the need for learning a specific induction technique. One can do an induction by talking about the process of a person sitting down in a chair or entering a meeting room. As long as the therapist promotes the five induction responses/goals, the surface level content of the induction patter is often secondary in relevance.

In traditional induction, technique is ritualized in another way. The induction lasts as long as the operator's script. In the Ericksonian subjective approach, induction time is variable. The induction is over when the patient responds consistently to minimal cues. This answers the question that beginning practitioners of hypnosis often ask, "How do I know when to stop the induction?" Well, induction is over when the patient develops responsiveness to minimal cues to the maximum extent possible. This could occur in sixty minutes or sixty seconds.

In traditional hypnosis, the end of the induction period is quite clear. There is no doubt when the operator stops induction and starts to deepen the trance and begin therapy. The frame is discretely separated from the picture. In Ericksonian induction, the lines are blurred; deepening and therapy are effected during induction.

This is similar to the process by which Erickson conducted hypnosis, therapy, and teaching. He blurred the lines between these three operations (Zeig, 1985). When he was teaching, he was doing therapy and hypnosis. When he was doing hypnosis, he was teaching and conducting therapy. It is justifiable to blur the lines between these operations because each has the same main goal, namely, influencing and eliciting behavior.

As has been maintained, induction is a ritual of change. Erickson was an expert at determining the parameters of human responsiveness in the individuals whom he contacted. Induction was a method to explore these parameters. He would learn how the patient responded, push to develop latent potentials, and help the patient pattern new, flexible, effective perspectives. The patient can learn new abilities in redefining situations, attending, varying intensity, and responding and experiencing.

Simply stated, induction *is* therapeutic; it does not have to be considered separate from therapy, or as a step *toward* therapy. Subjectively, *induction promotes flexibility in experience and response and offers new choices*—all of which are common therapeutic goals. Thinking about induction as therapy provides new opportunities for the practitioner, who can then use many different techniques within the induction (including symptom prescription, reframing, symbolic therapy, and humor).

Using technique within the induction works well because the patient is less resistant. He can think, "I can go along with this. It is merely induction. It isn't therapy." A good time to elicit more effective patterns is when the patient is not homeostatically defended against therapeutic pressures for compliance.

Having examined the nature of hypnotic induction, it is now appropriate to discuss the nature of psychological problems, and to compare or juxtapose the similarities between hypnotic induction and the maintenance of psychological problems.

THE NATURE OF PSYCHOLOGICAL PROBLEMS

What is the nature of problems? How does one define what a "problem" is? A process such as a problem can be defined objectively or subjectively. A problem can be defined by appearance, function, etiology, history, or its relationship to other things.

When are problems (symptoms) reported? Well, from the patient's phenomenology, problems are reported when there are: (1) Modified awareness, and/or (2) altered intensity from the normal/desired state, and/or (3) avolitional experience, or (4) responsiveness. They are also reported when (5) a particular situation is framed (defined) as a problem. It does not matter whether the symptom is individual, marital, or familial; to a noticeable degree, all symptoms have these five characteristics. For example, the patient can be intensely focused in his painful sensations and feel unable to ignore them, even though there are many other things in the environment to be aware of. Or, there can be an altered intensity of emotional experience; perhaps there is a change in mood, such as depression or fear. Or, there can be an avolitional experience so that "the symptom just happens." The patient doesn't feel like he does anything to cause it. Or, there can be avolitional responsiveness, for example, "It drives me crazy when my husband raises his voice!" Also, situations may be defined as problems ("I cannot take exams") when there is nothing intrinsically problematic in the situation. Clearly, a problem situation for one person can be merely an interesting challenge for another.

Symptoms are manifested in various patterns. In addition to defining the situation as a problem, the complaint may be stated in terms of some combination of awareness, intensity, avolitional experience, and/or avolitional response. Basically, problems (symptoms) occur when people feel deprived of choice and believe they have only limited ways to respond. They are lost in recursive patterns of limited choice and, more, have lost contact with their intrinsic ability to change.

SIMILARITIES BETWEEN INDUCTION AND
PROBLEM MAINTENANCE

It is commonly understood that hypnosis is a state to be induced and that it must be maintained as *foreground*. Otherwise, it will fade into the background and common everyday experience will re-emerge. If that were not the case, we would walk around in a trance all of the time because it is more pleasurable than customary experience. Essentially, something has to be done in order to maintain hypnosis, otherwise it dissipates. It is gone, and we are back to our "normal" selves. Hypnosis does not exist independently; it must be both induced *and* maintained.

Now, consider the nature of problems. In contradistinction to hypnosis, problems exist independently; it seems as if they do not have to be *maintained*. But, actually, problems *do* have to be maintained. It is just that the mechanism by which the problem is maintained is perceived as autonomous; it happens unconsciously and outside of awareness. But at some level, *active energy is needed to maintain the problem.* Therefore, a most important question the therapist can ask himself is, "How does the symptom persist?" or, better still, "By what mechanism does *the patient* maintain the symptom?" Once the therapist discovers the answer, he can better understand how to compose a therapeutic induction. *The therapist can proceed by using the same technique (process) that the patient uses to maintain the symptom.* In other words, *whatever the patient does to be a patient, the therapist can use to be a therapist.* The therapist can use the same method that maintains maladaption to induce and promote a more effective state.

In some ways, therapy is like gene-splicing. One uses the existing molecules to help make a few modifications that seem relatively minor. However, the effect is that the template is changed and new sequences are automatically composed by the altered gene.

The above concepts can be illustrated in clinical terms. Take a patient with a phobia. Postulate about what the patient does to maintain his phobia. One simple pattern is to visualize (hallucinate) Stephen King horror movies about the avoided situation; it is an easy way to maintain a phobia. How can one harness this process to create a therapeutic induction? Well, if the patient can picture Stephen King movies, he can also picture Stephen Spielberg movies. The existing process can be used, albeit in a slightly altered direction. Alternatively, if the patient agitates himself by playing a cha-cha inside his head, he can also play "The Blue Danube" or even "Rhapsody in Blue." Moreover, if a patient can pressure himself and create an undesirable state, that patient has the mechanism to pleasure himself and create a desirable state. Erickson summed this up succinctly. He said, "If you have phantom pain, you may also have phantom good feelings" (Erickson & Rossi, 1979, p. 107).

The therapist has at hand a usable mechanism that is inherent in each and every presenting problem. Thus, therapy can become a process of dehypnotization: One takes symptomatic people and modifies their own method of symptom maintenance to create a counterinduction. Their traditional choice is used to create new choice. However, simply telling the patient to modify the problematic mechanism is ineffective. It is here that indirection (multi-level communication/minimal cues/one-step-removed communicating/injunctions) holds sway. The patient is eased into the new pattern, and situations are composed whereby he voluntarily changes his previously held position by virtue of his own efforts.

The mechanism of the problem also can be used to create hypnotic induction. The induction of the trance can be structurally analogous to the mechanism that maintains the problem. They have similar outcomes—namely, focused awareness, altered intensity, avolitional experience, and avolitional responsiveness. Further, there is an intrinsic situational definition (e.g., "This situation is a problem"). However, the therapist's induction leads out of a rut, while the patient's maladaptive mechanism keeps him in the rut. The central idea is to use the well-developed channel that already exists in the direction of more functional adaptation. Also, inductions that use the existing mechanism of symptom maintenance may be even more effective than traditional inductions that use a therapist's preconceived script.

For example, in an interview a patient described the maintenance of his low self-esteem, which turned out to be a three-step process in difficult work and educational situations: (1) He would first wonder to himself if he had the necessary abilities to cope adequately; (2) then he customarily would decide, "No it's not present"; (3) finally, he would develop a series of physical symptoms, the first of which was a heavy feeling in his stomach, "like a stone."

The induction recapitulated this sequence, albeit with more positive

connotation. Also used was his description of times when he did have
self-esteem, which he described as his back becoming "stiff."

> Make yourself physically comfortable and then perhaps you *watch*
> . . . some spot and use that to *focus* your attention . . . all along
> just waiting, just waiting for a certain signal, a certain sensation,
> a certain sign in your body that you know will be there. A feeling
> I will name later.
>
> [1] But first, mentally, the process can interest you. Because you
> can be thinking to yourself about the eye changes, and you can
> be wondering to yourself, "Will my eye behavior change? Will
> that fluttering sensation be there? Will there be an alteration in
> my blink reflex?"
>
> [2] And then you can decide, "Yes, there can be that steadiness
> around the eye"; and, "Yes, there can be that pleasant fluttery
> feeling"; and, "Yes, there can be that change in reflex."
>
> [3] And, then there is that physical sensation. For example,
> there's a feeling that could be described as a kind of numbness
> that can happen in the center . . . of your hands. And later there
> can be an uplifting movement. But before that, there is that stiffness
> . . . down the spine of your hand. . . .

The same three steps used to maintain low self-esteem were used to
induce trance. The well-developed symptom mechanism was used, but
in the process a new value was subtly attached to the mechanism: It
could be used to promote a desirable, pleasant state, that of trance.
Hence, a hypnotic redefinition was accomplished.

Interestingly, in follow-up the patient reported an important effect—
that he had experienced "the strength of his internal eye." This was
taken as a positive sign reflecting his preconscious response to my
intended wordplay on the homonyms "eye" and "I." If he entered the
problem situation with a "strong I," he would effectively accomplish
his goals.

Another way of creating induction is to see how the patient emphasizes the five induction processes in his description of the symptom.
Is the symptom described more as modified awareness, altered intensity,
avolitional experience, or avolitional response, and how specifically is
it defined as a problem? Subsequently, the induction can be created to
emphasize the same aspect(s) as the one(s) emphasized by the patient.

As was seen, this process can be used well with formal hypnosis.

However, it can also be accomplished in strategic therapy without formal induction. Take a patient who is disturbing himself in certain social situations by repeatedly thinking, "I'm stupid. I will be rejected." When faced with a situation defined as a "problem," the patient avolitionally reacts in this manner. The patient will have a trigger-point. The more one knows about the trigger-point, the easier it is to devise the therapy. The trigger-point is one part of the mechanism (progression) that the patient uses in the process of maintaining a problem. An example of a trigger-point would be that when the patient notices others looking at him "critically," he finds himself thinking his repetitive phrase, "I am stupid. I will be rejected."

Now, how can one use the idea that the mechanism of the problem can be a mechanism of solution? What I have done successfully with this kind of patient is to explain that it is critical in his encounters with others that he closely notice the color of their eyes whenever he finds himself thinking his repetitive thought:

> When you see the other person's eyes, you can stop momentarily. Then, inside your head say three positive things about that person. I don't want you to say those things out loud, I merely want you to think three positive things.
>
> If you think about it, when you say to yourself "I am stupid; I will be rejected," you automatically create a certain body posture. Your thoughts influence your behavior. In hypnosis, we call this the *ideodynamic effect.*
>
> If, through your thinking, you are taking on a posture that indicates "I am stupid; I will be rejected," you are probably sending a signal to other people that influences their response to you. Actually, you might induce the very response you are trying to avoid, and thereby you will get confirmation of your original hypothesis.
>
> But, you can use that ideodynamic effect in a positive fashion by thinking to yourself three things that are positive about the other person. By doing so, unconsciously you will change your posture. As you change your behavior, you will get different responses from people. Then, that old constellation, "I am stupid; I will be rejected," will begin to dissolve.

While it is quite important for the therapist to ask himself, "How does the symptom persist?" it also can be valuable to ask that question of the patient. Pursuing in depth the issue of how the patient maintains the problem can create pattern disruption. It is akin to the old saw about querying a centipede regarding the pattern just before and immediately after the movement of leg 42. Invariably, it causes stumbling.

Sometimes making things conscious can be quite effective. However, the idea is not to make conscious the "underlying meaning," the psychodynamics of the symptom. Rather, one makes the mechanism of problem maintenance conscious—even uncomfortably conscious. When the actual steps are defined in great detail, the symptom state can lose some of its integrity. When the progressive steps are made conscious, often they become more volitional, and the avolitional nature of the symptom is disrupted.

To reiterate, *the mechanism of problem maintenance can be a mechanism of solution.* That mechanism is always benign. The end result—for example, the presenting complaint—may be problematic, but there is no sense in throwing out the baby with the bathwater. If the existing mechanism can be used, do not reject it. *Use it.*

SUMMARY

Induction is reported when five phenomena are established: modified awareness, altered intensity, avolitional experience, avolitional responsiveness, and when the situation is defined as hypnosis. Injunctive Ericksonian techniques such as ratification, incorporation, positive attribution, surprise, hypnotic definition, and seeding are used to elicit these responses. Rather than using a preset induction, the therapist establishes hypnosis by using the patient's well-developed symptom strategies. The technique used by the patient to maintain the symptom can be used to create effective inductions and effective therapy. Effective therapies and inductions mirror the process of symptom maintenance, but lead to positive outcomes. In Ericksonian approaches, induction is more than a means to a desirable state; it is a technique of therapy.

REFERENCES

Barber, T. X. (1969). *Hypnosis: A Scientific Approach.* New York: Brunner/Mazel.

Edmundston, W. E. (1984). *Hypnosis and Relaxation: Modern Verification of an Old Equation.* New York: Wiley.

Erickson, M. H., & Rossi, E. L. (1979). *Hypnotherapy: An Exploratory Casebook.* New York: Irvington.

Erickson, M. H., Rossi, E. L., & Rossi, S. (1976). *Hypnotic Realities.* New York: Irvington.

Gill, M. M., & Brenman, M. (1959). *Hypnosis and Related States: Psychoanalytic Studies in Regression.* New York: International Universities Press.

Haley, J. (1973). *Uncommon Therapy: The Psychiatric Techniques of Milton H. Erickson, M.D.* New York: Norton.

Hilgard, E. R. (1978). *Divided Consciousness: Multiple Controls in Human Thought and Action.* New York: Wiley.

Sarbin, T. R., & Coe, W. C. (1972). *Hypnosis: A Social Psychological Analysis of Influence Communication.* New York: Holt, Rinehart and Winston.

Watzlawick, P., Weakland, J., & Fisch, R. (1974). *Change: Principles of Problem Formation and Problem Resolution.* New York: Norton.

Weitzenhoffer, A. M. (1953). *Hypnotism: An Objective Study of Suggestibility.* New York: Wiley (paper edition, 1963).

Zeig, J. (Ed.) (1980). *A Teaching Seminar with Milton H. Erickson.* New York: Brunner/Mazel.

Zeig, J. (1985). *Experiencing Erickson: An Introduction to the Man and His Work.* New York: Brunner/Mazel.

SECTION TWO: PRACTICE

PART VIII

Tailoring Treatment

Chapter 21

One Method for Designing Short-Term Intervention- Oriented Ericksonian Therapy

Kristina K. Erickson

Kristina K. Erickson, M.D. (University of Missouri), is a family practitioner and emergency medicine specialist in the Baltimore area. A Board Member of The Milton H. Erickson Foundation and an Editorial Board Member of the Ericksonian Monographs, *she is the youngest child of Milton and Betty Erickson.*

Described and illustrated with four cases are three important principles of brief intervention-oriented therapy. Good therapy requires proper evaluation and creative planning, client commitment, emphasis on strengths, and tailoring to the individual.

Milton H. Erickson was my father. I was fortunate to have had the opportunity to closely observe his interactions with others and listen to his interpretations of behaviors, conversations and events. I continually discovered new and valuable information from watching and conversing with my father. He would relate case histories and describe patterns of thinking, interventions and therapies. He described people he had met and told many stories about life. His philosophies were reflected both in his homelife and in his practice. He was future oriented, optimistic and practical. He encouraged productivity and enjoyment of life. I would like to share my understanding of his approach and principles of brief therapy which has resulted from the close contact I had with him over the years.

The methodology of short-term interventional therapy is extremely complex. One may look at my father's teachings and interventions and see them as simplistic and straightforward. However, this apparent simplicity is an illusion of Ericksonian therapy. On close examination of my father's seemingly direct and commonsense therapeutic interventions, one finds incredible complexity. His therapeutic processes were created by a meticulous interweaving and integration of a multiplicity of factors. These factors include attention to the unique frame of reference inherent in the client, the client's own speech patterns and vocabulary, and the particular social and cultural background and beliefs of the client. Methods included hypnotic directives, interspersed suggestions, and specific therapeutic recommendations. While a discussion of these items would fill several books, the purpose of this chapter is to present and illustrate the application of three principles which form a foundation for the design of short-term interventions in Ericksonian therapy.

Seen another way, Ericksonian therapy can be viewed as an unending set of dominoes. The therapist guides the client to set up a vast array of dominoes, and then reaches out and tips one. The rest fall into place by the slight impact from the first domino. The key to successfully implementing this approach is the ability to set up the dominoes and the perceptiveness to know which to push and when.

Principles for developing effective short-term intervention-based therapy can be defined. I will describe a technique of developing such therapy and illustrate this by means of four case histories. The reader may find that this discussion overlaps with, and integrates the teachings of many other therapists while remaining fundamentally Ericksonian.

There are three principles that comprise the foundation of Ericksonian therapy. The first is careful and accurate assessment of the client. This includes not only what clients say, but how, when, and why they say it. The second principle is that therapists must secure a client's agreement to undergo change. Without a client's conscious and unconscious commitment and agreement, change is not readily achieved. Finally, therapy must be made compatible with the client's social and personal values and beliefs, and it must incorporate not merely management and resolution of the problem but also development of client strengths and resources.

Ericksonian therapy requires energy, ingenuity, and meticulous preparation to develop effective short-term interventions. Ironically, when the therapy is finally delivered, it often appears so logical and straightforward that clients frequently do not credit the therapist for helping them. Rather, they often report the concepts came to them solely on their own, unrelated to their visit to the therapist. Though this can be disconcerting to the therapist, it can be beneficial. Instead of losing power or autonomy when they are in therapy, clients gain from within themselves; their own sense of power and capability is enhanced. These points can be illustrated with case examples.

THE ANXIOUS PHARMACIST WHO JOGGED

This case involves a 38-year-old pharmacist residing and working in a rural community. Mr. Smith described his complaints in an uneasy and anxious fashion and explained that he was having "panic attacks." He described these as overpowering feelings of everything closing in on him and of feeling frightened, panicky and immobilized. He always had been ill at ease in crowds and at social functions, and had experienced these episodes since childhood. However, they had increased in frequency and intensity during the last few months. Now he was experiencing these anxiety attacks when alone, and he stated that these episodes were particularly frequent when he was driving to work. They had become so bad that he even had considered taking sedatives from his pharmaceutical stock without a prescription, but his integrity would not permit him to do so.

He had recently purchased the pharmacy, and it was clearly to his advantage in the small community to be personable and sociable to the townspeople. He was aware of this, yet due to the panic episodes, he was avoiding the public and spending an increasing amount of time alone in his stock room. His method of dealing with the panic episodes was to isolate himself. If unable to do that, then he would, in his words, "exert extreme willpower" and force himself to carry on with his activities.

A review of Mr. Smith's background indicated that he had a solid marriage, with two children, ages 12 and four. Mr. Smith was a bright and ambitious businessman. In addition to the recent acquisition of his pharmacy, he had built a new home. He felt some financial pressure, but assured me that basically he was doing satisfactorily. Although he enjoyed his family life, he also enjoyed solitude and long hikes in the country. For several years, he had enjoyed jogging three mornings a week, but, due to the panic attacks, he was curtailing this and other activities and becoming socially isolated. He described some recent difficulties with his 12-year-old daughter which appeared to be reasonably straightforward teenage-parent conflict.

The manner in which a therapist presents himself to clients can actually begin the process of change and problem resolution. My father exuded confidence to his clients and taught that a professional, self-assured manner served in itself to initiate therapeutic change. People tend to confer upon health professionals certain status, knowledge and privileges. My father recommended taking advantage of this phenomenon as a resource to be utilized. Hence, Ericksonian therapy with Mr. Smith was initiated as I listened to his story. I assured him that his problem was manageable, and then assigned him several tasks to perform prior to our next appointment. I recommended that he apply himself to improving his relationship with his daughter—a goal that he agreed was most worthy of his time.

I then reviewed some child management principles for him and his wife to consider. He promised me he would devote energy to these ideas. I also instructed him to purchase a detailed map of the area and to identify some locales that would offer potentially suitable hiking grounds.

These maneuvers served a dual purpose. Mr. Smith's attention was quite fixated on his panic attacks—including anticipating, dreading, and experiencing them and the aftermath which followed them. Part of his concentration would now be diverted to more rewarding activities—improving his relationship with his daughter and finding future hiking trails. In addition to this diversion of energy, Mr. Smith was being readied for future productive and rewarding activities—a setting up of the dominoes.

Finally, I requested that Mr. Smith attend carefully to the details of his panic attacks—where and when they occurred; their intensity, their duration and so forth. I asked him to note a great many details of the attacks. This last instruction incorporates the familiar Ericksonian concept of reframing and the redistribution of power. By studying details of the episodes, clients begin to gain control. No longer are they simply pawns of mysterious and elusive sensations. Rather, clients will begin to establish a semblance of control as they exhibit curiosity over symptom occurrence. Clients are often unaware of this subtle difference. However, by introducing new elements to the situation, the process of change is initiated. As this process continues, a shift in control and power naturally follows.

Having directed Mr. Smith in these preliminary steps, I dismissed him. Clients may be hesitant at this stage. They may feel that they have not been completely understood and that their therapist has been sidetracked to less important issues. A confident demeanor by the therapist, and assurances that the therapist will deal with all the problems will often suffice. Consequently, clients can be persuaded to depart with an agreement to follow instructions until the next session.

The next step is often the most difficult for the therapist. I call this step "Thinking Very Hard." This involves an intensive review of the data as well as researching texts and teachings. Additionally, therapists must invoke their own creativity and imagination. An intervention must be designed that is achievable, compatible with the client's lifestyle, effective in resolving the problem, and suitable in rechanneling energies to productive, fulfilling activities. A systematic review of the client's social, family and occupational situation will often prove a foundation the therapist can utilize to develop appropriate management. The meticulous study of available data additionally serves to bring to the therapist's attention client strengths and interests, thus providing a means for change. Discrepancies in a client's history also may be elucidated by contrasting spoken word against exhibited lifestyle and behavior. This may be particularly helpful in assessing client motivation.

For example, if a client verbalizes that clothing and personal appearance are of primary importance but consistently presents unkempt and disheveled grooming, there is clearly disharmony between spoken word and exhibited behavior. Importantly, if openly confronted with this contrasting material, clients may take offense or become defensive. Therapists should note closely both verbalized and exhibited behavior and design therapy which is acceptable and harmonious to the client's lifestyle.

Designing appropriate therapy can be extremely difficult and challenging. I recall my father spending hours reviewing data and writing out preliminary therapeutic strategies, only to rewrite them time after time before he was satisfied. Certainly, experience is an advantage and an asset. My father emphasized that although each client is unique in needs and situations, the therapist becomes more knowledgeable and thus more efficient with each client encounter.

After considerable review, research and effort, I developed a therapeutic strategy I believed would be effective for Mr. Smith. I was prepared to enter the phase of therapy in which one secures the client's agreement and readiness to accept therapy and change. However, clients must usually be carefully prepared and primed for the presentation of

the therapeutic solution. Appropriate time should be invested in soliciting a client's interest and commitment to undergo therapy. It may be
effective for therapists to express some curiosity as to whether a client
is ready for a change. Change requires effort, energy and time and has
consequences in one's life. The therapist can shift the patient's attention
and energies to contemplating his future without the problem.

Finally, the therapist should study the patient's history closely, and
review what the elimination of the problem may bring. Will the patient
be lost without his problem to fill his time and energies? Adequate
alternative activities must be provided, and client's energies must be
rechanneled productively. Prior to presenting Mr. Smith with a solution,
then, I needed to set the stage by preparing him for a life without
these demanding panic attacks. Additionally, the strength and import
of these attacks must be continually redefined and diminished.

Mr. Smith returned in a week, relating an improvement in his relationship with his daughter. As I had requested, he had located several
hiking grounds but told me frankly that his panic attacks were so bad
that he couldn't consider going. We spent the rest of the visit reviewing
his findings regarding the details of his panic attacks. We discussed
where, when, how long, and how intense. We discussed whether the
attacks started insidiously or if they arrived in full-blown intensity.
Could the ring of the telephone disrupt them? If he was driving, did
a passing car or a honk of a horn change them? Did the episodes come
in clusters or groups? Were there more at night or in the morning?
Before lunch or after? I questioned and queried, and we literally bored
ourselves dissecting and discussing those panic attacks—defusing them
and divesting them of much of their meaning and power. I was employing a technique of redefining by dissection and intense study of a
problem, which is a classical Ericksonian technique. My father repeatedly
demonstrated the effectiveness of reducing a problem in its significance
by the introduction of boredom, as I did in this case.

At this point, Mr. Smith was prepared for the presentation of a
solution. I expressed some curiosity as to whether Mr. Smith was ready
for a change. A change would require effort, energy, and time, and
have some consequences in his life. As the client offers a verbal or
nonverbal agreement to the therapist, he is committing himself not only
to accept change, but to relinquish symptoms. Focus is shifted from "is
there a solution?" to "I am willing to accept the work and consequences
of a solution." This latter focus presupposes that there *is* a solution.
Moreover, therapists should clearly ascertain that clients are committed
and not merely offering lip service.

After the discussion with Mr. Smith, I was satisfied that he was deeply motivated. Further, preliminary progress had already been achieved. His relationships with his family had improved, and he was beginning to explore areas of interest that had previously given him pleasure, such as hiking. However, in view of the intensity and long duration of his problem, I felt it prudent to allow further time for preparation and so I dismissed him for three days. He was instructed to review his decision, and if he continued to be committed to a change he was to wear a wristwatch with an accurate second hand on his return.

This last instruction is again typically Ericksonian. That is, taking advantage of natural assets, my father frequently invoked the human characteristic of curiosity. Clients can be influenced by provoking their curiosity, and this may enhance their receptiveness to information and therapeutic recommendations. Mr. Smith returned, wearing a fine-quality wristwatch with a second hand.

My recommendations were as follows: At the onset of a panic attack Mr. Smith was to excuse himself from wherever he was and go outside. He was to stride vigorously back and forth and use his wristwatch to time himself to the second. He was to continue the exercise for not less than two and no more than five minutes. He could use the back alley at work, the side or back lot at stores, and the backyard of homes. If he was in his car, he was to pull safely to the side of the road and walk off on the side grass. This exercise could be repeated as needed. Should someone make an inquiry—and social opinion was important in his situation—he was to respond with remarks in the nature of: "Well, you know I jog. I had a muscle cramp in my leg and I'm stretching out my leg." These could be seen as truthful statements and would satisfy any curious townspeople as they all knew Mr. Smith was a jogger.

This task was to be enforced at social events and even at dinner parties. At the onset of an attack, he was to get up, excuse himself, feel free to mutter his lines about leg cramps, and perform the exercise. He agreed a three- or four-minute absence, even from an important business or social function, would not be harmful. After receiving these instructions, Mr. Smith departed from my office, somewhat dubious, but with a solemn promise to adhere to the agreement. I made a telephone follow-up a week later which revealed that Mr. Smith was complying with the instructions. He did feel it quite inconvenient to pull his car over, park, get out and stride back and forth just for the required two minutes, but "a promise was a promise." He reported, in addition, that the back alley had proved convenient at work, and he had excused himself from a dinner party.

One week later another follow-up was made by telephone. He reported that the attacks were becoming less frequent. Mrs. Smith hastily explained this by the fact that his volume of work had increased, and he was so busy he scarcely had time for any extras. I asked to see him in a month.

In my office a month later, Mr. Smith demonstrated a phenomenon I call "Who me? I never had a problem." The concept was alluded to previously and is found frequently in Ericksonian therapy. Though the therapist must invest tremendous thought, energy and preparation into developing a solution, the transition for clients often flows smoothly and with such logic that credit is not openly and directly given to the therapist. Though at times this can be disconcerting, it is as it should be. My father stated that clients have the solutions within them and that the therapist is simply the guide. Clients frequently express their appreciation in an indirect fashion—and of course, the client's improvement and well-being are, in themselves, satisfactory rewards. My father rarely, if ever, recommended confronting clients or reviewing the now-resolved problem. He emphasized the client's inherent right to dignity and self-respect and his right to be normal.

Mr. Smith seemed almost impatient to be in the office. Things were going well and his pharmacy was very busy. He had hired a pharmacist to come in every other Saturday in order to free him from his six-day work week. He wanted to get some hiking in while the weather was still good. He informed me that he and his wife appreciated my advice regarding management of their daughter. The relationship had improved, their family unit had strengthened, and they were involved in more group activities and outings.

I asked Mr. Smith how his drive to work was each morning, as this morning drive had been a particularly problematic time. "Just fine," he replied with a puzzled air. He added that his car was getting a little old, but was still quite reliable. I terminated the visit by reminding Mr. Smith that he had strengths and solutions to call upon, encouraged him in his hikes and family life, and told him to feel free to call if he had need in the future.

My father consistently drew a conclusion to therapy and formally dismissed patients after such brief intervention-oriented therapy. While he believed the door must be left open for future contact, he believed that clients feel a sense of closure when termination is initiated by the therapist. Further, the formal conclusion gives clients a certain freedom to put the problem behind them and classify it as part of their past.

THE CASE OF ENURESIS AND THE BATHTUB

The second case study involves a girl who had enuresis, or bedwetting. This management again incorporates the three principles applied to the previous case. I will emphasize these again. Step one begins with , carefully assessing the client's personal, family, and social situation. This will be followed at step two by preparing the patient and family to cope productively and happily without the problem that had become the focus of their attention. Finally, step three is to introduce therapy that concomitantly deemphasizes the problem while maximizing strengths and positive interests with the client's life.

Kathy was seven years old and had wet the bed intermittently her entire life. Kathy's mother was a housewife, her father a laborer; she had three siblings. Neither parent had completed high school, but both were quite bright and had a lot of common sense. They were devoted to their children and were a close family unit. Kathy required remedial classes and special tutoring. The parents were diligent in seeking out these services and in involving themselves with her studies. They worked hard and scrimped financially in order to pay for needed services.

Kathy was quiet and timid. For two years she had been going to a state-supported counseling service. Various approaches had been recommended by the counseling service and had met with varying degrees of temporary success. The parents had devised a number of home remedies, including fluid restriction, awakening her at midnight, and paying her for dry nights. These methods had produced dry beds for up to six weeks, but never longer. She had been medically and urologically evaluated several times, and given a clean bill of health. Over the years, Kathy had, in her mother's words, "come a long way." She was more talkative and had made some friends—but she still wet the bed.

I had a good relationship with this family and had seen Kathy and her siblings in my office for the usual childhood illnesses. The mother was at her wit's end and asked if I had any recommendations. Because of Kathy's improvement in scholastic and social functionings, the state counseling center was now scheduling her at three-month intervals and the problem of her enuresis had been unresolved.

I believe I stepped into this case at an opportune time. The counseling center had been successful in improving Kathy's self-esteem, as well as contributing to an improvement in her studies. The family was interested, involved, and caring. I encouraged them to continue with the recommendations from the counseling center that were contributing to positive changes. I told them that Kathy had reached an age and a development that would change her pattern of bedwetting. The parents were pleased but doubtful. Kathy was silent. I scheduled a visit for one week hence and told them that at that time I would spend one-third of the time with the parents, one-third with Kathy, and one-third all together. This intrigued Kathy.

I will clarify that at this point, I was uncertain as to how to most effectively manage this problem. Intensive study was needed to design a regime that would redefine the enuresis as an entity without importance and simultaneously strengthen skills that would envelop Kathy in a fulfilling fashion.

Kathy's siblings included a nine-year-old brother who was of average intelligence, outgoing and athletic. His importance was built in—he was the only boy and the eldest child. Additionally, he and his father had a close bond in their enjoyment and skill in sports. Her sisters were four-year-old twins who were very bright. They were talkative, self-assured, vigorous and inseparable. They were good-humored and pleasant little girls, but it was pretty clear that anything Kathy could do, the twins could do better and faster. However, this was not true for bedwetting—Kathy was better at that. Kathy achieved recognition, attention, and individuality by wetting the bed.

I studied the family situation closely. In this age group, particularly in a tightly-knit family group, interpersonal relationships and self-esteem are closely interwoven and are of primary importance to the individual members. Consequently, therapy must result in an alternative source of recognition and self-esteem that would be both productive and enhancing. With considerable thought, a therapeutic plan was developed.

On their return, I saw Kathy first. We discussed some facts about people—that everyone is different, with different strengths, talents and skills; that everyone is special. I pointed out that Kathy was something the twins could never be. Nor could her brother. She was the eldest daughter—the first daughter her parents had ever had—*and* she was an older sister. She would be the first girl in the family to turn 8, 9, 10, 12, and 16, and so on. She giggled when I pointed out that the twins didn't even turn 5, 6, or 8 by themselves; they had to do it together. Continuing in terms and language to which she would relate, I told her that there were certain privileges and responsibilities befitting an eldest daughter and older sister. Kathy would need to set an example for her younger sisters and help them when she could. After all, she had lived longer. She would always be ahead of them in day-to-day living—she had eaten more meals, slept more nights, and played more days. She would be able to offer them wisdom and experience simply because she had lived longer.

Honesty in this type of therapy is mandatory. The statements made to Kathy were carefully phrased and were not debatable. The information was factual. My father cautioned against inaccurate information or praise; such maneuvers serve only to discredit the therapist or parents.

I did not discuss bedwetting during Kathy's session, but rather concentrated on alternative sources of self-esteem. By ignoring the enuresis, I initiated the process of diminishing its importance.

I spoke with her parents next and asked them to place emphasis on Kathy's strengths and role in the family. When I asked them what Kathy could do better or more easily than the twins, they couldn't think of anything. It is not unusual to find that negative qualities have been more evident than positive qualities. Indeed, it seems to be part of human nature to notice irregularities rather than to appreciate strengths. Teenagers as a group are often noted for negative behavior patterns, and parents of teens often must be assisted in identifying areas in which their children excel.

Truthfulness must be observed, and reliance on first person praise should be emphasized. For example, parents can say, "I enjoy your smile," or "I found you good company in the car today." Observations worded in this fashion are not debatable. Such comments, therefore, carry weight and significance. In Kathy's case, a number of skills and aspects were identified that could be complimented. For instance, she was kind and patient, she could match colors very well, she folded clothes neatly, her hands were graceful.

In preparing to discuss bedwetting, I obtained the parents' agreement to follow my upcoming recommendations for three months, at which time follow up would occur, if necessary. Then Kathy joined us and we discussed bedwetting.

I asked each person to tell me all the reasons why it was a problem. We all agreed that it didn't make her do poorly in school, stop her from growing up, or turn her into a frog. So exactly why was it a problem? Kathy didn't know. Her parents said it was a lot of work to change the bed and even if Kathy did it, it was extra trouble. The mother added that sleeping in all that wetness gave Kathy a rash. This discussion furthered the process of deemphasizing the bedwetting. It was redefined as a finite issue, and fantasies about it were deflated. Hence, it became less important.

I then made my recommendations. I suggested that Kathy spread a sheet in the bathtub and sleep there. Urine could run down the drain, keeping her drier, and cleanup would be minimal since they could throw the sheet in the wash and swish out the tub. Night time would no longer be a problem to anyone. Kathy could urinate all night, every night—or once a week or once a month. No one would care. I quickly ushered them out of the office.

My follow up after one week revealed that Kathy was sleeping in the bathtub and still urinating every night. Her parents had been discovering many areas in which Kathy excelled and were emphasizing these, as well as her role as older sister and eldest daughter.

It was developing that bedwetting was no longer of particular interest or significance to anyone but Kathy, who was in the cold, hard bathtub. Kathy's mother expressed some concerns regarding Kathy's comfort in the tub. However, she reconfirmed her decision to cheerfully continue with my recommendations. Perhaps another family would have had difficulty with these directives. However, these parents demonstrated an almost devout respect for health care professionals. It was this attitude to which I appealed in order to secure their further compliance.

At this point, treatment strategies had succeeded in getting Kathy to sleep in the bathtub, and the process of developing other productive activities and traits had been successfully initiated. For the following session, I had devised an intervention which I believed would help her graduate from the tub into a conventional bed and yet be free of her enuresis. I told Kathy that I suspected she would like to sleep in the bedroom with her sisters some nights and suggested she take a vacation from sleeping in the tub. However, according to my directions, she was to use the tub at least every Thursday.

Two weeks later, Kathy, content to be returned to her comfortable bed, was excelling in the role of being the oldest daughter and having skills and talents her sisters didn't have. She was wetting at night, but only on Thursday—when she was in the bathtub. In order to help her make the final shift from her symptom, I told Kathy that people vacation even on Thursdays. She could return to the tub any time and any night she wanted. After all, the tub was always there.

I saw Kathy's mother some months later for a minor health problem. At that time, I asked her about bedwetting. As Mr. Smith had done in the previous example, she looked puzzled and told me that none of her children wet the bed. Kathy *used* to, but that had been a long time ago.

At this point, I would like to add that although I have successfully managed a number of enuretic patients, Kathy is the only one for whom I recommended the bathtub bed. Interventions must be tailored to the individual and be consistent with individual, social, and environmental situations and mores. It is conceivable that a similar intervention could be applied to several clients; however, appropriate modifications would be necessary to fit each client and family.

The resolution of Kathy's enuresis demonstrated another of my father's favorite premises—particularly when applied to symptoms involving child-parent conflicts. He emphasized that when the parent didn't care so much, the child would stop the problem behavior. Consequently, he would develop therapy that would turn an issue into a non-issue. Kathy's bedwetting became a non-issue. It had been redefined and deemphasized.

THE CASE OF THE PERSISTENT SNIFFLER

The next case involves Mrs. V. and her four-year-old son, Nicholas. I was unsuccessful in the management of this case and present it to illustrate the importance of investing adequate time for a careful review of all available data. This case illustrates that information should be checked and crosschecked. And therapy must incorporate not only a resolution of the presenting problem, but a restructuring and rechanneling of client energies and strengths.

Mrs. V. was the wife of a prominent businessman in a small rural community. She reported a stable and good marriage even though her husband was involved in his business and often away evenings and weekends. They had two older children, aged 14 and 16, who were doing well and were busy and active in school.

She told me that she had been ready to return to work when, in her words, they "were blessed with Nicholas." I also thought Nicholas was a blessing: He had curly blond hair, a tremendous grin, twinkling eyes, was sharp as a tack and full of life.

I had seen Nicholas several times prior to Mrs. V.'s presentation with the problem which she defined as little Nicholas's "snorting." For almost a year, Nicholas had been sniffling. She had taken him to various physicians and then to referral centers. He had been examined and studied and tested by four highly reputable specialists. All had been reassuring and recommended various benign remedies—a vaporizer, a decongestant, saline nosedrops and so on. However, the snorting continued.

In retrospect, I erred in accepting the problem as Mrs. V. described it—a simple problem she wished resolved. Mrs. V. was an intelligent, competent, capable lady. I gave disproportionate credence to her spoken words without taking the time for a comprehensive review of information. Mrs. V. said she would try anything—all she wanted was for Nick to stop snorting. After all, the specialists had told her there was nothing wrong and it was just a habit. When I told her I had some recommendations, she seemed eager and interested.

My recommendations were as follows: Basically, it seemed Nicholas enjoyed snorting (he grinned and snorted), but she found it annoying. Therefore, when struck with an urge to snort, Nicholas was to go to his bathroom, close the door, and snort to his heart's content. His mother was to remind him to go to the bathroom if she found him snorting elsewhere. As Nicholas was an obedient child, an enforcement issue was unlikely.

Mrs. V. returned a week later, very pleased. Snorting was confined to the bathroom, and after a few occasions of his leaving his favorite television shows and toys, the snorting had diminished tremendously. In fact, she told me, it was no longer a problem.

Two weeks later, I unexpectedly heard from Mrs. V., who was quite upset. Nicholas's snorting had returned and had escalated. He would leave his favorite shows, his toys, meals, or his bed and go to his bathroom to snort. She knew that we—the doctors as a group—were wrong, and she was right. Something must be wrong with little Nick. It wasn't right or normal for a little boy to spend so much time snorting, she said. Nicholas sat there, listening with delight. She had insisted he be with her. He had a twinkle in his eye and so much power on his little shoulders that he couldn't shrug if he had tried.

I listened with dismay. I had not assimilated all the data this lady had given me. Her husband was gone many long hours in an active busy profession. She had been ready to return to her profession when she was thwarted by the birth of Nicholas. He may have been a blessing, but he was also an intrusion. She had been investing enormous energy each day, worrying about, listening to, and being annoyed by her young snorter. Much of her time and self-worth had been invested in searching for the cause of this affliction. When the snorting disappeared, she found herself at home with a four-year-old in a small rural community, a husband who was away much of the time, and many empty hours on her hands.

It seemed that little Nicholas, enjoying the pleasures of traveling about to various specialists and being fussed over, was more than willing to sacrifice a few television shows to regain his previous position of power. Simply by snorting he was able to monopolize his mother's time and attention, as well as the attention of many physicians.

Clearly, in review, this could not be reduced to a simple, easily controlled habit. Both Mrs. V. and Nicholas would need their energies rechanneled into more productive activities. Proper respect would need to be given to Mrs. V.'s year of effort in searching for a cure for Nicholas and to her strength and devout sense of mothering and duty. The relationship between the two needed restructuring. Activities such as enrollment in part-time nursery school for Nicholas and participation in community activities or part-time employment for Mrs. V. should be explored. Further information on the often absent Mr. V. and the building of family unity may be beneficial.

Under these circumstances, the family warranted guidance into more therapy. I accepted and agreed with Mrs. V.'s statements that this was more complex than a simple habit, and that, indeed, something was wrong. Two options were available: to readdress the problem or to make a high-power referral to a super-specialist who was expensive, a long drive away, and inconvenient to schedule. But he was superb with this type of problem, *if* Mrs. V. was willing to endure all the difficulties involved in seeing him. The phrasing of the referral was obviously geared to appeal to Mrs. V.'s profound commitment to the issue as a problem, and she was willingly referred to a colleague. The case of little Nicholas emphasized the need to address all three above mentioned principles when creating a therapeutic intervention, as well as illustrating some difficulties that may be encountered if the principles are not fully addressed.

THE CASE OF THE NOSEBLEED COVER-UP

The final case involves the unmasking of an underlying problem via the removal of a symptom. A 30-year-old auto mechanic, Mr. B., presented to the emergency room one evening. He was extremely anxious, ill at ease, and frightened. Two years prior, he had had a serious posterior nosebleed that required an uncomfortable packing procedure and a four-day hospitalization. Since that time, he had worried about bleeding again, even though his physician had assured him that such a situation was unlikely. Over the past six weeks, his worries had escalated and he was so convinced that he would bleed that he would continually put his thumb and finger in his mouth and then examine them for signs of bleeding. Posterior nosebleeds can drip into the back of the mouth and Mr. B. was checking for blood in his mouth.

He told me he knew this was crazy, but he couldn't help it. His boss and his wife were concerned and urged him to get help. Throughout his discussion with me, Mr. B. frequently and repeatedly put his finger in his mouth and then closely examined it for signs of blood. His repeated study of saliva-covered fingers was most annoying to watch and certainly would be an impediment in any social or personal relationship. The fact that his boss and his wife were supportive of this man indicated that behind this unsightly habit was a fine, decent individual who received loyalty and devotion from others. He reported a very solid marriage of seven years and had been at his same employment for over 10 years.

After I examined his nose and mouth and found him in good health, I withdrew and proceeded to the stage of therapy I call "Think Very Hard." This man had apparently had an exacerbation in his symptom some six weeks earlier. There were complexities that I could not fully understand in a single visit in the emergency room. I knew that in this setting management would necessarily be in stages. However, the advantages of the presenting situation could be used to initiate the process of change. Mr. B. was ready, willing and eager for an intervention. He was respectful of and in awe of the medical world—doctors had, in his opinion, saved his life. I had on my white coat and my stethoscope; we were in an emergency room; and the patient was receptive for an intervention. Utilizing the information I had available, I designed therapy to alter his presenting problem, anticipating that in its alteration, further data would present itself.

Mr. B. was a hardworking man who loved automobiles and mechanics. I commented on his outstanding ability to learn—he had gone from a handyman position to the master mechanic of the shop in 10 years. He now knew things he didn't even know existed 10 years ago. We talked about metals of which he was quite knowledgeable, and iron in particular. Iron is a component of blood, and I asked him if he had noticed that metallic taste when his nose bled. He had. I explained to him that in a posterior nosebleed, blood drips in the back of the throat prior to running out the nose. As there are taste buds in the back of the tongue, any blood from a posterior nosebleed would give an iron, metallic taste to the palate. I suspected that a man who was familiar with metals, as he was, would recognize it instantly.

The purpose of this discussion was to offer an alternative means for Mr. B. to detect blood in his mouth. He would no longer need to put his fingers in his mouth and examine them; rather, he could rely on his sense of taste. This would be far less distracting to others and would not interfere with his work.

As I was in the process of moving to another state, I then primed him for a referral. I commented that in the same way as auto mechanics, medical and psychotherapeutic sciences had made remarkable advances over the years. We had the technology to solve complex problems. These statements were logical, made sense to Mr. B., and prepared him to recognize and accept that his problems were solvable. My father repeatedly stressed that you must address a patient in his own terms. Mr. B. could clearly relate to the increased technologies, understandings and skills in the field of auto mechanics and accepted that other areas had similar advances.

Mr. B. left the emergency room with lightened shoulders. He felt assured his problem was manageable and in that assurance he took the first steps in resolution. The problem had already begun a process of redefinition and was losing its mysterious power.

I referred Mr. B. to a colleague. Although I made the appointment for him, I asked him to give his own history. I told him that a firsthand account is often more accurate than a secondhand one. Mr. B. could relate to this from his own work. An added factor was that I felt his present situation might alter considerably prior to his follow up.

My colleague saw Mr. B., who presented himself as a tearful, grieving man. Mr. B. said he had previously worried about nosebleeds, but the doctors had said his nose was fine. His problem, he related, was that of feeling sad and full of grief. Apparently, Mr. B.'s father had been ill and died while Mr. B. was hospitalized with his nosebleed. With his energies concentrated on his own problem, he had been unable to complete his mourning for his father. Six weeks earlier had been the second anniversary of his father's death and of his own nosebleed crisis. That would explain the exacerbation of the symptom prior to visiting me.

Mr. B. did well with therapy aimed at helping him resolve the grief reaction. My colleague, during follow-up conversation, was surprised to hear of the finger-in-mouth habit, as Mr. B. had never done this in his office. The suggestion to rely on his sense of taste had apparently been effective in freeing him from the need to visually search for signs of blood.

CONCLUSION

I agree with my father's philosophy that working with people is continually challenging, immensely informative, and most rewarding. It was his assertion that many clients can be successfully treated with short-term brief intervention-oriented therapy. I have illustrated this assertion by presenting four case studies from my work in family practice medicine. These cases depict a method for facilitating an Ericksonian approach to brief or short-term therapy. This method is founded on three principles: acquiring comprehensive information about each client's personal, social and environmental situations as well as about the presenting complaint or problem; soliciting commitment from clients to participate in therapy and change; and incorporating alternative avenues of productivity and enjoyable activity into the therapy itself. This Ericksonian style requires a personalization, or tailoring, of therapy to the individual needs of each client. Finally, I feel that the described techniques are malleable and render themselves readily adaptable both to the individual styles of many therapists and physicians and to a variety of therapeutic modalities and venues.

Chapter 22

Naturalistic Techniques with the "Difficult" Patient

Lynn D. Johnson

Lynn D. Johnson, Ph.D. (University of Utah), is in private practice in Salt Lake City. He has been an instructor in the Department of Educational Psychology at the University of Utah, and is founding President of the Utah Society of Clinical Hypnosis.

Johnson promotes a utilization approach based on accepting and utilizing the situation presented by the patient. Strategic techniques are the method of choice for difficult patients. Numerous case examples are provided.

It is generally accepted that between 65% and 80% of patients receiving psychotherapy will improve (Smith, Glass & Miller, 1980). The particular form of psychotherapy does not appear to make much difference in outcome studies, although it seems that techniques which focus on specific outcomes, such as behavior modification, tend to get better results with specific conditions, such as phobias. However, to my knowledge, there is no convincing evidence that any particular school of therapy will provide, across the board, better outcomes with a broad range of patients and problems.

This is partly because it is not the therapist who is the most important agent. Patients will improve in their complaints in over half of the cases, regardless of the intervention selected. The individual comes expecting help, and given appropriate warmth, understanding, and a credible ritual, they will improve (Frank, 1973).

However, the difficult patient—the patient who has tried professional help over and over to solve the problem—does not tend to get better with a credible ritual. We know this, because there are some patients who have seen numerous therapists and haven't benefitted. Thus, when a patient has tried several ways of solving the problem, and has failed, he or she becomes "difficult."

By "difficult patient," I do not refer to a patient the therapist does not like. That is a separate issue not addressed here. Also, this definition says nothing about the intrapsychic qualities of the difficult patient. If we ignore the issue of personality, the more important possibility emerges, namely, that if we can't blame "difficult" on the patient's personality, we are left with an exciting idea that the difficulty may lie in the class of solutions attempted to help the patient.

ERICKSON AND THE DIFFICULT PATIENT

In 1958, Erickson published a paper on "Naturalistic Techniques of Hypnosis" which consisted of a short introduction and six case histories (Rossi, 1980a). Four of the six cases were people who had sought help from others for their problem, including health professionals and religious resources. Erickson was able to help each person in a naturalistic way, that is, without requiring they learn anything new or foreign.

Erickson made reference in the paper on naturalistic techniques to some work reported in 1943 on psychophysiologic functioning (Rossi, 1980b). Erickson found that when profound hypnotic alterations of physical functioning such as deafness and color blindness were induced, often the subject would spontaneously manifest changes in other areas of functioning. For example, a subject who had been rendered hypnotically deaf would also experience altered vision. Erickson then concluded that a change in one area of functioning would affect other presumably independent areas.

Thus, in naturalistic techniques, we assume that an alteration in one area of behavior will tend to produce changes in other areas. We call this the "ripple effect" (Rabkin, 1977), i.e., a change in one area spreads like a ripple on a pond to affect other areas.

In 1973, I attended a training seminar with Mardi Horowitz, the noted psychoanalyst and stress response researcher. At that time, we were discussing treatment of the borderline personality, and I remember Horowitz mentioning that the classic interpretation did not work as well with the difficult patient as it does with the more neurotic patient. He said (as I remember), "This is one of the unfair things about life, that the best techniques work on the easy patients. If life were fair, it would be the other way around, the difficult patient would respond best to interpretations, while the neurotic patient would respond best to support, empathy, and confrontation."

That concept stayed firmly rooted in my mind for years, namely, that persons who needed psychotherapy the most, responded least positively to it. Since that time, I have struggled to learn what does help the difficult patient. I would like to share some of the incidents which help shape my thinking about that.

LEARNING TO WORK NATURALISTICALLY

In 1976, I was working at a mental health center. I had been studying *Uncommon Therapy* (Haley, 1973) and *Advanced Techniques of Hypnosis and Psychotherapy* (Haley, 1967). One of the things I learned from those volumes is that Erickson was a genius at accepting and using what the patient presented to him.

I had at that time a patient who could be called difficult. She complained of recurrent hallucinations, both auditory and visual. The hallucinations were of a persecutory, attacking nature, pointing out how totally useless and wicked she was. I thought the voices were being somewhat unreasonable, since there were other people I knew who were even more wicked and useless. Some of them were good friends of mine.

She could be called a difficult patient because she had been treated as both inpatient and outpatient many times, with no evidence of improvement. Her history suggested a continual state of seeking help without achieving any gains.

She was taking Thorazine at about 800 mg. a day, this having been prescribed by a psychiatrist in another state. She also took Stelazine on an as-needed basis, which she thought was every day, and was receiving a 1 cc injection of Prolixin decanoate every week. We thought she might be taking too much medicine and our consulting psychiatrist told me to get her to reduce her medication. This she refused to do, since she was firmly convinced that reduction would exacerbate the hallucinations. These were not constant but would occur in episodes, usually once or twice a week; each episode lasted around nine hours. During that time she would hear voices and see demonic figures insulting and persecuting her.

I thought of Erickson's work with the young schizophrenic who controlled her hallucinations through hypnosis. Erickson seemed to imply that one could relate to psychotic patients by assuming they were actually in some sort of personalized trance, complete with the classic trance phenomena of displacement, amnesia, time distortion, and so on.

I was part of a travelling clinic which visited her town every week. Therefore, I told her that it would be wonderful if she happened to have a hallucinatory episode while I was in town (as yet, I hadn't seen any of them). She was appalled, asking if I thought they were under her control. I said, "Of course not, but they are under the control of some part of you, and that part can have one when I am in town, so I can understand what they are like."

A few weeks later, she came in for her session and began to hallucinate. She was frightened, saying that each episode lasted nine hours, and she'd be out of control for all that time.

I was thrilled, of course, since my suggestion had some impact. But, now that I had what I wanted, what would I do? I immediately began to pace as best I could, and imbed suggestions about time distortion, suggesting the possibility of a nine-to-one ratio of distortion. After about 30 minutes, she seemed somewhat better, so I took her for a walk around the clinic, thinking that a more external orientation might be helpful.

I continued to utilize as best I could the extreme behavior, and when one hour had elapsed, she was quite recovered from the episode. She felt good about coming through the episode with me, but she said she could never afford a bill for nine hours of psychotherapy. I gravely assured her we were having a nine-for-one sale that week, and there was nothing to worry about. Following this, she was able to reduce her medication substantially. This was my introduction to Ericksonian psychotherapy.

In this case, I only asked her to experience something which she had felt many times before, namely, that time can pass quickly or slowly. Since I did that indirectly, by embedding the suggestions in such a way as to not call attention to them, she did not need to evaluate or resist. Acceptance of the present situation is the essence of the naturalistic approach.

ADVANTAGES OF WORKING NATURALISTICALLY

A great advantage of naturalistic techniques is the ease of change for the patient. In other words, psychotherapy itself is an unnatural process. Since this is so, it is courteous for therapists to require as little strange behavior as possible from patients. I believe they, in turn, appreciate that. I have often heard patients tell me on the second or third interview that therapy isn't as hard as they thought it would be.

When a change in patient behavior is needed, we should have a naturalistic explanation for it. This explanation should be highly believable to the therapist, more so than to the patient. When I first experimented with paradoxical techniques, I had poor results. I realized after a while that I was giving nonverbal messages of disqualification to the verbal message, conveying the idea that I was just kidding. Since I have come to believe in symptom prescription, I have much better results.

In a recent interview, Cloé Madanes (Simon, 1986) points out that the strategic therapist must strongly believe the symptom does have a purpose, whether in reality it does or not. She says, ". . . at the moment I'm supervising a case I'm absolutely sure the child is protecting the parent. I totally believe it. But ask me a few weeks later, and I'll say, 'Well, it was a useful hypothesis.' "

In this naturalistic approach to therapy, there is nothing for the patient to fight against. Key to it all is the utilization of the patient's behavior, and then redirection, rather than confrontation and forcing a change. It is like the difference between direct confrontation and the judo or aikido techniques in martial arts, where the attacker's own strength is used against him.

KEYS TO NATURALISTIC THERAPY

At the present time, I am director of a small group of clinicians who are working with the concept of brief therapy. Our experience so far is that about 75 to 80 percent of clients are appropriate for brief therapy. (See Cummings, 1986, who claims 85% are suitable for brief treatment.) We have also learned that the more difficult patients are the most suitable for strategic therapy. In the remainder of this chapter, I will attempt to illustrate certain principles of therapy which seem the most useful with difficult patients.

In work with patients who would be classified as borderline, the issue of being in tune with the patient is particularly difficult because the patient can become anxious. What it looks like is this: The therapist expresses an empathetic reflection of the patient's verbal content, and the patient denies the therapist is being empathic. Usually there is a statement to the effect that, "No, that is not what I mean . . ." and later the patient is unhappy with the therapist because he "did not understand."

Our group learned much from Yvonne Dolan (1985) about responding to these patients. She paces the patient completely nonverbally by making shifts of posture every time the patient shifts meanings or mood states. This is a form of nonverbal pacing which is completely outside the conscious awareness of the patient, and therefore undeniable.

We also have enjoyed the metaphors of these patients. They often tell stories which illustrate the hopelessness of their lives. Dolan has suggested we respond to each story with a matching story from our own lives, which incorporates a resource to deal with the problem. This is something like Richard Gardner's (1971) mutual storytelling technique. Dolan can tell such a story, and if the patient asks why she told that story, she can reply, "Well, it was just something interesting which happened to me lately."

John Weakland (personal communication, 1985) has helped us with the type of patient who blames all problems on people other than himself. In these cases, we completely agree with the patient, and suggest there is really no reason for psychotherapy to proceed, since they are not causing any of their own problems, but are simply the victims of malevolent others and damn bad luck. At this point, the patient is more motivated to tell us something which is his or her responsibility.

We have found that fairly simple modifications of our own responses can make a significant shift in relationships. A psychology graduate student had sought ongoing supervision for a difficult case. The patient complained of obsessive thoughts and compulsive acts. He also spoke with maddening slowness. From the audiotape, it was clear that after the therapist would make a comment, the patient would pause for 30 to 40 seconds. Then he would reply in a slow and deliberate way, never responding directly to what the therapist had said.

The patient was speaking around 80 words per minute when he was not pausing. The therapist described himself as being quite nervous during these pauses. As soon as the patient finished, the therapist would begin his next statement. The therapist rate of speech was around 150 words per minute.

I instructed the therapist to do two things: First, he should count the seconds while he was waiting for a reply from the patient. Then, when the patient was through speaking, the therapist would again count the seconds (silently, of course!) before he (the therapist) replied. This was to convey to the patient a sense of respect and courtesy.

The second thing was that the therapist should speak slowly and pedantically about the dangers of improvement. I pointed out to the therapist that we did not know what dangers improvement might bring, but asked him to trust the patient, who seemed to be indicating that improvement would be dangerous. Within the next hour, the patient began to speak within a few seconds of the therapist's last communication, and spoke more fluidly and closer to a normal rate of speech.

Our work with paradoxical techniques leads us in the direction suggested by de Shazer (1985): We do not believe paradoxical techniques are good for all patients. Instead we see the therapy relationship as a dance, and the patient lets us know by his response to assignments, what steps she or he is competent in. On first sessions, we always give assignments which are for information-gathering purposes. An example would be to ask for a comprehensive written list of all the pros and cons for getting over the problem.

On the next meeting, we inquire about compliance. Basically, the patient can comply, reject, or modify the assignment in some way. Each of those responses tells us what dance steps this patient can perform, and we adjust our music accordingly. Our steps are constantly being corrected by the responses of the patient.

We work paradoxically only with patients who reject the first assignment. It does not seem reasonable to us to give everyone paradoxical assignments. Rather, we give them only when the patient indicates through resistance that this is needed. In some cases we know before the end of the first session that a patient will resist.

SYMPTOM PRESCRIPTION WITH DIFFICULT PATIENTS

A man came to see me for problems with suicidal impulses. He felt hopeless about his life and wanted to end it all. His problems were considerable. He weighed 450 lbs. and was drinking over a quart of whiskey a day. He was intensely unhappy in his marriage and had gained the weight during the marriage. He reported he had been to several therapists, and mentioned them by name. I knew two of them and considered both to be competent at insight-oriented psychotherapy. With compliant patients, it is possible that insight therapy produces good results at almost the same rate as strategic therapy. I believe, however, that with a patient who resists everything the therapist says, it is counterproductive to use an approach such as insight, which is based on the notion that the patient is going to comply. My patient had been given the interpretations and challenges he should respond to if he were to change. The therapists had pointed out how necessary it was for him to lose weight and to stop his drinking. He agreed thoroughly, and became more suicidal. He couldn't or wouldn't comply.

With this patient, I did not need a week to tell that he would reject the help I might offer. Therefore, I began to focus on how we all need help at times, and I congratulated him on being wise enough to seek help. He had sought help from several therapists and now from me. He also sought help from his bottle of booze and from the rather substantial meals he prepared for himself at the restaurant he owned. I worried out loud that while competent mental health counselors had told him to quit overeating and drinking, I couldn't be sure they were on the right course. I thought that instead they might be taking away from him two crutches he desperately needed. In as kind a way as I could, I suggested that he might not be able to stand on his own two feet, and if he were to stop drinking, if he were to stop eating more than would be necessary to maintain him at about 350 lbs. or so, he would find himself in trouble without these crutches. He would be too weak if he just stopped suddenly, and as crazy as it sounded, I wondered about the wisdom of stopping suddenly.

The next week he announced he had stopped drinking. Naturally, I fretted about this, and cautioned him about making other changes. He eventually lost 250 lbs., divorced his wife, and made a lot of money in the weight loss business.

There are some noncompliant patients with whom we don't have the guts to prescribe the symptom. An example of this is a woman referred to me by a psychiatrist who said, "This woman really needs a social worker." I'm not sure what he meant by that, but in my office there was a social worker available and I suggested she see the patient. After one visit my colleague came to me and said, "Please take this patient, I can't stand to work with her."

In my interview with the patient, Susan, she complained that her husband was frequently beating her. He had recently lost his job and since then they were getting into bad fights and he would start slapping her around. Her counselors had all advised her to have him arrested, or at least to kick him out of the house. She would refuse to do this, but then continue to whine and complain. She also had a lot of complaints about how she was mistreated at work. Her husband was not interested in coming for therapy.

Susan had been raised in an abusive home and had spent four years in reform school. She was a hard worker and made a good living in a predominantly masculine occupation, but her personal life was chaotic. She had two children, but had lost custody of them to their father. She was a difficult person to be around. I think she made her counselors want to hit her; then they felt uncomfortable and guilty and referred her to someone else. Rejecting her was a better response than hitting her, I suppose.

I reviewed her life with her, pointing out all the suffering she had experienced. During this life review, she agreed she had experienced more suffering than the ordinary person. I pointed out that whatever we experience a lot of, we become able to cope with. If I hold my breath a lot, I get to where I can hold my breath for longer and longer times. By the same token, she had learned to experience more suffering and abuse than the usual person, and having experienced that abuse, she was better able than most to accept it. I congratulated her on her tolerance to suffering. In fact, I felt it was a great ability she had developed, which made her rather saint-like. While I did not approve of her husband hitting her, I did think that she could continue to practice her tolerance of suffering if he did it. She kicked him out the next week. He subsequently got a job and stopped the drinking which had preceded the beatings.

IS SYMPTOM PRESCRIPTION A LIE?

How can we justify saying something that is not true? The answer is that, at the time when I say it, it is true. In other words, the overweight patient does need the overeating and drinking, or he would already have changed it. Thus, when therapists ask patients to do things they cannot do, they ignore the reality of the situation. But when we state what is true, the patient can see it as truth, and, therefore, is free to move beyond it.

There is an ancient shaman chant used by Northwest Native Americans. In this chant, the doctor (e.g., the medicine man) says to the patient, "I don't lie, I don't talk shit. I will take thy illness on myself, and thou wilt see it." In symptom prescription, we take upon ourselves the illness, in a paradigmatic statement (Beier & Young, 1984). As we do that, the patient sees it. To do it in an accusing way by saying the patient should change would be to fail to take the illness, since we would be both accepting and rejecting it. The healing comes when we say, "This is you, and it is okay."

The objection to symptom prescription, therefore, ignores the factor of time. At the time, the statement is true, namely that no change should be attempted. As the statement is made, an effect is felt on the symptom, analogous to the way an electron is affected when we attempt to define (measure) it. If we try to measure an electron, our attempts to measure it change its position or its nature. Similarly, when we try, through a paradigmatic statement, to sum up where the patient is at the moment, the position changes.

APPLICATIONS TO COMPLIANCE-BASED PSYCHOTHERAPY

The skill of reframing negative symptoms in a positive way is obviously crucial to paradoxical psychotherapy. However, we also find the positive connotation of symptoms to be useful in compliance-based psychotherapy. For example, a man recently came for treatment complaining of very disturbing intrusive thoughts. He was hesitant to talk about it, but finally revealed to his therapist that he had intrusive, obsessional (involuntary) images of Jesus having sex with him.

He was horrified by the symptoms, especially so because he was a leader in his church. As a religious man devoted to his church and family, he considered himself completely unworthy to associate with anyone because of this obsessive thought.

His therapist sidestepped the obvious implications of secondary gain, that is, talking about the idea that these images really served the purpose of getting him away from family, and so on. Instead he congratulated him on being a very spiritual man. He pointed out that all spirituality is based on imagery and symbolism, such as the parables of Jesus in the New Testament. When Jesus teaches about the shepherd and the lost sheep, he does not want us to literally go out into the hills and look for lost sheep.

The therapist established his groundwork about religious feelings being symbolic, and then proposed that what he was seeking was a form of extreme closeness to God, and one in which he could feel personally fulfilled by that closeness. His deep longing for this had been transformed into that particular image by his unconscious mind, much as a deep longing might be transformed in a dream into some image which doesn't make immediate sense.

This reframe was comforting to the patient, and his symptoms decreased significantly. Further work centered around asking him to imagine the intrusive images (what might be thought of as symptom prescription) and repeating various meditations, such as "What I see does not mean anything." He would picture the intrusive images, and repeat, "This does not mean anything." The justification for this was that if that did not mean anything, then his unconscious would find a more acceptable way of expressing his need for closeness and spirituality. And this is exactly what happened. His spirituality found less disturbing ways to express itself. After six visits, he was free of the obsessive thought.

THE BARE BONES OF SKELETON KEYS

Our group has benefited from de Shazer's (1985) ideas about "skeleton key techniques." In strategic therapy we have followed Erickson's dictum about making up a new solution for every patient. This solution can be seen analogically as a key which fits a particular lock. We therapists are locksmiths, and our patients come to us having lost the key to their lock. We can make a new key for them. This is what we do with our individualized therapy. However, we can also use a skeleton key, one which fits many locks. A skeleton key, in psychotherapy, would be a common element which helps across the spectrum. Some of our favorite skeleton keys include reframing and symptom prescription.

Reframing

I have mentioned the reframing of all symptoms into positive frames. We take as positive a view as we are able to with all symptoms, like the positive connotation strategy of the Milan group.

Thus, in the case of the suicidal, overweight client, the positive connotation was that the overeating and drinking served to protect him against other, even worse, problems. In the case of the abused woman, I could not find a way to positively connote the abuse itself—but I could positively connote the suffering, thus unbalancing the system sufficiently to accomplish the therapeutic goal.

Standard First-Session Homework

Another skeleton key intervention I have enjoyed and which comes from de Shazer (1985) is the universal assignment. This assignment is to ask patients at the end of the first session to carefully note, so they can report next time, what positive changes they notice in the coming week. I tell them that the mind is very complex and often the act of talking over the problems in a new way produces deep levels of thought change. As a result, they may notice in the coming week some unusual positive changes. They should be sure and tell me about them, since I also do not know what to expect.

There are a number of possible responses to that assignment. If the patient reports spontaneous changes, independent of willpower, then subsequent assignments in therapy should emphasize the spontaneous nature of change. If there is, instead, a carefully planned improvement, then a more rational approach is appropriate. The patient may report that the symptom got worse, in which case a symptom-prescription strategy is indicated. Or the patient may report nothing at all happened, in which case "ambiguous function assignments" (Lankton & Lankton, 1986) are indicated.

Trance Ratification Challenges

A third skeleton key which I think bears more emphasis is the trance ratification through challenges. Traditional challenges as a part of hypnosis have usually been avoided in Ericksonian work. However, Erickson was in the habit of providing challenges after the trance, as a way of ratifying it. He would challenge patients to explain what had happened, for example. I remember in working with him that I experienced the best and most genuine trance I have ever experienced. At the conclusion (I thought) of the work, he questioned me carefully about childhood memories I had experienced. He suddenly challenged me to explain what he had done to cause me to have that memory. As I began to explain his steps, I suddenly had amnesia for that part of his work! As I stumbled to explain, he laughed delightedly and asked if I usually had such a hard time explaining things.

In working with patients, I find the same pattern useful. I like to find some way patients have responded to an indirect suggestion. I then ask them why they did that, and when they confabulate a reason, I reinterpret their motivation as their need to carry out indirect suggestions. This proves their unconscious is listening to what we do, and is able to help by carrying out suggestions without their being aware of doing so. This is a model for the unconscious helping them in other ways which they don't expect. An example of this pattern is seen in the recently released film edited by Haley (n.d.) in which Erickson is seen doing hypnotic training with a fairly naive subject. He consistently challenges and congratulates the subject for being able to respond to indirect suggestion. Erickson thus trains him to expect spontaneous behavior from himself, which will be in response to stimuli which he does not consciously recognize.

This pattern of challenges is a double bind, in that no matter what the patient does, it ratifies trance. The patient then has an expectancy created of further spontaneous change.

Steve Gilligan (personal communication, September 19, 1986) was working with a woman who had bothersome plantar warts (warts on the soles of the feet). Gilligan made metacomments which established the idea of spontaneous change outside of awareness.

Gilligan: What is your sense of relationship with the warts at this time?
Patient: Anger and disgust.
Gilligan: Anger and disgust. And a smile goes with that. And I'd like to ask you straightforwardly, what goes along with the smile?
Patient: They're so ridiculous. It's something kids are supposed to get, so it's incongruent. And I'm afraid of them.
Gilligan: . . . So I noticed that each time you mention your feet, they are tending to move. Are you aware of that?
Patient: No.
Gilligan: That's a nice skill to be able to have that ability to translate just a thought about some sense of involvement in the feet *to* the feet, and to have some action begin to develop without your really having to think about it.

Gilligan here challenges the patient to explain ideomotor behavior, and when she admits she is unaware of it, he congratulates her. This seeds the possibility of further out-of-awareness work.

I mention this challenge-type of trance ratification because in my supervision work I encounter the misconception that Ericksonian hypnotherapists never challenge their patients. I find that trance ratification challenges speed the hypnotic work.

Encourage Small Change

A fourth skeleton key is to always ask for and expect the smallest possible change, rather than the most. We take the position that change takes place best in small steps. Therefore, when large changes do happen, we can be sure they are spontaneous acts on the part of the patient and nothing that we ourselves have done. I have always thought of the words of Lao Tsu on this point: "As for the best leaders, the people say, 'We did it ourselves.' "

Regarding Therapeutic Obnoxiousness

Occasionally, we reframe negatively. For example, a woman I knew socially was going to commit suicide because a man she loved would not marry her. It was a bad situation because she had told her relatives that she and he were engaged. That was not true; John (as we will call him) had no intention of marrying her and was dating others. Her relatives were beginning to ask embarrassing questions, and she was furious at him.

I considered her suicide threat serious since her father had taken his life in her presence, in a violent manner. I went to see her. As we talked, she told me that John had embarrassed her to friends and relatives. I agreed that he certainly had hurt her badly. She began to imply that he would be sorry when she was dead. At that point, I began to talk about a scenario where she was lying in her coffin. John comes in, feeling terrible, and thinking it is all his fault. As she nodded about this idea, I suddenly said I couldn't help realizing something, but I didn't know whether to say it or not. She told me to go on, and I said I had a vivid picture of John at the funeral glancing at his watch and saying, "Well, I gotta go; I have a hot date in 20 minutes." Actually, this is exactly what John would have done, I am sure, since I also know him very well.

At that point her feelings changed dramatically, and she lost interest in suicide. She moved to another city, took a new job, and has continued to live successfully. I have used this challenging reframe with good results with other angry patients who image that someone will be sorry when they are dead.

TRUST ALL TO THE UNCONSCIOUS MIND

In 1978, I was able to study with Dr. Erickson for a week along with one other student. By the end of the week, I assumed he knew something about me. When I asked him to inscribe my copy of *Advanced Techniques*, he wrote, "To know and to use hypnosis, trust all to your unconscious mind." Those who know me well will recognize that there was not much overt pacing in that inscription. I did not have much of an idea about how to respond to the inscription, but I tried very hard by waiting for my unconscious to tell me something. It never did. So I learned about hypnosis and strategic therapy in a conscious way by obtaining supervision from some excellent therapists and continuing to go to workshops. It was this year that I began to notice that my work was becoming spontaneous. I would give some intervention during the hour, and maybe much later in the interview that would become valuable. This process began some nine years ago, which indicates how slow my unconscious is.

DISADVANTAGES OF NATURALISTIC PSYCHOTHERAPY

Many times I have been tempted to give up strategic therapy and go back to other styles. In fact, I was going to call this chapter, "Reasons for not doing therapy naturalistically." I can think of several. First, the naturalistic approach for the patient requires some unnatural behavior from the therapist. Essentially, the most intuitive response to a patient is always the one you don't want to do. (For an extensive discussion of this, see Beier & Young, 1984.) In working with borderline patients, for example, I sometimes feel angry and frustrated. To act on that feeling would make a therapeutic mess, whereas to construct a naturalistic intervention will improve the relationship. But it is hard work, requiring more from me.

A second reason for not doing naturalistic psychotherapy is that it requires help. I think I could do insight-oriented therapy pretty well all by myself. Strategic interventions need what Bateson (1979) called the "poly-ocular" view, or more than one set of eyes looking at the problem. So I have spent a lot of time and money in supervision and consultation. I think that if you want to do strategic therapy, you will be spending money on consultation that your colleagues may be spending on new cars.

A third reason is that there is little professional support for strategic interventions. I am a consultant to a large Employee Assistance Program, and was asked to review a case which had a definite strategic thumbprint. The point is, the supervisor who reviewed all the cases was upset since what the clinician had done did not make sense to her. This clinician has an excellent track record, and had been able to help in short-term therapy clients who would have been referred out to long-term therapy if they had seen some other counselor. In spite of the good record of success, though, the actual conduct of the case was upsetting to the supervisor. If you work in an agency and do strategic therapy, you will take some heat.

A fourth reason is that your patients, if you are successful as a strategic therapist, will give you less credit. They will admit you were helpful, but it will seem to them that they really did the work. Bill O'Hanlon recently reported (1986, personal communication) that he has learned from follow-up that some of his patients have amnesia for ever having seen him, and deny ever having had the problem they came for. In other words, their life is working very well, and they can't imagine they were ever in that situation for which they had sought treatment.

An additional problem now surfaces. If you do this long enough, you will be able to help some cases which other therapists had been unable to work with. Accordingly, you will be referred more and more "hard" cases, while your colleagues keep all the easy ones.

Finally, if you do strategic therapy long enough to accommodate to the problems I have already mentioned, one important problem will still loom: You will be asked to give papers at conferences like this one. This will require you spend long hours hunched over a keyboard, instead of living life in a more comfortable, relaxed way. I would really recommend you think long and hard before working to become a naturalistic, strategic therapist.

REFERENCES

Bateson, G. (1979). *Mind and Nature: A Necessary Unity.* New York: Dutton.

Beier, E. G., & Young, D. (1984). *The Silent Language of Psychotherapy, 2nd Ed.* New York: Aldine.

Cummings, N. A. (1986). The Dismantling of Our Health System: Strategies for the Survival of Psychological Practice. *American Psychologist, 41,* 4, 426–431.

de Shazer, S. (1985). *Keys to Solution in Brief Therapy.* New York: Norton.

Dolan, Y. M. (1985). *A Path with a Heart.* New York: Brunner/Mazel.

Frank, J. D. (1973). *Persuasion and Healing.* Baltimore, Md.: Johns Hopkins Press.

Gardner, R. (1971). *Therapeutic Communication with Children: The Mutual Storytelling Technique in Clinical Psychotherapy.* New York: Aronson.

Haley, J. (Ed.). (no date). *1958 Milton Erickson Hypnosis Induction.* Rockville, Md.: The Family Therapy Institute of Washington, D.C.

Haley, J. (1967). *Advanced Techniques of Hypnosis and Therapy: Selected Papers of Milton H. Erickson, M.D.* New York: Grune & Stratton.

Haley, J. (1973). *Uncommon Therapy.* New York: Norton.

Lankton, S. R., & Lankton, C. (1986). *Enchantment and Intervention in Family Therapy.* New York: Brunner/Mazel.

Rabkin, R. (1977). *Strategic Psychotherapy.* New York: Basic Books.

Rossi, E. L. (Ed.). (1980a). *The Collected Papers of Milton H. Erickson, Vol. II.* New York: Irvington.

Rossi, E. L. (Ed.). (1980b). *The Collected Papers of Milton H. Erickson, Vol. IV.* New York: Irvington.
Simon, R. (1986). Behind the One-Way Kaleidoscope. *The Family Therapy Networker,* September-October 1986, 25–29.
Smith, M. L., Glass, G. V., & Miller, T. I. (Eds.). (1980). *The Benefits of Psychotherapy.* Baltimore, Md.: Johns Hopkins Press.

SECTION TWO: PRACTICE

PART IX

Marital and Family Therapy

Chapter 23

Ericksonian Systems Approach

Stephen R. Lankton

Stephen R. Lankton, M.S.W. (University of Michigan), is founding Editor of the Ericksonian Monographs. *He maintains a private practice in Gulf Breeze, Florida, and travels internationally to teach Ericksonian psychotherapy and family therapy. Lankton is a fellow of the American Association of Marriage and Family Therapy. With his wife, Carol, Lankton has coauthored* The Answer Within: A Clinical Framework of Ericksonian Hypnotherapy *and* Enchantment and Intervention in Family Therapy. *He also authored* Practical Magic: A Translation of Basic Neuro-Linguistic Programming into Clinical Psychotherapy. *A talented practitioner and teacher of Ericksonian methods, he served as a Faculty Member at all of the Congresses and Seminars sponsored by The Milton H. Erickson Foundation.*

Lankton presents a framework by which to view the multilevel interactive dynamics of family experience. A matrix is proposed which demonstrates the relationship between stress on families due to transition through developmental stages and problem-solving skills available in the system. Problem-solving skills are viewed as determined and limited by a specific interaction of variables taking place on the four levels of family experience. While various schools of therapy intervene at one or another level on the matrix, an Ericksonian systems approach requires intervention at each level. Presenting problem/symptoms must be identified in relation to each level of family systems dynamics, and system-wide Ericksonian interventions are created that encompass and reflect unique contributions of each of these levels.

There are no entries entitled *family* or *systems*, in the indexes of Erickson's collected papers (Erickson, 1980), nor in Erickson's collected lectures and seminars (Rossi & Ryan, 1985; Rossi, Ryan & Sharp, 1983), nor in any book authored by him (Cooper & Erickson, 1954; Erickson, Hershman, & Secter, 1961; Erickson & Rossi, 1979, 1981; Erickson, Rossi, & Rossi, 1976). It is intriguing that Erickson is well known for his creative and pioneering contributions to family therapy in books by Bateson (1972, 1979), Fisch, Weakland, and Segal (1983), Haley (1973, 1985), Madanes (1983), Watzlawick (1976), and so on. Although Erickson himself never offered a family systems formulation of his work, his diagnostic and intervention strategies did, in fact, utilize an implicit general systems theory, or ecosystems theory, or cybernetic-type theory. It is therefore the purpose of this paper to provide a new schema for understanding Erickson's intervention strategies with individuals and families within the context of a systems framework.

Three volumes by Jay Haley—*Uncommon Therapy* (1973), *Conversations With Milton H. Erickson, Vol. 2: Changing Couples* (1985), and *Volume 3, Changing Children and Families* (1985)—are family therapy oriented books containing verbatim transcriptions of Erickson's work. They are noteworthy as rigorous attempts to place Erickson's work in a family developmental framework. While they make extensive reference to various aspects of the family by means of the cases presented, this is possibly more reflective of the editor's intention than of Erickson's original focus. Erickson's work in many areas, it seems, functions as a projection screen for theorists, the raw material or data which they frame in varying conceptual formulations. Certainly, this is true regarding his highly creative approaches to individuals and families which others have discussed in terms of specific systemic factors (Lankton & Lankton, 1983, 1986; Ritterman, 1983). In this chapter I will present an Ericksonian systems approach to working with individuals and their families by examining three main areas of concept and intervention. Part I presents a framework of family systems which identifies both the developmental factors and the interactive variables that create an ongoing feedback loop, characteristic of cybernetic systems, and culminates in the family's daily life experience. Part II discusses how presenting problems and symptoms can be identified in terms of the four levels that comprise the family's ongoing interaction dynamics. Part III discusses an Ericksonian approach to designing "system-wide interventions"—interventions that reflect and encompass the cybernetic dynamics that underlie all family experience.

PART I: A FRAMEWORK OF FAMILY SYSTEM DYNAMICS

Ongoing Developmental Issues

Illustrations 1 and 2 depict the impact of various interventions in different arenas of the individual and family system. These illustrations are intended to provide guidance for conceptualizing systemic intervention regardless of the number of clients being seen. A family, an individual, or an organization of any size can be viewed as going through continuous cycles of stability and instability (see Illustration 1, center portion). For example, at the family level the birth of a child or relocation of a home are periods of noticeable instability when contrasted with times that are characterized by homogeneous routines and a relative redundancy of daily living patterns. For the individual, graduation from college, a new job, or a physical illness are examples of such unstable periods.

There are stages of development through which a family will traverse over time (see Illustration 1, top portion). The family cycle of stability/instability is most often initiated by the changes brought on by requirements of particular developmental stages. At each new stage of development, novel experiences or alterations in the usual types of experiences and transactions must be learned. For instance, when the birth of a baby signals a change in the family to the child-raising stage of development, hundreds of new experiences, transactions, and behaviors must be learned: postponing one's gratifications for the sake of the child's needs, learning to ask for help with the child, being able to experience joy in the child's growth, acquiring a vast array of caretaking skills, and so forth.

If these experiences are readily available as resources due to previous learnings, the disorganization within the family system is relatively short and the transition to new organization is relatively easy. Conversely, to the extent that the resources are not available, the disorganization becomes more debilitating. Resolutions to the disorganization will come eventually with the implementation of problem-solving mechanisms and techniques used individually and collectively by the members of the family.

This process of problem solving is what takes the family system from a condition of instability to one of stability. I have depicted problem solving as the pivotal dynamic of the family system and have further detailed the levels of system dynamics (see bottom portion of Illustration

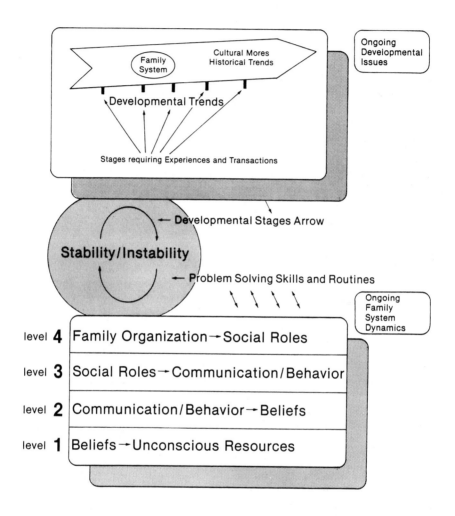

Illustration 1. Family systems dynamic chart. Illustration 1 depicts the multi-level cybernetic interaction taking place within individuals and their families. The developmental stages that influence the family cycle of stability/instability present problems to which the family must respond. The problem-solving skills that, in turn, must be marshalled will be a complex product of four interlocking levels of dynamic family interaction: On each level, the first variable determines the parameters and expression of the second variable. Family Organization delineates and delimits the roles each family member assumes; Social Role limitations, in turn, shape all forms of communication and behavior; Communication and Behavior then circumscribes the range and flexibility of beliefs that are acceptable; and these Beliefs, in turn, affect the accessibility of the individual's Unconscious Resources and processes.

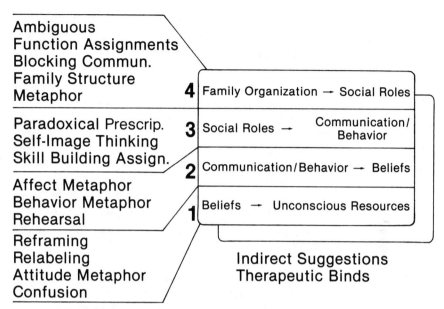

Illustration 2. System-wide interventions. Illustration 2 highlights the various forms of interventions that can be used at each level in designing a systems-wide approach to family therapy.

1 and expansion in Illustration 2) as the areas of primary emphasis in this chapter. The reader will notice that this discussion deals with only one direction of influence. Although it should be clear that there is a mutual influence between the entries on both sides of the chart, and the arrow points both ways, therapy deals with the social influence on experience and these arrows proceed from the social to the personal.

Ongoing Family Systems Dynamics

Illustration 1 shows how system dynamics relate at different levels of complexity. Specifically, it shows life experience interlocking in a matrix of developmental trends and interactive dynamics that can be understood to span the internal experience of single individuals, to coupled partners, to family structures, to informal social networks, socializing institutions, and social-cultural and economic environments. It depicts an ecosystemic approach to human problems, since the theory expands and extends a general systems theory by offering an understanding of the historical influences on populations of environments, families, and individual personality.

Personality can be seen as the natural dynamic of a system: It is the behavior which has the highest frequency of occurrence. Using this definition, it is understandable why the field of psychotherapy has been inclined to consider *personality*, a semantic *construct*, as a reality that is comprised of behaviors, roles, belief systems, thoughts, perceptions, sensations, and unconscious experiences. All these factors are, to me, different interactional aspects of human systems which reflect different levels of conception of the same system. These different conceptions are related to one another in a logical arrangement shown on the Family Systems Dynamics Chart.

Each level that is placed below another (Illustration 1, bottom) is relatively simpler in organization; each higher level is built in more complex ways from experiences below it. It is useful to remember that none of these levels of conceptualization gives a fully correct interpretation of the system. *Each level is constructed as an alternate perspective.*

Finally, since therapy is in the business of enhancing problem solving, it is necessary in this chapter to explain only the relationships which illustrate the greatest degree of social constraint and, hence, the greater impediments to problem solving. That is, this chapter is contending that family organization delimits social roles, despite the general awareness that the opposite is also true. The reason for this focus is simply that family organization is more complex—it is a larger category, it is a group of social roles. Change or lack of change at the organizational level can create broad alteration in many social roles, whereas a change in a single role may not have such a sweeping impact on the family organization.

In a similar hierarchical manner, social roles delimit communication. Yet, acquiring new communication can affect the way a role is played and the absence of an entire set of communication can limit the performance of a social role. However, social roles are themselves sets of communications and behaviors. Legitimizing a new social role has a pervasive affect on the relatively simpler subsets of communication and behavior. It might be accurate to say that first-order change to variables on the left-hand side of the chart (Illustration 1, bottom) creates second-order change in variables on the right-hand side of the chart. It is for this reason that unidirectional arrows have been used.

Let us use an example of a child being born into a family in order to trace this dynamic, interactive process through the entire chart.

Family organization shapes social roles

Level 4 of Illustration 1 begins with family organization which is, of course, a result of influences at a more complex level "above" the top of the chart—that is, the level of cultural mores and historical trends that dictate the range of family organizations that are acceptable. Societal values are in flux in many cultures. A representation of this flux in our current American society can be seen in the existence of group marriages, homosexual couples, single-parent families, serial monogamy, spouse swapping, "singles" condos, and so forth. This change of values loosens the controls on the organization of families and thus affects styles of decision-making and roles that are allowed within the families.

My four-year-old son has red hair. Nearly every stranger has one or two things to say to him, usually beginning with "Where did you get that red hair?" What's my son going to think as a result of such comments? Is he always going to be aware that everybody sees his red hair first? Some people are further moved to tell him what it means to have red hair: "Oh, you're going to be sensitive," "You're going to be handsome," "You're going to be angry," or, "You're going to be creative." This is an example of social structure from cultural norms reaching directly into the family and inducing (or trying to induce) a certain role as well as a receptive family order for that role. The comments may become roles that my son can learn to play.

Once a family organization is formed, it either begins to push at existing social boundaries or stays solidly in the middle. In both cases it *will delineate the degree of role diversity that is possible for its members.* An example: The statement, "Chris, you don't like potatoes. Give them to your brother," teaches Chris about what *she does not like and what she is supposed to do about it.* This type of transaction occurs countless times in a multitude of ways in most families. Transactions become conflicted when they violate the needs or the ecologically adaptive options of family members. Ackerman (1958) once wrote that *intra-psychic* conflicts originate as *interpersonal* conflicts. I think this is an example of what he meant. Parental conflict can occur in any number of arenas: verbally stated beliefs, perceptual predispositions, behavioral modeling, physical abuse, and so on.

As an example of shaping perceptions that become a role into which a child gets trained, let's imagine a parent who sees only the clumsy things his son does and then says, "I have a son who is a klutz." The parent would then "prove" the statement by continuing to perceive only clumsy movements in his son's active reporting of behavior. Those perceptions then would become true for the parent and true, to some extent, for the child. When this kind of transaction occurs, families often think they are commenting innocently on reality when in fact they are *inducing* reality. They are shaping roles so that their children will fit into the family structure of perceptions and action. They may even be shaping lifetime personality characteristics.

Social role shapes communication

The social role aspect of personality delimits the communications that individuals will make. Communications (verbal, nonverbal, emotional, behavioral, etc.) will most frequently occur as a part of a constellation of action. Behavior that is not a part of a constellation tends to not occur. The connection to the next two levels of beliefs and unconscious resources can be illustrated with a brief example of how roles limit communication options.

"Jane" is a girl we have sometimes employed for babysitting. She is from a strict religious family in which it is desirable for children to accept passively the parental beliefs and values. Because of the rigid rules in this family, the children have remained extremely dependent. They have been inculcated with injunctions against developing their own perspectives, and they have been shielded by the parents from the world of different opinions and beliefs. Of course, the children were not allowed to engage in any kind of assertive or aggressive behavior that resembled anger. For example, while Jane was babysitting for us, someone walked up and took a chair from the porch of our condominium on the beach. My wife, Carol, asked her what had happened to the chair. In response Jane whined, "Oh, that guy over there took it." When Carol asked, "Why didn't you tell him to give it back?" Jane said, "Oh, I couldn't do that."

Why couldn't she speak up to the intruder? She was never given a role for being assertive, aggressive or angry. None of the roles familiar to her included even the occasional option demanding anything from anyone, even in response to such blatant wrongdoing as the chair-stealing incident. Jane's engraved roles then delimited the range of communication available to her. She had learned to play an almost exclusive role of subservient victim and her communications were congruent with this role.

Communication shapes beliefs

Such *communications* are the interface between *roles* allowed by the family and the next level of the system—the level of *belief and unconscious resources*. The same girl, Jane, later tipped a plate of spaghetti onto one of our dining room chairs and said, "Oh, I always do that." The kinds of communication that she is allowed, that which she rehearses to herself, and for which she is reinforced for delivering, determines the kinds of belief systems she then formulates—for example, "I am the kind of person who always spills things and makes a horrible mess." We know this from the idea of cognitive consonance: Get a person to defend a position on a debate and he or she will modify previously held beliefs to be more consonant with what is being defended. (Modeling and attribution are, of course, still other ways of learning beliefs and cognitive structure. In this model, those learnings would usually affect the level of social roles.)

Once Jane has formulated such a belief system, unconscious resources which could mediate contrary experiences will not impinge upon her normal waking state. Or if they do, they are considered a conflict and an indication that therapy is needed. This is the way in which *beliefs* (lowest level of chart) delimit *unconscious resources* and unconscious experience. Even if Jane happens to feel aggressive impulses, she believes she is not the kind of person who can have them, so she denies having them. In the same way, a person who believes he cannot be confident in front of a group spends all of his time noticing his lack of confidence when he is in front of groups! Similarly, a person who believes he has ringing in his ears hears that background ringing that we all tend to ignore. A belief is a way of saying, in effect, "This range of experience is the only range of stimuli I can notice." Then, millions of other stimuli are not noticed. This is not to say that a simple change in beliefs is all that is necessary. Indeed, Erickson's work suggests that we should intervene at each level of the system, since each level contributes a reinforcing aspect to the situation.

Interface of Developmental Trends and Ongoing Family Systems Dynamic: A Case Example

A final example will show how developmental trends interface with family organization, role limitations, communication, and beliefs. This is the case of Paul, a 31-year-old man who came to therapy because of anxiety attacks. He was about to get married and wanted to be rid of the attacks that had plagued him intermittently since adolescence. Now that he was to marry, he wanted to "clean up these problems."

Interviewing revealed that he had been shy and unassertive throughout adolescence and young adulthood. Paul's wife-to-be was somewhat bossy and was now making all the choices about the wedding and giving him very little voice. For him, each stage of his development from adolescence to "about-to-be-wed" had been handled with the same general constellation of resources to solve problems—his shyness and unassertiveness. Thus, when developmental stress caused disruption in Paul's normal stability, his problem-solving resources failed to include appropriate assertiveness skills. Paul's consistently unassertive appearance and conduct produced an overall characteristic of consistency which one might call "personality." Here we see the cycle of stability/instability (middle of Illustration 1) being influenced simultaneously by the stress of developmental stages (top of Illustration 1) and by the use of problem-solving skills (at the bottom of Illustration 1).

The dynamics of this man's problem-solving abilities can be further discussed in terms of beliefs and unconscious resources (depicted at the bottom of Illustration 1 and 2). Both his family of origin and the family he was forming through the new marriage were organized around the placement of overt decision-making and assertiveness skills in the hands of others. Thus, his power to make changes in either family order would probably come as a result of his symptom formation. This symptom and its control would take shape over the years as the gap widens between his available assertiveness, and the need for using it.

Since role limits control the range of a person's communications (Illustration 2, level 3), his characteristic role of shyness did not allow for any random or occasional assertiveness. When his stress increases, so does his "symptom" of increased weakness or victim-like behavior (and not violent outbursts). At the next level (Illustration 1, level 2), communication/behavior form limits on beliefs; hence, we find that he has in fact formed a belief of himself as inadequate. He formed a self-concept that he consciously recalls from as early as adolescence. In these roles of shyness and inadequacy, he decided that he was inferior to several "normal" boys and did not compete in sports, academics, or social activities with them. This stance, according to him, led him later to drop out of college. Even upon returning to college several years later, he did not major in the field he truly desired due to thoughts that he could not handle it.

At the lowest level on the chart, again, we see that beliefs delimit unconscious resources. The beliefs he holds about his conduct and abilities make it difficult for him to perceive the assertiveness and aggressive impulses he might generate unconsciously in appropriate situations. It is very possible that the anxiety he experiences is his cognitive interpretation of his poorly formed perception of aggressive impulse.

The "Family Systems Dynamic Chart" helps clarify the interlocking levels of influence in the human system, as well as serving as a practical guide for therapeutic intervention. There are two ways to use this chart as a functional guide: 1) as a means of identifying and understanding presenting problems and symptoms, and 2) designing system-wide treatment. I'll discuss each area separately.

PART II: IDENTIFYING PRESENTING PROBLEMS AND SYMPTOMS

Problems brought to a therapist's office most often can be identified and located into one or another level on the Family Systems Chart. Problems are usually described in terms of conflicts taking place between coexisting elements on a particular level. For example, conflicts between *family organization* and *role limits* might be worded as, "Johnny is not fitting into the family due to his school behavior." Problems between *role limits* and *communication/behavior* might be expressed as, "I am so ashamed of my conduct," or, "Johnny has not been himself lately (he is influenced by his peers)." Another recently blossoming expression of conflict on this level is, "How can I balance my career and child-rearing demands?" Or, a converse conflict: "I don't know what to do with my time now that the children have left home."

Problems of incongruence between allowed communication/behavior and held beliefs might be expressed as, "I don't know how to be happy," "I'm anxious all the time," "It's just my nerves," and so on. Conflict on this level also includes the absence or presence of communication/behaviors (including emotional behaviors) that are not in keeping with the conscious belief system. An example is someone who believes he should perform better (absence of behavior) or a person who shows every sign of strongly suppressed emotional reactions (presence of behavior). Still another way of expressing such a conflict is, "I don't cry—I can't cry." In these statements we see the recurrence or absence of a behavior that in turn reinforces a belief and shapes a perceptual predisposition.

Problems exemplifying the lowest level of conflict in our system commonly occur as discrepancies between beliefs and unconscious resources and activity. An example would be, "I've been having these awful thoughts about harming people." Here the client is essentially saying that unconscious impulses are impinging on the disallowing belief system. Yet another way to express conflict on this level is in comments such as, "There is no emotional problem, but the doctor who treats my allergies says I should see a psychotherapist." Again, the belief system successfully denies the possibility of stimulated unconscious emotional factors contributing to the allergy.

At first glance, this chart helps us to make sense of a particular symptomatic conflict in the context of the broader *systems picture*. It appears to give us a sense of where to intervene: Identify the level and you've identified the point of intervention. Unfortunately, such a first glance would be misleading. Each of these levels of data organization gives, by itself, an incomplete picture of the human system of which it is a dynamic part. The entire range of events and experiences at all levels is, in fact, involved in the difficulty. The event is merely most conveniently characterized or measured at the one level where the conflict arises.

A therapist who is an ardent adherent of one or another therapeutic discipline might be quick to identify the existence of a problem at a particular level and perhaps overlook or underestimate the influence of other levels that are contributing to the problem. This is especially true of therapists who treat only symptoms and fail to consider their developmental context. I suspect this is why some psychotherapists devalue the importance of family therapy, or why radical family therapists say that we can't study or treat the individual outside of the family. Change the family organization and you change it all or you change the most important piece. In these instances, intervention at the family level of data organization is clearly emphasized.

Different therapeutic approaches tend to emphasize one or another level, without focusing on the interactive relationship actually taking place among all the levels. For example, Bob and Mary Goulding have suggested name changes for some of their clients (Goulding & Goulding, 1979). In following the therapeutic directive and changing their names, clients have a convenient symbol for indicating that they will present a different *role* to the world. I met a man whose name was "Twig." The Gouldings suggested a change and he decided to change "Twig" to "Forrest." These are examples of intervening at the level of social roles. Where Twig had been inconspicuous and unimpressive, Forrest is confident; Twig was dying and Forrest is living.

Some therapies have been greatly influenced by psychodrama which focuses on acting out emotional states and responses within various *social roles.* Gestalt therapy, for one, relies strongly upon intervention at this level of (emotional) *communications/behaviors.* I locate therapies that deal with emotion in the communications area because emotion is a form of relational communication or behavior. Emotion is movement outward. A careful reading of Perls shows that he believed primarily that "emotional explosion" and "organismic self-regulation" would solve an individual's problems (Perls, 1947, 1973; Perls, Hefferline & Goodman, 1951). The same is true to an even greater extreme for other "feeling therapists" (Hart, Corriere & Binder, 1975).

Proponents of this type of therapy tend to devalue the function of cognition belief systems. Perls called it "phony" (Perls, 1979, p. 59). In fact, his therapy goal was to break into and evoke an explosion of core feelings in order to change the way clients presented themselves. In this framework, clients' belief systems were only an inconvenience. But, is there a price to pay for "letting it all hang out" emotionally, to the exclusion of all other levels of psychosocial functioning? Doesn't the marathon attendee go home and bump headlong into a family that is at odds with the newly sanctioned conduct?

On the other hand, there are other therapies which emphasize change at the level of beliefs. Ellis (1973) skillfully convinces clients that problems are a result of irrational belief systems—and unconscious impulses, sociometric variables, family power dynamics, and other interactive factors are virtually ignored. Similarly for analytic therapists (Langs, 1973) an emphasis is placed on the cognitive level of organization; conscious thoughts are elevated as the pivotal point of behavior change.

The cognitive behaviorists, such as Lazarus (1976), however, have a systematic way of viewing belief and thought that gives them more breadth and scope. Thought is not regarded as rational or irrational, as contaminated or secondary, but rather as a discriminative stimulus that can determine the target for therapy when what follows the stimulus is maladaptive. Nevertheless, the primary interest of this type of therapy is located on the circumscribed level of cognition and belief in the individual and tends to again place "pathology" *in* the individual.

Conversely, body therapies, though obviously aware of the etiological influences from the family, tend to center their work on increasing the range of unconscious experience that is allowed into cognition-belief systems by manipulating the body in a variety of ways (Alexander, 1969; Baker, 1967; Feldenkrais, 1972; Lowen, 1958, 1965, 1972, 1975; Reich, 1945, 1951).

In this discussion it is not a matter of who is correct and who is incorrect. Every one of these is correct *in part*. It also may be partly correct to say that the proper answer is more than merely combining all of the psychosocial levels. The participant-observer dichotomy is only a semantic reality; any of these therapeutic frameworks constitutes a kind of participation—a therapist making these categorizations about a family also tends to induce that reality in the family or the individuals.

So the matter is not which approach is the truest, but rather *how we can best operate in a systemic manner with families and individuals*. It is here that the Ericksonian approach to psychotherapy makes the greatest contribution. Whereas most therapists tend to favor one or another level of psychosocial interaction as a means of conceptualizing presenting problems and creating appropriate interventions, Erickson perceived and intervened at each level of organization in a very large number of his reported cases and did not place "the problem" *in* the person or *in* the family.

PART III: DESIGNING SYSTEM-WIDE INTERVENTIONS

Erickson developed a range of interventions that accomplished different goals at different levels of the family system. In the course of therapy with any particular family, he used most of them. I have indicated these interventions along the left side of Illustration 2. Before discussing them, it would be useful to comment on Erickson's general ideas regarding the roles and interface of conscious and unconscious processes and resources as they impact both individuals and families.

Erickson seemed to value the unconscious mind more highly than the conscious mind because it was the conscious mind that concocted the limiting beliefs. Simply stated, this means that certain consciously held beliefs and thoughts stop people from searching for resources they may actually be able to use. For instance, the belief that "I can't be happy and trusting" will stop the individual from experiencing the components which make up *happy* and *trusting*. Another example is expressed in the cliché transaction: (Person A) "Why don't you try going dancing and getting out a little bit more?" (Person B) "Oh, I make such a fool of myself whenever I try to dance," or, "Oh I couldn't do that—I'm so uncoordinated." In this case the respondent will not allow the natural gracefulness of the body a chance to express itself because the belief system continually finds ways of choosing only those ungraceful moments to notice, remember, and recreate.

Although Erickson often sought to depotentiate or bypass the limitations of the patient's conscious mind, he nonetheless did not ignore or devaluate the subjective importance of consciously held beliefs. He honored the client's need to either receive an explanation regarding treatment or to not receive one. He worked *with* the conscious mind rather than through direct confrontation against it. This single element of his approach gave rise to techniques of communication that have been termed *reframing, relabeling,* and *therapeutic metaphor.* It is my intention to provide a more comprehensive overview of Erickson's techniques and to illustrate how specific types of techniques were used to intervene at specific levels of individual and family organization.

Level 1 Interventions

Level 1 of Illustration 2 shows unconscious resources interacting with beliefs. To effect changes at this level, Erickson used interventions that were based upon indirection. For retrieving unconscious resources, he recognized that interventions which stimulated unconscious search would be essential. The ambiguity inherent in metaphor, indirect suggestions, and various types of binds can stimulate unconscious activity in a therapeutic direction. Hearing a therapeutic metaphor, for example, activates types of cognition and behaviors that are difficult to delineate experimentally. These include: comparison, contrast, memory, association, congruity checking, identification, attributions selection, and so on. Similarly, indirect suggestions and binds (and the unconscious stimulation they create) constitute the "glue" that hold together a variety of internal associations. For example, indirect suggestions and binds about feeling confident might sound like this:

"Your conscious mind certainly knows a lot about confidence that you couldn't explain consciously. I doubt that anyone here could articulate consciously how to begin to feel a sense of confidence. Usually you don't notice. It may begin with an alteration of your body posture. Everyone has heard the phrase, 'breathing deeply, sigh of relief.' But a conscious mind never really knows how your unconscious can go about regulating your body experience and change it to be more comfortable."

Continued listening to such indirect verbalization results in continued unconscious associations to the words. Unconscious processes such as memory, association, anticipation, congruity checking, identification, and others continue too. Intervention at this level does not produce change in belief systems, nor in communication patterns, nor in roles the client commonly assumes. Unconscious resources are simply retrieved—in this case, it would be experiences of confidence.

Reframing, relabeling and attitude metaphors (Lankton & Lankton, 1986) are interventions that urge clients to conceptualize beliefs differently. A well-known example is that of the recently married couple who consulted Erickson because of the husband's failure to consummate the marriage despite his previously active sex life. The bride considered this situation to be a sign of his not loving her; to her it meant that the marriage had been a mistake. After two weeks the wife had consulted an attorney for an annulment. Erickson reframed the situation by asking her if she had considered what a compliment her husband had paid her: "Well, evidently he thought your body was so beautiful that he was overwhelmed by it. Completely overwhelmed. And you misunderstood that and felt he was incompetent. And he *was* incompetent, because he realized how little capacity he had to really appreciate the beauty of your body." Erickson explained separately to the husband that the fact that she overwhelmed him was proof that she was the right woman for him; and she was the one overwhelming girl for him (Haley, 1973, p. 157).

In this intervention, no retrieval of unconscious material was elicited for change. Rather, a new cognitive framework was presented to facilitate both family members' recognition of the potential for a loving experience (instead of feeling bitter and incompetent) in the future. The husband was then seen alone for further therapy to that exact end. A lengthy discussion of a metaphoric method used by Erickson to elicit change as an attitudinal level can be found elsewhere (Lankton & Lankton, 1986, pp. 193–198).

Level 2 Interventions

This brings us to the next level of Illustration 2—that of communication and the limits it places on beliefs. Interventions that affect this level include behavior protocols, affect protocols, behavioral rehearsal, and simple illustration. Erickson would sometimes have clients rehearse the very symptom that had brought them in for therapy. For instance, he had a girl who sucked her thumb learn in the office how to suck it better. There are numerous accounts throughout Erickson's *Collected Papers* (Erickson, 1980) illustrating in metaphorical ways the proper manner of shopping for presents, gift giving, standing up to a spouse in a quarrel, and so on.

In addition to these behavior-change metaphors, some metaphors are designed specifically to elicit emotions. Notable among these is the story of how Erickson helped his mother say goodbye to the farm and how this story evokes sadness in the listener (Lankton, 1978, and modified in Lankton & Lankton, 1986, pp. 285–288). Emotion can be aroused indirectly by metaphor (Lankton & Lankton, 1986, pp. 198–203) and non-emotional behaviors can also be brought into the foreground by the use of metaphor (Lankton & Lankton, 1986, pp. 203–205). Each of these techniques has the common goal of sensitizing the client to a new method of feeling, communicating, or behaving. This type of change is independent of the cognitive adjustment on Level 1 that may preclude or support it.

Level 3 Interventions

Interventions which exemplify Erickson's awareness of the social role level of dynamics (Level 3) include the interventions of building *self-image thinking* and prescribing *paradoxical prescriptions*. Roles become solidified when they are conceptualized as roles by the individuals who live the behaviors. Erickson frequently created changes in clients' self-image thinking (Lankton & Lankton, 1983, pp. 312–344).

One such case was that of a "dumb moron" named Harold (Haley, 1973) who was dealt with by being sent on a number of assignments. These assignments included learning to play the piano, taking dance lessons, and going to a barn dance to test his progress. Harold was not led to believe that these assignments would get him into the normal stage of courtship (which he needed to attain but which he found highly threatening); rather, he was allowed to believe that these tasks would further his goal of becoming a good manual laborer, a goal which did not threaten him. At the dance, Harold decided that he was "not so bad after all." At his next office session, Erickson used hypnosis to extend this sense of competency into the future where Harold would need it again and again. Changes in role conduct thus produced concomitant changes in self-image. Stories about the progress of Harold are, in fact, therapeutic metaphors that help clients create a change in their own self-image thinking.

Self-image thinking is another level of intervention aimed at the area of social role development and its influence on communication. Self-image thinking can be facilitated in metaphor with specific guided imagery, or with indirect suggestions and "assignments," as in Harold's case. Family members are taught to think about themselves in positive, goal-directed visual rehearsals as a method of problem solving. This may involve systematically building the body image of all family members by assisting to visualize themselves acting out certain capabilities and by helping them imagine scenarios of themselves playing different roles (Lankton & Lankton, 1983, pp. 312–344).

The use of paradox also belongs on this third level. The therapist using paradox tells a client to keep doing what he or she is doing (the presenting symptom or dynamic), but for a different reason. In this way, the role or the family organization can be changed to some degree. Consider the earlier case of the girl sucking her thumb (Haley, 1973, pp. 195–202). The parents bring her in to see Erickson after she has been labeled aggressive by a previous doctor for sucking her thumb. They are a very religious family and *aggressive* is a disturbing word to them. Erickson begins by telling the parents that no matter what the girl does, they should ignore her thumbsucking. Thus, he is setting limits on the family transactions. He then brought the girl into his office and, while the parent waited in the living room, he presented her with paradoxical instructions to continue sucking her thumb and to do it better! From her family she had acquired a role of having no control over her thumbsucking and, therefore, had acquired yet another role as a psychiatric patient. Erickson's use of paradox completely transformed this role. The paradoxical intervention—which was to keep doing the same behavior but to do it better—was to be done to "irk" her parents. That is, the same behavior would now be used for the role of making them angry, *and* there would be no way they could stop her from expressing this aggressive thumbsucking.

Let us take a closer look at how this intervention affected role limits within the girl's family. At first the girl's conduct says, "I'm a person who is accidentally sucking my thumb and can't help myself. It's my unconscious aggression." Then, she has to take the role of, "I'm going to really irk my parents with this and do it really well." So the same behavior becomes a different role because of a different motivation. Paradoxical interventions change the role that is being played by changing the context or the motivation for the behavior.

Level 4 Interventions

Blocking transactions, as when with the parents of the thumbsucker were told to ignore her, obviously affects the manner in which power can be channeled in a family. It is difficult to reestablish the rules in the family when normal avenues for communication are no longer open. This is a desirable situation that allows a learning of new social roles and congruent communications. Other interventions at this level include *ambiguous function assignment* (Lankton & Lankton, 1983, pp. 136–152) and *family structure change metaphors* (Lankton & Lankton, 1983, pp. 207–208). Both stimulate clients to begin to think about reorganizing the family structure.

A cogent example of intervention at this level was the case about the overprotected young woman whom Erickson ordered to move away from her mother and aunts without even telling them her whereabouts. In addition, she was told to get an apartment with three other girls and to regularly drive around with them in the car without regard for where they were going (Erickson & Rossi, 1979). Here we see an example of a very *direct* intervention, which is in contrast to the *indirect* approaches discussed as means of evoking change in the lower two levels of the chart. The family organization is literally disrupted by the girl's move; role selection is now confused as the disorganization affects and determines the boundaries of roles for each family member.

DISCUSSION

When a change in family organization creates a confusion about rules, there is also a flux regarding which roles will be tolerated. Further, once roles have become temporarily in flux, a tolerance for new communication arises. This new communication via behavior or emotion will be temporarily acceptable to the conscious mind to the degree that changes in attitude also have been stimulated. Finally, the entire package of small changes at each level can be interwoven via indirect suggestion and binds that create a set of operational changes which reverberate through the entire system at each level. This, indeed, constitutes my view of Erickson's systemic approach to therapy: he was capable of stimulating small changes at each level of the system, and each small change supported and reinforced the small changes at other levels.

This approach to therapy with a family system is analogous to assembling a toy spring horse: If all the screws in the frame and on the horse are loosened, the essential springs can be added easily.

However, if all the screws remain tightened, a great deal of resistance to proper construction is created. Without much resistance, then, Erickson's systemic approach allows the entire system to gradually shift to allow specific, new problem-solving resources to emerge which can help the client creatively adjust to the demands of developmental pressures.

I have attempted to focus specifically on Ericksonian interventions in regard to the variables depicted on the charts. Yet the reader will certainly recognize how interventions from Behavior Therapy, Psychodrama, Gestalt Therapy, Rational Emotive Therapy, and so on, will also apply. It is my intent to use learnings from Erickson's systemic approach as a means of furthering therapists' abilities to intervene effectively regardless of the "school of technique" used. To that end, this chapter has provided a latticework which relates interventions to different levels of psychosocial and familial organization. These levels of organization that occur within the entire family system are further related to the cycle of stability/instability that families experience as they traverse the various developmental stages in life. The usefulness of the chart can be evaluated operationally by how well it guides therapists to understand symptom formation and subsequently to intervene in an orderly way at all major levels of family experience.

REFERENCES

Ackerman, N. (1958). *The Psychodynamics of Family Life*. New York: Basic Books.
Alexander, F. (1969). *The Resurrection of the Body: The Writings of F. Matthias Alexander*. New York: Delta Books.
Baker, E. (1967). *Man in the Trap: The Causes of Blocked Sexual Energy*. New York: Avon Books.
Bandura, A. (1969). *Principles of Behavior Modification*. New York: Holt, Rinehart, & Winston, Inc.
Bateson, G. (1972). *Steps to Ecology of Mind*. New York: Ballantine.
Bateson, G. (1979). *Mind and Nature: A Necessary Unity*. New York: E. P. Dutton.
Berne, E. (1961). *Transactional Analysis in Psychotherapy*. New York: Ballantine.
Cooper, L., & Erickson, M. (1954). *Time Distortion on Hypnosis*. Baltimore: Williams & Wilkins.
Ellis, A. (1973). *Humanistic Psychotherapy*. New York: McGraw-Hill.
Erickson, M. (1980). *The Collected Papers of Milton H. Erickson on Hypnosis: Vol. 1. The Nature of Hypnosis and Suggestion; Vol. 2. Hypnotic Alteration of Sensory, Perceptual and Psychophysical Processes; Vol. 3. Hypnotic Investigation of Psychodynamic Processes; Vol. 4. Innovative Hypnotherapy*. Edited by Ernest Rossi. New York: Irvington.
Erickson, M., Hershman, S., & Secter, I. (1961). *The Practical Application of Medical and Dental Hypnosis*. New York: Julian Press.
Erickson, M., & Rossi, E. (1979). *Hypnotherapy: An Exploratory Casebook*. New York: Irvington.

Erickson, M., & Rossi, E. (1981). *Experiencing Hypnosis: Therapeutic Approaches to Altered States*. New York: Irvington.

Erickson, M., Rossi, E., & Rossi, S. (1976). *Hypnotic Realities: The Induction of Clinical Hypnosis and Forms of Indirect Suggestion*. New York: Irvington.

Feldenkrais, M. (1972). *Awareness through Movement: Health Exercises for Personal Growth*. New York: Harper & Row.

Fisch, R., Weakland, J., & Segal, L. (1983). *The Tactics of Change: Doing Therapy Briefly*. San Francisco: Jossey-Bass.

Goulding, M., & Goulding, R. (1979). *Changing Lives through Redecision Therapy*. New York: Brunner/Mazel.

Haley, J. (1973). *Uncommon Therapy: The Psychiatric Techniques of Milton H. Erickson, M.D.* New York: Norton.

Haley, J. (1985). *Conversations with Milton H. Erickson, M.D., Vol. 2: Changing Couples; Vol. 3: Changing children and families*. New York: Norton.

Hart, J., Corriere, R., & Binder, J. (1975). *Going Sane*. New York: Jason Aronson.

Keeney, B., & Ross, J. (1983). Cybernetics of brief family therapy. *Journal of Marital and Family Therapy, 9*, 375–392.

Langs, R. (1973). *The Technique of Psychoanalytic Psychotherapy: Vol. 1 & Vol. 2*. New York: Jason Aronson.

Lankton, S. (1978). Personal communication with Milton H. Erickson, August.

Lankton, S., & Lankton, C. (1983). *The Answer Within: A Clinical Framework of Ericksonian Hypnotherapy*. New York: Brunner/Mazel.

Lankton, S., & Lankton, C. (1986). *Enchantment and Intervention in Family Therapy: Training in Ericksonian Approaches*. New York: Brunner/Mazel.

Lazarus, A. (1976). *Multimodal Behavior Therapy*. New York: Springer.

Lowen, A. (1958). *The Language of the Body*. New York: Collier.

Lowen, A. (1965). *Love and Orgasm*. New York: Collier.

Lowen, A. (1972). *Depression and the Body: The Biological Basis of Faith and Reality*. New York: Coward, McCann & Geohegan.

Lowen, A. (1975). *Bioenergetics*. New York: Coward, McCann & Geohegan.

Madanes, C. (1983). *Strategic family therapy*. San Francisco: Jossey-Bass.

Perls, F. (1947). *Ego, Hunger and Aggression: The Beginning of Gestalt Therapy*. New York: Random House.

Perls, F. (1973). *Gestalt Approach and Eye Witness to Therapy*. Ben Lomond, CA: Science and Behavior Books.

Perls, F. (1979). *Gestalt Therapy Verbatim*. Lafayette, CA: Real People Press.

Perls, F., Hefferline, R., & Goodman, P. (1951). *Gestalt Therapy: Excitement and Growth in the Human Personality*. New York: Dell-Delta Books.

Reich, W. (1945). *Character Analysis*. New York: Simon and Schuster.

Reich, W. (1951). *Selected Writings: An Introduction to Orgonomy*. New York: Farrar, Straus and Giroux.

Ritterman, M. (1983). *Using Hypnosis in Family Therapy*. San Francisco: Jossey-Bass.

Rossi, E., & Ryan, M. (Eds.) (1985). *Life Reframing in Hypnosis: The Seminars, Workshops, and Lectures of Milton H. Erickson, Vol. 2*. New York: Irvington.

Rossi, E., Ryan, M., & Sharp, F. (Eds.) (1983). *Healing in Hypnosis: The Seminars, Workshops, and Lectures of Milton H. Erickson, Vol. 1*. New York: Irvington.

Satir, V. (1979). *Peoplemaking*. Palo Alto, CA: Science and Behavior Books.

Watzlawick, P. (1976). *How Real is Real? Confusion, Disinformation, Communication*. New York: Vintage Books.

Chapter 24

Human Sexuality, Hypnosis, and Therapy

Daniel L. Araoz

Daniel L. Araoz, Ed.D. (Columbia University), practices and consults in Malverne, New York. An internationally renowned trainer, he has published extensively in the areas of hypnosis, sex therapy, and family therapy. He is author of The New Hypnosis *and* Hypnosis and Sex Therapy *and co-author of* The New Hypnosis in Family Therapy. *He has served on a number of editorial boards and is founding editor of* The American Journal of Family Therapy.

In his chapter, Araoz demonstrates that hypnosis can be used in the diagnostic and preparatory stages of sex therapy to identify self-defeating patterns. Examples are provided of specific wording that can be used to hypnotically help patients define a clearer vision of good sex.

Two adults, respected in their own worlds, responsible and law-abiding citizens, are alone. They start taking off their clothes, smiles of enjoyment on their faces. They look at each other, they come closer, and their hands busy themselves touching each other. Their touch goes to bodily areas usually private. Their bodies respond with sexual arousal. Their activity becomes more intense. Passion. Desire. And soon they are connecting in ways that are intimate: touching, pressing, caressing, kissing. They move with more intense desire. They are overcome by passion, leading to carnal communion. Two bodies become one flesh in the ecstasy of sexual desire and carnal fulfillment. Then, their arms still intertwined, their breathing heavy, their bodies moist with perspiration, they rest, still gently caressing each other.

No matter how often we have experienced it or watched it in movies or in our own imagination, the scene is always attractive and interesting.

438

But those two respectable citizens who let themselves enjoy the pleasures of the flesh are not just two bodies responding to physical stimulation. Their emotions are involved; their spirits are engaged. Most humans don't just copulate. They make love. We express our desire, attraction, emotion, love through our physical selves. Our hands, our lips, our skin, our mucosa, our genitalia, our bodily orifices communicate. But communication in us humans involves inner realities: our beliefs, our values, our expectations, our fears, our yearnings, all our feelings.

Sex! America seems to be obsessed by it, either in the form of the multimillion-dollar smut industry or in the form of the moral watchdogs. The former deal with a spiritless sex: the latter deform and distort it in a moralistic chastity cage.

Neither monkeys nor angels, we humans have the delicate task of keeping a fragile balance between the flesh and the spirit in order to enjoy sex. That copulation—fucking—is an end in itself is as insulting to humans as the concept of "angelic virtue" designating an abstention from sexual activity still preached by some religious leaders who believe our bodies to be sinful.

Like all uniquely human realities such as art, music or heroism, sex in humans engages the soul as it transcends biology and physiology. And here is where hypnosis, self-hypnosis to be sure, comes into play. If it is true that in a valid sense we create our own reality, it is most evident in sex. On one extreme lies the reaction of guilt, embarrassment and shame connected with sexual activity. On the other are attitudes of pure physical satisfaction, conquest or power, leading to compulsive sex. Both extremes are the result of a form of self-hypnosis: As we believe, so we sex.

By the time we reach adulthood, we are usually operating under "post-hypnotic suggestions" regarding sex—suggestions given by our parents, society, religion, advertising and the media. We have incorporated these suggestions and made them our own. Many of us have never examined and revised them. And, as is often the case with post-hypnotic suggestions, we do not consciously know that we are operating under the influence of those suggestions.

We hypnotherapists often are asked to help people deal with sexual problems. Assuming that we are careful to diagnose *sexual* difficulties and to refer to medical practitioners those who truly suffer from medical problems, we are concentrating here on nonmedical sexual problems, the so-called psychogenic dysfunctions.

Even before concerning ourselves with a differential diagnosis of the sexual problem, we should be curious about the hypnotic suggestions at work in the individual or couple who requests our help. A good way to start is by asking clients to get into the fantasy of good sex. Encourage them to really get involved in this fantasy so that they become aware of what *they believe* is good sex. In this manner, the hypnotherapist will be able to understand the values, perceptions and beliefs of the client in order to help find a sexual fulfillment according to the client's, not the clinician's, goals and standards. This hypnotic fantasy of good sex should be encouraged in great detail, at first allowing the client "to be there" without reporting details of what is being experienced. Then, at the end of this exercise, it is imperative to discuss what happened in order to be able to proceed with the correction of any dysfunction. An example of the wording I use might further clarify this:

> Your memory keeps detailed files of everything you ever expe-
> rienced or of what you ever thought of experiencing. Relaxed as
> you are now, let your memory bring forth your true image of
> good sex. Perhaps you had a wonderful sexual experience in the
> past, perhaps you dreamed of it, perhaps you imagined it. Good
> sex, great sex, satisfying sex, enjoyable sex. Let the picture start
> slowly forming on your mind's screen. It's you in the midst of
> joyful sex, fully alive, all your senses fully awakened. Do you see
> yourself yet? No rush at all. Feel comfortable while your memory
> retrieves your personal picture of what is good, really good, sex.
> And as the picture slowly forms in your mind, you can see yourself
> having good sex . . . the way you know it can happen, the way
> it may have happened long ago, or in a way it might never have
> happened. But it can happen. You can now experience in your
> inner mind the wonderful sex you know you can have. Are you
> there? Be fully there. Enjoy every movement, every sensual aware-
> ness. Enjoy your partner: his (her) body, every part of it, kissing,
> touching, caressing, feeling. Every square inch of his (her) skin is
> exciting. Every sound, every smell, every awareness of closeness,
> warmth. And you feel progressively good. Everything you expe-
> rience makes you feel better and better about your own body,
> your own sex, your own flesh. Still with it? More turned on with
> every second that passes. Good sex. You and good sex. Fully alive.
> All your senses more and more into it as your sexual desire grows
> and your inner enjoyment grows and you want to join him (her)

totally, fully inside. You want to mix your wetness with his (hers). In the ecstasy of passion and sex you find satisfaction, pleasure, sexual fulfillment. And you take your time, allowing the whole experience of good sex to develop and come to a joyful fulfillment. Let it go on until it is completely finished and you are happy about it. . . .

Used judiciously, this kind of suggestion can help the client to focus on what she or he considers good sex. The discussion follows. At this point, the question of morality (what is good sex from a psychological, humanistic perspective) arises. What if the person views sex in either of the two extremes mentioned earlier? What if good sex is considered a sexual encounter devoid of feeling and caring? Are we as mental health workers valueless regarding what constitutes a wholesome sexual experience? What if the person views extreme forms of sado-masochism, hurtful things, as good sex? Do we as psychologists accept this as healthy sexuality?

Great minds have struggled with this issue of wholesome sex, yet we are still far from having a definite answer. I personally believe in full sexual freedom and enjoyment within a context of mutual respect, of caring. As Lady Chatterley's lover, Mellors, put it: "I believe in being warm-hearted in love; in fucking with a warm heart. I believe if men could fuck with warm hearts and the women take it warm-heartedly everything would come all right. It's all this cold-hearted fucking that is death and idiocy." Anthropological and psychosocial research as reviewed by Masters, Johnson and Kolodny (1982) seems to agree with Mellors.

The way I handle this "moral" question is always in terms of the specific client—what is understood to be good sex and how does this concept fit within the parameters of our culture. If a vision of good sex includes infants as sex objects, for instance, this does not fit into our cultural values. The client then is invited to examine a good sex vision in the light of our culture. We are not "moralists" in the sense of preaching *a priori* a specific type of "good sex." We are, however, moralists in the sense that we live and work within the parameters of this society at this point in history and as such cannot condone practices that our society has banned.

After the discussion, following the first hypnotic practice just mentioned, I suggest that clients ask themselves what might be behind their own nonacceptable good sex scene. They are instructed to focus hypnotically on a probable dichotomy by connecting with two internal "parts." One part brings up the tabu sexual scene, but another part recognizes its social unacceptability. Parenthetically, let me stress that I refer to "forbidden sex" as activities clearly condemned by current social mores and without informed consent of both parties, such as child pornography and forcible rape. Once these two inner parts have been identified, the client concentrates on one part at a time, later to experience both interacting. Usually, the part that wants the forbidden sex appears to the patient as immature or, generally, in a negative context. The part that recognizes the antisocial nature of the sex scene, on the other hand, usually comes up as "the voice of reason" and common sense.

It should be remembered, however, that tabu sexual scenes are very rare. In 25 years I have encountered only three cases of forbidden sex coming up as a good sex scene and none in the last 10 years. I interpret this first as indicative of the fact that people coming freely for therapy are socially aware to begin with, and as part of their developmental socialization have generally accepted our social mores. The other reason might be that people in our present society are informed about legislation condemning sexual abuses of different kinds and do not include "forbidden sex" among their free choices.

The two parts are kept in interaction until the client makes a choice in favor of what is not antisocial. My patter might sound like this: "Keep listening to that voice that wants it. But hear also, very clearly, the other voice in you. Pay attention to what this other voice says until your whole self accepts it."

The next step in this therapeutic process is to find out what is interfering with the attainment of "good sex." In order to bypass intellectualizations and phoney logical explanations, I suggest getting in touch with inner wisdom. I might say:

> Take a moment to be truthful with yourself. You have a clear idea of what good sex is for you. Yet, you are not having good sex these days. Ask the wise part in you to make you discover what's stopping you from good sex. Relax as much as you are able right now and listen to the wise part of you. You can become curious. What will come up? Will it come up now? Or will you be surprised by your inner wisdom when you dream tonight or when you are thinking of other things and the answer seems to come from nowhere? Trust in your inner mind's wisdom. You

know what good sex is for you. You want to enjoy sex and have good sex. Yet you don't. What is stopping you? Are you doing something or not doing something which could make a big difference?

This type of patter can continue until the person (or the couple) gets in touch with something that was ignored or denied before. During subsequent discussion, clients often start to see new connections between their sexual problem and other issues of performance anxiety, unhappy relationships, or unreasonable expectations.

The next step is to zero in on their negative self-hypnosis. Because in humans the mind and the soul are involved in sex as much as the body, we can conceptualize a quasi-fourth stage of sexual response. The first stage is desire, the second arousal, the third is resolution. But throughout these three, humans assess and evaluate their sexual experience, especially at the end of it. In fact their sexual processing seems to be crucial in determining sexual desire for the next encounter. "After the loving I'm still in love with you," the old song says, although it may be transposed to "I'm furious with you" or "I'm still ashamed of myself," or a million other reactions.

It seems that most people with psychogenic sexual problems are engaged in negative self-hypnosis, giving themselves negative suggestions about their sexual functioning. By asking clients to concentrate on what comes to mind when they think of their recent sexual experiences, you can easily uncover negative self-hypnosis. In most cases clients report mental images of repeated failure, of sexual frustration and tension, of fears of rejection or mockery. With these images, clients often use negative self-suggestions such as, "It's going to happen again," "I better avoid having sex for a while," "I won't be able to perform," and so on. Performance, by the way, is the death of sex. We must help clients to stop thinking in terms of performance and instead to concentrate on enjoyment of the whole experience.

Once they become aware of their negative self-hypnosis, I help them expand their focus of attention. I might ask, "What else can you be conscious of when you are having sex? What other sensations can you capture? Other than your genitalia, what other parts of your body are also involved?" Then I lead them to a hypnotic experience in which they focus on those other sensations. For instance, a man with erectile problems, overly conscious of the behavior of his penis, admitted that he also was aware of his lover's warm body and of her touching his legs and chest. In hypnosis, he was able to focus more sharply on those other sensations, ignoring his penis for a while. Through repetition of this exercise in self-hypnosis, he became more and more relaxed and comfortable during sex. The new focus on other sensations becomes, then, the new material for self-suggestions. In the case just mentioned, the person could say to himself, "I love to feel her warm, soft body next to me. I love the way she touches me," etc. He is encouraged to practice self-hypnosis daily and to use these self-suggestions throughout the day—during any lost moments—while driving the car or going to the bathroom.

The concentration on a differential diagnosis of sexual dysfunctions is appropriate only after this preliminary work. I have elsewhere (Araoz, 1982) described many hypnotic techniques for a variety of sexual dysfunctions. It is important to emphasize that any sex therapy technique, hypnotic or not, is going to be sabotaged by negative self-hypnosis. Not to deal with it first, before addressing ourselves to the specific sexual disorder, is a waste of time. If the person does not believe that he or she can enjoy sex, that sexual enjoyment is the right of an adult, that the human body's nature is sexual and pleasurable, then the efforts to improve sexual functioning will be in vain. Only through a change in attitude and beliefs can people recover from psychogenic sexual problems. Hypnosis is an effective way to change one's attitudes because, as we know, hypnosis goes directly to the unconscious source of attitudes. Since the nonconscious follows rules of personal inner experience and not those of logic and reason, the hypnotic approach is effective by fostering vivid imagery. Inner experience is essentially imaginative involvement. The more vivid the imagery, the more effective it is.

On the basis of the client's picture of "good sex," the clinician helps to develop the type of sexual experience possible for the client. After having separated the good sex image from unreasonable expectations—such as nonstop copulation for five hours for a man—or from culturally unaccepted behaviors, the client must start rehearsing hypnotically an enjoyable sexual scene. Mental rehearsal, therefore, is essential in sex therapy. I find it interesting that Masters and Johnson (1970) and Kaplan (1979) mention instances of negative self-hypnosis in their works without, however, giving specific directions on how to deal with it. Masters and Johnson refer to "spectatoring" and Kaplan, to the "turn-off mechanism." The former is a mental process by which the dysfunctional person allows the "observing ego" to interfere with the "experiencing ego," thus short-circuiting sexual enjoyment. The individual is so concerned with monitoring sexual functioning that actual sexual enjoyment (implying relaxation and spontaneity) is thwarted. In the case of the turn-off mechanism, the individual uses mental images and self-suggestions in order to cut off or derail sexual desire and interest.

Though both mental mechanisms are hypnotic in nature, neither of the works in which these are mentioned recognizes them as such, and neither helps the clinician deal effectively with them. My own experience has shown that the use of hypnosis as described in this chapter is an effective answer because all sexually dysfunctional people engage in negative self-hypnosis.

REFERENCES

Araoz, D. L. (1982). *Hypnosis and Sex Therapy.* New York: Brunner/Mazel.
Kaplan, H. S. (1979). *Disorders of Sexual Desire.* New York: Brunner/Mazel.
Masters, W. H., & Johnson, V. E. (1970). *Human Sexual Inadequacy.* Boston: Little, Brown.
Masters, W. H., Johnson, V. E., & Kolodny, R. C. (1982). *Human Sexuality.* Boston: Little, Brown.

Chapter 25

Ericksonian Techniques in Family Therapy

Jacques-Antoine Malarewicz

Jacques-Antoine Malarewicz, M.D. (Université René Descartes), is a trainer and practitioner of family therapy, and a director of one of the Erickson Institutes in France. He is coauthor of Milton Erickson: de l'hypnose Clinique à la Psychotherapie Stratégique, *the first book about Erickson originally published in French. He also translated into French* Healing in Hypnosis, *E. Rossi, M. Ryan and F. Sharp (Eds.).*

This chapter presents an interesting linking of group and individual hypnosis and the forces of pathology and change in individual family members.

Inevitably, there are several ways to use the hypnotic techniques of Milton H. Erickson in family therapy. Erickson was, historically, the originator of many of the techniques used in family therapy, such as symptom prescription, reframing, and use of metaphors.

On the other hand, one cannot state authoritatively that he was a family therapist in the sense of the term as it is currently used. He did not systematically work with the families of his patients and did not consider that every problem he encountered arose from family dynamics. He was among those who promoted the emergence of a particular psychotherapeutic practice, family therapy, without having directly and exclusively used it. He frequently worked with the individual first, while developing a particular technique based on the notion of a system of interactions between individuals.

However, a specific context is of particular interest—the use of formal group hypnosis by Erickson, as a demonstration and/or in therapy.

446

Formal hypnosis is understood as a situation where the hypnotic trance is overtly initiated by the therapist, who then induces certain hypnotic phenomena according to therapeutic objectives. This particular hypnotic practice is the one I use most often, especially with students in training.

When a trance state is induced in a group, certain elements can be observed. During such inductions, subjects seem to follow the same train of thought and to experience similar feelings. They claim to feel capable of remaining as much in contact with the hypnotist as with the other people present. This situation indicates that there is neither opposition nor mutual exclusion between two-party communication, and there is participation in a viable group. Multiple levels of communication are intertwined, and at any moment each subject can choose one of these levels to communicate with another member of the group, adjusting to his rhythm and establishing contact with him. After such an experience, the subject is able to describe how he could both deal with this context and remain independently involved in his own internal life.

This situation can, of course, be compared to that of the family therapist, with this difference: The goal is not to induce formal hypnosis with the family. For hypnosis, as Erickson conceived it, is much more than a simple technique for modifying the experience of one or more persons. From the experience afforded by hypnotic work with several people, two hypotheses can be retained for family therapists: 1) Any subject in a hypnotic trance amid other subjects also in trance can learn to increase modes of nonverbal and unconscious communication with the others by means of a multiplicity of interactions during this experience. 2) In this framework, the hypnotic state takes on a tone that differs from that familiar to the subject in the presence of the therapist alone, as a result of the constant give-and-take with the therapist and rapport with the group.

These are the communicational abilities therapists attempt to utilize in family therapy as they communicate on several levels with each member of the family. Then, too, the session, without corresponding to a hypnotic trance experience, nevertheless possesses dynamics more complex than the mere comprehension of a problem by the family.

It would be useful, at this point, to emphasize two questions:

1. On what level can therapists intervene in family therapy, i.e., how can they induce a change in the family's habitual interactions with the aid of Ericksonian hypnotic techniques?

2. Is it possible to transpose to the practice of family therapy a notion comparable to Milton H. Erickson's concept of the unconscious as a "storehouse of learnings"?

THE THERAPIST'S LEVEL OF INTERVENTION

A strange and most fascinating thing in hypnosis is the possibility it offers of making phenomena appear which closely resemble phenomena found in psychopathology. At times, the terms are identical, as in the case of dissociation or hallucination. The sensory and muscular modifications which can be induced in hypnosis, such as anesthesia, analgesia, and catalepsy, so closely resemble hysterical manifestation that, during the last century, the two entities often were confused. Since then, the notion of clients' "suggestibility" has prevailed and it has been said that hypnosis is impossible for a large number of patients. Erickson disregarded the notion of limited suggestibility and considerably extended the therapeutic field of hypnosis. He also altered our comprehension of psychopathological phenomena in cases of hysterical conversion and even beyond this diagnostic category.

The resemblance of hypnotically induced manifestations and observable psychopathology indicates that any pathological manifestation is the result of a multifaceted process which brings into play, simultaneously, the phenomena of auto-suggestion and heterohypnosis. Hysterical manifestations are an example. Insofar as they can be compared to an autohypnotic mechanism, we may assume that every symptom originates, in part, in the same dynamic. To this initial hypnotic process are added the interventions of the patient's social and family context, which, in addition to inducing the symptom, also reinforce it by giving it a relational dimension.

The family therapist can intervene on either of these two levels, using Ericksonian techniques which are founded upon communication at several levels. The promoted change responds to a multifaceted mechanism which, like the reality we construct for ourselves each moment, blends relational and internal experience.

For quite some time, one or the other of these two processes, inner or outer, has been favored by therapy. Any problem was thought to arise from either a personal dynamic or the social milieu. Erickson's work suggests a different epistemology which supercedes this polarity: An individual could develop a problem, symptom, or behavior both from an unconscious learning mechanism—self-hypnosis—and from stimuli generated by the family context, heterohypnosis. In the same way that family members are able to induce certain behaviors in the identified patient by unconsciously using double-binds, confusion, and other mechanisms used therapeutically by Erickson, so might any one of us be able to develop a symptom through a negative self-hypnosis mechanism based on individual capacity and specific physiology.

Erickson demystified hypnosis by demonstrating the frequency of common everyday trance and by giving numerous examples of hypnotic techniques that were used outside of the therapeutic context. The hypnotic state is a very ordinary phenomenon and yet allows us to change our subjective perception of time, or to forget pain. Hypnotic mechanisms can, of course, even be used by individuals outside of the experimental situation to set up a limiting and difficult psychophysiological process. Again, hypnosis can be a process families use for creating solutions or problems in life.

Therapists work with this complex situation by attempting to discover where to best intervene. Their selected interventions may be direct or paradoxical, and may address both conscious and unconscious parts of the subject. Let us examine this process.

THE NOTION OF THE UNCONSCIOUS

The idea of a collective or family unconscious is often disregarded in family therapy and attention is focused instead on the logic of the family system. However, certain characteristics of the unconscious, as defined by Erickson, can be compared to the idea of the family system's logic. Erickson believed the unconscious protects the individual. Similarly, the patient's symptom can be said to protect the homeostasis of the family. The unconscious has a logic of its own, a logic which does not necessarily have to become conscious. In the same way, a family therapist, without explaining the family's manner of functioning, can work to promote a change in that functioning.

Finally, the unconscious manifests itself with a great deal of economy and literalness. The redundant style of problem solving illustrated by symptom repetition and repetition of the family's interaction can be seen as economical, even though the problem-solving style is itself a part of the problem. Erickson communicated with the subject's unconscious to tap its unexplored potential. Similarly, family therapists can assume that the family system's logic contains resources capable of helping the family abandon the symptomatic situation.

There are two distinct levels of intervention for the family therapist to consider. The first level involves the microdynamics of the trance which corresponds to the microdynamics of the therapeutic session. The therapist is dealing with a series of dyads and is communicating with each person on different levels. For example, he may simultaneously address the father and mother, while adopting the designated patient's body language and using the brother's imagery and metaphors.

The second level concerns the confrontation with the idiosyncratic logic of the family system. The concept of logic can be related to the process of learning. System-specific logic evolves and is modified as it is used by the family to understand and act in the world. In family therapy, this type of learning allows the individual to develop a capacity for positive autohypnosis which facilitates giving up the symptom. Other members of the family can also be helped to develop capacity for positive heterohypnosis which reinforces alternative behavior. A transformation of the family system's logic results from this activation of the family's inventive capacities.

CASE HISTORY

A family of four (the parents and two children—a nine-year-old boy and a three-year-old girl) came to therapy as a result of the boy's disturbed behavior. John was terrified of the dark and had nightmares. He claimed to see skeletons everywhere. And he insisted upon walking with his mother in the cemetery at least half a day a week. This odd behavior may have resulted from an earlier family trauma: When he was five years old, he had accompanied his mother, six months pregnant at the time, to the gynecologist. An X-ray had revealed that the fetus was dead and she delivered a stillborn child several weeks later.

Family therapy was conducted in three sessions. During the first session I was able to establish rapport with each member of the family and to construct dyads on both an emotional and intellectual level. Hypnotic techniques proved useful in accomplishing this rapport. I also observed that John's little sister was protective of him and this prevented him from playing his proper role. The mother seemed closed to her son, both in the way she looked at him and in the tone of her voice when she questioned him.

She would ask every morning how he had slept and what he had dreamed. It was likely that, in this way, she had created a situation where she was inducing her son's nightmares. The father had taken a peripheral position.

This first session was concluded with a single prescription: Since John would be 10 years old in two months, it was suggested that he would be able to begin to play his role of big brother. But he still had two months left to have nightmares. This was a matter of reestablishing a correct hierarchy between the boy and the girl.

The second session is slightly more difficult to describe. During much of it I played with the little girl, hiding cushions from her which she had to find. This helped reinforce the reestablishment of the sibling hierarchy and evoked the idea, thanks to the cushions, of keeping things to oneself and hiding them from others. I asked John meanwhile to surprise his mother, to play a joke on her by, for example, telling her, "I met so-and-so" or "There is a skeleton in the closet." The idea was to transform the expectations of the mother into a game for the child. Finally, I asked the father to give a half-hour lesson on playing jokes to his son every day. Also, the paternal grandmother loved practical jokes. This brought the father back into the family by way of an enjoyable interaction and introduced a playful characteristic which the symptom could now reflect.

The third session consisted essentially, on my part, of refusing to believe John could improve. Even nine-year-old boys want to be right and have the therapist be wrong. He was, therefore, obliged to give up his nightmares. And that is exactly what happened.

Erickson has not only renewed the field of clinical hypnosis, but has also made possible a new orientation in family therapy. The significant characteristics are an emphasis on the "here" and "now" of the session, communication on several levels with every member of the family, the activation of potentialities contained in the family system's logic, and the enrichment of the therapist's creativity.

Chapter 26

Family Therapy with Adolescent Sex Offenders

Nancy J. Czech

Nancy Czech, M.A., is a psychotherapist in Seattle, Washington. She teaches and practices family therapy and hypnosis, and consults with local groups about sexual assault and sexual offenders.

Czech provides an account of the difficult work that accompanies treating families of sexual offenders. Common family dynamics are presented. She traces the application of several principles of an Ericksonian approach and provides a case example of her work.

Families where the presenting problem is an adolescent sexual offender present the therapist with multiple challenges. Once a sexual offense has been reported, there is the potential for several state and legal agencies to become involved in the family's life. The involvement of such agencies increases the complexity of the therapeutic task. Additionally, there are many obstacles that must be overcome for successful therapy. These include misconceptions about sex abuse which must be dealt with by both the family and the therapist; the family's reluctance to enter mandated therapy; and long-standing problems within the family in addition to the sexual abuse issues.

The basic principles of Ericksonian psychotherapy provide a structure and philosophy to work with these multiproblem families. This chapter provides a brief description of families where the presenting problem is an adolescent sexual offender, explains the misconceptions surrounding this issue, and illustrates how six Ericksonian principles aid the therapist in working with such families.

Several studies have shown that a significant proportion of all sexual offenses are committed by individuals under the age of 18 (Ageton, 1983; Amir, 1975; Polk et al., 1981). Further, nearly 50 percent of all adults who commit sexual offenses report that one or more offenses occurred during their adolescent years (Groth, Longo & McFadin, 1982).

In 1978, adolescents who committed sexual offenses were identified as a significant treatment population by mental health professionals. This identification led to the establishment of the Juvenile Sexual Offender Program (JSOP) at the Adolescent Clinic, The University of Washington, Seattle, Washington. The JSOP began by evaluating adolescents who had committed sexual offenses and later treated them. Prior to that time only the most violent adolescent sexual offenders were of interest to mental health professionals, the juvenile justice and correctional systems, and the general public.

The focus of this chapter is the use of Ericksonian principles when working with a family where the presenting problem is an adolescent who has committed a sexual offense. A sexual offense is defined as sexually aggressive, nonconsensual behavior that is characterized by the use of force, coercion, or difference in age or size between the adolescent and the victim. The victim may be a person of any age. Sexual offenses can be divided into two categories: hands-off or hands-on offenses. Hands-off cases include exhibitionism, voyeurism, fetishes (e.g., stealing underwear in conjunction with sexual behavior), making sexually obscene phone calls, and writing sexually threatening letters. The hands-on offenses are rape and indecent liberties.

In 1981, I began working at the JSOP, a community-based program for adolescent sexual offenders. The JSOP was founded to evaluate and treat adolescents, ages 12 to 18, who had committed sexual offenses. The majority of these adolescents were males. Their families were referred by juvenile court, agencies serving children, attorneys, school officials, and parents of the victim. The evaluation process included interviews with the adolescent and his family, psychological testing, and collaborative reports from juvenile court, schools, and other agencies that provide treatment and advocate services for victims. The evaluation consisted of determining the risk for repeating a sexual offense and making treatment recommendations. After the evaluation process was completed, many of the families began family therapy at the JSOP. Group therapy for adolescents was used as an adjunct to family therapy. None of the adolescents were self-referred, but they were pressured to complete the evaluation and to continue in therapy by juvenile court, Children's Protective Services, school officials, etc.

MISCONCEPTIONS ABOUT ADOLESCENTS WHO ARE SEXUAL OFFENDERS

There are several misconceptions consistently encountered when one works with adolescent sexual offenders. Typically, the misconceptions are held by the adolescent, his family, mental health agencies, and the juvenile justice system. These misconceptions result in the minimization or denial of the problem. Ultimately this may result in the lack of treatment for the adolescent and his family.

The first misconception is that the adolescent's sexual offense occurred once and will not be repeated. Data collected on a group of sex offenders over a period of 12 years indicate that this is false. Of 240 adolescents under the age of 18, each had committed an average of 6.75 offenses during their adolescence (Abel, Mittelman & Becker, 1984). Of the 297 males referred to JSOP for evaluation, 57.6 percent had committed at least one prior sexual offense (Fehrenbach et al., 1980). Since it is generally accepted that sexual offenses committed by adolescents are significantly underreported, it is likely that the percentages reported above are conservative estimates (Knopp, 1982).

The second misconception is that an adolescent will be stigmatized for life and is more likely to commit additional sexual offenses if his behavior is labeled as sexual abuse (James & Nasjleti, 1983). An example of this is a 16-year-old male who was caught masturbating while watching a female cashier in a store. Instead of being required to complete a thorough assessment, the adolescent was ordered by the juvenile justice department to complete one hour of therapy. Fortunately, he and his family agreed to go beyond the required court-ordered hour and complete the evaluation process. He admitted to peeping and masturbating in public approximately 300 times during a one-year period. Further, he reported having frequent fantasies of raping a woman and said he was afraid he would do so if the opportunity occurred. His legal status was reassessed, and instead of the one hour of therapy, he was sent to a residential facility for intensive treatment.

Another misconception is that "boys will be boys." In our society it is expected that adolescent boys will be preoccupied with sex and that there is no reason to scrutinize or evaluate their sexual behavior. A mother and father tried to convince me that their son had not committed a sexual offense because "All adolescent boys are interested in sex"; therefore, he had just done what all boys want to do, have sexual intercourse with a female. The female was a four-year-old for whom he was babysitting.

The fourth misconception is that the responsibility for the sexual abuse belongs to the victim or the victim's family; it is often said that the victim enticed, coerced, or seduced the sex offender. Sometimes the effect is downplayed. For example, in the presence of his family, a 14-year-old male admitted that he had fondled the genitals of the six-year-old girl that he had been babysitting. The 14-year-old and his family rationalized that the fondling did not have a negative impact on the six-year-old girl because the victim's mother had had two live-in boyfriends since her divorce five years earlier. Moreover, the six-year-old had been exposed to an unusual amount of adult sexual behavior and was accustomed to it.

FAMILY CHARACTERISTICS

The misconceptions described above and the constellation of family characteristics inherent in this population make these families a challenge. The families are usually involved with a number of agencies such as juvenile court, Children's Protective Services (CPS), the Department of Social and Health Services (DSHS) and mental health agencies. The families' histories with other agencies may have started when the sexual offenses were first reported or may have been even more longstanding.

The most pervasive and potentially lethal characteristic is the denial or degree of minimization of the seriousness of the sexual offense and other family problems. One father, whose 12-year-old son had just admitted to sexually abusing his five-year-old sister, claimed that he did not need to be involved in the evaluation or family therapy because he had no problems. He did not consider the incest or his wife's depression and thoughts of suicide to be problems that concerned him. In addition, the families will also minimize the severity of the sexual assault. Typically, a pattern of sexual abuse and/or incest in the family of the offender that spans two to five generations is found.

A generational pattern of social and/or physical isolation is frequently found in the families. Also, the roles of females amd males, both inside and outside of the family, are rigidly defined. This reduces or eliminates the flexibility that is required for families to respond to crises and developmental transitions. Given adequate time in family therapy, other problems related to sexuality will emerge. These problems include: 1) other family members who committed sexual offenses or were the victims of sexual abuse, 2) parents or grandparents with chronic or unresolved sexual concerns, or 3) the identified adolescent having been victimized. This particular combination of characteristics and their degree of severity results in a population that is uniquely difficult to treat. A case example will be used to illustrate the usefulness of Ericksonian principles when working with families where the presenting problem is an adolescent who has committed a sexual offense.

A CASE STUDY

Mrs. Smith had been sexually abused by two of her brothers; she has not maintained contact with her family of origin. Mrs. Smith's eldest child, 15-year-old Kevin, was born out of wedlock. Kevin's biological father has never been involved in Kevin's life, and his whereabouts are unknown. After Kevin was born, Mrs. Smith married her current husband, Mr. Smith. She did not have any information regarding Mr. Smith's family of origin. However, the DSHS record stated that he had grown up in a chaotic, troubled family and that he had spent considerable time in prison between the ages of 14 and 20.

The Smiths have three children: Tom, 14 years old, Anna, 13 years old, and Sara, 9 years old. Eighteen-month-old Linda was conceived about eight months after Mr. Smith was incarcerated for sexually abusing Anna and Sara. Mrs. Smith told her children that Linda's birth was the result of rape. However, Mrs. Smith reported spending the evening drinking in a neighborhood tavern and had asked a man that she did not know to go home with her. Their intercourse was consensual, and Linda was conceived.

At the time of the referral, Kevin had been residing in a youth shelter for the previous five months. He had been charged with raping his half-sisters, Anna and Sara. He was found guilty of raping Sara. Fourteen-year-old Tom had recently been sent to a permanent foster home after numerous incidents of physical abuse by his mother. Mrs. Smith was on probation with court-ordered therapy as a result of the last incident of abusing Tom.

Due to repeated incidents of neglect, as well as physical and sexual abuse, the four oldest children had been wards of the state for the past four years. In order for 13-year-old Anna and nine-year-old Sara to remain at home, family therapy was mandated by DSHS. The local mental health center informed the family and juvenile court that services would not be available because the family had repeatedly not followed through on previous treatment plans. The family had been ordered by the state, at three different levels, to begin family therapy and to continue for a period up to two years. In addition, the family's financial resources were severely limited. Mr. Smith had not contributed financially since his incarceration the previous year; Mrs. Smith had never been employed.

Information gathered during the JSOP evaluation indicated that a series of psychologists, juvenile court officials, CPS workers, adult probation officers, and DSHS case workers had informed the Smiths of their failure as individuals and as a family. In spite of data suggesting failure, incompetence, and the improbability of family change, I believed that family therapy using Ericksonian treatment principles could produce changes in this family.

The first principle used was that each family member made the "best choice possible for themselves at any given moment" (Lankton & Lankton, 1983, p. 12). Use of this principle did not in any way condone the abuse or neglect, it simply meant that I assumed that each family member was doing his or her very best in any given instance and that at times even abuse may have *seemed* the best possible choice. Considering the family history of repeated sexual and physical abuse and neglect, this principle provided a vital foundation, as will be shown, to implement the next principle, that of recognizing and building on the strengths of the family.

The second principle is that "the resources the client needs lie within his or her own personal history" (Lankton & Lankton, 1983, p. 12). When I initiated family therapy with the Smiths, they had been unable to convince any of the other agencies involved that, as a family, they had any resources on which they could rely to improve their family situation. All of the agencies had prescribed rigid schedules and set requirements that had to be met for a period of six months to two years. If the requirements were not met, Mrs. Smith's daughters would be moved to foster homes. Each agency had predicted that the family would be unable to fulfill the prescribed requirements. It was my intent to use the pessimistic stance of the other agencies and institutions to potentiate the Smiths' resources in the context of family therapy. To be more specific, the changes requested and suggested would be considered to be much less aversive than any of the requirements set up by the other agencies.

During therapy, the family presented frequent opportunities to discover ways of using their resources. For example, the first session was loud and chaotic. At one point, a colleague knocked on the door and asked that the session continue at a much quieter level. Mrs. Smith promptly asked me to make nine-year-old Sara stop yelling and leaving the room. By assuming that Mrs. Smith had the resources to become a competent, nonabusing parent, I responded by asking Mrs. Smith how she wanted me to convince Sara to be quieter and to stay in the room. Mrs. Smith then took charge of the matter in one of the only ways in which she was able: she yelled at Sara at the top of her voice, "Shut up and sit down so the lady can talk to us." I was able to emphasize her ability to be effective. During the first interview and for several months thereafter I used every opportunity to ask Mrs. Smith how she wanted to handle each situation. Gradually, Mrs. Smith demonstrated an ability to learn and to use her resources to become more competent as a mother.

"Respect all messages from the client" (Lankton & Lankton, 1983, p. 15) was the third principle. Ritterman (1983) describes this as accepting and respecting a "gift" which the family has to offer. For example, during a family therapy session, 13-year-old Anna told me, "Yuk, you stink." That message was accepted, and I responded to it on the level it was given by saying, "You are right, there is a definite smell in the room." This response also assumed Anna's message had several levels of meaning, including a desire not to be in family therapy. Throughout the course of therapy, every symptom and crisis was regarded as a "gift" from the family. As family therapy with the Smiths continued, my basic respect for the family deepened because of their resilience and sense of humor in the face of chronic and acute family problems.

The fourth principle, "If it's hard work, reduce it down," refers to setting small goals and working gradually toward larger ones (Lankton & Lankton, 1983). This was used on multiple levels. My primary concern was safety within the family. This meant the elimination of sexual and physical abuse and neglect. In addition to the sexual abuse described earlier, there were repeated incidents of physical abuse involving every family member except 18-month-old Linda. There was also a long history of neglect, including medical problems such as scoliosis, bronchitis, and bronchial pneumonia that were often untreated.

Every week for approximately six months, Sara and Anna directly, or more often indirectly, reported incidents of abuse or neglect that had occurred during the past week. After six months, Mrs. Smith began to report the few incidents that continued to occur as "family problems we need to talk about today." One by one the incidents were discussed. It was my intention to simplify each incident of abuse or neglect into components that Mrs. Smith found manageable. Concurrently, my efforts were directed toward finding ways to enhance Mrs. Smith's strengths as a competent parent as well as to challenge ways in which she assumed she was limited or incompetent. Within this framework, limit setting, discipline, increasing independence of the adolescents, appropriate supervision, sexuality, and school attendance and performance were addressed.

Working with the Smiths and the various agencies required significant flexibility on my part. The fifth principle employed was, "The person with the most flexibility will be the controlling element in the system" (Lankton & Lankton, 1983, p. 21). The Smiths' history, the severity of the sexual and physical abuse, and their responses during therapy sessions required considerable flexibility on my part so that change could be promoted within the family.

In spite of the progress the family made, the sessions were chaotic for six months. There was a crisis almost every week. There were also unpredictable moments. For example, there was the time nine-year-old Sara got up during the middle of a session, walked over and stood very close to me, and offered her left arm for inspection, asking, "Do you think these marks are from spider bites or lice or crabs?" I responded verbally and nonverbally with a combination of warmth, humor, concern, and curiosity, "Wait a minute, don't get those bugs on me!" Then Sara's arm was inspected; an appointment with a pediatrician was scheduled and a thorough discussion concerning the condition of their house was initiated. At that point in therapy, Anna's and Sara's responsibilities at home were important, but not as immediately relevant as were the bites on Sara's arm.

The sixth principle used was the recognition of the presence of limitations that therapy could not change (Haley, 1973). It was essential to realize and maintain acceptance of certain situations in the Smith family. Prior to the evaluation, two major decisions had been made. There was no possibility of negotiation or reversal. The first was that the four oldest children would continue to be wards of the state until they were 18. This decision was due to the extent and length of time there had been abuse and neglect in the family. However, it was understood that the children could live at home whenever there was no evidence of abuse and neglect.

The second decision was that Mr. Smith could never live with his daughters due to his long history of sexually abusing Sara and Anna. During the course of therapy, other limitations became obvious. Although Mrs. Smith was able to make great strides in the area of parenting her daughters, she was never able to do the same with either of her sons. Since Tom was in permanent foster care, this factor did not have the same implications as it did with Kevin. Every time plans for Kevin to visit home were carried out, Mrs. Smith became more specific about her limitations. After Kevin had visited home for Thanksgiving, she stated, "I just can't be the mother to boys. I don't know why, but I can't." Mrs. Smith's self-identified limitation was accepted and her request was respected. Instead of working to move 15-year-old Kevin back in with his family, we developed a new goal of finding ways to include Kevin in the family without his living at home.

Family therapy was terminated after 20 months. A definite change in the family situation had resulted. Mrs. Smith had learned to set limits, to discipline, and to supervise her daughters in ways that were age appropriate. All of the children remained in school and their grades markedly improved. Sexuality was an uncomfortable topic, but it was discussed. Family problems were identified, and Mrs. Smith found a part-time job, enjoying the contact with other adults. Kevin was in residential treatment and was scheduled to move into a semi-independent living situation within months.

In a two-year telephone follow up, Mrs. Smith reported both positive and negative information. All of the children had continued to improve in school. Mrs. Smith continued to enjoy her job. There was no evidence of additional sexual or physical abuse nor of medical neglect. However, 17-year-old Anna was two months pregnant. Mrs. Smith described Anna's pregnancy as a situation that she was unhappy about, but she was confident that the family would live through it.

In summary, it is my contention that the use of Ericksonian principles discussed in this chapter provided a way to conceive and conduct effective work with the Smith family. What in the past had been considered failures and limitations became the foundation of optimism and confidence in the family's ability to change.

REFERENCES

Abel, G., Mittelman, M., & Becker, J. (1984). *Sexual Offenders: Results of Assessment and Recommendations for Treatment*. Unpublished manuscript, New York State Psychiatric Institute, Sexual Behavior Clinic.

Ageton, S. (1983). *Sexual Assault Among Adolescents*. Lexington, MA: D.C. Heath.

Amir, M. (1975). *Forcible rape*. In L. Schultz (Ed.), *Rape Victimology*. Springfield, IL: Charles C. Thomas.

Erickson, M., Rossi, E., & Rossi, S. (1976). *Hypnotic Realities: The Introduction of Clinical Hypnosis and Forms of Indirect Suggestion.* New York: Irvington Publishers, Inc.

Fehrenbach, P., Smith, W., Monastersky, C., & Deisher, R. (1980). Adolescent sexual offenders: Offender and offense characteristics. *American Journal of Orthopsychiatry,* 56 (2), 225–233.

Groth, N.A., Longo, R.G., & McFadin, J.B. (1982). Undetected recidivism among rapists and child molesters. *Crime and Delinquency,* 28, 450–458.

James, B., & Nasjleti, M. (1983). *Treating Sexually Abused Children and Their Families.* Palo Alto, CA: Consulting Psychologists Press, Inc.

Haley, J. (1973). *Uncommon Therapy.* New York: W. W. Norton.

Knopp, F. (1982). *Remedial Intervention in Adolescent Sex Offenders: Nine Program Descriptions.* Syracuse, N.Y.: Safer Society Press.

Lankton, S., & Lankton, C. (1983). *The Answer Within: A Clinical Framework of Ericksonian Hypnotherapy.* New York: Brunner/Mazel.

Polk, K. et al. (1981). *Becoming Adults: An Analysis of Maturational Development from Age 16 to 30 of a Cohort of Young Men.* Final report of the Marion County Youth Study, University of Oregon, Eugene.

Ritterman, M. (1983). *Using Hypnosis in Family Therapy.* San Francisco: Jossey-Bass.

SECTION TWO: PRACTICE

PART X

Training with Erickson

Chapter 27

Reflections on Training by Erickson: The Mirror Within

Betty Alice Erickson Elliott

Betty Alice Erickson Elliott, Ed.D. Cand. (East Texas State University), reminds us that the behind-the-mirror team approach used to train psychotherapists has the benefit of objectivity and input from a number of observers. She describes how her father, Milton Erickson, had a utilization approach that harnessed some of the power of the team without relying on the technology of the observation room. New case descriptions shed light on Erickson's resourceful and perceptive approach.

I am Betty Alice Erickson Elliott, the fourth child of Milton H. Erickson. For purposes of clarity in this chapter, I will refer to my father as Erickson.

I am at this time a doctoral student in Counseling Psychology at East Texas State University. As such, I have spent many hours in front of the one-way mirror with my own clients, being watched and critiqued. There have been even more hours spent behind the mirror in the observation room, watching others work with their clients. I have also watched video tapes of my fellow students, of my instructors, and of myself, as well as tapes of such well-known clinicians as Rogers, Minuchin and Haley. Each of the tapes is fast-forwarded, freeze-framed, rolled backwards, and then replayed for second looks to discover new subtleties.

Not only am I trained with the advantages of the television camera and the replaying of an instant in time, but I have feedback from the team, a group of doctoral students and instructors behind the one-way mirror in the observation room of the clinic. We observe and talk among ourselves, discussing our hypotheses. We have the advantage of several other minds, each thinking differently, each with different perspectives and backgrounds, the combination of which is a multiplication of our individual abilities. Each team member is an integral part of the suggestions and thoughts that emerge.

When I am in front of the mirror, the team can call in to me by telephone, pointing out nuances I might have missed, suggesting directions and structuring interventions and homework. The team concept benefits therapists on both sides of the mirror by enhancing opportunities for learning. It enriches the client's environment as well. The proper use of a team and a one-way mirror can be invaluable in training. This approach has become so common and well-accepted that many universities include several semesters of behind-the-mirror training as part of their standard curriculum. Many institutes also use this approach and offer courses of training lasting from a few days to several months.

As I have gone through my schooling, I have wondered about the way Milton Erickson trained people. His training of others was successful—many can attest to that. At the time of his death, sessions in the "little house" were booked for almost a year ahead and would have been scheduled even further ahead except that his wife, Elizabeth, refused to do so.

And yet Erickson never used a one-way mirror. He did not have a team to call in suggestions. He didn't regularly test different hypotheses. Erickson never shied from new learnings. For him to reject the benefits of a team approach seems incongruous with his delight in trying new things. I would like to suggest that Erickson did, in fact, use many of the facets of a team. But as he did everything, he did it in his own way.

Upon examining the functions and benefits of a team, one can see that it does the following:

First, it gives a wide range of viewpoints. It provides multiples of realities, an overlapping of observations. A team has a cumulative wisdom enabling it to communicate in the reality most meaningful to the client.

A team provides for flexibility in approach. Because of its heterogeneity, it can move from one tactic to another. In a single session, a team can invite the therapist and the client to behave in a variety of ways and can share differing and different views.

With a team, objectivity is a more easily attainable goal. Despite some current views that objectivity is unattainable, most of us eschew the philosophical problem and attempt to deal in a world upon which we can agree. For want of a better term, that is referred to as "objectivity." A team of people can balance individual biases and skewed perceptions with those of other team members.

Erickson took the definitions of what the team does and then created his own team, using what was available to him—what is available to any practitioner. In his training sessions, he would tell and show his students how he used all the components without actually having them there.

He would use the client as the oppositional team member. One example is that of the woman who had had her stomach pain diagnosed as ulcers. She came to Erickson demanding to be freed of the pain. A nurse, she dominated everyone and everything; she had repeatedly lost jobs because she insisted on dictating to doctors as well as to the hospital administration. She ordered Erickson to hypnotize her and rid her of her ulcer. She said she knew he could do it, so he was to do it right then and there. She crossed her arms over her chest and waited.

Erickson told her that she could go into a light trance anytime she wanted; she was not the type of client a therapist would "put" into a trance. When she indicated that she was in a trance, Erickson burst into laughter. He chuckled and smiled and then laughed some more. The patient became openly angry. Finally, he stopped, and the patient naturally demanded to know why he had been laughing. Erickson gently explained that now she was in a position where *she* was going to be dictated to and she was going to be dictated to by her stomach whether she liked it or not. Immediately, the patient took the opposing view. She was *not* going to be dictated to and certainly not by her stomach! She began to plan ways in which she could control her ulcer. Before the sessions were terminated, Erickson and the patient had formulated and implemented plans for her; she soon brought the ulcer under control and suffered no more from pain despite her continuing to enjoy her favorite spicy foods. Now, one might say that Erickson merely utilized the resistance he knew this patient would show. Or one might say that he assessed her personality and modus operandi and used that knowledge to put the control of her well-being into a form compatible with her established behavior. I think it was all this and more.

After the woman went into a trance, she was given a new way of looking at what was happening. The trance helped her to hear and accept what was happening; it helped her to accept new information and receive it merely as a different perspective. It was a non-threatening, different point of view much as a team's different perspective is merely new information. It was pointless to argue with the new idea much as it is pointless to disagree with the ideas that a team sends in: The team doesn't really care whether or not the client agrees; the members are merely making an observation.

Erickson's amusement facilitated the intervention by focusing the client's attention on the absurdity of being dictated to *by a part of herself* in a way she didn't want. And like the team's new information, it was presented to her in a casual, almost take-it-or-leave-it manner.

Then she was presented with a challenge, unspoken but clearly a challenge, in much the same way that an oppositional team member will send in an addendum to an intervention designed to meet a particular goal. The intervention the patient wanted was that her ulcers be brought under control. The addendum was a "look at the fix you've got yourself into and you're stuck and I bet you can't get out of it." The challenge was by herself and to herself; the opposition was in herself and therefore could be defeated.

Erickson used the patient's own unrealized creativity to spur the patient. Like the creativity generated by a team and sent into the therapist, Erickson cared not from where it came nor did he try to become overly involved. He would set the stage and let the patient deliver the creative intervention to himself. Erickson would watch with real interest and complete confidence in the ability of this "other" member of his team, sure that the goal would be met.

Example: I used to be fearful of dentists, dental offices, dental examinations, and anything to do with sitting in a chair and opening my mouth for clinical inspection. Reality didn't matter; I had never had a dentist really hurt me, and I had had very little dental work done. Trembling knees, a rapidly beating heart, occasional fainting, and hours of concentrated pre-visit dread were certainly annoyances but evidently ones with which I was willing to live. Once I had children, however, it became a different matter. It was one thing for me to dread and tremble, but quite another for *them* to learn from me that way to behave. I was not willing to teach them that fear. So I told Erickson that I wanted to stop being afraid of the dentist.

He questioned me about the sincerity of my motives. I had been afraid, don't forget, for many years and had never before expressed a desire to rid myself of that fear. When he was convinced that I was indeed motivated, he told me he could cure me. No longer would I faint or even worry that I would faint. I might not enjoy visiting the dentist, but I wouldn't fear it and I certainly wouldn't pass any fear along to my children. I was all ears. He assured me repeatedly that if I did what he was going to suggest, I would overcome my fear. When I got so that I could hardly wait, he revealed the intervention. I was to make a sign and hang it around my neck. The sign was to say, "I faint at the dentist's office." Erickson told me that he would even call the dentist's office and enlist the cooperation of everyone there. He would get permission for me to sit in the waiting room all day, and he would even instruct the receptionist that if I did faint, she was to ignore me and to insist to the waiting patients that they also leave me alone. If I did this, he said, he would absolutely guarantee that I would overcome my fears in just a few sessions.

I was horrified! I would not for any reason, then or now, sit in a public, or even semi-public, place with a sign around my neck. Period. When I told him that, he just smiled. "Well," he said, "I've given you a way to overcome your fear and take care of your children, and you've turned it down." The conversation was over despite my best efforts to continue it.

I had two apparent and three real choices. I could continue being fearful, which I didn't want to do, or I could make a public spectacle of myself, which I wouldn't do. Or, the unspoken alternative—I could solve the problem myself. So I did. I don't know how. Years later when I was talking to him about it, I asked him how I had solved it. He didn't know either and he wasn't even very interested. He just knew that I had within me the ability to solve it, and he had provided me with two unpleasant and unwanted alternatives or the choice of using my own untapped ability.

Sidney Rosen (1982) says that story telling is an ancient art which can transmit moral and cultural values as well as giving instruction and guidance. Therapeutic suggestions can be woven into a story which hardly seems related to the problem at hand. Erickson was famed for his stories and for the powerful interventions carefully layered within. His stories could be heard on several levels and in several ways. He not only could give new ideas and expand horizons with his anecdotes, but he could convey any number of different possibilities for any given situation—just like a team of colleagues does. They can construct a possible reality that includes that already held by the client by using several ideas and interventions.

Some of Erickson's favorite stories are recounted in Rosen's book

(1982). In storytelling, Erickson would present different ways of expanding mind sets. In training his students, he often would begin by illustrating how we limit ourselves. "How many ways are there to get from this room to the one behind me?" he would ask. The students would struggle. Walk. Walk backwards. Hop, crawl or jump. A person could walk on his knees. One brave soul might say, "Walk out this door and in that door." Then the group would stop. How many ways are there? Walk around the house; tunnel underground; sit in the wheelchair with Erickson and have someone push both of you; climb out the window, walk on the roof, jump down and climb in the other window. You could even ride piggyback. Or hire a balloon to pick you up at this door, lift you high in the sky, move you over a few feet, and then gently settle you down next to the other way in. Erickson would go on and on with his examples, metaphors in themselves, and usually end with his favorite: You could step outside, catch a taxi, ride to the airport, purchase your ticket and fly around the world from Pheonix to Honolulu to Hong Kong, Rome, New York, Dallas and Pheonix. Then you could hire a taxi, drive to the house, and walk in the back door of the other room. During his recital of the different ways, students often would slip into trance, aided by their expectations as well as by Erickson's voice repeating over and over, "or you could, or you could, or you might. . . ." As some of you may have noticed, boredom, especially boredom suffered as a captive audience, is an excellent method by which trance can be induced. In trance, minds open to new ways of thinking; what could be perceived in the waking state as frivolous or impossible is considered literally in trance, examined, and then perhaps absorbed.

By using such mind puzzles, Erickson would begin to incorporate in his students the idea that their unconscious and their new ways of thinking would expand new abilities within themselves—multileveled, multireferenced and multioriginated. He taught students by example as well as by direct instruction how to construct internally some of the benefits of a team without actually having a team present.

One of the biggest benefits of training with a team and a one-way mirror is the enhanced powers of observation. While I, or any other therapist, am devoting my attention to one set of circumstances, the team has the freedom to observe in many directions. Erickson observed. He paid attention. He watched; he listened; he focused intense energy on what to most of us is simple and casual. He observed the whole person as well as the parts. He watched as people came into his office, how they sat down, the positions of their bodies, the tilts of their heads, the movements of their hands, the clothing they had chosen, the shoes they wore. He would also look carefully at the more subtle signs: How fast were they breathing? Were the pupils of their eyes dilated? Were they dilated equally? Erickson believed that in order to understand the unusual, first the usual must be understood. So he observed everyone—always and all ways.

He would demonstrate to his students the power of observation by weaving into the teaching for the day bits and pieces about each of them. There is an old story of the medical school instructor who dips his index finger into a beaker of urine and then puts his middle finger in his mouth to "taste." He then invites his students to do the same. Of course, each student dips his forefinger into the urine and then, with a shudder, puts that finger into his mouth. Sometimes I think that story originated with Erickson.

Havens (1985) describes how Erickson led a group of interns to a patient's room while telling them that this was to be an exercise in sharpening their observational skills. Erickson asked the interns to observe the patient silently, and without touching her, until they could come up with a possible diagnosis. I have heard this story from the time I was a little girl. Erickson told me that when he would lead the interns to the patient's bed, he would talk, for instance, about diseases of the lung. He would stand by the patient's head and look at her face and chest as he reminded them not to forget to notice the rate of her breathing and to listen carefully as she inhaled and exhaled. Could they notice any distinctive odor on her breath? He would go on and on, making his voice husky, even giving a cough or two. It's no wonder that none of the interns looked past the woman's chest. It's no wonder that none of them saw that the patient had had her leg amputated mid-thigh and that that, obviously, was the reason for her hospitalization. And it's no wonder that he used that story to emphasize the importance of observation. Observation must be open-minded and unfettered by misleading communications and misdirections, intentional or unintentional. Observation is not true observation when it is focused on a part to the exclusion of the whole.

Teaching others to observe is difficult. We all have our mindsets and assumptions; we all see through the spectacles of our past. In Erickson's speeches, lectures and writings, he emphasized again and again the importance of practice in observing. He never tired of making guesses about people and their behaviors based on his observations, and then waiting and watching to see if he was correct. He would tell story after story, giving the clues gleaned from his observations and then telling the conclusion so that the listeners could see just what cues they had missed. He would watch a man sitting on a bus, passing an apple orchard, looking out the window, his eyes moving over each row, his lips moving. Then he struck up a conversation with the man. Here was a farmer calculating the harvest from the trees—not for any purpose but because it was second nature.

I remember another example he loved. In an airport, a tired young mother with a babe in arms and an active three-year-old were seated next to Erickson; all of them were waiting for their flights. The little girl had spotted a doll in the gift shop window that she obviously wanted. Her eyes fixed on it, she looked at her mother, then back at the doll, and then she stood and thought. Now, how do you suppose she got the doll? This little girl was very smart. "I want a drink," she said, and tugged her mother to her feet. Off they went, with the little girl leading, on their way to the drinking fountain, in the opposite direction from the gift shop. The little girl stopped to look at interesting cracks on the plastered walls; she examined spots on the floor; she stood still peering in the ashtrays; she kicked the trash cans; and she paused to gaze at every interesting sign or poster along the way. Her mother trudged behind, carrying the baby and lugging her load of purse, hand luggage and diaper bag, weary and exhausted. The little girl had to be lifted to the fountain for her drink. Then they started their long journey circling back around the lobby. Of course, they passed in front of the gift shop window. The little girl slowed down and looked at the doll with interest. Then she started to walk on. It was a big lobby and there were a lot of interesting things to look at and trash cans to kick. As the mother passed the window, she saw the doll, and suddenly she had an idea. The little girl got her new doll, the mother got her rest, and Erickson got another example from his observations about how any of us can apply creative thinking to reach a goal.

He would ask his students: How can you plant ten cactus plants in five rows of four each? Actually, they had all seen such an arrangement as they came in. Yet they hadn't seen and Erickson wouldn't tell them. Some of them would go for days never seeing the arrangement at the front door.

He used the environment around him, his students and his patients in much the same way a therapist can use a team to provide differing realities to a client. To carry the comparison one step further, team members grow and learn from their experiences with the client as the client benefits from the team. The environment around Erickson was usually enriched by its interactions with the patient as the patient was also being enriched. His family was part of that environment. While a patient who did not have the funds to pay for therapy mulched our back yard, trading work for services received, we children were sent out to help him. We learned from him how to mulch a yard. He learned from our interactions with him that he was a worthy person and a teacher, and that he knew far more about some things than many other people. By accepting us as helpers, he accepted himself as a role model with all the implications of those words. When the yard was finished and we children cheered, delighted that the hard work was over, he saw another way of looking at completion. Completion and letting go could be a glorious thing, a time for rejoicing. This patient continued to visit us for years, even after he was no longer a patient, to check on our care of *his* yard, learning from the growth of that yard that a finishing can be a continuing. This was a new reality for him, overlapping and expanding both his former reality and the one presented by Erickson's own team.

As Erickson worked with his students, he would incorporate the environment to give them messages that they could interpret and accept in ways which suited them best, much as a team delivers messages in different ways to the client so that the one which fits best can be accepted. Many students climbed Squaw Peak at his direction. It meant different things to different people. Erickson usually framed it so that it meant whatever the student needed or wanted it to mean. There was a different reality for each.

He used his cacti and the plants in the yard as another voice of what I call his team. A night-blooming cereus blossom would be carefully saved in a bowl of water so that it could be shown to all. The plant blooming so seldomly, the flower so fragile, yet the beauty so intense . . . think of the different interpretations each of us can take from so rare, yet so common, an event. Erickson showed these blossoms as one might show a treasure. Most of his students had never seen any flower of any cactus, let alone a flower from a night-blooming cereus. The uniqueness of the experience, the anticipation that Erickson had that everyone would not only enjoy the beauty, but would realize the metaphor of the seldom-seen, unique and common beauty which is found and can be cherished in the most unusual places, I see as other voices that Erickson used and incorporated into his teaching.

The dogs Erickson always had were a part of his environment, too.

They were another "voice" of his team, and theirs were voices of simple honesty and earnestness. The dogs never wanted to be anything but dogs, content with their lot and joyful at the pleasures that came their way. I know Erickson used that analogy; I heard him more than once.

He also used his Basset hound, Roger Drasset, as a particular voice. Roger wrote letters to various people who studied with Erickson.* Some of the things which Roger advised or suggested were ideas about which Erickson claimed no knowledge and for which he certainly took no responsibility. Erickson could deliver whatever message he chose this way, yet in a way once removed—just as a team suggests a message or an intervention and the therapist, once removed, merely delivers it. Sometimes Erickson would remove himself even a step further: He would send letters from Roger to the other person's dog. Roger would explain that he felt a great kinship with the receiver. Yes, the other dog would sometimes reply, and then the two would carry on a great and lengthy correspondence. These letters would carry a great deal of fun and good humor; they could also carry a great deal of information. They were multilevel messages just as the several voices of a team are multilevel communications.

Roger was such an effective medium that even after his death at the ripe old age of almost 14, Erickson continued to use him. Then, however, the letters were signed "Ghost Roger." Ghost Roger resided, Erickson insisted, in The Great Bone Yard Up Yonder. Erickson was never one to let change hamper him; he always used it. As Ghost Roger in The Great Bone Yard Up Yonder he was an even more effective messenger. Think of the new vistas that being a ghost would open!

It would not be complete to discuss Erickson's way of training without talking about his abilities with and his uses of hypnosis. So much of what he did in his work with patients and students was part and parcel of hypnosis. Perhaps because of his long experience with hypnosis, Erickson used trance and his ability with hypnosis in almost every part of his work. He said that at times he didn't even know when he went into a trance. Neither did his students know when they were in a trance. Listening to the master, they would slip into a trance readily in response to the cadence of Erickson's voice, the expectant pauses, the choice of words with their messages and instructions embedded on multiple levels, the open-ended suggestions and phrases, and, far from

---

Editor's Note. For an example of Erickson corresponding through a dog, see *Experiencing Erickson* by J.K. Zeig (Brunner/Mazel, 1985).

least, the attitudes of the listeners that they would. It is beyond the scope of this chapter to analyze Erickson's abilities with hypnosis and the role these played in his therapy and teaching. Hypnosis and the mechanics of it were so much a part of him that it is difficult to separate Erickson from them. Hypnosis helped him in his observations which were basic keys to his therapy and teaching. It helped him structure stories and metaphors which would be the most meaningful to the listener and also helped him open his mind and creativity—no thought was too outlandish, all had to be considered—and it certainly helped him in the use of his voice and choice of words.

Erickson never let an opportunity pass that could be used in the instruction of his patients or his students. One of his students, Bob Gold, is now an instructor of mine at East Texas. I see so much of Erickson in him. He instructs in an indirect manner. He tells stories from which we may pluck a brick or two fitting the house we're constructing. When I told him that I could see Erickson in him, he said that, while Erickson was a great therapist, a master of hypnosis, and a consummate communicator, mastery of teaching was Erickson's greatest gift. Erickson taught everyone. Simply being in his presence gave him license to teach; all communication to him was an opportunity to instruct.

The way Erickson autographed books is an example. He would write a message that was personal, yet instructive and meaningful to the book's owner. One of my sons, Michael, has a streak of devil-may-care, "never mind tomorrow" in his personality. When we were living in Ethiopia, he raised pigeons. Shortly before our departure from that country, I reminded Michael that he must make plans to care for the fledglings; the adults could just be set free if necessary. It was all taken care of, he told me. He had no fledglings. Didn't I remember, he asked, how he had started eating pigeon eggs for breakfast a couple of months ago? Well, those would have been the birds who would have been fledglings when we left. I was astonished; Erickson was amused and pleased when I told him the story. One of Michael's books is autographed: "To Michael, whose brilliant and practical foresight was first manifested by eating pigeon eggs for months in anticipation of his departure from Addis Ababa." "First manifested." "Anticipation." Every word was chosen to be meaningful and rewarding to Michael; he has cherished and quoted this, the first of many recognitions of his foresight. Nobody knows how much encouragement that inscription has given him to this day.

My daughter is adopted; she is Vietnamese. Some of his inscriptions to her in her books refer to her as his gingerbread girl. Kim has always been a sweet yet spicy gingerbread girl in her mind and her dark skin proves it.

One of the most significant aspects of Erickson's teaching was his frequent references to the future. Sometimes the future was implied indirectly and references to it not stated openly; sometimes he spoke of it clearly. He believed and expected that the person would not only learn but would also have the capabilities to grow and to expand in a productive enjoyment of life.

It's easy for a team to inject the future in its messages to the client. Less personally involved, they have the freedom to survey a wider area that can include the future.

Erickson was raised on a farm and had a deep respect for the ability of sown seeds to sprout and grow, amazing all with the finished product. It isn't necessary to know how the seed interacted with the soil, water, fertilizer, and sun in order to appreciate and use the results. All seeds don't grow to maturity; wise farmers realize that. Nevertheless, the seeds continue to be sown, and sometimes even the farmer is pleasantly surprised by the fertility, and pleased by the fruits of the sowing. He trusts that the sun will rise, some rain will fall, and crops will grow.

Erickson's training of students took on a greater importance during his later years. Having limited and then finally eliminated his practice, he expended his energies on his students and, I think, a building of the future.

The training he gave was unique. By definition, however, the training that each of us receives is unique. Erickson used what was available to him, no more, no less. We each have what is available to us, no more, no less. He was able to access it and use it. We can do the same. Our training, while different, of course, from that offered by Erickson, encompasses much of the same territory. We each have a team within us and around us. Creativity is not limited; it is within us all.

REFERENCES

Havens, R. (1985). *The Wisdom of Milton H. Erickson.* New York: Irvington.
Rosen, S. (1982). *My Voice Will Go With You: The Teaching Tales of Milton H. Erickson.* New York: Norton.

Chapter 28

Modeling and Role-Modeling: Ericksonian Techniques Applied to Physiological Problems

Helen L. Erickson

Helen L. Erickson, Ph.D. (University of Michigan), is affiliated with the College of Nursing of the University of South Carolina in Columbia, South Carolina. Formerly, she was Assistant Professor of Nursing at the University of Michigan School of Nursing. She is the recipient of awards for teaching and excellence in nursing and is the co-author of Modeling and Role-Modeling: A Theory and Paradigm for Nursing.

Dr. Helen Erickson describes the personalized, utilization approach that she learned from her father-in-law, Milton H. Erickson. A practicing nurse and educator, her approach demonstrates that patients can access vast, often hidden, mental resources that can influence growth-directed physiological processes.

THE BACKGROUND STORY

About 30 years ago I waited anxiously in the lobby of a hotel in Detroit, hoping that I might be able to identify Dr. and Mrs. Erickson in the crowd of people that had gathered for a conference sponsored by the American Society for Clinical Hypnosis. It was late in the evening; I had arrived an hour or so earlier following instructions from my fiancé, Lance Erickson. He had called my residence hall and left a message for me to take the first possible bus to Detroit and go directly to the hotel where we were to meet so that I could be introduced to his parents.

As a 20-year-old woman from a small town in north-central Michigan, I found the mechanics of finding my way around the "big city" a challenge. Nevertheless, I located the hotel without difficulty, but soon learned that Lance would not arrive until the following day. After a few moments of panic, I decided that I would have to introduce myself that evening. As I waited and watched people go by, I observed each individual hoping that I could identify Dr. and Mrs. Erickson from pictures Lance had shown me earlier. When I spotted them across the lobby, I felt a strange mixture of relief and tension. I approached them hesitantly, introduced myself, and waited anxiously for their response.

Mrs. Erickson immediately responded with a big smile, and a warm welcome. Dr. Erickson focused his eyes on mine and then, in a very deep voice, stated, "Oh, yes," while he reached out, took my right wrist, lifted it to chest level and said, "There, isn't that comfortable?" Needless to say, I was very surprised and immediately in a trance. I remember Mrs. Erickson saying something like, "Not now, Milton, let her take her time," and Dr. Erickson saying, "Alright, Betty," as he proceeded to point out to me that a man coming across the lobby probably had suffered through the 1918 flu epidemic. When I asked if they were acquainted, he said no, but he could tell by the way the man walked and the way he carried his body. He said that there are so many things that we can tell about people if we would just observe them carefully—that we can learn about physical problems as they relate to the body and to the mind, as well as emotional problems as they relate to the body. He then reached out, lowered my wrist, and told me to go to my room, rest well, and we would meet in the morning.

The next few days were very exciting. I learned a great deal about "The Erickson Approach." Most important, I learned that there were inseparable mind-body relationships, and that these relationships would empower my practice as a nurse. I also learned that "The Erickson Approach" meant being creative and using one's own resources to help others use theirs.

When I returned to Saginaw General Hospital, I started practicing what I had learned. I was assigned to two women scheduled for hysterectomies the following day. Most women who had hysterectomies in the 50s had difficulty voiding postoperatively. In fact, the problem was so great that there were standard orders to catheterize if the patient had not voided within four hours postoperatively. Nearly every woman was catheterized; many had to be treated for secondary bladder infections. It seemed to me so simple: If an indirect suggestion could help them to void, then maybe catheterization and secondary complications could be avoided.

The night before surgery I went to the bedside of each patient and prepared her skin for surgery by shaving and cleansing. I talked with each about postop recovery—coughing, ambulation, and so forth. Then, as I rubbed the back of the first, I quietly leaned down and told her that she could "relax, completely relax, breathe in and out regularly, and as you do, you will know that tomorrow you will be able to relax when I rub your back and you will know that rivers run easily without resistance and you can enjoy an easy flowing river." As I rubbed the back of the second patient, I said nothing.

The following day both patients went off to surgery. Neither had difficulty in surgery. After a few hours of routine postoperative care, I approached the first patient, rubbed her back, and quietly stated that she might remember how she had been able to completely relax the evening before, and that she might want to do that again now. I instructed her to relax, starting with her face and continuing down her torso as I continued to rub her back and periodically suggested that she breathe in deeply and blow out deeply. As I finished, I asked her if there was anything that I might be able to do to help her. I was delighted when she said she wanted the bedpan, that she needed to urinate. I was even more pleased when she proceeded to do so without difficulty. Although I rubbed the back of the second patient and made the same statements to her, this second patient had to be catheterized. Interestingly, the first patient commented later on the value of learning how to relax and stated that she was sure that it had helped her get through a difficult experience!

During the next several years I often tried various techniques with my patients. Sometimes I was successful, sometimes not. Often when I tried to identify specific factors that might serve as predictors for success, I would ask Dr. Erickson what I might do that would be most helpful. He would often reply with a story that demonstrated the need to fully understand the patient's unique perception of the situation, coupled with new evidence that mind-body relationships existed. In the later years he often would say, "Model and role-model. That's all that you have to do." The more I asked for specific details, the more I was told to consider the individual's situation and to understand people holistically. He offered many suggestions that enabled me to do this and repeatedly encouraged any initiative that I showed. Often he would help me gain insight by commenting on the behaviors of our children or by telling stories about clients. Other times, he would mention such things as Maslow's peak experiences or Erikson's developmental stages. Nevertheless, it took me nearly 15 years to gain a conscious awareness of what he had patiently, bit by bit, tried to teach me. Slowly but surely I was able to aggregate and synthesize what I had learned through the years.

My first attempt to put a language to my understanding was in the early 70s when I developed the adaptive-potential model (Erickson, 1976; Erickson & Swain, 1982). This model was developed in an effort to more clearly specify an individual's ability to mobilize resources needed to contend with stressors. Since I had become familiar with the holistic nature of people, this model was a snythesis of the work of a biophysiologist (Hans Selye) and a psychologist (George Engel). When I sent my manuscript to Dr Erickson, he reinforced his hypnotic suggestion of the 50s by telling me that "knowing" that mind-body relationships existed was important. I was also told that I should continue to work on these thoughts. An earlier indirect suggestion had now become an overt embedded command! I was hooked, and I loved it!

The approach that I purposefully use today was a natural outcome of those repeated lessons. While my practice occasionally includes patients that have apparent psychological or mental health problems, the majority of my clientele are individuals who have either physio-psychological or psychophysiological problems. The rest of this chapter will provide a synopsis of the Modeling and Role-Modeling paradigm (Erickson, H., Tomlin, E., & Swain, M. A., 1983) and related philosophical assumptions. Following this will be a general discussion of therapeutic issues and a few select cases that I have treated using this approach.

PHILOSOPHICAL ASSUMPTIONS

There are several basic assumptions that relate to the practice of Modeling and Role-Modeling that warrant discussion. The first set of assumptions relates to the nature of people in general. The second set relates to the role of the practitioner.

Nature of People

People experience stressors as a part of everyday life. Their ability to mobilize resources will determine their ability to adapt or contend with stressors. Numerous factors determine an individual's ability to mobilize resources. For example, it is possible that resources needed to contend with the stressors simply are nonexistent. It is equally possible that resources exist, but are compartmentalized in such a way that it is difficult or impossible for the individual to access them. Under these circumstances, the therapist uses techniques that will "unfreeze" or adapt the resources so that they match the identified stressors. Generally speaking, when individuals perceive that stressors are challenging, they are able to mobilize some appropriate resources. On the other hand, when stressors are perceived as threatening, there is greater difficulty in mobilizing appropriate resources. However, since the human organism is extremely resourceful, people often mobilize secondary resources in order to maintain some degree of equilibrium in the whole of the biophysical-psychosocial self. Unfortunately, when resources don't exist or are compartmentalized in a way that they are not available for use, then the self may overtax the physical system in order to maintain a sense of equilibrium in the whole. Thus, there is the proverbial headache due to too much stress, the tight throat because of feeling sad, the onset of a "bad cold" because of one too many arguments with the spouse, or the heart attack because of too much pressure at work.

A second belief is that people are holistic, rather than wholistic. Holism implies that the total is *greater than* the sum of the parts and that there are interactions among the subsystems whereas in wholism there is the connotation that the total is *equal to* the sum of the parts, and that interactions among the subsystems do not necessarily exist. Holistically, stressors related to a psychological or social subsystem may cause added symptoms of stress in that subsystem or may result in new symptoms in other areas. Thus, physical problems such as hypertension or coronary infarcts can be related to psychological stressors. When treating persons from a wholistic perspective, mind-body relations are neither expected nor considered on a routine basis.

Mind-body relations can be understood from a wide range of perspectives. From the broadest view one might use as an example the individual who has a sudden outburst of anger followed by a coronary infarct, or the person who becomes very depressed following the onset of a physical illness. From a more limited viewpoint, one can consider the relationships described in the current psychoneuroendocrine literature. This later view takes into consideration the hypothalamus-pituitary-adrenal axes, including the affect and effect of psychosocial stressors on these biological responses. These relationships were described and expanded upon by Rossi (1986) when he illustrated the possible linkage between psychosocial stressors and the DNA/RNA recombinant mechanisms of cell reproduction. These linkages also demonstrate the depth of the problem.

Another assumption inherent in the Modeling and Role-Modeling approach is that people have an inherent need to be associated with others, while they simultaneously have an inherent need to maintain individuality and seek self-actualization. This drive for affiliated individuation is related to needs that are innate and instinctual, needs that cross the life span and drive behavior. As needs are repeatedly met, attachment occurs to the object meeting those needs, resources are developed, and growth follows. Real, threatened, or perceived loss of the attachment object can interfere with need satisfaction and growth.

A final basic assumption is that people go through patterned, sequential developmental stages across the life span. Each stage can be described by specific developmental tasks and associated life crises (Erikson, 1963). Continuous growth is necessary for development to occur. When growth is impeded by unavailable, inadequate or inappropriate resources, the outcome of the developmental crisis leaves the individual with a residual that impedes further growth. While individuals have the same type of needs across the life span, the way that these needs are satisfied is dependent upon the developmental task related to the unmet needs. Since the developmental process is both time-related and dependent upon satisfying needs, it is possible that patients will experience stressors that are related to the chronological, age-related task at the same time that they experience stressors related to tasks from a much earlier developmental stage.

Role of Practitioner

The concept of modeling requires that the practitioner step into the world of the patient, build a model or image of that world, and interpret that world within some context. Role-Modeling is the planning and implementing of interventions that help the patient mobilize or build resources needed to grow and to move to a higher level of health and development. Role-Modeling is always contingent upon the practitioner's modeling the patient's world and planning interventions that match the patient's unique model and needs.

Inherent in this approach is the assumption that the practitioner's major responsibility is to facilitate individuals in mobilizing or building their own resources. It is not assumed that the practitioner has control over these processes. (An analogy may be seen in the method that Erickson used in helping individual practitioners develop their own special approaches.) Planned interventions are based on an assessment of the individual's needs, developmental residue, object relationships, and ability to mobilize coping resources. Strategies used in the Modeling and Role-Modeling approach are similar to those described by numerous others advocating the Erickson approach. These include pacing and leading, use of indirect suggestions, embedded commands, and reframing.

CASE REPORTS

Case I: Mrs. A.

As I walked down the hall of a medical-surgical unit of a large midwest teaching hospital, I heard a strange chanting sound coming from a nearby room. Entering the room, I noted that the curtains were drawn and the room was barren of personal objects. The patient was lying flat in bed with the sheet pulled up to her nose. The medical diagnosis for this 59-year-old lady was "Headaches of unknown origin." Admitted for medical workup and diagnosis, she had been in excellent health until approximately five months before when she experienced an insidious onset of headaches that were now incapacitating. She had been married for 36 years, had three healthy children, and her relationship with her husband was positive. She was active in the community and in her church. In essence, she was a healthy woman except for her disabling headaches. She had been hospitalized for three days. Several tests had been run, but nothing had been found. In the meantime, she was receiving Empirin and codeine every four hours, without much effect. The nurses on the unit had suggested that this lady might need a psychiatric consultant, but were advised that she was a healthy woman who needed only to have her headaches treated.

I noticed as I approached her bed that her chanting tones reminded me of someone in a deep grieving process, someone trying to console herself. While her chant lacked coherence, there was rhythm, tone, and volume attached to the words that symbolized deep pain. I asked where her pain came from. She immediately told me that it came from the wall at the foot of her bed, and that the pain entered her feet, moved up her legs, circled several times in her lower abdomen, proceeded up her body, and settled in her right temporal area. I then asked her why that pain came from the wall. She launched into a description of her life during World War II, stating that she had been in a German concentration camp where her parents and siblings had been killed. She had been forced to walk over their bodies. Later she was raped. When she got pregnant, she used self-inflicted methods to cause an abortion. After telling me about the abortion, she reverted to her chanting and pulled the sheet back up over her mouth.

I stated that she had suffered long enough and it was now time for her to find a way to enjoy her life, children, grandchildren, and all living loved ones. I then asked her if she would like to give her headaches away. First she said yes, she'd give them to the ambulance driver because he had driven too fast and hit too many bumps, making her headache worse. But then she withdrew that statement, saying that this would be unfair since he hadn't meant to hurt her. Noting her need to maintain control over her symptom, I suggested that rather than give her headaches away, she place them in a small square space that I had marked out on the bulletin board at the foot of her bed. I suggested that she would probably want to leave them there for 23 or 23½ hours of the day. The rest of the day she could decide what she wanted to do with them. I then suggested that she take a short nap, and that she would rest well, and awaken feeling rested.

During the next few days, this lady underwent several additional tests to diagnosis the source of her headaches. Interestingly, the headaches seemed to disappear with the exception of late afternoon. She would call for her medication and be quite uncomfortable for 30–45 minutes, but would be fine the rest of the time. The day of discharge, her physicians were trying to explain that they had been unable to diagnose her problem, but it didn't matter since her condition seemed to have changed considerably without treatment. They were sending her home. She was very upset and repeatedly stated, "But my headaches." With that I took an envelope and wrote her name and the word "headaches" on it. Handing it to her, I told her to put her headaches in it and take them out only when she needed them. She happily tucked the envelope into her purse and was discharged. I received a letter from her daughter several weeks later stating that her mother was "back to her old self" and doing well.

Case II: Miss L.

Miss L. was brought to my attention when I was asked to consult with the nursing staff about management of "a very difficult patient."

The nurses reported her as a demanding, unlikable 28-year-old college-trained nurse who had been admitted three weeks before for "diabetic management." She typically turned her call light on every half hour and then demanded that the nurse spend the next 10 to 15 minutes with her, straightening her bed, her hair, her chair, and so on. She made up excuses for the nurses to be with her, but when they were there, she was obnoxious, rude, and sometimes abusive. She had thrown things at them and thrown her trays on the floor. Frequently, when a new nurse would go into the room, the patient would yell at her, warning her to get out. Needless to say, most of the nurses would flee the room and no one wanted to take her as a patient. Her medical history showed that she had been doing well for years, but had suddenly decided that she needed to be admitted for diabetic management. Medically she had deteriorated from the day of admission. She experienced repeated insulin reactions during those three weeks, with alternating episodes of hyperglycemia. She developed urinary tract infections and phlebitis, and seemed to have a continuous runny nose.

When I walked into her room, she immediately threw a pillow at me and screeched at the top of her lungs, demanding that I get out of her room. I caught the pillow in midair, looked her straight in the eyes, and threw it back with equal force, saying in a firm but quiet voice that I had absolutely no intention of leaving and that I expected her to be quiet while I came over to sit down to talk. She looked quite surprised, settled back, and waited. I walked over to her and took hold of her wrist. I lifted it into the air, said that would do, and then sat down beside her bed. I told her to tell me what was going on.

She proceeded to tell me that she was a baccalaureate-trained nurse who had been working for several years, and who had been living with a young physician. She said that the night before she came to the hospital she had confronted him with their future, insisting that he either agree to marry her or move out. He moved out. She then decided that she needed to come to the hospital to "get her diabetes taken care of." I asked her to tell me more about herself. She said that her mother had gotten pregnant when she was barely 17 and had married and kept the baby (i.e., L) unwillingly because she was Catholic. A second baby was born when L was 18 months old. She stated that she remembered developing an attachment to a blanket at that time, and that she carried her blanket everywhere as a child. When she was four her father decided that the blanket was too dirty and worn, and that she was too big to carry a blanket around, so he threw it in a trash fire. She stated that from that time on she was always "doing things" in order to get attention. For example, she purposely burned herself, cut her finger, and even lay down in the street hoping to get run over. At the age of eight she developed diabetes. From that day until she entered nursing school, she was taken care of by her mother. She did not learn to give her own shots, manage her diet, or regulate her life until she left home.

She reported that since her hospitalization she and her mother had had many arguments. At one point her mother told her in a very angry voice that she would never walk out of the hospital on her own two feet. She screamed back that she didn't need two feet.

When she had finished, I told her that it was wonderful that she had learned how to control her body, and that now she was going to learn how to make it work *for* her, not *against* her. As I lowered her wrist, I told her that she was a special person, that many people wanted to help her, and that she would soon know that she could get her needs met and be independent too.

Over the next few weeks L had a number of interesting physical complications. First it was noted that she hadn't had a bowel movement for nearly two weeks. She had been given stool softeners, laxatives, and even enemas. She retained them all; the physicians were preparing to take her for a sigmoidoscopy to determine if there was a physical obstruction. When I heard about this, I went to her immediately. By now we had established a working relationship so that she would settle into a trance almost as soon as I entered her room. As I entered I said, "L, take a deep breath. Now. It is time in your life for you to get your shit together, and to let it go." She said "Yes," and went into the bathroom and filled the stool.

Another time the physicians were discussing her case, stating that they didn't think that they would be able to get her diabetes under better control, so they might as well discharge her home. Within a few hours she had developed a serious cough that was followed by pneumonia, and then serious respiratory distress. She was transferred to the intensive care unit. The following day I visited her and learned that she did not seem to be responding to the medical regime. The doctors were worried that she might go into fulminating pulmonary edema.

When I went to her bedside and identified myself, she barely responded. Nevertheless I told her that I was there and that she could *remember* that she had control over her body. That she could make her body work *for* her, not *against* her. I then put her hand on her chest and told her that she could feel her heart beat, that she had *such wonderful control* and that soon she would be *well enough* to leave the intensive care unit. She was transferred back to her room that afternoon.

The next day her left foot was gray, cold and lacking in pedal pulse. The diagnosis was possible thrombus; an angiogram was ordered. When I once again approached her and told her that she had control over her body and that she could *let her foot be healthy and still get her needs met*, a visible change occurred in her foot. The color gradually improved and the pulse returned, but, her great toe continued to be cool and gray.

Since I planned to leave town for an extended period of time, I had arranged for another therapist to take over this case. She became very upset, insisted that she was being abandoned, and that the new therapist (a female psychiatrist) didn't like her. When I returned from my trip, I learned that she had taken an overdose of sleeping pills. Later she had been discharged to her mother's home. She was confined to a wheelchair due to a gangrenous great toe.

Case III: Mr. G.

Mr. G., a 32-year-old male, was referred to me by his physician for assistance with persistent hypertension (158/104) that was unresponsive to medication and unrelated to known causes. The physician had become particularly frustrated following two admissions to the emergency room over the past two weeks. Mr. G.'s symptoms were chest pain, vertigo and dyspnea. The medical assessment in the emergency room had yielded diagnoses of hypertension, angina, and hyperventilation. Whereas his electrocardiograms were abnormal, his enzymes indicated that no muscular damage had occurred.

During our first visit I instructed him to make himself completely comfortable, to relax, and to know that he would be safe in my office. Using a progressive relaxation approach, I assisted him in acquiring a trance state. I then asked him to describe his experience, how he felt, and what he thought had caused his *physical distress and high blood pressure*. (I asked for both since patients generally deny conscious awareness of physical sensations related to high-blood pressure.)

Mr. G. launched into a discussion about his work as a carpenter and his experience in roofing houses. He said that he had been in the business for a number of years, and roofed many houses. Recently, however, when he was on top of a house he was building and looked down, he suddenly became very dizzy. He had noticeable chest pain and difficulty in breathing. As a result, he was taken to the hospital. This was the first of his emergency room visits.

When hypnotized and asked if this had happened to him before, he stated that he had had a similar experience two years before. At that time, in addition to the physical symptoms, he had felt as if he were "rolling down a hill and couldn't get up." Encouraged to consider whether those feelings could be associated with other experiences, he described a time when he was in Vietnam. He had been ordered to lead a group of men up a hill in combat. As he approached the top of the hill, he turned around, looked down, and saw several of his men stepping on mines and being blown up. He tried to go to one, but stepped on a mine and rolled down the hill. He was hospitalized for four months with severe leg injuries. He stated that he had felt guilty the entire time he was hospitalized and for some time after his medical discharge. He felt that he had been "irresponsible" and hadn't thought through his strategies sufficiently well. As he was recounting this, he began to hyperventilate. He was reminded that he was in my office and was safe, that he could relax, breathe normally and enjoy his body being healthy.

As he regained a slow, deep breathing pattern I told him that his unhappy feelings were normal and that he had experienced a terrible tragedy that he was not responsible for and could not have avoided. I also told him that he would probably *soon find some new ways to be healthy* so that he could enjoy life and his family. He was then told that he could rest until he was ready to wake up and that when he did awaken he would feel strong and invigorated. He sat quietly for a few minutes, then slowly stretched. He commented that he felt pretty good and thought he would be on his way.

The following week, immediately after I had taken his blood pressure and reported to him that it was 136/90, he took a deep breath, settled back into his chair and began to talk. He stated that he had been thinking about his father who, like himself, had been a carpenter. Seven years before in this same month, his mother had called him, told him that his father didn't feel well, and asked him to come over to see his father. He was "fooling around" and didn't go immediately. When he arrived, his mother met him at the door and told him his father had just slumped to the floor unconscious. He ran to his father, decided he needed to do cardiac massage, and pushed on his chest. His father made a terrible noise, "like his life being pushed out of him." They rushed him to the hospital, but he was dead on arrival from a heart attack. Mr. G. described feeling unable to breathe, dizzy, and having a tight chest for days after. When asked how he felt about his father's death, he stated that he shouldn't have pushed on his chest, that he had killed his father. As he stated that he should have gotten there sooner, he began to hyperventilate again.

I reminded him that he was in my office, that he was *working hard and responsibly,* and that he could breathe easily and enjoy it. I then told him that he had had a terrible experience, that he had lost someone very important to him, and that his sad and angry feelings were normal symptoms of the grief response. I then made several factual statements about heart attacks, describing the physiological responses of a coronary occlusion and infarct. I stated that no one was responsible for this sad event and that we can only do what we think is best under the circumstances. He began to cry, so I again told him that his *feelings and behaviors* were perfectly normal, that crying often helped people express feelings, and that soon he would probably feel much better. As he quieted down, I commented that he was very fortunate because he would always have a part of his *father and friends* with him, and that those *good memories* which he would *always retain and enjoy* would help him feel happy and healthy. I then told him that he could rest in my office until he felt peaceful and healthy, and that he would know that when he had finished his rest, *he would fully understand that he was a very* responsible, healthy young man. He sat quietly for a few moments, then straightened up and smiled. He stated that he felt better and was ready to leave. His blood pressure was 124/84.

Although I have not seen this young man since this second visit which was seven years ago, his physician reports that he has been healthy and happy and has not required additional care other than routine checkups.

CONCLUSIONS

The above cases are presented to provide examples of mind-body relationships and possible intervention strategies. The variance in the severity of these cases can be understood if the histories are compared. The earlier the stressors, the more severe the problem. The first case, Mrs. A., had experienced major stressors during early adolescence, while the last case, Mr. G., had experienced major stressors in later adolescence. Both cases demonstrated the availability of resources needed to contend with earlier residual stress as well as with current life stressors.

They simply needed assistance in mobilizing their own resources. Both cases were able to return to fairly healthy lifestyles. The second case, Miss L., had carried negative residues since early infancy. These were difficult to overcome and left her feeling vulnerable and abandoned. Since the infant's early needs are strongly linked to physiological dynamics of the body, stressors at this time of life leave the individual vulnerable to physical illness throughout the lifespan. Examples of other cases that can be considered in this category include the failure-to-thrive child and the anorexic patient.

Others may have less obvious medical problems. For example, through the years a number of people have told me that they have repeatedly done things to make themselves sick. Being sick means getting away from the pressures of life. I have also had many clients directly state that they cannot let themselves get well, because if they do, they can't come to see me. Unless we learn how to treat clients who are sick as *people who happen to have an illness or disease*, rather than *as a disease that must be cured*, we reinforce their sick role behaviors. It helps to remember that it is the person who must be cured, not the disease. Otherwise, symptoms merely travel from one system of the person to another, as in the case of Miss L.

The above patients are dramatic examples selected to make a point. However, less complicated cases also benefit from the Ericksonian approach. There are those who give up hope because of chronic illness, others who become acutely ill due to chronic psychosocial stress, and some who develop patterns of minor illnesses due to acute psychosocial stress. Probably, the key principle to keep in mind is that with every physical problem there is an associated mental health response, and with every mental health problem there is an associated physical response. The degree of the response will be determined by the developmental residue, available resources, and availability of attachment objects.

REFERENCES

Erickson, H. (1976). *Identification of States of Coping Utilizing Physiological and Psychological Data.* University Microfilms, Ann Arbor, Michigan.

Erickson, H., & Swain, M. A. (1982). A model for assessing potential adaptation to stress. *Research in Nursing and Health, 5,* 93–101.

Erickson, H., Tomlin, E., & Swain, M. A. (1983). *Modeling and Role-Modeling: A Theory and Paradigm for Nurses.* Englewood Cliffs, NJ: Prentice-Hall.

Erikson, E. (1963). *Childhood and Society.* New York: W.W. Norton.

Rossi, E. (1986). Mind/body communication and the new language of human facilitation. In J.K. Zeig (Ed.), *The Evolution of Psychotherapy.* New York: Brunner/Mazel.

SECTION THREE

Panel

Chapter 29

How Milton H. Erickson Encouraged Individuality in His Children

Panel: Lance Erickson, Ph.D., Robert Erickson, M.A., and Betty Alice Erickson Elliott, Ed.D. Cand. Betty Alice serves as moderator; Mrs. Milton Erickson, Kristina Erickson, M.D., and Roxanna Erickson Klein, M.S., were in the audience and contributed during the question and answer period.

Betty Alice: I am Betty Alice, the fourth of Milton Erickson's eight children. All of us eight children have many of the same values. Honesty to self and to others, and the desire to live a fulfilled and productive life in a way that is considerate of, and productive to, the world at large.

Now, we don't believe that those values are unique to us, nor was our general family life unique. However, each of us does feel that Dad and Mom did have some unique ways in which our developing individuality was fostered. Each of us has selected views and concepts which were important to us. We will begin with Lance, who is the second oldest.

Lance: I am Lance Erickson, the second of Milton Erickson's children. We Erickson children are as much in the dark about our development as anyone else might be. We don't always know what we were supposed to learn and we sometimes don't know how we learned it, but we learned it. I think it was to a large extent through the very carefully thought-out interventions that occurred in our lives relative to our individuality. I attended a workshop at this Congress

that David Gordon gave on metaphors. He was talking about analogies in a way that I appreciated.

The mind is like the soil of the earth; it receives everything that
comes into it. Sensations of all kinds are transmitted in different
ways. The earth receives dirt, chemicals, whatever, and the earth
provides, through some means, some organization of appropriate
chemicals or elements, like water or fertilizer, whatever is necessary
to bring forth really creative things like plants, blades of grass, or
flowers. A mind is similar because it, too, brings forth ideas and
behaviors of an individual and his personality, each of which is
different and all of which are the result of the individual and peculiar
elements that went into that particular mind. Dad certainly believed
that and practiced it always. It would be completely incongruous for
him to treat us the same because he knew how different we were,
certainly from his observations of our day-to-day activities, but also
because of his concept of people in general.

The following are a few of the incidents that occurred in my
developmental years and some of the reactions that we got from
Dad.

One of the things that he attempted to do was to find a physical
aspect of each of us that was different from the other children. He
felt it was important for each of us to have a good self-concept,
both physically and psychologically. I have rather prominent bumps,
if you will, on my forehead and I worried some about this. Would
they go away? Would they get bigger? If they got bigger, I thought
I would surely be a monstrosity, and nobody would care to deal
with me. He knew that I was concerned about my appearance. He
set up a number of occasions, appropriate occasions, to let me know
what a wonderful thing it was that I had these bumps, these knowledge bumps that nobody else in the family had developed so well.
They would not only stand me in good stead, but someday I would
meet a girl who thought those were just delightful, a wonderful
physical asset, and they would endear me to her. I am sure that
this is what actually occurred, but his remarks helped me to accept
a part of me that I might have rejected.

Along these same lines, I was tall and gangly. He called me a
"stringbean" or "high pockets," in a teasing way, but I was concerned.
When was I going to stop growing up and start growing out? I was
all skin and bones during my early adolescence, and in typical
adolescent thinking I was concerned with that. At first Dad teased

me about how I was growing, how tall I was compared to everybody else, and how thin I was until he realized I was really concerned. Then he changed.

He brought it to my attention that everybody in the family, all the males, were relatively short. Dad was about 5'6" and his brother was about 5'8", so it was clear to him that I was going to be the tallest male in the whole family, on either side. I would have an advantage that nobody else had. He said that when I did become so tall, I would also widen out and have an appearance that would be fully acceptable to me. Again, that was a successful intervention that relieved how I felt about myself. I could concentrate on other things.

With regard to our behavior, Dad left us a wide range of latitude. We knew what was right and wrong in his sense and what our limits were. But we lived on the grounds of state hospitals, and there were all kinds of wonderful things to do, like learning mental patients' vocabularies. We didn't realize that some of the things we did would be beneficial to us in the long run. I remember one incident. Dad and Mom had gone to Detroit to celebrate their anniversary. It was a pleasant June night. Dad had been encouraging Bert's interest in trapping. Dad had done trapping when he was a boy. While Bert thought it was wonderful to trap muskrats and skin them for the pelts, he thought skunk pelts looked better than muskrat. He had trapped a skunk that night, and he and I went out to get it. The skunk wasn't quite dead when we retrieved it. Then came the major error in judgment. We took it home. We lived in Eloise at that time on the grounds of a very large county mental hospital in one of the buildings that also served patient needs. It never occurred to us that there was anything wrong with taking the skunk to the washtub down in the patients' area of the basement. It was there that Bert skinned it, and this was the error in judgment. On their way back (about 5 miles away) Mom and Dad smelled the skunk odor and said, very lightly, "I hope that isn't something Bert's been involved in." The closer they got, the more they worried. When they got home, the building stunk awfully. Dad had to go see the superintendent of the hospital the next day. He returned with orders to curb some of our instincts.

Dad did it in a very nice way but was firm with both of us. My lesson was indirect. I ended up very angry with Bert, because my best flashlight was buried along with a lot of other things, clothes and so forth, because of the skunk smell. Bert's portion of blame was more direct . . . several days of work such as groundskeeping for the involved building. Although it was a very constructive kind of punishment, Bert didn't really feel it was right at the time because he couldn't quite see that he had done anything wrong. If anything, it was the skunk's problem. But we both learned the necessary lesson.

We had an enjoyable life growing up. The kinds of interventions that we had from our parents were constructive and individualized. The longer I live, the more I appreciate what we had.

Robert: I am the sixth of Milton Erickson's children. In our household, we all had responsibilities that were rather carefully structured for each of us. But within that structure each child was allowed and encouraged to do family chores in his own fashion and thereby express his individuality in completing them.

What follows is a picture of my growing up and how I now perceive that my individuality was influenced by my parents. Our parents, especially my father, treated my brothers and sisters and me as individuals throughout our lives. He usually used a simple, straightforward approach which was very effective. We were treated differently—as individuals, and for the most part we never really felt that we were being treated unfairly. We grew up in an environment in which we each had an assortment of jobs or tasks which we were responsible for completing. The number of jobs, the complexity or difficulty, and the types of jobs were fairly and reasonably apportioned; at various ages we would either be reassigned a job or we would just gradually accept a new responsibility and take over a new job. I remember how I did my chores in our home in Phoenix, on Cypress Street, where for the most part we children all grew up. We lived in a three bedroom, one bathroom house. During our growing up years, there would usually be seven or eight people living there. By today's standards, it was a rather small house, but it was warm and comfortable. I sometimes wonder, in retrospect, how we as a family managed to cooperate as well as we did. As children, we had been taught from the very beginning that we all had the responsibility of working, sharing, and planning together as a family. We all had numerous tasks to perform and we each developed our own personal schedules and plans.

I was the early riser in the family, along with my father. At a very early age I might be found up and about playing, reading, or doing some chores an hour or two before my brothers and sisters would be up and active. During the summer when I turned 14 years, I had a newspaper route in my neighborhood which included early Sunday morning deliveries. Thus, I would be up and out of the house long before it was even light outside. Upon the completion of my route, I would then do chores—tend to the yard, edge the lawn, trim bushes, take the dog for a walk, clean up after the dog, then take care of some of the other pets. I would serve myself some breakfast. Then I would bike to my older brother's house to tend to his plants and do a few minor chores. (My brother, his wife and family were out of state for much of that summer, and I was more or less house-sitting for them.) After biking home, which was a rather lengthy ride, I would complete any of my jobs that I had not been able to complete. I mention all these things—my accomplishments for the day—not to brag but to demonstrate my thesis, which is, with our responsibilities came a certain freedom of choice—choice of method, choice of time, and choice of order.

After completing Sunday's jobs I would then be ready for what I considered to be my favorite pastime—going to the movies. This was a very important form of entertainment for me at that time in my life, because we grew up in a house that did not have a television set in it until I was 18 years old. This is not to suggest, however, that we children didn't watch TV, nor were we ever forbidden to watch TV. Each of us had friends with whom we would see some programs, and on some occasions my parents would make special arrangements so that we could see a particular program. We grew up with the understanding that we did not *need* television since we all had so many diverse interests, both those assigned and those we chose to take part in. Only recently, in a discussion with my mother, did I learn that the reason my parents decided not to have television in our house during our growing up years was because they wanted to encourage us to read as a relaxed activity. And we did read endlessly. And now I understand why my brothers and sisters and I are all such avid readers on so many different subjects.

To continue, upon returning home I would clean up, eat a snack, and then set out to a movie theatre, walking or biking with a friend or by myself. Such a Sunday morning as I have just described would begin at 4:30 or 5:00 AM. Delivering the newspapers, tending to the yard, trimming, edging, various chores, the bike ride to and from my brother's house, and any other jobs would easily take up as much as seven hours. So then it would be as late as 11:30 or noon; and, I was ready to go to the movies and I would do so.

Except for my parents, I would usually be the only one in the household who was up and active until about 10:00 or 10:30 in the morning. Sunday at our house was the day my brothers and sisters liked to sleep late and they were allowed to do so. As I mentioned earlier, my brothers and sisters had their own tasks to perform, and each would carry out his or her responsibilities. They would simply operate on a later schedule—their own schedule. They had their own way of doing things.

For me the early morning was the ideal time to do my chores. Not only did I enjoy doing my work at that time because of the freshness of the day, but I could get things done the way I wanted to without having any brother or sister telling me how to do it, when to do it, in what way to do it, and then to later criticize that I was doing it the wrong way. By the time my brothers and sisters had risen, I had already completed my chores by myself. I had escaped their interference—I had escaped their influence—and I had escaped their criticism. I had done my work—my way.

In conclusion, I realize now that our parents had encouraged us to find satisfaction in our control over our own lives. That satisfaction and control were important aspects which helped to shape our respective individuality.

Roxanna Erickson Klein: I'm Roxanna, the seventh of Milton Erickson's children. Our parents communicated clear values to us: consideration for others, appreciation of differences, the idea that every life experience presents opportunities. They also encouraged the sharing of assets.

As a parent myself, I communicate these values to my children. I don't think they are unique values. I'm not even convinced that raising eight children to be very different individuals is unique. But if anything *is* unique, I think it was the creative problem-solving that our parents encouraged.

I don't think that any of us let problems hang around for long. If we are unhappy with the status quo of anything, we usually initiate a positive change. If we can't think up one, we seek advice. We don't always follow the advice, but we do explore the alternatives and make an active decision as to what we will or will not do. We may even decide that status quo isn't so bad after all.

When we sought advice from Daddy, he would indirectly direct us toward actions that would resolve the problem. He rarely would address the problem outright.

I will illustrate this indirect approach with two examples. One is from my own childhood, and the second is an occasion where I have used a similar approach with my own children.

When I was 12 years old, in the sixth grade, the grammar school I attended merged with another and the population shifted from 100% white to 30% Hispanic. The sixth graders coming in had already dealt with most of the problems associated with coming from a Spanish-speaking home into an English-speaking school. The only concession the school made, that I was aware of, was the introduction of an elective "Spanish as a Second Language" which was available only to those students in the highest reading groups. Although I was very interested in taking the class, my reading scores were not high enough for me to be admitted.

My first approach to solving this problem was to speak with the instructor. I tried hard to convince her that I was so highly motivated that the minimum requirements should be waived. This approach was unsuccessful.

Next, I went to Daddy and described the problem. At first, he seemed very interested and asked all sorts of pertinent questions. Why was I so interested in taking the class? Had I considered waiting till next year and working on reading this year? What did I expect to gain from the class? The answers were clear to me. I was satisfied with my reading abilities, even if I wasn't in the accelerated group. I liked the sound of Spanish and I was fascinated with the idea of being able to talk in a foreign language.

Then his questions became less relevant. "Where do the Spanish-speaking children live?" "What did they do after school and during the lunch hour?" Both of these questions were dead ends from my perspective. They lived too far away for after-school activities, and at lunchtime, they all participated in the free lunch program. They ate separately at tables reserved for the cafeteria workers.

Suddenly Daddy lost all interest in my problem. Instead, he launched a money-saving campaign. He proposed that I join the lunch work program, but he would continue to provide me with lunch money (25¢ per day) on those days. That would amount to $1.25 a week, and if I was a real good saver and put it in the bank, he would match it! At $2.50 a week, my savings would grow fast. And he went on to speculate what I might like to buy after I had saved my money for several months.

I wasn't entirely satisfied with what I thought was the "distraction" technique, but nevertheless the new project might take my mind off the problem. So I decided to do it.

It wasn't until years later that I recognized his suggestion as an intervention dealing directly with the problem described. Eating lunch every day at a table where only Spanish was spoken provided me with a perfect opportunity to learn Spanish. The outcome of that intervention was successful. I did learn Spanish and perhaps more fluently than did my classmates in the advanced reading group.

As a child, I promised myself that when I grew up and had children of my own, I would always answer their questions directly. But as we grow, our perspectives change. Now, as a parent, I find that sometimes the indirect approach is far more effective.

My second example is how Ethan used his imagination.

My son, Ethan, is five years old now. He was only a baby when it became apparent that he was one of those unfortunate children to have ear canals shaped in such a way that earaches and ear infections become a fact of life. As parents, we learned to be alert to the earliest symptoms, to keep antibiotics in the refrigerator, and to hope that the child would grow in such a way that the problem resolves itself.

The hardest part is those long hours between the time the infection is recognized and when the antibiotics gain sufficient foothold to diminish the swelling and the pain. It was during one of those endless spans of time when Ethan, then three years old, sat on the sofa with tears running down his little face. Somehow my comforting embrace seemed insufficient. "What if I'm not around when this happens?" "What if he outgrows his faith in me, faster than he outgrows his earaches?" I wanted him to learn to accept pain and to gain control over it; that skill would be with him throughout his life.

I snuggled close to him and slowly removed my shielding arm while we talked. "It's really sad to have an earache, Ethan." I affirmed his unfortunate status. "I hope that none of your pals in the bedroom has an earache." Ethan giggled thinking whether any of his stuffed toys might have a problem similar to his own. At three, it's hard to figure these things out.

There on the sofa, we let our imaginations carry us around the

bedroom, examining each stuffed animal and speculating on the possibilities. "The giraffe has little-bitty ears, and if one did hurt, would the pain make it all the way down that long neck?"

"And poor Fred! If he had an earache, it would really be something!" Ethan agreed that the toy basset with the long ears and the sad face would have the biggest problem of all.

The game seemed to capture Ethan and enfold him in the possibilities. Pain is experienced differently by each individual.

Then we came to Milton, a very special teddy bear. Ethan named Milton after his own middle name. The remarkable thing about Milton is that he can unzip his fur coat and underneath he has a pair of bright red longjohns!

"I wonder if Milton ever has any ow's?" It seemed a reasonable possibility. "I wonder what Milton does when he has an ow?"

I wondered, but Ethan knew. "He unzips his coat and puts it on the chair. Then he goes to bed." We both sat there several minutes marveling over what a wonderful bear Milton is.

"Ethan, I wonder what it would be like if you had a zipper that ran all around your face, down to your tummy, that unzipped *your* skin?" I ran my finger along the path of the imaginary zipper. At first, he collapsed in laughter, but as I slowly, intently, continued, he became quiet. We pretended to slowly remove Ethan's skin, back from around his face, over his head. Then we pulled his arms and legs out like one would remove a snowsuit. I carefully took the imaginary garment and placed it on the far end of the sofa. Ethan was blissfully relaxed.

Whereas I helped Ethan and guided him through his first lesson, he picked it up from there. Ethan and Milton have shared a lot. Ethan continues to use Milton and the lesson that Milton taught him whenever he has an earache or any of the other "ows" that are an inevitable part of childhood.

Can parents encourage their children to be individuals, or does it just turn out that way?

THE ENCOURAGEMENT OF INDIVIDUALITY

Betty Alice: How did Milton Erickson encourage individuality in his children? It may sound like an easy question for one of his children to answer. In fact, when several of us were discussing ideas for this panel, I thought up this topic and was pleased when everyone agreed on it. This will be a breeze, I thought. But the more I thought about it, the more specific I tried to be, the more I tried to narrow it down, the harder and more complex the question became.

Please realize I include our mother, Elizabeth Erickson, in all that I say. She was equally involved in our raising. So, how did they teach us to become happily individualistic?

I have thought off and on about this topic ever since I had to make a genogram of my family of origin for a class. For that genogram, I had to think about each of my brothers and sisters—draw comparisons and make distinctions between them. It was then that I was first struck by the differences in each of us even though we're similar in so many ways. I guess individuality can be defined as following your own course, as knowing that your differences from others are not only okay, but a part of what makes you and life enjoyable. Another part of that definition is, I think, that appreciating your own differences enables you to accept and appreciate and even seek out differences in other people—in all areas of your life.

After I had defined individuality in my own way, I began to think about how that had been encouraged in me as I grew up. First, perhaps foremost, was that we were never compared to each other or to anyone else. I don't remember it ever happening. Now, that is not to say that I wasn't given specific instructions on how to behave: Good girls do the dishes without complaining, curfew is at 10 o'clock on school nights, and arguing with brothers and sisters is not the way to act.

It's not as though I was never praised. I made most of my own clothes and some of my sisters', I got good grades, and I was a great cook. I was praised for all those things and more.

Each instruction, however, each expectation, each acknowledgement, each piece of appreciation or praise that I received was especially for me. It was given as though I were an only child, the only person in the world, almost. The expectations, the discipline, the praise—none of them had anything to do with anyone else. This was so firm a precept that even now, I can hardly *imagine* Daddy or Mama comparing me with anyone else. I was, and am, me—good, bad or indifferent.

Added to and part of that was the carefully taught appreciation of the uniqueness of my brothers and sisters. We were encouraged to ask each other for help. Each of us had areas of strength; we were always encouraged to take advantage of the expertise available to us in our family. We still do that. This is not to say that we always use the expertise or take the advice that is offered. Far from it. I may decide the other person is not so expert after all, and that my way is better. Or I may recognize that the other person's ideas are better than mine, but I *like* my way better. The important thing, to me, is that I have them available to me just as they have me, with no obligation implied that I must do as they recommend. I am an individual, they are individuals, and who's to say who is the wiser.

Another way individuality and the appreciation of individuality were taught to me was through the relationships I had with the variety of people around me as I grew up. When I was a little girl, the family lived on the grounds of mental hospitals. Some of my best friends were patients. I can still remember my brother, Robert, sharing his tricycle with one of his patient friends. When I was a little older, Daddy had his office in our house. His patients sat in our living room. A large number of people passed through our house, and our lives, and some of them, believe me, were unusual. However, their differences and unusualness were accepted outright. They may have been Daddy's patients, but many of them became our friends.

I think a basic condition for developing individuality in yourself is a belief that differences in people are to be accepted and, more than that, valued. Without that belief, it would be almost impossible to develop your own individuality and be comfortable with your differences from other people. Daddy's patients helped to teach me to accept and value differences.

Another way in which I believe individuality was fostered in me was the way that Daddy liked an outcome which incorporated all sorts of benefits on the path to that outcome. Usually, those pathways were not straight-line paths; they curved and meandered about as they picked up an advantage here and a good point there. (This is not nearly as complicated as it sounds.)

For example, Daddy enjoyed a fire in the fireplace. To get to that outcome, he traveled the path of benefit to all. There is a lot of waste wood around, even in cities. People prune their trees and trim their shrubs; branches fall from trees in storms. This wood just creates problems for everyone—the street sweeper, the trashmen, and those in charge of the city dump. So we children, certainly the ones who grew up in Arizona, kept sharp eyes out for recent tree trimmings and fallen branches. If you were to look for these, and I still do, you'd be amazed at how much there is. Whenever we found some wood, we would hurry home and get our wagon, pull it back and load it up. We would have huge piles of wood balanced precariously on the wagon. It would usually take two of us—one to tug the wagon, the other to walk along beside, balancing the load which was always topheavy. We'd drag it home, unload the wagon, saw the wood into neat lengths and then stack it in tidy piles for use in the fireplace. A fireplace can burn a *lot* of wood, even in Arizona, and Daddy like to have plenty on hand in case lean times came. So these trips were frequent occurrences.

As I got older, I began to hate to go get wood. Once, when I complained that I didn't want to do it, Daddy seemed puzzled: I was getting exercise; I felt pride when I saw the neat rows of stacked firewood; I enjoyed the fire; I was even cleaning up the environment. Best of all, it was all for free. What more could I want out of life? (I never could think of a good enough answer, though I assure you I racked my brain every time I pulled that wagon along.)

Now that I'm grown, I've thought about the wood-gathering expeditions in a different way. I think that experience of doing something that was so very different from anything my friends did and doing it in such a natural and matter-of-fact way, with an emphasis on the end result, carried a powerful message to me. I'm not trying to convince anyone, including myself, that Daddy was not interested in getting firewood. To the contrary. The use of waste wood for our fireplace was another important consideration. But Daddy loved to have multiple meanings attached to any act. Nothing pleased him more than having several benefits happen from one piece of behavior, and it was especially pleasing if the end results could hardly be traced directly. Now I am certain he knew then that we would gain a base of security from our wood-gathering trips. I do know that today I can do things very differently from my friends and feel quite comfortable doing so. I can tease them—look at what I've got just because I'm not afraid to do things that others think odd.

Another way in which I was helped to be confident in my individuality was through my parents' reactions to goals I set. When I decided over 20 years ago that I wanted to move to Australia, Daddy was able to look at the move through my eyes and anticipate the adventure with me. He made no judgments and offered no advice. He respected my individuality enough to accept what I had decided to do. He was proud of the fact that I had sold almost everything

I owned in order to get enough money to move to Australia just for fun. He was proud because I was pleased with what I was doing. He would have been just as proud, I'm sure, had I decided to stay and continue to teach school in Michigan. I think his pride in my accomplishments was not so much a pride in the accomplishment itself as it was something else. Pride in a particular accomplishment carries with it a certain burden. I think Daddy was proud of me because I was doing what I wanted, and I was doing it happily and productively. I think the kind of respect, acceptance and pride that he demonstrated is an extraordinarily powerful tool to teach a person acceptance of, respect for, and pride in one's own individuality.

Daddy was never afraid to be different. In fact, he enjoyed it. He conveyed that to me as a value worth having. He would look for opportunities to show all of us the pleasures of trying the different. There are so many ways to teach children that. For instance, I've eaten beaver, elk, squirrel, rattlesnake, thousand-year-old eggs, poi, Rocky Mountain oysters, squid, and countless other unusual foods. Some of them were pretty good; some of them were just awful. But I always enjoyed the new and different experience.

There is a price for everything. What was the cost of individuality for me? Sometimes I feel a little removed—some of the things which are very important to many of the people I'm around are not that important to me. Sometimes I feel as if I'm regarded as different when I don't really want to be seen as the odd one.

But I think the enjoyment of life I have gained from my sense of secure individuality far outweighs any inconveniences it may have brought, and I have tried to instill individuality in my own children. Sometimes when I look at them, adults now, going their own ways, doing what they want to do, I think that I have succeeded. I hope so.

Question: If your Dad was always seeing patients, how much time did he have to spend with the family? If the patients were in your home, how could you have dinner together? Tell us more about quality time you had with your Dad.

Betty Alice: I have wondered about that myself because, as Kristi mentioned at a previous meeting, Daddy did not attend our graduations, and he didn't do some of the things that you might think parents should do. He did spend time with us. We did lawn work with him; we dug in the gardens with him; he admired our "stupid" firewood. He used to lie down in the time between his patient appointments, and I can remember sitting on the foot of the bed when he was lying there and just talking to him. I think because his office was in our house it gave him the opportunity to spend bits and pieces of time which probably added up. I also think that when he paid attention to us, he really paid attention.

Lance: I remember Dad spending a great deal of time with us, or so it seemed; maybe there is a time distortion factor there. In our early years he would play ball with us, despite the fact that he would have to play ball while using a cane. Bert and I enjoyed this play immensely. He would also come out and review the work we had done in the garden, which we didn't enjoy. That was one of the ways we learned that when you do a job, you should do it well, because we knew what his expectations were, but not because he would tell us directly. When we worked in the garden, he, having lived on a farm, really didn't expect to see any weeds when we got through hoeing. Bert and I didn't think it was that important. However, after his going back two or three times and saying, "Did you notice that little weed in the row of beans there?" we worried that he would think maybe we should do all the beans again because we might have missed other weeds. We got the idea that he wanted us to do the job well, so we were more careful about it.

I think the evening meals were examples of family time when we would all be included in what was going on. The conversation might be with one individual or just be general playfulness. We were always expected to be there and, of course, if one didn't show up on time, one did without dessert—added incentive to be on time. So everybody would be there at mealtimes. Afterwards, Dad would tell White Tummy or other stories. This was very high quality time in our memories and quite sufficient.

He might stay up until midnight or later, working or writing. Sometimes he stayed up because of his allergies or physical pain when he could not sleep anyway. He kept long hours, and the time he spent with us was valued a lot.

Question: I seem to recall in an article I read there was a story where somebody, one of the males of the family, cut his leg severely and had to have stitches in it. Your father used a distraction technique which I have found very helpful with my own son.

Mrs. Erickson: That was the first summer we spent in Arizona. Allan fell and cut his leg quite badly. We were very new here, of course, but we did know there was a doctor's office nearby, so we took him over there. It so happened that his older sister sometime previously had had to have quite a few stitches for an injury. Somehow Dad appealed to Allan to make sure he had more stitches than his sister. He was instructed to count them. Allan was seven years old at the time and tended to be a very bossy little boy. So when he got to the doctor's office, he ordered the doctor to put in stitches and use black thread so they would show. And he was to be sure to put a lot of stitches. This was the distraction. Looking back, I can just see Allan doing all this because that was the kind of little boy he was.

Question: Was this use of distraction a frequent pain intervention that your Dad used?

Betty Alice: All of us, I think, learned how to use hypnosis and self-hypnosis on pain, and all of us have taught it to our children. Roxie gave an example of teaching it very specifically. My children can all do it. I don't know how they learned, but they can turn off pain. My one son has had root canal work, and he read a comic book as the dentist worked on his mouth. He doesn't have any pain. So, all of us benefitted by that learning from Daddy.

Kristi: Another distraction in our home regarding injuries with cuts was that we weren't supposed to bleed on the carpet because bloodstains are hard to get out. So a concern was not only that one had a cut, but also that it was necessary to get this situation under control . . . keep the cut from dripping until whoever was hurt could get to the sink. I can remember that I had this bad cut from gathering firewood. The log had fallen on my leg. My brother carried me into the house. He laid me on the floor, then they pulled Dad out of the office. (You know, Dad's a doctor and he would look at it and tell us what to do.) He looked at me on the floor, and he said, "Get her off the rug." I tell you, it took me aback. So I got up, cut and all. Then he said, "Get that wrapped up and have her go get some stitches." I walked out to get it taken care of, but it really took me aback. He changed our perspective. Then, we worried about the rug.

Roxie: One more comment on the pain control: All of the females in the family have been taught to use hypnosis during childbirth. We are all very comfortable in that area.

Lance: I probably learned this from Dad, but I don't know when or how. We used to go to the dentist, and in the old days it wasn't as pleasant as it is today. The techniques, the drills, everything; I mean, you felt everything. They didn't always use a shot to ease the pain. I learned at quite an early age a technique that I have used ever since. It is very effective for me, especially when having dental work. I psych myself up in advance. Just prior to or on the trip over to the dentist's office, I build up horrible, awful sensations of how much pain there is involved in going to the dentist. I imagine just how much this can possibly hurt me. When I actually get to the dentist and he starts drilling, it's not that bad. It's always minimal compared to the expectation.

Regarding vocational directions: People have often asked me how Dad influenced our directions in life. Kristi has answered that she never felt pushed to go into any particular area. I was undecided at one point between law, medicine, psychology, or something in business. One way or another, I narrowed all these down to nothing and didn't go into any of them for various reasons. But I got the distinct impression from Dad and Mom that whatever I chose would be fine as long as it was something that would give me personal satisfaction. That was the major criterion in determining what we did with our lives: that we gain satisfaction from what we did. We were to be happy with it.

I changed careers once, although I was not particularly dissatisfied with my first choice. I liked it, but I found some undesirable aspects related to the business aspect of that vocation. I ended up in education, which gave me more satisfaction. The only thing I remember Dad instilling is the idea that if you get into something, business or a job or whatever, you want to do it as well as you can. I think we all have had the idea instilled in us in various ways—often by the reinforcement we got for what we accomplished. Even when we were very young, we would work like crazy to build or make things for Christmas presents for Mom and Dad. They really appreciated that, and they gave us strong reinforcement. It might have been a god-awful, put-together thing that a kid might make, but it was the best we could do. Because we would spend hours and hours on it, we got a great deal of reinforcement for that. I think that has helped us a great deal in our present lives.

Question: How did Dr. Erickson handle any type of agitation or fighting amongst yourselves?
Lance: Shall we quarrel over who answers this? I will be glad to start.

When we lived at Eloise, Bert and I lived in a room apart. The family had an apartment but it was located on four different floors of the building . . . the basement, the first floor, the second floor, and the third floor. We had bedrooms apart simply because there wasn't enough room in the building. It was a mental hospital, and we lived in a part of one of the buildings where the patients lived. Mom and Dad would come down when Bert and I had a bedroom on the first floor and say goodnight to us. On occasion, they might come down even later and note evidence of destruction in the room, but kind of ignore it. Because Bert and I had differences of opinion, we got into some very disagreeable fights. He was stronger, but I was taller. We would break things, like furniture. I know they couldn't avoid noticing the damage, but Dad seemed to accept that as a normal part of growing up, as long as we weren't breaking arms or causing wounds. We needed to learn on our own about getting along with each other. So, he would let us do it. And, we never did cause each other any permanent damage. Maybe he was just risking that, or maybe it was due to his trust in a natural kind of holding back. On lots of occasions he would allow us to fight it out and just ignore us.

Roxie: I have four small children under the age of seven. They fight quite a bit. My parents and I did not handle these problems in the way that I see most of my peer group handling their children. That is, we are not interested in who started the fight or even who is really at fault. The children are fighting, they are going to have to settle it on their own in their own way, but not break the basic rules. They are not to disrupt the household, they are not to break objects in the household, they are not to injure each other, but they can just go off and settle the fight in whatever way, between the two of them, they are able to do that. And with those rules, it is very rare that parental intervention is really necessary.

Kristi: I can remember hiding the fights that I had with my sister and brother from my parents. They didn't seem to know that we fought. As for the hurting each other, the basic rules were, you could not be cruel to each other. It is all right to say, "You are tall and skinny," but not to say something cruel. I can remember receiving a severe lecture about that on the one occasion I transgressed.

Question: Was discipline handled exclusively by your father, and if not, did your father and mother agree on your discipline?

Answers from various Ericksons at one time: They always agreed, they always supported one another. No, they did not always agree, they always supported each other.

Lance: Please recognize we are not always in agreement, but I do agree our parents did support each other very well when a decision was made about discipline. But they did not take the same type of actions in disciplining us. In fact, Mom would stick up for us on numerous occasions when she felt that Dad's punishment was too severe. Mom did punish us and did use the same kinds of techniques as Dad, but hers seemed more benign than Dad's.

Question: Then, evidently, Dr. Erickson usually directed the disciplining?
Lance: It was simply a matter of who would discover the situation— whether it was Mom who saw us quarreling or whether it was Dad.
Betty Alice: And I can remember one thing which worked for us, and I did it with my children. We used to like to read the Oz books. I can remember, if I were mean to my brother, or my sister was mean to me, the quarreling pair had to sit down together and the oldest had to read to the youngest. And by the time we got done reading half the story, the fight was over. We liked each other again, and we got to finish the book or the chapter in a nice, warm way. And I thought that was a very good way to handle some of our arguments.
Lance: With respect to punishments, I think our parents were very creative about making them constructive and beneficial. For example, if we had transgressed in some way, one of the things that we often had to do was to crack nuts. We enjoyed gathering walnuts, black walnuts, and hickory nuts, even though we knew what would happen in the long run. When we did something bad, we would have to crack a certain amount of nuts. But we loved what Mom made with those walnuts and hickory nuts, hickory nut bread and things like that. They were great. So, we enjoyed the results but the punishment was tedious. To get a half cup of hickory nut meats is many hours of work. We didn't always appreciate doing it, but I think it was a very positive way to approach punishment. Everything our parents did for and with their children was intended to be creative and constructive. We all appreciate that even more as we grow older.

Invocation: Keynote Address

Chapter 30

The Tools of the Therapist

Virginia M. Satir

Virginia M. Satir, M.A., A.C.S.W. (University of Chicago), for over forty years has practiced and extensively taught psychotherapy, her primary interest being family systems. She is often considered the "Columbus" of family therapy. She has coauthored four books and authored five. Additionally, there are a number of books about her work. She is recipient of the Distinguished Family Therapy Award from the American Association of Marriage and Family Therapy. Cofounder of the Mental Research Institute, past president of the Association of Humanistic Psychology, she is socially active and works at the policy level to improve the lot of disadvantaged populations.

Satir describes essential aspects of her humanistic treatment approach based in fostering self-worth. After developing factors which are universal to every therapy and any human problem, she describes five stages of therapy. Finally, she presents therapists with a "self-esteem maintenance kit." This was a warm, inspiring presentation which was one of the most highly rated at the Congress.

This chapter is about the tools and resources that I as a therapist use to accomplish therapeutic outcomes. It is the backbone of what I teach to my students.

At this writing my lifetime spans 70 years. For 43 of these years I have worked as a psychotherapist, part of the time disguised as a social worker.* For 35 of these years, I focused on the family unit as the

---

* This refers to a long standing argument about whether social workers do psychotherapy.

physical, psychological, and social home of individuals. The family* is the place where babies grow into adults and where they learn how to be in the world. This learning becomes the foundation upon which later life is built. When these learnings are negative, they reflect themselves in symptoms. My aim is to help people get new, more effective learnings. The following is presented to tell you a bit about my experience.

The population with whom I have worked includes such labels as: mentally ill, schizophrenic, poor, psychosomatic, delinquent, criminal, drug abusers, alcoholic, physical and sex abusers, learning disabled, anorectic and bulimic, deaf, blind, handicapped—all of these seen in children, adults and older age persons of varying racial, national, and income groups. The human being is the common denominator for all of the above. Because I have been around so long, I have had ample time for follow-up, which helped me to develop further confidence in my work, and also to open up new vistas to explore.

I mention my experience to indicate the variety of forms of human malfunction, pain, and destruction that I have seen. My experience over time has shown me that all the human agonies are variations coming from the same root—namely, a lack of worth and value of the self by the self and toward others. This psychology makes up the society as well.

In short, we do not teach children how to value themselves. Instead we teach obedience and conformity. This breeds fear and robotic response and paves the way for all our psychologically expensive defenses—denial, ignoring, projection, and distortion—with their often tragic results. These defenses are accompanied by fear and anxiety which have a high cost in physical erosion and are often later reflected as physical illness.

What we need are well-developed feelings of value about ourselves which we can extend to ourselves and to others. Human beings are manifestations of life and, therefore, of divinity. I believe that human life is sacred. It needs to be treated that way.

We need opportunities to experience responsibility from a perspective of love, understanding and purpose. We need to know that we have power and impact which we can use consciously and constructively.

---

*Family is used here to refer to all contexts where children grow up, including institutions.

We need to discover our creativity, to develop our ability to see options and choices.

All the above are undeveloped or unmanifest in people who have symptoms. It is as though they were wearing straightjackets that keep their energies in check. Just as there are universals that underlie the development of symptoms, there are universals that can be successfully applied to their change. I am using this in the context of therapy which I define as follows: *Therapy consists of a process of change, consciously and deliberately entered into between a therapist and client to achieve mutually desired results.*

In the following pages, I want to tease out those factors which I consider to be universal and applicable to therapy around any human problem. In the next part I will use the format of an imaginary interview with myself.

THE INTERVIEW

"What do I have to offer you, my client,* to assist you to become well, whole, and symptom free?"

First, "I have faith in your ability to grow. This comes from my knowledge of life rather than from your behavior. I have faith and confidence in my ability to connect with your growth potential so it can flourish.

"I have ways to help you access your resources. I work on the certainty that you have everything you need. It has only to be accessed.

"To this end, I offer you

My human presence.
My awareness of the present.
My learnings from my experience.
My ability to make contact.
My knowledge, gleaned from specialized study.
My creativity in your behalf.
My leadership in the change process.
My companionship in your struggle.

---

* Client is a word I am using to indicate those who come for help, whether individually, couple or family.

My modelling of taking risks with you.
My congruence."

(The Interview Continues)

Second, "I am prepared to really see and hear you in ways you cannot hear and see yourself. Only those outside of you can see your back. You can't. You are a unique being with similarities to and differences from every other human being, which includes myself. You are the only one exactly like you in the whole world. While I have experiences and knowledge which allow me to make inferences and have hunches in relation to you, I need to check these out with you. What I hold in my mind concerning the who and what I am seeing in you defines my perspective and directs my approach."

I ask myself, "From what perspective am I seeing this person/these persons in trouble?" (Is this person a specimen, a treatment category, good, bad?)

When I see persons, I see them as human beings who are showing me through their words, affect, and behavior what they have learned about being a person. Often, in my mind's eye, I see an infant being born and then fill in the experiences about how this individual learned what he or she is now showing me. How was this person initiated in the first place? How received? Who was there? How did those present interact with one another? What were the rules in the system in which this person grew up?

Third, "What do I know that you don't? Perhaps nothing. However, I may know things in a way that allows you to see them better. Sometimes I think of myself as a midwife assisting in the birth of your self-worth, your new possibilities and consequent released energy.

"One thing I am quite sure of is that I don't put anything into you. What I do is help you open those parts that are closed, find those parts that are present but unnoticed, nourish those parts that are starving, bring freedom to those parts that are suffocating and oppressed. Then I offer you ways to integrate and mediate among your parts."

This is a process. The underlying assumption is that when a self freely has access to all its parts, the behavior will reflect that harmony.

Fourth, "I offer you my willingness to be aware of myself well enough so I don't get in your way. For example: I don't want to mistake my ambitions for you with what you want for yourself."

Fifth, "I can offer my kindness, courtesy, and humor, as well as my competence."

Some time ago, I ran across a statement describing the criteria for hiring personnel in businesses led by enlightened leadership. They were as follows:*

First—Kind
Second—Fun to be around
Third—Competent

I was immediately impressed by how those same criteria characterize my idea of a good therapist. It would be unlikely that such a therapist would suffer much from burnout.

If I am kind, I do not need to use my precious energy to blame, complain and look for scapegoats. I can instead use myself to give positive energy and messages to myself and my clients. I can breathe comfortably while I am doing this.

If I am fun to be around, the chances are good that I do not make a practice of carrying other people's burdens—I carry only my own. I know that the most important learnings occur when things are light, not heavy.

If I have a fine sense of humor, I can laugh at myself and find ways to laugh with others. I can also find the humor in heavy situations.

If I can make mistakes, admit them and learn from them, I demonstrate that the world does not fall apart when I make a mistake. This is a marvelous model for others.

Unfortunately, kindness and humor have been largely ignored as a tool for therapy. This may have come about because kindness was equated with weakness or lack of objectivity. Humor was probably associated with unprofessional behavior. Professional behavior is seen by many as objective and heavy. Kindness and humor are irrelevant to this perspective, yet I see these two factors are essential to any therapeutic success. *(end of interview)*

---

* I learned about this in a new idea seminar on reinventing work at Telluride, Colorado, August 1985. This idea is used by Gore-Tex.

THE CHANGE PROCESS (THE CORE OF THERAPY)

I keep remembering that changing one's self is a monumental task, perhaps more difficult than major surgery. Anything that difficult has to be handled with care.

There are five basic steps to my change process:

1. The first is recognizing and owning the status quo.
2. The second is the introduction of a foreign element that is powerful enough to produce an effect, causing the system to respond.
3. The third is the manifestation of chaos.
4. The fourth is the practice period.
5. The fifth is the integration and development of a new status quo.

Each step is accompanied by anxiety and has a body response. Each stage has to experience a new comfort or there will not be any support for going on to the next stage.

All these steps can be completed in as short a time as five minutes or as long as forever. My goal is to complete one set, on some level, at each interview.

The presence of trust is what enables the frightened, angry, submissive, and/or lost inner self to let down the barriers and permit vulnerability to have a voice and free energy to go forward.

Change is also a delicate matter. It means that one must go from where one is (the familiar) to where one has never been (the unknown). This is very scary. However, the first step in change (healing) is to confront the fear of risking and move into the abyss of the unknown. Within the therapeutic context, the therapist is the companion on that journey.

Stage I

The starting point for all change is the status quo. This represents an established system which is strong, automatic, familiar and rooted in a reliable and predictable set of expectations and which is synonymous with survival.

When one tries to change the status quo, one always encounters resistance. The resistance, itself, tells me about the degree of fear of going forward. It is the system's effort to protect the familiar. Therefore, it deserves my respect. To the degree that I respect and support this resistance, I have the opportunity to create trust, and am therefore preparing the goundwork for taking the risks necessary to going toward the unknown. When the familiar results in defeating and destructive behavior, the therapist has to find other ways which are nurturing to protect that self. That takes a little time. Then one can build a new foundation upon which one can take the risk to go in new directions.

It is natural for the status quo to attempt to repel any change agent. This is what resistance is all about. It doesn't seem to matter much whether the motivation is positive or negative. I have found that, generally speaking, the familiar will always exert a strong pull toward itself even in the face of desire and comfort.

We underestimate the power of the familiar. Our very security is bound up in it. This is the reason that I am prepared to have patience and be compassionate about unsuccessful attempts by both the client and myself to meet goals as soon as I would like.

We all know the pitfalls between the promise and the delivery, especially if the promise is new. For example, I tell myself I want to break this or that habit. I am not successful right away. I fall by the wayside many times. The status quo is solid, practically written in blood, and grounded in concrete. Moving from there is a major thrust of therapy.

Something really mighty has to happen to alert the necessity for change. I need to remember that people do not resist change because they are perverse. They do so because their survival is tied to the familiar. To move to the unknown, we have to establish a new base for security.

Stage II—The Introduction of a Foreign Element

In the context of therapy, the therapist is the first foreign element. Because of the need to maintain the status quo, the foreign element, by the nature of its presence, invites the ongoing system to repel it and expel it. It is much the same process as an organ transplant. The same care needs to be taken by the therapist to enter into the system and become part of its healthy potential without being overtaken by its unhealthy operation.

The therapist has to stand completely alone at this stage. I, the therapist, need to recognize that I am also the personification of that which is causing the step into the unknown. The therapist needs to understand that this is a projection and treat it accordingly.

I have found it wise to set up a context in which I am clearly in charge of the treatment process, but I am not in charge of the persons who are within that process. I treat the client as an equal and I expect that the client respond to me as an equal. I will do what I have to do to lead the client in ways so there will be feelings of equality in relation to me. That could be the main thrust for the treatment. My role defines our treatment task, not my personhood. My personhood may be one of the main factors in getting the task completed, however.

Sometimes the survival is so rooted in the status quo that further attempts at changing are self-defeating. I have found this only rarely, however. The therapist faces two traps in this stage which can defeat the attempts to change.

The first has to do with the development of so much anxiety that the therapist joins the dysfunctional system to escape that anxiety. Once that happens, the therapist's power to change greatly diminishes.

The second trap deals with setting up oneself in the person or family as though it was one's own. In this case, the differentiation between therapist and client is blurred. This also ends in diminishing your power.

Stage III—Chaos

Successfully holding your own in Stage II automatically catapults you into the next stage, that of chaos.

The manifestation of chaos is the evidence that the system is responding. It is open.

I see the place between leaving the known and going into the unknown as being "in limbo." There is as yet no place to anchor one's self. New predictions and expectations have not yet had time to develop, and the old ones are no longer valid. During this limbo period, the therapist needs to offer a safe, loving context in which the client can risk taking the steps into the unknown, dealing with the panic and anxiety which sometimes are present.

This is the period that I call the crisis period. It is always accompanied by chaos. It is a situation of danger which, appropriately handled, becomes an opportunity, a new door to growth.

This crisis period is the time when everything looks and feels like it is falling apart (chaos). The push is to return to a former status quo. Weathering this storm is the beginning of new possibilities.

It is in the chaos period that real changes have a chance to take place. This is the time when vulnerability is present. This is where centeredness, ethics, and congruence are essential. I need to keep myself open, responsive, undefended, but not vulnerable. In this stage, I discourage any decisions that cannot be made and carried out within 10 to 15 seconds. This is not the time one decides to divorce, marry, or have surgery. The decisions would not be made on solid ground. I call this stage the second chance for learning anew.

In this period, catastrophic expectations can be verbalized, even acted out with new endings. This is the place where old fears can be confronted, and where deeper levels of pain will emerge. This is the place where new possibilities emerge, get tried out, and begin to form new expectations for the coming of the new status quo. They are like new buds that can be nourished only by love and energy.

I love gardening and plants. One thing I have noticed is that my plants thrive only when they have love, care, nurturance, moisture, the right degree of sun or shade. They respond negatively if I tell them I won't love them unless they grow.

I think people are the same: Love and nurturance are the ingredients of growth. Threat and fear bring only apparent growth.

Stage IV—The Stage of Practice

As soon as new possibilities have been experienced and are obviously going in the direction hoped for by head and heart, we are ready for stage four.

My feeling of what is right is often ahead of my awareness. For instance, when I learn something I really want to use, I have to surround myself with reminders to help me remember my new direction. I need to be able to intervene with a spontaneous, automatic reaction of the past.

In this practice period I take the fledgling node of a new conscious direction and nurture it until I have built up enough new experience to fade out the old.

As reminders, I suggest posters, slogans, notes on the medicine cabinet, and special remembering meditations. This is just another awareness regarding the pull of the familiar. Change is a conscious process, subject to continuing awareness, nurturing and practice. No one gets to be good at anything without practice and use of the new. Changes in ourselves need the same care and attention.

Stage V—The New Status Quo

Now, as we have practiced and effectively used our possibilities, we can begin to rely on new expectations and predictions. What we have hoped for has been accomplished and now we can create a new status quo.

We soon find out that the changes we have made require, and make possible, changes in other areas. For example, when one has lost a lot of weight, one has to make changes in self-image, food habits and clothes. These stages could be pictured as shown in Figure 1.

Once this first set of steps has been completed, the chances are good that the symptom has begun to disappear. The energy that was invested in the symptom has now begun to transform into a more positive use.

Anxiety is at a 100% level, with comfort at zero, at the beginning—the first time around. By the time the last stage is reached, the ratio has changed to 50% anxiety and 50% comfort. The inner self of the person has begun to show itself and becomes more bold in expressing itself. This heralds the second cycle of the same five stages.

We then start at the new status quo, with a ratio of 50% anxiety, 50% comfort. After going through the five stages, we end up with a new status quo, with a ratio of 25% anxiety and 75% comfort.

By the end of the third cycle, that new status quo no longer represents anxiety, but excitement and vitality. Now clients just keep on going. This might be described as a second birth.

At each stage in the change process, I approach it through congruence in communication, deepening trust and consequent risk-taking, making body pictures which I call sculpting, and attending to breathing and other physical responses.

Throughout all this, I carry a self-esteem maintenance kit which I encourage people to use. It has a detective hat to remind people to look and explore before they judge. It has a beautiful medallion, jeweled

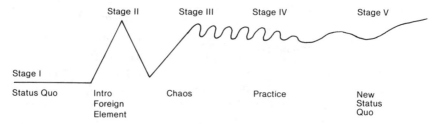

Figure 1

on both sides. One side has "NO," with the words underneath, "Thank you for noticing me. What you ask does not fit. The answer is no."

On the other side is "YES." Underneath are the words, "Thank you for noticing me. What you ask fits just fine. The answer is yes."

This medallion is to remind us to say our real yes's and no's. We know that to say "yes" when we feel "no," or vice versa, is inviting trouble to our bodies. We are compromising our integrity.

The next item is a wishing wand/courage stick which gives us the power to move ahead even when we are afraid.

The fourth item is a golden key which enables us to unlock any doors.

The fifth item is a wisdom box which is located two inches behind our navel, halfway between our heart and our navel. Like a thought or a feeling, it will never be found on an operating table. That doesn't mean you don't have it. This is the place where our sense of fitness and our connection with the intelligence of the universe abide. This is not anxiety, which takes place directly behind the navel.

As I come to the end of this discussion, I realize that my tools of therapy are all the human dimensions brought into play in colorful and dramatic ways to develop high self-worth and introduce the self to its energy and vitality.

YOUR TREASUREHOOD*

Feel your treasurehood.
The miracle that you are
not only because you are you
but because you are a manifestation
of the universal laws
of
the
UNIVERSE

We do not make ourselves.
We are only co-creators.

Love yourself,
for you are
a member of
the universe.
